HANDBOOK OF ISLAMIC BANKING

Handbook of Islamic Banking

Edited by

M. Kabir Hassan

University of New Orleans, USA

Mervyn K. Lewis

Professor of Banking and Finance,
University of South Australia,
Adelaide, Australia

ELGAR ORIGINAL REFERENCE

Edward Elgar
Cheltenham, UK • Northampton, MA, USA

Published by
Edward Elgar Publishing Limited
Glensanda House
Montpellier Parade
Cheltenham
Glos GL50 1UA
UK

Edward Elgar Publishing, Inc.
William Pratt House
9 Dewey Court
Northampton
Massachusetts 01060
USA

A catalogue record for this book
is available from the British Library

Library of Congress Control Number: 2006934135

ISBN 978 1 84542 083 3 (cased)

Printed and bound in Great Britain by MPG Books Ltd, Bodmin, Cornwall

Contents

Figures

Tables

Contributors

Habib Ahmed joined the Islamic Research and Training Institute of the Islamic Development Bank in 1999. Prior to this he taught at the University of Connecticut, USA, the National University of Singapore and the University of Bahrain. He has an MA (Economics) from the University of Chittagong, Bangladesh, Cand. Oecon. from the University of Oslo, Norway, and a PhD from University of Connecticut, USA. Dr Ahmed has more than 30 publications, the most recent including *The Islamic Financial System and Economic Development, Operational Structure of Islamic Equity Finance, A Microeconomic Model of an Islamic Bank, Exchange Rate Stability: Theory and Policies from an Islamic Perspective*, *Corporate Governance in Islamic Financial Institutions* (with M. Umer Chapra) and *Risk Management: An Analysis of Issues in Islamic Financial Industry* (with Tariqullah Khan).

Zafar U. Ahmed has the Chair of Marketing and International Business at the Texas A&M University at Commerce, Texas, USA. He received a BBA in International Business from the University of the State of New York's Regents College at Albany, New York, an MBA in International Business from the Texas A&M International University, Laredo, Texas, and a PhD from the Utah State University. Professor Ahmed has more than 100 scholarly publications and is the President, Academy for Global Business Advancement, Editor-in-Chief, *Journal for Global Business Advancement* and Editor-in Chief, *Journal for International Business and Entrepreneurship Development.* He was awarded a Doctor of Literature (D.Litt) degree in 1997 by the Aligarh Muslim University of India in recognition of his scholarship in Business Administration.

Latifa M. Algaoud is Director of Human and Financial Resources, Ministry of Finance, Manama, Bahrain. Previously she held the position of Director of Administration and Finance in the Ministry of Finance and National Economy, Bahrain. She has a Bachelor of Business Administration (International Trade) from the University of Hellwan, Cairo, Egypt and an MBA in Financial Studies from the University of Nottingham, England. Miss Algaoud is the joint author (with M.K. Lewis) of several journal articles on Islamic banking and finance and the volume *Islamic Banking* (Edward Elgar, 2001).

Simon Archer is Professor of Financial Management at the University of Surrey, England. Previously, he was Midland Bank Professor of Financial Sector Accounting at the University of Wales, Bangor. He studied Philosophy, Politics and Economics at the University of Oxford. He then qualified as a Chartered Accountant with Arthur Andersen in London, and then moved to Price Waterhouse in Paris, where he became partner in charge of Management Consultancy Services in France and Scandinavia. Professor Archer is now Consultant at the Islamic Financial Services Board, Kuala Lumpur, Malaysia. He is the author (with Rifaat Karim) of *Islamic Finance: Innovation and Growth* (Euromoney Institutional Investor, 2002). He has published many academic papers on international accounting and on accounting and finance issues in Islamic financial institutions.

Ricardo Baba is Associate Professor in the School of International Business and Finance, University of Malaysia Sabah, Labuan International Campus. He holds a BBA degree in Management from Ohio University, an MBA degree in Marketing and International Business from the University of New Haven, and a DBA degree in International Banking from the University of South Australia. He has worked for the Central Bank of Malaysia, Standard Chartered Bank and Rabobank Nederland, and has conducted research on offshore financial centres and offshore banking. Dr Baba is the author of *Introduction to Offshore Banking* (Pearson/Prentice-Hall, 2005).

Mohd Ma'sum Billah is Professor of Islamic Applied Finance and Dean, Faculty of Islamic Finance, University of Camden, USA (Malaysian Center). Dr Billah is the Founder, Global Center for Applied Islamic Finance and Group Chairman, K-Professional Development Academy, Malaysia. Author of *Manual of Principles and Practices of Takaful and Re-Takaful* (International Islamic University Malaysia), he is an Islamic Corporate Advisor on *shari'a* compliance, investment, corporate *mu'amalat* and e-Commerce, and a variety of Islamic financial instruments and applications.

Kym Brown is Assistant Lecturer in Banking at Monash University, Australia. Previously she was employed by Deakin University and worked in a number of small businesses. Her research interests predominantly relate to banking and development of financial systems, particularly in developing markets. This includes the performance of Asian and Islamic banks. Kym is a Certified Public Accountant and has an Honours degree in Commerce, a Graduate Diploma in Management Information Systems, and is completing a PhD on Asian bank efficiency. She has over ten publications.

M. Umer Chapra is Research Advisor at the Islamic Research and Training Institute (IRTI) of the Islamic Development Bank. Dr Chapra joined IRTI after retiring as Senior Economic Advisor of the Saudi Arabian Monetary Agency. He received the Doctor's degree in Economics in 1961 from the University of Minnesota, Minneapolis. He has made seminal contributions to Islamic economics and finance over more than three decades and has lectured widely on various aspects of Islam and Islamic economics at a number of academic institutions in different countries. Dr Chapra is a member of the Technical Committee of the Islamic Financial Services Board and has received a number of awards, including the Islamic Development Bank Award for Islamic Economics, and the prestigious King Faysal International Award for Islamic Studies, both in 1989.

Masudul Alam Choudhury is Professor of Economics at the School of Business, University College of Cape Breton, Sydney, Nova Scotia, Canada. Professor Choudhury is the International Chair of the Postgraduate Program in Islamic Economics and Finance at Trisakti University Jakarta, Indonesia and is Director-General of the Center of Comparative Political Economy in the International Islamic University, Chittagong, Bangladesh. He has published widely and his most recent books are *An Advanced Exposition of Islamic Economics and Finance* (with M.Z. Hoque) (Edwin Mellen Press, 2004); *The Islamic World-System, a Study in Polity–Market Interaction* (RoutledgeCurzon, 2004).

Humayon A. Dar is the Vice-President of Dar al Istithmar, UK, a London-based subsidiary of Deutsche Bank and a global think-tank for Islamic finance. Previously he was a lecturer at the Department of Economics at Loughborough University and an Assistant Professor and Head of the Economics Department at the Lahore College of Arts and Sciences, a Visiting Lecturer at the Imperial College of Business Studies, Lahore and also at the Markfield Institute of Higher Education. Dr Dar holds a BSc and MSc in economics from the International Islamic University, Islamabad, Pakistan, and received an M.Phil in 1992 and a PhD in 1997 from the University of Cambridge, England. He has published widely in Islamic banking and finance.

Said M. Elfakhani is Professor of Finance and Associate Dean, Olayan School of Business at the American University of Beirut, Lebanon. He has a BBA from the Lebanese University, an MBA from the University of Texas at Arlington, and an MSc and PhD in Finance from the University of Texas at Dallas. Previously he taught for ten years at the University of Saskatchewan, and has held visiting appointments at Indiana State University and King Fahad University of Petroleum and Minerals, Saudi Arabia. Dr Elfakhani has published 23 academic papers in international refereed journals, 12 papers in international proceedings, and presented 30 academic papers in international conferences held in the US, Europe and worldwide. He is an International Scholar in Finance with the Organization of Arab Academic Leaders for the Advancement of Business and Economic Knowledge.

Mahmoud A. El-Gamal is Professor of Economics and Statistics at Rice University, where he holds the endowed Chair in Islamic Economics, Finance and Management. Prior to joining Rice University, he had been Associate Professor at the University of Wisconsin at Madison, and Assistant Professor at Caltech and the University of Rochester. He also served in the Middle East Department of the IMF (1995–6), and was the first Scholar in Residence on Islamic Finance at the US Department of Treasury (2004). He has published extensively in the areas of econometrics, finance, experimental economics, and Islamic law and finance.

Sam R. Hakim is Adjunct Professor of Finance at Pepperdine University in Malibu, California. He is a Vice President of Risk Management at Energetix LLP, an energy company in Los Angeles CA. Previously he was Director of Risk Control at Williams, an oil and gas company in Houston. Dr Hakim was also financial economist at Federal Home Loan Bank in Washington, DC. Between 1989 and 1998 Dr Hakim was an Associate Professor of Finance and Banking at the University of Nebraska at Omaha. He is an Ayres fellow with the American Bankers Association in Washington, DC and author of over 40 articles and publications. He holds a PhD in Economics from the University of Southern California.

M. Kabir Hassan is a tenured Professor in the Department of Economics and Finance at the University of New Orleans, Louisiana, USA and currently holds a Visiting Research Professorship at Drexel University in Pennsylvania, USA. He is editor of *The Global Journal of Finance and Economics*. Dr Hassan has edited and published many books, along with articles in refereed academic journals, and is co-editor (with M.K. Lewis) of

Islamic Finance, The International Library of Critical Writings in Economics (Edward Elgar, 2007). A frequent traveller, Dr Hassan gives lectures and workshops in the US and abroad, and has presented over 100 research papers at professional conferences.

Munawar Iqbal is Chief of Research, Islamic Banking and Finance, Islamic Development Bank. He has worked as Senior Research Economist, Pakistan Institute of Development Economics, Islamabad; Dean, Faculty of Social Sciences, International Islamic University, Islamabad; Director, International Institute of Islamic Economics, Islamabad, and Economic Adviser, Al-Rajhi Banking and Investment Corporation, Saudi Arabia. Dr Iqbal holds an MA (Economics) degree from McMaster University and a PhD from Simon Fraser University, Canada. His recent publications include *Islamic Banking and Finance: Current Developments in Theory and Practice* (Islamic Foundation, 2001), *Financing Public Expenditure: An Islamic Perspective*, co-authored (IRTI 2004), *Thirty Years of Islamic Banking: History, Performance and Prospects*, co-authored (Palgrave Macmillan, USA, 2005), *Banking and Financial Systems in the Arab World*, 2005, co-authored (Palgrave Macmillan, USA, 2005), *Islamic Finance and Economic Development*, co-edited (Palgrave Macmillan, USA, 2005), *Financial Engineering and Islamic Contracts*, co-edited (Palgrave Macmillan, USA, 2005).

Monzer Kahf is Professor of Islamic Economics and Banking in the graduate programme of Islamic economics and banking, School of Shari'ah, Yarmouk University, Jordan. Previously he held the posts of Senior Research Economist and Head of Research Division of the Islamic Research and Training Institute of the Islamic Development Bank, Jeddah, Saudi Arabia, and Director of Finance, Islamic Society of North America, Plainfield, Indiana. Dr Kahf has a BA (Business), University of Damascus, Syria, a PhD in Economics from the University of Utah, Salt Lake City, and is a Certified Public Accountant in Syria. He is the author of more than 50 articles and 25 books and booklets on *Awqaf, Zakah*, Islamic finance and banking and other areas of Islamic economics, and was awarded the IDB Prize for Islamic Economics in 2001.

Rifaat Ahmed Abdel Karim is Secretary-General of the Islamic Financial Services Board (IFSB), Kuala Lumpur, Malaysia. Previously he was the Secretary-General of the Accounting and Auditing Organization for Islamic Financial Institutions (AAOIFI), Manama, Bahrain. Professor Karim is Honorary Professor in the Faculty of Business and Economics at Monash University, Australia, and is currently a member of the Standards Advisory Council of the International Accounting Standards Board, and a member of the Consultative Advisory Group of the International Auditing and Assurance Standards Board. He has published extensively on accounting, ethics and Islamic finance.

M. Fahim Khan is Chief, Islamic Economics, Cooperation and Development Division, the Islamic Research and Training Institute, Islamic Development Bank. Previously he was Deputy Chief of the Ministry of Planning, Government of Pakistan, Professor and Director in the International Institute of Islamic Economics, International Islamic University, Islamabad and was seconded to the State Bank of Pakistan as Advisor on Transformation of the Financial System. Dr Khan holds a BA and MA (Statistics) from Punjab University, Pakistan, and an MA and PhD in Economics from Boston University,

USA. He has over 15 articles in refereed journals, and he has published or edited ten books on Islamic economics, banking and finance, including *Money and Banking in Islam, Fiscal Policy and Resource Allocation in Islam*, jointly edited with Ziauddin Ahmed and Munawar Iqbal, and *Essays in Islamic Economics* published by the Islamic Foundation, Leicester, UK.

Tariqullah Khan is currently Senior Economist and officiating Chief, Islamic Banking and Finance Division at Islamic Research and Training Institute (IRTI), the Islamic Development Bank. He is also a member of the Risk Management Working Group of the Islamic Financial Services Board (IFSB), and Coordinator of the Malaysian Ten-Year Master Plan for the Islamic Financial Services Industry. Before joining IRTI he held faculty positions in universities in Pakistan. He holds an MA (Economics) degree from the University of Karachi, Pakistan, and a PhD degree from Loughborough University, England. His recent publications include *Islamic Financial Architecture: Risk Management and Financial Stability* (2005) co-edited, *Islamic Financial Engineering* (2005) co-edited, and *Financing Public Expenditure: An Islamic Perspective* (2004).

Mervyn K. Lewis is Professor of Banking and Finance, University of South Australia. Previously he was Midland Bank Professor of Money and Banking at the University of Nottingham, a Consultant to the Australian Financial System Inquiry, and Visiting Scholar at the Bank of England. He was elected a Fellow of the Academy of the Social Sciences in Australia, Canberra in 1986. Professor Lewis has authored or co-authored 18 books and over one hundred articles or chapters. The latest volume, edited with Kabir Hassan, is *Islamic Finance* (Edward Elgar, 2007). Other recent co-authored books include *Islamic Banking* (Edward Elgar, 2001), *Public Private Partnerships* (Edward Elgar, 2004), *The Economics of Public Private Partnerships* (Edward Elgar, 2005) and *Reforming China's state-owned enterprises and banks* (Edward Elgar, 2006). Professor Lewis is a foundation member of the Australian Research Council Islam Node Network.

Michael J.T. McMillen is a Partner with the law firm of Dechert LLP and works in the firm's New York, London and Philadelphia offices. He also teaches Islamic finance at the University of Pennsylvania Law School. His law practice focuses primarily on Islamic finance and international and domestic project finance, leasing and structured finance. He has been active in the Islamic finance field since 1996 and in the project finance field since 1985. Mr McMillen has developed numerous innovative Islamic finance structures and products, and he also works closely with the Islamic Financial Services Board and the International Swaps and Derivatives Association on a broad range of global Islamic finance initiatives. His project finance experience includes some of the largest and most innovative project financings in the world, primarily in the electricity, petrochemical, mining and infrastructure sectors. Mr McMillen received a Bachelor of Business Administration from the University of Wisconsin in 1972, his Juris Doctor from the University of Wisconsin School of Law in 1976, and his Doctor of Medicine from the Albert Einstein College of Medicine in 1983.

Abbas Mirakhor is the Executive Director for Afghanistan, Algeria, Ghana, Islamic Republic of Iran, Morocco, Pakistan and Tunisia at the International Monetary Fund,

Washington, DC. Born in Tehran, Islamic Republic of Iran, Dr Mirakhor attended Kansas State University where he received his PhD in economics in 1969. He has authored a large number of articles, books, publications and conference proceedings, and is the co-editor of *Essays on Iqtisad: Islamic Approach to Economic Problems* (1989), and *Theoretical Studies in Islamic Banking and Finance* (1987). Dr Mirakhor has received several awards, including the Islamic Development Bank Annual Prize for Research in Islamic Economics, shared with Mohsin Khan in 2003.

Volker Nienhaus is President of the University of Marburg, Germany, and Honorary Professor of the University of Bochum, and a member of academic advisory committees of the German Orient-Foundation, the Federal Ministry of Economic Cooperation and Development and the Federal Agency for Civic Education. Previously he held Chairs in economics at the German universities of Trier and Bochum. He has had a longstanding interest in Islamic economics and finance. Other areas of interest are service sector economics, economic systems, transformation economics and international economics.

Mohammed Obaidullah is Associate Professor at the Islamic Economics Research Center, King Abdulaziz University, Jeddah, Saudi Arabia. Previously he worked at the International Islamic University Malaysia and the Xavier Institute of Management, India. Dr Obaidullah is the Editor of the *International Journal of Islamic Financial Services* and *IBF Review*. He is the Founder Director of IBF Net: The Islamic Business and Finance Network, and is Secretary-General of the International Association of Islamic Economics (IAIE). Dr Obaidullah is the author of *Indian Stock Markets: Theories and Evidence* (Institute of Chartered Financial Analysts of India, Hyderabad) and has published in a wide range of refereed journals. His areas of interest include Islamic finance, security markets and development finance.

Ridha Saadallah is Professor of Economics at the University of Sfax in Tunisia. Previously he worked with the Islamic Research and Training Institute of the Islamic Development Bank, Jeddah for a number of years before moving to academia. Dr Saadallah has published widely in Islamic economics, banking and finance. His research monograph *Financing Trade in an Islamic Economy* was published by the Islamic Research Training Institute in 1999.

Yusuf M. Sidani is a member of the faculty at the Suliman S. Olayan School of Business at the American University of Beirut. His earlier appointments include the Lebanese University (School of Economic Sciences and Business Administration), and the University of Armenia. Dr Sidani has over 30 contributions to academic and professional journals, academic and professional conferences and book chapters, and has been involved in managerial and financial education, training and consulting for companies and individuals in the private and the public sectors in various areas of the Middle East. He is an active member of the Lebanese Accounting and Auditing Corporate Governance Taskforce and the Lebanese Association of Certified Public Accountants.

Michael Skully is Professor of Banking at Monash University, Victoria, Australia. Prior to becoming an academic, he worked in the investment banking industry and in corporate finance with General Electric. Professor Skully is a fellow of CPA Australia and the Australasian Institute of Banking and Finance, an associate of the Securities Institute of Australia, a director and vice president of the Asia Pacific Finance Association and a member of the Victorian government's Finance Industry Consultative Committee. He has published widely in the areas of financial institutions and corporate finance and his books include *Merchant Banking in Australia*, co-author of *Management of Financial Institutions*, and general editor of the *Handbook of Australian Corporate Finance*. Professor Skully has a longstanding research interest in Islamic banking and is a foundation member of Australia's Islam Node Network of academic researchers.

Seif El-Din Tag El-Din is Associate Professor at the Markfield Institute of Higher Education, UK. He is editor of the *Review of Islamic Economics*, and a member of the Advisory Board, *Journal of Islamic Studies*. Previously he worked for the Tadamum Islamic Bank, Khartoum, as lecturer at Khartoum University, Centre of Research in Islamic Economics, and lecturer at King Abdul Azziz University, Jeddah, Ministry of Planning, Riyadh, Al-Barakah Development and Investment Company and the National Management Consultancy Centre, Jeddah. Dr Tag El-Din has a BSc (Hons), Khartoum University, an MSc, Glasgow University and PhD, Edinburgh University. Dr Tag El-Din has published many research papers in refereed journals on Islamic economics and finance.

Rodney Wilson is Professor of Economics and Director of Postgraduate Studies, School of Government and International Affairs, the University of Durham. He currently chairs the academic committee of the Institute of Islamic Banking and Insurance in London and has acted as Director for courses in Islamic finance for Euromoney Training in London and Singapore, the Financial Training Company of Singapore and the Institute of Banking Studies in Kuwait. Professor Wilson's recent academic publications include *The Politics of Islamic Finance* (edited with Clement Henry), Edinburgh University Press and Columbia University Press, 2004; and *Economic Development in Saudi Arabia* (Routledge/Curzon, 2004). His latest book, edited with Munawar Iqbal, is *Islamic Perspectives on Wealth Creation* (Edinburgh University Press, 2005).

Iqbal Zaidi is Senior Advisor to the Executive Director, International Monetary Fund. Dr Zaidi has worked for the IMF for over 25 years, including being Resident Representative in Ghana (1992–4) and Kyrgyzstan (1999–2001), and has participated in numerous IMF missions. He was an Advisor to the Governor of the State Bank of Pakistan (1995–7), in which capacity he served on the Open Market Operations Committee of the State Bank and was also a member of the High Level Task Force for Bank Restructuring set up by the Government of Pakistan. Dr Zaidi graduated *magna cum laude* with a BA Honours in Economics from Haverford College, and an MA and PhD in Economics from Princeton University. He has published widely in professional journals.

Imad J. Zbib is Chairman of the Management, Marketing and Entrepreneurship Track in the Olayan School of Business at the American University of Beirut, Lebanon. He obtained his MSc in Managerial and Cost Accounting in 1986 and a PhD in Operations Management from the University of North Texas in 1991. Dr Zbib has authored and co-authored over 40 articles in refereed journals, books and conference proceedings. He is a frequent speaker and consultant on such issues as Strategic Executive Leadership, Strategic Management, Strategic Marketing, International Business and Supply Chain Management, and holds the position of Assistant Vice President for Regional External Programs at the American University of Beirut.

Glossary

This section explains some Arabic words and terms occurring in the volume.

Arbun is a non-refundable deposit to secure the right to cancel or proceed with a sale during a certain period of time.

Bai'al-dayn means the sale of debt or a liability at a discount or negotiated price.

Bai'al-inah is a contract that involves the sale and buy back of assets by a seller.

Bai bi-thamin ajil is deferred payment sale by instalments.

Bai'muajjal is deferred payment sale.

Bai'salam is pre-paid purchase.

Bay (bai) is a comprehensive term that applies to sale transactions, exchange.

Fiqh is Islamic jurisprudence, the science of religious law, which is the interpretation of the Sacred Law, *shari'a*.

Gharar is uncertainty, speculation.

Hadith (plural *ahadith*) is the technical term for the source related to the *sunna*, the sayings – and doings – of the Prophet, his traditions.

Halal means permitted according to *shari'a*.

Haram means forbidden according to *shari'a*.

Hiyal (plural of *hila*) are 'permissions' or legal manipulations, evasions.

Ijara contract is a leasing contract.

Ijara wa iqtina is a lease-purchase contract, whereby the client has the option of purchasing the item.

Ijma means consensus among jurists based on the Holy Qur'an and *sunna*, and one of the four sources of law in Sunni Islam.

Ijtihad means the act of independent reasoning by a qualified jurist in order to reach new legal rules.

Islam is submission or surrender to the will of God.

Istijrar refers to a sale in which an asset is supplied on a continuing basis at an agreed price payable at a future date.

Istisnaa is a contract to manufacture.

Ju'alah is the stipulated price (commission) for performing any service.

Kafala is a contract of guarantee or taking of responsibility for a liability provided by a guarantor, *kafeel*.

Maysir means gambling, from a pre-Islamic game of hazard.

Mudaraba contract is a trustee financing contract, where one party, the financier, entrusts funds to the other party, the entrepreneur, for undertaking an activity.

Mudarib means an entrepreneur or a manager of a *mudaraba* project.

Murabaha is resale with a stated profit; for example the bank purchases a certain asset and sells it to the client on the basis of a cost plus mark-up profit principle.

Musharaka contract is an equity participation contract, whereby two or more partners contribute with funds to carry out an investment.

Muslim is one who professes the faith of Islam or is born to a Muslim family.

Nisab is the minimum acceptable standard of living.

Qard hasan is a benevolent loan (interest-free).

Qiyas means analogical deduction.

Qur'an is the Holy Book, the revealed word of God, followed by all Muslims.

Rabb al-mal refers to the owner of capital or financier in a *mudaraba* partnership agreement (also *sahib al-mal*).

Riba is literally 'excess' or 'increase', and covers both interest and usury.

Shari'a is Islamic religious law derived from the Holy Qur'an and the *sunna*.

Shirkah (or *sharika*) is a society or partnership.

Sukuk is a freely tradeable Islamic participation certificate based on the ownership and exchange of an approved asset.

Sunna is a source of information concerning the practices of the Prophet Muhammad and his Companions, and is the second most authoritative source of Islamic law.

Sura (pl. *surat*) is a chapter of the Holy Qur'an. There are 114 *suras* of varying length and in all references to the Holy Qur'an (for example 30:39) the first number refers to the *sura* and the second to the *aya* or verse.

Tabarru means charity or donation. In *takaful*, it is a voluntary pooled fund for the benefit of all members.

Takaful refers to mutual support which is the basis of the concept of insurance or solidarity among Muslims.

Ulama are the learned class, especially those learned in religious matters.

Umma means the community; the body of Muslims.

Wadia means safe custody or deposit.

Wakala involves a contract of agency on a fee-for-services basis with an agent, *wakil*.

Waqf is a trust or pious foundation.

Zakat is a religious levy or almsgiving as required in the Holy Qur'an and is one of the five pillars of Islam.

1 Islamic banking: an introduction and overview
M. Kabir Hassan and Mervyn K. Lewis

Introduction

From a situation nearly 30 years ago when it was virtually unknown, Islamic banking has expanded to become a distinctive and fast growing segment of the international banking and capital markets. There are well over 200 Islamic banks operating in over 70 countries comprising most of the Muslim world and many Western countries. Not included in these figures are the 50 Islamic insurance (*takaful*) companies operating in 22 countries, Islamic investment houses, mutual funds, leasing companies and commodity trading companies. Also excluded are the very largest Islamic banks engaged at a multilateral level. To these numbers must be added the many hundreds of small Islamic financial institutions such as rural and urban cooperative credit societies, Islamic welfare societies and financial associations operating at a local level and dealing with rural entities, small business firms and individual households.

Many people are interested in the phenomenon of Islamic banking and in the question of how it differs from conventional banking, yet, despite the expansion over the last 30 years, Islamic banking remains poorly understood in many parts of the Muslim world and continues to be a mystery in much of the West. Our aim in this volume is to provide a succinct analysis of the workings of Islamic banking and finance, accessible to a wide range of readers.

There is now a considerable amount of research on the topic and, in what can be considered as a companion to this volume, we have collected together some of the most significant previously published articles on the subject covering the last four decades (Hassan and Lewis, 2007). Inevitably, however, there were large gaps in the coverage of topics (notably in the treatment of operational efficiency, marketing, project finance, risk management, mutual funds, the stock market, government financing, multilateral institutions and financial centres) and a narrow number of themes were pursued in these journal articles written, in most cases, for specialist researchers in the field.

This volume seeks to bring the research agenda and the main issues on Islamic banking before a wider audience. For this reason we invited leading scholars to write chapters on various aspects of Islamic banking and report on the current state of play, and the debates, involved. The essays aim to provide a clearly accessible source of reference material on current practice and research.

Before introducing the individual contributions, a word of explanation is needed about the title. When the subject matter first began to be written about, it was usual to use the terms 'Islamic banks' and 'Islamic banking'. Nowadays, it has become more commonplace to talk of Islamic finance and Islamic financial institutions, reflecting in part the shift – evident in Western markets as well as Islamic ones – away from what used to be banking activities to financing activities more generally, previously carried out by investment companies and assorted non-banking intermediaries. Nevertheless, so long as this wider agenda is recognized, we prefer the simplicity of the original terms.

Foundations of Islamic banking

An Islamic banking and financial system exists to provide a variety of religiously accept-able financial services to the Muslim communities. In addition to this special function, the banking and financial institutions, like all other aspects of Islamic society, are expected to 'contribute richly to the achievement of the major socio-economic goals of Islam' (Chapra, 1985, p. 34). The most important of these are economic well-being with full employment and a high rate of economic growth, socioeconomic justice and an equitable distribution of income and wealth, stability in the value of money, and the mobilization and investment of savings for economic development in such a way that a just (profit-sharing) return is ensured to all parties involved. Perhaps the religious dimension should be presented as a further explicit goal, in the sense that the opportunity to conduct reli-giously legitimate financial operations has a value far beyond that of the mode of the financial operation itself.

In Chapter 2, Masudul Choudhury notes that Islamic banks have mushroomed under an Islamization agenda, but the system has not developed a comprehensive vision of an interest-free system, nor has it mobilized financial resources for enhancing social wellbe-ing by promoting economic development along Islamic lines. These omissions, he argues, are shared more generally by Islamic economic thinking and social thought which has produced no truly Qur'anic worldview and has failed to understand the dynamics of Islamic transformation within an equitable and participatory framework. Choudhury comes to this conclusion after reviewing the social theory developed from the early years of Islam to the present day. In advocating the rediscovery of a worldview founded on the doctrine of *Tawhid* (the oneness of God) as enunciated by the Holy Qur'an and *sunna*, Choudhury envisages a social wellbeing function for Islamic banks in terms of social security, protection of individual rights and resource mobilization in keeping with the Islamic faith.

Financial systems based in Islamic tenets are dedicated to the elimination of the payment and receipt of interest in all forms. It is this taboo that makes Islamic banks and other financial institutions different in principle from their Western counterparts. The fundamental sources of Islam are the Holy Qur'an and the *sunna*, a term which in Ancient Arabia meant 'ancestral precedent' or the 'custom of the tribe', but which is now syn-onymous with the teachings and traditions of the Prophet Muhammad as transmitted by the relators of authentic tradition. Both of these sources treat interest as an act of exploitation and injustice and as such it is inconsistent with Islamic notions of fairness and property rights. Islamic banking thus derives its specific *raison d'être* from the fact that there is no place for the institution of interest in the Islamic order.

Some scholars have put forward economic reasons to explain why interest is banned in Islam. Anwar Iqbal Qureshi ([1946] 1991) believes that it is not necessary to offer intel-lectual arguments in favour of the Qur'anic injunction against *riba*. The real question, however, is not about *riba* but about the definition of *riba*. Latifa Algaoud and Mervyn Lewis in Chapter 3 examine the nature of *riba,* distinguishing between *riba* that relates to loans and *riba* that involves trade, before going on to consider the divergent positions taken by traditionalists and modernists on the definition of *riba.* They also point out that the Islamic critique is based on more than the prohibition on interest, even if we over-look the broader social charter recommended by Choudhury and others. There is also the prohibition in Islam of *maysir* (gambling, speculation) and *gharar* (unreasonable uncertainty), the need to ensure that investment be undertaken on the basis of *halal* (permitted) activities, and the requirement to benefit society through the collection of *zakat* (almsgiving) overseen by a special religious supervisory board.

This rejection of interest by Islam poses the question of what replaces the interest rate mechanism in an Islamic framework. If the paying and receiving of interest is prohibited, how do Islamic banks operate? Here PLS comes in, substituting profit-and-loss-sharing for interest as a method of resource allocation. Although a large number of different contracts feature in Islamic financing, certain types of transaction are central: trustee finance (*mudaraba*), equity participation (*musharaka*) and 'mark-up' methods. Some of these profit-sharing arrangements such as *mudaraba* and *musharaka* almost certainly pre-date the genesis of Islam. Business partnerships based on what was in essence the *mudaraba* concept coexisted in the pre-Islamic Middle East along with interest loans as a means of financing economic activities (Crone, 1987; Kazarian, 1991; Cizaka, 1995). Following the birth of Islam, interest-based financial transactions were forbidden and all finance had to be conducted on a profit-sharing basis. The business partnership technique, utilizing the *mudaraba* principle, was employed by the Prophet Muhammad himself when acting as agent (*mudarib*) for his wife Khadija, while his second successor Umar ibn al-Khattab invested the money of orphans with merchants engaged in trade between Medina and Iraq. Simple profit-sharing business partnerships of this type continued in virtually unchanged form over the centuries, but they did not develop into vehicles for large-scale investment involving the collection of large amounts of funds from large numbers of individual savers. This development did not happen until the growth of Islamic financial institutions.

This leads us to Chapter 4, by Abbas Mirakhor and Iqbal Zaidi which provides an account of both the traditional financial instruments, *mudaraba, musharaka* and mark-up (*murabaha, ijara, salam, bai bi-thamin ajil, istisnaa*), along with the newly developed *sukuks.* Mirakhor and Zaidi explain in detail the features that make these instruments acceptable from an Islamic viewpoint, and the implications which follow from an agency theory perspective for the contractual relationships involved. They then consider some practical issues involved in the development of Islamic structured finance in the form of asset-backed securities, covered bonds, *sukuks* and collateralized securitization. Finally, the authors review the future of the profit-and-loss sharing principle in the light of these innovative financing arrangements.

Following on from these analyses of the economic and social principles underlying Islamic financing, the nature of the Islamic critique of conventional financial systems, and the present-day Islamic alternative, the last chapter in this section brings a different perspective to the issues, for Islam is not the only (or indeed the first) religion to prohibit usury (interest). In Ancient India, laws based on the Veda, the oldest scriptures of Hinduism, condemned usury as a major sin and restricted the operation of interest rates (Gopal, 1935; Rangaswami, 1927). In Judaism, the Torah (the Hebrew name of the Law of Moses or the Pentateuch, the first five books of the Old Testament) prohibited usury amongst the Jews, while at least one authority sees in the Talmud (the Oral Law which supplements the Written Scriptures for orthodox Jews) a consistent bias against 'the appearance of usury or profit' (Neusner, 1990). Under Christianity, prohibitions or severe restrictions upon usury operated for over 1400 years, but gradually the Christian Church bowed to the pressures of reformist theologians and the needs of commerce and came to see only exorbitant interest as usurious.

The Islamic ban on usury rests on the unparalleled authority of the Holy Qur'an in which the prohibition is frequently and clearly enunciated. What was the authority for the Christian opposition to usury? What rationale was provided by the clerical authorities? How do these compare with those of Islamic jurists? How was the Christian ban enforced? Was it honoured more in the breach than in the practice? What devices were used to avoid the ban? Why did the Christian Church shift its stand on the nature of usury? These are the questions examined in Chapter 5 by Mervyn Lewis. The answers provided to these questions shed new light on the achievements of Islamic banking methods, while at the same time revealing a number of interesting parallels with present-day Islamic financing techniques. The author argues that Islam has succeeded in sustaining its prohibition on interest, where Christianity relented, because of the efforts made by Islamic bankers and jurists to fashion instruments that conform to *shari'a* principles. Nevertheless, a question mark still exists, because there are many within the Islamic community and outside who consider that some of the techniques (such as mark-up and *sukuks*) are more successful in meeting the letter of the law, rather than the spirit, of the Qur'anic injunctions on *riba*. Chapters by Chapra and Nienhaus take up this point, and we return to it at the end of this chapter.

Operations of Islamic banks
This section of the volume examines a number of aspects of the workings of Islamic banks. In Chapter 6, Humayon Dar considers incentive compatibility problems. First, he examines the traditional contracts offered by Islamic banks which are divided into fixed return (*murabaha, ijira, salam, istisnaa* and so on) and variable return methods (*mudaraba* and *musharaka*). Incentive compatibility relates to the in-built inducements that exist for the transacting parties to honour the terms of the contract. This is an area in which there are conflicting views (Khan, 1985, 1987; Ahmed, 1989; Presley and Sessions, 1994). Dar argues that the benefits of improved productivity from the variable-return modes of financing are likely to be outweighed by the moral hazard and adverse selection problems vis-à-vis the fixed-return contracts, perhaps explaining the dominance of the latter in bank portfolios. However, while incentive compatibility is relevant for all forms of financing, it is particularly so for modern markets based on derivatives such as options, futures and forward contracts that exceed, on some measures, the markets in the underlying assets (Stulz, 2004). In the remainder of his chapter, Dar focuses on the incentive structures of the Islamic methods of financial engineering based on *arbun, bai' salam* and *istijrar*.

Dar observes that the relative dearness of Islamic financial products has proved to be a disincentive to their use in comparison with the less expensive conventional banking products. To some extent this difference may be a result of the incentive compatibility problems, necessitating larger outlays on monitoring costs. However, it is also inseparable from the question of the operational efficiency of Islamic banks, examined in Chapter 7 by Kym Brown, M. Kabir Hassan and Michael Skully. What exactly is operational efficiency and how is it measured? This is the first issue to be addressed but it does not beg an easy answer. There is no single measure of operating performance or of efficiency, and the small number of Islamic banks in each country means other benchmarks are needed. A number of approaches have been followed in the literature, and it is difficult to ascertain to what extent different research findings reflect differences in research methodology and data. Nevertheless, where a direct comparison is possible, it would seem that Islamic banks compare favourably in terms of profitability measures vis-à-vis conventional banks, despite the fact that their social charter may lead them into areas (such as *qard hasan* loans) and responsibilities (such as *zakat*) that conflict with profit maximization. In terms of efficiency, there would seem to be some potential to cut operating costs and exploit scale economics. A feature of the chapter is the extensive data provided of the structure of Islamic bank activities.

Islamic financial products need to be more than offered to customers, they need to be actively marketed. For those Islamic banks operating in fully Islamicized financial systems this may not be needed. For those in mixed financial systems it is certainly the case. When these banks were initially established, they relied heavily on their religious appeal to gain deposits. This emphasis has continued. To give one example, Saeed (1995) reports that the Faisal Islamic Bank of Egypt (FIBE) is actively involved in attracting Muslims, particularly those who believe in the unlawfulness of interest, to its deposit mobilization schemes. To attract such customers in an increasingly competitive financial environment, FIBE utilizes several means:

- Encouraging leading *'ulama* (religious scholars) to propagate the prohibition of interest.
- Emphasizing its Islamic credentials by means of the collection and distribution of *zakat*.
- Convening seminars and conferences to propagate the merits of Islamic banking.
- Offering modern banking facilities such as automatic teller machines and fast banking services by means of installing the latest computer technology in banking operations.
- Giving depositors a return comparable to that given to the depositors of traditional banks.

While all of these factors are relevant, the last two are critical. The Islamic financial market is no longer in its infancy, and an Islamic bank cannot take its clients for granted. There are many institutions, including Western banks, competing with the original Islamic banks by means of Islamic 'windows', and the general lesson in financial, as in other, markets is that profit spreads and profit margins fall as new financial institutions enter the market. In this competitive milieu, a clearly targeted marketing strategy is important. Few banks can be all things to all people. Islamic banks must use market research to identify their market segments and reach them with innovative products. This is the message of Chapter 8, on the marketing of Islamic financial services by Elfakhani, Zbib and Ahmed.

Corporate governance is an important issue for all corporations, but especially so for an Islamic bank. This is the topic of Chapter 9, by Volker Nienhaus. Normally, corporate governance is seen as revolving around the conflict of interest between shareholders and management. When corporate governance is discussed in the context of banking, depositors are usually brought into the picture because of the fact that banks are so highly geared and it is they (depositors) who can suffer, along with shareholders, when a bank fails. With an Islamic bank there is an extra dimension arising from its religious charter, and an additional layer of governance stemming from the role of the *Shar'ia* Supervisory Board (SSB) that monitors its adherence to Islamic principles.

Nienhaus makes the very interesting observation that the behaviour of most SSBs has altered markedly over the years. When the system of *shari'a* supervision was first established in the formative period of Islamic banking, the *shari'a* scholars were thought to be overcautious, and perhaps even obstructive, by the bankers. Nowadays, they have allowed, as permissible, instruments that would perhaps have been seen earlier as *hiyal*, legal fictions, obeying only the letter of the law. The development of the *sukuk* is an example that comes readily to mind. Nienhaus wonders why the change from overly-conservative to permissive has taken place. He advances reasons that essentially parallel the 'capture' theory of regulation (Stigler, 1971). If the members of the SSB wish to be reappointed and continue their SSB membership, it is in their interest to foster good relations with the management of the Islamic bank, and give the managers the benefit of the doubt when approving new product innovations, blurring the distinctiveness (and ideological purity) of the Islamic banking system. To this end, Nienhaus recommends the establishment of a National *Shari'a* Board for each country that would be independent of management.

It is now recognized that risk management is an indispensable part of good corporate governance, and most major corporations today will have a Board committee to oversee internal risk management systems. For a bank, this function is vital, for the management of risks lies at the heart of banking activities. Risk management is the topic of Chapter 10, by Habib Ahmed and Tariqullah Khan, who approach the issue properly in an orderly and systematic manner. The authors first examine the special risk characteristics of Islamic banking operations, identifying the unique credit risks, market risks, liquidity risks, fiduciary and other risks faced by Islamic bankers. They then consider the risk mitigation and risk transfer options open to Islamic banks. Conventional banks make much use of derivatives for these purposes, but many of these instruments need extensive modification or re-engineering to be suitable for Islamic financial institutions. Finally, the authors provide an analysis of capital adequacy requirements, and expected loss recognition for the Islamic institutions.

Instruments and markets

So far, in the chapters reviewed, the volume has examined the religious underpinnings of Islamic finance and the general operations of Islamic banks. The focus in this part of the book is a range of specialist applications of the general principles and practices.

Management of liquidity has traditionally been a problem area for Islamic financial institutions. Conventional banks use a variety of methods to manage liquidity. Like any enterprise, banks use asset and liability management techniques to manage cash flows on both sides of the balance sheet, revolving around the repricing and duration of assets and liabilities (Lewis, 1992a, provides an overview of the measures employed). However, it is inevitable that imbalances will arise, and banks make extensive use of two markets in these circumstances. One is the secondary market for debt instruments where bills and bonds can be readily bought and sold. The other is the inter-bank market where banks lend and borrow at interest on an overnight or longer-term basis. Together these venues constitute what is known as the 'call money market' (Lewis, 1992b).

For many years Islamic banks were hampered in liquidity management by the absence of an equivalent infrastructure. Islamic law has restrictions on the sale of debt that inhibit *shari'a* acceptable secondary markets, while the institutional framework for a money market was undeveloped. That situation has changed markedly over the last decade, as is made apparent in Chapter 11, by Sam Hakim, who reviews the range of Islamic money market instruments. One major development comes from the engineering, and rapid expansion, of Islamic tradeable securities, especially *sukuk*. Another has come from the establishment of an Islamic inter-bank money market in Malaysia in 1994 and the number of instruments that have developed in its wake. There is also an important international dimension to these initiatives which is discussed in Chapter 23.

Muslims are instructed by the Holy Qur'an to shun *riba*. At the same time, however, they are encouraged by the Holy Qur'an to pursue trade. However, trade invariably creates the need for trade financing. This occurs when the buyer of goods wishes to defer the payment of the goods acquired to a future date or wishes to pay for the goods by instalment over a number of future periods. Financing of trade is thus a major component of Islamic banking but, in order to adhere to the prohibition on *riba,* this financing cannot be done by the extension of credit at interest, and other Islamically acceptable financing techniques must be developed. These are very extensive indeed and are examined in detail in Chapter 12 by Ridha Saadallah. He outlines first the transition of the *murabaha* concept into an Islamic financial or credit instrument, before considering longer-term trade financing instruments employed by the banks, including the participatory instruments and the securities based on them. This leads us to the next chapter.

Chapter 13 is devoted to the securitization of Islamic financial instruments. The author, Mohammed Obaidullah, points out that securitization has a relatively short history in the West but has grown spectacularly in the last five years. The chapter begins with an outline of the basic structure of structured financing, as it is now commonly called (Fender and Mitchell, 2005), which is then followed by an explanation of what is wrong with conventional securitization from an Islamic point of view. From this base, Obaidullah goes on to analyse the Islamic alternatives in theory and in practice. There are controversial *fiqh* issues in terms of both the form (pay-through, pass-through or asset-backed) and the underlying assets (trade receivables, leasing) that need to be resolved if the market is to expand along Western lines. At this juncture, the *sukuk-al-ijara* offers the most acceptable basis for a strong secondary market to evolve.

Project finance is also a form of structured finance, since it involves structuring the financing, typically via a special purpose vehicle, to suit the cash flows of an underlying asset, invariably an infrastructure project. If Muslim countries follow trends elsewhere, this area seems likely to be of considerable importance in the future. For most of the post-war period, government has been the principal provider of infrastructure (at least outside the United States). Over the last decade, that position has begun to change. Faced with pressure to reduce public sector debt and, at the same time, expand and improve public facilities, governments have looked to private sector finance, and have invited private sector entities to enter into long-term contractual agreements which may take the form of construction or management of public sector infrastructure facilities by the private sector entity, or the provision of services (using infrastructure facilities) by the private sector entity to the community on behalf of a public sector body (Grimsey and Lewis, 2004).

The budgetary pressures which have forced the pace in the West seem particularly strong for countries such as Pakistan, seeking greater Islamization of the financial system and looking for replacements to cover the removal of *riba*-based government borrowing. From the viewpoint of the private sector bodies, public–private sector financing arrangements are essentially project financing, characterized by the low capitalization of the project vehicle company and consequently a reliance on direct revenues to pay for operating costs and cover financing while giving the desired return on risk capital. The senior financier of private finance looks to the cash flow and earnings of the project as the source of funds for repayments. The key principle for such projects is to achieve a financial structure with as little recourse as possible to the sponsors, while at the same time providing sufficient support so that the financiers are satisfied with the risks. Successful project design requires expert analysis of all of the attendant risks and then the design of contractual arrangements prior to competitive tendering that allocate risk burdens appropriately, and meet the financing needs.

In the case of Islamic project financing there is an additional test that is needed, for the financing must be *shari'a*-compliant, and this is the topic of Chapter 14, by Michael McMillen, which gives a detailed account of the techniques and structures involved in this very complex area of Islamic financing. From the Islamic viewpoint a number of structure forms are possible, based on *istisnaa, ijara, mudaraba, murabaha* and *sukuk* financing vehicles. Thus there are a number of different ways in which the revenue stream from an Islamically acceptable project can support project financing contracts which accord with the *shari'a*. Such instruments would enable the large sums that are currently held mainly in short-term Islamic investments to be harnessed for investment in long-term infrastructure projects. Not only would this mobilization be valuable in resolving the problems of public sector financing in Islamic countries, it is entirely consistent with Islamic precepts. By providing basic social goods such as power, water, transport and communications services, infrastructure projects fit comfortably with the social responsibility ethos that is an essential feature of Islamic finance. In addition, limited recourse or non-recourse project financing structures are a form of asset-based financing that seem entirely consistent with Islamic law. When the complex financial structures that constitute these arrangements are stripped away, what is apparent is that project investors are sharing in the asset and cash flow risks of projects in ways that financiers are required to do under Islamic law.

The final two chapters of Part III deal with different aspects of stock market investment. The stock market poses particular problems from an Islamic point of view. The basic difficulty is the absence in Islamic law of the concept of a corporation, although Muslim jurists now agree on the permissibility of trading common stocks, which are similar to the shares in a *mudaraba*, so long as other requirements of Islamic law are not contravened. One such constraint posed by Islamic law concerns the principles of investment. In terms of the spirit of Islam, all Muslim shareholders are expected to take a personal interest in the management of each one of the companies in which their funds are invested. They cannot be disinterested investors. The *shari'a* emphasizes the importance of knowing the nature of the item to be bought. To many Muslims, the anonymity of a Western stock exchange offends Islamic notions of the responsible use of wealth. The assumption that investors may not be concerned about the detailed operations of a business in which they have invested money is a source of criticism. Muslim stockholders have a responsibility to acquaint themselves with what is taking place in the organization.

Another constraint is imposed on stock market investment because of the strong prohibitions on speculation in Islamically acceptable forms of financing. The question, however, is what is speculation in the context of the stock market? This is one issue considered by Seif El-Din Tag El-Din and M. Kabir Hassan in Chapter 15. The authors begin with the standard classification of transactors in the market as hedgers, arbitrateguers and speculators. Obviously the first two categories pose no problems from a juristic position. In the case of speculators, the issue is whether the activities of speculators constitute gambling and involve undue *gharar* (excessive uncertainty). There is little doubt that if a liquid investment market is desired, it will be necessary to accommodate speculative activity in some form, where such activity is based on differences in opinion and beliefs. Accordingly, Tag El-Din and Hassan seek to develop a definition of excessive speculation within the context of what is called a Normative Islamic Stock Exchange (purely equity-based, free of interest and guarded against *gharar*). This then leads to a comparison of Islamic views on money making with those of the Aristotelian tradition. Shifting then to the empirical evidence, the authors look at the available evidence of speculation and market efficiency in the context of the behaviour of various Islamic stock market indices.

Chapter 16, by Said Elfakhani, M. Kabir Hassan and Yusuf Sidani, focuses upon Islamic mutual funds. Islamic banks have long offered special investment accounts under an individual restricted *mudaraba* basis for high net worth individuals investing, say, $500 000 or more, as well as the unrestricted *mudaraba* for ordinary depositors. It was a short step to combine elements of these two investment modes in the form of closed-ended or open-ended unit trusts or, in the American terminology, investment companies and mutual funds. These investment vehicles can be classified according to the types of investments made by the pooled funds. These can be divided into three groups:

1. *Islamic transactions*. A number of long-established funds have concentrated on a variety of Islamic portfolios. Thus, for example, the Al-Tawfeek Company for the Investment of Funds and the Al-Amin Company for Securities and Investment Funds, both part of the Al-Baraka group, were established in Bahrain in 1987. Both issue shares which participate in profits and can be bought and sold. Investments are made in a number of countries such as Morocco, Mauritania, Algeria, Turkey and Saudi Arabia, and comprise instruments such as lease contracts, *murabahas* and Islamic deposits.
2. *Specialized funds*. A number of funds specialize in particular activities such as leasing whereby the Trust finances equipment, a building or an entire project for a third party against an agreed rental. For example, in June 1998, the Kuwait Finance House launched a leasing fund in the United States, to invest in industrial equipment and machinery. There are also specialized real estate and commodity funds.
3. *Equity funds*. These are simply trusts, both closed and open-ended, which invest funds in stocks and shares. Those funds investing in international equities cover the world's major stock markets.

It is the latter type of fund which is the topic of Elfakhani, Hassan and Sidani's chapter. In considering equity funds, the principal question from the Islamic point of view is whether investments in international equity markets are acceptable under the *shari'a*. There is no doubt that dealing in the supply, manufacture or service of things prohibited by Islam (*haram*), such as *riba*, pork meat, alcohol, gambling and so on cannot be acceptable. But companies which are not involved in the above *haram* activities could be considered acceptable. The main objection against them is that in their own internal accounting and financial dealings they lend and borrow from *riba* banks and other institutions, but the fact remains that their main business operations do not involve prohibited activities.

In order for the returns from such companies to quality for inclusion in the mutual fund, quoted companies are classified according to a number of screens. After removing companies with unacceptable core business activities, the remaining lists are tested by a financial-ratio 'filter', the purpose of which is to remove companies with an unacceptable debt ratio. Those left in the fund must then be assessed according to 'tainted dividends' and 'cleansed'. Here 'tainted dividend' receipts relate to the portion, if any, of a dividend paid by a constituent company that has been determined to be attributable to activities that are not in accordance with *shari'a* principles and therefore should be donated to a proper charity or charities. However, such 'cleansing' cannot be counted as part of *zakat* obligations, but merely as a way of ensuring that investments are ethically sound.

There are obvious parallels in this selection process with the Western ethical investment movement. A number of investment advisers have been providing investment advice for over three decades to clients who want to invest in ethical funds, that is, those which do not invest in the shares of companies trading in tobacco, alcohol, gambling or the arms trade. The main difference is that the determination of whether an investment is ethical or unethical is made by the fund managers, based on information received from various professional bodies and other specially constituted committees of reference. In the case of Islamic funds, the ultimate approval comes from the Boards of Religious Advisers, and their rulings are binding on the fund managers.

After reviewing these procedures, Elfakhani, Hassan and Sidani examine the performance of the Islamic mutual funds. In the case of the Western ethical funds it would seem that ethics 'pay', although this may be largely because these funds have excluded tobacco companies, which have been hit by large compensation payouts. For the Islamic funds the results would seem to be more mixed. The authors conclude, overall, that the behaviour of Islamic mutual funds does not greatly differ from that of other conventional funds, with some *shari'a*-compliant mutual funds outperforming their relevant benchmarks and others underperforming them. However, it would seem that the Islamic mutual funds performed more strongly than their conventional equivalents during the recessionary period of the stock market, potentially opening up some possibilities for diversification across Islamic and conventional equity portfolios as a hedging strategy for downswing phases of the market.

Islamic systems
The chapters in this part of the book look at some system-wide regulatory and accounting issues facing Islamic banks. The first two chapters examine, in their different ways, the economic development 'charter' of Islamic banks.

Chapter 17, by Monzer Kahf, considers Islamic banking and economic development. He begins with a strong defence and restatement of the guiding precepts of Islamic financing which he argues is basically very simple, since the banks rely on a combination of three principles (sharing, leasing and sale) and funds are channelled to entrepreneurs through sale, sharing and lease contracts. Three features of this process are conducive to development. First, there are direct links to the real economy through the profit participation, the sale and purchase of commodities and the acquisition and leasing of assets. Second, ethical and moral values are integrated with the financing so that gambling and other illicit activities do not get funded, while resources are devoted to charity and welfare needs. Third, participatory financing replaces lending, leading to a relationship between the financier and entrepreneur based on profit-generating activities.

In conventional financial systems, government borrowing plays a central role in a number of respects. First, the interest rates on Treasury bills and bonds underpin the structure of short-term and long-term interest rates in the economy. They are typically the benchmark low-risk rates against which other securities are priced. Second, there are normally active secondary markets in government securities which impart liquidity to banks' asset portfolios. Third, bill and bond markets have traditionally been the venues through which monetary policy in the form of open market operations has been conducted (although, at the short end, the 'money market' in a broad sense, including private bills, commercial paper and especially the market for inter-bank borrowing and lending, has assumed more significance). Fourth, long-term government bonds play a leading role in financing infrastructure, despite the fact that private sector project financing and public–private financing arrangements are a growing trend (see Chapter 14 and the comments earlier in this chapter).

M. Fahim Khan, in Chapter 18, reviews the Islamic alternatives for government borrowing. This is another area in which product innovation has been extensive. Where once government borrowing in Islamically acceptable ways was seen as a major problem in attempts to move to a more complete Islamicization of financial systems in Muslim countries, this is no longer the case. There are now many instruments available. Moreover, they are able to offer in many cases fixed returns at very low risk, so meeting the requirement for Islamic benchmark rates. Some can be traded on secondary markets, meeting the second condition sought after. Third, they offer the potential for central bank operations. Fourth, because these instruments are based on assets valued as infrastructure, the final requirement is also met. We return to his analysis later in this chapter.

As we saw in Chapter 10, Islamic banks are required to meet capital adequacy regulations and other standards applied to conventional banks. Accounting standards are the subject of Chapter 19, by Simon Archer and Rifaat Karim. Accounting is an important issue for Muslims because certain Islamic ethical principles have a direct impact on accounting policy and principles. The Holy Qur'an and *sunna*, from which ethical principles are derived, have defined clearly what is true, fair and just, what are society's preferences and priorities, what are the corporate roles and responsibilities, and also, in some aspects, spell out specific accounting standards for accounting practices (Lewis, 2001).

In an Islamic society, the development of accounting theory should be based on the provisions of Islamic law along with other necessary principles and postulates which are not in conflict with Islamic law. Two approaches suggest themselves: first, establish objectives based on the spirit of Islam and its teaching and then consider these established objectives in relation to contemporary accounting thought; second, start with objectives established in contemporary accounting thought, test them against Islamic *shari'a*, accept those that are consistent with *shari'a* and reject those that are not.

Bodies such as the Accounting and Auditing Organisation for Islamic Financial Institutions (AAOIFI) (2000) have followed the second approach when formulating accounting, auditing and governance standards for Islamic financial institutions. Archer and Karim favour the first approach on the grounds that accounting rules can only give a faithful representation of transactions reported if they are accounted for in a way that gives the substance as well as the form of the *shari'a* contractual arrangements that govern the Islamic acceptability of the transactions. They examine a number of issues involved in developing such an agenda when there is a paucity of research on this topic.

In Chapter 20, Mahmoud El-Gamal argues that the appropriate regulatory model for Islamic banks turns on the conception of the role of depositors. Should they be regarded as receiving implicit capital guarantees like depositors in conventional banks by virtue of the relatively fixed-return, low-risk assets acquired by the banks under mark-up methods? Or are depositors to be regarded as shareholders because, as holders of investment accounts, they share in the profits earned by the banks, albeit in ways different from ordinary shareholders since the investment account 'shareholders' do not have a voting right? El-Gamal argues that this dilemma might have been avoided if Islamic banking had evolved within a different framework, and argues a strong case for the system to be based on the mutuality principle. Whether, at a practical level, this alternative paradigm would solve the regulatory treatment issue would remain to be seen. In particular, it might not avoid the Islamic institutions being put on a par with other institutions when regulations are applied. Certainly, mutual insurance companies are subject to the same solvency standards as proprietary companies. Also credit unions and other mutual ownership financial enterprises in countries like Australia are subject to much the same regulatory framework as the privately funded banks.

Regulation and the treatment of depositors are topics raised also by M. Umer Chapra in Chapter 21. Dr Chapra, one of the visionaries who forged the system of Islamic banking, reflects on the challenges facing the Islamic financial industry. Looking back at the original ideals that drove the system to be established, he notes a disconcerting gap between the dream and the reality because the Islamic financial system has not been able to escape from the straitjacket of conventional banking. Instead of using equity participation and profit-and-loss sharing modes of finance, along with appropriate monitoring systems, the bankers prefer to adopt different legal stratagems (*hiyal*) to transfer the entire financing and asset risk to lessees or those acquiring the assets, so violating the first principle of justice underpinning the system, namely that there be an equitable distribution of risks between the parties. Against this background he outlines a reform agenda to implement the original vision.

Globalization of Islamic banking
Islamic banking has always had a global orientation. Many investment accounts, especially in the Gulf, are denominated in US dollars. Because trade financing makes up so much of the asset portfolio of the Islamic banks, there is a natural vehicle available for the finance of international trade. There are many Islamic banks, business groups and investment houses controlled by the two large Islamic groups, DMI and Al-Baraka, that have a worldwide presence. Oil-related wealth provided the capital resources behind the establishment of many Islamic banks, and the Islamic Development Bank (IDB) based in Jeddah, and created in 1974, was the first institution to benefit from the inflow of oil money.

Its formation with the support of the Saudi Arabian government and the Organization of Islamic Countries (OIC) as a multilateral organization nevertheless gave momentum to the Islamic banking movement generally, being followed soon afterwards by both private institutions (for example, Dubai Islamic Bank, 1975, Faisal Islamic Bank of Egypt, 1977, Bahrain Islamic Bank, 1979) and government institutions (for example, Kuwait Finance House, 1977).

The IDB is the first of the international Islamic financial institutions examined by Munawar Iqbal in Chapter 22. It is primarily an intergovernmental bank aimed at providing funds for development projects in member countries. The IDB provides fee-based financial services and profit-sharing financial assistance to member countries. Operations are free of interest and are explicitly based on *shari'a* principles. From these beginnings, the IDB has grown to a large group, incorporating ICIEC providing insurance services and export credit, ICD providing corporate finance, structured finance and advisory services for private sector entities and projects in key priority areas with a developmental impact, and IRTI with a mandate for research and training. Other international financial institutions studied in the chapter are those involved with accounting standards, financial services, financial markets, credit rating, arbitration and promotion of the concept of Islamic banks and financial institutions.

One of the institutions covered in Chapter 22 is the International Islamic Financial Market, created in 2002 to facilitate international trading in Islamic financial instruments across a number of financial centres. Islamic financial centres are the topic of Chapter 23, by Ricardo Baba. The value of having an international centre for Islamic finance can be argued by analogy to the role of international financial centres in conventional banking operations. At any time, there are banks with 'surplus' deposits which can be on-lent to an international finance centre which could act as a funnel for the funds. For each individual bank participating in such a market, the funds provided might be on a short-term basis. But a series of such short-term funds by different banks when combined would exhibit greater stability and provide resources which could be channelled into longer-term investments. At the same time, the existence of this pool of resources would attract long-term investment vehicles, and so act as a magnet for investment avenues in need of funding. Thus at the aggregate level the existence of the market would enable a succession of short-term surpluses to be transformed into longer-term investments. This is exactly what happened with the London market and international syndicated credits and much the same sort of process could occur with Islamic finance, although, in this particular instance, the new instruments and financial innovations required need to be equity or equity-based and real asset-based and not debt instruments.

A number of factors seem relevant to the location of such an international centre: regulatory environment, range of markets, track record of innovation, availability of complementary services, presence of foreign institutions, time zone, language, political and economic stability, communications infrastructure, business tax regime, staffing and office costs and quality of life. In addition to these factors, an international Islamic financing centre raises further issues such as compliance with *shari'a* requirements and the ability of the location concerned to attract a sizable share both of Islamic investment money and of international financing activities which would qualify as being Islamically acceptable. Of course, there need not be only one centre. There is not one centre in conventional banking (witness London, New York, Frankfurt, Tokyo, Singapore, Hong Kong) and there seems no reason why there would not be several international centres for Islamic financing. Baba focuses on three. He sees Bahrain as the global Islamic finance centre, Malaysia (Kuala Lumpur, Labuan) as the regional centre for S.E. Asia, and London as the Western centre for Islamic financing activities. The different roles of these locations is considered in his chapter.

Islamic insurance (*takaful*) has developed hand-in-hand with the global expansion of Islamic banking because Islamic banks have been instrumental in the establishment of about one-half of the *takaful* companies and in promoting the concept. *Takaful* is examined in Chapter 24, by Mohd Ma'sum Billah. The nature of *takaful* business is not widely understood, in part because family *takaful* (life insurance) is so different from conventional life insurance business in the United States. However there are much closer parallels between family *takaful* and the unit-linked policies that operate in the UK and Australia (Lewis, 2005). (In the United States, such insurance policies are called 'variable life'.) There are some differences, especially in nomenclature where the minimum life cover of the unit-linked policy becomes a *tabarru* (donation) and the policy holders' special fund (unit trust or mutual fund) becomes a participation account.

Substitute these name changes and the basic structures are remarkably similar, with differences in payout and inheritance rules and investment methods in line with Islamic law. Another important difference is that *takaful* operates more like a mutual insurance operation with the *takaful* company handling investment, business and administration. There are also three different models governing the relationship between participants and the operator. These are *ta'awuni* (cooperative insurance), *wakala* (agency) and *tijari* (business/commercial) which operate in different Islamic countries. Billah examines these three different models. Although all three are in line with *shari'a* principles, these differences may be impeding the development of a globalized *takaful* market.

Finally, in Chapter 25, Rodney Wilson looks at Islamic banking in the West. There are over six million Muslims living in the United States, nearly two million in the UK and perhaps another ten million in the rest of Europe. A number of Islamic institutions have grown up to provide these communities with financial services in an Islamically acceptable way. Because of the relatively wealthy financial situation of some of these Muslims, and their aspirations to follow the lifestyle choices of many of their fellow citizens, housing finance has been a large part of the operations of these financial institutions. In order to conform to Islamic law, this finance has been provided in a number of *shari'a*-compliant modes such as *ijara* (leasing) and diminishing *musharaka* (participation finance). Islamic institutions also offer investment services, although many of these are aimed at international clients in the Gulf rather then local customers. The growth of this international orientation is one way in which London in particular has emerged as a centre for Islamic finance.

Concluding remarks
We conclude this introduction with some observations on product innovation. The success of Islamic banking, like any other system, rests on innovation and designing products that meet customer needs. Certainly, recent innovations in Islamic financing pass this particular test. Many innovative new products such as *sukuks* built around mark-up financing methods have allowed banks and their clients to engage in investment, hedging and trading activities that would have been unthinkable not so long ago. But do these instruments go too far? Unlike other financial arrangements, the Islamic system must meet another test, the religious test, and remain within the scope of Islamic law.

Consider, for example, the innovations that have taken place in the area of government financing. Fahim Khan in Chapter 18 is convinced that fixed interest rate government debt along conventional lines has to be replicated with fixed return, negligible risk, Islamic securities, based upon mark-up arrangements, if a successful secondary market is to develop that can rival those in conventional financial systems. He may well be correct in this judgment. But the question then becomes one of whether, in the process of achieving this objective, the 'baby is thrown out with the bathwater'.

Let us consider the reasons given for Islamic fixed-return contracts being regarded as acceptable, as explained by Khan in Chapter 18.

> The pricing mechanism of Islamic financial instruments, including those of government securities would, basically, be similar to that for conventional financial instruments. The time value of money in economic and financial transactions is recognized in Islam. The only difference is that the time value of money cannot be realized as a part of the loan contract. It can be realized only as an integral part of a real transaction. Thus, in a trade transaction, if the payment of price is deferred, then the time value of money will be included in the price of the commodity. Similarly, in a leasing contract, time value is an integral part of the rent that parties agree upon.

But is this really a trade transaction, or is it a loan in disguise masquerading as a commodity deal to conform to legal rules? Saadallah in Chapter 12 talks of a credit *murabaha*, which seems to be an accurate description of such a transaction since credit is an integral part of the transaction. Moreover, one is then led to ask how this 'bundling' of the time value of money and the commodity side really differs in substance from the bill of exchange route used by bankers in the Middle Ages to get round the Christian prohibition on usury. Consider the example given in Chapter 4:

> . . . a medieval bill of exchange transaction consisted of the sale for local currency of an obligation to pay a specified sum in another currency at a future date. It thus involved both an extension of credit and an exchange of currency. A modern-day bank would handle this transaction by converting the foreign into the local currency at the ruling spot rate of exchange, and then charging a rate of discount for the credit extended when paying out cash now for cash later. To do so in the Middle Ages would have been usurious, for discounting was not an allowable activity. Consequently, by not separating the two elements involved, the medieval banker bought the bill at a price which incorporated both an element of interest and a charge for his services as an exchange dealer . . .
> . . . the Medieval banker then had an open book which had to be closed by reversing the transaction and buying a bill in the foreign location, and receiving payment in his own currency. The fluctuation of exchange rates provided a convincing case of risk, since the terms at which the reverse deal could be undertaken would not be guaranteed at the time of the original transaction. It was this risk that reconciled bill dealing with the laws.

In what ways do the two examples differ? It would be a great pity for the reputation of the Islamic financial system if outsiders concluded that, if there is a difference, then it is that the medieval banker seemingly felt some guilt about the subterfuge (as indicated by the amount left to charity in their wills and testaments), whereas Islamic bankers today are absolved of such guilt because they have received approval from the *Shari'a* Supervisory Boards (SSBs) for their replication of fixed-rate returns. One is then led to ask the question: do these instruments such as *sukuks* obey the letter but not the spirit of the law? Is it any wonder that one of the 'founding fathers' of Islamic banking, Umer Chapra, describes these techniques in Chapter 21 as 'legal stratagems (*hiyal*) . . . in violation of the first condition of justice . . .'?

In Chapter 9 in this collection, Volker Nienhaus, who first contributed to the topic of Islamic banking over 20 years ago (Nienhaus, 1983), advanced reasons for the present day permissiveness of the SSBs that revolved around the 'capture' theory of regulation first advanced by George Stigler (1971). His observations prompt a number of questions. Is Nienhaus correct in surmising that many SSBs may have been 'captured' by the bankers? Has the Islamic ban on usury (*riba*) effectively been lost with the bankers' success? Has Islam, unlike Christianity, maintained the rhetoric on usury, while admitting the practice? Perhaps, after all, the modernist or revisionist views on *riba* outlined in Chapter 3 may have triumphed in the end, in this roundabout way, over the views of the traditionalists. Or can it be argued in defence of the SSBs that an important principle, namely that there be at least some risk in financial transactions, however small, to justify reward, has been maintained under Islam?

These are questions that we leave readers to ponder while working their way through the chapters that follow. When doing so, it may be worth keeping in mind that the Islamic financial system is still passing through the growing pains of developing into a legitimate and equitable financial method in world capital markets. In that sense the system is still engaged in the search for, and debates about, answers to questions such as those posed in previous paragraphs. Nevertheless, it is our belief that this process of product innovation and development, which necessarily involves a sequence of trial and error, will eventually lead to truly Islamic financial products that will enable the system to achieve its original intent of meeting the legitimate financial needs of those sharing Islamic ideals.

References

Accounting and Auditing Organisation for Islamic Financial Institutions (AAOIFI) (2000), *Accounting, Auditing and Governance Standards for Islamic Financial Institutions*, Bahrain: Accounting and Auditing Organisation for Islamic Financial Institutions
Ahmed, Shaghil (1989), 'Islamic banking and finance. A review essay', *Journal of Monetary Economics*, **24**, 157–67.
Chapra, M.U. (1985), *Towards a Just Monetary System*, Leicester: The Islamic Foundation.
Cizaka, M. (1995), 'Historical background', *Encyclopedia of Islamic Banking and Insurance,* London: Institute of Islamic Banking and Insurance, pp. 10–14.
Crone, P. (1987), *Meccan Trade and the Rise of Islam*, Oxford: Basil Blackwell.
Fender, I. and J. Mitchell (2005), 'Structured finance: complexity, risk and the use of ratings', *BIS Quarterly Review,* June, 67–79.
Gopal, M.H. (1935), *Mauryan Public Finance,* London: George Allen & Unwin.
Grimsey, D. and M.K. Lewis (2004), *Public Private Partnerships: the Worldwide Revolution in Infrastructure Provision and Project Finance*, Cheltenham, UK and Northampton, MA, USA: Edward Elgar.
Hassan, M.K. and M.K. Lewis (2007), *Islamic Finance*, Cheltenham, UK and Northampton, MA, USA: Edward Elgar (forthcoming).
Kazarian, E. (1991), 'Finance and economic development, Islamic banking in Egypt', Lund Economic Studies Number 45, Lund: University of Lund.
Khan, W.M. (1985), *Towards an Interest-Free Islamic Economic System*, Leicester: The Islamic Foundation.
Khan, W.M. (1987), 'Towards an interest-free economic system', in M.S. Khan and A. Mirakhor (eds), *Theoretical Studies in Islamic Banking and Finance*, Houston: Institute for Research and Islamic Studies.
Lewis, M.K. (1992a), 'Asset and liability management', in P. Newman, M. Milgate and J. Eatwell (eds), *New Palgrave Dictionary of Money and Finance*, vol.1, London: Macmillan, pp. 70–4.
Lewis (1992b), 'Call money market', in P. Newman, M. Milgate and J. Eatwell (eds), *New Palgrave Dictionary of Money and Finance,* vol.1, London: Macmillan, pp. 271–4.
Lewis, M.K. (2001), 'Islam and accounting', *Accounting Forum*, **25** (2), 103–27.
Lewis, M.K. (2005), 'Wealth creation through takaful (Islamic insurance), in M. Iqbal and R. Wilson (eds), *Islamic Perspectives on Wealth Creation*, Edinburgh: Edinburgh University Press, pp. 167–87.
Neusner, Jacob, trans. (1990), *The Talmud of Babylonia: An American Translation*, Atlanta: Scholar's Press.

Nienhaus, V. (1983), 'Profitability of Islamic banks competing with interest banks: problems and prospects', *Journal of Research in Islamic Economics*, **1**, 37–47.

Presley, J. and J. Sessions (1994), 'Islamic economics: the emergence of a new paradigm', *The Economic Journal*, **104**, 584–96.

Qureshi, Anwar Iqbal ([1946] 1991), *Islam and the Theory of Interest*, Lahore: Sh. Md. Ashraf.

Rangaswami, K. (1927), *Aspects of Ancient Indian Economic Thought*, Mylapore: Madras Law Journal Press.

Saeed, A. (1995), 'Islamic banking in practice: the case of Faisal Islamic Bank of Egypt', *Journal of Arabic, Islamic and Middle Eastern Studies*, **2** (1), 28–46.

Stigler, G.J. (1971), 'The theory of economic regulation', *Bell Journal of Economics and Management*, **2** (1), 1–21.

Stulz, R.M. (2004), 'Should we fear derivatives?', *Journal of Economic Perspectives*, **18** (3), 173–92.

PART I

FOUNDATIONS OF ISLAMIC FINANCING

2 Development of Islamic economic and social thought

Masudul Alam Choudhury

Introduction

Has there been a development in Islamic thought beyond a mere deepening subservience to neo-liberal economic and social doctrines, that those who enter a so-called project of Islamic economics, finance and social thinking borrow from their Western education lineage? Is there such a dichotomous and linear nature of thinking in Islam as exists between differentiated economic and social phenomena? Conversely, is there a substantive paradigm premised on Islamic epistemology that builds on the foundations of the Qur'an and the *sunna* that renders to the intellectual and practitioner world-system a worldview that is distinct, revolutionary and universal? What is the nature of such a foundational worldview that evaluates the contemporary Muslim mindset and compares it with the historical background of Muslim scholasticism? Instead, how does the worldview establish a revolutionary and distinctive world-system? These questions will be investigated in this chapter in an uncompromising note of criticism founded in the epistemological worldview of unity of knowledge emanating from the Qur'an and the *sunna*.

Critical thinking: Islam v. rationalism

Islamic scholarly activity has gone in waves of intellectualism over four cross-currents and conflicts through history. Such a historical trend is succinctly summarized in the words of Imam Al-Ghazzali in his Tahafut al-Falsafah (trans. Marmura, 1997, p. 217):

> [Man] must imitate the law, advancing or holding back [action] not as he chooses, [but] according to what [the law] directs, his moral dispositions becoming educated thereby. Whoever is deprived of this virtue in both moral disposition and knowledge is the one who perishes. . . . Whoever combines both virtues, the epistemological and the practical, is the worshipping 'knower', the absolutely blissful one. Whoever has the epistemological virtue but not the practical is the knowledgeable [believing] sinner who will be tormented for a period, which [torment] will not last because his soul has been perfected through knowledge but bodily occurrences had tarnished [it] in an accidental manner opposed to the substance of the soul. . . . He who has practical virtue but not the epistemological is saved and delivered, but does not attain perfect bliss.

The first category belonging to the rationalist tradition belongs to people who are spiritually damned. This is the tradition to be found in the Hellenic Muslim philosophers that marked the Muslim scholastic history (Qadir, 1988). Today it is found in the Muslim mindset based on the rationalist and liberal and neoliberal doctrines of Occidentalism. In it the Muslim homage to Western tradition increases as *taqlid* (blind submission to [Western] authority) (Asad, 1987). The second category of the Muslim mindset is rare in contemporary Islamic intellectualism, yet it existed powerfully in cultivating Islamic intellectual and spiritual contribution to the world (Ghazzali trans. Karim, undated).

To this class belong the high watermarks of the *mujtahid*, who have derived and developed the Islamic Law, the *shari'a*, on the premise of the Oneness of Allah as the supreme knowledge. They placed such divine knowledge as primal and original foundations from which faith emanates and deepens. The third category of intellectualism mentioned by Ghazzali comprises the rationalist mendicants of Muslims. They indulged in speculative philosophy without a worldly meaning of practicality. The fourth category of intellectualism comprises common members of the Muslim community called the *umma*. They are led out of darkness into truth by the collective action and law-abiding practitioners of the divine law. They are guided and led but are not leaders and revolutionary thinkers. To this category belong the present day's Muslim imitators and superficial proponents of the principle of *tawhid* (Oneness of God). They understand neither the universally functional logical formalism of *tawhid* nor its application in constructing the Qur'anic world-system. The functional knowledge and application of *tawhid* in constructing the Islamic world-view and its application to the construction of the *umma* have become dim in the hands of such imitators.

The wave of change that swept through the above four categories of intellectualism in the Muslim mindset as pointed out by Ghazzali is a repetition of scholastic experience in contemporary times. The difference though is this: while the scholastic Muslim mindset thought of an epistemological understanding in the world-system as a coherent universality, the present generation of Muslim scholars has designed a partitioned and segmented view of the natural and social sciences, indeed of all thought process. The latter category partitioned thinking between matter and mind, the natural and social sciences, and segmented the academic disciplines within these.

Political economy and world-system theory (Choudhury, 2004a) is of a more recent genre in the tradition of the epistemological and ontological contexts of the Qur'anic worldview premised on the divine law, cognitive world and materiality. But, by and large, these mark a revolutionary rebirth that remains distanced and shunned by the Muslim mind today as it embarks and deepens in rationalism and has merely a superficial understanding of *tawhid* and the Islamic–occidental world-system divide. Such a thought process accepts fully the Western model of neoliberal thought, methodology, perceptions, social contractibility and institutionalism. Let us examine this claim more closely.

The epistemological roots of Muslim rationalism: the scholastic period
The rationalism of the Mutazzilah, Ibn Rushd, Ibn Sina and Al-Farabi
The above-mentioned names were among the rationalist Muslim philosophers who perceived the nature of the world in the light of ideas of deductive syllogism derived from Greek thought. They then applied such ideas to the discussion of the nature of the universe. They both derived as well as embedded the ethical and moral ideas in their rationally construed philosophy. Such Hellenic philosophers did not premise their precepts on the Qur'an and the *sunna*. The metaphysical and rationalist nature of such inquiry rendered Muslim beliefs speculative philosophy. The final result was that a body of speculative philosophy arose that hinged on syllogistic deduction of the existence of God, predestination and the nature of the universe, the Qur'an and their functions.

The above-mentioned rationalist thinking was the harbinger of the eighteenth-century utilitarianism. Muslim rationalists relied on the cognitive worth of a concept. Al-Farabi's theory of the universe, for instance, was limited by the extent of matter (Walzer, 1985).

There was no existence of the universe outside the field of matter. This idea was grandly extended by Einstein's (Einstein, 1954) problem of space and time. Within his conception of material universe bounded by materiality, Al-Farabi assigned his meaning to justice and freedom while reconstructing his Greek allegiance to these concepts (Aristotle, trans. Welldon, 1987). While Aristotle thought of happiness and freedom as being non-material in nature, Al-Farabi, like the latter-days' utilitarian, saw the ethical attributes as having meaning within material substance (such as beauty and human needs). To Al-Farabi the way towards the discovery of this ethical substance was reason. He thus placed reason above revelation and thought of the Prophet Muhammad as philosopher–king.

As in the case of latter days' utilitarianism, social ordering was thought of in terms of rationally motivated self-interested agents aiming at optimization of decision and power. Such agents had to be self-seeking and individualistic owing to their maximizing objectives with the associated analytical, self and institutional perceptions. In economics, the function of resource allocation, market exchange and the pricing of goods, services and productive factors were thereby governed by the principle of economic rationality as the cause and effect of the precepts of optimality and steady-state equilibrium. Since economic rationality assumes the existence of full information in making rational choices the utilitarian precept, this idea induces a sequence of preference pre-ordering defining institutional and individual perceptions coherently. We thus find that the various ramifications of neoclassical utilitarianism existed in Al-Farabi's model of the perfect state, which exists solely in human cognition, not reality (Walzer, 1985).

The Mutazzilites, Al-Farabi, Ibn Rushd, Ibn Sina, the Ikhwan as-Safa and many other Muslim rationalists were dialecticians belonging to the school of ethical egoism. Man was elevated to the higher level of an evolutionary category rising above the mineral kingdom, the vegetable kingdom and the animal kingdom. The ethical interaction between these subsystems of total reality was marginalized to partitioned views of existence. This echoed early Darwinian beginnings in which the mind was perceptually partitioned between matter and spirit.

When such dialectical thought is applied to themes such as the philosophy of history, we come to perceive something of Hegelian-Marxism in it. The continuous rise of the human and worldly order towards God can be interpreted in the same way as the rise of the World-Spirit, about which Hegel wrote in his philosophy of history (Hegel, trans. Sibree, 1956). On the other hand, understanding the basis of the universe as a field of matter invoking ethical egoism belongs to the Marxist genre. Marx premised his idea of political economy on sheer economics and made this the explanatory social field of his overdetermination praxis, where everything remains in a perpetual flux of conflict and disequilibrium (Resnick and Wolff, 1987; Staniland, 1985).

Furthermore, like Kant, the Muslim dialecticians believed in the deductive process of causation arising from the divine will. Hence predestination was strongly upheld by this school. Nor did the dialecticians believe in the inductive possibility that God's Law could be comprehended by inferences from the cumulative sensations of the evidential world. We thereby infer that the dialecticians did not develop any model of knowledge at all in terms of its essential parts: epistemology, ontology and the ontic (evidential) stages that go interactively together in a coherent model of the knowledge-centred universe. The effects of the otherwise rationalist models were transmitted to the social, economic, political and scientific thought of the Muslim dialecticians.

According to the tenets of natural liberty, the structure of society in relation to states of equilibrium, optimality and ethical egoism was provided in terms of the law of natural liberty. The theory of justice and fairness conceptualized in terms of rationalism rather than in terms of the divine episteme was subsequently introduced into theories of markets and institutions. Such an approach to the study of society, institutions and scientific phenomena caused the latter day Muslim rationalists to remain oblivious to the *Shar'ia* and an orthodox interpretation of the Qur'an on these issues.

Ibn Khaldun (1332AD–1406AD)
Ibn Khaldun (1332AD–1406AD) also belonged to the rationalist and empiricist school (Ibn Khaldun, trans. Rozenthal, 1958). His conceptual philosophy of history was not premised on a Qur'anic understanding of historicism. Contrarily, Ibn Khaldun's ideas on historical change were premised on his observation of North African society of his time. He saw in such historical change the variations in different stages of social evolution from the hard and frugal life of the early years of a city-state to the emerging process of civilization (*umran*). During the frugal periods of social evolution, Ibn Khaldun saw a strong sense of Islamic belief and solidarity within its rank and file. This social state was further pampered as the *umran* neared.

Ibn Khaldun also brought into his analysis of social change the concept of a science of culture (Mahdi, 1964). He associated with this science the prevalence of a divine will in the conduct of worldly affairs, and saw in it the causes of a predestined pattern of social change. To Ibn Khaldun the science of culture meant a methodological understanding of an indelible path of change governed by divine will.

Ibn Khaldun, though, failed to explain the following questions of historical dynamics: how were the cycles of history determined endogenously by a conscious recognition, understanding and methodological application of the divine will as the framework of the science of culture? Can a civilization revert to the path of moral advance after its decadences in the ascent to material acquisition?

Thus one fails to find in Ibn Khaldun a substantive formulation of the philosophy of history pertaining to the Qur'anic principle of civilization cycle. Note the understanding of historical evolutionary cycles in following Qur'anic verse:

> It is He who begins the process of creation, and repeats it, that He may reward with justice those who believe and work righteousness . . . (9:4)

Ibn Khaldun did not contribute to this very important Qur'anic principle of creative evolution, *khalq in-jadid* (or *khalqa summa yue'id*).

Being unable to explain the Qur'anic cycle of change and progress, Ibn Khaldun was equally unable to formalize a methodological theory of the *shari'a* as a social contract embedded in the historical semblance of universal equilibrium and meaning. For instance, Ibn Khaldun argued that, although the *shari'a* was the golden rule for mankind to emulate, the imperfect human communities were not running according to these sublime precepts. Hence Ibn Khaldun's *Muqaddimah* (Rozenthal, 1958) became simply a study of empirical facts underlying observed changes. He did not go deeper into the normative content and possibility of the *shari'a* in the context of interaction between *shari'a* and historicism.

Likewise, Ibn Khaldun's economic ideas on the social division of labour and his two-sector analysis of urban and agricultural development were based on a 'perfect competition' model of efficient allocation of resources and ownership. Such a model became the abiding one for latter days' occidental thought, particularly following the classical economic school in the development of both individual and social preferences and in the theory of division of labour. The result was the occidental socioscientific legacy of methodological independence and individualism. Ibn Khaldun's sociological and historical study of the state, governance, development and social change rested upon a similar view of North African sociological reality.

Ibn Khaldun did not consider the issue of the endogeneity of values. While he pointed out that overindulgence of a city, state and civilization (*umran*) brings about the decay of social solidarity and commitment to the community (*asabiyya*), he did not consider whether there could be a reversal of such a decadent condition after its failure. In other words, Ibn Khaldun's historicity does not consider the possibility of the *shari'a* being established in a progressive modern nation that could reverse the process of social decadence.

Thus no circular dynamics of historicism is explainable by the Khaldunian social theory. Ibn Khaldun had given a rationalist interpretation of historical change based on empirical observations of societies in North Africa during his time. Khaldunian historicism began a positivistic root in empirical facts. There was no permanently underlying epistemology driving the process of historical change. Ibn Khaldun's calling on divine reality in his science of culture remained an exogenous invocation of *tawhid* in social theory. He failed to derive an essentially Qur'anic philosophy of history, wherein the process of change is endogenously explained by interaction between moral and ethical forces that learn by the law of divine unity with historical and social dynamics. At best we find in Ibn Khaldun the emergence of a dichotomy between the epistemic roots of divine law, which like Kant's impossibility of pure reason, remains outside comprehensive socioscientific reality. On the other hand, like Hume's ontological sense perception, Ibn Khaldun's empirical social science was his analytical premise.

Al-Kindi (801AD–873AD)
Atiyeh (1985, p. 23) points out that Al-Kindi had no consistent way of treating the subject matter of revelation and reason. The philosophical thought of the rationalist scholastics as exemplified by Al-Kindi manifested a separation of reason from revelation or a tenuous link between the two. The precept of divine unity was thus simply invoked but not epistemologically integrated with the Qur'anic interpretation of the matter–mind–spirit interrelationship.

The Muslim rationalists like Al-Kindi merged philosophy with religious or theological inquiry. The result was blurring of a clear vision as to which comes first, revelation or reason, since reason is simply an instrument and therefore subservient to what Al-Kindi called the First Philosophy. This Al-Kindi reasoning was an Aristotelian consequence. Atiyeh (1985, p. 23) explains the problem of certainty between philosophy (reason) and religion (revelation) as the source of the ultimate knowledge for the quest of *tawhid*: 'Al-Kindi's inclusion of theology in philosophy confronts us with a problem. If philosophy's main purpose is to strengthen the position of religion, philosophy should be a handmaiden to theology and not vice versa. What strikes one particularly is that this inclusion of theology in philosophy is a direct Aristotelian borrowing and therefore points towards a higher esteem for philosophy than for religion' (*tawhid* from the Qur'an).

Contemporary Muslim socioscientific scholars have been caught in this same Al-Kindi *problématique*. The desire for Islamization of knowledge fell into a trap: what are they Islamizing? Is it Islamic knowledge, or Western knowledge, lock stock and barrel, to Islamize with a palliative of Islamic values?

The continuing criticism of this chapter is that the *tawhidi* worldview, which is the fundamental epistemology of Islamic worldview, was only uttered but never understood as a substantive formal logic entering formalism of the *tawhidi* epistemological worldview. Contrarily, this is the premise where the Islamic transformation of all socioscientific thinking and world-system must begin and take shape and form as the divinely revealed episteme singularly above reason interacting and driving experience.

Almost all Muslim scholars working in the socioscientific fields and claiming *tawhid* have not enquired into the epistemological foundations (Al-Faruqi, 1982; AbuSulayman, 1988; Siddiqui, 1979; Chapra, 1992, p. 202). I will elaborate on my criticism of a few Muslim scholars later. The project of Islamization remains deadlocked as the Western epistemological and methods programme with a palliative of Islamic values without the *tawhidi* analytical content.

Such was the age of the Muslim rationalists. It is still the age of rationalism devoid of the *tawhidi* epistemology in the socioscientific realm today. Rationalism at all levels was opposed powerfully by the second category of Muslims. In the scholastic epoch the intellectual opposition was championed by Imam Ghazzali. What was the nature of scholarship in this category as expressed by the epistemologists of the *tawhidi* worldview?

Islamic epistemologists and the world-system

Imam Ghazzali's social theory (1058AD–1111AD)
Ghazzali was by and large a sociopsychologist searching for the source of spiritual solace for the individual soul. Within this field he thought of society. The spiritual capability of attaining moral eminence conveyed the real meaning of freedom to him. Such a state of freedom was to rescue the soul from material limitations of life. Self-actualization was possible in the perfect state of *fana'*, the highest state of spiritual realization that the individual could attain by coming nearest to God. Such a state was possible only through the understanding of *tawhid* at its highest level transcending the 70 veils of divine light. Ghazzali thought the human soul or cognizance advances by means of and toward spirituality. To Ghazzali such a perfect state could be humanly experienced through complete submission to God's will (trans. Buchman, 1998).

Ghazzali's social theory was premised profoundly on the episteme of Oneness of God. In economic theory, the implication of Ghazzali's concept of *fana'* and the aggregation of preference is equivalent to the invisible hand principle of atomistic market order governed by economic rationality (full information). The market equilibrium price is now formed by such an invisible hand principle. This kind of completeness of information and knowledge is the reflected manifestation of the act of God in the scheme of things.

Ibn Al-Arabi on divine unity (1165AD–1240AD)
Ibn al-Arabi's (1165AD–1240AD) ideas on divine unity as the sole foundation of knowledge are noteworthy. Al-Arabi pointed out that knowledge can be derived in just two ways and there is no third way. He writes in his *Futuhat* (Chittick,1989):

The first way is by way of unveiling. It is an incontrovertible knowledge which is actualized through unveiling and which man finds in himself. He receives no obfuscation along with it and is not able to repel it . . . . The second way is the way of reflection and reasoning (*istidlal*) through rational demonstration (*burhan 'aqli*). This way is lower than the first way, since he who bases his consideration upon proof can be visited by obfuscations which detract from the proof, and only with difficulty can he remove them.

Imam Ibn Taimiyyah's social theory (1263AD–1328AD)

Ibn Taimiyyah's significant contribution to the field of political economy was his theory of social guidance and regulation of the market order when this proved to be unjust, unfair and inimical to the *shari'a*. In his small but important work, *Al-Hisbah fil Islam* (Ibn Taimiyyah, trans. Holland, 1983) Ibn Taimiyyah recommended the establishment of an agency to oversee the proper guidance of markets to minimize unjust and unfair practice. The work was written during the reign of the Mamluk Dynasty in Egypt, where he found gross inequity and unfair practices contradicting the tenets of the *shari'a* in the market order. Thus both Imam Taimiyyah and his contemporary, Al-Markizi, opposed the Mamluk policies of unjust and unfair market practices. They opposed the conversion of the monetary standard from gold to copper (*fulus*), the effect of which was phenomenal inflationary pressure. 'Bad money' drove out 'good money' from usage. Hyperinflationary conditions of the time brought about economic hardship and poverty in the nation. Hence price control, fair dealing and appropriate measures to revert back to the gold standard were prescribed in Ibn Taimiyyah's social regulatory and guiding study, *Al-Hisbah fil Islam*.

The theory of *Al-Hisbah fil Islam* proved to be an institutionalist approach based on the legal framework of the *shari'a* calling for reversal to *shari'a*-driven policies as measures of compensation principle. Such issues were only recently considered by Ronald Coase (1960). But in keeping with the tenets of the *shari'a*, *Al-Hisbah* did not prescribe the compensation principle to be realized out of tax revenue, for Ibn Taimiyyah, in accordance with the *ahadith* (guidance) of the Prophet Muhammad, promoted sovereignty of the market process in terms of its self-organizing force. Market intervention was necessary only when market behaviour contravened the *shari'a*. The *Al-Hisbah* as a social institution was meant to return a corrupt market order to the true values of market exchange. Ibn Taimiyyah's market order comprised an endogenously embedded social and economic system governed by ethical values and legal precepts. To Ibn Taimiyyah, the concept of value in exchange was inextricably made out of ethical and material worth.

Such theories of market and endogenous social value are not to be found in an occidental history of economic thought. Smith (reprinted 1976), Marx (Resnick and Wolff, 1987) and Walras (trans. Jaffe 1954) wanted to introduce such ideals. Yet Smith's attempt contradicted his concept of *laissez faire* or non-intervention. Marx's epistemological concept of overdetermination of a social system resulted in an early form of social Darwinism. Walras's general equilibrium system was premised on an exogenous monetary unit as the *numéraire* of his general equilibrium system. This caused competition between money and real economy as two opposing sector activities. The result was the inevitable prevalence of the interest rate as the price of money in contradistinction to the price of goods. Even in the ethical theory of moral sentiment, Smith's precept of natural liberty working in the rationalist human order lost its fervour when it was applied to the invisible hands of the market order as in Smith's *Wealth of Nations*.

We note Ibn Taimiyyah's combination of the ontology of the *shari'a* in terms of the Prophet's *sunna* with the social necessity to correct adverse market consequences. This was a strong manifestation of the circular relationship between the ethical values as deductive rule, and the world-system, which stands in need of policy and institutionally induced reformation. The same integrative conception is also to be interpreted as a methodological approach in combining the normative with the positive elements of social thought.

Imam Shatibi's social theory (d. 1388AD)
A similar theory of social contract was expounded by Imam Shatibi, who was a contemporary of Imam Ibn Taimiyyah. The two developed and applied the dynamic tenets of the *shari'a* to practical social, economic and institutional issues and problems of the time.

Imam Shatibi was an original thinker on the development of the *shari'a* in the light of individual preference and social preference and their relationship with the institutional tenets of public purpose. Imam Shatibi thus brought the Islamic discursive process (*shura* and rule making) to the centre of the very important issue of development of the *shari'a* through discourse, *ijtihad* and *ijma* (Shatibi, trans. Abdullah Draz, undated). Imam Shatibi's preference theory, called *Al-Maslaha Wa-Istihsan*, is a forerunner of the profound concept of social wellbeing in most recent times (Sen, 1990). In the perspective of this concept, Imam Shatibi took up his principles on which the *shari'a* can be developed (Masud, 1994).

These principles are (1) universal intelligibility; (2) linking the possibility of action to the degree of physical efforts rendered; (3) adaptation of the *shari'a* to the natural and regional differentiation of customs and practices. By combining these attributes in the development of the *shari'a*, Imam Shatibi was able to deliver a comprehensive theory of social wellbeing. The social wellbeing criterion explained the aggregate view of preference in society within the tenets of the *shari'a*.

By combining the above principles, Imam Shatibi examined both the core and the instrumental aspects of the *shari'a*. According to his 'theory of meaning' of the core of the *shari'a* (*Usul al-shari'a*), Imam Shatibi 'dismisses the existence of conflict, contradiction and difference in the divine law, arguing that at the fundamental level there is unity. Variety and disagreement, apparent at the second level are not the intention and objective of the law' (Masud, 1994). This aspect of Shatibi's perspective on the *shari'a* adds a dynamic spirit to the moral law. Through such universality and the dynamic nature of the moral law, Imam Shatibi was aiming at a universal theory of social wellbeing.

Using the integrative perspective of social preference made out of the interactive preferences of members of society, Imam Shatibi thought of the necessities of life as fundamental life-fulfilling goods. To incorporate basic needs into dynamic evolution of life-sustaining regimes, he subsequently introduced basic-needs regimes into his analysis. These were the social needs for comfort and refinements of life. All the components, namely basic needs, comfort and refinement, were for life-fulfilment at the advancing levels of a basic-needs regime of socioeconomic development. On the basis of the dynamic basic-needs regime of socioeconomic development, Imam Shatibi constructed his social wellbeing criterion, and thereby, his theory of preference and the public purpose, *Al-Maslaha Wa-Istihsan*. These ideas proved to be far in advance of their time in the social meaning and preferences of life.

Shah Waliullah's social theory (1703AD–1763AD)

Shah Waliullah was a sociologist and a historian. His approach in explaining Islamic social theory took its roots from the Qur'an. In his study he saw the need for an independent body of knowledge to study all the worldly and intricate problems of life and thought. As one of the great scholars of the *shari'a*, Shah Waliullah combined reason, discourse and extension by *ijtihad* (rule making by consensus and epistemological reference to the Qur'an and the *sunna*) in the understanding and application of the Islamic law.

Shah Waliullah's methodology on the commentary of the Qur'an was based on diverse approaches. He held the view that the study of the Qur'an can embrace viewpoints which are traditionalist, dialectical, legalist, grammarian, those of a lexicographer, a man of letters, a mystic or an independent reader. Yet in all of these approaches the integrity of the Qur'anic foundational meaning cannot be dispensed with. In this regard Shah Waliullah wrote, 'I am a student of the Qur'an without any intermediary' (Jalbani, 1967 p. 67). He thus combined all of the above-mentioned approaches to render his own independent exegesis of the Qur'an pertaining to worldly issues and the study of the Qur'an.

Shah Waliullah's outstanding contribution comprised his Qur'anic interpretation of sociological change in the light of historicism. According to him, history is a movement across phases of social arrangements starting from primitive stages and then advancing in stages through feudal, medieval and higher levels of civilization. But, unlike Ibn Khaldun, Shah Waliullah thought of a continuous possibility for moral reformation and decline in the process of civilization change. According to Shah Waliullah, it was possible for a civilization even at the highest stage of its advance not to be pampered by the softness of that life, as claimed by Ibn Khaldun in his theory of *asabiyyah* (community) and *umran* (nation state). The determinant of a civilization going through cycles of prosperity and decline was seen as a function of the perspective of the moral and social order according to the *shari'a*. Thus Shah Waliullah had a truly evolutionary understanding of historical change, which was missing in Ibn Khaldun's *Muqaddimah*.

Shah Waliullah used the principle of *irtifaq* (Jalbani, 1967), meaning social cooperation, to explain the hierarchical movement of society across its four stages of development. These stages are, first, the jungle life characterized by crude basic needs of life. Within this stage Waliullah also considers dynamic necessities of man in a growing social environment, such as the stage of comforts evolving to refinements. The second stage of human development according to Waliullah is the development of social laws and mutual coexistence. The third stage is nationalism marked by institutional development and well-knit organization with mutual cooperation among various parts of the organizational structure. The need for a just ruler becomes predominant in establishing social cohesion. Government collects fair taxes for its social functions and defence. The fourth stage in Waliullah's theory of human development is internationalism. Precepts of trade, development, war and peace are taken up within the purview of an international order. Law and order is seen to require adequate government treasury for meeting war needs.

According to Waliullah, the guarantee of basic needs was a mandatory social function. Such basic needs were seen to be dynamic in satisfying the ever-changing needs of society over its distinct evolutionary phases and functions.

Malek Ben Nabi's social and scientific theory
A significant use of the interdisciplinary approach to Qur'anic exegesis in developing *shari'a* rules as a dynamic law was undertaken by Malek Ben Nabi in his phenomenological study of the Qur'an (Nabi, trans. Kirkary, 1983). Within his phenomenological theory, Malek Ben Nabi could not reject evolutionary theory. He placed the precept of the Oneness of God at the centre of all causation. He then introduced the guidance of the *sunna* as the medium for comprehending and disseminating the episteme of divine unity in the world-system. Thus the ontological and ontic (evidential) derivations of the latter category comprised Nabi's phenomenological consequences on the premise of the epistemology of divine unity. This integration between God, man and the world carries the message of causal interrelationship between the normative and positive laws, deductive and inductive reasoning.

Nabi's evolutionary phenomenology was a reflection of his Qur'anic interpretation of historical change. In this respect he shared the views of Shah Waliullah on this topic, respecting the unfolding of human development in consonance with the levels of deliverance of the prophetic message and social change. But Nabi extended his evolutionary argument beyond simply the social arena. He also examined the problem of scientific phenomenology in the light of the Qur'an. Nabi wrote (Kirkary, 1983 pp. 23–4):

> The evolution of this matter would be regulated by an intelligence which assures equilibrium and harmony and whose unchangeable laws human science can establish. But certain steps in this evolution will escape the usual assertion of men of science, without which there would be a lacuna in the system. In these exceptional cases, one allows for the intervention of a metaphysical determinism, an intervention which contradicts nothing since it is compatible with the nature of the axiom. Where there would have been lacuna in the preceding system, here there is an intervention of a voluntary, conscious, and creative cause.

History, according to Malek Ben Nabi, is thus a movement of events that is determined by and in turn reinforces the principle of cause and effect on the moral plane. Such is the interrelationship between God, man and the world through the divine law. To this *tawhidi* foundation conform the social and natural laws (sciences) in the Islamic worldview.

Contemporary Muslim reaction: devoid of epistemology
The Islamizing agenda
In recent times, to get out of the human resource development enigma of Muslims, Ismail Al-Raji Faruqi led the way in the so-called 'Islamization' of knowledge. Rahman and Faruqi formed opposite opinions on this project (Rahman, 1958). Al-Faruqi (1982) thought of the Islamization of knowledge in terms of introducing Western learning into received Islamic values and vice versa. This proved to be a mere peripheral treatment of Islamic values in relation to Western knowledge. It is true that out of the programme of Islamization of knowledge arose Islamic universities in many Muslim countries. Yet the academic programmes of these universities were not founded upon a substantive understanding and application of the *tawhidi* epistemology. The theory of knowledge with a substantive integrated content remains absent in Islamic institutional development.

This last approach mentioned above could otherwise have been introduced into the study of complex endogenous relations in and among scientific theory, development, social and economic issues and political inquiry. The Islamic universities remained silent

on these complex issues as they became subservient to the will and requirements of political establishments that fund their activities and allow such universities to exist in the first
place. Thus the same mainstream thinking by Muslim scholars went on to be imitated
under an externally enunciated and exogenously driven Islamic way of thinking. The
bearing of the Qur'anic worldview in all the essentials of learning remained marginalized
and weak.

Islamization and Islamic banks
In the financial and economic field, Islamic banks have mushroomed under an Islamization agenda, yet the foundation and principles of Islamic banks give no comprehensive vision of a background intellectual mass of ways to transform the prevailing
environment of interest transactions into an interest-free system. How do the economic
and financial economies determine risk diversification and prospective diversity of investment and production, thus mobilizing financial resources in the real economy along
shari'a-determined opportunities?

The financial reports of Islamic banks show an inordinately large proportion of assets
floating in foreign trade financing. These portfolios have only to do with sheer mercan-
tilist business returns from charging a mark-up on merchandise, called *murabaha*. Such a
mark-up has nothing in common with real economic returns arising from the use of trade
financing. Consequently the mobilization of resources through foreign trade financing
alone has helped neither to increase intercommunal trade financing in Muslim countries
nor to increase returns through development prospects in the real economic sectors of
undertaking foreign trade financing.

Islamic banks have not constructed a programme of comprehensive development by
rethinking the nature of money in Islam in terms of the intrinsic relationship between
money as a moral and social necessity linked endogenously with real economic activities.
Here endogenous money value is reflected only in the returns obtained from the mobilization of real sectoral resources that money uses to monetize real economic activities
according to the *shari'a*. Money does not have any intrinsic value of its own apart from
the value of the precious metals that are to be found in real sector production of such
items. The structural change leading to such money, society, finance and economic transformation has not been possible in Islamic banks. Contrarily, Islamic banks today are
simply pursuing goals of efficiency and profitability within the globalization agenda as
sponsored by the West and the international development finance organizations. Thus,
Islamic banks are found to have launched a competitive programme in the midst of privatization, market openness, rent-seeking economic behaviour and financial competition,
contrary to promoting cooperation between them and other financial institutions.

A study carried out by Choudhury (1999) showed that, although deposits have risen
phenomenally in Islamic banks as a whole, the rate of profitability (distributed divi-
dends/deposit) remained low, at 1.66 per cent. The investment portfolio of Islamic banks
is overly biased toward foreign trade financing and equity financing. Yet, as is known,
equity financing is destined to be highly risky when adequate sectoral diversification and
progressive production and investments remain impossible for Islamic financial and
non-banking institutions. We therefore infer that the high level of deposits in Islamic
banks comes from the sincere desire by Muslims to turn to meaningful modes of Islamic
financing. The dynamics of Islamic transformation and an equitable and participatory

framework of business operations as forms of Islamic relations have received marginal attention at the social and institutional levels and in reference to Islamic socioeconomic transformation of the Muslim world.

Logical faults of Western thinking: resource allocation concept and its Muslim imitation
In the end, we find that the clamour of Islamic economic thinking over the last 70 years or so has remained subdued. It has produced no truly Qur'anic worldview to develop ideas, and thereby to contribute to a new era of social and economic thinking and experience.

The principle of marginal rate of substitution that remains dominant in all of Western economic, financial and scientific thought has entered the entire framework of Islamic social, economic and financing reasoning. This has resulted in a complete absence of the praxis of unity of knowledge as expressed by social, economic and institutional complementarities at the epistemological, analytical and applied levels. No structural change other than perpetuation of mechanical methods at the expense of the Qur'anic worldview arises from incongruent relations. The Qur'anic methodological praxis rejects such an incongruent mixture of belief mixed with disbelief.

By a similar argument, the neoclassical marginal substitution agenda of development planning is found to enter the imitative growth-led economic prescription of all Muslim countries. Recently, such growth and marginalist thinking has received unquestioned support by Muslim economists like Chapra (1993) and Naqvi (1994). Siddiqui (undated) does not recognize the fundamental role of interest rates in the macroeconomic savings function as opposed to the resource mobilization function and, thereby, the consequential conflicting relationship between the real and financial sectors. He thereby endorses 'saving' in an Islamic economy. These Muslim economists follow the macroeconomic arguments of capital accumulation via 'savings' as opposed to the substantive meaning of resource mobilization (Ventelou, 2005) according to the Qur'anic principle interlinking spending, trade, charity and the consequential abolition of interest (*riba*) (Qur'an, 2:264–80). The Muslim economists failed to understand the system of evolutionary circular causation between these Qur'anic recommended activities underlying the process of phasing out interest rates through the medium of a money–real economy interrelationship (Choudhury, 1998, 2005).

The concept of financial 'saving' in both the macroeconomic and microeconomic sense carries with it an inherent price for deferred spending. Such a price of deferment caused by 'saving' is the rate of interest on savings. Likewise, savings and thereby also the underlying interest motive in it, generate capital accumulation (Nitzan and Bichler, 2000). Capital accumulation so generated, in turn plays a central role in economic growth. These, together with the consequent pricing areas of factors of production in an economic growth model, have simply been misunderstood by Islamic economists while applying classical and neoclassical reasoning and analytical models to Islamic economic, financial and social issues (Bashir and Darrat, 1992; Metwally, 1991). The nearest that Islamic economists have come to applying alternative theories of economic growth is by using an endogenous growth model (Romer, 1986). Yet the neoclassical marginal substitution roots of such a growth model have been kept intact. Thus the methodology of circular causation in the light of *tawhidi* epistemology remained unknown to contemporary Muslim scholars.

The future of Islamic transformation
In the light of the above discussion we note the deeply partitioned views in the develop-ment of Muslim thought from two distinct angles – Islamic epistemology and Muslim rationalism. This conflict started at the time of the Mutazzilah, about a hundred years after the Prophet Muhammad, followed by the scholastics. The same train of thought is being pursued today by a blind acceptance of economic, social and institutional neolib-eralism. As a result of such imitation (*taqlid*) in Muslim thinking, no overwhelming attempt has been made to bridge the gap between the Qur'anic epistemological thinking and Occidental rationalism. The totality of a *tawhidi* unified worldview according to the Qur'an could not be introduced into the body framework of Muslim thinking. The rise of the *umma* that would be led by the *tawhidi* epistemology for guidance and change fell apart.

Our discussion brings out the important focus on the deep and long-standing problem of the Muslim world. This is the lack of a clear and unified vision premised on the praxis of *tawhidi* unity of knowledge. How can science, society, economy, state, development and social contract be formalized within the framework of the Qur'anic episteme of unity of life and its world-system? There are burning questions that need to be addressed. It is the indifference and division between the Muslim rationalists and Islamic epistemologists over a long period of time historically that has left the Muslim world 'floundering in a flood of confusion', as the Qur'an declares.

The *tawhidi* methodology in Islamic reconstruction
In this chapter we have argued that only along the epistemological, ontological and ontic circular causal interrelations of the *tawhidi* knowledge-centred worldview is it possible to establish a truly Qur'anic methodology for all the sciences. We point out the nature of the *tawhidi* approach using creative evolution for the realization of an Islamic transformation.

Discourse along lines of *tawhidi* epistemology and its ontologically constructed world-system needs to prevail in all sectors between Muslim nations. According to the learning impetus within a maturing transformation process, consensus on such interactive venues can be attained. Thereby, the Muslim world as a whole and her communities would come to evaluate the level of social wellbeing determined through the participatory and com-plementary process of development in the light of the *shari'a*. The evaluation of such a social wellbeing criterion, within the interactive institutions of economy, markets, society, governments and the extended Muslim community, gives rise to consensus and creative evolution. This in turn leads to heightened understanding and implementation of the cir-cular causation and continuity framework of the knowledge-centred worldview. In this way, the worldview of *tawhidi* unity of knowledge is generated through a cycle of human resource development and participation – a complex symbiosis (Choudhury, 1998).

From the nature of economic and social transformation that has been traced above arises the interrelated realization of distributive equity and economic efficiency as a socioeconomic example of the complementary relations of participation, organization and methodology. The complementary realization of the two socioeconomic goals results in social justice. An appropriate form of development, with endogenous participation at all levels and sustained by appropriate economic, financial and institutional instruments and organization, determines sustainability for the Islamic world. There is no need to feverishly imitate Occidentalism in the *tawhidi* paradigm.

Social wellbeing criterion for Islamic banks
The social wellbeing function as the objective criterion of Islamic banks serving the *shari'a* tenets of social security, protection of individual rights and progeny, and preservation of the Islamic State, ought to become a description of ways and means of stimulating resource mobilization that establishes sustainability and the high ideals of the Islamic faith. This goal involves the principle of *tawhid*. That is, the Oneness of God as the highest principle of Islam. The model implementing the principle of *tawhid* in the socioeconomic, financial and institutional order involves organizing the modes of resource mobilization, production and financing these in ways that bring about complementary linkages between these and other *shari'a*-determined possibilities. In this way, there will appear co-determination among the choices and the evolution of the instruments to be selected and implemented by many agencies in society at large through discourse. Islamic banks ought to form a part and parcel interconnecting medium of a lively developmental organism of the *umma*.

Development possibilities are realized both by the networking of discourse between management and shareholders of an Islamic bank as well as in concert with other Islamic banks, the central bank, enterprises, government and the community at large. This construction is extended across the Muslim world. In this way, a vast network of discourse-related networking and relational systems is established between Islamic banks and the socioeconomic and socioinstitutional order as a whole. Such unifying relations as participatory linkages in the economy and society-wide sense convey the systemic meaning of unity of knowledge. This in turn represents the epistemology of *tawhid* in the organic order of things. In the present case such a complementing and circular causation interrelationship is understood by their unifying interrelationships with the socioeconomic and socioinstitutional order in terms of the choice of cooperative financing instruments. The literal meaning of *tawhid* is thus explained in terms of an increasingly relational, participatory and complementary development, wherein events such as money, finance, markets, society and institutions unify. In the end, by combining the totality of the *shari'a* precepts with financing instruments, Islamic banks become investment-oriented financial intermediaries and agencies of sustainability of the socioeconomic order, the sociopolitical order and institutions of preservation of community assets and wellbeing.

The nature of money now turns out to be endogenous. Endogenous money is a systemic instrument that establishes complementarities between socioeconomic, financial, social and institutional possibilities towards sustaining circular causation between money, finance, spending on the good things of life and the real economy. Money in such a systemic sense of complementary linkages between itself, financial instruments and the real economic and social needs according to the *shari'a* assumes the properties of a 'quantity of money' (Friedman, 1989) as in the monetary equation of exchange. In the endogenous interrelationships between money and the real economy, the quantity of money is determined and valued in terms of the value of spending in *shari'a* goods and services in exchange. Money cannot have an exchange value of its own, which otherwise would result in a price for money as the rate of interest. Money does not have a market and hence no conceptions of demand and supply linked to such endogenous money in Islam.

The *shari'a riba* rule forbids interest transactions. Thus, instead of a market for money and the corresponding supporting financial instruments, there are now simply markets of exchangeables in the light of the *shari'a*. In this sense, the quantity of endogenous money and the returns on it are determined by the real economic value of the exchange between *shari'a* goods and services in demand and supply.

Besides, such real exchangeable goods and services being those that are recommended by the *shari'a* enter a social wellbeing criterion to evaluate the degree of attained complementarities between the *shari'a*-determined possibilities via a dynamic circular causation between such evolving possibilities. Such a social wellbeing function is the criterion that evaluates the degree to which complementary linkages are generated and sustained between various possibilities as *shari'a*-determined choices. On the basis of valuation of exchange of goods and services, the real financial returns are measured as a function of prices, output and net profits and private as well as social returns on spending. Islamic banks ought to become important links between the national central banks, financial intermediaries, the economy and community in realizing the regime of such endogenous money, finance and market interrelations through the formalism of evolutionary circular causation as strong economic, social and developmental causality driven by the principle of universal complementarities as the worldly mark of *tawhidi* unity of knowledge in systems.

Conclusion
The dividing line between current understanding of Islamic–Occidental connection and the *tawhidi* worldview as the methodological and logical formalism of unity of divine knowledge in thought and its ontologically constructed world-system spells out the dualism caused by rationalism. With this are carried the two contrasting perceptions, social contractibility and institutionalism. The distinction is also between the emptiness of Islamic theology (Nasr, 1992) and *tawhidi* formalism with its application in the truly Islamic world-system and its dynamics. On the distinct themes between *tawhid* and rationalism there are several contrasting views.

Imam Ghazzali wrote (trans. Buchman, 1998, p. 107) on the *tawhidi* contrariness to rationalism:

> The rational faculties of the unbelievers are inverted, and so the rest of their faculties of perception and these faculties help one another in leading them astray. Hence, a similitude of them is like a man 'in a fathomless ocean covered by a wave, which is a wave above which are clouds, darkness piled one upon the other'. (Qur'an, 24:40)

Recently Buchanan and Tullock (1999) wrote on the neoliberal order of rationalism, upon which all of the so-called 'Islamic economic and sociopolitical paradigm' rests:

> Concomitant with methodological individualism as a component of the hard core is the postulate of rational choice, a postulate that is shared over all research programs in economics. (p. 391)

Regarding the Occidental world-system, Buchanan and Tullock (ibid., p. 390) write on the nature of liberalism in constitutional economics.

> For constitutional economics, the foundational position is summarized in methodological individualism. Unless those who would be participants in the scientific dialogue are willing to locate the exercise in the choice calculus of individuals, *qua* individuals, there can be no departure from the starting gate. The autonomous individual is a *sine qua non* for any initiation of serious inquiry in the research program.

In respect of speculative rationalism of theological inquiry, Ghazzali (Buchman, 1998, p. 107) wrote (edited):

> On your impotence [to know] becomes manifest, then [one must point out that] there are among people those who hold that the realities of divine matters are not attained through rational reflection – indeed, that it is not within human power to know them. For this reason, the giver of the law has said, 'Think of God's creation and do not think on God's essence.'

In the end, the *tawhidi* epistemological and ontological precepts present the ontic economic and social phenomena as integral and complementary parts of the whole of socio-scientific reality. In the case of Islamic banking as a financial institution, the conception of money in Islam together with the embedded views of social, economic and institutional perspectives of development as sustainability and wellbeing are to be studied according to the principle and logic of complementariness. The emerging study of such complex and rich interaction in the light of *tawhid* and its learning dynamics rejects the study of the economic, financial, social and institutional domains as segmented parts within dichotomous fields despite what the mainstream analytics and neoliberal reasoning prompts.

In the light of the arguments cited in this chapter the development of economic and social thought in the contemporary Muslim mindset has been a sorry replay of the dichotomous divide of Islamic scholasticism. It is high time to reconstruct, and reform and return to the *tawhidi* foundational worldview as enunciated by the Qur'an and the *sunna* through the *shuratic* process of discourse, participation and creative evolution in the scheme of all things.

Bibliography

AbuSulayman, A.A. (1988), 'The Islamization of knowledge: a new approach toward reform on contemporary knowledge', *Proceedings & Selected Papers of the Second Conference on Islamization of Knowledge*, Herndon, VA: International Institute of Islamic Thought, pp. 91–118.

Ahmad, K. (2004), 'The challenge of global capitalism – an Islamic perspective,' in J.H. Dunning (ed.), *Making Globalization Good*, Oxford: Oxford University Press.

Al-Faruqi, I.R. (1982), *Islamization of Knowledge: General Principles and Workplan*, Herndon, VA: International Institute of Islamic Thought.

Al-Faruqi, I.R. (1988), 'Islamization of knowledge: problems, principles, and prospective', *Proceedings & Selected Papers of the Second Conference on Islamization of Knowledge*, Herndon, VA: International Institute of Islamic Thought, pp. 13–64.

Aristotle, trans. J.E.C. Welldon (1987), *The Nicomachean Ethics*, Buffalo, NY: Prometheus Books.

Asad, M. (1987), *This Law of Ours*, Gibraltar: Dar al-Andalus.

Atiyeh, G.R. (1985), *Al-Kindi: The Philosopher of the Arabs*, Islamabad, Pakistan: The Islamic Research Institute.

Bashir, A.H. and A.F. Darrat (1992), 'Equity participation contracts and investment', *American Journal of Islamic Social Sciences*, **9** (2), 219–32.

Buchanan, J.M. (1999), 'The domain of constitutional economics', *The Collected Works of James M. Buchanan, Vol. 1*, Indianapolis: Liberty Fund.

Buchanan, J.M. and G. Tullock (1999), 'Individual rationality in social choice', *The Collected Works of James M. Buchanan, Vol. 1*, Indianapolis: Liberty Fund.

Chapra, M.U. (1992), *Islam and the Economic Challenge*, Leicester, UK: Islamic Foundation & Herndon, NY: International Institute of Islamic Thought.

Chapra, M.U. (1993), *Islam and Economic Development*, Islamabad, Pakistan: International Institute of Islamic Thought and Islamic Research Institute.

Chittick, W.C. (1989), *Sufi Path of Knowledge*, Albany, NY: The State University of New York Press.

Choudhury, M.A. (1998), 'Human resource development in the Islamic perspective,' in M.A. Choudhury (ed.), *Studies in Islamic Social Sciences*, London: Macmillan and New York: St Martin's.

Choudhury, M.A. (1999), 'Resource mobilization and development goals for Islamic banks', *Proceedings of the*

Second Harvard University Forum on Islamic Finance: Islamic Finance into the 21st Century, Cambridge, MA: Harvard Islamic Finance and Investment Program, Center for Middle Eastern Studies, Harvard University, pp. 31–50.

Choudhury, M.A. (2004a), *The Islamic World-System, a Study in Polity–Market Interaction*, London: Routledge Curzon.

Choudhury, M.A. (2004b), 'Learning systems', *Kybernetes: International Journal of Systems & Cybernetics*, **33** (1), 26–47.

Choudhury, M.A. (ed.) (2005), *Money and Real Economy*, Leeds, New York, New Delhi: Wisdom House Academic Publication.

Coase, R.H. (1960), 'The problem of social cost', *Journal of Law and Economics*, **3**, 1–45.

Einstein, A. (1954), 'Relativity and the problem of space', in A. Einstein (ed.), *Relativity*, London: Methuen, pp. 135–57.

Friedman, M. (1989), 'Quantity theory of money', in J. Eatwell, M. Milgate and P. Newman (eds), *The New Palgrave: Money*, New York: W.W. Norton.

[Imam] Al-Ghazzali, trans. D. Buchman (1998), *The Niche of Lights*, Provo, Utah: Brigham University Press.

[Imam] Al-Ghazzali, trans. F. Karim (undated), *Ihya Ulum-Id-Din*, vol. 1, Lahore, Pakistan: Shah Muhammad Ashraf Press.

[Imam] Al-Ghazzali, trans. M.E. Marmura (1997), *The Incoherence of the Philosophers*, Provo, Utah: Brigham University Press.

Hegel, G.W.F., trans. J. Sibree (1956), *The Philosophy of History*, New York: Dover Publications.

Ibn Khaldun, trans. F. Rozenthal (1958), *Muqaddimah, an Introduction to History*, 3 vols, London: Routledge and Kegan Paul.

[Imam] Ibn Taimiyyah, trans. M. Holland (1983), *Al-Hisbah fil Islam (Public Duties in Islam: The Institution of the Hisba)*, Leicester: The Islamic Foundation.

Jalbani, G.N. (1967), *Teachings of Shah Waliyullah of Delhi*, Lahore, Pakistan: Shah Muhammad Ashraf Press.

Mahdi, M. (1964), *Ibn Khaldun's Philosophy of History*, Chicago: University of Chicago Press.

Masud, M.K. (1994), *Shatibi's Theory of Meaning*, Islamabad, Pakistan: Islamic Research Institute, International Islamic University.

Metwally, M. (1991), 'The humanomics of a Muslim consumer', *Humanomics*, **7** (3), 63–72.

Nabi, Malik B., trans. A.B. Kirkary (1983), *The Qur'anic Phenomenon*, Indianapolis: American Trust Publications.

Naqvi, S.N.H (1994), 'The problem of abolishing interest: I', in S.N.H. Naqvi (ed.), *Islam, Economics, and Society*, London: Kegan Paul International.

Nasr, S.H. (1992), 'The Gnostic tradition', in S.H. Nasr (ed.), *Science and Civilization in Islam*, New York: Barnes & Noble.

Nitzan, J. and S. Bichler (2000), 'Capital accumulation: breaking the dualism of "economics" and "politics"', in R. Palan (ed.), *Global Political Economy*, London: Routledge.

Qadir, C.A. (1988), *Philosophy and Science in the Islamic World*, London: Routledge.

Rahman, F. (1958), *Prophecy in Islam, Philosophy and Orthodoxy*, London: George Allen and Unwin.

Resnick, S.A. and R.D. Wolff (1987), 'Marxian epistemology: the critique of economic determinism,' in S.A. Resnick and R.D. Wolff (eds), *Knowledge and Class*, Chicago: University of Chicago Press.

Romer, P.M. (1986), 'Increasing returns and long-run growth', *Journal of Political Economy*, **94**, 1002–37.

Sen, A. (1990), 'Economic judgements and moral philosophy', in A. Sen (ed.), *On Ethics and Economics*, Oxford: Basil Blackwell Ltd.

[Imam] Shatibi, trans. Abdallah Draz (undated), *Muwafaqat al-Usul al-S hari'ah*, Cairo, Egypt: Al-Maktabah al-Tijariyyah al-Kubra.

Siddiqui, M.N. (undated), *Partnership and Profit-Sharing in Islamic Law*, Leicester: The Islamic Foundation.

Siddiqui, M.N. (1979), 'Tawhid: the concept and the process', in K. Ahmad and Z.I. Ansari (eds), *Islamic Perspectives*, London: Islamic Foundation.

Smith, A. (ed. E. Cannan) (1976), *An Inquiry into the Nature and Causes of the Wealth of Nations*, Chicago: The University of Chicago Press.

Staniland, M. (1985), 'The fall and rise of political economy', in M. Staniland, *What is Political Economy? A Study of Social Theory and Underdevelopment*, New Haven: Yale University Press.

Ventelou, B. (2005), 'Economic thought on the eve of the General Theory', in B. Ventelou (ed.), *Millennial Keynes*, London: M.E. Sharpe.

Walras, L., trans. W. Jaffe (1954), *Elements of Pure Economics*, Homewood: Richard D. Irwin.

Walzer, R. (1985), *Al-Farabi on the Perfect State*, Oxford: Clarendon Press.

3 Islamic critique of conventional financing
Latifa M. Algaoud and Mervyn K. Lewis

The significance of Islamic law

By definition, an Islamic bank abides by Islamic law, the *shari'a* (formally *shari'a Islami'iah* but generally abbreviated to *shari'ah* or *shari'a*). The literal meaning of the Arabic word *shari'a* is 'the way to the source of life' and, in a technical sense, it is now used to refer to a legal system in keeping with the code of behaviour called for by the Holy Qur'an and the *hadith* (the authentic tradition). Muslims cannot, in good faith, compartmentalize their behaviour into religious and secular dimensions, and their actions are always bound by the *shari'a*. Islamic law thus embodies an encompassing set of duties and practices including worship, prayer, manners and morals, marriage, inheritance, crime and commercial transactions.

The unique validity of Islamic law comes from its being the manifested will of God, who at a certain point in history revealed it to mankind through his prophet Muhammad; as such it does not rely on the authority of any earthly lawmaker. Its origins, in addition to the Holy Qur'an, are to be found in the judgments given by the Prophet himself, reflecting the application of rules, principles and injunctions already enunciated in the Holy Qur'an. As the centuries passed, these rules grew into a complete system of law, both public and private, as well as prescriptions for the practice of religion.

Just as Islam regulates and influences all other spheres of life, so it also governs the conduct of business and commerce. The basic principles of the law are laid down in the four root transactions of (1) sales (*bay*), transfer of the ownership or corpus of property for a consideration; (2) hire (*ijâra*), transfer of the usufruct (right to use) of property for a consideration; (3) gift (*hiba*), gratuitous transfer of the corpus of property; and (4) loan (*ariyah*), gratuitous transfer of the usufruct of property. These basic principles are then applied to the various specific transactions of, for example, pledge, deposit, guarantee, agency, assignment, land tenancy, *waqf* foundations (religious or charitable bodies) and partnerships, which play an important role in Islamic financing and form the backbone of Islamic banking practices.

As the preceding paragraph indicates, there are strict rules applying to finance under Islamic law, and it is to these that we now turn. In order to conform to Islamic rules and norms, five religious features, which are well documented in the literature, must be followed in investment behaviour (Lewis and Algaoud, 2001):

a. *riba* is prohibited in all transactions;
b. business and investment are undertaken on the basis of *halal* (legal, permitted) activities;
c. *maysir* (gambling) is prohibited and transactions should be free from *gharar* (speculation or unreasonable uncertainty);
d. *zakat* is to be paid by the bank to benefit society;
e. all activities should be in line with Islamic principles, with a special *shari'a* board to supervise and advise the bank on the propriety of transactions.

Islamic financing rules
The five elements mentioned above give Islamic banking and finance its distinctive religious identity, and we now briefly explain each in turn.

Riba
Perhaps the most far-reaching and controversial aspect of Islamic economics, in terms of its implications from a Western perspective, is the prohibition of interest (*riba*). The payment of *riba* and the taking of interest as occurs in a conventional banking system is explicitly prohibited by the Holy Qur'an, and thus investors must be compensated by other means. It is further stated in the Holy Qur'an that those who disregard the prohibition of interest are at war with God and His Prophet Muhammad.

Haram/halal
A strict code of 'ethical investments' operates for Islamic financial activities. Hence Islamic banks cannot finance activities or items forbidden (that is, *haram*) in Islam, such as trade of alcoholic beverages and pork meat. Furthermore, as the fulfilment of material needs assures a religious freedom for Muslims, Islamic banks are encouraged to give priority to the production of essential goods which satisfy the needs of the majority of the Muslim community. As a guide, participation in the production and marketing of luxury activities, *israf wa traf*, is considered as unacceptable from a religious viewpoint when Muslim societies suffer from a lack of essential goods and services such as food, clothing, shelter, health and education.

Gharar/maysir
Prohibition of games of chance is explicit in the Holy Qur'an (S5: 90–91). It uses the word *maysir* for games of hazard, derived from *usr* (ease and convenience), implying that the gambler strives to amass wealth without effort, and the term is now applied generally to all gambling activities. Gambling in all its forms is forbidden in Islamic jurisprudence. Along with explicit forms of gambling, Islamic law also forbids any business activities which contain any element of gambling (Siddiqi, 1985). The *shari'a* determined that, in the interests of fair, ethical dealing in commutative contracts, unjustified enrichment through games of pure chance should be prohibited.

Another feature condemned by Islam is economic transactions involving elements of speculation, *gharar* (literally 'hazard'). While *riba* and *maysir* are condemned in the Holy Qur'an, condemnation of *gharar* is supported by *ahadith*. In business terms, *gharar* means to undertake a venture blindly without sufficient knowledge or to undertake an excessively risky transaction, although minor uncertainties can be permitted when there is some necessity. In a general context, the unanimous view of the jurists held that, in any transaction, by failing or neglecting to define any of the essential pillars of contract relating to the consideration or measure of the object, the parties undertake a risk which is not indispensable for them. This kind of risk was deemed unacceptable and tantamount to speculation because of its inherent uncertainty. Speculative transactions with these characteristics are therefore prohibited.

This prohibition applies in a number of circumstances, such as when the seller is not in a position to hand over the goods to the buyer or when the subject matter of the sale is incapable of acquisition, for example the sale of fruit which is not yet ripened, or fish or birds not yet caught; that is, short-selling. Speculative business, like buying goods or shares at low prices and selling them for higher prices in the future, is considered to be illicit (Mannan [1970] 1986, p. 289).

Gharar applies also for investments such as trading in futures on the stock market; indeed, *gharar* is present in all future (*mudhaf*) sales and, according to the consensus of scholars, a *gharar* contract is null and void (*batil*). The position of jurisprudence on a future sale is explained by Sheikh Dhareer (1997):

> In this variety of sale the offer (to sell something) is shifted from the present to a future date; for instance, one person would say to another 'I sell you this house of mine at such a price as of the beginning of next year' and the other replies: 'I accept'. The majority of jurists are of the view that the sale contract cannot accept clauses of this nature; if the sale is shifted to a future date the contract becomes invalid . . .
>
> . . . *gharar* in a future contract lies in the possible lapse of the interest of either party and to his consent with the contract when the time set therein comes. If someone buys something by a '*mudhaf*' contract and his circumstances change or the market changes bringing its price down at the time set for fulfilment of contract, he will undoubtedly be averse to its fulfilment and will regret entering into it. Indeed, the object in question may itself change and the two parties may dispute over it.
>
> Thus, we can say that *gharar* infiltrates the *mudhaf* contract from the viewpoint of uncertainty over the time, that is, when the parties conclude the contract they do not know whether they will still be in agreement and have continued interest in that contract when it falls due. (pp. 18–19)

The rejection of *gharar* has led to the condemnation of some or all types of insurance by Muslim scholars, since insurance involves an unknown risk. Further, an element of *maysir* arises as a consequence of the presence of *gharar*. This has led to the development of *Takaful* (cooperative) insurance, considered in Chapter 24 below.

Zakat

According to the Holy Qur'an, God owns all wealth, and private property is seen as a trust from God. Property has a social function in Islam, and must be used for the benefit of society. Moreover, there is a divine duty to work. Social justice is the result of organizing society on Islamic social and legal precepts, including employment of productive labour and equal opportunities, such that everyone can use all of their abilities in work and gain just rewards from that work effort. Justice and equality in Islam means that people should have equal opportunity and does not imply that they should be equal either in poverty or in riches (Chapra, 1985). However, it is incumbent on the Islamic state to guarantee a subsistence level to its citizens, in the form of a minimum level of food, clothing, shelter, medical care and education (Holy Qur'an 58: 11). The major purpose here is to moderate social variances in Islamic society, and to enable the poor to lead a normal, spiritual and material life in dignity and contentment.

A mechanism for the redistribution of income and wealth is inherent in Islam, so that every Muslim is guaranteed a fair standard of living, *nisab. Zakat* is the most important instrument for the redistribution of wealth. This almsgiving is a compulsory levy, and constitutes one of the five basic tenets of Islam. The generally accepted amount of the *zakat* is a one-fortieth (2.5 per cent) assessment on assets held for a full year (after a small initial exclusion, *nisab*), the purpose of which is to transfer income from the wealthy to the needy.

Consequently, in countries where *zakat* is not collected by the state, every Islamic bank or financial institution has to establish a *zakat* fund for collecting the funds and distributing them exclusively to the poor directly or through other religious institutions. This religious levy is applied to the initial capital of the bank, on the reserves and on the profits.

Shari'a board
In order to ensure that the practices and activities of Islamic banks do not contradict the Islamic ethics, Islamic banks are expected to establish a Religious Supervisory Board. This board consists of Muslim jurists, who act as independent *Shari'a* auditors and advisers to the banks, and are involved in vetting all new contracts, auditing existing contracts, and approving new product developments. Also the *Shari'a* Board oversees the collection and distribution of *zakat*. This additional layer of governance is quite different from that for a conventional bank (Algaoud and Lewis, 1999).

The prohibition of *riba*
The prohibition of *riba* is mentioned in four different verses in the Holy Qur'an. These are *Surah al-Rum* (Chapter 30, verse 39); *Surah al-Nisa* (Chapter 4, verse 161); *Surah al-Imran* (Chapter 3, verses 130–32); *Surah al-Baqarah* (Chapter 2, verses 275–81). The verses, as given below, are from the English translation of the Holy Qur'an revised and edited by The Presidency of Islamic Researches, 1413:

> That which you give in usury
> For increase through the property
> Of (other) people, will have
> No increase with Allah:
> But that which you give
> For charity, seeking
> The Countenance of Allah. (*Surah al-Rum*, 30:39)

> That they took usury,
> Though they were forbidden:
> And that they devoured
> Men's wealth wrongfully; –
> We have prepared for those
> Among them who reject Faith
> A grievous chastisement. (*Surah al-Nisa*, 4:161)

> O ye who believe!
> Devour not Usury,
> Doubled and multiplied;
> But fear Allah; that
> Ye may (really) prosper. (*Surah al-Imran*, 3:130)

> Those who devour usury
> Will not stand except
> As stands one whom
> The Satan by his touch
> Hath driven to madness.
> That is because they say:
> 'Trade is like usury,'
> But Allah hath permitted trade

> And forbidden usury.
> Those who after receiving
> Admonition from their Lord,
> Desist, shall be pardoned
> For the past; their case
> Is for Allah (to judge);
> But those who repeat
> (The offence) are Companions
> Of the Fire: they will
> Abide therein (for ever).
>
> Allah will deprive
> Usury of all blessing,
> But will give increase
> For deeds of charity:
> For He loveth not
> Any ungrateful Sinner.
>
> O ye who believe!
> Fear Allah, and give up
> What remains of your demand
> For usury, if ye are
> Indeed believers. (*Surah al-Baqarah*, 2:275–8)

The first of the verses quoted above emphasizes that interest deprives wealth of God's blessings. The second condemns it, placing interest in juxtaposition with wrongful appropriation of property belonging to others. The third enjoins Muslims to stay clear of interest for the sake of their own welfare. The fourth establishes a clear distinction between interest and trade, urging Muslims, first, to take only the principal sum and second, to forgo even this sum if the borrower is unable to repay. The ban on interest is also cited in unequivocal terms in the *hadith* or *sunna*.

Quite clearly, this prohibition is central. Islamic finance, like Islamic commercial law in general, is dominated by the doctrine of *riba*. It is important that we understand the nature of, and reasons for, this prohibition.

Nature of riba
A general principle of Islamic law, based on a number of passages in the Holy Qur'an, is that unjustified enrichment, or 'receiving a monetary advantage without giving a countervalue', is forbidden on ethical grounds. According to Schacht (1964), *riba* is simply a special case of unjustified enrichment or, in the terms of the Holy Qur'an, consuming (that is, appropriating for one's own use) the property of others for no good reason, which is prohibited. *Riba* can be defined formally as 'a monetary advantage without a countervalue which has been stipulated in favour of one of the two contracting parties in an exchange of two monetary values' (p. 145).

The literal meaning of the Arabic word *riba* is 'increase', 'excess', 'growth' or 'addition'. Saeed (1996, p. 20) notes that the root *r-b-w* from which *riba* is derived, is used in the Holy Qur'an 20 times. The root *r-b-w* has the sense in the Holy Qur'an of 'growing', 'increasing', 'rising', 'swelling', 'raising' and 'being big and great'. It is also used in the sense of 'hillock'. These usages appear to have one meaning in common, that of 'increase', in a qualitative or quantitative sense.

The actual meaning of *riba* has been debated since the earliest Muslim times. Umar, the second Caliph, regretted that the Prophet died before having given a more detailed account of what constituted *riba*. Amongst Westerners, the term 'usury' is now generally reserved for only 'exorbitant' or 'excessive' interest. But the evidence from the Holy Qur'an would seem to be that all interest is to be condemned: 'But if ye repent, ye shall have your capital sums [that is principal]' (S2: 279).

On this basis, most Islamic scholars have argued that *riba* embraces not only usury, but all interest (*riba*). This is reminiscent of arguments by medieval Western scholars that all interest is usurious (see Chapter 4 below). *Riba* comes from the root *rab-a* meaning to increase (or exceed), while *rib.h* comes from the root *rabi.ha* meaning to gain (or profit). Certainly the above verse makes it clear that profit is not a form of *rib-a*, and Islamic banking rests on this foundation (Ahmad, 1982, p. 478).

The concept of *riba* is not limited to interest. Two forms of *riba* are identified in Islamic law. They are *riba al-qarud*, which relates to usury involving loans, and *riba al-buyu*, which relates to usury involving trade. The latter can take two forms. *Riba al-fadl* involves an exchange of unequal qualities or quantities of the same commodity simultaneously, whilst *riba al-nisa* involves the non-simultaneous exchange of equal qualities and quantities of the same commodity. The prohibition applies to objects which can be measured or weighed and which, in addition, belong to the same species. Forbidden are both an excess in quantity and a delay in performance. Figure 3.1, based on El Diwany (2003), illustrates the forms of *riba* that are defined in Islam.

Riba al-qarud, the usury of loans, involves a charge on a loan arising with the passage of time, in other words a loan at interest, and is sometimes referred to as *riba al-nasia*, the usury of waiting or delay. It arises where a user of another's wealth, in any form, is contracted by the other to pay a specified increase in addition to the principal amount in repayment. If the increase is predetermined as a specified amount at the outset of the transaction, however this increase occurs, then the loan becomes a usurious one. The prohibition has been extended to all loans and debts where an increase accrues to the creditor.

It is this last form, *riba al-nasia*, in which money is exchanged for money with deferment, that forms the basis of the Western financial system, and is so abhorrent to

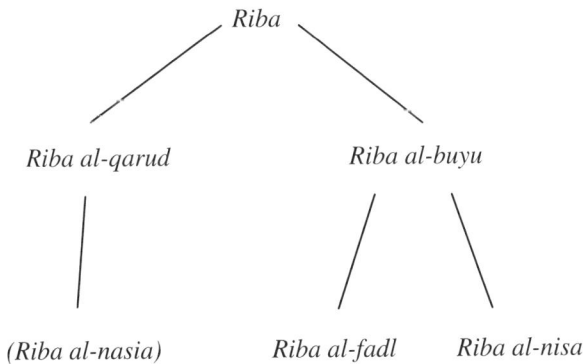

Source: El Diwany (2003).

Figure 3.1   Different forms of riba

Muslims. In the conventional banking system, financial intermediation takes place with lending, and the time value of money is built into interest payments made by the borrower. From an Islamic viewpoint, this practice is *riba,* which is unequivocally condemned.

That all *riba* is banned absolutely by the Holy Qur'an, the central source of Islamic law, is apparent from the verses reproduced earlier. Similarly, in the *ahadith,* the next most authoritative source, the Prophet Muhammad condemns the one who takes it, the one who pays it, the one who writes the agreement for it and the witnesses to the agreement. Nevertheless, despite these clear injunctions, some scholars have questioned the circumstances surrounding the ban in the Holy Qur'an and have wondered whether the objection to *riba* applies (or ought to apply) with equal force today. Fazlur Rahman (1964), in particular, argues as a dissenting view that there has been a disregard of what *riba* was historically, why the Holy Qur'an banned it so categorically, and the function of bank interest in a modern economy.

Revisionist views
The essence of Rahman's position is that *sunna* is not fixed, but dynamic. The prohibition on *riba* clearly does extend back to the Holy Qur'an and the Prophet, but the particular definition given to *riba,* as formalized by earlier generations and enshrined in the *hadith* – namely that it represents any amount of interest – need not be applied. What is needed instead, according to Rahman, is to study *hadith* in a situational context in order to understand the true meaning and extract the real moral value. Rather than apply *ahadith* directly, these should be studied for clues to the spirit of the injunction.

On this basis, it might be argued that the interest prohibition relates only to exorbitant interest rates and not to all forms of interest. The reference quoted earlier from the Holy Qur'an to *riba* 'doubled and multiplied' (S3: 130) may reflect the fact that at the rise of Islam the practice of lending money was being exploited so as to reap excessive gains from the interest charged on loans. If borrowers could not meet the due date by which to return the capital borrowed, the lenders would double and then redouble the interest rates, thus reducing the debtor to penury. Such practices were deemed intimidatory, unjust and against social and economic welfare. The Islamic interdiction of *riba* therefore fell into the net of social reform instituted by the Prophet upon pre-Islamic practices. Certainly, the Islamic code urges leniency towards debtors, and the Holy Qur'an specifies no punishment for unpaid debts.

Similarly, the characteristics of Arab society at the time should be recalled – a largely agricultural, partly nomadic, civilization living as settled communities in walled towns (to protect themselves from marauding Bedouins), linked by caravan routes to each other and Asia Minor. In such an environment, the need for borrowing often arose, not from normal commercial expansion, but from misfortune: famine, crop failure, loss of a caravan and so on. To charge interest to kin, under such circumstances, would be to violate tribal loyalty. Since crop failure and so on may occur to anyone, through no fault of their own, a system of lending freely without interest could be seen as a sort of mutual-help insurance system.

Drawing on some of these points, modernists have raised a number of issues about the definition of *riba.* Some have claimed that Islam has prohibited 'exploitative' or 'usurious' *riba* rather than interest per se, thereby allowing for a 'fair' return on loanable funds (Rida, 1959). Others, like the Syrian Doualibi, would differentiate between 'consumption' loans and 'production' loans on the grounds that the verses in the Holy Qur'an relating to *riba* go hand-in-hand with injunctions to alleviate the condition of the poor, needy and weaker sections of the community (cited in Abu Zahra, 1970). There has also been advanced the view that the prohibition of *riba* covers only individuals, not the giving or taking of interest among corporate entities, such as companies, banks or governments. Some, such as Tantawi, the Sheikh of al-Azhar in Cairo, even argue that bank interest is a sharing of the bank's commercial profit and, being a profit share, is therefore permissible. This view, like the other modernist views, has been almost unanimously rejected.

Also rejected have been those arguments that see fixed interest rates to be *haram* and variable interest rates *halal*. It is said that, if the rate of interest is allowed to vary, this is permissible since the actual rate of return is not fixed in advance. While it is true that the absolute amount of interest under a floating rate contract is not fixed, the formula is specified (for example, LIBOR plus a set spread) and in this sense the payment is predetermined. In effect, both fixed and variable loan contracts require interest to be paid and only the method of determining the amount of interest differs.

'Zeros' have also been rejected. When these were first introduced, some commentators argued that the zero-coupon bonds are 'Islamic' because no interest is paid during their lifetime. A bond is a 'zero coupon bond' if no coupons (that is, interest instalments) are due to the bondholder during the life of that bond. Investors therefore are only prepared to buy zero-coupon bonds at a price that is below face value so that, when the bond matures, the difference between the purchase price and the face value is realized as a gain of waiting. Again, interest is paid; it is just that it is all paid at the maturity date instead of in instalments over the life of the bond.

Thus, despite the modernist views on the meaning of *riba* and how it should justifiably be defined, the dominant position remains intact. One of the most important documents on Islamic banking, the CII (Council of Islamic Ideology) Report (1983), is explicit: 'There is complete unanimity among all schools of thought in Islam that the term *riba* stands for interest in all its types and forms' (p. 7).

Razi's five reasons

This leaves the question: why? Razi ([1872]1938), a Persian/Arab scholar who died in 1209, set forth some of the reasons as to the prohibition of *riba*:

1. That *riba* is but the exacting of another's property without any countervalue while according to the saying of the Prophet a man's property is unlawful to the other as his blood. It is argued that *riba* should be lawful to the creditor in return for the use of money and the profit which the debtor derives from it. Had this been in the possession of the creditor he would have earned profit by investing it in some business. But it should be noted that profit in business is uncertain while the excess amount which the creditor gets towards interest is certain. Hence insistence upon a sum which is certain in return for what is uncertain is but harm done to the debtor.
2. That *riba* is forbidden because it prevents men from taking part in active professions. The moneyed man, if he gets income through *riba*, depends upon this easy means and abandons the idea of taking pains and earning his livelihood by way of trade or industry, which serves to retard the progress and prosperity of the people.
3. That the contract of *riba* leads to a strained relationship between man and man. If it is made illegal there will be no difficulty in lending and getting back what has been

lent, but if it is made legal, people, in order to gratify their desires, will borrow even at an exorbitant rate of interest, which results in friction and strife and strips society of its goodliness.

4. That the contract of *riba* is a contrivance to enable the rich to take in excess of the principal which is unlawful and against justice and equity. As a consequence of it, the rich grow still richer and the poor still poorer.

5. That the illegality of *riba* is proved by the text of the Holy Qur'an and it is not necessary that men should know the reasons for it. We have to discard it as illegal though we are unaware of the reasons (vol. 2, p. 531).

For most scholars the last is sufficient. The meaning and scope of *riba* and its grave nature have been brought to light in the Holy Qur'an (S2: 225). Its prohibition cannot be questioned, as the verse 'God permitteth trading and forbideth *riba*' is quite clear. When the text is clear on this point there is no need for further clarification. Because the Holy Qur'an has stated that only the principal should be taken, there is no alternative but to interpret *riba* according to that wording. Therefore the existence or otherwise of injustice in a loan transaction is irrelevant. Whatever the circumstances are, the lender has no right to receive any increase over and above the principal.

The basis of Islamic financing
In banning *riba*, Islam seeks to establish a society based upon fairness and justice (Holy Qur'an 2:239). A loan provides the lender with a fixed return irrespective of the outcome of the borrower's venture. It is much fairer to have a sharing of the profits and losses. Fairness in this context has two dimensions: the supplier of capital possesses a right to reward, but this reward should be commensurate with the risk and effort involved and thus be governed by the return on the individual project for which funds are supplied (Presley, 1988). Hence what is forbidden in Islam is the predetermined return. The sharing of profit is legitimate and the acceptability of that practice has provided the foundation for the development and implementation of Islamic banking. In Islam, the owner of capital can legitimately share the profits made by the entrepreneur. What makes profit-sharing permissible in Islam, while interest is not, is that in the case of the former it is only the profit-sharing ratio, not the rate of return itself, that is predetermined.

A banking system in which interest is not allowed may appear strange to those accustomed to conventional Western banking practices. In this respect, it is necessary to distinguish between the expressions 'rate of interest' and 'rate of return'. Whereas Islam clearly forbids the former, it not only permits, but rather encourages, trade and the profit motive. The difference is that in trade there is always the risk of loss or low returns. What is eschewed is the guaranteed rate of interest: the pre-agreed, fixed return or amount for the use of money (Khan, 1986).

In the interest-free system sought by adherents to Muslim principles, people are able to earn a return on their money only by subjecting themselves to the risk involved in profit sharing. According to the Hanafi school, profit can be earned in three ways. The first is to use one's capital. The second is to employ one's labour. The third is to employ one's judgment, which amounts to taking a risk. Al-Kásâni, the Hanafi jurist, states: 'The rule, in our view, is that entitlement to profit is either due to wealth (*mal*) or work (*'amal*) or by bearing a liability for loss (*daman*)' ([1910]1968, vol. 7, p. 3545).

With the use of interest rates in financial transactions excluded, Islamic banks are expected to undertake operations only on the basis of profit-and-loss sharing (PLS) arrangements or other acceptable modes of financing. Gafoor (1995) considers the concept of profit-and-loss sharing to be of recent origin:

> The earliest references to the reorganisation of banking on the basis of profit-sharing rather than interest are found in Anwar Qureshi ([1946]1991), Naiem Siddiqi (1948) and Ahmad (1952) in the late forties, followed by a more elaborate exposition by Mawdudi in 1950 (1961) . . . They have all recognised the need for commercial banks and the evil of interest in that enterprise, and have proposed a banking system based on the concept of *Mudarabha* – profit and loss sharing. (pp. 37–8)

But, of course, the idea has earlier origins:

> This situation was envisaged by Islam 1400 years ago. The Islamic law asserted that there should be no pre-agreed rates of interest on loans. Uzair ([1955]1978) says that Islam emphasises agreed ratios of profit sharing rather than fixed and predetermined percentages. Instead, the transactions should be on a profit and loss sharing basis. (Siddiqui, 1994, p. 28)

Under Islamic commercial law, partnerships and all other forms of business organization are set up primarily for a single objective: the sharing of profits through joint participation. These techniques are explored in the following chapter.

References

Abu Zahra, Muhammad (1970), *Buhuth fi al-Riba,* Kuwait: Dar al-Buhuth al-'Ilmiyya.
Ahmad, S.M. (1952), *Economics of Islam,* Lahore: Institute of Islamic Culture.
Ahmad, I. (1982), 'Islamic Social Thought', in W. Block and I. Hexham (eds), *Religion, Economics and Social Thought: Proceedings of an International Symposium,* Vancouver, BC: The Fraser Institute, pp. 465–91.
Algaoud, L.M. and M.K. Lewis (1999), 'Corporate governance in Islamic banking: the case of Bahrain', *International Journal of Business Studies,* **7**(1), 56–86.
Al-Kâsâni, Abu Bakr ibn Mas'ud ([1910] 1968), (d.587/1191), *Bada'I' al-Sana'I fi Tartib al-Shara'i',* 10 vols, Cairo: Al-Galia Press.
Chapra, M.U. (1985), *Towards a Just Monetary System,* Leicester: Islamic Foundation.
Council of Islamic Ideology (Pakistan) (1983), 'Elimination of interest from the economy', in Z. Ahmed, M. Iqbal and M.F. Khan (eds), *Money and Banking in Islam,* International Centre for Research in Islamic Economics, Jeddah and Institute of Policy Studies, Islamabad, pp. 103–211.
Dhareer, Al Siddiq Mohammad Al-Ameen (1997), *Al-Gharar in Contracts and its Effects on Contemporary Transactions,* Jeddah: Islamic Development Bank, Islamic Research and Training Institute.
El Diwany, Tarek (2003), *The Problem with Interest,* London: Kreatoc Ltd.
Gafoor, Abdul A.L.M. (1995), *Interest-free Commercial Banking,* Groningen, The Netherlands: Apptec Publications
Khan, M.S. (1986), 'Islamic interest-free banking: a theoretical analysis', *IMF Staff Papers,* **33** (1), 1–25.
Lewis, M.K. and L.M. Algaoud (2001), *Islamic Banking,* Cheltenham, UK and Northampton, MA, USA: Edward Elgar.
Mannan, M.A. ([1970] 1986), *Islamic Economics: Theories and Practice* (originally Lahore: Islamic Publications, 1970), Sevenoaks, Kent: Hodder and Stoughton.
Mawdudi, Sayyed Abul A'la ([1950]1961), *Sud* (Interest), Lahore: Islamic Publications.
Presley, J.H. (1988), *Directory of Islamic Financial Institutions,* London: Croom Helm.
Qureshi, Anwar Iqbal ([1946]1991), *Islam and the Theory of Interest,* Lahore: Sh. Md. Ashraf.
Rahman, Fazlur G. (1964), 'Riba and Interest', *Islamic Studies,* **3** (1), 1–43.
Razi, Muhammad Fakr al-Din ([1872]1938), *Mafatih al-Ghayb*, known as *al-Tafsir al-Kabir,* Bulaq Cairo: Dar Ibya al-Kutub al-Bahiyya.
Rida, Muhammad Rashid (1959), *al-Riba wa al-Mu'amalat fi al-Islam,* Cairo: Maktabat al-Qahira.
Saeed, A. (1996), *Islamic Banking and Interest,* Leiden: E.J. Brill.
Schacht, J. (1964), *An Introduction to Islamic Law,* Oxford: Oxford University Press.

Siddiqi, M.N. (1985), *Insurance in an Islamic Economy*, Leicester: The Islamic Foundation.
Siddiqi, Naiem (1948), 'Islami usual par banking' (Banking according to Islamic principles), paper in the Urdu monthly, *Chiragh-e-Rah* (Karachi), **1** (11 & 12), Nov. & Dec., 24–8 and 60–64.
Siddiqui, S.H. (1994), *Islamic Banking: Genesis, Rationale, Evaluation and Review, Prospects and Challenges*, Karachi: Royal Book Company.
Uzair, M. ([1955] 1978), *An Outline of Interest-Free Banking,* Karachi: Royal Book Company.

4 Profit-and-loss sharing contracts in Islamic finance
Abbas Mirakhor and Iqbal Zaidi

Profit-sharing contracts

Islamic finance has grown rapidly over the last several years, in terms both of the volume of lending and of the range of financial products that are available at institutional and retail levels. The main characteristic of these financial instruments is that they are compliant with the *shari'a* – the Islamic legal system.[1] Since the Islamic financial system differs in important ways from the conventional interest-based lending system, there is a need to devote more attention to the particular issues raised by Islamic finance. This chapter discusses some key insights from an agency theory perspective, and illustrates how the insights from this literature can be employed to provide a framework for the design of Islamic financial contracts and control mechanisms for the regulation of Islamic financial institutions. The agency theory concepts of incentives, outcome uncertainty, risk and information systems are particularly germane to the discussion of compensation and control problems in Islamic financial contracting.[2]

The main difference between an Islamic or interest-free banking system and the conventional interest-based banking system is that, under the latter, the interest rate is either fixed in advance or is a simple linear function of some other benchmark rate, whereas, in the former, the profits and losses on a physical investment are shared between the creditor and the borrower according to a formula that reflects their respective levels of participation. In Islamic finance, interest-bearing contracts are replaced by a return-bearing contract, which often takes the form of partnerships. Islamic banks provide savers with financial instruments that are akin to equity called *mudaraba* and *musharaka* (discussed below). In these lending arrangements, profits are shared between the investors and the bank on a predetermined basis.[3] The profit-and-loss sharing concept implies a direct concern with regard to the profitability of the physical investment on the part of the creditor (the Islamic bank). Needless to say, the conventional bank is also concerned about the profitability of the project, because of concerns about potential default on the loan. However, the conventional bank puts the emphasis on receiving the interest payments according to some set time intervals and, so long as this condition is being met, the bank's own profitability is not directly affected by whether the project has a particularly high or a rather low rate of return. In contrast to the interest-based system, the Islamic bank has to focus on the return on the physical investment, because its own profitability is directly linked to the real rate of return.

The direct links between the payment to the creditor and the profitability of the investment project is of considerable importance to the entrepreneur. Most importantly, profit-sharing contracts have superior properties for risk management, because the payment the entrepreneur has to make to the creditor is reduced in bad states of nature. Also, if the entrepreneur experiences temporary debt-servicing difficulties in the interest-based system, say, on account of a short-run adverse demand shock, there is the risk of a magnification effect; that is, his credit channels might dry up because of lenders overreacting to the bad news. This is due to the fact that the bank's own profitability is not affected by the fluctuating fortunes of the client's investment, except only when there is a regime change from regular interest payments to a default problem. In other words, interest payments are due irrespective of profitability of the physical investment, and the conventional bank experiences a change in its fortunes only when there are debt-servicing difficulties. But a temporary cash-flow problem of the entrepreneur, and just a few delayed payments, might be seen to be a regime change, which could blow up into a 'sudden stop' in lending. In the Islamic model, these temporary shocks would generate a different response from the bank, because the lenders regularly receive information on the ups and downs of the client's business in order to calculate their share of the profits, which provides the important advantage that the flow of information, as indeed the payment from the borrower to the lender, is more or less on a continuous basis, and not in some discrete steps.

For this and other reasons, Muslim scholars have emphasized that profit-and-loss sharing contracts promote greater stability in financial markets. Islamic financial contracting encourages banks to focus on the long run in their relationships with their clients. However, this focus on long-term relationships in profit-and-loss sharing arrangements means that there might be higher costs in some areas, particularly with regard to the need for monitoring performance of the entrepreneur. Traditional banks are not obliged to oversee projects as closely as Islamic banks, because the former do not act as if they were partners in the physical investment. To the extent that Islamic banks provide something akin to equity financing as against debt financing, they need to invest relatively more in managerial skills and expertise in overseeing different investment projects. This is one reason why there is a tendency amongst Islamic banks to rely on financial instruments that are acceptable under Islamic principles, but are not the best in terms of risk-sharing properties, because in some respects they are closer to debt than to equity. This chapter focuses on this tendency that has been evident in both domestic and international Islamic finance, and comments on what steps could be taken to foster the development of profit-and-loss sharing contracts, which should be given the pride of place under the *shari'a*. The remainder of the chapter is structured as follows. The next section provides a brief overview of Islamic financial principles, and discusses the structure of a few popular Islamic financial instruments. Following this, in the third section, there is a discussion of agency relationship in Islamic financial contracting, namely, the issues that arise when one party (the principal) contracts with another party (the agent) to perform some actions on the principal's behalf and the decision-making authority is with the agent. The fourth section provides a rapprochement between the theory and practice of Islamic financial contracting, including a discussion of what steps could be taken to promote profit-sharing contracts. Finally, an assessment is made in the fifth section.

Overview of Islamic financial contracts
The prohibition of interest (*riba* in Arabic) is the most significant principle of Islamic finance.[4] *Riba* comes from the Arabic root for an increase, or accretion, and the concept in Islamic finance extends beyond just a ban on interest rate to encompass the broader principle that money should not be used to generate unjustified income. As a *shari'a* term, *riba* refers to the premium that the borrower must pay to the lender on top of the principal, and it is sometimes put in simple terms as a 'return of money on money' to emphasize the point between interest rate and rate of return on a financial investment: *riba* is

prohibited in Islam, but profits from trade and productive investment are actually encouraged. The objection is not to the payment of profits but to a predetermined payment that is not a function of the profits and losses incurred by the firm or entrepreneur. Since the Islamic financial system stresses partnership arrangements, the entrepreneur and the creditor (bank) alike face an uncertain rate of return or profit. The Islamic financial system is equity-based, and without any debt: deposits in the banks are not guaranteed the face value of their deposits, because the returns depend on the profits and losses of the bank. Thus, on the liability side, depositors are similar to shareholders in a limited-liability company, while, on the asset side, the bank earns a return that depends on its shares in the businesses it helps to finance.

One well-known Islamic banking model is known as the two-tiered *mudaraba* to emphasize the point that the bank enters into a profit-and-loss sharing contract on both sides of the balance sheet. On the asset side, the bank has a contract with an entrepreneur to receive a predetermined share of his profit in lieu of an interest rate. On the liability side, the bank has a contract with the depositor in which there is an agreement to share the profits accruing to the bank. In the interest rate-based system, depositors expect to receive either a predetermined return or one that is linked to some benchmark interest rate, but there is the risk that, in an extreme scenario or a very bad state of nature event, these expectations might not be fulfilled and the bank will not meet its obligations. However, in Islamic banking, the depositors know that it is the real sector that determines the rate of return that the bank will give to them, because from the very outset, and in all states of nature, the contract between the two parties is one of profit sharing. As such, the depositors expect to receive a return that is closely aligned with the ex post return on physical investment, including the possibility that there might be no or negative return.

There are certain basic types of financial contracts, which have been approved by various *shari'a* boards as being in compliance with the principles of Islamic finance, which are briefly discussed next.[5]

Musharaka *(partnership)*
This is often perceived to be the preferred Islamic mode of financing, because it adheres most closely to the principle of profit and loss sharing. Partners contribute capital to a project and share its risks and rewards. Profits are shared between partners on a pre-agreed ratio, but losses are shared in exact proportion to the capital invested by each party. Thus a financial institution provides a percentage of the capital needed by its customer with the understanding that the financial institution and customer will proportionately share in profits and losses in accordance with a formula agreed upon before the transaction is consummated. This gives an incentive to invest wisely and take an active interest in the investment. In *musharaka*, all partners have the right but not the obligation to participate in the management of the project, which explains why the profit-sharing ratio is mutually agreed upon and may be different from the investment in the total capital.

Mudaraba *(finance by way of trust)*
Mudaraba is a form of partnership in which one partner (*rabb al-mal*) finances the project, while the other party (*mudarib*) manages it. Although similar to a *musharaka*, this mode of financing does not require that a company be created; the financial institution provides all of the capital and the customer is responsible for the management of the project. Profits

from the investment are distributed according to a fixed, predetermined ratio. The *rabb al-mal* has possession of the assets, but the *mudarib* has the option to buy out the *rabb al-mal's* investment. *Mudaraba* may be concluded between an Islamic bank, as provider of funds, on behalf of itself or on behalf of its depositors as a trustee of their funds, and its business–owner clients. In the latter case, the bank acts as a *mudarib* for a fee. The bank also acts as a *mudarib* in relation to its depositors, as it invests the deposits in various schemes.

Murabaha *(cost-plus financing)*

In a *murabaha* contract, the bank agrees to buy an asset or goods from a third party, and then resells the goods to its client with a mark-up. The client purchases the goods against either immediate or deferred payment. Some observers see this mode of Islamic finance to be very close to a conventional interest-based lending operation. However, a major difference between *murabaha* and interest-based lending is that the mark-up in *murabaha* is for the services the bank provides (for example, seeking and purchasing the required goods at the best price) and the mark-up is not stipulated in terms of a time period. Thus, if the client fails to make a deferred payment on time, the mark-up does not increase from the agreed price owing to delay. Also the bank owns the goods between the two sales, which means it carries the associated risks.

Ijara *(leasing)*

Like a conventional lease, *ijara* is the sale of *manfa'a* (the right to use goods) for a specific period. In Muslim countries, leasing originated as a trading activity and later on became a mode of finance. *Ijara* is a contract under which a bank buys and leases out an asset or equipment required by its client for a rental fee. Responsibility for maintenance/insurance rests with the lessor. During a predetermined period, the ownership of the asset remains with the lessor (that is, the bank) who is responsible for its maintenance, which means that it assumes the risk of ownership. Under an *ijara* contract, the lessor has the right to re-negotiate the terms of the lease payment at agreed intervals. This is to ensure that the rental remains in line with market leasing rates and the residual value of the leased asset. Under this contract, the lessee (that is, the client) does not have the option to purchase the asset during or at the end of the lease term. However this objective may be achieved through a similar type of contract, *ijara wa iqtina* (hire-purchase). In *ijara wa iqtina*, the lessee commits himself to buying the asset at the end of the rental period, at an agreed price. For example, the bank purchases a building, equipment or an entire project and rents it to the client, but with the latter's agreement to make payments into an account, which will eventually result in the lessee's purchase of the physical asset from the lessor. Leased assets must have productive usages, like buildings, aircrafts or cars, and rent should be pre-agreed to avoid speculation.

Salam *(advance purchase)*

Salam is purchase of specified goods for forward payment. This contract is regularly used for financing agricultural production.

Bai bi-thamin ajil *(deferred payment financing)*

Bai bi-thamin ajil involves a credit sale of goods on a deferred payment basis. At the request of its customer, the bank purchases an existing contract to buy certain goods on a deferred payment schedule, and then sells the goods back to the customer at an agreed price. The bank pays the original supplier upon delivery of the goods, while the bank's customer can repay in a lump sum or make instalment payments over an agreed period.

Istisnaa *(commissioned manufacture)*
Although similar to *bai bi-thamin ajil* transactions, *istisnaa* offers greater future structuring possibilities for trading and financing. One party buys the goods and the other party undertakes to manufacture them, according to agreed specifications. Islamic banks frequently use *istisnaa* to finance construction and manufacturing projects.

Sukuk *(participation securities)*
Sukuk were introduced recently for the same reasons that led to the establishment of interest-free banking, which was to meet the requirements of those investors who wanted to invest their savings in *shari'a*-compliant financial instruments. As mentioned earlier, interest-based transactions and certain unlawful business activities (such as trading in alcoholic beverages) are ruled out in the Islamic mode of financing. However, this does not mean that the possibility of bond issuance is forbidden in Islamic finance as well. Recognizing that trading in bonds is an important element of the modern financial system, Muslim jurists and economists have focused on developing Islamic alternatives, and the *sukuk* have generated the most attention amongst these financial innovations.

The basic difference between conventional bonds and *sukuk* lies in the way they are structured and floated. In the conventional system of bond issue and trading, the interest rate is at the core of all transactions. In contrast, the Islamic *sukuk* are structured in such a way that the issue is based on the exchange of an approved asset (for example, the underlying assets could include buildings, hire cars, oil and gas pipelines and other infrastructure components) for a specified financial consideration. In other words, *sukuk* are based on an exchange of an underlying asset but with the proviso that they are *shari'a*-compliant; that is, the financial transaction is based on the application of various Islamic commercial contracts. Thus, the equity-based nature of *mudaraba* and *musharaka sukuk* exposes investors to the risks connected with the performance of the project or venture for which the financing was raised. On the other hand, the issuance of *sukuk* on principles of *ijara* (leasing) and *murabaha* (cost plus sale) provides predictable and in some respects even a fixed return for the prospective investors. Under the *shari'a*, a financial instrument is eligible for trading in primary as well as secondary markets only if it assumes the role of *al-mal* or property. Insofar as a bond certificate is supported by an asset, and is transformed into an object of value, it qualifies to become an object of trade. The investor can sell the bond to the issuer or even to the third party if a secondary market for Islamic bonds exists. Therefore asset securitization is essential for Islamic bond issuance.[6]

Implications of agency theory for Islamic financial contracting
In an agency relationship, one party (the principal) contracts with another party (the agent) to perform some actions on the principal's behalf, and the agent has the decision-making authority.[7] Agency relationships are ubiquitous: for example, agency relationships exist among firms and their employees, banks and borrowers, and shareholders and managers. Agency theory has generated considerable interest in financial economics, including

Islamic banking.[8] This section uses agency theory to examine contractual relationships between financiers (principals) and entrepreneurs (agents) in the different types of *sukuks*.

Jensen and Meckling (1976) developed the agency model of the firm to demonstrate that there is a principal–agent problem (or agency conflict) embedded in the modern corporation because the decision-making and risk-bearing functions of the firm are carried out by different individuals. They noted that managers have a tendency to engage in excessive perquisite consumption and other opportunistic behaviour because they receive the full benefit from these acts but bear less than the full share of the costs to the firm. The authors termed this the 'agency cost of equity', and point out that it could be mitigated by increasing the manager's stake in the ownership of the firm. In the principal–agent approach, this is modelled as the incentive-compatibility constraint for the agent, and an important insight from this literature is that forcing managers to bear more of the wealth consequences of their actions is a better contract for the shareholders. However increasing managerial ownership in the firm serves to align managers' interests with external shareholders', but there is another problem in that the extent to which managers can invest in the firm is constrained by their personal wealth and diversification considerations.

The agency literature suggests that, under certain conditions, debt might be useful in reducing agency conflicts. Jensen (1986) argues that, insofar as debt bonds the firm to make periodic payments of interest and principal, it reduces the control managers have over the firm's cash flow, which in turn acts as an incentive-compatibility constraint; that is, it reduces the incentive to engage in non-optimal activities such as the consumption of perks. Grossman and Hart (1986) argue that the existence of debt forces managers to consume fewer perks and become more efficient because this lessens the probability of bankruptcy and the loss of control and reputation. To the extent that lenders were particularly concerned about these issues, the *ijara sukuk* would serve the purpose of imposing these borrowing constraints on the firm's managers.

Ijara sukuk

Ijara sukuk are the most popular type of *sukuk*, and investors of various types – both conventional and Islamic, individual and institutions – have shown interest in this instrument. In particular, the *ijara* concept is the most popular amongst issuers of global Islamic *sukuk*. *Ijara sukuk* are securities of equal denomination of each issue, representing physical durable assets that are tied to an *ijara* contract as defined by the *shari'a*. The *ijara sukuk* are based on leased assets, and the *sukuk* holders are not directly linked to any particular company or institution. These *sukuk* represent the undivided pro rata ownership by the holder of the underlying asset; they are freely tradable at par, premium or discount in primary as well as secondary markets.

To fix ideas about the structure of an *ijara sukuk*, consider a corporation that wants to raise funds amounting to $50 million for the purchase of land or equipment. It can issue *ijara sukuk* totalling that amount in small denominations of $10 000 each. The firm then either purchases the asset on behalf of the *sukuk* holders or transfers the ownership of the already acquired asset to certificate holders who will be the real owners of the asset. The asset is then leased back to the firm and the lease proceeds from the asset are distributed to the *sukuk* holders as dividend. For the issuance of the certificate the *ijara* certificate issuer transfers the ownership of the asset to a Special Purpose Vehicle (SPV), then sells investor shares in the SPV. Since the returns on the certificates, which come from leasing out the assets owned by the SPV, could be either fixed or floating, it is clear that the expected returns are as predictable as a coupon on a conventional bond. *Ijara sukuk* can be issued through a financial intermediary (bank) or directly by the users of the lease assets. A third party can also guarantee rental payments, and since the yield is predetermined and the underlying assets are tangible and secured, the *ijara* certificate can be traded in the secondary market.

However, too high a level of debt subjects the firm to agency costs of debt, especially in the form of distorting the risk-sharing properties. Risk shifting means that, as debt is increased to a large proportion of the total value of the firm, shareholders will prefer riskier projects. By accepting riskier projects, they can pay off the debt holders at the contracted rate and capture the residual gain if the projects are successful. However, if the projects fail, the bond holders bear the cost of the higher risk. Similar considerations apply in the bank–borrower relationship. Indeed, one of the most important lessons of the numerous banking crises is the problem of 'moral hazard' that arises when banks are such an important part of the payments system and the need to protect the depositors is a major political constraint. Under such circumstances, some banks felt that they were too big to fail. The incentives for bank managers had become distorted in the difficult times. In good times, managers are unlikely to take huge risks with depositors' and shareholders' money, because they have their jobs and reputations to protect. However the manager's attitude could change if the bank is close to insolvency. By raising rates to attract new deposits and then betting everything on a few risky investments, the managers can try to turn the banks' dire situation around. This 'gambling for resurrection' is what may have happened to some of the troubled banks during some of the financial crises, which may have tried to avoid insolvency by continuing to lend at very high rates to the same clients. The profit-sharing modes of financing mitigate these types of problems in Islamic finance, because of the close linkages between the assets and liabilities sides of Islamic banks. These are precisely the sort of reasons why one would encourage the use of *mudaraba* or *musharaka sukuk*s.

Mudaraba sukuk

Mudaraba or *muqaradah sukuk* have as an underlying instrument a *mudaraba* contract in which, as discussed above, one party provides the capital, while the other party brings its labour to the partnership, and the profit is to be shared between them according to an agreed ratio. The issuer of the certificate is called a *mudarib*, the subscribers are the capital owners, and the realized funds are the *mudaraba* capital. The certificate holders own the assets of the modaraba operation and share the profit and losses as specified in the agreement. Thus the *mudaraba sukuk* give their owner the right to receive their capital at the time the *sukuk* are surrendered, and an annual proportion of the realized profits as mentioned in the issuance publication. *Mudaraba sukuk* may be issued by an existing company (which acts as *mudarib*) to investors (who act as partners, or *rab al-mal*) for the purpose of financing a specific project or activity, which can be separated for accounting purposes from the company's general activities. The profits from this separate activity are split according to an agreed percentage amongst the certificate holders. The contract may provide for future retirement of the *sukuk* at the then market price, and often stipulates that a specific percentage of the *mudarib's* profit share is paid periodically to the *sukuk*-holders to withdraw their investment in stages.

Musharaka sukuk

Musharaka sukuk are based on an underlying *musharaka* contract, and are quite similar to *mudarada sukuk*. The only major difference is that the intermediary will be a partner of the group of subscribers or the *musharaka sukuk* holders in much the same way as the owners of a joint stock company. Almost all of the criteria applied to a *mudaraba sukuk* are also applicable to the *musharaka sukuk*, but in the *mudaraba sukuk* the capital is from just one party. The issuer of the certificate is the inviter to a partnership in a specific project or activity, the subscribers are the partners in the *musharaka* contract, and the realized funds are the contributions of the subscribers in the *musharaka* capital. The certificate holders own the assets of partnership and share the profits and losses.

Agency theory recognizes that principals and agents often have different goals, and that the agent may not be motivated to act in the interests of the principal when there is goal conflict. In such cases, the principal needs to make sure that a contract is drawn up appropriately and that there are enforcement mechanisms to ensure that its interests are served. However, it is practically impossible to draw up a contract that considers all possible future contingencies. There is outcome uncertainty, which means that outcomes are influenced by unpredictable factors that are beyond the agent's control. For this reason, it is not always possible to infer the quality of the agent's effort by examination of outcomes and to determine unambiguously whether the agent or external factors are to blame if outcomes are poor.[9] If one takes these factors into consideration in financial contracting, it appears that, for short-term and medium-term lending, principals would prefer the *murabaha sukuk*.

Murabaha sukuk

Murabaha sukuk are issued on the basis of *murabaha* sale for short-term and medium-term financing. As mentioned earlier, the term *murabaha* refers to sale of goods at a price covering the purchase price plus a margin of profit agreed upon by both parties concerned. The advantage of this mode of financing is that, if the required commodity in the *murabaha* is too expensive for an individual or a banking institution to buy from its own resources, it is possible in this mode to seek additional financiers. The financing of a project costing $50 million could be mobilized on an understanding with the would-be ultimate owner that the final price of the project would be $70 million, which would be repaid in equal instalments over five years. The various financiers may share the $20 million *murabaha* profit in proportion to their financial contributions to the operation. According to *shari'a* experts, the *murabaha sukuk* certificate represents a monetary obligation from a third party that arises out of a *murabaha* transaction, which means that it is a *dayn*, and it cannot be traded except at face value because any difference in value would be tantamount to *riba*. Accordingly, *murabaha*-based *sukuk* can be sold only in the primary market, which limits its scope because of the lack of liquidity. To allow the trading of the *murabaha sukuk* in the secondary market, Islamic finance experts have suggested that, if the security represents a mixed portfolio consisting of a number of transactions, then this portfolio may be issued as negotiable certificates.

The problem of moral hazard arises because the principal has imperfect information about the agent's actions.[10] Consequently, the agent may be tempted by self-interest to take advantage of the principal. (Actually, the threats of bankruptcy and sudden stops in lending may deliver at least a certain minimum quality of entrepreneurial effort. Unfortunately, they do not necessarily encourage the most effective environment.) In order to protect its interests, the principal may offer the agent a contract that indicates the extent to which his or her compensation is contingent upon certain specified behaviour and outcomes. Control systems that include contracts in which compensation is contingent primarily upon specified outcomes are referred to in the agency literature as 'outcome-based' control systems. On the other hand, control systems that include contracts in which compensation is contingent primarily upon specified behaviour are referred to in the agency literature as 'behaviour-based' control systems.

The advantage of outcome-based contracts is that they may be structured so that they align the goals of the two parties; if entrepreneurs are motivated to maximize income because of profit sharing, they will attempt to produce outcomes that the principal specifies. Consequently, such contracts require the principal to monitor outcomes but reduces the need to monitor entrepreneurs' behaviour. Unfortunately, outcome-based contracts may not be efficient in lending. Their inefficiency may arise, in part, because it is practically impossible for a principal to write a contract that considers all possible future contingencies (supply and demand shocks, wage) that can influence outcomes. Outcome-based contracts may also be inefficient because outcomes may be influenced not just by an entrepreneur's actions but also by factors that are beyond his control.

Thus there may be considerable variation in profits even when the amount and quality of the entrepreneur's effort are high. In such cases, the relative risk aversion of individual entrepreneurs may reduce the efficiency of outcome-based control systems that force them to absorb the risk that their income may vary owing to factors beyond their control. Entrepreneurs will only accept such a risky contract if the expected income from this contract will be greater than that from a contract in which compensation is not dependent upon factors that are outside their control. Also outcome-based compensation systems may discourage entrepreneurs from investing in projects when they feel that these projects may not have favourable outcomes.

Theory and practice in profit sharing
Reflecting the need for a rapprochement between theory and practice in Islamic finance, bankers and policymakers have focused on the problem that, despite several years of experience by now in the countries that have adopted Islamic banking, it is still the case that a high percentage of the assets of the domestic banking system have remained concentrated in short-term or trade-related modes of financing rather than in the more bona fide modes of *musharaka* and *mudaraba*. The weaker Islamic modes are permissible under the *shari'a*, but unfortunately they do not provide the same advantages as the profit-sharing modes, including incentives for financing longer-term investment projects and improved risk management. In the international context, *sukuk* is somewhat similar to a conventional bond in that it is a security instrument, and provides a predictable level of return. However, a fundamental difference is that a bond represents pure debt on the issuer but a *sukuk* represents in addition to the risk on creditworthiness of the issuer, an ownership stake in an existing or well-defined asset or project. Also, while a bond creates a lender/borrower relationship, the subject of a *sukuk* is frequently a lease, creating a lessee/lessor relationship.

Asset-backed securities
Both asset-backed securities (ABS) and project finance loans can be used to create Islamic structures, since the underlying assets generate the return on investment that is not directly linked to a predetermined interest rate. When compared to ABS, project financings are complex to arrange, and moreover, they come to the market at unpredictable intervals, depending on the project cycle in a given country. Thus banks and arrangers have focused on the *sukuk*, which has emerged as the most popular and fastest-growing new product in Islamic finance. However, whereas Islamic finance generally incorporates a degree of risk sharing, the modelling of rental payments can in practice result in a highly predictable rate of return. For example, the *sukuk* can be backed by the underlying cash flows from a portfolio of *ijara* (lease contracts), or other Islamic agreements such as *istisnaa* (financing for manufactured goods during the production period). If the rental payments are calculated on some floating rate benchmark, say the six-month US Dollar Libor, then the end-product will not differ all that much from a debt obligation. Furthermore, to achieve the same ratings as assigned to the sovereign, *sukuks* might include unconditional, irrevocable guarantees and/or purchase agreements from the issuer. In the Bahrain, Malaysia and Qatar deals there was a commitment from the government to buy back the leased assets at a price sufficient to meet the *sukuk* obligations. These guarantees by the borrowers are so central to the credit enhancement of the *sukuk* that the credit rating agencies do not look very closely at the assets in the underlying pool. This may be contrasted to what would be expected in a conventional asset-backed deal, which suggests that *sukuk* are more similar to covered bonds than to securitizations. In a covered bond offering, investors have full recourse to the borrower and, by way of example, in the Malaysian government's inaugural Islamic offering in 2002, the five-year global *sukuk* was backed by government-owned land and buildings, and the offering was structured like a sale-and-leaseback arrangement to accommodate the Islamic prohibition on interest payments.

Covered bonds
Covered bonds are securities backed by mortgages or public sector loans, and in some respects are a form of fixed-rate debt that remain on the lenders' balance sheet. The market was invented in Germany, where mortgage lenders use the bonds, known as Pfandbriefe, to recapitalize and to finance new lending. Issuers like covered bonds because they offer a reliable source of liquidity, while investors like them because they offer a more highly rated investment product than a straight institutional bond. This reflects the fact that the ratings for the covered bond are relatively more independent from issuer, event and credit risk than for the institutional bond. Thus issuers find the covered bond market appealing because they can refinance their asset pools much more cheaply and, because investors feel more secure with mortgage-backed or public sector-backed bonds, they are willing to accept lower returns.

A covered bond generally constitutes a full recourse debt instrument of an issuing bank that is unsecured against the bank, but has a priority claim over a pool of mortgages or public sector assets (cover pool). For instance, covered bonds are backed by pools of mortgages that remain on the issuer's balance sheet, as opposed to mortgage-backed securities, where the assets are taken off the balance sheet. Despite similarities between a covered bond structure and a securitization, the covered bond involves the bank, rather than the SPV (special purpose vehicle), issuing the bonds. Bondholders thus have recourse to the bank as well as to the security over the assets. Unlike a securitization, where the bonds are financed by the cash flows from the assets, the cash flow that supports covered bonds is only used to service the bonds if the bank defaults and there is a call on the guarantee.

Sukuks

Investors also like the fact that covered bond issuers are on a very tight leash, and have strong controls on what they may and may not do. In contrast, borrowers may or may not live within their budget limits. To the extent that *sukuks* are akin to covered bonds, they ought to lower monitoring costs, but this comes at the expense of less efficient risk sharing than in the traditional *mudaraba* or *musharaka* contracts. It should also be noted that monitoring costs are not eliminated altogether in *sukuks*. A potential problem of adverse selection remains with such a contract, because borrowers may be tempted to exaggerate competence, ability or willingness to provide the effort required by the principal in order to obtain a contract or to obtain a contract with more favourable terms. In such cases, the principal, in order to protect its interests, often requires that borrowers should present some evidence of their competence, ability and willingness to provide the necessary effort. Such evidence may include past performance. In order to protect principals from adverse selection, principals may enter into contracts with entrepreneurs who have the necessary credentials with assurance that these agents are able and willing to provide the considerable effort required to obtain the credentials. The threat of terminating the lending also serves as a deterrent to entrepreneurs who wish to misrepresent their abilities and engage in contracts that require practice beyond the scope of their training. In a competitive market, it also may be desirable for principals to ensure that the entrepreneurs are able to deliver high levels of customer satisfaction. To this end, customer evaluations of the firms may be useful data for principals who wish to ensure that they do not enter into contracts with entrepreneurs who are less able to satisfy their customers. Thus customer evaluations of entrepreneurs or firms may be useful information for principals who wish to minimize the problem of adverse selection.

Above and beyond these considerations, some observers have also pointed to the possible advantages of *sukuks* over traditional *musharaka* in terms of securitization and credit enhancement possibilities that are available with *sukuks*. The arguments advanced in this connection are similar to those that were made for using guarantees on certain external debt-servicing payments of indebted developing countries. Those proposals had been motivated by the desire to reduce some of the difficulties that heavily indebted countries had faced in restoring normal market access, which reflected in part the perceptions of market participants concerning the credit risks involved in financial transactions with indebted developing countries. It had been argued that the use of new collateralized financial instruments to securitize existing and new bank claims in the indebted developing countries could play a role in reducing these credit risks.

Structured finance

The securitization of bank claims – that is, the conversion of such claims into readily negotiable bonds that could be held by either bank or non-bank investors – could be facilitated by establishing collateral that would be used to partially guarantee future interest payments or principal repayments on the new bonds. Some countries have undertaken securitization schemes, which collateralized the principal of new bonds. Such a collateralized securitization can result in a reduction in contractual indebtedness since investors will exchange existing claims for new claims bearing a smaller face value when the prospect of future payments is more certain on the new claims. Moreover, it is also possible that the availability of securitized and collateralized claims will stimulate non-bank investor interest in the external obligations of developing countries. Both the reduction in contractual indebtedness and the possible increased involvement of non-bank investors have been viewed as means to foster increased access to international financial markets for countries with debt-servicing difficulties.

To be sure, the downside of structured finance should also be mentioned, because collateralization can result in shifting the financing risk to the country. One technique to mitigate transfer and exchange rate risks has been to establish escrow accounts and to use future export receivables as collateral for the commercial loan. As is well known, however, these techniques may have negative macroeconomic implications if pursued too vigorously or if risk-sharing attributes are skewed too heavily against the borrowing country. The earmarking of foreign exchange revenues for particular creditors may reduce the country's flexibility in responding to a balance of payments crisis. Such contracts may also set prices at significantly below market levels. Finally, they may have large up-front fees, which can undermine a country's foreign exchange position.

An assessment
Three broad approaches that might be considered for invigorating the role of profit-sharing arrangements in Islamic finance in the near term or over the longer term should be mentioned. The first approach could focus on ways to improve the links between the real and financial sides of the economy and to lower the monitoring costs in Islamic financing. The key point is that, when a firm's revenues and/or profits or a country's GDP growth turn out to be lower than what would be the typical case, debt payments due will also be lower than in the absence of Islamic financing. This is a very important advantage of Islamic finance, because it will help maintain the firm's debt/revenue or a country's debt/GDP ratio at sustainable levels, and avoid what could be a costly bankruptcy for a firm, or a politically difficult adjustment in the primary balance at a time of recession for a country. Conversely, when GDP growth turns out higher than usual, the country will pay more than it would have without Islamic financing, thus reducing its debt/GDP ratio less than it would have otherwise. In sum, this insurance scheme embedded in Islamic finance keeps the debt/GDP ratio within a narrower range for the borrowing country.

A second approach to invigorating the profit sharing modes of financing might be to encourage a greater role in the securitization and collateralization of claims on firms or countries, which is done in structured finance or *sukuk*s. However, it should be stressed, at the risk of repetition, that transformation of banking from an interest-based system to one that relies on profit sharing makes the Islamic banking system an essentially equity-based system, and the returns on bank deposits cannot be determined ex ante. Therefore an important difference between interest-based bank lending and Islamic modes of financing is that, whereas the former banking system makes interest payments to depositors regardless of the actual returns on the physical investment, the latter system determines the returns to depositors on the basis of profit sharing, which is linked to the productivity of the investment. However, *sukuk*s do not focus on the close linkages with the real rates of return for a particular firm or for the GDP of the economy at large, which makes them less attractive than the traditional *mudaraba* or *musharaka* contracts. In this connection, it should also be noted that an Islamic financial system has a number of features which distinguish it from the interest-based system, and the absence of a fixed or predetermined interest rate is only one such feature. Indeed, one of the most important characteristics of an Islamic financial system is that there is a close link between the real sector and the financial sector, and *sukuk*s are not the natural instrument for strengthening such linkages.

A third approach to invigorating profit sharing could focus on ways to promote the usability and liquidity of Islamic financial instruments. One way of catalyzing such an expansion could concentrate on the establishment of some form of clearinghouse mechanism for various types of Islamic modes of financing. In this connection, it should be emphasized that, when outcomes are strongly influenced by factors beyond an agent's control, and agents are risk-averse and are reluctant to accept contracts in which their compensation is contingent upon these outcomes, principals may be better off if they offer their agents a contract in which compensation is contingent upon certain specified behaviour. In other words, Islamic financing would complement profit sharing (that is, outcome-based monitoring) with additional incentives for appropriate behaviour. Such a behaviour-based control system, however, is most desirable if principals can specify clearly, a priori, what behaviour an agent should perform and can inexpensively acquire information to ensure that the agent actually performs the contractually agreed-upon behaviour. Unfortunately, there are several potential problems with such control systems. First, it may be very difficult for principals clearly to specify an entrepreneur's behaviour in every possible situation. This is especially likely if an entrepreneur's behaviour must be contingent upon specific aspects of the firm or particular market and there is considerable heterogeneity in these markets. Second, it may be difficult and expensive for principals to monitor entrepreneurs' behaviour. Typically, direct observation of individual actions is usually infeasible. Thus behaviour is usually monitored by examination of the records in major cost categories, that often are required from entrepreneurs to justify their recommendations for increased borrowing. It is likely to be quite expensive to determine whether the right actions were taken by the entrepreneurs. Such data-checking control systems would require highly skilled personnel and even then the evaluations might be rather ambiguous.[11] Be that as it may, this is an area worth further consideration.

Notes

1. See, for example, Iqbal and Mirakhor (1987) and Mirakhor (2005). The body of Islamic law is known as *shari'a*, which means a clear path to be followed and observed.
2. Mirakhor and Zaidi (2005) provide principal–agent models to examine certain key issues in Islamic financial contracting.
3. One example of this partnership would be that the bank provides the financing and the entrepreneur gives his expertise and time to the project. The profits are split according to an agreed ratio, and if the business venture incurs a loss or fails, the bank loses the capital it spent on the project, while the entrepreneur has nothing to show for his time and effort. There can be other types of arrangements in which there are multiple partners and different levels of capital investments, but the main principle of profit sharing remains the same; that is, unlike conventional finance, there is no guaranteed rate of return, and banks should not be nominal or detached creditors in an investment, but serve as partners in the business.

4. There is little or no disagreement amongst scholars when it comes to the very basic tenets of Islamic finance (e.g., prohibition of *riba*, the obligation to be fair and transparent in financial contracting, the principle of profit-and-loss sharing, exclusion of sectors such as alcoholic beverages and casinos from lending operations) but there are some differences in certain detailed issues. For example, interest, either paid or received, is not permitted, but does this mean that an Islamic bank cannot hold any shares in a company that has part of its funding as debt rather than equity? However, to exclude a company that pays interest on any portion of its debt could lead to an adverse selection problem for Islamic banks, because they will be obliged to deal only with those companies that are unable to raise debt.
5. A *shari'a* board is the committee of Islamic scholars available to an Islamic financial institution for guidance and supervision.
6. Securitization is defined as the process of pooling assets, packaging them into securities, and making them marketable to investors. It is a process of dividing the ownership of tangible assets into units of equal value and issuing securities as per their value.
7. Ross (1973) and Jensen and Meckling (1976).
8. See Haque and Mirakhor (1987).
9. The principal has to incur costs in order to draw up contracts and to acquire reliable information either about outcomes or about the nature and quality of the agent's actions. Unfortunately, if such costs are not incurred, the agent may be tempted to provide misinformation about its actions if such behaviour serves the agent's interests. It usually is assumed that perfect information is prohibitively expensive and so principals inevitably have imperfect information about their agents' actions.
10. See Akerlof (1970).
11. This example illustrates well the potential problems of a behaviour-based control system for financial contracting. A control system for investment programmes would be costly because of the need to obtain second opinions from outside managers/entrepreneurs, which runs the risk of giving out important information about the firm to potential competitors. Also, because of the inevitability of disagreements, such a system may not be very effective in detecting any subtle biases in recommendations for particular investments. In summary, monitoring individual entrepreneurs' behaviour to determine the quality or the cost-effectiveness of their investment plans may be expensive and yet may not be very effective.

Bibliography

Aghion, P. and P. Bolton (1992), 'An incomplete contracts approach to financial contracting', *Review of Economic Studies*, **77**, 338–401.
Akerlof, G. (1970), 'The market for "Lemons": quality and the market mechanism', *Quarterly Journal of Economics*, **84**(August), 488–500.
Chapra, M. Umer (1992), *Islam and the Economic Challenge*, Leicester: The Islamic Foundation.
Fama, E. and M.C. Jensen (1983), 'Separation of ownership and control', *Journal of Law and Economics*, **June**, 301–25.
Grossman, S. and O. Hart (1986), 'The costs and benefits of ownership: a theory of vertical and lateral integration', *Journal of Political Economy*, **94**, 691–719.
Haque, Nadeem ul and Abbas Mirakhor (1987), 'Optimal profit-sharing contracts and investment in an interest-free economy', in Mohsin S. Khan and Abbas Mirakhor (eds), *Theoretical Studies in Islamic Banking and Finance*, Houston: The Institute for Research and Islamic Studies.
Hart, O. (2001), 'Financial contracting', *Journal of Economic Literature*, **39**(4), 1079–1100.
Hart, O. and J. Moore (1994), 'A theory of debt based on the inalienability of human capital', *Quarterly Journal of Economics*, **109**, 841–79.
Hart, O. and J. Moore (1998), 'Default and renegotiation: a dynamic model of debt', *Quarterly Journal of Economics*, **113**, 1–41.
Holmstrom, B. (1979), 'Moral hazard and observability', *Bell Journal of Economics*, **10** (Spring), 74–91.
Iqbal, Zubair and Abbas Mirakhor (1987), 'Islamic banking', International Monetary Fund Occasional Paper 49, IMF, Washington, DC.
Jensen, M.C. (1986), 'Agency costs of free cash flow, corporate finance, and the market for takeovers', *American Economic Review*, **May**, 323–9.
Jensen, M.C. and W. Meckling (1976), 'Theory of the firm: managerial behavior, agency costs, and capital structure', *Journal of Financial Economics*, **3**, 305–60.
Mirakhor, Abbas (2005), 'A note on Islamic economics', International Monetary Fund, mimeograph.
Mirakhor, Abbas and Iqbal Zaidi (2005), 'Islamic financial contracts between principal and agent', International Monetary Fund mimeograph.
Ross, S. (1973), 'The economic theory of agency: the principal's problem', *American Economic Review*, **63**(2), 134–9.

Rothschild, M. and J.E. Stiglitz (1976), 'Equilibrium in competitive insurance markets: an essay on the economics of imperfect information', *Quarterly Journal of Economics*, **XC**, 629–49.

Shleifer, A. and R.W. Vishny (1989), 'Management entrenchment: the case of manager-specific investments,' *Journal of Financial Economics*, **June**, 123–40.

Stiglitz, Joseph E. (1974), 'Incentives and risk sharing in sharecropping', *Review of Economic Studies*, **XLI**, 219–55.

Stiglitz, J.E. and A. Weiss (1981), 'Credit rationing in markets with imperfect information', *American Economic Review*, **LXXI**, 393–410.

Stulz, R.M. (1990), 'Managerial discretion and optimal financing policies', *Journal of Financial Economics*, **26**(1), 3–27.

5 Comparing Islamic and Christian attitudes to usury
Mervyn K. Lewis

The Christian attitude to interest

Islam is today the only major religion that maintains a prohibition on usury, yet this distinctiveness was not always the case. Hinduism, Judaism and Christianity have all opposed usury. Under Christianity, prohibitions or severe restrictions upon usury operated for over 1400 years. Generally, these controls meant that any taking of interest was forbidden. But gradually only exorbitant interest came to be considered usurious, and in this particular form usury laws of some sort preventing excessive interest remain in force today in many Western countries (and some Muslim ones). This chapter examines the attitudes of the Christian Church to usury, and compares Christian doctrine and practice with the Islamic position.[1]

To medieval Christians, the taking of what we would now call interest was usury, and usury was a sin, condemned in the strongest terms. Usury comes from the Latin *usura*, meaning enjoyment, denoting money paid for the use of money, and under medieval canon law meant the intention of the lender to obtain more in return from a loan than the principal amount due. It equates to what we would today call interest, measured by the difference between the amount that a borrower repays and the principal amount that is originally received from the lender (Patinkin, 1968). Both usury and interest also correspond to *riba* which, as we saw in Chapter 2, literally means 'increase' or in excess of the original sum. On the face of it, the Islamic stance on usury would seem to be little different from the official Christian position in the Middle Ages.[2]

Doctrinal sources

Christian doctrine derived from three basic sources. First, there were the scriptures, especially the Gospels and the teachings of Jesus. Second, as the Middle Ages progressed and the Church became increasingly institutionalized, the words of Jesus were not sufficient to cover all eventualities and were supplemented, and to a large degree supplanted, by canon law based on the rulings of ecumenical councils and Church courts. Third, schoolmen and theologians laid the foundations of Christian theology, drawing on ethical principles developed by Greek philosophers such as Plato and Aristotle.

Biblical sources

The New Testament has three references to usury, and the Old Testament has four. Of the three passages on usury in the New Testament, two are identical and relate to the parable of the talents (Matthew 25: 14–30; Luke 19: 12–27). Both, it must be said, are decidedly ambiguous on the question of usury (Gordon, 1982). The servant who returns the talents as he received them is castigated by the nobleman for not having 'put my money to the exchanges, and then at my coming I should have received my own with usury' (Mt. 25: 2–7). If interpreted literally, this verse would appear to condone the taking of usury, yet at the same time the recipient is criticized for 'reaping that thou didst not sow' (Luke 19: 21).

However, the other reference in the New Testament is clear: 'But love ye your enemies, and do good, and lend, hoping for nothing again; and your reward shall be great, and ye shall be the children of the Highest' (Luke 6: 35).[3] Jesus himself exhibited a distinctly anti-usury attitude when he cast the money-lenders from the temple, while the Sermon on the Mount revealed strongly anti-wealth sentiments as well.

In the case of the Old Testament, three references to usury come from the Pentateuch, the Law of Moses, the other from Psalms and attributed to David. In historical order:

> If thou lend money to any of my people *that* is poor by thee, thou shalt not be to him as a usurer, neither shall thou lay upon him usury. (Exodus 22: 25).

> And if thy brother be waxen poor, and fallen in decay with thee; then thou shalt relieve him: *yea, though he be* a stranger, or a sojourner: that he may live with thee.
> Take thou no usury of him, or increase: but fear thy God; that thy brother may live with thee.
> Thou shalt not give him thy money upon usury, nor lend him thy victuals for increase. (Leviticus 25: 35–7)

> Thou shalt not lend upon usury to thy brother; usury of money, usury of victuals, usury of any thing that is lent upon usury:
> Unto a stranger thou mayest lend upon usury; but unto thy brother thou shalt not lend upon usury. (Deuteronomy 23: 19–20)

> Lord, who shall abide in thy tabernacle, who shall dwell in thy holy hill?
> He that putteth not out his money to usury, nor taketh reward against the innocent. He that doeth these things shall never be moved. (Psalm 15: 1,5)

In Exodus and Deuteronomy, the biblical (Hebrew) term for interest is *neshekh*, although in Leviticus the term *neshekh* occurs alongside *tarbit* or *marbit*. In the *Encyclopedia Judaica* it is argued that *neshekh*, meaning 'bite', was the term used for the exaction of interest from the point of view of the debtor, and *tarbit* or *marbit*, meaning 'increase', was the term used for the recovery of interest by the creditor (Cohn, 1971, p. 28). In both meanings, it seems to be the case that the prohibition on interest is not a prohibition on usury in the modern sense of the term, that is, excessive interest, but of all, even minimal, interest. Cohn concludes that there is no difference in law between various rates of interest, as all interest is prohibited.

Three other features of the Mosaic injunctions are notable. First, in at least two cases, the ban on usury is connected to poverty and consumption loans (likely the main form of loan at that time). Second, two of the passages extend the ban to any form of loan, not just of money, by including food given for profit. Any time-contingent contract might therefore be regarded as usurious. Third, all three make clear that the prohibition refers to loans to 'brothers', that is, fellow members of the tribe or adherents to the common faith. Charging interest to 'foreigners' was acceptable. In this way, the Jews justified taking interest from Gentiles, and Christians charged interest to 'Saracens' (as Arabs and, by extension, Muslims in general were called in the Middle Ages).[4]

These three qualifications were to prove instrumental to the later removal of the ban. Even at the time, the 'Deuteronomic double standard', as Nelson (1949) termed it, was difficult to explain away by Christians, since Jesus had preached the oneness of friend and foe alike. In addition, the idea that usury to any group could be considered religiously sound was contradicted by the passage from the Psalms quoted above.

Canon law
Canon law was fashioned by the ecumenical councils, the popes and the bishops. The early Church first condemned usury by the 44th of the Apostolic Canons at the Council of Arles, 314, followed by Nicea in 325, and Laodicia in 372. The first Canon law ruling against usury was the Papal Encyclia *Nec hoc quoque* of Saint Leo the Great, pope from 440 to 461. The last Papal Encyclical against usury, *Vix pervenit*, was issued in 1745 by Pope Benedict xiv (although it was not an infallible decree). In between, the Catholic Church maintained its opposition to the practice, although the emphasis did change over time.

At first, the Church's prohibition on usury did not go beyond the clergy, although more general disapproval was expressed to laity by the first Council of Carthage (345). Roll (1953) argues that a wider prohibition was unnecessary. In the absence of a developed money economy and capital market, with most feudal dues rendered in kind, the Church was not only the largest production unit but also virtually the only recipient of large sums of money. Irrespective of the scriptures, for the Church to charge interest on consumption loans to the needy would rightly be seen as exploitation. Glaeser and Scheinkman (1998) suggest that interest-free loans were 'good business' in that they generated enthusiasm amongst the people for religion, and acted as a form of insurance by transferring resources from situations when households were well off to situations when they were in need of help.

As trade and commerce expanded in the later Middle Ages, and the demand for loans increased, to combat 'the insatiable rapacity of usurers' the Church's prohibition was extended to laymen in ever more strident and stringent forms (Divine, 1967). These condemnations came from the great Lateran Councils, Lyon II and Vienne. The Second Lateran Council (1139) condemned usury as 'ignominious'. Lateran III (1179) introduced excommunication (exclusion from the Christian community) for open usurers. Lateran IV (1215) censured Christians who associated with Jewish usurers. Lyon II (1274) extended the condemnations to foreign usurers. Finally, the Council of Vienne (1311) allowed excommunication of princes, legislators and public authorities who either utilized or protected usurers, or who sought to distinguish between allowable interest and usury.[5]

It was thus with good reason that Tawney (1926) described this period as the 'high-water mark' of the ecclesiastical attack on usury. It was also at this time that an extra dimension was added to the Church's arguments against usury in the revival of Aristotelian logic and its combination with Roman law by St Thomas Aquinas (1225–74).

Aquinas and Aristotle
The third influence upon the Church's view on usury came from the medieval Schoolmen and in particular the most important of them, Saint Thomas Aquinas, who is generally acknowledged as the greatest of the scholastic philosophers, ranking in status as a philosopher alongside Plato, Aristotle, Kant and Hegel (Russell, 1946). St Thomas succeeded in persuading the Church fathers that Aristotle's views should form the basis of Christian philosophy, and that the Arab philosophers, especially Ibn Rushd (1126–98) the Spanish–Arabian and his Christian followers, the Averroists, had misinterpreted Aristotle

when developing their views on immortality. Consequently, St Thomas's *Summa Theologica* sought to undo this close adherence to Arabian doctrines.

In the process, St Thomas resurrected Aristotle's views on usury. The Greeks themselves (like the Romans later) exhibited no compunction about the taking of interest, but Plato disliked usury and *The Republic*, his ideal state, was opposed to all credit transactions except those undertaken on the basis of friendship and brotherhood, and explicitly prohibited lending at interest.[6] Plato's pupil Aristotle also opposed interest, based on a distinction between natural and unnatural modes of production, the latter including income from money lending. Interest thus violates natural law, a position with which St Thomas and the Church concurred.

Why did Christians abhor usury?
Having examined the sources of the Christian doctrine on usury in terms of the Bible, the canon law and the writings of the Fathers and Schoolmen overlaid on Greek philosophy, it is now time to pull the threads together. At least ten justifications could be offered by the medieval Churchmen for the ban on usury.

First, usury contravened the teachings of Jesus. Although the passages in the Gospels can be variously interpreted, the absence of a specific condemnation cannot disguise the fact that on the basis of Jesus's casting out of the moneylenders and the principle 'actions speak louder than words', the lending out of money at interest was regarded as the very worst form of gain.

Second, Hebrew law prohibited usury unambiguously. The only point at issue was to whom and how widely the ban applied. However, from the very earliest years, Christians at least should have had few illusions on that score. St Jerome (340–420) and St Ambrose (340–97) claimed that 'brothers' in Deuteronomy had been universalized by the prophets and the New Testament ('love thine enemies'). Consequently, there was no scriptural warrant for taking usury from anyone.

Third, the Scriptures also severely restricted loan-related activities. Much lending of money occurred against objects held in trust (a pawn or pledge) by the lender. The prohibition of usury also extended to the types of collateral which could be used. The usury restriction in Exodus is immediately followed by the injunction: 'If thou at all take thy neighbour's raiment to pledge, thou shalt deliver it unto him by that the sun goeth down' (Exodus 22: 26).

This and other limitations on pledges are given in Deuteronomy 24, and there are restrictions on collateral in the *Halakha* (Rabinovich, 1993). These presumably had the intention of reducing the power of the creditor, and preventing the debtor from having to observe usurious contracts (and thus himself commit a sin). Under Talmudic law, it is not only the creditor who takes interest who is violating the biblical prohibition, but also the debtor who agrees to pay interest, the guarantor who guarantees the debt which bears interest, the witnesses who attest the creation of an interest-bearing debt, and even the scribe who writes out the deed (Cohn, 1971).

Fourth, usury was contrary to Aristotle. Once canonists accepted Aristotle's distinction between the natural economy and the unnatural art of moneymaking, then it followed that the science of economics had to be seen as a body of laws designed to ensure the moral soundness of economic activity. Money, according to Aristotle, arose as a means of facilitating the legitimate exchange of natural goods in order to provide utility to consumers. As such, money was barren. Interest was the unnatural fruit of a barren parent, money.

> The most hated sort [of wealth], and with the greatest reason, is usury, which makes gain out of money itself, and not from the natural object of it. For money was intended to be used in exchange, and not to increase at interest . . . Of all modes of getting wealth, this is the most unnatural. (*Politics*, 1258)

In fact, usury (which of course meant all lending at interest) was doubly condemned. Through usury, the accumulation of money becomes an end in itself, and the satisfaction of wants is lost from sight. Those doing so are rendered 'deficient in higher qualities' (*Politics*, 1323).

Fifth, St Thomas Aquinas augmented the Aristotelian view with the doctrine of Roman law which divided commodities into those which are consumed in use (consumptibles) and those which are not (fungibles). Wine is an example of the former (although perhaps not a good one to use in this context). 'If a man wanted to sell wine separately from the use of wine, he would be selling the same thing twice, or he would be selling what does not exist: wherefore he would evidently commit a sin of injustice.' Since 'the proper and principal use of money is its consumption', 'it is by very nature unlawful to take payment for the use of money lent, which payment is known as interest' (*Summa Theologica*, II, 78).

Sixth, closely related was the view that usury violated natural justice. When a loan of money is made, the ownership of the thing that is lent passes to the borrower. Why should the creditor demand payment from a person who is, in effect, merely using what is now his own property? To do so would be to rob from those who make profitable use of the money. Profits should rightly belong to those who make the money profitable.

Seventh, St Thomas also condemned usury because it 'leads to inequality which is contrary to justice'. The Biblical admonitions on usury are surrounded by references to the 'poor', 'widows and orphans' and those in poverty to whom one is encouraged to 'lend freely, hoping for nothing thereby'. Prohibitions on usury were allied to the notion of a 'just price', which featured in Aristotle's *Ethics* (Thomson, 1953). The moral justification for trade, and wealth derived from trade, depended on whether the exchange which was effected is just. A 'proportionate equality' between the parties prior to exchange is essential if justice is to underlie commercial transactions (*Ethics*, Book V, Ch. 5, p. 152). This was unlikely to be the case when money was lent to needy persons for the purposes of consumption. Usury, and the search for gain for its own sake, was the basest aspect of trade, leading men to the desire for limitless accumulation. In this respect, usury laws were 'commands to be lenient, merciful and kind to the needy' (Maimonides, 1956).

Eighth, since interest was regarded as the means by which the wealthy received an 'unearned income' from the unfortunate, it cut across medieval views on work. Work was a positive virtue and supplied the only justification for any kind of economic increment and profit. Consider the scriptures: 'In the sweat of thy face shalt thou eat bread, till thou return unto the ground' (Genesis 3:19). A university professor, for example, who might otherwise be accused of selling knowledge, which belongs only to God and cannot be sold, could at least argue on this basis that he is working and therefore merits a salary (Le Goff, 1979). But this defence did not help the usurer: 'The creditor becomes rich by the sweat of the debtor, and the debtor does not reap the reward of his labour' (Tawney, 1926,

p. 115). Not only does the usurer not work, but he makes his money work for him. Even in his sleep, the usurer's money is at work and is making a profit. Nor does money observe the Sabbath. Even the peasant lets his cattle rest on Sundays. But the usurer does not let his money respect the day of rest (Baldwin, 1970, vol. 2, p. 191).

Ninth, to the canonists, time was an important consideration in the sin of usury. Interest was a payment for the passage of time. Moreover, usury was defined broadly. Under Charlemagne, who first extended the usury laws to the laity, usury was defined in 806 CE as 'where more is asked than is given' (Glaeser and Scheinkman, 1998, p. 33), while in the thirteenth century usury or profit on a loan (*mutuum*) was distinct from other contracting arrangements. A usurer, in fact, was anyone who allowed for an element of time in a transaction, such as by asking for a higher price when selling on credit or, because of the lapse of time, goods bought cheaper and sold dearer (Tawney, 1926, pp. 59–61).[7] The sin was in exploiting time itself. Time belongs to God, a divine possession. Usurers were selling something that did not belong to them. They were robbers of time, medieval gangsters (Le Goff, 1979, pp. 34–5).

Finally, most damning of all was that interest was fixed and certain. It was a fixed payment stipulated in advance for a loan of money or wares without risk to the lender. It was certain in that whether or not the borrower gained or lost, the usurer took his pound of flesh (Tawney, 1926, p. 55). What delineated usury from other commercial transactions was in its being a contract for the repayment of more than the principal amount of the loan 'without risk to the lender' (Jones, 1989, p. 4).

It was this last point which created an unbridgeable divide between commercial motives and divine precepts. According to Tawney, medieval opinion, by and large, had no objection as such to rent and profits, provided that they were not unreasonable and exploitive. In addition, the ecumenical authorities had endeavoured to formulate the prohibition upon usury in such a way as to not unnecessarily conflict with legitimate trade and commerce. But no mercy was to be shown to the usurer. In many areas of economic activity, temporally based returns were permitted because they involved the taking of a certain amount of risk. But where no risk was considered to be involved, interest taking was strictly forbidden. The usurer's crime was in the taking of a payment for money which was fixed and certain:

> The primary test for usury was whether or not the lender had contracted to lend at interest without assuming a share of the risk inherent to the transaction. If the lender could collect interest regardless of the debtor's fortunes he was a usurer. (Jones, 1989, pp. 118–19)

Comparing Islamic and Christian views
The parallels
The similarities between the views in the previous section and those of Islam outlined in other chapters of this book are striking. These parallels are hardly surprising since Islam builds on, and sustains and fulfils, the message of its two monotheist antecedents, Judaism and Christianity, and a Muslim is not a Muslim unless he or she believes in Jesus, as a messenger of God, and all of the prophets of Allah.

Consider the similarities on the topic of interest. The Christian attitudes seeing usury as the worst form of gain, as lacking any scriptural warrant whatsoever, as involving unjustified collateral, forcing the debtor to sin, as unnatural and barren, as an unwarranted expropriation of property, as devoid of true work, and fixed, certain and lacking in risk sharing, are echoed in (or echo) Islamic views. This parallel is especially so in the case of the last mentioned reason, in that a loan provides the lender with a fixed predetermined return irrespective of the outcome of the borrower's venture, whereas the reward to capital should instead be commensurate with the risk and effort involved and thus be governed by the return on the individual project for which funds are supplied.

There are other parallels as well. Islam comprises a set of principles and doctrines that guide and regulate a Muslim's relationship with God and with society. In this respect, Islam is not only a divine service, but also incorporates a code of conduct which regulates and organizes mankind in both spiritual and material life. The Aristotelian idea that ethics should govern the science of economics would sit comfortably with an adherent, as would the view that the Church (Muslims would of course substitute God) has command over the totality of human relations.

Yusuf al-Qaradawi (1989) gives four reasons for the Islamic prohibition of interest (*riba*), similar to those quoted earlier in Chapter 2 of Razi ([1872]1938):

- Taking interest implies taking another person's property without giving him anything in exchange. The lender receives something for nothing.
- Dependence on interest discourages people from working to earn money. Money lent at interest will not be used in industry, trade or commerce, all of which need capital, thus depriving society of benefits.
- Permitting the taking of interest discourages people from doing good. If interest is prohibited people will lend to each other with goodwill expecting nothing more back than they have loaned.
- The lender is likely to be wealthy and the borrower poor. The poor will be exploited by the wealthy through the charging of interest on loans.

These points are virtually identical to some of the early Christian views. There is also a shared concern about the time element in contracting. Compensation from licit forms of Islamic financing must differ from interest not only by being calculated on a pre-transaction basis but also by not being explicitly related to the duration of the finance.

The differences
However, there are differences too. The first, and most obvious, concerns the central scriptural authority. In the case of the Bible, there are enough ambiguities – New versus Old Testament, Mosaic versus later Hebrew law, and a very parabolic parable[8] – to keep an army of scholars employed (as indeed they did), whereas the injunctions in the Holy Qur'an are forthright. Second, while canon law and scholastic philosophy sought to augment scripture, the essential feature of that source was that it could – and did – change in response to the temper of the times and new religious thinking, whereas the Holy Qur'an provided a fixed and certain point of reference. Third, to the extent that Christian doctrine rested on an Aristotelian foundation it was vulnerable to the charge of being, at heart, anti-trade and commerce. Aristotle adopted the view, later followed by the Physiocrats, that the natural way to get wealth is by skilful management of house and land. Usury was diabolical and clearly the worst way of making money. But there was also something degraded about trading and exchanging things rather than actually making

them, as summed up in the medieval saying, '*Homo mercator vix aut numquam Deo placere potest*' – the merchant can scarcely or never be pleasing to God. By contrast, the Holy Qur'an endorsed trade, so long as it was not usurious.

On all three counts, where Christianity was somewhat equivocal in comparison with Islam, its stand on usury was subject to erosion. Perhaps ironically, the one aspect on which Christianity was more forthright than Islam probably served to reinforce that trend. This was in the area of punishment.

Christian sanctions on usurers
A Christian usurer faced five sanctions. First, he had eventually to face his Maker, and the Church left him in no doubt that he faced the fiercest of the fires of hell.[9] In the scale of values, the usurer was linked with the worst evildoers, the worst occupations, the worst sins and the worst vices. Indeed, the prohibition of usury is even more rigorous than the commandment against murder; murder could be condoned in some circumstances, but nothing could excuse usury. Also, echoing Talmudic law, the sin is shared by all of those who conspire in the acts: public officials who sanction usury and even the debtors themselves. Debtors who contract to pay usury without explicitly demurring in some way are declared to share the creditor's sin. Without the addict, the dealer could not survive.

Second, disclosure meant becoming a social outcast. It has been said that the usurer was 'tolerated on earth but earmarked for hell' (Lopez, 1979, p. 7), but this was not so. Public opinion was that usurers should be exterminated like wolves, and their bodies thrown on the dung hill. They should be condemned to death and hanged, or at the very least banished from the country and their property confiscated.[10] They were fit only to associate with Jews, robbers, rapists and prostitutes, but were worse than all of them. Thirteenth-century society was classified according to two groupings: a classification by sins and vices, and a classification according to social rank and occupation. On both lists, usurers were at the bottom of the heap. They were publicly preached at, shamed, taunted and reviled.

Third, the usurer would be punished by the Church, and by the orders of the Church. The Lateran Councils laid down clear rules for offenders: they were to be refused communion or a Christian burial, their offerings were not to be accepted, and open usurers were to be excommunicated. There could be no absolution for them and their wills were to be invalid. Those who let houses to usurers were themselves to be excommunicated. No usurer could hold public office. Church courts and civil courts fought over the lucrative business of who would levy the fines.

Fourth, the only salvation for the usurer lay in restitution. Restitution had to be made to each and every person from whom interest or increase had been taken, or to their heirs. Were that not possible, the money had to be given to the poor. All property that had been pawned had to be restored, without deduction of interest or charges. And the ecclesiastical authorities could move against the usurers and their accomplices even if the debtors would not.

Fifth, the usurer risked condemning his wife and heirs to penury, for the same penalties were applied to them as to the original offender. They also faced a lifetime of humility and devotion. Certain actions of the living (alms, prayers, masses) could aid in the posthumous redemption of the usurer: the sinful husband might be saved by the faithful wife. By becoming recluses, and engaging in alms, fasts and prayers, the wife and children might move God to favour the usurer's soul.

Islamic sanctions
In comparison with these punitive measures, the sanctions imposed on the Islamic usurer seem less extreme. That the usurer will not fare well on the Day of Judgement is clear enough. Consider Zamakhshari on Sura 2: 275–6:

> Those who consume interest (*ar-riba*) shall not rise again (on the day of resurrection), except as one arises whom Satan has prostrated by the touch (that is, one who is demon-possessed): that is because they have said: 'Bargaining is just the same as interest, even though God has permitted bargaining but has forbidden interest. Now whoever receives an admonition from his Lord and then desists (from the practice), he shall retain his past gains, and his affair is committed to God. But whoever repeats (the offence) – those are the inhabitants of the fire, therein dwelling forever.[11]

However, no specific penalty on usurers was laid down in the Holy Qur'an, and it was left to the jurists to determine the scale of punishment, qualification and legal validity (Schacht, 1964, p. 12). According to Islamic law, *riba* falls into the category of those violations against the command of God for which discretionary punishment (*al-ta'zir*) is determined by judges of the *shari'a* courts. There is in these cases (which include usury) neither fixed punishment nor penance, and the ruler or the judge is completely free in the determination of the offences or sanctions (El-Awa, 1983).

As for the legal status of *riba* transactions, Islamic law recognizes, first, a scale of religious qualifications and, second, a scale of legal validity. Interest is forbidden (*haram*), but on Schacht's (1964, p. 145) interpretation a contract concluded in contravention of the rules concerning *riba* is defective (*fasid*) or voidable rather than null and void (*batil*). Nevertheless, this distinction between the two is not recognized by all schools of Islamic law, and since *riba* is a special case of 'unjustified enrichment' by which the property of others is consumed (or appropriated for one's own use) for no good reason, the *riba* element cannot be enforced. It is a general principle of Islamic law, based on a number of passages in the Holy Qur'an, that unjustified enrichment, or 'receiving a monetary advantage without giving a countervalue', is forbidden, and he who receives it must give it to the poor as a charitable gift. The latter condition is the practice of Islamic banks when extant transactions are found to have violated the ban on interest, and the earnings are distributed by *shari'a* boards to various *zakat* funds.

The Christian usury ban in practice
Usury was clearly a sin but it was one that many Christians found difficult to resist, despite the severe temporal penalties exacted by the ecclesiastical authorities. To what extent the prohibition on usury was followed is a matter of debate. Some consider that the usury laws were rarely obeyed, others contend that evasion was difficult and rare (Temin and Voth, 2004). However, if evasion was to take place, it was much better for the interest element to be concealed and many a technique was developed in order to come to gain, while not violating the letter of the law. Of course, it hardly needs to be said that such stratagems are not unknown in Muslim economic life.

Our examination of these arrangements in medieval Christianity is grouped under six headings. First, there are the variations upon *interesse*. Second, there are those transactions which took advantage of the international dimension. Third, interest income could be converted into other permissible forms of income. Fourth, some of the legal fictions that were employed borrowed directly from those being used contemporaneously by the early Muslim community to circumvent the ban on *riba* (as others did from Jewish evasions). However, it is the fifth and sixth categories – partnerships and *mudaraba*-type investments – which are particularly interesting. Some practices followed seem virtually identical to those which have gained approval today in Islamic financing.

Interesse

A number of techniques rested on the distinction between *usura*, which was unlawful, and *interesse*, compensation for loss, which was lawful. Under the doctrine of *damnum emergens*, the suffering of loss, the lender was entitled to exact a penalty from the borrower if he failed to return the principal at the agreed time, that is if he defaulted. Thus, while a person was prevented from charging money for a loan, he could demand compensation (*damna et interesse*) if he was not repaid on time. *Interesse* referred to the compensation made by a debtor to a creditor for damages caused to the creditor as a result of default or delays in the repayment of the principal, corresponding to any loss incurred or gain forgone on the creditor's part.[12] This provision opened the door to the taking of interest, since the courts assumed that there had been a genuine delay and that a *bona fide* loss had occurred. By making very short-term loans and simulating delay (*mora*) in repayment, interest could be concealed.

Payment could also be demanded under the doctrine relating to *lucrum cessans*. As well as compensation for damage suffered, the lender could be compensated for the gain that had been sacrificed when money was lent. A creditor with capital invested in a business could claim compensation on this account, and the growing opportunities for trade made it easier to prove that gain had escaped him. A wide range of financial transactions could be legitimized in this way, especially since a special reward could be claimed by the lender because of the risk which had been incurred.

International transactions

The international dimension could also be utilized. If the asset concerned was a foreign one, the price at which the sale was concluded could be used to conceal that the transaction was really the combination of a loan with a foreign exchange transaction. The most typical case was that of the bill of exchange, and special 'foreign exchange fairs' which operated between 1553 and 1763 were held at regular intervals, usually four times a year, largely for the purpose of issuing bills payable there and organizing foreign exchange clearing (Kindleberger, 1984; de Cecco, 1992).

Usually a medieval bill of exchange transaction consisted of the sale for local currency of an obligation to pay a specified sum in another currency at a future date. It thus involved both an extension of credit and an exchange of currency. A present-day bank would handle this transaction by converting the foreign into the local currency at the ruling spot rate of exchange, and then charging a rate of discount for the credit extended when paying out cash now for cash later. To do so in the Middle Ages would have been usurious, for discounting was not an allowable activity. Consequently, by not separating the two elements involved, the medieval banker bought the bill at a price which incorporated both an element of interest and a charge for his services as an exchange dealer. Many Islamic scholars would contend that much the same concealment underlies the *murabaha* (or mark-up) techniques used by Islamic banks today where the mark-up is meant to incorporate service fees alone, but has the appearance of interest.

Of course, the Medieval banker then had an open book which had to be closed by reversing the transaction and buying a bill in the foreign location, and receiving payment in his own currency. The fluctuation of exchange rates provided a convincing case of risk, since the terms at which the reverse deal could be undertaken would not be guaranteed at the time of the original transaction. It was this risk that reconciled bill dealing with the laws.[13]

Once the bill of exchange became admissible, it was a short step to lend money domestically by means of fictitious exchange transactions involving drafts and redrafts between two places. For example, a merchant needing cash would get it from an Italian banker by drawing a bill on the banker's own correspondent at the fairs of Lyons or Frankfurt. When this bill matured, it would be cancelled by a redraft issued by the correspondent and payable by the borrowing merchant to his creditor, the banker. Thus the latter would recover the money which he had lent. To confuse the theologian, the real nature of the *cambio con la ricorsa*, as it was called, was clouded in technical jargon and was further obscured by clever manipulations in the books of the banker and of his correspondent. But once these trimmings were stripped away, it was simply discounting taking place under the cover of fictitious currency exchanges (de Roover, 1954, 1963).

Many bankers had a guilty conscience about getting around the usury laws in this way, as reflected by those of their number who included in their wills and testaments a distribution to the Church or to the needy in restitution for their illicit returns (Galassi, 1992). Other bankers institutionalized their attempt to buy 'a passport to heaven'. In fourteenth-century Florence, the Bardi and Peruzzi banks regularly set aside part of their annual profits for distribution to the poor, holding the funds in an account under the name of *Messer Domineddio*, Mr God-Our-Lord (ibid., p. 314).

Income conversions
Converting interest income into permitted sources of earnings lay at the heart of all of the techniques, including those above. Land provided the vehicle for the one form of investment that was widely understood and universally practised, even by the Church itself. This was the rent charge. Those with funds to lend could purchase a contract to pay so much from the rents of certain lands or houses or premises in return for the sum outlaid. For example, around 1500 CE, £10 a year for £100 down was about a normal rate in England. Such an investment was not regarded as usurious, despite being as fixed, certain and safe in medieval conditions as any loan. As in most legal systems, observance of the letter rather than the spirit of the law often took precedence.

Islamic hiyal
Not surprisingly, the same pressures to follow 'form' over 'substance' in commercial dealings existed in the Islamic countries, and at much the same time. Commercial practice was brought into conformity with the requirements of the *shari'a* by the *hiyal* or 'legal devices' which were often legal fictions (Schacht, 1964). It seems quite likely that many of these *hiyal* were conveyed to medieval Europe by Muslim traders, presumably through the principles and practice of the triangular international trade and commerce which connected the Islamic countries, Byzantium and (at that stage) the relatively undeveloped West.

Muslim merchants, like those in the West, utilized the potential of the bill of exchange to (and perhaps beyond) the limits of the law. Another device consisted of giving real property as a security for the debt and allowing the creditor to use it, so that its use represented the interest. This arrangement was not dissimilar to the rent charge. Closely related to this transaction was the sale of property with the right of redemption (*bay' al-wafa', bay' al-'uhda*).

A popular technique consisted of the double sale (*bay 'atan fi bay'a*). For example, the (prospective) debtor sells to the (prospective) creditor an item for cash, and immediately buys it back from him for a greater amount payable at a future date. This amounts to a loan with the particular item concerned as security, and the difference between the two prices represents the interest. Schacht claims that there were 'hundreds' of such devices used by traders cum moneylenders, all with a scrupulous regard for the letter of the law.[14] It goes without saying, of course, that from an Islamic perspective these legal fictions or *hiyal* are strictly prohibited.

Partnerships

Some of the more approved modes of Islamic financing also featured in medieval Europe. Since the legal form of the financing was what ultimately mattered, the owner and the prospective user of funds could, as an alternative to arranging a loan, form a partnership (*nomine societatis palliatum*), with profit and loss divided among them in various ways. What was of crucial importance, theologically, was that the provider of funds had to share in the partner's risk. That proviso rendered the arrangement broadly equivalent to that of the Islamic *musharaka*, under which an entrepreneur and investor jointly contribute funds to a venture, and divide up the profits and losses according to a predetermined ratio. Finance-based partnerships involving merchants find mention in Islamic sources around 700 CE, but the origins in the West (the *commenda* and the *compagnia*) go back no further than the tenth century (Lopez, 1979).

Of course, it was also possible to use the partnership form as a legal fiction to cloak what was really interest rate lending in all but name. For example, a person might have lent money to a merchant on the condition that he be a partner in the gains, but not in the losses. Another favourite method, used particularly in the City of London, was for the 'partner' providing funds to be a 'sleeping one' to conceal the borrowing and lending of money. Even more complicated devices such as the *contractus trinus* (triple contract) were devised which, while approved by custom and law, caused much theological strife.[15]

Mudaraba-type investments

More interesting still was the existence in Middle Ages Europe of *mudaraba*-type arrangements when the medieval banks took in funds from depositors. Under these types of account no fixed return was specified but the depositor was offered a share or participation in the profits of the bank. For example, on 17 November 1190, a servant of the famous Fieschi family entrusted 'capital' of £7 Genoese to the banker Rubeus upon condition that he could withdraw his deposit on 15 days' notice and that he would receive a 'suitable' return on his money (de Roover, 1954, p. 39). Much closer to present-day *mudaraba* were the investment modes offered by the Medici Bank. For example, the famous diplomat and chronicler Philippe de Commines (1447–1511) placed with the Lyons branch of Medici a time deposit which, instead of yielding a fixed percentage, entitled him to participate in the profits 'at the discretion' of the bank (*depositi a discrezione*). As another illustration, the contract between this same bank and Ymbert de Batarnay, Seigneur du Bouchage, concerning a deposit in 1490 of 10 000 écus does not mention any fixed rate, but states, on the contrary, that this sum was to be employed in lawful trade and the profits accruing therefrom were to be shared equally between the contracting parties (de Roover, 1948, p. 56).

The historian Raymond de Roover called this 'strange behaviour' and dismissed the practice as merely a legal deception to skirt the usury laws. Viewed from the perspective of current Islamic banking, however, the arrangement seems an entirely appropriate response, valid in its own right. It would thus be fascinating to know how widespread this type of contract was (it was obviously in operation for over 300 years), and why it later fell into disuse.

The Christian retreat

With the advent of the mercantile era (c.1500–1700) the practice of the taking of interest, which had been forbidden by the Church, gradually came to be accepted (although cases involving usury were still being heard in England in the reign of Elizabeth I) and eventually sanctioned. Why did the prohibition on usury break down throughout Europe?

Growth in commerce
Tawney was the first to connect this shift in religious thought with the rise in commerce. He argued that economic growth swelled the channels for profitable investment to such an extent that the divorce between theory and reality had become almost unbridgeable. Greater investment opportunities made the usury laws more costly and tiresome to enforce, while the devices to get around the prohibition had become so numerous that everyone was concerned with the form rather than the substance of transactions. In effect, the ban had become unworkable and the rulings themselves were brought into disrepute.

When the bans were introduced in the early Middle Ages, the Church itself was the centre of economic life, and canon law was concerned with ensuring that its own representatives were kept in line. As the outside market grew and commerce expanded, more and more activity moved outside the controlled (that is non-usury) sector. At first, the Church extended the ban on usury to the non-controlled activities. When the market continued to expand, and the legal devices to circumvent the regulations expanded also, the Church's condemnations became at first more strident and its penalties more severe as it tried to keep a lid on the expansion of interest transactions. But at some point the tide turned. As the thinly disguised interest economy continued to grow, more and more were willing to seek immediate gains in the present world and take their chances in the hereafter, hoping that a deathbed confession and token restitution would ensure an easier route to salvation. The Church itself was forced to devote more of its energies to examining the accounts of moneylenders and merchants in order to root out the various subterfuges used to conceal usury. In short, the cost of maintaining and policing the prohibition increased to such an extent that it became desirable all round to remove the irksome controls.

Then the problem, of course, was how to save face and break from the past, particularly when so much intellectual capital and moral fervour had been devoted to the issue. It was necessary to avoid the charge of hypocrisy or moral backsliding. In this case the solution came in the form of the challenge to the orthodoxy of Catholicism from the rise of Protestantism associated with the names of Luther and Calvin.

Calvin and the rise of Protestantism

Luther was rather ambivalent on the topic of usury, but Calvin was not. His stand (in a series of letters beginning in 1547) denying that the taking of payment for the use of money was in itself sinful has been hailed as a 'turning point in the history of European thought' (Ashley [1888, 1893]1913), as the foundation stone of the 'spirit of capitalism' (Weber, 1930) and the 'Gospel of the modern era' (Nelson, 1949). Much earlier, St Paul had declared that the 'New Convenant' between Jesus and the people had superseded the old covenant of Mosaic law, so that Judaic law was no longer binding on Christian society (Letter to the Romans, ch.3). Calvin went further. He argued that neither the old Halakic code nor the rulings of the Gospels were universally applicable and binding for all time, because they were shaped by and designed for conditions that no longer exist. Rather they should be interpreted in the light of individual conscience, the equity of the 'golden rule' (do unto others as you would have them do unto you) and the needs of society.[16]

Thus under Calvin's reformation the lender is no longer a pariah but a useful part of society. Usury does not conflict with the law of God in all cases and, provided that the interest rate is reasonable, lending at interest is no more unjust than any other economic transaction; for example, it is as reasonable as the payment of rent for land. Although Calvin repudiated the Aristotelian doctrine that money was infertile, he nonetheless identified instances in which the taking of interest would be an act of sinful usury, as in the case of needy borrowers oppressed by circumstances and faced with exorbitant interest rates. But these are problems inherent in the social relations of a Christian community, to be solved in the light of existing circumstances and the dictates of natural law and the will of God, not by blanket prohibition.

Redefining usury

Calvin's doctrine has become the language of modern (or at least non-evangelical) Protestant Christianity. However, in terms of usury laws, the practical reality of the time was that everyone who sought a more liberal approach to usury turned to Calvin for support. Throughout Protestant Europe, governments embraced his views to abolish the legal prohibition of interest. Somewhat earlier, after Henry VIII's break with Rome, a statute was enacted in England in 1545 legalizing interest but limiting it to a legal maximum of 10 per cent, and legislation laying down a maximum rate in place of a prohibition of interest was made permanent by law in 1571. Such 'usury laws' became the norm thereafter in Protestant Europe.

The retreat of Catholic canon law was in general slower and involved the concession of exceptions while clinging to the principle. Nevertheless, in the nineteenth century, the Roman Catholic authorities also relented by the issuance of some 14 decisions of the Congregations of the Holy Office, the Penitentiary and the Propaganda stating that the faithful who lend money at moderate rates of interest are 'not to be disturbed', provided that they are willing to abide by any future decisions of the Holy See. Nonetheless, the Church still provides in the Code of Canon Law (c.2354) severe penalties for those convicted of usury in the modern sense, that is excessive interest (Nelson, 1949: Divine, 1967).

Consequently, from a modernist perspective, the great achievement of Calvin and his followers was, in effect, to have turned Deuteronomy on its head. Finding a solution to the troublesome 'Deuteronomic double standard' had long worried Christian theologians imbued with ideas of universal fraternity. Amongst the early Church, the distasteful implication that usury was lawful when levied upon some ('foreigners') but unlawful and sinful when applied to others ('brothers') was initially resolved by not charging interest to anyone. Following Calvin, the resolution came about instead by charging usury to all, but at a rate deemed to be not injurious.

Can Islam sustain its ban on usury?
This chapter has shown that the Christian Church maintained a prohibition on usury (interest) for over 1400 years and, once the terminological differences are sorted out and the doctrinal sources examined, it is apparent that the official Christian objection to usury was almost identical to the Islamic position. Moreover, some of the financing methods used by Christians to conform with the Church's opposition to usury were quite consistent with the spirit of the law and similar to the preferred modes of Islamic financing, such as *musharaka* and *mudaraba*. This raises a question. Will Islam, nearly 1400 years after the Prophet's revelations, go the same way as Christianity and relax its ban on interest?

Notwithstanding the similarities between the Christian and the Islamic positions on interest, there were differences, too. In fact, the divergences between the two religions on their stance about usury go a long way to explaining why Christianity relaxed and eventually retreated from the ban on usury, while Islam has not. One factor was the lack in the Christian creed of an overriding injunction on the subject like that in the Holy Qur'an. That deficiency, along with ambiguities on related issues such as the acceptability of trade, opened up Catholicism to the inroads of Protestant revisionist interpretations on usury.

Another difference came from the severity of the temporal penalties applied to usurers by the Christian ecclesiastical courts. These inhibited much legitimate trade and at the same time raised the incentive to evade the prohibition in the form of taking advantage of various legal loopholes, which brought the institution itself into disrepute because of the transparency of some of the devices.

At the same time, however, it can also be claimed with considerable justification that in medieval Christendom too much time was devoted to evasion, and by the Church to condemning and rooting out the evaders, than to finding acceptable non-interest alternatives to usury. In Islam, compliance has been left as a matter for the individual (and his Maker), but the Islamic community and the Islamic bankers have spent much effort examining the legitimacy of particular transactions and formalizing procedures which have enabled everyday banking, finance and commerce to be conducted on an *halal* basis.

On this interpretation, a key factor governing the success of Islamic banking and finance is product innovation – fashioning instruments which remain genuinely legitimate, in the sense of meeting the spirit as well as the letter of the law, while responding to the ever-changing financial needs of business and commerce. Many examples of such product innovation are given in later chapters.

Nevertheless, there are also some dissenting voices in the Islamic community on the legitimacy of many of these products. These critics feel uneasy with many of the directions that Islamic financing has taken. In this respect, they wonder whether the battle against *riba* may have already been lost because many of the activities, such as mark-up techniques and *sukuk*, essentially replicate, with some modifications, interest rate banking and, to this degree, amount to *hiyal,* legal fictions. The critics hold to this view because these financial instruments are seen to be structured in such a way that they generate virtually fixed returns to investors, with little risk, violating the spirit, if not the letter, of the Qur'anic injunction. These criticisms of Islamic banking practices are also matters that are explored in later chapters.

Notes

1. The chapter draws extensively upon Lewis (1999).
2. The Middle Ages usually refers to the period in Europe, between the disintegration of the Western Roman Empire in 476 CE and the onset of the Italian Renaissance, and covering an area stretching from Sweden to the Mediterranean. This was the period when the Church had vast secular and religious authority and was a universal and unifying force across Christian countries. For our purposes, we need to extend the analysis to at least the sixteenth century, for the great medieval unity of Christendom – and its views on usury – went largely unchallenged until the Protestant Reformation and the rise of Calvinism.
3. This and other passages below come from the Authorised Version or King James Version of 1611 prepared by scholars in England.
4. This practice was often rationalized as an instrument of warfare. Pope Alexander III in 1159 argued that 'Saracens and heretics' whom it had not been possible to conquer by force of arms would be compelled under the weight of usury to yield to the Church (Nelson, 1949, p. 15).
5. The Church's position is outlined in Jones (1989), Le Goff (1979, 1984), Nelson (1949), Noonan (1957).
6. Platonic and Greek economic thought is explained by Trever (1916) and Langholm (1984).
7. There is similarity here to the Rabbinic rulings in the Mishna, the collection of legal interpretations of Exodus, Leviticus, Numbers and Deuteronomy. Loans of goods and speculative trading in wheat are ruled as morally equivalent to usury (Baba Mesia 5:1) (Levine, 1987).
8. The description owes to Keen (1997).
9. For example, a special place is reserved for the usurer in the *Inferno*, volume 1 of the classic by Dante Alighieri (1265–1321). See Dante ([1314] 1984).
10. All of these actions were recommended in Thomas Wilson's *Discourse upon Usury* (1572) quoted in Nelson (1949).
11. From the commentary of the Persian–Arab scholar Abul-Qasim Mahmud ibn Umar az-Zamakhshari completed in 1134 CE, as reported in Gätje (1997).
12. The compensation originated from *id quod interest* of Roman law, which was the payment for damages due to the nonfulfilment of a contractual obligation (*Encyclopedia Britannica*, 1947 edn).
13. Owing to the slowness of communications at that time, even a sight draft was a credit instrument, since time elapsed while it was travelling from the place where it was issued to the place where it was payable. The theologians insisted upon the observance of the *distantia loci* (difference in place), but they tended to play down the fact that the difference in place necessarily incorporated a difference in time (*dilatio temporis*). As the jurist Raphael de Turri, or Raffaele della Torre (c.1578–1666), put it succinctly: *distantia localis in cambio involvit temporis dilationem* (distance in space also involves distance in time). Although he could not deny that a *cambium* (exchange) contract was a loan mixed with other elements, he wrote a treatise full of references to Aristotle, Aquinas and a host of scholastic doctors in order to establish that exchange dealings were not tainted with any usury. In other words, the exchange transaction was used to justify profit on a credit transaction (de Roover, 1967).
14. The first and simplest *hiyal* were probably thought out by the interested parties who felt the need for them, the merchants in particular, but it was quite beyond them to invent and apply the more complicated ones. They would have had to have recourse to specialists with knowledge of the *shari'a*. The early development of Islamic law is examined by Lindholm (1996).
15. The kind of loan which the Church condemned – a loan in which the creditor claimed interest from the beginning of the loan and stipulated the return of his principal, whether the enterprise was successful or not – could be considered a combination of three separate contracts. The components were a *commenda* in the form of a sleeping partnership, an insurance contract against the loss of the principal, and an insurance contract against fluctuations in the rate of profit. What clearly was legal was that A could enter into partnership with B; he could further insure the principal against loss with C and contract with D against loss caused by fluctuations in profits. The essence of the triple contract was that it combined three separate contracts which were legal when struck in isolation between different parties, but when combined and made between just two parties had the effect of contracting for an advance of money at a fixed rate of interest. If it was lawful for A to make these three contracts separately with B, C and D, why was it not possible for A to make all three of them with B? This was the dilemma posed by the triple contract. Pope Sixtus V denounced the triple contract in 1585 in response to Luther's offensive against the Church's position in his *Tract on Trade and Usury*. Nevertheless, it led to a religious quandary and perhaps even hastened along the removal of the ban on usury (Nelson, 1949; Anwar, 1987; Taylor and Evans, 1987).
16. There are some obvious parallels to be drawn here in terms of the 'modernist' or 'revisionist' views on *riba*, associated with the name of Fazlur Rahman. See Chapter 2 above.

References

al-Qaradawi, Yusuf (1989), *The Lawful and the Prohibited in Islam,* Kuwait: International Islamic Federation of Student Organisations.
Anwar, Muhammad (1987), *Modelling Interest-Free Economy: A Study in Macroeconomics and Development,* Herndon, Virginia: International Institute of Islamic Thought.
Aquinas, Thomas, trans. (1955), *Summa Theologica,* London: Oxford University Press.
Ashley, W.J. ([1888, 1893]1913), *An Introduction to English Economic History and Theory,* 2 vols, London.
Baldwin, J.W. (1970), *Masters, Printers and Merchants,* vol. 2, Princeton: Princeton University Press.
Cohn, H.H. (1971), Sv 'Usury', *Encyclopedia Judaica,* Jerusalem: Keter Publishing House, pp. 17–33.
Dante, Alighieri ([1314]1984), *The Divine Comedy,* vol. 1, *Inferno,* trans. Mark Musa, Harmondsworth: Penguin Books Ltd.
De Cecco, M. (1992), 'Genoese exchange fairs', in P. Newman, M. Milgate and J. Eatwell (eds), *The New Palgrave Dictionary of Money and Finance,* vol. 3, London: Macmillan.
De Roover, Raymond (1948), *The Medici Bank: its Organisation, Management, Operations and Decline,* New York: New York University Press.
De Roover, Raymond (1954), 'New interpretations of the history of banking', *Journal of World History,* Paris: Librairie des Mieridiens, pp. 38–76.
De Roover, Raymond (1963), *The Rise and Decline of the Medici Bank, 1397–1494,* Cambridge, Mass.: Harvard University Press.
De Roover, Raymond (1967), 'The Scholastics, usury and foreign exchange', *Business History Review,* **43,** 257–71.
Divine, T.F. (1967), Sv 'Usury', *New Catholic Encyclopedia,* New York: McGraw-Hill, pp. 498–500.
El-Awa, M.S. (1983), *Punishment in Islamic Law: A Comparative Study,* Delhi: Marzi Maktaba Islami.
Galassi, F.L. (1992), 'Buying a passport to heaven: usury, restitution and the merchants of medieval Genoa', *Religion,* **22,** 313–26.
Gätje, Helmut (1997), *The Qur'an and its Exegesis,* Oxford: Oneworld Publications.
Glaeser, E.L. and J.A. Scheinkman (1998), 'Neither a borrower nor a lender be: an economic analysis of interest restrictions and usury laws', *Journal of Law and Economics,* **41** (1), 1–36.
Gordon, B. (1982), 'Lending at interest: some Jewish, Greek and Christian approaches. 800 BC–AD 100', *History of Political Economy,* **14,** 406–26.
Jones, N. (1989), *God and the Moneylenders,* Oxford: Basil Blackwell.
Keen, S. (1997), 'From prohibition to depression: the Western attitude to usury', *Accounting, Commerce and Finance: The Islamic Perspective Journal,* **1** (1), 26–55.
Kindleberger, C.P. (1974), *The Formation of Financial Centres: a Study in Comparative Economic History,* Princeton Studies in International Finance, No. 36, and Princeton, NJ: Princeton University Press.
Kindleberger, C.P. (1984), *A Financial History of Western Europe,* London: George Allen & Unwin.
Langholm, O. (1984), *The Aristotelian Analysis of Usury,* Bergen: Bergen Universitetsforiaget; distributed in the USA by Columbia University Press, New York.
Le Goff, Jacques (1979), 'The usurer and purgatory', *The Dawn of Modern Banking,* Los Angeles: Center for Medieval & Renaissance Studies, University of California, pp. 25–52.
Le Goff, Jacques (1984), *The Birth of Purgatory,* trans. A. Goldhammer, Chicago: University of Chicago Press.
Levine, Aaaron (1987), *Economics and Jewish Law: Halakhic Perspective,* Hoboken: Ktav and Yeshiva University Press.
Lewis, M.K. (1999), 'The cross and the crescent: comparing Islamic and Christian attitudes to usury', *AL-IQTISHAD, Journal of Islamic Economics,* **1** (1), Nuharram, 1420H/April, 1–23.
Lindholm, C. (1996), *The Islamic Middle East. An Historical Anthropology,* Oxford: Basil Blackwell.
Lopez, Robert Sabatino (1979), 'The dawn of medieval banking', *The Dawn of Modern Banking,* Los Angeles Center for Medieval & Renaissance Studies, University of California, pp. 1–24.
Maimonides, Moses (1956), *The Guide for the Perplexed,* New York: Dover Publications.
Nelson, Benjamin (1949), *The Idea of Usury: From Tribal Brotherhood to Universal Otherhood,* Princeton: Princeton University Press.
Noonan, John T. (1957), *The Scholastic Analysis of Usury,* Cambridge, Mass.: Harvard University Press.
Patinkin, D. (1968), 'Interest', *International Encyclopedia of the Social Sciences,* London: Macmillan.
Rabinovich, L. (1993), 'Introduction to secured transactions in Halakha and common law', *Tradition,* **27**(3), 36–50.
Razi, Muhammad Fakr al-Din ([1872] 1938), *Mafatih al-Ghayb* known as *al-Tafsir al-Kabir,* Bulaq Cairo: Dar Ibya al-Kutub al-Bahiyya.
Roll, E. (1953), *A History of Economic Thought,* London: George Allen & Unwin.
Russell, Bertrand (1946), *History of Western Philosophy,* London: George Allen & Unwin.
Schacht, J. (1964), *An Introduction to Islamic Law,* Oxford: Oxford University Press.

Sinclair, T. (1962) (trans.), *The Politics of Aristotle*, revised T. Saunders (1981), Penguin Classics, London: George Allen and Unwin Ltd.

Tawney, R.H. (1926), *Religion and the Rise of Capitalism*, London and New York: Harcourt Brace.

Taylor, T.W. and J.W. Evans (1987), 'Islamic banking and the prohibition of usury in Western economic thought', *National Westminster Bank Quarterly Review,* November, 15–27.

Temin, Peter and Hans-Joachim Voth (2004), 'Financial repression in a natural experiment: loan allocation and the change in the usury laws in 1714', available from the SSRN Electronic Paper Collection: CEPR Discussion Paper No. 4452, June.

Thomson, J.A.K. (1953) (trans.), *The Ethics of Aristotle*, Penguin Classics, London: George Allen and Unwin Ltd.

Trever, Albert (1916), *Greek Economic Thought*, Chicago: University of Chicago Press.

Weber, Max (1930), *Die protestantische Ethik und der Geist des Kapitalismus*, in *Gesammelte Aufsazte zur Religionssoziologic*, I. Originally appeared in the *Archiv fur Sozialwissenschaft und Sozialpolitik*, xx–xxi, 1904–05. English trans. Talcott Parsons with a Foreword by R.H. Tawney, The *Protestant Ethic and the Spirit of Capitalism*, London: Collins.

PART II

OPERATIONS OF ISLAMIC BANKS

6 Incentive compatibility of Islamic financing
Humayon A. Dar

Islamic financing modes

Islamic modes of financing are classified into fixed-return (such as *murabaha*, *ijara*, *salam* and *istisnaa*) and variable-return (mainly *mudaraba* and *musharaka*). The two classes provide different sets of incentives to providers of capital and its users in Islamic financial arrangements. Fixed-return modes, for example, offer residual rights of control and management to users of the capital or funds made available by investors. Consequently, Islamic financial institutions are inclined to offer financing based on fixed-return modes of financing like *murabaha* and *ijara* (the two most widely used contracts in Islamic banking and finance the world over) because they offer built-in incentives to the users of funds to maximize their economic interests by keeping on honouring their financial commitment to the financier. This, in turn, minimizes possibility of default on the part of the businesses or individuals acquiring finance on the basis of fixed-return modes. A specific example of such a financial arrangement is *ijara*-based and *murabaha*-based mortgages offered by Islamic banks and financial institutions. The households/individuals acquiring houses with the help of such mortgages exclusively benefit from capital gains accruing from appreciation in the property value during the mortgage period.[1] This is a sufficient incentive for such customers to keep on honouring their financial commitment to the financing institution.

The variable-return mode of financing, on the other hand, offers the possibility of sharing residual financial rights between the financier and the user of funds. While it may offer some benefits in terms of improved productivity and profitability, it is also subject to the agency problem giving rise to moral hazard and adverse selection problems (see Dar and Presley, 1999). More specifically, the *mudaraba* contract is essentially a skewed contract that favours the user of funds more than the capital provider. This creates imbalances in management and control functions, a technical reason for lack of its popularity as a mode of financing (see Dar and Presley, 2000). Although *mudaraba* remains the most dominant way of collecting deposits by Islamic banks, it requires close scrutiny and additional regulation to impose the required discipline on the management of banks (see Muljawan, Dar and Hall, 2004).

Consequently, variable-return modes of financing have seen rather limited application especially in Islamic retail banking. Islamic investment accounts, based on *mudaraba*, although fair and just to both savers and banks, do not cater for relatively risk-averse individuals who prefer the schemes generating regular streams of income. While Islamic savings accounts, based on the concept of *wadi'a* (safe custody), tend to fill this vacuum, they require rather a liberal juristic application of Islamic financial principles to offer contractually ensured regular return to investors. There are very few Islamic saving vehicles that are genuinely Islamic in the sense that they do not offer capital protection and regular income while remaining within the Islamic framework. For example, Islamic savings accounts offering capital protection do so by the use of *wadi'a*, but a contractual regular income is offered only as a compromised solution.

The incentive compatibility of Islamic modes of financing is indeed important for further development of viable Islamic structures for Islamic financial institutions. In the absence of two-way incentive compatibility, it is difficult to develop *shari'a*-compliant structures for options, forward, futures and other complex derivative contracts. This chapter discusses the issue of incentive compatibility in detail to derive some implications for financial engineering in Islamic finance.

Incentive compatibility: an introduction
For a financial structure to work on its own, the transacting parties involved should have sufficient incentives to stick to the terms of the contract; otherwise the structure will make little sense. For example, a simple sale contract between a buyer and a seller takes place only if there is synchronization of needs and agreement on price. In a conventional loan contract, stipulation of interest ensures that the borrower returns the principal sum plus the agreed interest on it. In the event of default, the borrower faces an accumulation of interest, which in fact is a major deterrent to default. In a *murabaha*-based sale contract for deferred payment, such a deterrent is less effective in the absence of a penalty clause. However, it offers less protection to the financier as they cannot benefit from the proceeds of penalty, which are paid out to some designated charities. This less favourable treatment of the financier may in fact result in higher pricing of Islamic products based on *murabaha*. As a matter of fact, this is actually the case in the widespread use of *murabaha* in the Islamic finance industry. The relative dearness of Islamic financial products has proved to be a disincentive to the use of such services in well-informed and competitive environments.[2] This interrelatedness of different incentives/disincentives complicates the matter further. Therefore it is important to understand the root-cause of incentive compatibility (wherever it exists in Islamic banking) to develop products/structures that may provide better incentives to the transacting parties.

Other than the differences in terms of incentive compatibility, fixed-return Islamic modes and conventional modes like interest are quite comparable. There are certain cases in which classical Islamic arrangements do not offer sufficient incentives to the transacting parties to enter into meaningful economic transactions. For example, conventional options provide compatible incentives to writers as well as buyers of options, who mutually benefit in terms of risk reduction and hedging. The Islamic concept of undertaking (or what is known as *wa'd*) on the other hand, does not offer sufficient economic incentives to the two parties to enter into arrangements similar to conventional options. The undertaking offers incentive compatibility in a number of financial arrangements, when used in conjunction with other contracts. For example, *murabaha*-based sales cannot work in the absence of a purchase order by the client (buyer) of an Islamic financial institution. The purchase order in this context is nothing more than an undertaking to buy the asset-to-be-financed from the bank once it has purchased it from the market. This is a binding promise on behalf of the buyer who cannot renege on it without facing financial implications. In the absence of such an undertaking, *murabaha*-based sales contain too large a legal risk to be used as a mode of financing. Similarly, Islamic mortgages based on *ijara wa iqtina* and diminishing *musharaka* are not very useful in the absence of an undertaking on the part of the financing institution to sell the house/property to the client at the end of the mortgage period.

Other Islamic contracts also offer relatively less compatible incentives to one of the

Table 6.1   Incentive features of some Islamic financing modes

Modes	Residual rights	Control rights	Incentive compatibility	Remedial measures
Murabaha	Fund user	Fund user	Marginally less	Penalty clause, undertaking from buyer
Ijara wa iqtina	Fund user	Financier	Moderately less	Undertaking from financier
Salam	Financier	Fund user	Moderately less	Parallel *salam*
Istisnaa	Shared	Shared	Moderately less	Parallel *istisnaa*
Mudaraba	Shared	Fund user	Significantly less	Strong monitoring and supervision
Musharaka	Shared	Shared	Significantly less	Strong monitoring and supervision

parties, especially when they are used in their traditional (classical) form. *Salam*, for example, is proposed to be used mainly for financing of agriculture,[3] which exposes the financier to the price risk of the underlying asset – a feature less attractive as compared with a straightforward (but prohibited) interest-based loan (for relative inefficiency of *salam* contracts, see Ebrahim and Rahman, 2005). This incentive incompatibility of *salam* is reduced by allowing the financier to enter into a parallel *salam* contract with a third party to hedge against price risk. A similar argument holds for creating sufficiently compatible *istisnaa* structures, which also requires entering into a parallel *istisnaa* contract.

Incentive incompatibilities are most significant in the case of the variable-return modes, which require extensive measures to reduce them to a tolerable level. These measures include (1) ensuring creditworthiness of the users of funds and their proven record of successful business experience; (2) investing in highly credit-rated businesses; (3) stipulating additional conditions in the *mudaraba* contract to minimize risks for the fund providers; (4) stage financing; (5) periodic progress reports to minimize informational asymmetries; (6) the use of restricted *mudaraba* rather than unrestricted financing; and (7) third-party guarantees (see Yousri Ahmad, 2005). Table 6.1 provides a summary of residual rights, control rights, nature of incentives and remedial measures of incentive incompatibility for different Islamic modes of financing, as compared to interest-based financing. While these measures may make Islamic financing more efficient, it appears as if this will widen the gulf between the developmental objective of Islamic finance and its actual practice.

Incentive compatibility in options, forward and derivative contracts
Although incentive compatibility is relevant to all financial contracts, it is particularly important in writing incentive-compatible contracts for modern financial institutions and

markets. Modern financial markets in options, futures and forward contracts provide sufficient incentives for transacting parties to enter voluntarily into financial contracts. Islamic alternatives are either linked to real (physical) trading or do not provide sufficient incentives for voluntary transacting. For example, a put option gives its holder the right to sell a certain quantity of an underlying security to the writer of the option at a strike price. The holder of the put option pays a premium for this option. Similarly, the holder of a call option pays a premium to have the right to buy an underlying security at the agreed strike price. Both parties in such option contracts have compatible incentives: one party getting a premium and the other party receiving a right. Islamic alternatives of *arbun* and *wa'd* either provide incompatible incentives or have rather limited applicability to financial options. *Arbun* is a non-refundable deposit paid by a buyer to retain a right to cancel or confirm the sale during a certain period of time. Although tipped as a candidate for an Islamic call option, *arbun* does not offer sufficient incentives for voluntary transacting, as compared to a conventional call. The requirement that the deposit should be considered as a part of the settlement price dilutes incentives for the writer of the *arbun*-based call because, in the event of the confirmation of sale, the writer is worse off as compared with a writer of the conventional call. The writer of the *arbun*-based call, however, benefits when the option holder does not exercise his option, in which case the writer retains the deposit. One possible way of increasing incentives for the writer of an *arbun*-based call is to contract on a price higher than the market price of the security, but this may cause dilution of incentives for the buyer who will have less freedom of choice in exercising his option. To make *arbun* offer compatible incentives to buyers and sellers, there must be institutional mechanisms to enter into parallel *arbun* contracts to hedge against price risks accruing to the seller. This, however, complicates the overall structure, which requires enabling legal frameworks. Such legal and institutional provisions do not exist at present, although some initial work is being undertaken by the law firms specializing in Islamic finance. A government-level or industry-level effort in this direction has yet to take place.

Wa'd, which is less complicated than other alternatives including *arbun*, is a simple undertaking on the part of a seller or a buyer to sell/buy on a future date (or during a certain time period) for a contractually agreed price. This is binding on the undertaker subject to the following conditions: (a) the promise should be unilateral; (b) it must have caused the promisee to incur some costs/liabilities; (c) if the promise is to purchase something, the actual sale must take place at the appointed time by the exchange of offer and acceptance. Mere promise itself should not be taken as a concluded sale; (d) if the promisor reneges on their promise, the court may force them either to purchase the commodity or to pay actual damages to the seller. The actual damages will include the actual monetary loss suffered by the promisee, and must not include the opportunity cost.

However, in the absence of a premium, merely undertaking to buy or sell does not provide sufficient incentives to the transacting parties to enter into meaningful financial arrangements.

Creating incentive-compatible structures

Given the conditions attached with *wa'd*, it can be used to develop innovative structures incorporating characteristics of option contracts. For example, a Party A buys a stock/index

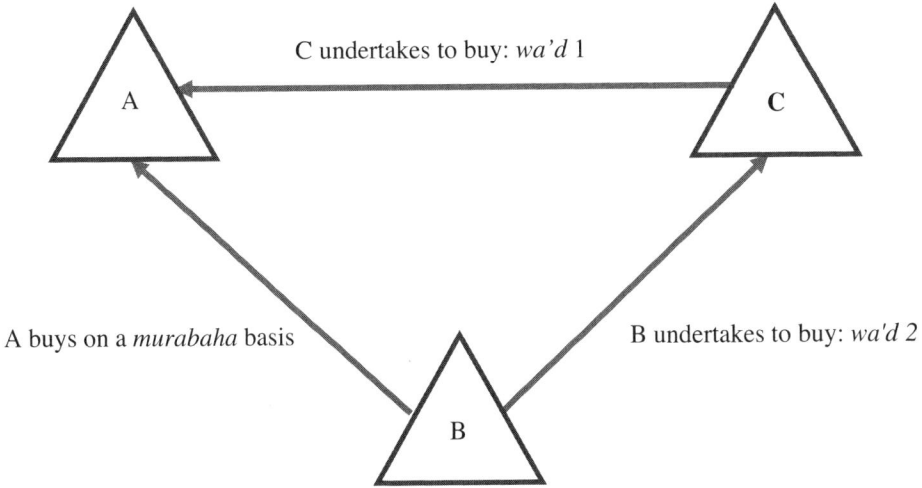

Figure 6.1   Structure of a murabaha-*based option contract*

Table 6.2   Payoffs under a murabaha-*based option contract*

When $P_f > P_{mar}$	When $P_f < P_{mar}$
A: $P_f - P_{mur} > 0$	A: $- P_{mur} < 0$
B: $- (P_f - P_{mur}) < 0$	B: $P_{mur} > 0$
C: 0	C: 0

from a Party B on a *murabaha* basis whereby price is deferred to a future date. Another Party, C, unilaterally undertakes to buy (*wa'd* 1) the asset from A for a specified price during a certain time period (American 'put') or at a specified future date (European 'put') and B unilaterally undertakes to buy (*wa'd* 2) the asset from C for a specified price during a certain time period or at a specified future date. The two promises are binding as they fulfil all the requirements imposed by the Organisation of Islamic Countries (OIC) *Fiqh* Academy for a binding promise. This structure (depicted in Figure 6.1) gives rise to an option contract between Parties A and B, if they hold the respective parties to their promises.

Suppose the agreed future price (P_f) is equal to P_{mur}, *murabaha* price (which may include a premium to cover the cost of a put), then, in the future, if the agreed future price is greater than the then prevailing price (P_{mar}), A will make C honour its promise to buy the asset for a price of P_f and C will hold B to its promise to buy the asset for a price of P_f. If $P_f < P_{mar}$, A will not be interested in the promise given by C, as it will make no economic sense for A to sell the asset at a price lower than its purchase price.

Given the payoffs of A (shown in Table 6.2), the structure gives downward protection to the buyer of the asset (A) who also benefits from any upward changes in the stock price. Similarly, Party B is protected against downward changes in price of the stock. However, Party C's net gain is zero (assuming no transaction costs). In practice, Party C may serve as broker or a clearing house and should be allowed to charge a fixed fee for its services to the other two parties. This fee should be governed by separate independent contracts with the parties, somewhat akin to a membership fee.

This is only a simple example of developing Islamic option contracts by using the concept of *wa'd* and *murabaha*. In fact, this methodology allows us to develop numerous tailor-made structures allowing options, futures and forward trading in a *shari'a*-compliant manner. Frequent use of these innovative structures and their acceptance in the market is expected to contribute to the development of Islamic markets for options, future and forward contracts, thus providing liquidity in the Islamic finance industry.

While developing Islamic options contracts is relatively straightforward, the same cannot be said about futures contracts, as they need to meet more stringent conditions attached to short selling that is deemed *shari'a*-repugnant. This is one of the reasons for Islamic hedge funds in the past not having been very popular amongst *shari'a* scholars as well as Islamic investors. However, the methodology outlined in this chapter makes it relatively easy to develop Islamic hedge funds that allow short-selling in a *shari'a*-compliant manner.

Incentive compatibility issues in Islamic hedge funds
Numerous strategies are used by hedge fund managers, including, but not limited to, long–short, global macro, arbitrage, distressed securities, opportunistic and aggressive growth. However, long–short strategy (also known as market-neutral) happens to be most widely used. Almost all attempts to set up Islamic hedge funds have tried to replicate shorting in a *shari'a*-compliant way. The contracts of *arbun* and *salam* have so far been used to replicate a short position in an Islamic framework. The question arises if these contracts provide sufficiently compatible incentives to the transacting parties. To understand this issue, we must explain how *salam* and *arbun* may be used for shorting as part of a market-neutral strategy. We also discuss the contract of *istijrar*, albeit briefly.

The use of salam *for shorting*
Salam is a sale whereby the seller undertakes to provide some specific commodities to the buyer at a future date for an advance, mutually agreed price paid in full. Although the Accounting and Auditing Organisation for Islamic Financial Institutions (AAOIFI) disallows using *salam* for buying shares, there are many practitioners in the Islamic finance industry who believe that *salam* can be used for implementing shorting strategy in a hedge fund.

Suppose an Islamic hedge fund (IHF) identifies a basket of *shari'a*-compliant commodities the market price of which it expects to fall in future. Therefore, at T_0, the IHF promises to sell such commodities to a party, called XXX, for an upfront payment in full to deliver the commodities in future, at date T_1. Usually such a price is lower than the market price. At T_1, the IHF will buy the promised commodities (to deliver to XXX) at a price that would be expected to be lower than the price charged at T_0. The difference between the two prices determines the profit.

In a conventional short, however, the hedge fund would borrow the undervalued commodities from the market to sell them to a party for the current market price, expecting that the future market price would be less. If so, the hedge fund would buy such commodities from the market in future to pay them back to the lender. The price differential (after allowing for the borrowing costs) would determine the return for the hedge fund on such a short position.

The IHF may hedge its risk exposure from this *salam* contract, in case the price expectation reverses, resulting in possible loss for the IHF at T_1. For this purpose, the IHF may enter a parallel *salam* at any time during T_0–T_1 with another party (YYY) on similar commodities. This time, the IHF will be a buyer and will have the promised commodities delivered to it by YYY at T_1.

This structure does indeed provide sufficiently compatible incentives to all the transacting parties, and is comparable in terms of its incentive structure with a conventional short strategy in a hedge fund. An alternative strategy, based on the concept of *arbun*, is equally effective.

The use of arbun *for shorting*

Arbun is a sale in which the buyer deposits earnest money with the seller as part-payment of the price in advance, but agrees to forfeit the deposit if he fails to ratify the contract during a specified time period. The strategy works as follows. At T_0, the IHF enters into an *arbun* contract with XXX and promises to deliver the contracted stocks (that IHF considers overvalued at T_0) in exchange for a mutually agreed part-price at T_0. XXX would pay the remaining price to IHF at T_1. This is another *shari'a*-compliant way of replicating a conventional short. The IHF can use the money received upfront to generate further income from other *shari'a*-compliant strategies. At T_1, the IHF buys the promised stocks (to deliver to XXX) at a price that is expected to be lower than the price charged at T_0. The difference in the two prices gives rise to the IHF's profit. As in the case of *salam*, the IHF may in fact hedge its risk exposure from the *arbun* contract by entering into a parallel *arbun* contract with a third party during T_0–T_1.

The use of istijrar *for shorting*

Istijrar is an innovative arrangement which offers a variety of flexible *shari'a*-compliant solutions. It is a supply sale whereby the supplier agrees to supply a particular asset (commodities, stocks and so on) on a continual basis at an agreed price to be paid at a future date when the repeated purchases of the buyer from the single seller are completed. It allows purchase/sale of a commodity at a future date (or during a period), enabling the buyer to take delivery of the commodity to pay for it later. In order to short, the IHF must take into account a number of *shari'a* considerations, as *istijrar* is not a universally accepted contract in Islamic jurisprudence. The following is only an example of the use of *istijrar* as a shorting strategy.

At T_0, the IHF enters into an *istijrar* facility with XXX to sell *shari'a*-compliant shares as and when XXX requires. In such an arrangement, XXX pays upfront the then market price of shares it intends to buy from IHF over the *istijrar* period. The IHF has the liberty to invest this sum in another *shari'a*-compliant portfolio, including a possibility of going long on some other shares. The master agreement spells out the following:

- The allowable range of price movement (upper (P_U) and lower (P_L) bound around the initial purchase price of the shares, P_0). P_U is set so as the parties expect that the *istijrar* price, P^*, never reaches it during the *istijrar* period. P_L is, however, set at P_0 or a price marginally less than P_0.
- The *istijrar* price, P^*, which may be linked to a market index (e.g., Dow Jones Islamic Market Index).

- The settlement price can either be the *istijrar* price (P^*) or P_0, depending on exercise of the option available to both parties.
- The XXX's option to fix the price at P_0 is activated when the mutually agreed P^* touches P_U.
- The IHF's option to fix the price at P_0 is activated when P^* touches P_L.
- If a party does not exercise its option following a trigger point in its favour and the opposite bound is pierced in the meantime, the right of the first party will be replaced by the second party's right of option.

At T_1, depending on the price movements, one of the transacting parties exercises its option. A series of such transactions may take place during the *istijrar* period, which must be settled by a chosen date (for a detailed discussion on the structure, see Obaidullah, 1996; Bacha, 1999). This is a sophisticated structure that offers compatible incentives to the transacting parties to behave in such a way as gives rise to a conventional short.

All these strategies based on *salam*, *arbun* and *istijrar* offer advantages of a conventional short in a *shari'a*-compliant way. Innovations in Islamic finance in the recent past have thus enabled Islamic investors to benefit from a range of products and strategies, which make Islamic financing as efficient as conventional methods of finance. The four strategies are summarized in Table 6.3. While *salam* and *arbun* are comparable to a commercial short, the hedging against price risk requires entering into parallel *salam* and *arbun*. *Istijrar*, on the other hand, is more flexible, allowing the benefits of short selling to be shared between the buyer and the seller.

Table 6.3   A comparison of conventional and Islamic shorting strategies

Type of short	T_0	T_1	T_S	Incentives
Conventional short	A borrows *overvalued* stocks from B and sells in the market for the prevailing market price, P_0	A buys the stock from the market for a price (P_1) lower than P_0 and returns them to B		If the strategy works, A earns $P_0 - P_1 -$ borrowing cost
Salam-based short	A sells an *overvalued* commodity for P_0 to B, to be delivered at T_1; B makes the payment upfront	A buys the commodity from the market for $P_1 < P_0$ and delivers them to B		If the strategy works, A earns $P_1 - P_0$ and possible income generated by the price received in advance B apparently attempts to hedge against future price fluctuations If the price expectations do not materialize and A

Table 6.3   (continued)

Type of short	T_0	T_1	T_S	Incentives
				has to enter into a parallel *salam*, then A may not earn any positive return or may in fact incur some loss, depending on the price at which parallel *salam* was made

Arbun-based short	A sells *overvalued* stocks to B for P_0; B advances a deposit as a part-payment	A buys stocks from the market for $P_1 < P_0$ (subject to B's demand)		If the strategy works, A benefits from the price differential and the additional income that may come from investing the earnest money (deposit received from B)
				
				  B apparently attempts to hedge itself against future upward price fluctuations
				
				  If the price goes down sufficiently so that B decides in favour of forfeiting the deposit, A earns the deposit plus income generated from investing it

Istijrar-based short	A undertakes to sell stocks/ commodities to B as and when B demands them during T_0–T_1 (subject to conditions set out in the master agreement); B pays an advance sum	If the price increases to touch the upper bound, B exercises its option of fixing the price at $P_{mur} < P_{mar}$ and gets the asset delivered by A, who buys it from the market (in practice, the upper bound is set too high to	A and B settle the account	This structure allows short selling, capping benefits to the transacting parties, as defined by the upper and lower bounds

Table 6.3   (continued)

Type of short	T_0	T_1	T_S	Incentives
	(called a facility)	be breached) If the price decreases to touch the lower bound, A exercises its option of fixing the price at $P_{mur} > P_{mar}$	A and B settle the account	

Conclusions

Although Islamic modes of financing in their original forms suffer from some incentive compatibility problems, their modern use and the consequent modifications have addressed a number of such issues successfully. The classical contracts of *murabaha*, *ijara*, *salam*, *istisnaa*, *mudaraba* and *musharaka* have seen a lot of modifications in light of the practical problems faced by the contemporary Islamic finance industry. However, pricing of Islamic financial products has yet to internalize the issue of incentive compatibility, as most Islamic banks remain more expensive than their conventional counterparts.

Hybridization of contracts reduces incentive incompatibilities, and this is the route adopted by the Islamic finance industry. This chapter discusses a number of hybrid structures that offer compatible incentives for the transacting parties, as compared with the conventional structures. Organized markets in such hybridized contracts/structures are expected to increase incentive compatibility in Islamic finance.

Notes

1. Although some of the existing Islamic mortgages apply the principle of diminishing *musharaka*, they, however, use it for the gradual transfer of ownership of property to the customer without allowing a sharing of capital gains that may arise as a result of appreciation in the property value.
2. This is probably one of the reasons for potential Islamic clients not having reacted as positively as was expected by an increasing number of providers of Islamic financial services in the UK and other competitive environments. In less competitive environments where Islamic banking has flourished, it is not necessarily due to the economic benefits it offers to its clients; rather it is mainly influenced by religious motivation of the users of Islamic financial services.
3. *Salam*'s use is not limited to farming. This, in fact, can be used for financing of other *shari'a*-compliant assets.

References

Bacha, O.I. (1999), 'Derivative instruments and Islamic finance: some thoughts for a reconstruction', *International Journal of Islamic Financial Services*, **1** (1).

Dar, H.A. and J.R. Presley (1999), 'Islamic finance: a Western perspective', *International Journal of Islamic Financial Services*, **1** (1).

Dar, H.A. and J.R. Presley (2000), 'Lack of profit/loss sharing in Islamic finance: management and control imbalances', *International Journal of Islamic Financial Services*, **2** (2).

Ebrahim, M.S. and S. Rahman (2005), 'On the Pareto-optimality of conventional futures over Islamic: implications for emerging Muslim economies', *Journal of Economic Behaviour and Organisation*, **56** (2), 273–95.

Muljawan, D., H.A. Dar and M.J.B. Hall (2004), 'A capital adequacy framework for Islamic banks: the need to reconcile depositors' risk-aversion with managers' risk-taking', *Applied Financial Economics*, **14** (6), 429–41.

Obaidullah, M. (1996), 'Anatomy of *Istijrar*: a product of Islamic financial engineering', *Journal of Objective Studies*, **8** (2), 37–51.

Yousri Ahmad, A.R. (2005), 'Islamic banking modes of finance: proposals for further evolution', in M. Iqbal and R. Wilson (eds), *Islamic Perspectives on Wealth Creation*, Edinburgh: Edinburgh University Press, pp. 26–46.

7 Operational efficiency and performance of Islamic banks
Kym Brown, M. Kabir Hassan and Michael Skully

Introduction

Islamic banks have expanded rapidly over the last three decades, but with the exception of some countries, such as Brunei and Iran, they are often in a minority compared with conventional banks even in countries such as Indonesia which have large Muslim populations (Brown, 2003). Nevertheless, Islamic banks are now becoming more accepted and competitive with their commercial counterparts, with approximately US$250 billion in assets and a healthy growth rate of 10–15 per cent p.a. (Hasan, 2004). New Islamic banks are being established, such as the Bank Islami Pakistan Limited in 2005, and existing banks are opening more branches (State Bank of Pakistan, 2005). Conventional financial institutions are now realizing the value of Islamic financing techniques and beginning to incorporate them, either in their lending practices or via separate Islamic departments (or 'windows'). Hence conventional banks now compete with Islamic institutions both directly and through their own Islamic operations. This raises the question as to how Islamic banks perform compared to their conventional counterparts. This chapter will examine structural and performance differences.

Differences between an Islamic bank and a conventional bank may include their ultimate goals. An Islamic bank aims to follow the social requirements of the Qur'an. The relationship an Islamic bank has with its clients is also different. It may offer finance via equity relationships in projects. An Islamic bank is able to undertake direct investments and participate in the management of projects. Indeed, this process can potentially help people even if they reside in developing countries with limited funds but with good projects and ideas to obtain finance. Another common financing technique is the purchase and resale agreement where the Islamic bank effectively purchases the product and then resells it to the client with a specific repayment schedule including a set mark-up. The latter type of transaction is less risky than conventional loans, however equity financing is much more risky because of the potential for the Islamic bank also to share in losses from the project.

Our starting point is to examine the operational efficiency and performance of Islamic banks. But what is operational efficiency and why is it an important issue for the Islamic banking system? Islamic bank operations have often been limited in size within most financial systems. Hence, when comparing the performance of these banks, there are few peer banks within a particular country. So, although a number of single country studies exist (e.g. Hassan, 1999; Sarker and Hassan, 2005; Ahmad and Hassan, 2005, examining Bangladesh), there are advantages in examining Islamic bank performance across country borders. Efficiency shows how well a bank performs. During the 1990s especially, there was a fundamental push for banks to lower costs. Hence measures of 'cost' efficiency were seen as important. Regulation and other operational aspects of Islamic banking also influence performance. Therefore these will all be examined.

Conceptual differences between Islamic and conventional banking

Conventional banking is based upon financing profitable projects with interest lending. Islamic banks avoid interest or *riba*, and instead invest on a profit or loss basis. Typical types of transactions include leasing, purchase and resale transactions (*murabaha* and *ijara*) or profit and loss sharing (*mudaraba*), trust financing or limited partnership and *musharaka*, joint venture investment. These techniques were examined in earlier chapters of this *Handbook*. Part of the social significance of an Islamic bank, relative to a conventional bank, is its social objectives. Conventional banks usually require a person with a business idea also to have some collateral or capital before finance will be granted. Regardless of whether the project is profitable or not, interest will always be levied. The aim of a conventional bank is to fund the most efficient and productive projects. Obviously, from the viewpoint of building 'relationship banking', the banker would like the project to succeed. However, even if it does not, the interest and principal has some chance of being recovered. Islamic bank funding, however, can be structured so that the bank's success can be tied directly to that of the client. They can share in the profits, but also in any losses, hence taking on a more active role. Amongst conventional banks a variety of off-balance sheet activities have assumed considerable importance over the years (Lewis, 1988, 1992). As with conventional banks, Islamic banks can run a banking book and a trading book (Hassan and Choudhury, 2004). This means that they can also deal with off-balance sheet contracts such as letters of credit, foreign exchange and financial advising. Sources of funds for Islamic banks include deposits. Islamic current accounts do not pay any reward and are only used for liquidity purposes, hence there are no profits to share. Savings accounts holders may be able to receive a return called *hiba* for their investments. An investment account attracts a higher return for depositors, but they also share in the risk of losing money if the bank makes a loss. Money must be deposited for a minimum period of time also. For large investors or institutions further investment accounts may exist. These are usually for a specified large project.

In contrast to conventional banks, Islamic banks have an ethical investment charter. Unethical investments in gambling, alcohol or pornography are avoided in line with the Qur'an. As part of their social responsibility, Islamic banks will arrange the payment of *zakat*, or donations to charitable purposes, which is often listed on their financial statements. This may motivate further supportive *zakat* payments by other parties when the Islamic bank clearly nominates charitable donations. Muslim consumers are able to gain comfort from investing/borrowing via principles that follow the Qur'an and therefore can help consumers ensure their religious compliance (Ahmad and Hassan, 2007; Sarker and Hassan, 2005). Typically Islamic banks have a *shari'a* board to ensure that practices comply with the Qur'an.

A stronger social standing is therefore required for Islamic banks in society than for conventional banking (see Table 7.1). Ahmad and Hassan (2005) note that, given that *shari'a* principles require social justice, Islamic banks also take on this responsibility because of the following:

a.   Islamic banking has certain philosophical missions to achieve. That is, since God is the Creator and Ultimate Owner of all resources, institutions or persons have a vicegerency role to play in society. Therefore Islamic banks are not free to do as they wish; rather they have to integrate moral values with economic action;

Table 7.1   Fundamental differences between Islamic and conventional banking

	Islamic banking	Conventional banking
1.	An advance step toward achievement of Islamic economics	Part of the capitalistic interest-based financial system
2.	Try to ensure social justice/ welfare or the objectives of *shari'a*	Not concerned
3.	Flow of financial resources is in favour of the poor and disadvantaged sections of society	Not concerned
4.	Prepare and implement investment plans to reduce the income inequality and wealth disparity between the rich and poor	Increase the gap
5.	Make arrangements for investment funds for assetless, poor but physically fit people	All plans are taken out for the rich
6.	Observe the legitimate and illegitimate criteria fixed by the *shari'a* in the case of production and investment	No such rules and regulations
7.	Implement investment plans on *mudaraba* and *musharaka* to stimulate the income of the people below the poverty line	No such programme
8.	Interest and usury is avoided at all levels of financial transactions	The basis of all financial transactions is interest and high-level usury
9.	Depositors bear the risk, no need for deposit insurance	Depositors do not bear any risk, moreover the bank is inclined to pay back principal with a guaranteed interest amount
10.	The relationship between depositors and entrepreneurs is friendly and cooperative	Creditor–debtor relationship
11.	Socially needed investment projects are considered	Projects below the fixed interest level are not considered
12.	Elimination of the exploitation of interest and its hegemony	Helps to increase capital of the capitalists
13.	Islamic banks become partner in the business of the client after sanctioning the credit and bear loss	Do not bear any loss of client
14.	Islamic bank can absorb any endogenous or exogenous shock	Cannot absorb any shock because of the ex ante commitment
15.	Islamic banking is committed to implementing welfare-oriented principles of financing	No such commitment; extend oppression and exploitation
16.	Inter-bank transactions are on a profit and loss sharing basis	On interest basis and create unusual bubble in the market, i.e. exorbitant increase in the call money rate
17.	Islamic banks work under the surveillance of the *Shari'a* Supervisory Boards	No such surveillance
18.	Lower rate of moral hazard problem because of the brotherhood relationship between the bank and customers	High moral hazard problem because relation is based only on monetary transactions
19.	Avoids speculation-related financial activites	Main functions are speculation-related

Table 7.1 (continued)

	Islamic banking	Conventional banking
20.	Bank pays *zakat* on income and inspires clients to pay *zakat*, which ensures redistribution of income in favour of the poor	No *zakat* system for the benefit of the poor
21.	The basis of business policy is socioeconomic uplifting of the disadvantaged groups of the society	Profit is the main target of business, or the prime duty is to maximize the shareholders' value
22.	Dual target: implementation of the objectives of *shari'a* and profit	Profit making is the sole objective
23	Islamic banks sell and purchase foreign currency on a spot basis, not on forward looking or future basis	Spot and forward are both used

Source: Ahmad and Hassan (2005).

b. The ability to provide credit to those who have the talent and the expertise but cannot provide collateral to the conventional financial institutions, thereby strengthening the grass-root foundations of society; and

c. The duty to create harmony in society based on the Islamic concept of sharing and caring in order to achieve economic, financial and political stability.

Comparing the operational performance analysis of Islamic banking versus conventional banking

This section considers performance figures of the two types of banks. Initially data are compared at the aggregate bank-type level and then more specifically by country and bank type. Given Islamic banks' 'social' significance it may be expected that profitability is lower. Data were collected from the Bankscope database which contains bank level data. The period examined is from 1998 to 2003. The same banks and countries were used for both groups of data.

The two main sources of funds for a bank are equity and debt. Banks usually operate with a high leverage ratio (in relation to other non-financial businesses), meaning that they borrow high levels of funds, in relation to equity, to be able to lend out more funds and therefore to increase returns to equity holders. Results indicate that the Islamic banks had a conservative level of equity in relation to liabilities and equity over the period (see Table 7.2). From the figures for 2003, it would seem that the Islamic banks' structure was converging or reducing to conventional bank levels. However a 4.5 per cent difference in equity to total assets ratio remained. Perhaps the conservative structure relates to the social standing of Islamic banks and could also relate to the fact that Islamic banks are more exposed to business risks than conventional banks. Given the higher equity levels, it might be expected that returns or profitability will also be lower for Islamic banks.

Financial institutions need access to funds for net new investment (new financing less repayments of existing finance) and net withdrawals by depositors (when withdrawals exceed new deposits). And, as with any other business form, banks require funds for

Table 7.2 Aggregate performance data for 11 countries: Islamic v. conventional banks (1998–2003)

		2003	2002	2001	2000	1999	1998
Structure	Capital funds/liabilities						
	Islamic	20.10	23.64	62.26	35.98	42.90	46.00
	Conventional	13.50	18.66	16.29	17.22	15.93	15.94
	Equity/total assets						
	Islamic	15.40	18.49	20.77	20.22	21.62	20.08
	Conventional	10.88	11.60	11.48	11.80	10.55	12.34
Liquidity	Liquid assets/cust. and ST funding						
	Islamic	33.46	35.52	66.83	42.13	40.31	42.93
	Conventional	46.00	52.92	63.68	55.06	55.45	54.60
Lending	Net 'loans'/total assets						
	Islamic	54.28	50.71	53.58	53.81	50.52	50.79
	Conventional	44.28	39.96	40.72	42.18	43.41	44.38
	Net 'loans'/cust. and ST funding						
	Islamic	74.30	66.72	99.09	85.85	81.09	111.04
	Conventional	56.81	50.46	50.60	51.85	54.51	58.30
Performance	Cost to income ratio						
	Islamic	81.06	60.71	73.30	54.12	58.38	58.94
	Conventional	52.89	60.23	67.53	63.47	62.42	58.29
Profitability	Return on average equity						
	Islamic	12.04	12.44	6.76	17.48	14.82	13.05
	Conventional	15.04	8.42	1.46	9.76	11.56	12.78
	Return on average assets						
	Islamic	2.22	2.37	2.35	2.96	1.76	1.47
	Conventional	1.63	1.00	0.22	0.74	−0.02	0.98

Source: Bankscope database.

100

day-to-day expenses. Liquidity risk is the possibility that the bank will not have enough funds on hand to be able to meet obligations as they fall due. Returns on liquid assets are generally much lower than returns from funds invested in long-term assets such as loans. The conundrum a bank faces is that holding smaller levels of liquidity increases liquidity risk, whereas, if the bank holds a higher proportion of liquid assets, liquidity risk is minimized but returns such as return on assets (ROA) are likely to be much lower. Liquidity is proxied by liquid assets to customer and short-term funding. Conventional bank operations had a higher level of liquidity. Given that Islamic banks have limited access to Islamic products to use for liquidity purposes, such as Islamic securities, it might have been expected that Islamic banks would have had higher liquidity levels than conventional banks.

The mainstay business of a bank is providing new financing. Nevertheless, banks are able to balance their asset portfolio with other investments, such as in securities or bonds. Government bonds are commonly purchased because of lower credit risk (risk of default of repayment) and liquidity or ability to sell in the secondary markets (conversion to cash when the banks are short on cash). It could be reasonably expected that Islamic banks would provide finance to customers at levels similar to conventional banks. The ratio results of net loans or financing (referred to as 'loans' in the tables) to total assets show that Islamic banks have higher levels of financing provided in all years. The other measurement of loan or financing levels is net loans or financing to customers and short-term funding; Islamic banks obtained higher results in all years, but the level fluctuated from 66 per cent to 111 per cent. The conventional banks had a much more stable loan portfolio at about 55 per cent of customer and short-term funding or 42 per cent of total assets. Perhaps this highlights more consistent management practices of conventional banks which may stem from the fact that conventional banks have been in existence for a longer period and have more competition than Islamic banks. Islamic banks had a much more consistent result for net financing to total assets, at around 51 per cent for all years. Islamic banks therefore provided financing at a rate about 9 per cent higher than conventional banks when compared to total assets. Part of this could be due to equity financing where Islamic banks take a position in the project as a joint partner or perhaps in the purchase and resale types of transactions. If the Islamic banks had higher risk equity, this would be expected to be offset by lower risk assets, such as low-risk loans or government securities. Perhaps purchase and resale funding is considered sufficiently low-risk to lend out at higher levels. This will be examined later.

Conventional banks are seen to have the advantage of being able to pool funds and lend out monies to the most productive users of funds. Without an effective banking system some money may be hoarded in a household for instance, which is then not invested for the good of the economy. Hence banks are able to assist in economic output and growth by collecting funds and then financing suitable projects. To gain the most potential economic output, however, banks must be working efficiently. A traditional ratio measurement of efficiency for banks is cost to income. Hence the emphasis is on minimizing costs to maximize efficiency. Although this is a reasonable assumption, it must also be noted that a more profit-efficient bank may incur higher costs to look after their high-end customers, but meanwhile make a higher margin. From 2001 to 2003, Islamic banks had higher cost to income ratios, at around 70 per cent, but still in line with worldwide conventional bank average figures. Given the different arrangements with Islamic finance which often require more 'work' on the part of the bank, such as with purchase-and-resale or mark-up trans-actions, it would be expected that Islamic banks incur higher costs as compared to conventional banks. When Islamic banks take equity investments in a new project it is reasonable to consider that costs in the initial years would be high. With time, however, the expected return would hopefully be higher and associated costs lower. Conventional banks obtained a measure around 55–60 per cent, which is considered quite low. Nevertheless, many of the countries used in our sample are from the Middle East region and that region is noted for the lowest cost efficiency levels worldwide (Brown and Skully, 2004).

For most financial institutions, the ultimate aim is to maximize shareholder wealth. Islamic banks have a broader covenant, and they may be willing to sacrifice profitability for utilitarian aspects of social lending. Nevertheless, the continued financial health and existence of a bank requires that the capital be maintained. Equity investors will also be concerned that returns are adequate to cover the risks they are taking in their investment in the bank. In this case profitability is measured by return on average equity and return on average assets. Interestingly, for both profitability measures the Islamic banks outperformed conventional banks, although note that the results were calculated on specific country data only and not on a worldwide basis. Equity levels are much smaller than total assets because on the source of funds side of a bank's balance sheet there is also the debt. Hence profitability figures will always be higher in relation to equity than to total assets.

Next, the specific country data are examined. These are set out in the Appendix to this chapter for 11 countries: Bahrain, Egypt, Iran, Jordan, Lebanon, Oman, Qatar, Saudi Arabia, Tunisia, Turkey and Yemen. It must be noted that banks in the different countries operate under different conditions. Although both the conventional and Islamic banks within a particular country will have similar economic, social and financial conditions, they may work within different banking regulations. The very nature of Islamic banking, with purchase and resale and profit-sharing contracts, is different from lending in conventional banks. Hence the applicable regulation in regard to Islamic banks may be different. Some Islamic banks have previously been able to operate outside the conventional bank regulatory boundaries.

Bank regulations exist to minimize the risk of financial failure of banks within an economy and the costs to society that this might entail. Regulators typically require banks to hold capital to protect depositors from these costs. Under Basel I, an international banking standard set by G10 countries, banks are required to hold at least 4 per cent Tier 1 capital and some Tier 2 capital which must add to 8 per cent capital requirement as a minimum. Regulators typically prefer banks to hold higher levels of capital to minimize risks. Bank management, however, prefer to maximize returns. Investing in liquid or short-term assets offers lower returns. Hence they prefer to minimize capital held, although they will not want the bank to fail either. Note that an Islamic bank version of Basel I was not developed and meanwhile the Islamic Financial Services Industry (IFSI) is examining the ramifications of Basel II for Islamic banks.

Although the specific regulatory capital held is not reported here, we do have proxies via the structure ratios. Generally the Islamic banks hold higher levels of equity or capital than conventional banks. Notable exceptions are Egypt and Qatar. Islamic banks in Egypt did not even seem to hold capital equivalent to the minimum regulatory level under Basel I of 8 per cent. Their capital levels were about 5.3 per cent in relation to total assets. Thus Egyptian Islamic banks would seem to be operating in a much more risky manner compared to other Islamic and conventional banks. Similarly, in Qatar, the Islamic banks operate with higher capital risk. Capital risk is the risk that the bank will not have enough capital to absorb losses. Results to 2002 were around 7.5 per cent for the Islamic banks, but seemingly much improved by 2003, at 9.82 per cent for equity to total assets. At the other extreme, Islamic banks from Bahrain had seemingly the least capital risk, with results ranging from around 27 per cent to 50 per cent for equity to total assets. This may be because some banks treat investment accounts as off-balance sheet funds under management. However the conventional banks in Bahrain also held higher levels of equity in comparison to peer conventional banks elsewhere.

Cost efficiency measures were generally considered low and consistent for most countries. Results of the cost to income ratio were in the vicinity of 45–55 per cent. One exception was Turkey. Turkish banks have needed to cope with high inflation levels that could lead to higher costs. Conventional banks in Turkey had low net loans to customer and short-term funding owing to the fact that they often invested in the safer option of inflation-adjusted government bonds rather than risking lending to businesses which were also trying to cope with the high inflation. Islamic banks in Turkey, however, were able to maintain a much higher proportion of financing. Again this is directly related to the risks involved in lending. Lending to a sovereign government is considered less risky than lending to corporations or individuals. In the years 2002 and 2003, the conventional banks made a correspondingly higher return whereas the Islamic banks in Turkey had much lower results. Hence Islamic banks in Turkey seemingly were able to maintain customer lending in an ethical manner, whilst the conventional banks minimized their risks and lent predominantly to the government.

Liquidity results, however, were very different. These results should also be considered in the light of profitability results. Banks with lower liquidity could be expected to have invested in more long-term higher earning assets. Therefore, if low liquidity results were reported, it would be expected that a corresponding higher level of profit would also arise: that is, higher return from taking on higher risk levels. Alternatively, if these banks did not have a correspondingly high profit figure, it could be suggested that they perhaps had to pay higher costs to get adequate liquidity, as was required. Hence you would then expect that the cost to income ratio would be higher.

Banks in Qatar and (sometimes) Bahrain generally held low levels of liquidity. The profitability levels were still considered excellent for Return on Equity (ROE) for both countries, but Bahrain reported higher profit levels for Return on Asset (ROA). For the measure net financing ('loans') to total assets, the results for both types of banks were around 40–55 per cent, with Islamic banks usually having higher levels. However, for net financing to customer and short-term funding, the results for the Islamic banks in Bahrain were often above 100 per cent. This means that Islamic banks in Bahrain were also outlaying funds not always categorized as financing to customers. Future research could examine this point. The most profitable banks at a consistent level were located in Iran, Qatar and Saudi Arabia. Islamic banks often recorded higher profitability levels in these countries.

Efficiency studies of Islamic banking
Efficiency is an important factor for banks to remain competitive. Islamic banks are no exception, with increased competition from conventional banks, despite often only having

a few Islamic banks within any one country. In addition, the Basel capital regulations intend to foster global competition and therefore bank management and regulators should look to place their performance in an international context. Bank efficiency can be defined as the relative performance of a bank given its inputs or outputs to other banks with the same input or output limitations. In its basic output context, 'efficiency' measures the given output from a firm using a given input of resources. More efficient firms will produce more output from a given set of inputs. An efficient bank will score 1 (or 100 per cent). The other banks in the sample are compared relative to the best bank and will often have an efficiency score of less than 1.

Under the ratio analysis as used earlier, there was no single best measurement of performance. Using linear programming techniques, however, multiple 'inputs' and 'outputs' into the intermediation process can be interpreted to give a single-figure result. Given that banks or financial institutions have a number of variables that input into their 'intermediation' process and a number of outputs that use linear models such as the non-parametric Data Envelopment Analysis (DEA) for small data sets, or, for larger data sets, a parametric model such as Stochastic Frontier Analysis, were able to be used (SFA). Caution needs to be taken when comparing results. As a new sample is taken to study, a new 'frontier' of best practice banks then exists. Hence the most efficient bank in one sample may not replicate that result for that bank in a different sample.

Further research into Islamic bank performance has been necessary to aid in the analysis of such institutions (Zaher and Hassan, 2001). Country borders no longer hinder the measurement of the performance of banks. Efficiency studies for conventional banks began in America. Further data sets then expanded to include the European region, given increased competition due to the Second Banking Directive within the European Union (EU). Since then, developing countries' banks have been examined (Brown and Skully, 2004). Latest developments in efficiency research include the use of variations on the standard statistical techniques. Empirical measurement of the performance of Islamic banks began slowly, owing to a lack of data. Initial studies examined individual banks. Given the corresponding growth in performance studies of conventional banks and the expansion of Islamic banks, it was only a matter of time before Islamic banks would be more thoroughly investigated.

Hassan (2003a) reported that the Islamic banks were relatively less efficient than conventional banks elsewhere. Efficiency results produced from both parametric and non-parametric methods were highly correlated with ROE and ROA, suggesting that ratio analysis was also suitable for performance measurement. Cost efficiencies for Sudan, Pakistan and Iran averaged 52 per cent, whilst profit efficiency was 34 per cent. Allocative efficiency which measures how well management resources are applied to the intermediation process was 79 per cent, whereas technical efficiency, or how well technology is applied to the intermediation process, was much lower, at 66 per cent. Hence Islamic banks in these economies could readily improve their efficiency by better use of technology. Efficiency for Islamic banks has generally improved with the expansion of business rather than improvement in the use of inputs and outputs into or out of the production process. As might be expected, larger banks and more profitable banks were generally also more efficient.

Specific environmental differences for each country were included in a cost-efficiency study of Islamic banks by Brown and Skully (2004). Sudanese banks had the lowest cost efficiency, as could be expected owing to agricultural financing rather than cost-plus for retail expenditures-type transactions; however they had a higher compensating net interest margin. At a regional level, Middle Eastern banks were the most cost-efficient, followed by Asian and then African Islamic banks. Hassan and Hussein (2003) examined Sudanese banks alone (note that the Sudanese financial system is Islamic in nature). The decline in efficiency was attributed to poorer use of technology and not operating at a sufficient size or scale to be optimally efficient in the presence of scale economies (see Davis and Lewis, 1982; Lewis and Davis, 1987, ch. 7, for an analysis of scale economies in banking).

The profitability of Islamic banks is positively influenced by high capital and loan-to-asset ratios, favourable macroeconomic conditions, and negatively to taxes (Hassan and Bashir, 2005). Larger banking markets, and hence increased competition, negatively affected interest income, but was of no effect on non-interest income.

Using a panel of Islamic banks from 22 countries, and using multiple efficiency techniques including parametric and non-parametric methods, Hassan (2005) found that the average cost efficiency was 74 per cent, whilst the average profit efficiency was 84 per cent. This suggests that these Islamic banks could improve efficiency most via cutting costs. Further analysis of allocative efficiency suggested that inefficiency was due to the way resources were allocated rather than to the use of technology. Reasons suggested for such results were that Islamic banks often face regulation not conducive to Islamic transactions in most countries. This of course will then have a negative effect on efficiency. As with Hassan (2003a), banks of a larger size and profitability were generally more efficient, suggesting economies of scale (size of bank).

Foreign bank entry and Islamic banking
A source of competition for Islamic banks is the possibility of local entry of Islamic banks from other countries. Foreign bank entry provides the impetus for improved efficiency performance of domestic Islamic banks. An example of an Islamic bank foreign entry is Qatar Islamic Bank, which entered the Malaysian Islamic market in 2006. The new bank will be called the Asian Finance Bank, which will also service clients from Brunei and Indonesia. Also in Bangladesh, Shamil Bank of Bahrain E.C. operates as a foreign Islamic bank.

Why do banks move overseas? It is often to follow their market, that is, clients, or to expand their business (Lewis and Davis, 1987, ch. 8; Williams, 1997). Further advantages beyond efficiency improvements for allowing the entry of foreign banks include the expansion of products or services in the market, perhaps improved technology and improved training for staff. A disadvantage cited is that the home regulator can be appearing to lose power over the market, depending on the foreign bank entry mode (local joint venture, wholly owned subsidiary or branch office and so on).

In view of the lack of literature on Islamic foreign bank entry, a study of the Middle Eastern region is instructive. Analysing both domestic and foreign commercial banks in the Middle Eastern region, Hassan (2004) found evidence that foreign banks had higher margins, non-interest income and profits. This was deemed due to better quality management and operations. As the per capita GDP increased, however, net interest margins and ROE declined, perhaps because of the sophistication and availability of finance: as GDP per capita increased, it would be expected that further financial services would be offered and hence increased competition. Taxation appeared not to be a determining factor alone as to which markets banks entered. Customer and short-term funding levels appeared to be higher for foreign banks, perhaps indicating their preference for loan investments.

An issue Islamic banks face when trying to enter other countries is that of regulation. Except for Malaysia, the Islamic banking regulations are often different from those of conventional banks. Hence regulations can be a limiting factor if they are not conducive to Islamic beliefs (Ahmad and Hassan, 2005).

Market risk measurements and regulation in Islamic banking
Market risk is defined as the potential for losses due to changes in the market prices. This could occur in the bank trading book or it may relate to commodity prices or foreign exchanges' rate changes that can have a negative impact on the bank (either on- or off-balance sheet). The initial Basel regulations in 1988 predominantly were intended to avoid credit risk. Amendments in 1998, however, required a capital charge for market risk. Two methods of measuring market risk for a bank are via value at risk (VaR) and stress testing. Stress testing is used to measure possible outcomes under extreme market conditions. Risk testing under normal market conditions is tested via VaR. VaR measures the worst possible loss that a bank could make over a given period under normal trading conditions at a given confidence level, for example 95 per cent or 99 per cent. There are a number of different VaR methods that may vary, depending on assumptions of the portfolio returns and ease of implementation, including expected time required to implement.

Hassan (2003b) notes that Islamic banks' liabilities or debt differs from conventional banks' balance sheet debt. There are non-investment deposits where the risk-averse depositor may have their funds invested. There are also unrestricted profit-sharing investment deposits (UPLSID) and restricted profit-sharing investment deposits (RPLSID). Islamic banks share the profits or losses with UPLSID but they only play an administrative role under RPLSID. Hence Islamic banks can play two roles either as a fiduciary arrangement for risk-averse depositors or as an agency for risk-taking investors. The Accounting and Audit Organization for Islamic Banks (AAOIFI) has argued that, on the liability side of an Islamic bank's balance sheet, there should be an account called a Profit-Sharing Investment Account (PSIA) that should be capable of being included in capital calculations because of risk-absorbing capabilities. Hassan (2003b) suggests that regulatory capital charged for risk-adverse depositors needs to be separate and distinct from capital allocation from UPLSID where the bank takes on an equity stake in the investment. Currently most Islamic banks have mainly short-term investments not of an equity-type investment. After applying a number of different VaR models to various Islamic banks, the highest VaR estimates were obtained using the Non-affine Stochastic Volatility Jump-Diffusion (NASVJ) method.

In the banking arena at present the most pressing issue is the theoretical and operational aspect of implementing Basel II capital regulation. Fundamentally, the question is whether Islamic banks need to be regulated if they operate with equity capital and investment deposits as their source of funds. Since depositors share profits and losses with the bank, they can be considered to be in effect quasi-shareholders (Hassan and Chowdhury, 2004). Profit and loss-sharing investments could be considered as part of Tier 2 capital under Basel I. The problem, however, is that they are not permanent in nature and so remain risky because of liquidity concerns. Hence profit/loss-sharing investments need to be included in capital risk calculations, but perhaps as a lower risk category (Hassan and Dicle, 2005).

With the implementation of Basel II, it is expected that most Islamic banks will opt for the Standardized Approach to risk assessment. However, the impetus will be provided for improved internal risk measurement techniques, and actual reporting, when banks are able to hold lower levels of capital, hence leading to lower costs. Basel II needs to be implemented by Islamic banks, even if not required by their bank regulator, to provide confidence in operations and capability to borrow from non-conventional streams for liquidity/funding purposes. Islamic banks have higher levels of demand deposits, and undertake profit/loss sharing in projects via *mudaraba* and *musharaka*, which leads to the possibility that they perhaps require higher capital levels to compensate. Hassan and Choudhury (2004) suggest that capital requirements for demand deposits and investment deposits be applied differently than for conventional banks. One option is to put demand deposits on the balance sheet in the banking book and report investment deposits off balance sheet via the trading book. This, it would seem, is the practice of the Faisal Islamic Bank Bahrain (Lewis and Algaoud, 2001, ch. 7). A second option is to 'pool' investments and run them via a subsidiary of the bank and hence apply separate capital standards. The AAOIFI supports the notion that investment deposits be reported on balance sheet rather than off balance sheet. This discrepancy between Islamic banks has made analytical comparisons of performance limited to those banks that comply with transparency.

Problems and prospects of Islamic banking
A number of aspects add to the dilemma of Islamic banks (Ahmad and Hassan, 2005). First, many people do not understand Islamic banking; this includes both Muslims and non-Muslims. The fact that *shari'a* boards, which oversee the transactions in relation to the Qur'an, are often at the individual bank level, can lead to many interpretations of what is and what is not a suitable 'Islamic' transaction. Also the nomenclature is often not consistent. Islamic bankers have often modified the Islamic transaction to suit the requirements of the current transaction. Islamic investments are not always palatable to investors, but this may be related to their limited knowledge of Islamic finance. Second, although Islamic banking was able to develop rapidly in the Middle East oil-rich countries in the 1980s, many people, companies and governments in that region still use only conventional banks. Third, it is difficult for Islamic banks to manage liquidity risk with Islamic products where interest-free capital markets do not exist. This is also related to the shortage of Islamic investment instruments.

Next there is a conflict of interest within Islamic banks to balance achievement of a high ROE, but also to meet customers' needs in an Islamic and 'social' manner by perhaps providing *qard hasan* in a low-value contract, which may not lead to maximizing ROE. In addition, the social aspect of Islamic banking such as making *zakat* donations to charities is seen as an important aspect to maintain.

Other problems include a lack of suitable trained staff able to perform adequate credit analysis on projects, as well as suitable managers, rather than just the owner. Latest technologies as used in conventional banks are often not used by Islamic banks. Under conventional banking systems, risk is priced according to interest rates, whereas Islamic finance often requires a mark-up or profit-sharing amount to be determined before the transaction begins. Often Islamic banks do not fall under the lender of last resort facility, where the central bank can lend money to the bank in times of low liquidity, except in Malaysia. Another point at issue is regulation. Islamic banks came into existence when conventional banks, which charged interest, were well established. Some regulations need to be amended before an Islamic bank can operate within a particular economy, an example being stamp duties. The Islamic bank will purchase a product on behalf of a client and then resell it. Double stamp duties should not be charged in such circumstances. In the non-Muslim world, new banks also need to meet economic requirements such as a certain size requirement and may be limited as regards areas of the economy in which they can operate. Sudanese Islamic banks, for instance, are so restricted.

Islamic banks are in a privileged position to gain access to customers from large Muslim populations around the world, thanks to the philosophy of the Qur'an. However, they also have a social obligation to finance via equity, or profit or loss mode, projects that may initially lack capital funds. This could also see the emergence of countries with large Muslim populations financially expanding at a more rapid rate. Perhaps then the social equity of an Islamic bank is best supported through finding a good project that does not have sufficient equity or capital for a conventional bank to lend to. Table 7.3 examines some broad statistics for individual Islamic banks. Data are examined at bank level, given that many Islamic banks do not report specific details. In most instances, Islamic operational assets are over half the total assets. In Kuwait the International Investor Company reports very low levels. The two Sudanese Islamic banks have low levels of Islamic assets; however, to their credit, they have the highest percentage of equity investments, at over 20 per cent of their total assets. More profit and loss-sharing lending, such as *mudaraba* and *musharaka*, should ethically be undertaken by more Islamic banks that could include further investments with people with new ideas but limited capital.

Conclusions

A major aim of this chapter was to compare the performance of Islamic banks with conventional banks. Two fundamental differences between these two forms of banking are related to financing techniques with or without interest usage and social objectives. Islamic banks typically held higher levels of equity and it was initially suggested that this might be due to equity investments such as with *mudaraba* and *musharaka* transactions. Further analysis, however, showed that only Sudanese banks had significant levels of equity investments. Given the attention Islamic bank equity investments receive, one might have expected Islamic banks to be a major source of long-term capital for their clients. This was not the case. Islamic banks also seemingly lent out to customers at a higher level to total assets than conventional banks. This again could be related to social aspects.

More recent periods show the cost efficiency of Islamic banks to be higher than local conventional banks but similar to conventional banks elsewhere. It would be expected for the additional labour required to perform Islamic transactions to lead to higher costs. Islamic financing has instead tended to be short-term in nature. For the future, obviously the development of new Islamic products and services is imperative. The most profitable banks were found in Iran, Qatar and Saudi Arabia, with Islamic banks often achieving higher levels than conventional banks. Prior efficiency studies found that Islamic banks

Table 7.3   Financial results of Islamic banks (2004)

Country	Bank	Islamic operations/ total assets	Equity investments/ total assets	Income from Islamic transactions/ total assets	Total assets $US millions
Bahrain	Al Amin Bank	65.2	n.a.	6.4	270.6
Bahrain	Arcapita Bank BSC	23.9	22.9	n.a.	1 228.3
Bahrain	Bahrain Islamic Bank	66.4	n.a.	2.5	677.7
Bahrain	Gulf Finance House	n.a.	n.a.	0.3	501.6
Bahrain	Kuwait Finance House (BHD)	53.4	n.a.	2.7	466.40
Bahrain	Shamil Bank of Bahrain	24.5	n.a.	2.7	1 613.7
Egypt	Faisal Islamic Bank of Egypt	79.8	14.7	3.5	2 546.90
Iran	Bank Sepah	59.6	n.a.	5.4	13 913.50
Jordan	Jordan Islamic Bank for Finance and Investment	48.4	0.2	2.4	1 591.8
Kuwait	International Investor Company	9.9	1.2	0.1	279.60
Kuwait	Kuwait Finance House (Kuwait)	46.5	n.a.	3.9	11 734.30
Malaysia	Bank Islam	60.9	0.6*	n.a.	3 410.1
Pakistan	Meezan Bank Limited	62.6	7.3	2.7	333.2
Qatar	Qatar International Islamic Bank	53.6	7.1	3.8	1 363.3
Qatar	Qatar Islamic Bank	57.8	n.a.	4.4	2 111.8
Russia	Badr Forte Bank	33.7	0.0	n.a.	26.20
Sudan	Sudanese Islamic Bank	12.8	n.a.	n.a.	100.40
Sudan	Tadamon Islamic Bank	17.4	28.3	1.4	173.30
UAE	Abu Dhabi Islamic Bank	61.4	6.0	3.4	3 454.60
UAE	Dubai Islamic Bank plc	59.5	1.1	3.8	8 335.80
UAE	Emirates Islamic Bank	79.5	n.a.	0.2	628.7

Note: Islamic operations include all types of Islamic investments; * based on *mudahraba* (profit sharing) and *musyaraka* (profit and loss sharing).

Source: Bankscope database.

often achieved efficiency through expanding their markets and that a larger scale or size and higher levels of capital were desirable. Efficiency levels could most readily be improved if Islamic banks took more care with input costs. Banks were generally profit-efficient.

Meanwhile regulators around the world have a better understanding of specific Islamic requirements, but further change will be required to accommodate Islamic banks. Improved risk assessment techniques should be implemented, including VaR for market risk measurements. Consumers and investors need further education in Islamic finance. Ahmad and Hassan (2005) suggest that Islamic banks need to ensure high-quality services for customers. For banks to operate efficiently, and hence help economic growth of an economy, banks need to be trusted by both the general public and regulators alike. As stated initially, Islamic banks are now competing with conventional banks offering Islamic windows or services. It is important for Islamic banks to develop common reporting standards, or harmonization, as promulgated by Basel II, the Accounting and Auditing Organization for Islamic Financial Institution (AAOIFI) and the Islamic Financial Services Industry (IFSI). This could include following International Financial Reporting Standards (IFRS) and employing International Accounting Standards (IAS). With continued globalization of financial services, the outlook is for continued growth of Islamic banks. However, compliance with Basel II, and resultant effective market discipline, will be a mitigating factor, owing to special problems of investment accounts and the role of depositors, explored further later in this volume.

References

Ahmad, A.U.F. and M.K. Hassan (2007), 'Regulation and performance of Islamic banking in Bangladesh', *Thunderbird International Business Review* (forthcoming).

Brown, K. (2003), 'Islamic banking comparative analysis', *Arab Bank Review*, **5** (2), 43–50.

Brown, K. and M. Skully (2004), 'Islamic banks: a cross-country study of cost efficiency performance', *Accounting, Commerce and Finance: The Islamic Perspective Journal*, **8** (1 & 2), 43–79.

Davis, K.T. and M.K. Lewis (1982), 'Economies of scale in financial institutions', Technical Paper 24, in Australian Financial System Inquiry, *Commissioned Studies and Selected Papers,* part 1, Canberra: Australian Government Publishing Service, pp. 645–701.

Hasan, Z. (2004), 'Measuring the efficiency of Islamic banks: criteria, methods and social priorities', *Review of Islamic Economics*, **8** (2), 5–30.

Hassan, M. Kabir (1999), 'Islamic banking in theory and practice: the experience of Bangladesh', *Managerial Finance*, **25** (5), 60–113.

Hassan M.K. (2003a), 'Cost, profit and X-efficiency of Islamic banks in Pakistan, Iran and Sudan', International Seminar on Islamic Banking: 'Risk Management, Regulation and Supervision', 30 September–2 October, Jakarta, Indonesia.

Hassan, M.K. (2003b), 'VaR analysis of Islamic banks', paper presented in an International Conference on Islamic Banking: 'Risk Management, Regulation and Supervision, Towards an International Regulatory Convergence', 30 September–2 October, Jakarta, Indonesia.

Hassan, M.K. (2004), 'Financial liberalization and foreign bank entry on Islamic banking performance', working paper (mimeo), University of New Orleans.

Hassan, M.K. (2005), 'The X-efficiency of Islamic banks', paper presented at the 12th ERF Conference in Cairo, 19–21 August, Cairo, Egypt.

Hassan, M.K. and A.H. Bashir (2005), 'Determinants of Islamic banking profitability', in Munawar Iqbal and Rodney Wilson (eds), *Islamic Perspectives on Wealth Creation*, Edinburgh: Edinburgh University Press.

Hassan, M.K. and Mannan Choudhury (2004), 'Islamic banking regulations in light of Basel II', paper presented at the Sixth Harvard University Forum in Islamic Finance, 8 May, Cambridge, Mass.

Hassan, M.K. and Mehmet Dicle (2005), 'Basel II and capital requirements of Islamic banks', paper presented at the Sixth International Conference of Islamic Banking and Finance, 21–24 November, Jakarta, Indonesia.

Hassan, M.K. and K.A. Hussein (2003), 'Static and dynamic efficiency in the Sudanese banking system', *Review of Islamic Economics*, **14**, 5–48.

Lewis, M.K. (1988), 'Off balance sheet activities and financial innovation in banking', *Banca Nazionale del Lavoro Quarterly Review*, **167**, 387–410.

Lewis, M.K. (1992), 'Off-the-balance-sheet activities', in P. Newman, M. Milgate and J. Eatwell (eds), *New Palgrave Dictionary of Money and Finance*, vol 3, London: Macmillan, pp. 67–72.

Lewis, M.K. and L.M. Algaoud (2001), *Islamic Banking*, Cheltenham, UK and Northampton, MA, USA: Edward Elgar.

Lewis, M.K. and K.T. Davis (1987), *Domestic and International Banking,* Oxford: Philip Allan.

Sarker, Abdul Awwal and M. Kabir Hassan (2005), 'Islamic banking in Bangladesh: background, methodology and present status', working paper, Bangladesh Bank, Dhaka, Bangladesh, December.

State Bank of Pakistan (2005), *Quarterly performance review of the state banking system*, State Bank of Pakistan, 22–24 March.

Williams, B. (1997), 'Positive theories of multinational banking: eclectic theory versus internalisation theory', *Journal of Economic Surveys*, **11** (1), 71–100.

Zaher, Tarek and M. Kabir Hassan (2001), 'A comparative literature survey of Islamic finance and banking', *Financial Markets, Institutions and Instruments*, **10** (4), 155–99.

Appendix   Country-specific performance results

		2003	2002	2001	2000	1999	1998
Bahrain							
Islamic	Capital funds/liabilities	39.59	72.69	173.35	127.35	84.18	121.81
Conventional		20.31	69.99	32.98	32.43	21.07	16.40
Islamic	Equity/total assets	26.77	47.93	47.44	50.12	43.17	39.35
Conventional		14.40	20.23	17.98	17.19	15.11	13.59
Islamic	Cost to income ratio	47.26	53.05	45.06	52.10	58.98	58.30
Conventional		42.03	50.75	47.51	49.04	52.67	45.34
Islamic	Liquid assets/cust. and ST funding	8.68	14.72	129.35	44.58	19.17	17.75
Conventional		15.99	18.88	81.67	74.54	27.31	28.67
Islamic	Net 'loans'/total assets	59.13	48.00	56.94	57.24	48.16	57.83
Conventional		38.26	41.85	43.67	49.91	50.18	48.24
Islamic	Net 'loans'/cust. and ST funding	106.39	82.56	212.35	145.94	111.41	225.51
Conventional		48.42	51.55	53.98	60.38	64.09	58.94
Islamic	Return on average equity	16.66	12.11	12.72	11.46	5.50	5.20
Conventional		14.09	7.50	13.23	12.87	9.43	9.79
Islamic	Return on average assets	5.52	6.32	7.78	7.35	2.58	2.42
Conventional		2.15	2.27	3.08	3.01	1.12	1.27
Egypt							
Islamic	Capital funds/liabilities	—	4.97	5.44	5.85	5.75	6.12
Conventional		9.12	10.43	11.00	11.41	12.58	12.62
Islamic	Equity/total assets	—	4.72	5.13	5.50	5.39	5.75
Conventional		8.20	9.00	9.46	9.70	10.62	10.58
Islamic	Cost to income ratio	—	57.41	49.04	42.58	49.40	40.72
Conventional		50.36	59.68	49.03	47.90	43.81	43.10
Islamic	Liquid assets/cust. and ST funding	—	8.38	9.36	10.56	11.02	9.34
Conventional		20.86	19.42	19.46	18.26	17.31	20.45
Islamic	Net 'loans'/total assets	—	40.84	41.63	41.74	41.49	42.92
Conventional		39.42	48.71	51.26	52.52	55.62	54.16
Islamic	Net 'loans'/cust. and ST funding	—	43.91	45.26	45.97	46.54	48.31
Conventional		45.31	57.98	62.14	62.76	67.59	65.81
Islamic	Return on average equity	—	2.41	9.34	9.98	7.83	13.71
Conventional		11.66	5.01	8.59	11.50	15.74	16.30
Islamic	Return on average assets	—	0.08	0.47	0.56	0.40	0.87
Conventional		1.16	0.53	0.77	1.14	1.73	1.67
Iran*							
Islamic	Capital funds / liabilities	—	18.45	78.21	20.31	44.78	17.89
	Equity / total assets	—	13.75	20.41	14.08	15.77	10.75
	Cost to income ratio	—	50.02	58.36	60.39	62.86	67.04
	Liquid assets / cust. and ST funding	—	44.58	66.06	48.90	49.21	56.17

		2003	2002	2001	2000	1999	1998
	Net 'loans' / total assets	—	51.31	52.61	53.70	52.91	47.77
	Net 'loans' / cust. and ST funding	—	72.83	96.15	91.18	91.44	104.80
	Return on average equity	—	22.02	20.65	23.91	20.04	11.15
	Return on average assets	—	3.40	2.52	2.28	1.29	0.40
Jordan							
Islamic	Capital funds / liabilities	—	12.35	14.00	18.13	15.79	24.88
Conventional		10.72	10.28	9.70	9.36	9.01	9.92
Islamic	Equity / total assets	—	10.80	11.86	14.53	13.19	18.39
Conventional		9.62	9.04	8.63	8.29	7.60	8.12
Islamic	Cost to income ratio	—	55.00	60.99	53.69	61.69	67.72
Conventional		55.69	53.92	53.22	58.90	61.01	61.19
Islamic	Liquid assets / cust. and ST funding	—	52.90	50.04	50.07	35.84	41.03
Conventional		40.81	44.92	46.11	47.28	52.58	48.53
Islamic	Net 'loans' / total assets	—	35.61	32.21	31.24	31.04	32.97
Conventional		36.95	37.77	41.57	41.50	44.20	46.44
Islamic	Net 'loans' / cust. and ST funding	—	40.15	37.86	37.37	36.16	39.82
Conventional		43.92	47.04	54.95	52.59	55.94	59.12
Islamic	Return on average equity	—	3.89	4.24	5.65	3.56	3.89
Conventional		9.79	8.81	8.15	8.48	4.33	8.84
Islamic	Return on average assets	—	0.63	0.71	0.89	0.55	0.43
Conventional		1.00	0.94	0.86	0.76	0.41	0.74
Lebanon							
Islamic	Capital funds / liabilities	—	—	—	11.38	82.56	101.72
Conventional		8.02	10.25	11.26	12.51	13.71	16.85
Islamic	Equity / total assets	—	—	—	10.22	36.42	40.11
Conventional		6.83	8.54	9.41	10.33	11.00	12.53
Islamic	Cost to income ratio	—	—	—	44.89	60.65	64.54
Conventional		55.44	65.84	71.96	77.23	85.29	69.01
Islamic	Liquid assets / cust. and ST funding	—	—	—	69.27	119.86	114.03
Conventional		80.25	71.37	69.76	72.73	71.27	75.60
Islamic	Net 'loans' / total assets	—	—	—	38.84	20.68	25.19
Conventional		21.91	26.06	28.60	30.02	32.27	31.10
Islamic	Net 'loans' / cust. and ST funding	—	—	—	46.50	27.09	35.61
Conventional		24.81	29.54	32.71	35.17	38.31	38.48
Islamic	Return on average equity	—	—	—	22.56	7.74	11.62
Conventional		13.38	1.21	6.69	5.54	7.69	9.26
Islamic	Return on average assets	—	—	—	2.54	2.51	2.21
Conventional		0.93	0.55	0.51	0.61	0.63	2.41
Oman							
Islamic	Capital funds / liabilities	—	—	—	—	—	—
Conventional		14.86	14.39	16.13	30.49	48.48	35.46
Islamic	Equity / total assets	—	—	—	—	—	—

		2003	2002	2001	2000	1999	1998
Conventional		11.47	11.32	12.80	19.56	23.00	31.52
Islamic	Cost to income ratio	—	—	—	—	—	—
Conventional		47.84	44.65	48.50	47.25	47.83	44.97
Islamic	Liquid assets / cust. and ST funding	—	—	—	—	—	—
Conventional		—	—	—	—	—	—
Islamic	Net 'loans' / total assets	—	—	—	—	—	—
Conventional		69.83	72.56	75.24	74.71	73.34	69.52
Islamic	Net 'loans' / cust. and ST funding	—	—	—	—	—	—
Conventional		85.74	87.96	91.84	103.02	117.08	98.00
Islamic	Return on average equity	—	—	—	—	—	—
Conventional		5.03	15.71	1.82	10.98	11.39	14.33
Islamic	Return on average assets	—	—	—	—	—	—
Conventional		0.50	1.81	−0.15	1.88	1.99	2.58
Qatar							
Islamic	Capital funds / liabilities	10.88	8.08	7.81	8.47	8.28	8.14
Conventional		14.00	13.24	12.42	91.06	52.01	63.77
Islamic	Equity / total assets	9.82	7.46	7.24	7.81	7.65	7.53
Conventional		12.27	25.27	25.34	24.44	23.16	24.10
Islamic	Cost to income ratio	30.96	40.33	41.37	44.42	48.79	45.50
Conventional		33.19	36.49	42.71	43.52	40.37	39.10
Islamic	Liquid assets / cust. and ST funding	15.89	13.20	11.69	9.02	10.52	8.36
Conventional		—	—	—	—	—	—
Islamic	Net 'loans' / total assets	68.00	82.22	84.28	86.04	82.98	82.98
Conventional		56.78	46.77	45.87	41.87	44.59	49.74
Islamic	Net 'loans' / cust. and ST funding	79.84	95.74	101.21	105.13	99.87	99.68
Conventional		69.78	95.13	62.79	58.14	55.41	60.66
Islamic	Return on average equity	34.74	26.89	22.47	17.78	20.77	24.23
Conventional		21.68	19.46	11.76	−0.33	15.62	16.69
Islamic	Return on average assets	3.21	1.99	1.69	1.38	1.58	1.81
Conventional		2.62	2.49	1.86	0.77	2.12	2.04
Saudi Arabia							
Islamic	Capital funds / liabilities	12.62	13.01	14.93	15.35	15.30	16.71
Conventional		10.48	11.13	10.89	10.33	10.35	11.07
Islamic	Equity / total assets	11.21	11.51	12.99	13.31	13.27	14.32
Conventional		9.47	9.97	9.76	9.29	9.30	9.94
Islamic	Cost to income ratio	—	—	—	—	—	—
Conventional		41.18	44.32	44.05	46.88	52.00	48.12
Islamic	Liquid assets / cust. and ST funding	68.83	72.51	62.38	70.84	56.26	60.48
Conventional		47.97	55.08	38.85	26.29	21.60	24.34
Islamic	Net 'loans' / total assets	40.67	36.47	41.97	37.61	48.53	45.76
Conventional		46.89	41.73	39.54	38.92	40.34	40.28

		2003	2002	2001	2000	1999	1998
Islamic	Net 'loans' / cust. and ST funding	52.70	46.66	53.45	48.78	62.01	58.81
Conventional		54.33	48.90	45.91	44.89	46.31	46.49
Islamic	Return on average equity	28.94	20.85	22.79	30.45	26.96	26.60
Conventional		22.70	21.59	22.02	20.80	−0.17	15.53
Islamic	Return on average assets	3.29	2.54	2.99	4.05	3.71	3.86
Conventional		2.14	2.02	1.94	1.72	0.48	1.53
Tunisia							
Islamic	Capital funds / liabilities	—	43.75	48.27	46.83	51.40	54.63
Conventional		11.34	14.73	16.44	19.16	29.21	17.71
Islamic	Equity / total assets	—	30.43	32.55	31.89	33.95	35.33
Conventional		10.09	11.85	12.63	14.21	17.68	19.30
Islamic	Cost to income ratio	—	46.38	39.73	41.43	45.07	51.61
Conventional		63.22	58.71	55.31	56.73	55.74	54.76
Islamic	Liquid assets / cust. and ST funding	—	2.22	3.29	1.91	2.17	2.27
Conventional		12.41	20.91	33.01	29.80	54.64	28.25
Islamic	Net 'loans' / total assets	—	59.96	54.05	32.12	43.10	46.45
Conventional		74.48	71.11	63.73	62.35	63.03	62.97
Islamic	Net 'loans' / cust. and ST funding	—	89.13	89.18	52.00	71.18	77.69
Conventional		102.30	97.80	82.79	78.65	81.11	118.34
Islamic	Return on average equity	—	4.21	5.27	4.93	4.39	4.09
Conventional		8.38	5.93	11.75	12.05	11.74	8.59
Islamic	Return on average assets	—	1.32	1.70	1.62	1.52	1.40
Conventional		0.86	0.68	1.29	1.25	1.42	1.17
Turkey							
Islamic	Capital funds / liabilities	12.17	10.56	8.59	7.51	5.93	3.03
Conventional		19.85	39.09	12.12	17.72	8.87	8.00
Islamic	Equity / total assets	10.68	9.52	7.78	6.97	5.55	2.94
Conventional		14.58	15.45	10.30	12.93	3.23	4.03
Islamic	Cost to income ratio	122.18	82.71	178.05	71.73	61.00	47.57
Conventional		58.73	75.12	143.34	82.26	65.74	80.82
Islamic	Liquid assets / cust. and ST funding	25.92	30.25	38.49	21.95	21.93	—
Conventional		62.67	67.56	75.20	66.86	60.25	42.14
Islamic	Net 'loans' / total assets	66.68	64.74	58.04	72.75	78.43	85.78
Conventional		37.29	28.89	25.07	30.88	31.12	39.35
Islamic	Net 'loans' / cust. and ST funding	78.56	75.49	66.07	80.98	87.05	97.36
Conventional		55.22	37.25	33.97	41.40	39.51	47.04
Islamic	Return on average equity	2.09	2.48	−46.29	19.59	36.04	67.41
Conventional		22.52	15.88	−42.10	12.59	23.56	25.77
Islamic	Return on average assets	0.28	0.07	−2.71	1.08	1.42	1.98
Conventional		2.67	1.15	−4.31	−1.21	−4.24	−5.41

		2003	2002	2001	2000	1999	1998
Yemen							
Islamic	Capital funds / liabilities	15.08	17.63	13.22	14.90	15.45	19.96
Conventional		7.80	10.45	15.24	8.52	9.75	9.44
Islamic	Equity / total assets	12.66	13.89	11.55	12.95	13.38	16.60
Conventional		7.17	8.96	11.68	7.81	8.83	8.39
Islamic	Cost to income ratio	74.58	80.64	48.70	46.99	53.21	51.02
Conventional		62.81	59.69	59.53	49.75	51.53	55.17
Islamic	Liquid assets / cust. and ST funding	73.06	61.51	46.93	43.27	48.84	52.64
Conventional		68.93	71.44	77.26	70.48	64.07	66.72
Islamic	Net 'loans' / total assets	22.17	27.97	46.30	54.09	49.55	49.58
Conventional		27.98	27.37	25.36	25.92	31.28	34.78
Islamic	Net 'loans' / cust. and ST funding	25.65	31.58	56.84	65.51	61.68	66.06
Conventional		30.94	31.33	29.20	28.82	35.32	39.73
Islamic	Return on average equity	5.20	10.24	15.10	14.28	18.64	14.44
Conventional		5.09	5.18	4.30	3.37	6.41	9.67
Islamic	Return on average assets	0.12	0.22	1.90	1.84	2.73	2.60
Conventional		0.39	0.41	−0.05	0.28	0.40	0.44

* Iran has a full Islamic financial system, hence no conventional banks reported.

Source: Bankscope database.

8 Marketing of Islamic financial products
Said M. Elfakhani, Imad J. Zbib and Zafar U. Ahmed

Introduction

Islamic financial products offer new opportunities for institutions to address previously unexplored consumer and business segments. Institutions offering Islamic financial services have increased in number and availability thanks to a growing demand by certain segments of the world's 1.3 billion Muslims for *shari'a*-compliant products. Currently, more than 265 Islamic banks and other financial institutions are operating across the world, from Jakarta (Indonesia) to Jeddah (Saudi Arabia), with total assets of more than $262 billion, as detailed in Tables 8.1 to 8.3. Table 8.1 lists some major Islamic banks in the Middle East. Table 8.2 ranks the largest Islamic banks in the Arab world. Table 8.3 lists the leading Islamic debt managers (2004–2005). Islamic banks aim at addressing the needs of new segments by creating a range of Islamically acceptable products, the development of which pose significant challenges arising from the need for *shari'a* compliance in addition to regulatory complexities. Marketing such products is another challenge in light of competition from conventional banks and the need for innovative products.

Table 8.1   Prominent Islamic banks in the Middle East

Country	Islamic financial institutions
Algeria	Banque Al Baraka D'Algérie (1991)
Bahrain	ABC Islamic Bank (1995)
	Al Amin Co. for Securities and Investment Funds (1987)
	Albaraka Islamic Investment Bank (1984)
	Al Tawfeek Company for Investment Funds (1987)
	Arab Islamic Bank (1990)
	Bahrain Islamic Bank (1979)
	Bahrain Islamic Investment Co. (1981)
	Citi Islamic Investment Bank (1996)
	Faysal Investment Bank of Bahrain (1984)
	Faysal Islamic Bank of Bahrain (1982)
	First Islamic Investment Bank (1996)
	Gulf Finance House (1999)
	Islamic Investment Co. of the Gulf (1983)
	Islamic Leasing Company
Egypt	Alwatany Bank of Egypt, Cairo (1980) (one Islamic branch)
	Arab Investment Bank (Islamic Banking operations), Cairo
	Bank Misr (Islamic Branches), Cairo (window opened 1980)
	Egyptian Saudi Finance Bank (1980)
	Faisal Islamic Bank of Egypt, Cairo (1977)
	International Islamic Bank for Investment and Development, Cairo (1980)
	Islamic Investment and Development Company, Cairo (1983)
	Nasir Social Bank, Cairo (1971)

Table 8.1   (continued)

Country	Islamic financial institutions
Iraq	Iraqi Islamic Bank for Investment and Development (1993)
Jordan	Beit El-Mal Saving and Investment Co. (1983) Islamic International Arab Bank (1998) Jordan Islamic Bank for Finance and Investment (1978)
Kuwait	International Investment Group (1993) Kuwait Finance House, Safat (1977) The International Investor (1992)
Lebanon	Al Baraka Bank Lebanon (1992) Arab Finance House (2004)
Mauritania	Al Baraka Islamic Bank, Mauritania (1985)
Qatar	Al-Jazeera Investment Company, Doha (1989) Qatar International Islamic Bank (1990) Qatar Islamic Bank (SAQ) (1983)
Saudi Arabia	Al Baraka Investment and Development Company, Jeddah (1982) Al Rajihi Banking and Investment Corporation (1988) Islamic Development Bank, Jeddah (1975)
Tunisia	Bank Al Tamwil Al Saudi Al Tunisi (1983)
UAE	Abu Dhabi Islamic Bank (1977) Dubai Islamic Bank, Dubai (1975) Islamic Investment Company of the Gulf, Sharjah (1977)
Yemen	Saba Islamic Bank (1996) Tadhom Islamic Bank (1996) Yemen Islamic Bank for Finance and Investment (1996)

Note: date in brackets is the date of formation.

Source: Lewis and Algaoud (2001).

Contemporary environment

The introduction of Islamic financial products across the world has been in response to the growing need of a significant segment of the marketplace that refused to deal with interest-based instruments. This development has helped finance the operations of small and medium enterprises that were unable to gain access to credit facilities owing to their lack of collateral and the small size of these loans, making costs higher. Conventional banks rely extensively on the creditworthiness of clients before granting a loan, while Islamic banks emphasize the projected cash flows of a project being funded, culminating in the emergence of various Islamic financial services as a significant contributor to the development of local economies and meeting consumers' needs.

In certain societies, conventional banks are viewed as depriving the society of economic balance and equity because the interest-based system is security-oriented rather than growth-oriented, thereby depriving resources to a large number of potential entrepreneurs who do not possess sufficient collateral to pledge with banks. There are many

Table 8.2   Ranking of top Islamic banks in the Arab world

Bank	Type of operation
National Commercial Bank (Jeddah, Saudi Arabia)	Islamic window
Riyadh Bank (Riyadh, Saudi Arabia)	Islamic window
Arab Banking Corporation (Manama, Bahrain)	Islamic window
Al Rajihi Banking & Investment Corp. (Riyadh, Saudi Arabia)	Islamic bank
National Bank of Egypt (Cairo, Egypt)	Islamic window
Saudi British Bank (Riyadh, Saudi Arabia)	Islamic window
Gulf International Bank (Manama, Bahrain)	Islamic window
Kuwait Finance House (Safat, Kuwait)	Islamic bank
Saudi International Bank (London, UK)	Islamic window
Banque Du Caire (Cairo, Egypt)	Islamic window
United Bank of Kuwait (London, UK)	Islamic window
Dubai Islamic Bank (Dubai, UAE)	Islamic bank
Faisal Islamic Bank of Bahrain (Manama, Bahrain)	Islamic bank
Faisal Islamic Bank of Egypt (Cairo, Egypt)	Islamic bank
Jordan Islamic Bank for Finance and Investment (Amman, Jordan)	Islamic bank
Qatar Islamic Bank (Doha, Qatar)	Islamic bank
Al Baraka Islamic Investment Bank (Manama, Bahrain)	Islamic bank
Bank of Oman, Bahrain & Kuwait (Ruwi, Oman)	N.A.

Source: *The Banker*, November 1997.

Table 8.3   Top Islamic debt managers (July 2004–May 2005)

Manager	Amt, US$ m.	Iss.	Share (%)
HSBC	866	28	15.00
Citigroup	753	3	13.05
RHB Capital Bhd	582	4	10.08
AmMerchant Bank Bhd	551	19	9.54
Dubai Islamic Bank	433	2	7.5
Commerce International Merchant Bankers Bhd	427	9	7.39
UBS	350	1	6.06
United Overseas Bank Ltd	285	3	4.94
Aseambankers Malaysia Bhd	279	27	4.84
Government bond/no bookrunner	263	3	4.56
Total	4789	99	82.96

Source: Islamic Financial News (available in *Executive Magazine*, June 2005, Issue 72).

individual consumers and entrepreneurs in Islamic societies who believe that the interest-based conventional banking system leads to a misallocation of resources. It is believed that conventional banks are more interested in the pledge of collateral and in securing interest payment regardless of the profitability of the project funded.

Islamic banking is now a global phenomenon and is gaining regulatory approval to operate alongside conventional Western-style institutions. For example, the British regulatory body, the Financial Services Authority (FSA), has been playing a proactive role in promoting Islamic banking across the UK, leading to the establishment of the Islamic Bank of Britain. In order to respond to this expansion, Islamic bankers began developing new products to reach out to this broader client base. Among the innovations have been the development of fixed-return instruments such as Islamic bonds (*sukuk*) and the creation of the global Islamic money market. Corporate and sovereign *sukuk* issues totalled $6.7 billion in 2004, up from $1.9 billion in 2003.

Funds generated within certain rich Muslim countries such as the six member Gulf Cooperation Council countries (consisting of Saudi Arabia, United Arab Emirates, Oman, Kuwait, Qatar and Bahrain) have motivated Western banks to establish Islamic subsidiaries ('windows') and cater for this new need. Banks such as Citibank, Chase Manhattan, HSBC, Deutsche Bank, ABN Amro, Société Générale, BNP Paribas, Bank of America, Standard Chartered and Barclays have been offering Islamic financial products through their subsidiaries to tap into this lucrative market. A subsidiary of Citigroup now operates what is effectively the world's largest Islamic bank in terms of transactions. About $6 billion worth of Islamic financial products have been marketed by Citibank worldwide since 1996.

Islamic financial products
Islamic financial systems are based on five major tenets founded on the *shari'a* bans and commandments (Iqbal, 1997). They are the prohibition of *riba*, profit and loss sharing, the absence of *gharar* (speculation and gambling-like transactions), disallowing the derivation of money on money, and the avoidance of *haram* (forbidden) activities. These have been examined in earlier chapters.

Financial instruments based on these principles have been developed to facilitate everyday banking activities by providing *halal* (*shari'a*-compliant) methods of lending or borrowing money and still offering some acceptable returns for investors. Listed below are some popular Islamic financial products being marketed worldwide by Islamic banks and financial institutions.

Murabaha
Murabaha (trade with mark-up cost) is one of the most widely used instruments for short-term financing and accounts for nearly 75 per cent of Islamic financial products marketed worldwide. Referring to 'cost-plus sale ', *murabaha* is the sale of a commodity at a price that includes a set profit of which both the vendor (marketer) and the consumer are aware.

Ijara
Ijara (leasing) permits the client to purchase assets for subsequent leasing for a certain period of time and at a mutually agreed upon amount of rent, and represents approximately 10 per cent of Islamic financial products marketed worldwide.

Mudaraba
Mudaraba or trust financing is a contract conducted between two parties, a capital owner *(rabb al-mal)* and an investment manager *(mudarib)*, and is similar to an investment fund.

The *rabb al-mal* (beneficial owner or sleeping partner) lends money to the *mudarib* (managing trustee or labour partner), who then has to return the money to the *rabb al-mal* in the form of principal with profits shared in a pre-agreed ratio.

Musharaka

Musharaka literally means sharing derived from *shirkah*. *Shirkat-ul-milk* means a joint ownership of two or more persons of a particular property through inheritance or joint purchase, and *shirkat-ul-aqd* means a partnership established through a contract. *Musharaka* is basically a joint contract by which all the partners share the profit or loss of the joint venture, which resembles *mudaraba*, except that the provider of capital or financier takes equity stakes in the venture along with the entrepreneur.

Muqarada

Muqarada (bonds) allows a bank to issue Islamic bonds to finance a specific project. Investors who buy *muqarada* bonds take a share of the profits generated by the project as well as assuming the risks of losses.

Salam

Salam literally means 'futures'. A buyer pays in advance for a designated quantity and quality of a certain commodity to be delivered at a certain agreed date and price. It is limited to fungible commodities and is mostly used for the purpose of agricultural products by providing needed capital prior to delivery. Generally, Islamic banks use a *salam* contract to buy a commodity and pay the supplier in advance for it, specifying the chosen date for delivery. The bank then sells this commodity to a third party on a *salam* or instalment basis. With two *salam* contracts, the second should entail delivery of the same quantity and description as the first contract and is concluded after the first contract (El-Gamal, 2000).

Istisnaa

Istisnaa is a contract in which a party (for example a consumer) demands the production of a commodity according to certain specifications and then the delivery of it from another party, with payment dates and price specified in the contract. The contract can be cancelled at any time by any party given a prior notification time before starting the manufacturing process, but not later than that. Such an arrangement is widely used for real estate mortgage. Consider a family who would like to buy a $100 000 house and want to finance this purchase with the help of an Islamic bank. It may make an up-front payment equalling 20 per cent ($20 000), leaving the bank to invest 80 per cent, or $80 000, in the house. The family's monthly payment will comprise paying back rent to the bank plus a purchase of a certain portion of shares from the bank, until they effectively 'buy it out'. The rent payments are legitimate because they are used to get a tangible asset that the family does not completely own, and are not paid to return borrowed money with interest.

Sales contracts

In the *fiqh* literature, there are frequently used sales contracts called *bai'muajal* and *bai' salam* or conducting credit sales, that are similar to mortgage instruments. *Bai'muajal* refers to the sale of commodities or real estate against deferred payment and permits the immediate delivery of the product, while payment is delayed or pushed forward for an agreed-upon period without extra penalty, that could be made as a lump sum or in instalments. The distinguishing feature of this contract from any regular cash sale is the deferral of the payment. *Bai'salam* is also a deferred-delivery sale, and resembles a forward contract where the delivery of the product takes place in future in exchange for a spot payment.

Strategic marketing approaches
Besides using the regular marketing tools employed by conventional banks, Islamic banks have also developed their own marketing strategies to attract their target clientele. Some of these strategies are discussed next.

Focus on believers
The main niche for Islamic banks is target adherents to Islamic faith. They appeal to Muslim consumers' basic capital needs. Islamic banks have been able to introduce a variety of financial products that are compliant with *shari'a*, while at the same time offering alternatives to conventional interest-based lending.

Shari'a *supervision*
A *Shari'a* Supervisory Board (SSB) guides *shari'a* compliance on behalf of the clients. The SSB is made up of distinguished Islamic legal scholars who assume responsibility for auditing *shari'a* compliance of a bank, including its marketing strategies, thereby functioning as a customer advocate representing the religious interest of investors (DeLorenzo, 2000).

Special attributes of Islamic banks
Hegazy (1995) investigated bank selection criteria for both Islamic and conventional banks, and concluded that the selection attributes for Islamic banks are different from conventional banks. For example, the most important factor used by Muslim consumers seeking Islamic financial products was the advice and recommendations made by relatives and friends. Convenience of location, friendliness of the personnel, and the bank's vision of serving the Islamic community regardless of the expected profitability were also found to play important roles in the decision-making processes of individual and business clients. Identifying such features allows Islamic banks and institutions to develop appropriate marketing strategies to ensure high levels of customer satisfaction and retention by striving to develop appropriate marketing strategies (Metawa and Almossawi, 1998).

Competing with conventional banks
Marketing of Islamic financial products is faced with various types of competitive pressures from conventional banks. In this environment, Islamic banks have to formulate and implement successful marketing strategies in which a key ingredient is a clear understanding of the behaviour, attitudes and perceptions of their clients. This is achieved through identifying behavioural profiles encompassing banking habits, selection criteria used by target markets, risk-tolerance levels, awareness, preferences and usage patterns of various Islamic bank products (Metawa and Almossawi, 1998). Also Islamic banks offer many of the conventional banking services such as ATM machines, and credit cards to their clients at competitive prices.

Conveying trust and piety
Among the more important attractions Islamic banks aim to portray are the characteristic traits of trust and piety. As Islamic-based institutions, the banks foster a God-abiding, trustworthy and pious image, that is well recognized and appreciated by religious consumers, offering a sense of reassurance that their investments are lawful (*halal*).

Conveying credibility and experience
Like conventional banks, Islamic banks aim to convince customers of their investment experience. An inexperienced customer, seeking a way to invest his/her savings, strongly appreciates evidence of credibility and past investment performance. In this way, the perhaps daunting task of investing is made easier and within reach.

Complementing regular banks
Islamic banks' marketing strategy can be complementary to that of conventional banks. Services not offered by Islamic banks may be acquired from regular conventional banks while maintaining a sense of religious peace and trust by continuing the relationship with the Islamic banks.

Marketing challenges
Islamic banks share the same marketing challenges faced by regular (conventional) banks. However, they also have their own challenges that are related to their business line and constraints. Some of these challenges are discussed next.

Competition from conventional banks
The biggest challenge to Islamic banks, most less than three decades old, is to compete with a well developed and mature conventional banking industry evolving over the past many centuries. They need to know how to market their products successfully. While there are areas where Islamic and conventional banks pursue similar marketing strategies, there are also areas where Islamic banks pursue different strategies. Many individual and business consumers wish to have a guaranteed return on their investments and would thus have recourse to conventional banks based on zero-default interest payment, a factor that does not have a corresponding substitute in Islamic banks (Awad, 2000).

Dealing with non-Islamic financial institutions
Islamic banks often operate in a business environment where laws, institutions, attitudes, rules, regulations and norms serve an economy based on interest. They are faced with the problem of investing short-term deposits and paying returns on them to depositors, while conventional banks have no constraint, dealing with overnight or short-term deposits as well as charging interest on overdrafts. Delineating an appropriate target market is a prerequisite for the successful execution of marketing strategies by Islamic financial institutions.

Maintaining competitive profits
Low profit ratios could hurt Islamic banks as they rely solely on the profit and loss sharing (PLS) principle to market their financial products. PLS is a form of partnership, whereby owners and investors serve as business partners by sharing profits and losses on the basis of their capital share, labour and managerial expertise invested. There can be no guaranteed

rate of return in such a case, although some investments (such as mark-up) provide more stable returns than others (such as *mudaraba*). The justification for the PLS financier's share in profit is their efforts and the risks undertaken, making it legitimate in Islamic *shari'a*.

Supervision and transparency
Islamic institutions need to have some kind of regulatory supervision in day-to-day operations in order to protect their depositors and clients. Because of the differences in their nature and operations, Islamic banks require more strict supervision of the firms' operations after the disbursement of funds. Banks' supervision, scrutiny and examination, and sometimes participatory management in the conduct of firms' operations, are important components of the Islamic financial marketing system set in place, because of the greater risks that the Islamic banks shoulder. In most countries there are no coherent standards of Islamic marketing regulations, and the lack of uniformity in accounting principles and *shari'a* guidelines makes it difficult for central bankers to regulate such an industry (Awaida, 1998). Thanks to the new standards adopted, such as auditing rules in Bahrain, new international standards are now applied by all Islamic banks, enhancing their transparency significantly.

Regulatory hurdles
Because Islamic banking operates on a risk-sharing basis, it may not be necessary to have the same obligation as conventional banks to carry certain levels of capital. However, some regulators take the view that, since Islamic banks are conducting new and unexplored financial pursuits with illiquid assets, they should perhaps have a greater safety margin than conventional banks (Awaida, 1998). In these cases an additional burden is placed on Islamic banks.

Need for adequate human resources
Marketing success hinges on having a highly-qualified and trained marketing team. Many problems in Islamic banks arise because of insufficient training of their marketing personnel (Kahf, 1999). Greater professionalism and competence instituted by proper training programmes are key ingredients for forging successful relationships with clients (Metawa and Almossawi, 1998).

Developing new products
Islamic banks must strive to provide specific products tailored to satisfy different segments of individual and business consumers. They can do so by employing strategies ranging from re-engineering products to focusing on some specific services (see Metawa and Almossawi, 1998), *vis-à-vis* conventional banks, which is seen as one of the biggest challenges to a broader acceptance of new Islamic financial products (Montagu-Pollock and Wright, 2002).

Developing successful marketing strategies
Success in marketing relies on the information retrieved from complete and up-to-date consumer profiles. The availability of such a database is needed for making plausible and effective decisions regarding the marketing of Islamic financial products. Moreover, Islamic financial institutions need recourse to periodic customer surveys to investigate whether clients are aware of new products and to ascertain how many of those products are being used on a regular basis and what benefits are sought by consumers.

Islamic institutions ought to pursue integrated promotion strategies that allow consumers to have adequate information about various products offered that, if properly carried out, will speed up the consumers' learning about various Islamic products and attract new potential segments. Specific promotional and educational activities may need to be undertaken to increase the level of customer awareness and to narrow the gap in customer usage of these products caused by lack of proper awareness (Metawa and Almossawi, 1998).

Balancing profit and development
Islamic banks have presented themselves as providers of capital for entrepreneurs and business adventurers. In fact, most of their products (for example, *murabaha, mudaraba, musharaka, salam* and *istisnaa*) are investment banking-type products. To the disappointment of many Muslim consumers, most of the banks have focused on consumers' loans and mortgages using variations of the above-named products rather than financing new ventures and capital expansion projects. Islamic banks argue that they were pressured to perform to offer a viable alternative to conventional banks during the formative years of their operations. Hence they focused on short-term lending rather than supporting long-term profit-sharing activities. Now that these banks are more stable and mature, there is a the potential for them to carry out their intended responsibilities to fund longer-term projects.

Promoting new client profiles
Islamic banks generally target the following segments: younger generation, female consumers, educated consumers, wealthy consumers, and non-Muslim consumers. Each of these segments requires different marketing strategies, and a certain percentage of annual revenue should be set aside to cover them. Most Islamic banks devote insufficient funds for marketing in comparison with the millions of dollars invested by conventional banks to promote an image. The idea of an Islamic bank, as seen today, was non-existent not so many years ago and there are still many questions among customers, Muslims and non-Muslims alike.

Industrial marketing: business to business marketing
A large contribution to Islamic banking's increasing global success may have been made by major global multinationals (MNCs), operating throughout the Muslim world, which have begun to turn to Islamic financial products as an alternative source of funding for everything from trade finance to equipment leasing. Examples include IBM, General Motors and Xerox, which have raised money through a US-based Islamic Leasing Fund set up by the United Bank of Kuwait, while international oil giants such as Enron and Shell have used Islamic banks to finance their global operations across the Arab Gulf region and Malaysia. Islamic financial institutions are marketing their products across 15 major non-Muslim countries, encompassing the US, Canada, Switzerland, the UK, Denmark and Australia (Martin, 1997, 2005).

Although Islamic financial institutions employ classical marketing tools encompassing the four Ps of marketing-mix (product, price, promotion and place/distribution), their marketing strategies employ different orientations. This is due to the unique attributes of Islamic financial products, on one hand, and the distinctive psychographic (lifestyle and personality) profiles of its consumer market, on the other, as reflected in consumers' religious belief structures influencing their behavioural attitudes and dispositions. For instance, these institutions avoid using sexy models in their promotional campaigns while promoting their products. Many do not aggressively market their Islamic products, but rather depend largely on word of mouth for promotion and distribution of flyers among attendees of mosques, Islamic educational institutions and Islamic centres. Similarly, Citibank does not necessarily employ an aggressive promotional campaign for the successful execution of its marketing strategy, but rather relies on its globally renowned brand for generating awareness among its consumer and business segments.

Non-Muslims as a target market
Another factor contributing to the current surge in the Islamic financial industry is the innovative, competitive and risk-sharing nature of Islamic financial products, providing non-Muslims with attractive and viable alternatives to conventional Western banking instruments. Hence, global financial professionals such as Montagu-Pollock and Wright (2002) believe that the crux of the industry lies in non-Muslim companies and investors taking an interest in tapping it like any other pool of liquidity, or investing in it for no other reason than something that presents a good investment opportunity. Dudley (1998) believes that the future of Islamic banking lies in the idea not to sell Islamic products to Muslims, but rather to sell them to anybody, on the basis of its inherent advantages over other financial alternatives.

Critical evaluation
A vocal and assertive segment of 'ultrareligious Muslim consumers' has serious reservations about non-Islamic banks' involvement in marketing Islamic financial products. They have demonstrated resentment towards the entry of Western and traditional banks in the foray of Islamic banking industry as their vast and traditional operations are contrary to the tenets of Islamic piety. In their opinion, this would not be dissimilar to the Johnny Walker Whisky Company introducing 'Halal Zamzam' bottled water, as a part of its brand extension strategy, to the dismay of a large Muslim population. On another front, funds of these regular banks are drawn, at least partially, from earnings sources that are Islamically doubtful, and are carried over into the Islamic financial products. Purifying or cleansing these assets originating from prohibited earnings is an almost insurmountable challenge, as well as shifting the burden of purification to Muslim users. Hence regular banks, practising both Islamic and non-Islamic banking, generally concentrate on more liberal segments of Muslim consumers, who are more lenient about the Western versus Islamic bank distinction, and ignore the ultrareligious segments who resent conventional banks' entering the Islamic financial industry, as they cannot meet their strict religious criteria. The bottom line is that the regular and non-Islamic banks are perceived as not having entered this industry to serve 'Muslim Umma', but to make money under the pretext of 'Islamic banking'. Ultrareligious Muslims do not wish to ban these banks from serving Islamic financial products when these products are sought by fund users (Muslims and non-Muslims); they simply do not themselves deal with them.

Future scenarios
Islamic banking cannot rest on its laurels. With the advent of the Islamic windows of conventional banks and on-line banking, strong competition has to be faced. The current

marketing challenge for Islamic institutions is to orchestrate strategies promoting competitive, dynamic and sustainable Islamic financial products in order to respond to the requirements of local economies and the international financial market, via innovation of products (Aziz, 2005). Innovation is the key to sustainable and competitive marketing advantage for the future growth of Islamic financial markets. Both innovation speed and innovation magnitude have beneficial effects on an institution's financial performance. Hence Islamic financial marketers should be responsive to the evolving needs of Islamic investors and borrowers (Edwardes, 1995).

Although Islamic banks have been able to grow quickly, their growth has been constrained by a lack of innovation. Developing new Islamic financial products in compliance with the *shari'a* is challenging. Failure to provide the full range and the right quality of products according to *shari'a* will defeat the very purpose behind Islamic banks' existence and will lead to difficulties in retaining current customers and attracting new ones. However, a successful implementation of quality systems, involving *shari'a* scholars and modern corporate finance experts in a Total Quality Management (TQM) exercise, for instance, can help enhance institutional creativity, leading to innovations. The Islamic banks can learn from successful conventional banks by employing appropriate Customer Relationship Management (CRM) strategies. There should also be intensive collaborative efforts among Islamic 'financial engineers' and *shari'a* scholars to accelerate the pace of innovation.

Islamic institutions should also promote knowledge and awareness of their products among their employees by employing internal marketing strategies. This awareness is an important tool as Islamic banks strive to develop close relationships with individual and business clients. They might thereby gain a competitive advantage based on superior customer relationships (Rice and Essam, 2001) and at the same time gain insights, through customer collaboration and feedback, into new customer needs and wants. Education and awareness programmes in the general Islamic community will generate a higher demand for Islamic financial products that could then be customized to the requirements of better informed consumers. This would also help Islamic banks craft specific strategies aimed at capturing unexplored market segments. Collaboration efforts between Islamic banks and conventional banks could bring Islamic products to the mass-market and ultimately develop global distribution capabilities. The IT revolution might also help the Islamic institutions, creating new information portals enabling them to deliver products to consumers through different distribution channels at reduced cost and competitive prices (Aziz, 2004).

Thus advances need to be made on a number of fronts. A qualified and skilled workforce well versed in both *shari'a* and modern corporate financial management is indispensable for innovation. Widening the product range calls for substantial and continuous investment in research and development (R&D). In this context, an industry-sponsored research and training institute, Islamic Banking and Finance Institute Malaysia (IBFIM), deserves special mention, for it has been established to undertake collaborative research with academics at the Malaysian universities aimed at developing unique and innovative Islamic financial offerings across Malaysia (www.ibfim.com). Tomorrow's successful marketers of Islamic financial products will be those who identify and anticipate the evolving needs of the Islamic consumer and pioneer product innovations and improvements to meet those needs (Edwardes, 1995) and should also be able to address non-Muslim financing needs.

References

Awad, Y. (2000), 'Reality and problems of Islamic banking', unpublished MBA dissertation, AUB Librairies, American University of Beirut.

Awaida, H. (1998), 'Islamic banking in perspective', unpublished MBA dissertation, AUB Libraries, American University of Beirut.

Aziz Akhtar, Z. (2004), 'The future prospects of Islamic financial services industry', speech by Governor of the Central Bank of Malaysia, at the IFSB interactive session, Bali, 31 March.

Aziz Akhtar, Z. (2005), 'Islamic finance: promoting the competitive advantage', Governor's keynote address at the Islamic Bankers' Forum, Putrajaya, Malaysia, 21 June.

DeLorenzo, Y.T. (2000), 'Sharia supervision of Islamic mutual funds', *Proceedings of the 4th Harvard Forum on Islamic Finance*, Cambridge: Harvard Islamic Finance Information Program, Center for Middle Eastern Studies, Harvard University, http://www. azzadfund.com (accessed July 2002).

Dudley, N. (1998), 'Islamic banks aim for the mainstream', *Euromoney,* **349**, 113.

Edwardes, Warren (1995), 'Competitive pricing of Islamic financial products', *New Horizon,* May, **39**, 4–6.

El-Gamal, Mahmoud A. (2000), *A Basic Guide to Contemporary Islamic Banking and Finance*, Indiana: Islamic Banking & Finance America.

Hegazy, I.A. (1995), 'An empirical comparative study between Islamic and commercial banks' selection criteria in Egypt', *International Journal of Contemporary Management*, **5** (3), 46–61.

Iqbal, Z. (1997), 'Islamic financial systems', *Finance & Development*, **34** (2), 42–4.

Kahf, Monzer (1999), 'Islamic banks at the threshold of the third millennium', *Thunderbird International Business Review*, **41**, 445–60.

Lewis, Mervyn K. and Latifa M. Algaoud (2001), *Islamic Banking*, Cheltenham, UK and Northampton, MA, USA: Edward Elgar Publishing.

Martin, J. (1997), 'Islamic banking raises interest', *Management Review*, **86** (10), 25.

Martin, J. (2005), 'Islamic banking goes global', *Middle East,* **357**, 50.

Metawa, Saad A. and M. Almossawi (1998), 'Banking behavior of Islamic bank customers: perspectives and implications', *The International Journal of Bank Marketing*, **16** (7), 299–313.

Montagu-Pollock, M. and C. Wright (2002), 'The many faces of Islamic finance', *Asiamoney*, **13** (7), 31.

Rice, G. and M. Essam (2001), 'Integrating quality management, creativity and innovation in Islamic banks', paper presented at the American Finance House – Lariba 8th Annual International Conference, Pasadena, CA, 16 June.

9 Governance of Islamic banks
Volker Nienhaus

Opaqueness and agency problems in banking

Today it is the exception rather than the rule that owners manage their companies. Usually ownership and management are separated, and managers who control the resources of a company have a better knowledge of its status, risks and opportunities than the owners. The separation of ownership and control combined with information asymmetries gives rise to various agency problems. The core issue of governance of a corporation is how to ensure that managers will use a company's resources in the interest of the shareholders.

Because of banks' specifics, governance issues are more relevant in this sector than in other industries. It is widely accepted that banks are opaque institutions and that information asymmetries between insiders and outsiders are pronounced, especially with respect to the risk characteristics and the quality of the assets (especially the loan portfolio). The peculiarities of the financing business make it at best very difficult and costly or at worst factually impossible for outsiders to monitor effectively and in timely fashion the performance of bank managers. The usual remedy for agency problems – incentive contracts – does not go well in banking: not only are outcomes difficult to measure, but they are also relatively easy to influence or to manipulate by managers. For example, if compensations are linked to the interest income earned by a bank, managers may extend high interest loans to borrowers in trouble, thus increasing the risk exposure of the bank. For outsiders such a practice is nearly impossible to detect. If the compensation is linked to asset prices, managers may have sufficient resources at their disposal to move the prices in a favourable direction, at least for a limited period of time. 'Furthermore, since managers frequently control the boards of directors that write the incentive contracts, managers of opaque banks can often design compensation packages that allow managers to benefit at the expense of the long-run health of the bank' (Levine, 2004, p. 8). Finally the strong information asymmetries make hostile takeovers far less probable in banking than in other industries. This limits the effectiveness of competition as an instrument for the protection of shareholders' interests.

However, not only may the shareholders' capital be put at risk by management decisions, but – in the case of insolvency – also outside capital provided by debt holders (creditors) and, in particular, depositors. Depositors may be protected by deposit insurance schemes (which create incentives for bank managers to take even more risk), but this only shifts financial burdens to other outsiders in a case of bankruptcy. Therefore the scope of corporate governance has been enlarged for banking to include not only shareholders but also depositors. Corporate governance shall be seen 'as the methods by which suppliers of finance control managers in order to ensure that their capital cannot be expropriated and that they earn a return on their investment . . . [B]ecause of the peculiar contractual form of banking, corporate governance mechanisms for banks should encapsulate depositors as well as shareholders' (Arun and Turner, 2003, p. 5).

These statements for conventional banks are even more relevant for Islamic banks because for them depositors are exposed to a much higher risk than in conventional banks. Strictly speaking, most funds credited to customer accounts in Islamic banks are legally not deposits. A main characteristic of a deposit is the unconditional claim for full repayment of the principal amount. In Islamic banks, this claim holds true only for money paid into current accounts which are intended for payment transactions and do not generate any income for the account holders. *Shari'a*-compliant accounts which are intended to generate an income (usually named savings or investment accounts) are not vested with an unconditional claim for full repayment. Investment accounts are based on a *mudaraba* type of contract. This implies a participation in the financial results of the employment of funds – be it profit or loss. In the case of loss, the investment account holders cannot claim the full repayment of their principal amount. Investment account holders of Islamic banks bear risks very similar to those of the shareholders, but they do not have any right to monitor and control the management. This provides a strong justification for adopting the broad view of corporate governance for Islamic banks and to include the interests of investment account holders (that is, 'Islamic depositors') in corporate governance mechanisms.

Governance structures of conventional and Islamic banks do not only differ with respect to the status of the depositors. In most Islamic financial institutions, an additional body is part of the governance structure which has no counterpart in conventional banks, namely the *Shari'a* Supervisory Board (SSB). Figure 9.1 summarizes the stylized governance structures of conventional and Islamic banks.

In conventional banks, the classical agency problem is that between management and shareholders. Internal solutions may be found through procedural rules and incentive contracts. External support could come from banking regulations, especially prudential

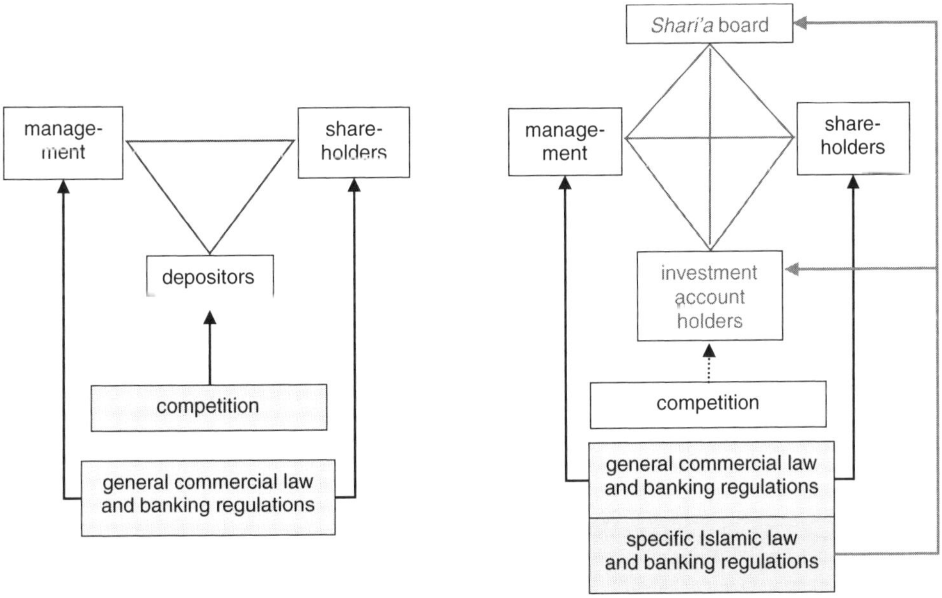

Figure 9.1 Stylized governance structures of conventional and Islamic banks

regulations dealing with reporting and disclosure rules, early warning systems and state supervision.

Profit-and-loss sharing 'deposits' (investment accounts)
In a conventional banking system with effective competition for depositors' funds, the income interests of depositors are safeguarded by this competition, and regulations dealing with capital adequacy and deposit insurance protect the principal amount of their deposits. Thus the resolution of conflicts of interest between depositors and management on the one hand and depositors and shareholders on the other hand does not require too many 'benevolent' discretionary decisions by managers and shareholders but is widely enacted by market forces and state regulations.

   This is very different in Islamic banks. First, there is a fundamental conflict of interest between Islamic depositors and shareholders: both parties share (substantial parts of) the bank's profit, and this implies a distribution conflict. The ratio by which the profit is shared is numerically not defined in the Islamic deposit contracts. It is set by management decision. The management's discretionary margin would be limited by an effective competition amongst banks for Islamic deposits, but it cannot be taken for granted that such a competition does exist. In many Islamic countries where conventional and Islamic financial institutions coexist, the market is dominated by conventional banks, the number of domestic Islamic financial institutions is very small (often fewer than five), and the regulated financial markets are not open for an outflow of funds or for an inflow of international competitors (with only a few exceptions such as Bahrain, the United Arab Emirates and Pakistan). Very often the benchmarks for Islamic products, including Islamic deposits, are taken from the conventional interest-based sector and are applied in analogy to Islamic products. For example, the return on Islamic deposits is roughly kept in line by management decisions with interest earned on conventional deposits. Such a practice, however, does not take into consideration the different risk positions of insured conventional and uninsured Islamic depositors, and it does not reflect the risk profile of the assets of the Islamic bank.

a. Islamic depositors may not be fully aware of the risk and therefore are satisfied with a rate of return equivalent to the prevailing interest rate. In this case the management of an Islamic bank would exploit the depositors' lack of information either to cover higher operating costs (which could include compensation packages for the management itself) or to increase the residual income (profit share) of the shareholders.
b. A similar situation could emerge even if the Islamic depositors were aware of the higher risks but did not have an Islamic alternative in a mixed system without competition in the Islamic segment (because only one or very few non-competing Islamic banks offer Islamic deposits). In this case the management of Islamic banks could exploit the 'Islam-mindedness' of the depositors and pay a return which is less than what would be risk-equivalent in the conventional system.

Smoothing returns
Another practice deserves attention from a governance perspective: the returns for Islamic deposits seemingly fluctuate less than the income generated by the employment of the funds on Islamic deposit accounts. The reason is that the management has recourse to

smoothing techniques which allow it to delink the profits allocated to depositors in a given period from the investment returns of the same period and to keep the Islamic returns in line with movements of the benchmark interest rate. Smoothing can be achieved by two different techniques: the variation of reserves and the commingling of funds.

a.   Islamic banks can create a profit equalization reserve. In a period of high returns, the management can decide to transfer parts of the income and profits from the investment of Islamic deposits to the reserve in that period. In the opposite case, that is, in a period of low returns, the management can decide to reduce the reserve, thus increasing the amount available for distribution in that period.
b.   Many Islamic banks dispose of a relatively large volume of return-free deposits on current accounts. After catering for a sufficient liquidity reserve, the bank may invest the remainder and generate an income. This income is not due to the depositors; rather it increases the profits due to the shareholders. The current account deposits must not be invested separately but can be commingled with investment account deposits or/and shareholders' funds. It is at the discretion of the management to transfer parts of the income from the current account funds to the profits to be shared with the Islamic depositors. This allows a return on Islamic deposits which is above the level which would be possible if only the income from the investment of the Islamic deposits were distributed. This stabilizes the return on Islamic deposits without a reduction of the profit equalization reserve.

Both the use of profit equalization reserves and the commingling of funds are recognized practices of Islamic banks which are deemed *shari'a*-compliant (although there are some different opinions on specific terms and details, especially with respect to the commingling of funds), and at first glance they seem to be in the interests of depositors. But a closer look reveals some conceptual and governance issues of these practices.

   The commingling of funds can work in favour of the Islamic depositors only as long as the Islamic banks dispose of an above-average level of funds in current accounts. There are reasons to expect that in the long run – especially after depositors have gained more experience with Islamic banks, more credible regulations of Islamic banks have been enacted, and competition within the Islamic banking sector has been established – the level of funds in current accounts will be reduced to a lower level comparable to that of current accounts in conventional banks. This will severely restrict or even eliminate the potentials for a stabilization of Islamic depositors' returns through the allocation of profits generated from the investment of current accounts. But as long as this technique is applied, the criticism is valid that it is not well documented and cannot be monitored and assessed by outsiders from the information published in reports of Islamic banks. This clearly adds to the opaqueness of Islamic banks and to the information asymmetries.

   While the effects of the commingling of funds seem to be in the interest of the Islamic depositors, this is far less clear with respect to the profit equalization reserve. If, in the long run, the effect of the smoothing is that the returns on Islamic deposits keep in line with benchmark interest rates, this may not be to the advantage of the Islamic depositors who bear a higher risk than their conventional counterparts.

   If one does not look at the long run but at shorter periods, then the practice of smoothing through appropriations to or from reserves has the effect that depositors do not fully participate in the income or profit generated by the investment of their funds. If they held Islamic deposits during a period of a net increase of reserves, they share a smaller percentage of the income or profit generated by the employment of the funds at the disposal of the Islamic bank during the respective period than those who held their Islamic deposits during a period of a net reduction of reserves. This is a kind of 'intergenerational' shift of portions of income or profit to be shared which was not to be found in the traditional *mudaraba* or *musharaka* contracts (which assumed a definite termination of a transaction whose profits were to be shared).

The *mudaraba*-inspired modern Islamic deposit contracts which allow such practices have been sanctioned by *shari'a* experts, and AAOIFI has issued accounting standards for profit equalization reserves. Furthermore each Islamic depositor accepts the terms for investment accounts. Thus there is no doubt about the legality of the smoothing of returns, but that is no guarantee that the smoothing is done in the interests of depositors. One could argue that smoothing is in harmony with the preferences of risk-averse Islamic depositors (who are willing to forgo some profit shares for a reduced volatility of the expected return). But, unless a bank offers different investment accounts which differ in their risk/return profiles, the empirical relevance of this argument is hard to assess. And even if the preference argument is basically correct, one has to consider that the decision on the concrete figures for the appropriations to or from reserves is at the discretion of the management. It is possible that the decision is guided by the interests of the Islamic depositors, the shareholders or the management. Outside observers will not be able to prove or disprove any specific assumption: neither calculation methods nor concrete figures are open to the public. From balance sheets and income statements outsiders can only see the appropriations to or from reserves, while the underlying income from the employment of current account deposits and investment account deposits is usually not disclosed. Therefore it is hardly possible to assess the sustainability of a given return on Islamic deposits.

Erosion of Islamic distinctiveness and systemic opaqueness
Smoothing of investment account returns implies a governance problem at the systemic level, assuming that shareholders and Islamic depositors are interested in an Islamic financial system which is clearly distinct from conventional banking and which follows its own logic.

A core concept of Islamic finance is that of an equitable sharing of profits and losses or of risks and chances between the providers and the users of funds. The practice of smoothing returns moves the system in the opposite direction. It is not only that smoothing emulates fixed returns on deposits, it also links the Islamic deposit business economically to the interest-based system. If depositors are aware of smoothing practices in the past which kept the returns on Islamic deposits roughly in line with the prevailing market rate for interest-bearing deposits,[1] and if they expect the same practice in the future, they will form expectations on the future returns which are based on interest rates. These interest rates reflect, inter alia, the profitability of investments in the interest-based financial sector (including government bonds), the demand for and supply of money market funds, exchange rate speculations and hedging activities, as well as the competitive situation in the conventional financial sector. At least conceptually, Islamic financial institutions should not be involved in such types of transactions and markets, and their profitability should be determined by other types of (asset-backed) transactions (trade, production, construction). The profitability of these transactions must not go parallel to the conventional interest rates, and there is no guarantee that Islamic investments are consistently more profitable than conventional ones. For systemic reasons, conventional financial institutions are not as restricted in their repertoire of financing modes and techniques and can enter into a much wider range of financial deals than can Islamic banks. Conventional banks can offer Islamic products or establish Islamic subsidiaries, but this does not work the other way round, for Islamic banks must not offer conventional products or establish *riba* windows.

If Islamic banks expand from small niche markets and develop highly profitable new investment avenues, conventional banks will soon be attracted, and any competitive advantage of Islamic banks will be eroded. During the niche market period the profitability of Islamic capital may be higher, but it will decrease with further expansion and more competition. Thus, it is difficult to compare the profitability of Islamic and conventional banks in a mixed financial system.

The smoothing creates expectations which cannot be ignored by the management of Islamic banks. The expectations and according management decisions (that is, self-fulfilling expectations) factually link the returns of Islamic deposits to the development of the non-Islamic financial sector.

a.   This is not justified if the Islamic and conventional segments differ markedly in projects, transactions, competition and so on.
b.   Further, the linking blurs the distinction between the Islamic and the conventional sector.
c.   It can also create significant problems for Islamic banks if competition compresses their profitability and if current account deposits shrink to a lower ('normal') average level comparable to that of conventional banks.

Against this background it is plausible to assume that the management of Islamic banks have a strong incentive to keep the profitability of Islamic capital as well as operational details as opaque as possible. And the management have another strong incentive. If restrictions in the financial toolbox and a lack of instruments do limit the scope of permissible transactions with high profitability, the toolbox has to be extended and new techniques and Islamic products must be developed. However, this implies two governance problems.

a.   In order to gain or keep a competitive edge, not all the details of the new instruments should be disclosed. Transparency may help to spread innovations, and this is positive for the economy and society as a whole, but it must not be in the interest of those stakeholders of the innovative bank who participate in the profits generated by the innovation.
b.   The direction of financial innovations in Islamic banking does not favour an economically independent and distinct Islamic financial system. On the contrary, new tools will level out economic differences and allow Islamic banks to emulate conventional interest-based instruments and fixed-income products much better than now. Even speculative instruments may come within the reach of Islamic banks. Amongst

the 'hot topics' in Islamic finance are the launch of Islamic hedge funds and the design of Islamic options and futures. Economic differences will vanish, only the underlying contracts will legally distinguish Islamic from conventional financial products and arrangements. It is an open question whether such a development, driven by managers of Islamic banks, is in the interest of Islamic depositors and shareholders. If not, then a large number of new agency problems and governance issues will come up in the course of the further development of Islamic banking.

Indications for increasing emulation of conventional finance
The argument above conveys a rather sceptical assessment of the evolution of Islamic finance. Its core hypothesis is an inherent tendency towards an emulation of conventional interest-based techniques and products. Some examples will illustrate the trend in this direction.[2]

The Islamization of the finance sector started in Pakistan in 1979 by order of the military government. The top-down introduction of Islamic banking was officially completed (with the exception of public debt finance) in 1985. The State Bank of Pakistan had published an exclusive list of all permissible *shari'a*-compliant modes of finance. The banks combined two individually approved modes of financing which were intended for very different purposes, namely mark-up financing (intended for trade financing) and the purchase of property with a buy-back agreement (intended for the creation of securities in long-term fixed asset and real estate financing), in such a way that they clearly circumvented the prohibition of *riba* (Akhtar, 1988, p. 185): For example, a bank buys property from a client at a cash price of 100 and resells the same property immediately to the client with a mark-up of 10 per cent, payable after six months. This is nothing other than an interest loan with an interest rate of 20 per cent p.a. even though the transaction can be broken down into three individually permissible contracts (a sales contract, a buy-back agreement, mark-up trade financing). Because of the widely used circumvention techniques, the Federal Shari'at Court passed a judgment in 1991 and declared that the Islamized financial system of the country was un-Islamic. This was confirmed by a judgment of the Shari'a Appellate Bench of the Supreme Court in 1999 (with a very extensive justification of more than a thousand typewritten pages). The judgments of 1991 and 1999 were reversed by a verdict of the Supreme Court in 2002 (with an extremely short and formalistic justification) and the case was referred back to the Federal Shari'at Court.

Islamic banking was introduced in Iran by the Law on Usury-Free Banking in 1983 (Aryan, 1990; Taheri, 2004). This law allows transactions which are deemed interest-based in other parts of the world, as the discounting of trade bills, the charging of service fees proportional to the amount of a financing, the obligation of banks to repay the principals of interest-free savings deposits and the possibility to insure the principals of term investment deposits. In addition, Islamic deposits receive factually fixed returns (interest) because the announced 'anticipated' rates of return (meanwhile even called 'interest' in English Internet advertisements of Iranian banks) were always identical with the realized rates, irrespective of the profits or losses of the banks.

Banks in Sudan applied for a couple of years' *murabaha* financing without a fixed respondent with a variable mark-up and with flexible redemption periods so that the costs of financing were determined by the length of time to maturity, which comes close to interest-based loans (Stiansen, 2004).

The first Islamic bank in Malaysia was established in 1983, and a dual banking system was introduced from 1993 onwards. A dual banking system means that all conventional banks have the opportunity to open Islamic windows. Islamic banking in Malaysia is encouraged and supported by the government (Hassan and Musa, 2004; Salamon, 2004). The *shari'a* framework is set by a National Shari'a Advisory Council at the Bank Negara Malaysia (the central bank). This *shari'a* council has approved several financing techniques and capital market instruments which are very controversial and rejected by many *shari'a* experts in the Arab world. Among the disputed transactions is the widely used *bay' al-inah*, a sale and buy-back arrangement with fixed mark-ups (that is, factually interest), which is very similar to the dismissed technique in Pakistan (Rosly and Sanusi, 1999). A buy-back agreement (*bay' al-inah*) with a fixed price is also used for the construction of a commercial paper: a company securitizes claims against its assets and issues bonds with a specified face value and a given maturity. These asset-backed securities do not bear any returns, but the company will buy back the papers at maturity at a fixed price above the face value. By this arrangement, the fixed nominal interest rate (the *pro rata* difference between the issue or purchase price of the paper and the guaranteed buy-back price) can be (poorly) disguised as a profit from trade. What is further noteworthy with respect to Malaysia is the broad spectrum of consumer-related financial products, on the one hand,[3] and the efforts to create an Islamic capital and money market and an interest-free inter-bank market, on the other. Malaysia obviously endeavours to emulate the conventional financial system as far and as closely as possible in all market segments and with a comprehensive set of financial products.

A new financial product is gaining rapidly in popularity amongst Islamic banks in the Arab world and the Islamic departments of Western financial institutions: *sukuks*. The idea behind *sukuks* is to create standardized asset-backed securities with predictable nominal returns to be issued by private or public entities and traded on a secondary market. Obviously there is a need for a *shari'a*-compliant substitute for interest-bearing bonds (Al-Amine, 2001). In an extreme form, as applied in principle for the recent *sukuk* issue of a highly indebted German state, the construction could be as follows. First, the government G sets up a legally independent but wholly owned business unit B (for tax reasons in a tax haven abroad). There are no *shari'a* objections to this transaction. Second, G concludes a *shari'a*-compliant sales contract with deferred payment for office buildings with B. Third, the office buildings are rented by G from B on the basis of a long-term lease contract with a fixed rental income for B. Leasing (*ijara*) is a preferred mode for the *shari'a*-compliant long-term financing of fixed assets. Fourth, B will issue a commercial paper which documents a standardized (temporary) partial ownership of the office buildings purchased from and rented to G. From a *shari'a* point of view, there are no objections to this type of securitization if the market value of the paper is due, not to a buy-back guarantee of the issuer (as in the case of the Malaysian Islamic bonds), but to the participation in a rental income. This rental income is nominally fixed and predictable for a specified period which factually gives the *sukuk* the economic characteristics of an interest-bearing bond. Fifth, since *sukuks* represent partial ownership of real assets, they can be traded legitimately on a secondary market at prices determined by supply and demand.

The approval of the *sukuk* model by *Shari'a* supervisory boards (SSBs) will have far-reaching consequences for the further development of Islamic finance. With this model,

Islamic financial institutions as well as private companies and indebted governments can replicate a large variety of interest-based financing techniques and securities. The basic ploy is that the bank, company or government creates a legally independent but wholly owned business unit as a partner for legally effective, but commercially fictitious, sale and lease transactions. By this technique all types of productive and unproductive assets can be mobilized. Non-marketable assets can be marketed and generate a 'market income' where no market exists. This can be illustrated with an extreme example. The government could create the 'Public Defence Ltd', sell to it all its defence assets and lease them back at fixed rates. The issue of *sukuks* by the Public Defence Ltd allows the government to finance budget deficits of almost any size at fixed costs. The calculation of leasing rates and issue prices will tie the Islamic sector to the interest-based economy.

Independence of shari'a *supervisory boards*
Given that Islamic law bans interest and speculation and that the management of nearly all Islamic banks operates under the supervision and with the guidance of a board of *shari'a* experts, one wonders how the evolution of the Islamic system could take such a dubious course as that indicated above. The answer to this puzzle requires a more detailed assessment of the role of the *shari'a* supervisory boards (SSBs) in the governance structure of Islamic banks (Bakar, 2002).

The Accounting and Auditing Organisation for Islamic Financial Institutions (AAOIFI) has issued the Governance Standard No. 1 on the *'shari'a* supervisory board: appointment, composition and report'. According to this standard, every Islamic financial institution will have an SSB which

a.   'is an independent body of specialized jurists in *fiqh almua'malat* (Islamic commercial jurisprudence)',
b.   'is entrusted with the duty of directing, reviewing and supervising the activities of the Islamic financial institution in order to ensure that they are in compliance with Islamic *Shari'a* rules and principles',
c.   can issue *fatwas* and rulings which 'shall be binding on the Islamic financial institution',
d.   'shall consist of at least three members' who are 'appointed by the shareholders . . . upon the recommendation of the board of directors (not including 'directors or significant shareholders of the Islamic financial institution'),
e.   shall prepare a report on the compliance of all contracts, transactions and dealings with the *shari'a* rules and principles,
f.   shall state that 'the allocation of profit and charging of losses related to investment accounts conform to the basis that has been approved' by the SSB; finally,
g.   'shareholders may authorize the board of directors to fix the remuneration of the *Shari'a* Supervisory Board.'

The 'management is responsible for ensuring that the financing institution conducts its business in accordance with Islamic *Shari'a* Rules and Principles'. The responsibility of the SSB is 'to form an independent opinion' on *shari'a* compliance.

It should be noted that the AAOIFI standard does not contain any information about the duration of a SSB membership or on the possibilities and procedures of dismissal and reappointment. Despite the AAOIFI standard, the specific rules and criteria for the selection and appointment of SSB members (regarding, for example, the relevance and the relative weight of their Islamic and secular qualifications, their scholarly reputation and general popularity, their doctrinal strictness or intellectual flexibility, their main occupation and source of income, the duration of their SSB membership and the criteria for reappointment and so on) as well as the quantitative and qualitative dimension of their financial and non-financial rewards are not well documented in sources open to the general public. Empirical research on the selection process of SSB members and their professional careers (before, during and after the membership) is still lacking. There are also no case studies on causes and consequences of multiple memberships of individual scholars in different SSBs. Following the guidelines of AAOIFI, the board of directors suggests the candidates for the SSB and determines their remuneration. Very often the management has a strong influence on decisions of the board of directors. Therefore it is plausible to assume that top executives will have a strong influence on the composition of the SSB and on the financial and non-financial rewards for SSB members.

As an independent body, the SSB is not subject to instructions by the management, the board of directors or the shareholders. SSB members are free to express their opinion and to sanction or decline banking practices, techniques, contracts, dealings and transactions.[4] This, however, does not mean that they are totally untouched by economic, social, political and intellectual trends and developments. In addition, it has to be borne in mind that SSB members had an initial motivation to accept their appointment (whatever that motivation was, whether scholarly reputation, the sake of Islam, financial reward or public visibility). If the membership of a SSB does promote the achievement of individual goals, it is a plausible assumption that the SSB members are interested in a continuing membership respondent in a reappointment. This creates a factual dependence on the board of directors which nominates SSB members and on the shareholders who appoint them. In addition, if the interests of the management are well represented in the board of directors, the SSB members have to take these into consideration. As long as the management is supported by the board of directors and the shareholders, this boils down to the hypothesis that SSB members will not ignore the interests of the management when they apply their interpretation of *shari'a* principles to the activities, contracts and transactions of their Islamic bank. This does not mean that they will always find ways to accept whatever new financial product or transaction is submitted by the management. It must be a prime concern of the SSB that the Islamic character of the institution is recognized by the general public. But the SSB must also bear in mind the survival and commercial success of the institution. Given this simple set of behavioural assumptions for SSB members, a changing external environment can explain the obvious change of attitudes of SSBs towards financial innovations which imply new governance issues. The attitude of SSBs has indeed changed over the years, from being rather restrictive to becoming quite permissive.

Changing attitudes of shari'a *supervisory boards*
The early years of Islamic finance – the 1970s and 1980s – can be characterized as high expectations and little experience. When Islamic finance was introduced, not only to Muslims but also to the rest of the world, it was often heralded as a unique financial system based on Qur'an and *sunna*. It claimed superiority over the conventional *riba*-based system with respect to allocation, distribution and stability. This claim was put

forward not only by Muslim economists but also by Islamic banking groups such as Dar al-Maal al-Islami. During these initial years, most *shari'a* scholars were not very familiar with techniques, contracts and procedures of modern (conventional) financial institutions and markets, and they were trained neither in economics and finance nor in contemporary business law. The economic world of traditional Islamic law was based on trade, handicrafts and agriculture, but not on industrial production, resource extraction, personal and commercial services, multiple currencies on fiat money, international capital flows, global competition, and so on.

To underline the distinctiveness and the divine origin on the one hand, and owing to a lack of knowledge and experience on the other, SSB members often referred to the early Islamic period and recommended old legal constructs without much sophistication. This early approach was retrospective and in many ways restrictive. It created tensions between *shari'a* scholars (and ideological proponents of Islamic finance) and the management of Islamic banks. Islamic bank managers had to struggle with too conservative SSBs which did not sanction financial instruments deemed necessary by the management. Executives designed products and techniques which were better adapted to an economy which had become much more diversified than that of Arabia in the formative years of Islamic commercial law.[5] Trade-related contracts do not go well with the needs of the manufacturing and (non-trade) service sector. It may be owing to a lack of more appropriate financing instruments that disputable commodity transactions were quite common in this period. In the early years of Islamic finance it was a formidable challenge to adapt the commercial law of past centuries to the needs of complex and diversified modern economies.

After a decade Islamic banks had firmly established themselves in market niches. They heavily relied on trade-related modes of finance. Profit and loss sharing arrangements were extremely rare because of high transaction and monitoring costs, the danger of adverse selection (attracting projects with above-average probabilities of loss) and insufficient demand from the entrepreneurial customers. The discrepancy between the ideology and the practice of Islamic banking became increasingly visible.

With the passing of time it had become apparent that traditional contracts could not be applied directly but had to be modified considerably (as with *musharaka* for continuing concerns instead of terminated deals) and that some of the most highly esteemed contracts (*mudaraba, musharaka*) implied an adverse selection and were in low demand, while new instruments had to be designed for new and more complex financing tasks which were unknown to the traditional Islamic law (for example, project or infrastructure financing, financing of working capital, consumer finance). Furthermore, instruments for a more efficient liquidity management and the development of interest-free capital (and money) markets were in urgent need.

During the 1980s, *shari'a* scholars had accumulated more practical knowledge and had to recognize (together with Muslim economists) that the banking practice deviated widely from the ideological ideal. SSBs were confronted with requests – growing in number and urgency – of Islamic bank executives to sanction modifications of traditional contracts and financial innovations.

Other changes in the environment of Islamic finance have occurred. While most Islamic banks held monopoly positions in their countries during the 1970s and 1980s, this has changed considerably since the mid-1990s. Today customers have a choice between several

Islamic financial institutions in many Islamic countries (such as Bahrain, the United Arab Emirates, Sudan, Pakistan and Malaysia). In addition, in many countries, conventional banks do offer Islamic products or have established Islamic subsidiaries. Furthermore, in countries with few restrictions on international capital movements, the range of Islamic products is enhanced by internationally operating Islamic financial institutions. In sum, competition has increased substantially between the conventional and the Islamic finance sector as well as within the Islamic sector. Also, with the growth of the Islamic financial sector, central banks and regulatory authorities paid more attention to this sector. These institutions, which previously dealt with conventional banks, strongly supported the activities of organizations such as AAOIFI, and established in the early 2000s the Islamic Financial Services Board (IFSB) in Kuala Lumpur, in order to create a coherent legal and regulatory framework.

The standardization of Islamic contracts and techniques implies that the importance of the individual SSBs of Islamic banks is considerably reduced, at least for established (standard) transactions. When standard techniques are part of everyday life, financial innovations become the major instrument for Islamic banks in their competition amongst each other and with Islamic products or subsidiaries of conventional banks. Standardization of traditional techniques and financial innovations as the main vehicle of competition does have far-reaching implications for the role and relevance of SSBs:

a.   Standardization curtails the importance of individual SSBs for the 'daily business' of Islamic banks.
b.   Financial innovations are basically designed and engineered by the management and put forward to the SSB for a *shari'a* assessment.
c.   In a highly competitive environment, the prosperity of a bank will depend crucially on its innovative potential.
d.   If an SSB wants to maintain its importance, its members must adopt an attitude towards financial engineering and product innovations which is less retrospective and restrictive but more prospective and permissive.

Innovations create new business opportunities, as long as the innovator has a competitive edge. When imitation sets in, temporary 'monopoly profits' (or 'innovation rents') will dwindle away. Therefore neither the management nor the SSB has an interest in too much disclosure of the Islamic qualities of financial innovations as this could speed up imitation by other banks. Islamic banking is by its character more complicated (because it has to meet the requirements of the secular and the Islamic legal system) and less transparent than conventional banking. The need to keep 'Islamic business secrets' makes it even more opaque than *riba*-based banking. Credibility of the Islamic qualities of the products and transactions is achieved, not by disclosure, but by the reputation and public recognition of the members of the SSB.

The technical details of new transactions and innovative products can be quite complicated. A well-founded *shari'a* analysis and assessment requires much financial expertise by the *shari'a* experts. Distinguished and well-known *shari'a* scholars with a profound understanding of financial techniques are in short supply. This explains why the names of some outstanding *shari'a* scholars are found in the SSBs of several Islamic financial institutions, and in addition in advisory boards or committees of regulatory authorities and standard-setting organizations (such as AAOIFI or IFSB). This raises several governance issues at the macro or policy level. For example, if prominent members of SSBs determine the Islamic framework of Islamic banks, set the tone of public opinion and give advice to regulatory agencies, how will the independence of regulators be assured?

It seems that SSBs no longer impede the progress of financial technology. Instead, a legalistic view has become dominant which deconstructs complex financial techniques, products and contracts into a number of more basic components which resemble (or are identical with) legal figures of the traditional Islamic commercial law. The *shari'a* quality of these components is then assessed for each component separately. If no objections are raised against a component, the total product is sanctioned. This method seemingly supports financial engineering and product innovation in the Islamic segment of the financial market, but it has one very serious weakness: elements which are perfectly legitimate separately may interact in such a way that the result comes into contradiction of fundamental principles of Islamic law. The dispute over the legitimacy of banking practices in Pakistan is a well documented historical case, and questionable public debt issues in the form of *sukuks* are more recent examples.

Besides the structural (external) factors for the change from a rather restrictive to a very permissive attitude of SSBs, some personal (internal) factors may also be of relevance. First, if membership of an SSB is desirable for a *shari'a* expert, he will avoid as far as possible whatever may endanger his reappointment. The attraction of SSB membership can have various reasons, ranging from idealistic objectives (participating in the shaping of the Islamic finance system) to material considerations (substantial financial compensation for SSB members).

Second, it seems that a sufficiently large number of clients of Islamic banks and public opinion leaders do not require a very strict adherence to instruments and techniques of the traditional Islamic business law. They are satisfied with the observance of legal minimum requirements. The ideological impetus of the early years has become a minority position. If this is a correct picture of the public and political environment in many Muslim countries, then a too restrictive stance of SSB members could provoke much public criticism which would endanger the reputation of SSB members and put them in a defensive position. This is a serious problem particularly if other (more) eminent *shari'a* scholars outside the given SSB approve similar techniques or products.

External and internal factors can explain why SSBs have adopted a more permissive attitude towards financial innovations. This seems to be the best way to maintain the importance of the SSB and its individual members. If the bulk of Islamic financial techniques and products become standardized, an SSB is relevant only with respect to non-standard products and procedures, and these are usually financial innovations. A restrictive stance against innovations which are proposed by the Islamic bank's management could cause a conflict with the management, the board of directors and also with shareholders who want a 'progressive' or innovative bank or see a threat to the profitability of the bank. Without innovative products, the bank may suffer a competitive setback, and the relevant question becomes what the SSB is good for. It is welcome only if it does not block, but facilitates, innovations.

The SSB is a unique element in the governance structure of Islamic banks (compared to conventional banks) which follows its own logic. Its members are no advocates for the interests of Islamic depositors:

a.   SSBs have sanctioned smoothing techniques which give much discretionary power to the management and imply various distribution conflicts (between shareholders and Islamic depositors as well as among different 'generations' of depositors).
b.   The members of the SSBs, though formally independent, do have many strong incentives to foster good relations with the management of the Islamic bank, at least if they are interested in continuing membership of the SSB. One implication is that SSBs nowadays have become definitely permissive with regard to financial innovations.
c.   The SSB issues statements and reports on the Islamic qualities of the transactions and products of its Islamic bank. But when it comes to the specifics of the financial innovations, the informational content of these publications is very limited.
d.   It is not despite, but because of, the activities of SSBs that the economic (and ideological) distinctiveness of Islamic banking becomes blurred.

Although the SSBs are unique elements in the governance structure, they do not contribute to the solution of old governance problems. Instead, they add new governance issues at the macro and political level.

Conclusions
Although the SSB has a unique position in the governance structure of Islamic banks, it is not an effective body to ensure that the Islamic depositors will earn a return which is adequate to the risks they bear. If neither internal structures nor the external competition are currently sufficient to protect Islamic depositors' interests, this points to a kind of market failure which may justify state action. Given the specifics of Islamic banking today, this action cannot be of an interventionist regulatory type.

a.   Market imperfections as such are no justification for the correction of market performance and market results by public authorities. This can only be the last resort if no other instruments are available.
b.   For an assessment of the risk profile of the assets of an Islamic bank, much more information is needed than is currently disclosed. Accounting, reporting and disclosure rules are still in the process of evolution. In particular, the risk characteristics of Islamic financial innovations are difficult to assess because the concept is new and practical experience is lacking.
c.   Even if the relevant risk information were available to a regulator, no 'objective formula' for the calculation of adequate returns for the risk-sharing depositors is at hand.

The right type of state action would be to create a legal environment which supports Islamic depositors by inducing a wider range of Islamic products and by facilitating better-informed customer choices.

a.   Many Islamic depositors may not be aware of the inherent risks of Islamic deposits. The risks and their determinants would become more apparent if Islamic banks had to offer at least two or three separate types of investment accounts with different risk–return positions. This would also be a contribution to the education of depositors who then have to make a choice, which implies that they have to think about the alternatives. The other side of the coin is that a broader range of deposits will facilitate choices which are more in line with depositors' preferences and risk appetites.

b. The supervisory authorities will ensure the comparability of the different types of investment accounts of the different Islamic banks. Accounting and reporting standardization is progressing only gradually. At present rating agencies focus on Islamic capital market instruments. With a growing diversity of Islamic retail banking products and with more educated Islamic depositors, rating agencies or similar enterprises (including media and publishers) should find a market for comparisons of Islamic products, consultancy services and rankings of Islamic finance products and Islamic banks.

c. In countries where only one Islamic bank exists and where domestic entrepreneurs do not show any interest in the establishment of a competing institution, a liberalization and opening of a protected national market for Islamic banks from abroad could be a suitable policy.

d. Competition spurs innovation but hampers transparency. This is in the interests of individual banks respondent their management and shareholder but not necessarily also in the interests of depositors and the development of the Islamic finance sector as a whole. To avoid a capture of SSB members by the management and to prevent too permissive *shari'a* compliance rulings by individual SSBs, a National Shari'a Board (NSB) should be installed. It should issue binding *shari'a* standards for all Islamic banks of a country, and assess all financial innovations submitted by the banks. Its members must be recognized scholars, and they should be appointed in a transparent procedure for one non-renewable term of several years. The NSB members will enjoy the intellectual and financial independence of high court judges.

At present and in the near future, Islamic banking is and will be plagued with more governance issues than conventional banking and with the conflict between efficiency and distinctiveness of Islamic finance. It seems that the dynamism of market imperfections requires a more proactive role of legislators in order to solve the most serious governance problems and to preserve the distinctiveness of Islamic banking. Bahrain and Malaysia have taken up this challenge, and a few other countries such as Pakistan and Indonesia have followed. It remains to be seen how non-Muslim states will react when Islamic finance spreads into their territories.

Notes

1. It is hard to imagine a smoothing of Islamic deposits' returns at a level consistently below the market interest rate.
2. The design of instruments with inherently speculative elements has not yet found broad support.
3. This does not only include the financing of durable consumer goods but also covers, for example, Islamic financing of holidays.
4. It is not clear whether SSBs are supposed to deliver *fatwas*, rulings, reports and opinions on the basis of a majority or a unanimous vote of their members.
5. The Islamic commercial law stagnated more or less following the rise of the West and the decline of the Islamic empires in the Middle East, Central Asia and South East Asia. For economic development this was a crucial period, with a huge number of technical, social and institutional innovations. Many new phenomena of the business world came into existence (from joint stock companies to new modes of finance), which were not covered by the traditional Islamic commercial law.

References

Akhtar, A.R. (1988), *The Law and Practice of Interest-Free Banking with Banking Tribunals Ordinance (LVIII of 1984)*, Lahore: Mansoor Book House.

Al-Amine, M.A.M. (2001), 'The Islamic bonds market – possibilities and challenges', *International Journal of Islamic Financial Services*, **3** (1) (http://islamic-finance. net/ journals/ journal9/albashir.pdf).

Arun, T.G. and J.D. Turner (2003), 'Corporate governance of banks in developing economies – concepts and issues', University of Manchester, School of Environment and Development – development economics and public policy: working paper No. 2/2003 (http://www.sed.manchester.ac.uk/idpm/publications/wp/depp/ depp_wp02.pdf).

Aryan, Hossein (1990), 'Iran – the impact of Islamization on the financial system', in R. Wilson (ed.), *Islamic Financial Markets*, London, New York: Routledge.

Bakar, Mohd Daud (2002), 'The *Shari'a* supervisory board and issues of *Shari'a* rulings and the their harmonisation in Islamic banking and finance', in Simon Archer and Rifaat Ahmed Abdul Karim (eds), *Islamic Finance: Innovation and Growth*, London: Euromoney Books and Accounting and Auditing Association for Islamic Finance Institutions.

Hassan, Nik Mustapha Hj. Nik and Mazilan Musa (2004), 'An evaluation of Islamic banking development in Malaysia', in B. Shanmugam, V. Perumal and A.H. Ridzwa (eds), *Islamic Banking – An International Perspective*, Serdang: Universiti Putra Malaysia Press.

Levine, Ross (2004), 'The corporate governance of banks – a concise discussion of concepts and evidence', World Bank Policy Research working paper 3404, Washington, September (http://wdsbeta.worldbank.org/ external/default/WDSContentServer/IW3P/IB/2004/10/08/000012009_20041008124126/Rendered/PDF/WPS3 404.pdf)

Rosly, S.A. and M.M. Sanusi (1999), 'The application of *bay' al-'inah* and *bay' al-dayn* in Malaysian Islamic bonds – an Islamic analysis', *International Journal of Islamic Financial Services*, **1** (2) (http://islamic-finance. net/journals/journal2/art1.pdf).

Salamon, Hussin (2004), 'The Islamic banking system in Malaysia – concept, operation, challenges and prospects', in B. Shanmugam, V. Perumal and A.H. Ridzwa (eds) *Islamic Banking – An International Perspective*, Serdang: Universiti Putra Malaysia Press.

Stiansen, Endre (2004), 'Interest politics – Islamic finance in the Sudan, 1977–2001', in C. Henry and R. Wilson (eds), *The Politics of Islamic Finance,* Edinburgh: Edinburgh University Press.

Taheri, Mohammad Reza (2004), 'A comparison of Islamic banking in Iran with other Islamic countries', in B. Shanmugam, V. Perumal and A.H. Ridzwa (eds), *Islamic Banking – An International Perspective*, Serdang: Universiti Putra Malaysia Press.

10 Risk management in Islamic banking
Habib Ahmed and Tariqullah Khan

Introduction

Risk entails both vulnerability of asset values and opportunities of income growth. Successful firms take advantage of these opportunities (Damodaran, 2005). An important element of management of risk is to understand the risk–return trade-off of different assets and investors. Investors can expect a higher rate of return only by increasing their exposure to risks. As the objective of financial institutions is to create value for the shareholders by acquiring assets in multiples of shareholder-owned funds, managing the resulting risks faced by the equity becomes an important function of these institutions.

As Islamic banking is relatively new, the risks inherent in the instruments used are not well comprehended. Islamic banks can be expected to face two types of risks: risks that are similar to those faced by traditional financial intermediaries and risks that are unique owing to their compliance with the *shari'a*. Furthermore, Islamic banks are constrained in using some of the risk mitigation instruments that their conventional counterparts use as these are not allowed under Islamic commercial law. This chapter discusses some of the unique risks that arise owing to compliance with the *shari'a* and the special nature of risk mitigation enforced on Islamic financial institutions by the *shari'a* mandate.

The chapter is organized as follows. First we examine the nature of risks in Islamic banks. After defining and identifying different risks, we report on the status of risk management processes in Islamic banks. Then specific issues related to risk measurement and mitigation in Islamic banks are discussed. The last section draws some conclusions.

Risks in Islamic banks

The asset and liability sides of Islamic banks have unique risk characteristics. The Islamic banking model has evolved to one-tier *mudaraba* with multiple investment tools. On the liability side of Islamic banks, saving and investment deposits take the form of profit-sharing investment accounts. Investment accounts can be further classified as restricted and unrestricted, the former having restrictions on withdrawals before maturity date. Demand deposits or checking/current accounts in Islamic banks take the nature of *qard hasan* (interest-free loans) that are returned fully on demand. On the asset side, banks use *murabaha* (cost-plus or mark-up sale), instalment sale (medium/long-term *murabaha*), *bai-muajjal* (price-deferred sale), *istisnaa/salam* (object deferred sale or pre-paid sale) and *ijara* (leasing) and profit-sharing modes of financing (*musharaka* and *mudaraba*).[1] These instruments on the asset side, using the profit-sharing principle to reward depositors, are a unique feature of Islamic banks. Such instruments change the nature of risks that Islamic banks face. Some of the key risks faced by Islamic banks are discussed below.

Credit risk

Credit risk is the loss of income arising as a result of the counterparty's delay in payment on time or in full as contractually agreed. Such an eventuality can underlie all Islamic modes of finance. For example, credit risk in *murabaha* contracts arises in the form of the counterparty defaulting in paying the debts in full and in time. The non-performance can be due to external systematic sources or to internal financial causes, or be a result of moral hazard (wilful default). Wilful default needs to be identified clearly as Islam does not allow debt restructuring based on compensations except in the case of wilful default. In the case of profit-sharing modes of financing (like *mudaraba* and *musharaka*) the credit risk will be non-payment of the share of the bank by the entrepreneur when it is due. This problem may arise for banks in these cases because of the asymmetric information problem where they do not have sufficient information on the actual profit of the firm.

Market risk
Market risks can be systematic, arising from macro sources, or unsystematic, being asset- or instrument-specific. For example, currency and equity price risks would fall under the systematic category and movement in prices of commodity or asset the bank is dealing with will fall under specific market risk. We discuss a key systematic and one unsystematic risk relevant to Islamic banks below.

Mark-up risk   Islamic financial institutions use a benchmark rate to price different financial instruments. For example, in a *murabaha* contract the mark-up is determined by adding the risk premium to the benchmark rate (usually the LIBOR). The nature of a *murabaha* is such that the mark-up is fixed for the duration of the contract. Consequently, if the benchmark rate changes, the mark-up rates on these fixed income contracts cannot be adjusted. As a result Islamic banks face risks arising from movements in market interest rate. Mark-up risk can also appear in profit-sharing modes of financing like *mudaraba* and *musharaka* as the profit-sharing ratio depends on, among other things, a benchmark rate like LIBOR.[2]

Commodity/asset price risk   The *murabaha* price risk and commodity/asset price risk must be clearly distinguished. As pointed out, the basis of the mark-up price risk is changes in LIBOR. Furthermore, it arises as a result of the financing, not the trading process. In contrast to mark-up risk, commodity price risk arises as a result of the bank holding commodities or durable assets as in *salam*, *ijara* and *mudaraba/musharaka*. Note that both the mark-up risk and commodity/asset price risk can exist in a single contract. For example, under leasing, the equipment itself is exposed to commodity price risk and the fixed or overdue rentals are exposed to mark-up risks.

Liquidity risk
Liquidity risk arises from either difficulties in obtaining cash at reasonable cost from borrowings (funding liquidity risk) or sale of assets (asset liquidity risk). The liquidity risk arising from both sources is critical for Islamic banks. For a number of reasons, Islamic banks are prone to facing serious liquidity risks. First, there is a *fiqh* restriction on the securitization of the existing assets of Islamic banks, which are predominantly debt in nature. Second, because of slow development of financial instruments, Islamic banks are also unable to raise funds quickly from the markets. This problem becomes more serious because there is no inter-Islamic bank money market. Third, the lender of last resort (LLR) provides emergency liquidity facility to banks whenever needed. The existing LLR facilities are based on interest, therefore Islamic banks cannot benefit from these.

Operational risk
Operational risk is the 'risk of direct or indirect loss resulting from inadequate or failed internal processes, people, and technology or from external events' (BCBS, 2001, p. 2). Given the newness of Islamic banks, operational risk in terms of personal risk can be acute in these institutions. Operation risk in this respect particularly arises as the banks may not have enough qualified professionals (capacity and capability) to conduct the Islamic financial operations. Given the different nature of business, the computer software available in the market for conventional banks may not be appropriate for Islamic banks. This gives rise to system risks of developing and using informational technologies in Islamic banks.

Legal risk
Legal risks for Islamic banks are also significant and arise for various reasons. First, as most countries have adopted either the common law or civil law framework, their legal systems do not have specific laws/statutes that support the unique features of Islamic financial products. For example, whereas Islamic banks' main activity is in trading (*murabaha*) and investing in equities (*musharaka* and *mudaraba*), current banking law and regulations in most jurisdictions forbid commercial banks undertaking such activities. Second, non-standardization of contracts makes the whole process of negotiating different aspects of a transaction more difficult and costly. Financial institutions are not protected against risks that they cannot anticipate or that may not be enforceable. Use of standardized contracts can also make transactions easier to administer and monitor after the contract is signed. Finally, lack of Islamic courts that can enforce Islamic contracts increases the legal risks of using these contracts.

Withdrawal risk
A variable rate of return on saving/investment deposits introduces uncertainty regarding the real value of deposits. Asset preservation in terms of minimizing the risk of loss due to a lower rate of return may be an important factor in depositors' withdrawal decisions. From the bank's perspective, this introduces a 'withdrawal risk' that is linked to the lower rate of return relative to other financial institutions.[3]

Fiduciary risk
Fiduciary risk can be caused by breach of contract by the Islamic bank. For example, the bank may not be able to comply fully with the *shari'a* requirements of various contracts. Inability to comply fully with Islamic *shari'a* either knowingly or unknowingly leads to a lack of confidence among the depositors and hence causes withdrawal of deposits. Similarly, a lower rate of return than the market can also introduce fiduciary risk, when depositors/investors interpret a low rate of return as breaching an investment contract or mismanagement of funds by the bank (AAOIFI, 1999).

Displaced commercial risk
This is the transfer of the risk associated with deposits to equity holders. This arises when, under commercial pressure, banks forgo a part of their profit to pay the depositors to prevent withdrawals due to a lower return (AAOIFI, 1999). Displaced commercial risk implies that the bank may operate in full compliance with the *shari'a* requirements, yet

may not be able to pay competitive rates of return as compared to its peer group Islamic banks and other competitors. Depositors will again have the incentive to seek withdrawal. To prevent withdrawal, the owners of the bank will need to apportion part of their own share in profits to the investment depositors.

Bundled risks
It is uncommon for the various risks to be bundled together. However, in the case of most Islamic modes of finance, more than one risk coexists. For example, in *salam*, once the bank has made an advance payment, it has started to take the counterparty risk concerning delivery of the right commodity on time, the market risk of the commodity, the liquidity risk of its conversion into cash, the operational risk of its storing and movement and so on. The same is the case with *istisnaa*, financial *murabaha*, *ijara* and *musharaka/mudaraba*.

Risks in different Islamic modes of financing
Risks in Islamic modes of financing are complex and evolve. Table 10.1 reports the perceptions of 18 Islamic bankers on some important risks inherent in various Islamic modes of financing.[4] The figures in the table show the ranking of seriousness of risks, with higher figures indicating the relative severity of risks.

Credit risk appears to be the least in *murabaha* (2.47) and the most in *musharaka* (3.71), followed by diminishing *musharaka* (3.43) and *mudaraba* (3.38). It appears that profit-sharing modes of financing are perceived by the bankers to have higher credit risk. *Ijara* ranks second (2.64) after *murabaha* as having the least credit risks. Like the *murabaha* contract, the *ijara* contract gives the banks a relatively certain income and the ownership of the leased asset remains with the bank. *Istisnaa* and *salam*, ranked 3.13 and 3.20 respectively, are relatively more risky. These product-deferred modes of financing are perceived to be riskier than price-deferred sale (*murabaha*). This may arise as the value of the product (and hence the return) at the end of the contract period is uncertain. There are chances that the counterparty may not be able to deliver the goods on time. This may arise for different reasons, such as natural disasters (for commodities in a *salam* contract) and production failure (for products in *istisnaa* contract). Even if the good is delivered, there

Table 10.1   Risk perception: risks in different modes of financing

	Credit risk	Market risk	Liquidity risk	Operational risk
Murabaha	2.47 (17)	2.75 (12)	2.62 (16)	2.8 (15)
Mudaraba	3.38 (13)	3.56 (9)	2.57 (14)	2.92 (13)
Musharaka	3.71 (14)	3.67 (9)	3.0 (13)	3.08 (12)
Ijara	2.64 (14)	3.17 (6)	3.1 (10)	2.9 (10)
Istisnaa	3.13 (8)	2.75 (4)	3.0 (6)	3.29 (7)
Salam	3.20 (5)	3.25 (4)	3.2 (5)	3.25 (4)
Diminishing *musharaka*	3.43 (7)	3.5 (6)	3.43 (7)	3.17 (6)

Note: The numbers in parentheses indicate the number of respondents; the scale is 1 to 5, with 1 indicating 'not serious' and 5 denoting 'critically serious'.

can be uncertainty regarding the price of the good upon delivery affecting the rate of return.

Market risk is relatively high in most modes of finance. It is among the highest ranked in terms of severity for profit-sharing modes of financing with the highest for *musharaka* (3.67) followed by *mudaraba* (3.56) and diminishing *musharaka* (ranked at 3.5). *Murabaha* and *istisnaa* are considered to have the least market risk (2.75) followed by *ijara* (3.17). Liquidity risk of instruments will be smaller if the assets can be sold in the markets and/or have short-term maturity. The bankers consider *mudaraba* to have the least liquidity risk (2.57), followed by *murabaha* (2.62). Note that both of these instruments are usually used for short-term financing. Other instruments are perceived as relatively more risky, with diminishing *musharaka* showing the highest liquidity risk (with a rank of 3.43) and product-deferred instruments of *salam* and *istisnaa* following at 3.2 and 3.0, respectively. *Ijara* is also perceived to have a relatively higher liquidity risk (3.1).

The rankings showing the operational risk for different instruments should include these concerns. *Murabaha, ijara* and *mudaraba* are considered to have relatively lower operational risk (2.8, 2.9 and 2.92 respectively). The product-deferred sale contracts of *salam* and *istisnaa* are considered most serious in terms of operational risk (3.25 and 3.29 repectively). Profit-sharing modes of financing of *musharaka* and diminishing *musharaka* follow closely, ranked 3.08 and 3.17 respectively. The relatively higher rankings of the instruments indicate that banks find these contracts complex and difficult to implement.

Risk management systems in Islamic banks
The nature of risks faced by Islamic banks is complex and difficult to mitigate, for different reasons. First, unlike the conventional banks, given the trading-based instruments and equity financing, there are significant market risks along with credit risks in the banking book of Islamic banks. Second, risks intermingle and change from one kind to another at different stages of a transaction. For example, trade-based contracts (*murabaha, salam* and *istisnaa*) and leasing are exposed to both credit and market risks.[5] For example, during the transaction period of a *salam* contract, the bank is exposed to credit risk and at the conclusion of the contract it is exposed to commodity price risk. Third, because of rigidities and deficiencies in the infrastructure, institutions and instruments, the risks faced are magnified and/or difficult to mitigate. For example, there are objections to the use of foreign exchange futures to hedge against foreign exchange risk and there are no *shari'a*-compatible short-term securities for liquidity risk management in most jurisdictions.

Table 10.2 reports an assessment of the overall risk management system in 17 Islamic banks.[6] Each bank was asked about the various aspects of the risk management system and process described above. Specifically there were six questions related to 'Establishing an appropriate risk management system and environment', nine questions on 'Maintaining an appropriate risk measurement system' and five questions on 'Adequate internal controls'. The figures reported in the table are the sum of affirmative answers as a percentage of the total possible answers in each component.

The figures in Table 10.2 indicate that Islamic banks have been able to establish better risk management policies and procedures (82.4 per cent) than measuring, mitigating and monitoring risks (69.3 per cent), with internal controls somewhere in the middle (76.5 per cent). The relative percentages indicate that Islamic financial institutions have to upgrade

Table 10.2   Scores of aspects of risk management systems for Islamic banks

Risk management components	Score (total)	Percentage
Establishing an appropriate risk management system and environment	84 (102)	82.4
Maintaining an appropriate risk measurement system	106 (153)	69.3
Adequate internal controls	65 (85)	76.5

their measuring, mitigating and monitoring process, followed by internal controls to improve their risk management system.

Risk mitigation in Islamic banks

The techniques of risk identification and management available to the Islamic banks could be of two types. The first type comprises standard techniques, such as risk reporting, internal and external audit, GAP analysis, RAROC, internal rating and so on, which are consistent with the Islamic principles of finance. The second type consists of techniques that need to be developed or adapted, keeping in mind the requirements for *shari'a* compliance. Hence the discussion of risk management techniques for Islamic banking is a challenging one. While all these challenges cannot be identified and fully discussed in this chapter, we focus on some of the issues that have relevance to *shari'a* and avoid the details of standard techniques. We discuss the risk mitigation techniques and challenges under the headings of risk avoidance/elimination, risk transfer and risk absorption/management below.

Risk avoidance/elimination

Risk avoidance techniques would include the standardization of all business-related activities and processes, construction of a diversified portfolio and implementation of an incentive-compatible scheme with accountability of actions (Santomero, 1997). Some risks that banks have can be reduced or eliminated by transferring or selling these in well-defined markets. The ways in which some risks can be reduced or eliminated in Islamic banks are discussed below.

Contractual risk mitigation

As Islamic banks use unique modes of finance, some risks need to be mitigated by proper documentation of products. *Gharar* (uncertainty of outcome caused by ambiguous conditions in contracts of deferred exchange) could be mild and unavoidable but could also be excessive and cause injustices, contract failures and defaults. Appropriate contractual agreements between counterparties work as risk control techniques. A number of these can be cited as examples.

a.   To overcome the counterparty risks arising from the non-binding nature of the contract in *murabaha*, up-front payment of a substantial commitment fee has become a permanent feature of the contract. To avoid fulfilling the promise made by a client in taking possession of the ordered goods (in the case of *murabaha*), the contract should be binding on the client and not binding on the bank. This suggestion assumes that the bank will honour the contract and supply the goods as contractually agreed, even if the contract is not binding on it.

b.   Since the *murabaha* contract is approved on the condition that the bank will take possession of the asset, at least theoretically the bank holds the asset for some time. This holding period is more or less eliminated by the Islamic banks by appointing the client as an agent for the bank to buy the asset.

c.   In an *istisnaa* contract, enforceability becomes a problem particularly with respect to fulfilling the qualitative specifications. To overcome such counterparty risks, *fiqh* scholars have allowed *band al-jazaa* (a penalty clause). Again in *istisnaa* financing, disbursement of funds can be agreed on a staggered basis subject to different phases of the construction instead of lumping them towards the beginning of the construction work.

d.   In several contracts, a rebate on the remaining amount of mark-up is given as an incentive for enhancing repayment.

e.   Fixed-rate contracts such as long maturity instalment sale are normally exposed to more risks as compared to floating-rate contracts such as operating leases.

f.   In an environment with no Islamic courts or formal litigation system, dispute settlement is one of the serious risk factors in Islamic banking. To overcome such risks, the counterparties can contractually agree on a process to be followed if disputes become inevitable. Specifically, Islamic financial contracts include choice-of-law and dispute settlement clauses (Vogel and Hayes, 1998, p. 51). This is particularly significant with respect to settlement of defaults, as rescheduling similar to interest-based debt is not possible.

Many of these features of contracts serve to mitigate counterparty default risks. Similar features can enhance the credit quality of contracts in different circumstances.

Two-step/parallel contracts
One of the most common and reliable tools to manage interest rate risk is the GAP analysis.[7] The effectiveness of a GAP management strategy depends on the repriceability of assets and liabilities. In Islamic banks, investment deposits are perfectly repriceable as the expected rate of return depends on the market rate of return. Most of the assets of Islamic banks, however, are fixed-income and non-repriceable. One way to mitigate the rate of return risk in Islamic banks is to use two-step contracts. In these, the Islamic bank can play the role of a guarantor in facilitating funds to the users. Since a guarantee cannot be provided as a commercial activity under *shari'a*, in a two-step contract, it can be provided by the Islamic bank's participation in the funding process as an actual buyer. In the two-step contract, the bank will have two *murabaha* contracts, one as a supplier with the client and the other as a buyer with the actual supplier. Hence the bank will not make an up-front payment to the actual supplier, but do so when it receives payment from the buyer.

On-balance sheet netting
On-balance sheet netting implies the matching of mutual gross financial obligations and accounting for only the net positions of the mutual obligations. For example, bank A owes to bank B $2 million resulting from a previous transaction. Independent of this obligation, bank B owes to A $2.2 million. In a netting arrangement, the $2 million mutual

obligations will match each other so that $0.2 million will be settled by B as a net amount. There could be several considerations in this arrangement including the maturity of the two obligations, and the currencies and financial instruments involved. The netting process could therefore include discounting, selling and swapping the gross obligations. On-balance sheet netting can minimize the exposure of risks to the net amount between the receivables and payables to the counterparty. Netting is more suitable for payments between two subsidiaries of a company. With non-subsidiary counterparties, the currency position of receivables and payables can generally be matched so that the mutual exposures are minimized.

Carefully prepared, netting can overcome credit risk exposures between the two parties. With the participation of a third party, playing as a clearinghouse for the obligations, the arrangement becomes a powerful risk-mitigating technique. The Islamic banks, so far, have not designed any such mechanism. This may be considered as an important area for future cooperation between the Islamic banks particularly, if the market for two-step contracts as discussed in this section expands, with banks having more mutual obligations.

Immunization

Once the net exposure of foreign currency is minimized the possibility exists that the exposure can be hedged. Suppose an Islamic bank has to pay a net amount of $1 million in three months' time and the current spot exchange rate is Rs.60/$. The risk is that, after three months, the dollar will have appreciated compared to the current exchange rate. The bank can protect against this risk, by raising three months' profit and loss sharing (PLS) deposit in rupees for the value of $1million and buying dollars with this amount at the spot rate. These dollars can then be kept in a dollar account for three months. After the three months, and at the time of making the payment, the PLS deposit will mature and the bank can share the earnings on the dollar deposit with the rupee deposit holders. Thus the dollar exchange rate risk for the three months' period is fully hedged by the bank.

Risk transfer

Risk-transferring techniques include, among others, use of derivatives for hedging, selling or buying of financial claims and changing borrowing terms. It is important to note that most of the conventional derivative instruments do not conform to *shari'a*. Some instruments that can be used to transfer risks in Islamic banks and other related issues are discussed below.

Credit derivatives

Credit derivatives are one of the newest tools for managing credit risks.[8] In these instruments the underlying risk of a credit is separated from the credit itself and sold to possible investors whose individual risk profile may be such that the default risk attracts their investment decision. This can be done by packaging, securitization and marketing credit risk exposures with a variety of credit risk features (Crouhy et al., 2001, p. 442). Islamic banks are not using any equivalent of credit derivatives, as sale of debts is prohibited, almost by a consensus, except in Malaysia. Some studies, however, call for making a distinction between a fully secured debt and an unsecured debt. It is argued that external credit assessment makes the quality of a debt transparent. Moreover, credit valuation techniques have improved drastically. Furthermore, all Islamic debt financing is asset-based and secured financing. In view of these developments, restrictions on sale of debt may be reconsidered (Chapra and Khan, 2000).

Some scholars suggest that, although sale of debt is not possible as such, the owner of a debt can appoint a debt collector. For example, if the due debt is $5 million and the owner considers that, as a result of default, $0.5 million may be lost, the owner can offer some amount less than this estimated loss, say, for example, $0.4 million, to a debt col-lector. The arrangement will be organized on the basis of *wakalah* (agency contract) or *ju'alah* (service contract). There seems to be no *fiqh* objection to this.

Swaps
In a swap agreement, parties agree to exchange sets of cash flows over a period in the future (Kolb, 1997, p. 613). By using swaps both parties end up with a net financial gain as the cash flows become consistent with their own asset and liability structures. Given that, by using swaps, both parties are better off and there is a great need for these con-tracts, there should not be any objections to using these as long as they are compatible with *shari'a*. One of the most common swaps involves swapping fixed return with vari-able. Since fixed-rent and adjustable-rent *sukuk* have recently been introduced in the markets, this may pave the way for further financial engineering in the form of *shari'a*-compatible swap arrangements. Some other swaps that can be used by Islamic banks to mitigate various risks are discussed below.

Debt–asset swap   While debt cannot be sold, it can be used as a price to buy real assets. Suppose bank A owes debts worth $1m to bank B, which are due after two years. Meanwhile bank B needs liquidity to buy real assets worth $1m from a supplier C on deferred basis for two years. In this case, subject to the acceptance of C, the payments for bank B's instalment purchase can be made by bank A. Because of the instalment sale from C to B, C will charge *murabaha* profit of, say, 5 per cent. This profit can be adjusted in two ways. First, upon mutual agreement the supplier may supply goods worth $0.95 million to bank B and the supplier will receive $1m cash from bank A in two years. As a second option, C will receive $1million from A and $0.05m directly from B. The impli-cation of this is important. B receives assets worth $1million at the present time instead of receiving $1million after two years, but after paying 5 per cent. As a result, in net terms, B receives $0.95million today for $1million after two years. Thus the arrangement facilitates a *fiqh*-compatible discount facility and can be used by Islamic banks to miti-gate liquidity risks.

Swap of liabilities   Exchange of liabilities can minimize exposure to foreign exchange risk. For instance, a Turkish company needs to import rice from Pakistan, and a Pakistani company needs to import steel from Turkey. The two parties can agree to buy the com-modities for each other, bypassing the currency markets. If the dollar amount of the two commodities is the same, this arrangement can eliminate transaction risk for both parties. If the ratings of the two companies are good in their own home countries as compared to the other country, this swap will also save them some of the cost of finance.

Deposit swap   Islamic banks have been using the technique of deposit swaps to mitigate foreign exchange risk. In this method two banks, in accordance with their own expected risk exposure, agree to maintain mutual deposits of two currencies at an agreed exchange rate for an agreed period of time. For example, a Saudi bank will open a six months account for SR 50m. in a counterpart Bangladeshi bank. The Bangladeshi bank will open the TK amount of the SR deposit in the Saudi bank for the same period. The SR/TK exchange rate will be mutually agreed and will be effective for the deposit period. After the six months, both banks will withdraw their deposits. In this way the risk exposure for the value of the deposits for the currency involved is minimized according to the two banks' own perceptions.

There are, however, at least two *shari'a* objections to this contract. The exchange rate cannot be any rate except the spot rate. In this case the rate is fixed for a period during which there could be a number of spot rates, not only one. The exchange of deposits is also questionable. These deposits are supposed to be current accounts, which are treated as *qard*. There cannot be mutual *qard*. Further, *qard* in two different currencies cannot be exchanged.

Forwards/futures

Contemporary futures contracts in which both payment and receipt of good/asset are post-poned are prohibited under Islamic law because of the presence of *gharar* and elements of *riba*. Some types of forwards and futures that are used by Islamic banks are given below.

Salam and commodity futures   The potential of futures contracts in risk management and control is tremendous. Conventional banks manage risks by utilizing commodity forwards and futures contracts. In these contracts, unlike *salam*, payment of the price of the commodity is postponed to a future date. In the traditional *fiqh*, postponing both the price and the object of sale is not allowed. Therefore the Islamic banks at the present do not utilize the commodity futures contracts on a large scale. Nevertheless, by virtue of a number of *fiqh* resolutions, conventions and new research, the scope for commodity futures is widening in Islamic financing. For example, Kamali (2005) argues that, if new technology can eliminate *gharar* in the contract, then it may be reconsidered. He asserts that the implementation of a contemporary futures contract removes *gharar* that is the basis of forbidding these contracts and, consequently, may be allowed. In the future these contracts may prove to be instrumental in managing the risks of commodities.

Another argument given to accept the postponement of both the price and the object of sale is the occurrence of many transactions in real life. One such transaction is a continuous supply–purchase relationship with known but deferred price and object of sale (*bai' al-tawrid*). For example, public utilities are consumed and the bill is paid when it comes at a future date. The postponement of the price and delivery actually enhances efficiency and convenience and sometimes the postponement in fact becomes inevitable.

Currency forwards and futures   Forwards and futures are the most effective instruments for hedging against currency risks. Most Islamic banks which have significant exposure to the foreign exchange risk do use currency forwards and futures for hedging purposes as required by regulators. However, all *fiqh* scholars unanimously agree that such contracts are not allowed in the *shari'a*. Keeping this apparent contradiction in view and the tremendous difference between the stability of the present and past markets, Chapra and

Khan (2000) make a suggestion to the *fiqh* scholars to review their position and allow the Islamic banks to use these contracts for hedging. Such a change in position will remove the contradiction between the practices of Islamic banks and the existing *fiqh* positions, on one hand, and will empower the Islamic banks, on the other. Furthermore, it may be noted that hedging is not an income-earning activity. Since *riba* is a source of income and hedging does not generate income, there is no question of involvement of *riba*. On the other hand hedging actually reduces *gharar*. It is important to note that the consensus among *fiqh* scholars is that currency futures and forwards are another form of *riba* which has been prohibited by the *shari'a*.

Options
Options are another powerful risk management instrument. However a resolution of the Islamic *Fiqh* Academy prohibits the trading in options.[9] Therefore the scope for the utilization of options by the Islamic banks as risk management tools is limited at the present. However, some other forms of options that can be used are discussed next.

Bai' al-tawrid with khiyar al-shart   In *bai' al-tawrid* contracts both parties are exposed to price risk. The risk is that, immediately after the contract of fixed price and quantity is signed, the parties may experience a noticeable change in the market price of the commodity. If the market price declines, the buyer will be at a loss as regards continuing with the contract. If market price rises, the seller will lose by continuing with the contract. Thus, in such contracts of continuous-supply purchase, a *khiyar al-shart* (option of condition) for rescinding the contract will make the contract more just and will reduce the risk for both parties. Beyond these boundaries they can agree to rescind the contracts.[10]

Another, similar, way of using an option is to minimize the risks of price fluctuations in a *salam* contract. For example, after signing the contract and receiving the price in advance, if the price of wheat appreciates substantially at the time of delivery the wheat grower may have an incentive to default on the contract. The risk can be minimized by a clause in the contract showing an agreement between the two parties that a certain level of price fluctuation will be acceptable, but beyond that point the gaining party shall compensate the party which is adversely affected by the price movements. In Sudan, such a contractual arrangement, known as *band al-ihsan* (beneficence clause), has now become a regular feature of the *salam* contract. These options can be used by Islamic banks not only as incentives, but also as instruments to hedge against price fluctuations.

Embedded options   Khan (1999, 2000) argues that there are no *fiqh* objections to using non-detachable embedded options. As mentioned, use of debts in buying goods, services and other real assets is allowed. This permission can further be extended to design quasi debt (equity) financial instruments by embedding convertibility options. For instance, in writing an Islamic debt contract, the user of funds can inscribe a non-detachable option in the contract that, subject to the preference of the financier, the receivables can be used to buy real assets or shares from the beneficiary. This option in fact changes the nature of collateral from a limited recourse to a full recourse as the option can be utilized according to the will of the financier. In this manner, it enhances the quality of credit facility by reducing its risk. The potential of these instruments increases in the framework of two-step contracts. However, the Islamic banks at present do not write such instruments.

Bay al-arbun   Islamic funds have successfully utilized *arbun* (down payment with an option to rescind the contract by forgoing the payment as a penalty) to minimize portfolio risks in what are now popularly known in the Islamic financial markets as the principal protected funds (PPFs). The PPF arrangement roughly works in the following manner: 97 per cent of the total funds raised are invested in low-risk (low-return) but liquid *murabaha* transactions. The remaining 3 per cent of the funds are used as a down payment for *arbun* to purchase common stock at a future date. If the future price of the stock increases as expected by the fund manager, the *arbun* is utilized by liquidating the *murabaha* transactions. Otherwise the *arbun* lapses, incurring a 3 per cent cost on the funds. This cost is, however, covered by the return on the *murabaha* transactions. Thus the principal of the fund is fully protected. In this way, *arbun* is utilized effectively in protecting investors against undesirable downside risks of investing in stocks while at the same time keeping an opportunity for gains from favourable market conditions.

Parallel contracts
Price risk can be due either to transitory changes in prices of specific commodities and non-financial assets or to a change in the general price level or inflation. Inflation poses a risk to the real values of debts (receivables), which are generated as a result of *murabaha* transactions. However, as a result of inflation, it is expected that the prices of the real goods and commodities, which the banks acquire as a result of *salam* transactions, will appreciate. This divergent movement of asset values created as a result of *murabaha* and *salam* has the potential to mitigate the price risks underlying these transactions. Although permanent shifts in asset prices cannot be hedged against, however, the composition of receivable assets on the balance sheet can be systematically adjusted in such a way that the adverse impact of inflation is minimized.

Supposing that an Islamic bank has sold assets worth $100 on a *murabaha* basis for six months, it can fully hedge against inflation by buying $100 worth on a *salam* basis. If, for example, 10 per cent of the value of the previous assets is wiped out by inflation, its *salam*-based receivables can become valuable by the same percentage. Moreover, as far as the *salam* is concerned, it can be fully hedged by the bank by adopting an equivalent parallel *salam* contract as a supplier.

Risk absorption/management
Some risks cannot be eliminated or transferred and must be absorbed by the banks. The first is due to the complexity of the risk and difficulty in separating it from assets. Second, risk is accepted by the financial institutions as these are central to their business. These risks are accepted because the banks specialize in dealing with them and are rewarded accordingly. Examples of these risks are the credit risk inherent in banking book activities and market risks in the trading book activities of banks. Some issues related to managing risks in Islamic banks are given below.

Collateral
Collateral is also one of the most important securities against credit loss. Islamic banks use collateral to secure finance, because *al-rahn* (an asset as a security in a deferred obligation) is allowed in the *shari'a*. According to the principles of Islamic finance, a debt due from a third party, perishable commodities and something which is not protected by the

Islamic law as an asset, such as an interest-based financial instrument, is not eligible for use as collateral. On the other hand, cash, tangible assets, gold, silver and other precious commodities, shares in equities and debt due from the finance provider to the finance user are assets eligible for collateral. The industry-wide general quality of collateral depends on a number of institutional characteristics of the environment as well as the products offered by the industry. An improvement in the institutional infrastructures and a refinement of the Islamic banking products can be instrumental in enhancing the collateral quality and reducing credit risks.

Guarantees
Guarantees supplement collateral in improving the quality of credit. Commercial guarantees are extremely important tools to control credit risk in conventional banks. Although some Islamic banks also use commercial guarantees, the general *fiqh* understanding goes against their use. In accordance with the *fiqh*, only a third party can provide guarantees as a benevolent act and on the basis of a service charge for actual expenses. Owing to this lack of consensus, therefore, the tool is not effectively used in the Islamic banking industry.

Loan loss reserves
Sufficient loan loss reserves offer protection against expected credit losses. The effectiveness of these reserves depends on the credibility of the systems in place for calculating the expected losses. Recent developments in credit risk management techniques have enabled large traditional banks to identify their expected losses accurately. The Islamic banks are also required to maintain the mandatory loan loss reserves subject to the regulatory requirements in different jurisdictions. However, as discussed above, the Islamic modes of finance are diverse and heterogeneous as compared to the interest-based credit. These require more rigorous and credible systems for expected loss calculation. Furthermore, for comparability of the risks of different institutions, there is also a need for uniform standards for loss recognition across modes of finance, financial institutions and regulatory jurisdictions. The AAOIFI Standards No. 1 provides for the basis of income and loss recognition for the Islamic modes of finance. However, except for a few institutions, banks and regulatory organizations do not apply these standards.

   In addition to the mandatory reserves, some Islamic banks have established investment protection reserves. The Jordan Islamic Bank has pioneered the establishment of these reserves, which are established with the contributions of investment depositors and bank owners. The reserves are aimed at providing protection to capital as well as investment deposits against any risk of loss including default, thereby minimizing withdrawal risk.

Allocating capital
The basic concept of risk-adjusted return on capital (RAROC) is used to provide a 'decision rule that allocates capital to projects/investments according to risk' (Thomson, 2001). RAROC can be used for allocating capital among different classes of assets and across business units by examining their associated risk–return factors. An application of RAROC in Islamic finance would be to assign capital for various modes of financing. Islamic financial instruments have different risk profiles. For example, *murabaha* is considered less risky than profit-sharing modes of financing like *mudaraba* and *musharaka*.

Using historical data on different modes of financing for investments, one can estimate the expected loss and maximum loss at a certain level of confidence for a given period for different financial instruments. Then this information can be used to assign risk capital for different modes of financing by Islamic financial instruments.

The concept of RAROC can also be used to determine the rate of return or profit rate on different instruments ex ante by equating their RAROCs as shown below:

$$RAROC_i = RAROC_j,$$

or

$$(\text{risk adjusted return})_i / (\text{risk capital})_i = (\text{risk adjusted return})_j / (\text{risk capital})_j,$$

where i and j represent different modes of financing (*mudaraba* and *musharaka*, respectively). Thus if instrument j is more risky (that is, has a larger denominator) then the financial institution can ask for a higher return to equate RAROC of the instrument with that of instrument i.

Conclusion

Islamic banks face additional risks due to the nature of their balance sheet and *shari'a* compliance. Non-availability of financial instruments to Islamic banks is a major hindrance in their way to manage market risks as compared to the conventional banks. While some of the *fiqh*-related issues have to be resolved by *shari'a* scholars, setting up of infrastructure institutions needs to be done by the government and regulatory authorities in different countries. Obviously, owing to religious restrictions, the Islamic banks cannot enter the conventional banking market, but the conventional banks are offering the Islamic products simultaneously with their own products. Competition no doubt enhances efficiency and a level playing field is a prerequisite for a healthy competitive environment. A more level playing field for competition between Islamic and conventional banks in this regard cannot be ensured unless the Islamic banks have similar supporting infrastructure institutions.

There is a need to introduce a risk management culture in Islamic banks. One way to introduce this culture is to initiate some form of internal rating system. Specifically, risk weighting of all their assets separately is needed. In the medium and longer-run these could evolve into more sophisticated systems. Initiation of such a system can be instrumental in filling the gaps in the risk management system and hence enhancing the rating of these by the regulatory authorities and external credit assessment agencies.

Notes

1. For a discussion on these modes of financing see Ahmad (1993), Kahf and Khan (1992) and Khan (1991).
2. For a discussion on the determining profit-sharing ratio for project financing, see Ahmed (2001).
3. See Ahmed (2005) and Chapra and Ahmed (2002) for results from a survey of depositors showing evidence of withdrawal risk.
4. The results are based on a survey conducted in 2001 and reported in Khan and Ahmed (2001). Note, however, that the results reported here are different from those of Khan and Ahmed (2001). The number of banks used here has one more bank in the sample than that in the former and also the market risk results are reported here instead of mark-up risks in the former.

5. See IFSB (2005) for risks in different Islamic financial instruments and the accompanying regulatory capital allocation.
6. The results reported in Khan and Ahmed (2001) are based on a survey conducted in 2001.
7. See Koch (1995) for a discussion.
8. See Das (2000) for a detailed discussion on the topic.
9. For the resolution prohibiting conventional futures see Islamic *Fiqh* Academy Ruling no. 63/1/7 (IRTI and IFA, 2000, p. 127).
10. For more detailed discussion, see Obaidullah (1998).

References

AAOIFI – Accounting and Auditing Organization for Islamic Financial Institutions (1999), *Statement on the Purpose and Calculation of the Capital Adequacy Ratio for Islamic Banks*, Bahrain: AAOIFI.
Ahmad, Ausaf (1993), 'Contemporary practices of Islamic financing techniques', research paper no. 20, Islamic Research and Training Institute, Islamic Development Bank, Jeddah.
Ahmed, Habib (2001), 'Determinants of profit-sharing ratio in project financing: a note', *Islamic Economic Studies*, 9 (1), 41–5.
Ahmed, Habib (2005), 'Withdrawal risk, market discipline and efficiency in Islamic banking', in Tariqullah Khan and Dadang Muljawan (eds), *Islamic Banking Stability: The Role of Risk Management, Regulation and Supervision*, Islamic Research and Training Institute, Jeddah: Islamic Development Bank.
BCBS (Basel Committee on Banking Supervision) (2001), *Operational Risk,* consultative document, Basel: Bank for International Settlements.
Chapra, M. Umer and Habib Ahmed (2002), 'Corporate governance in Islamic financial institutions', occasional paper no. 6, Islamic Research and Training Institute, Islamic Development Bank, Jeddah.
Chapra, M. Umer and Tariqullah Khan (2000), 'Regulation and supervision of Islamic banks', occasional paper no. 3, Islamic Research and Training Institute, Islamic Development Bank, Jeddah.
Crouhy, Michel, Dan Galai and Robert Mark (2001), *Risk Management*, New York: McGraw-Hill.
Damodaran, Aswath (2005), 'Value and risk: beyond betas', *Financial Analysts Journal*, 61 (2), 38–45.
Das, Satyajit (ed.) (2000), *Credit Derivatives and Credit Linked Notes*, 2nd edn, Singapore : John Wiley and Sons.
IFSB (Islamic Financial Services Board) (2005), 'Capital adequacy standard for institutions (other than insurance institutions) offering only Islamic financial services', Exposure Draft no. 2, Islamic Financial Services Board, Kuala Lumpur.
IRTI and IFA (2000), 'Resolutions and recommendations of the Council of the Islamic Fiqh Academy', Islamic Research and Training Institute, Islamic Development Bank, Jeddah.
Kahf, Monzer and Tariqullah Khan (1992), 'Principles of Islamic financing', research paper no. 16, Islamic Research and Training Institute, Islamic Development Bank, Jeddah.
Kamali, M.H. (2005), '*Fiqhi* issues in commodity futures', in Munawar Iqbal and Tariqullah Khan (eds), *Financial Engineering and Islamic Contracts*, London: Palgrave Macmillan.
Khan, M. Fahim (1991), 'Comparative economics of some Islamic financing techniques', research paper no. 12, Islamic Research and Training Institute, Islamic Development Bank, Jeddah.
Khan, Tariqullah (1999), 'Islamic quasi equity (debt) instruments and the challenges of balance sheet hedging: an exploratory analysis', *Islamic Economic Studies*, 7 (1), 1–32.
Khan, Tariqullah (2000), 'Islamic quasi equity (debt) instruments and the challenges of balance sheet hedging: an exploratory analysis', *Islamic Economic Studies*, 7 (2), 1–32.
Khan, Tariqullah and Habib Ahmed (2001), 'Risk management: an analysis of issues in Islamic financial industry', occasional paper no. 5, Islamic Research and Training Institute, Islamic Development Bank, Jeddah.
Koch, Timothy (1995), *Bank Management*, Orlando: The Dryden Press.
Kolb, Robert W. (1997), *Futures Options and Swaps*, Malden, MA: Blackwell Publishers.
Obaidullah, Mohammad (1998), 'Financial engineering with Islamic options', *Islamic Economic Studies*, 6 (1), 73–103.
Santomero, Anthony M. (1997), 'Commercial bank risk management: an analysis of the process', *Journal of Financial Services Research*, 12, 83–115.
Thomson, James B. (2001), 'PSAF, economic capital and the new Basel Accord', working paper 01-11, Federal Reserve Bank of Cleveland.
Vogel, Frank E. and Samuel L. Hayes (1998), *Islamic Law and Finance: Religion, Risk, and Return*, The Hague, The Netherlands: Kluwer Law International.

PART III

INSTRUMENTS AND MARKETS

11 Islamic money market instruments
Sam R. Hakim

Introduction

The Islamic financial system broadly refers to financial market transactions, operations and services that comply with Islamic rules, principles and codes of practice. The laws and rules of the religion require certain types of activities, risks or rewards to be either prohibited or promoted. While Muslims undertaking financial transactions are encouraged to use financial instruments that comply with these rules, other investors may find that these instruments have appeal from an ethical standpoint.

Islamic laws and rules are known as *shari'a* and the study of them is Islamic jurisprudence. *Shari'a* governs all aspects of Islamic matters including faith, worship, economic, social, political and cultural aspects of Islamic societies. The rules and laws are derived from three important sources, namely the Holy Qur'an, *sunna* (the practice and tradition of the Prophet Muhammad s.a.w.) and *ijtihad* (the reasoning of qualified scholars). Further elaboration and interpretation of the rules dictated by the Holy Qur'an and *sunna* are provided by qualified scholars in Islamic jurisprudence via *ijtihad*, an interpretative process which is carried out within the framework of the Qur'an and *sunna*.

Modern Islamic financial products and services are developed using two different approaches. The first approach is by identifying existing conventional products and services that are generally acceptable to Islam, and modifying as well as removing any prohibited elements so that they are able to comply with *shari'a* principles. The second approach involves the application of various *shari'a* principles to facilitate the origination and innovation of new products and services (Warde, 2000).

Basic principles of Islamic finance

The basis of Islamic commercial law[1] is predicated on *fiqh al-mu'amalat* (literally the *fiqh* of human interrelations) which advocates the principles of *shari'a* with respect to civil liberties, economic freedom, social equity, justice, transparency and accountability in all financial matters. In *shari'a*, the moral dictum that governs financial transactions and agreements is that all are permissible, provided that they do not include a prohibited gain, activity or commodity, such as *riba, gharar, maysir* (gambling), specific foods and beverages and indecent activities. By integrating religious doctrine and ethical conduct in financial transactions, Islamic finance offers an alternative framework to the Western model and sets boundaries to permissible activities (Hakim and Rashidian, 2004).

For example, *riba* is generally recognized to represent the return or interest expense charged on a loan agreement although the literal translation suggests that it indicates an excess value realized on a loan, the sale or exchange of a commodity. Similarly, *gharar* is inherent in transactions that involve excessive uncertainty, or deception. Examples include the case where a reasonable buyer has a significant lack of confidence about the price or quality of a good or service or when there is outright deception of the buyer by a person hiding the true risks or benefits (Vogel and Hayes, 1998). In addition, alcoholic beverages, pork-based foods, harmful products such as tobacco and guns, and indecent activities such as casinos and adult entertainment are acknowledged to be un-Islamic because they defy the principles of *shari'a*.

While there may only be a handful of differences between conventional and Islamic financial products, the distinctions are fundamental to the structure and the risk/return profile of these instruments. For example, Islamic finance promotes risk sharing through partnerships and eschews interest-based charges. This fundamental difference distances Islamic banking from conventional finance (Wilson, 1997). For a long time, equity financing was the dominant financial product being offered to depositors and investors (Siddiqi, 2000; Anwar, 2003). These are based on the concepts of profit-sharing in the form of *mudaraba* and profit-and-loss sharing *musharaka* (Ayub, 2002). Flanking these were *murabaha* contracts that have constituted the cornerstone for working capital and short-term financing (AAOIFI, 2003; Islamic Financial Services Board, 2005a, 2005b). As the market evolved, *shari'a* rules were introduced to chart the designs of debt financing. Here the challenge was particularly onerous because conventional debt is not necessarily asset-specific, whereas the *shari'a* requires the existence of an underlying asset or assets to back the transaction (DeLorenzo, 1997; Khan, 2000; Bahrain Monetary Agency, 2002).

Traditional money markets instruments
The 'money market' is a collective term that refers to the markets where short-term high-quality credit instruments are traded. Securities with maturities within one year fit in this category and are generally issued in the primary market through a telecommunications network by banks, corporations and governments to obtain short-term funds. Those purchasing these securities generally sell them on in the secondary market to financial institutions and government agencies that have funds available for a short-term period. Most financial institutions and firms maintain some holdings of money market securities. The securities enhance liquidity in two ways. First, newly issued securities generate cash. The institutions that issue new securities have created a short-term liability in order to boost their cash balance. Second, institutions that previously purchased money market securities will generate cash upon sale or liquidation. In this case, one type of asset (the security) is replaced by another (cash). Below we cite three of the most popular money market instruments that have been replicated by Islamic banks to conform to Islamic principles.

Treasury bills
Treasury bills are short-term obligations issued by a government and represent one of the most popular money market instruments because of their marketability, safety and short-term maturity (typically three months). They are attractive as investment instruments for a number of reasons: there is no default risk per se, they are highly liquid and they benefit from a well-developed secondary market. Treasury bills are also used to mop up excess cash from the banking sector and help the government to borrow from banks to meet its budgetary shortfall. In many countries, they represent a major instrument to carry out monetary policy. When a central bank feels that that the economy is too liquid with surplus funds, it sells Treasury bills to sop up the excess liquidity. But when there is a shortage of funds in the economy, it pumps funds back into the economy by buying back Treasury bills. When issued, Treasury bills are sold at a discount to their face value. So the

yield on Treasury bills is closely monitored because the rate that the central bank uses when it sells the Treasury bills is also a leading indicator of where it wants short-term interest rates to go.

Call money market

Call money is a key component of the money market, in which banks primarily participate on a daily basis mainly to wipe out the temporary mismatch in their assets and liabilities. As there is no brokerage house or intermediary organization in most call money markets, the transactions usually take place on the basis of bilateral negotiations. Since call loans are unsecured, lending institutions/banks are always cautious in the selection of borrowing banks/institutions.

The call money market allows banks to effectively lend or borrow short-term funds from each other. In the US, these loans are referred to as Federal funds and the rate charged on these transactions, the Federal funds rate, is one of the most closely watched interest rates since other key interest rates depend on it. The call money market is influenced by the supply of and demand for overnight funds. In addition, through open market operations, the central bank can directly adjust the amount of funds available in the bank system in order to influence the call money rate and several other short-term interest rates. Because the Treasury bill rate embodies no default risk, the call money rate is generally slightly higher at any point in time. The inter-bank market is often the centre of the call money market where the negotiations between two banks may take place over a communication network or occur through a broker. Once an inter-bank loan transaction is agreed upon, the lending institution can instruct the central bank to debit its reserve account and to credit the borrowing institution's reserve account by the amount of the loan.

In smaller countries, foreign banks are often the main source of liquidity in the call money market. Costs of funds for foreign banks are often lower than those of local banks. As a result, they can hold a substantial amount of excess liquidity for lending in the call money market.

Certificates of deposit

Negotiable certificates of deposit (CDs) are large-denomination negotiable liabilities issued at a discount by banks to businesses and government units with a fixed maturity and interest rate. Because of their size, these CDs are issued primarily by the largest banks and have a liquid secondary market. By selling a CD, the holder can effectively redeem the deposit before maturity without loss of funds to the bank. Their marketability feature makes CDs attractive to temporary holders of substantial funds and permits banks to tap the money market for quick access to borrowed funds. Interest rates on CDs must be competitive with market rates on comparable money market instruments. Using liability management, a bank can increase its deposits quickly and substantially by offering a slightly higher rate of interest than its competitors.

Islamic money market instruments

Islamic banks have been expanding the scope and scale of their activities where traditional investment and financing products are restructured to conform to *shari'a* principles. One impetus of change has been attributed to the growing needs of Islamic banks to cope with liquidity issues (Sundararajan and Errico, 2002). In response several countries (Malaysia,

Bahrain, Kuwait, Sudan and Iran) have taken the lead to back new instruments aimed at facilitating asset management by Islamic banks (Abdul Majid, 2003).

In a parallel effort, governments with a dominant Muslim population have introduced new laws and provided the necessary legal framework for these financial instruments to evolve. Two important developments are worth mentioning here. The first milestone was Malaysia's issuance of the first Islamic Bond in 1983 and which at the time was known as a Government Investment Certificate (or GIC). This instrument was introduced with the goal of providing liquidity to the growing Islamic banking system at the time. The instrument was non-tradeable because it represented a non-interest-bearing loan based on the Islamic principle of *qard hasan*. More recently, the definition was expanded, based on the concept of *bai'al-inah*, which permits secondary market trading.

Another milestone was the issuance of interest-free bonds to finance properties by the Central Bank of Kuwait. The concept was also appealing to Iran which later introduced several participation bonds based on *mudaraba*. It is important to note that the success of these early developments rested on the backing of individual governments. However, as the market developed, these issues gained their own momentum and permitted this infant market to grow. Today, these instruments provide a tangible alternative to traditional financing.

These early developments would not have been possible without the regulatory legal framework that ensured their legitimacy (Yaacob and Ibrahim, 1999). Table 11.1 at the end of this chapter provides a comparison between the main Islamic money market instruments and their traditional counterparts where they exist. More recent Islamic money market securities include the following.

Tradeable Islamic financial assets
Mudaraba *certificates*   These represent certificates of permanent ownership in a project or company where the holder is not entitled to exercise management control or voting rights.

Musharaka *certificates*   These are defined as with the *mudaraba* certificates, with the notable exception that the bearer holds management and voting rights.

Musharaka *term finance certificates*   These represent certificates that entitle the holder to a temporary ownership of a project or company. The certificates may include or exclude management control and/or voting rights.

There are two other types of certificates based on the concept of *ijara* (rent) for a durable asset. However, these certificates are typically considered as capital market instruments.

Other certificates
Murabaha *and* istisnaa *certificates* are debt securities arising from standard *istisnaa* or *murabaha* contracts. The periodic repayment of the debt under these certificates is not broken up between principal or coupons and the total debt or any portion therefrom cannot be traded in compliance with the ban *shari'a* imposes on debt trading. The certificates are similar to a zero coupon security. As a result these securities have limited appeal because of the absence of a secondary market. There is an apparent conflict of opinion on the tradeability restriction of these certificates. In Malaysia, *murabaha* and *istisnaa* certificates are very popular and are tradeable in the domestic bond market.

Salam certificates These securities arise from *salam* contracts which require pre-payment for the future delivery of a commodity. The pre-paid funds can represent debt certificates for a commodity. However, the certificates are non-tradeable for the same reason as the *murabaha* and *istisnaa* certificates.

Sukuk *structures*
Sukuks represent *shari'a*-compliant securities that are backed by tangible assets. Conceptually, *sukuks* are similar to traditional asset-backed securities with the notable exception that the backing cannot be solely comprised of debt. The stipulation applies irrespective of the contractual form of debt, and regardless of whether such debt was based on *murabaha* or *istisnaa*. Instead, the issuing entity should possess a tangible asset (or group of assets).

Traditionally *sukuk* structures have varying terms. Their classification into money or capital markets will hinge on the term of a specific structure. They are equivalent to the asset-backed securities which are pervasive in non-Islamic financial markets. Below we discuss various *sukuk* certificates and identify the key aspects of their risk profile.[2]

Ijara sukuk These are certificates backed by lease agreements of land, buildings or equipment. The underlying lease payments, which determine the return on the *sukuk* certificates, can be fixed or variable. The terms of the certificates cannot exceed the term of the underlying leases but there is no compelling reason why the *sukuk* cannot have a shorter term.

Hybrid sukuk If the underlying revenues are not solely dependent on revenues from leases, but include *istisnaa* or *murabaha* receivables, the *sukuk* certificates are designated as hybrids provided that the proportion of lease-based assets exceeds 50 per cent.

Variable rate sukuk In some cases, the issuer may be willing to step in by pledging some assets that are beyond the underlying leases in order to collaterize the *sukuk* certificates. Such action has the advantage of enhancing the credit quality of the certificates and realizing a more stable cash flow to the certificate holders who are no longer solely dependent on the dividend payout from the leases but also on the direct profitability of the issuer. Consequently, these *sukuk* are referred to as *Musharaka* term finance certificates (MTFCs).

Zero-coupon non-tradeable sukuk When the backing assets do not yet exist or are not completed at the time the *sukuks* are issued, the *sukuks* are then similar to *murabaha* and *istisnaa* certificates. In this case, these *sukuks* are subject to the same restriction on secondary market tradeability imposed by the *shari'a* as the certificates.

Malaysian Islamic Inter-bank Money Market (IIMM)
A centrepiece for the healthy operation of an Islamic banking system is the existence of a liquid money market that affords financial institutions the ability to adjust their portfolios in the short term through a funding facility. This was the prime objective of the Islamic Inter-bank Money Market (IIMM) which was introduced in January 1994 in Malaysia.

In this respect, the Islamic inter-bank market creates incentives for surplus banks to channel funds to deficit banks, thereby maintaining the funding and liquidity mechanism necessary to promote stability in the system. The IIMM is structured as a short-term intermediary to provide a ready source of short-term investment outlets based on *shari'a* principles. Through the IIMM, all financial institutions participating in the Islamic banking scheme match their funding requirements. The IIMM is equivalent to a traditional call money market where bank deposits at the central bank are loaned to other banks. The main instruments traded in the IIMM include *mudaraba*-based inter-bank investment and inter-bank trading of Islamic financial instruments (Institute of Islamic Banking & Insurance, 2000). These instruments include the following.[3]

Mudaraba *inter-bank investment (MII)*   MII refers to a mechanism whereby a deficit Islamic banking institution (investee bank) can obtain investment from a surplus Islamic banking institution based on *mudaraba*. The period of investment is from overnight to 12 months, while the rate of return is based on the rate of gross profit before distribution for investment of one year of the investee bank. The profit-sharing ratio is negotiable between both parties. At the time of negotiation, the investor bank does not guarantee the rate of return, which is known at the end of the investment period. The principal invested is repaid at the end of the period, together with a share of the profit arising from the uses of the fund by the investee bank. The MII is an instrument equivalent to the traditional bank CD. Islamic banks purchase these securities in order simultaneously to earn a return and maintain adequate liquidity. In turn, they issue MII securities when experiencing a temporary shortage of cash.

Wadia *inter-bank acceptance*   This is an inter-bank transaction between the Malaysian Central Bank and the Islamic banking institutions. The instrument represents a mechanism whereby the Islamic banking institutions place their surplus fund in the custody of the Central Bank. Under this concept, the acceptor of funds is viewed as the custodian of the funds without any obligation to pay a specific return. Any dividend paid by the custodian is perceived as a gift (*hiba*). The *Wadia* inter-bank acceptance facilitates liquidity management by giving the central bank the flexibility to declare a dividend without the obligation to invest the funds received.

Under the liquidity management operation, the Central Bank uses the *Wadia* inter-bank acceptance to absorb excess liquidity from the IIMM by accepting overnight money or fixed-tenure *wadia*.

Government investment issues (GII)   When the first Islamic bank in Malaysia began operations in 1983, the bank could not, among other things, purchase or trade in Malaysian government securities, Malaysian Treasury bills or other interest-bearing instruments. However, Islamic banks had a serious need to hold liquid securities to meet their statutory liquidity requirements and to park their idle funds. To meet their needs, the Malaysian Parliament passed the Government Investment Act in 1983 which permitted the issuance of non-interest bearing certificates known as Government Investment Certificates (GIC). These certificates have since been replaced by Government Investment Issues (GII) under the concept of *qard hasan* (Haron, 1997).

The concept of *qard hasan* does not permit trading the GII in the secondary market. To address this shortfall, the Central Bank opened a window to facilitate the purchase and sale of the securities by market participants. The security prices are set by the Central Bank which maintains a system that keeps track of the movement in the GII.

In June 2001, Malaysia issued three-year GIIs under the concept of *bai'al-inah*. The move was designed to add depth to the Islamic inter-bank money market by permitting the tradeability of the GII on the secondary market via the concept of *bai'al-dayn* (debt trading). At the end of 2003, the outstanding amount of GIIs issued was about US$2 billion (Bank Negara Malaysia, 2004).

Bank Negara negotiable notes   These notes represent short-term instruments issued by the Central Bank predicated on the concept of *bai'al-inah*. These notes were introduced in November 2000 and are tradeable in the secondary market. The price of the notes is determined on a discount basis and issued by the Central Bank for a maximum term of one year. The notes are an effective tool used by the Central Bank to manage liquidity (Bank Negara Malaysia, 1999, 2001, 2004). These negotiable notes play the role of Treasury bills in traditional banking, and are highly attractive for three main reasons: they are default risk free; highly liquid with a relatively deep secondary market; and are sold at a pure discount to their face value. They thus exhibit characteristics identical to Treasury bills and represent the instrument of choice by the Central Bank to soak up or inject liquidity into an Islamic banking system or conduct open market operations.

Sale and buy-back agreement   These represent an Islamic money market transaction entered between two parties in which one counterparty sells an asset at an agreed price with the obligation to buy it back in the future at a predetermined and higher price.

Cagamas mudaraba *bonds*   These were introduced in March 1994 to finance the purchase of Islamic housing debts from financial institutions that provide Islamic house financing to the public (Bank Islam Malaysia, 1994). The *mudaraba* bonds are structured under the concept of *mudaraba* where the bondholders and Cagamas share the profits according to predetermined profit-sharing ratios.

When issue (WI)   When Issue is a transaction for the sale and purchase of debt securities before they are issued. The Malaysian National *Shari'a* Advisory Council ruled that the WI transactions are allowed, according to the permissibility of sale and buy-back agreements.

Islamic Accepted Bills   An Islamic Accepted Bill (also known as Interest-Free Accepted Bill) was introduced in 1991 with the objective to promote domestic and foreign trades by providing merchants with an attractive Islamic trade finance product. The instrument is formulated on the Islamic notion of *murabaha* (deferred lump-sum sale or cost-plus) and *bai'al-dayn* (debt trading). The Islamic Accepted Bills are equivalent to the traditional banker's acceptance, a money market instrument used primarily to finance foreign trade. There are two types of financing under the Islamic Accepted Bills facility: imports and local purchases, and exports and local sales.

Imports and local purchases are transactions financed under a *murabaha* working capital financing mechanism. Under this concept, the commercial bank appoints the customer as the purchasing agent for the bank. The customer then purchases the required goods from the seller on behalf of the bank, which will then pay the seller and resell the goods to the customer at a price, inclusive of a profit margin. The customer is allowed a deferred payment term of up to 200 days. Upon maturity of the *murabaha* financing, the customer pays the bank the cost of goods plus a profit margin.

The sale of goods by the bank on a deferred payment term basis constitutes the creation of debt. This is securitized in the form of a bill of exchange drawn by the bank and accepted by the customer for the full amount of the bank's selling price payable at maturity. If the bank decides to sell the Islamic Accepted Bill to a third party, then the concept of *bai'al-dayn* will apply, whereby the bank will sell the security at the agreed price.

Exports and local sales are the second type of Islamic bill facility. The bills supporting these transactions are traded under the concept of *bai'al-dayn*. An exporter who has been approved for an Islamic Accepted Bill facility prepares the export documentation as required under the sale contract or letter of credit. The export documents are sent to the importer's bank. The exporter draws on the commercial bank a new bill of exchange as a substitution bill which then becomes the Islamic Accepted Bill. The bank purchases the security at a mutually agreed price using the concept of *bai'al-dayn* and the proceeds are credited to the exporter's account. Domestic sales are treated in a similar manner.

Islamic negotiable instruments These instruments take two separate forms. The first is Islamic Negotiable Instruments of Deposit (INID). For these, the applicable concept is *mudaraba*. It refers to a sum of money deposited with an Islamic banking institution and repayable to the bearer on a specified future date at the nominal value of INID plus declared dividend. The second instrument is the Negotiable Islamic Debt Certificate (NIDC). This transaction involves the sale of a pro rata share in the bank's assets to the customer at an agreed price on a cash basis. Subsequently the pro rata share is purchased back from the customer at a principal value plus profit and settled at an agreed future date.

Islamic private debt securities These securities were introduced in Malaysia in 1990. Current securities in the market are issued based on the *shari'a*-compliant concepts of *bai bi-thaman ajil*, *murabaha* and *mudaraba*.

Rahn agreement Under this structure, the lender provides a loan to the borrower, based on the concept of *qard hasan*. The borrower pledges its securities as collateral against the loan. Should the borrower fail to repay the loan on the maturity date, the lender has the right to sell the pledged securities and use the proceeds to settle the loan. If there is surplus money, the lender will return the balance to the borrower. The Rahn agreement is predicated on the concept of a repurchase agreement (or Repo), a very popular instrument in traditional money markets, though its use by Islamic banks is more limited. The Central Bank uses these instruments as a tool for liquidity management for money market operations. Any returns realized from these securities are considered a gift (*hiba*) and determined according to the average inter-bank money market rates.

Conclusion
This chapter has profiled the role and function of Islamic money market instruments used by the Islamic financial institutions today and has discussed the role of the Islamic money

Table 11.1   Some Islamic money market instruments

	Objective	Non-Islamic security equivalent	Popularity
Sukuk structures	Create a secondary market and liquidity for debt collaterized by real and financial assets	Asset-backed securities	High
Mudaraba Inter-bank Investment (MII)	Inter-bank borrowing and lending	Negotiable Certificates of Deposit (CDs)	Medium
Wadia Inter-bank Acceptance	Liquidity management facility between the Central Bank and an Islamic bank	Islamic bank reserves at the Central Bank	Medium
Bank Negara negotiable notes	Manage liquidity of the Islamic banking system	Treasury bills	High
Islamic Accepted Bills	Finance foreign trade transactions	Bankers' acceptances	Medium
Islamic Negotiable Instruments of Deposit (INID)	Provide a return on maturity time deposits	Time deposit with fixed maturity	High
Rahn Agreement	Liquidity management	Repurchase agreement	Low

market within the broader Islamic financial services industry. It has also assessed the extent to which Islamic money market products and services are offered in various jurisdictions (with special emphasis upon Malaysia) and identified potential regulatory issues specific to Islamic money and capital markets.

While conventional principles of securities regulation may be applied to the Islamic financial market instruments, in certain instances individual jurisdictions may perceive a need for more specific guidelines in order to ensure that the unique aspects of Islamic money market products are appropriately regulated. However, it is important to note that there are currently no global best practices for regulation concerning significant areas such as *shari'a* certification, the establishment of *shari'a* boards, qualifications of *shari'a* advisors and enhanced disclosure relating to Islamic money and capital market products. A set of uniform regulation practices would be valuable. Such a development is necessary to achieve clarity for market participants and meet the needs of investor demands more effectively. Consistency on the basis and foundations of regulatory approaches would instil greater investor confidence and enhance their understanding of the scope of the products being offered. This will encourage further cross-border activity and greatly expand the size of this market in the future.

Finally, the availability of and access to information about an individual security is critical to ensure proper market functioning and smooth operations. Here, both the cost and quality of the information is important to the orderly expansion of the Islamic financial market and for the protection of market participants.

Notes

1. For a summary of Islamic commercial law, see Kamali (2002), Al-Qaradawi (1985). Bakir Haji (2004) relates the Islamic money market to *fiqhi* issues in businesses practices.
2. For a detailed discussion of the underlying risks of *sukuks*, see Tariq (2004).
3. For a summary of the genesis of securities traded on the IIMM, see Securities Commission for Malaysia (2001, 2003, 2004).

References

AAOIFI (2003), *Shari'a Standards*, Manama, Bahrain: The Accounting & Auditing Organization for Islamic Financial Institutions.
Abdul Majid, Abdul Rais (2003), 'Development of liquidity management instruments', International Conference on Islamic Banking, Risk Management, Regulation and Supervision, Jakarta, September.
Al-Qaradawi, Yusuf (1985), *The Lawful and the Prohibited In Islam*, Kuala Lumpur: Islamic Book Trust.
Anwar, Muhammad (2003), 'Islamicity of banking and modes of Islamic banking', *Arab Law Quarterly*, **18** (1), 62–80.
Ayub, Muhammad (2002), *Islamic Banking and Finance: Theory and Practice*, Karachi: State Bank Printing Press.
Bahrain Monetary Agency (2002), *Islamic Banking & Finance in the Kingdom of Bahrain*, Bahrain: Arabian Printing Press.
Bakir Haji Mansor, Mohd (2004), 'Islamic money market: shari'ah perspective', Centre for Fiqh Muamalat, Islamic Banking and Finance Institute, Malaysia.
Bank Islam Malaysia Bhd (1994), *Islamic Banking Practice: From the Practitioner's Perspective*, Kuala Lumpur: Bank Islam Malaysia Bhd.
Bank Negara Malaysia (1999), *The Central Bank and the Financial System in Malaysia*, Kuala Lumpur: Bank Negara Malaysia.
Bank Negara Malaysia (2001), *Financial Sector Masterplan*, Kuala Lumpur: Bank Negara Malaysia.
Bank Negara Malaysia (2004), 'Implementing Islamic Money Market – Issues and Challenges', Asian Islamic Banking Summit, September.
DeLorenzo, Yusuf Talal (ed.) (1997), *A Compendium of Legal Opinions on the Operations of Islamic Banks: Murabaha, Mudaraba and Musharaka*, London: Institute of Islamic Banking and Insurance.
Hakim, Sam and Manochehr Rashidian (2004), 'How costly is investor's compliance to *Shari'a*?', Economic Research Forum Annual Conference, Beirut, December.
Haqqi, Abdurrahman Raden Aji (1999), *The Philosophy of Islamic Law of Transactions*, Selangor, Malaysia: Univision Press.
Haron, Sudin (1997), *Islamic Banking: Rules & Regulations*, Selangor, Malaysia: Pelanduk Publications.
Institute of Islamic Banking & Insurance (2000), *Islamic Banking and its Operations*, London: Institute of Islamic Banking & Insurance.
Islamic Financial Services Board (2005a), 'Guiding principles of risk management, for institutions offering only Islamic financial services', Exposure Draft no. 1, March, Kuala Lumpur, Malaysia.
Islamic Financial Services Board (2005b), 'Capital Adequacy Standards for Institutions Offering Only Islamic Financial Services', Exposure Draft no. 2, March, Kuala Lumpur, Malaysia.
Kamali, Mohammad H. (2002), *Islamic Commercial Law: An Analysis of Futures and Options*, Cambridge: The Islamic Texts Society.
Khan, Zafar Ahmad (2000), *Islamic Banking and its Operations*, London: Institute of Islamic Banking & Insurance.
Securities Commission (2001), *Capital Market Masterplan*, Kuala Lumpur: Securities Commission.
Securities Commission (2003), *Resolutions of the Securities Commission Syariah Advisory Council*, Kuala Lumpur: Securities Commission.
Securities Commission (2004), *Guidelines on the Offerings of Islamic Securities*, 26 July, Kuala Lumpur: Securities Commission.
Siddiqi, Asma (ed.) (2000), *Anthology of Islamic Banking*, London: Institute of Islamic Banking & Insurance.
Sundararajan, V. and Luca Errico (2002), 'Islamic financial institutions and products in the global financial system: key issues in risk management and challenges ahead', IMF Working Paper 02/192 (www.imf.org/external/pubs/ft/wp/2002/wp02192.pdf).
Tariq, Ali Arsalan (2004), 'Managing financial risks of *sukuk* structures', Loughborough University, UK, September (mimeo).
Vogel, F.E and S.L. Hayes (1998), *Islamic Law and Finance: Religion, Risk and Return*, Boston, MA: Kluwer Law International.

Warde, Ibrahim (2000), *Islamic Finance in the Global Economy*, Edinburgh: Edinburgh University Press.

Wilson, Rodney (1997), 'Parallels between Islamic and ethical banking', Centre for Middle Eastern and Islamic Studies, University of Durham, UK (www.islamonline.net/english/Contemporary/2004/02/Article01.shtml).

Yaacob, Abdul Monir and Hamiza Ibrahim (eds) (1999), *Islamic Financial Services and Products*, Kuala Lumpur: Institute of Islamic Understanding Malaysia (IKIM).

12 Trade financing in Islam
Ridha Saadallah

Nature of trade financing

Definition

Trade financing is tied to the acquisition of goods, either through purchase transactions or through leasing operations where the rented goods are ultimately owned by the lessee. The need for trade financing arises when the buyer of goods wishes to defer the payment of the price or, less frequently, when the seller requires the advance payment of money. When the financing involves a promise of a future payment of the exchange value, the price or the purchased good, it takes the form of credit.[1] In an interest-based environment, trade transactions are financed exclusively through credit, whether it is tied or untied to the commercial transaction. In an Islamic economy, trade operations may still be financed through credit. But, since the consensus view of contemporary Muslim jurists identifies interest with the prohibited *riba*, there is a need to develop alternative credit techniques which conform to Islamic *shari'a*. Trade operations may also be financed through profit and loss sharing (PLS) techniques. This is the case whenever the good is acquired against the participation in future profits that may be earned from putting it into productive use. We will refer to this form of financing as 'participatory finance' because the exchange value is a share in future profits.

Trade financing may thus be defined as the provision of funds by all permissible means, on credit or on a participatory basis, for the purpose of acquiring all kinds of goods, domestic as well as foreign.

Demand for trade financing

The demand for financing emanates from both households and business concerns. A major part of households' demand is to finance the purchase of houses. Consumer credit is used by households to finance major purchases, such as cars and durables, as well as other purchases of consumer goods, particularly through the use of credit cards. Refinancing of debts incurred for such purposes is also considered as consumer credit. Most of consumer credit is on an instalment basis. Business concerns demand short-term finance to pay for their inventories or to refinance their accounts receivable. They may also need medium to long-term finance to acquire capital goods. Business firms engaged in international trade transactions demand financing to cover the price of their imports or to refinance the credit they would have extended to their foreign customers.

Supply of trade financing in an interest-based environment

Financial intermediaries are the first source of trade financing. Credit needs of both consumers and business firms are primarily met through a variety of financial intermediaries: commercial banks, savings institutions, insurance and pension organizations, finance companies and credit unions. Business firms constitute the second source of trade financing. On the one hand, consumers may get their purchase of consumer goods financed directly by retailers. On the other hand, a major part of short-term borrowing by business concerns is extended by other business firms. This inter-firm credit, also known as trade credit, is used by almost all firms, but more substantially by small businesses. It accounts for a substantial portion of their short-term liabilities as well as of their total assets. Sometimes, it far exceeds their short-term liabilities to banks. Trade credit is usually extended on very short to short terms. The credit terms typically leave to the buyer the choice between a discount for an early payment within a very short period (such as seven days) and a full payment for a longer credit period (such as 30 days). Sellers may also offer terms whereby cash is due within a specified period with no discount for prompt payment (for example, net 30). An interest cost is usually, though sometimes only implicitly, charged on trade credit. The interest cost is explicitly charged on trade credit when it is materialized in a bill of exchange or a promissory note. This form of trade credit is more frequently used in international trade.

Financing needs may also be satisfied directly in the market, without the intervention of financial intermediaries. Firstly, large and creditworthy firms operating in developed financial markets may raise short-term funds directly from the money market by issuing commercial paper for the purpose of financing the purchase of inputs or the refinancing of the credit extended to their customers. These firms and, to a lesser extent, smaller size business concerns may also issue corporate bonds to raise long-term funds to finance the purchase of equipment.

Supply of trade financing in an Islamic framework
In an Islamic system, trade transactions may be financed either on credit or on a participatory basis. Credit involves the deferment of the price or of the delivery of the purchased commodities. Credit may be extended either by business firms or by banks and financial intermediaries. Participatory finance involves the participation of the financier in the profits and losses brought in by the means of either reselling the financed goods or incorporating them into an income-generating production process. Participatory finance is normally the preserve of financial intermediaries, because business firms would, in normal circumstances, prefer to provide their customers with the required credit rather than sharing with them the risks inherent in their activities. Financial institutions may provide participatory finance either to the buyers of the goods or to the sellers. In the latter case it is considered as a form of refinancing in the sense that it provides the sellers with financial support which allows them to extend credit to their customers over and above their own resources.

Financial markets may also be used by business firms to finance their acquisitions of capital goods or to refinance their credit activity.

Islamic credit techniques for financing trade operations
Credit, whether extended by banks or by business firms, may be of different maturities. Business credit is usually short-term, while bank credit may be short-term as well as medium-term. As for long-term finance, Islamic banks would not be in a position to provide it directly to any significant extent, owing to the short run-dominated structure of their resources. They may, however, contribute indirectly through participation in investment funds.

Different credit techniques may be needed to finance different types of commodities. While *murabaha*, instalment sale, *salam* and *ijara-wa-iqtina* are appropriate to finance the acquisition of standard and divisible goods, it will be shown that large and buyer-specific capital goods are most effectively financed via the *istisnaa* technique.[2]

Murabaha

From murabaha *to financial* murabaha   Murabaha, as inherited from Islamic jurisprudence, was not tailored to fit readily the needs of bankers and other financiers for a substitute financing technique. As a financial technique used by Islamic financial institutions, murabaha has evolved from the original contract of the same name. *Murabaha* simply means 'mark-up sale'. It is a particular type of sale that Islamic jurisprudence considers as a trust contract, because the seller and the buyer do not negotiate the price, but rather agree on a certain profit margin added to the cost, as faithfully declared by the seller.

Originally, *murabaha* was not conceived of as a mode of finance, since it was not necessarily concluded on the basis of deferred payment. *Murabaha* sale for cash was the rule rather than the exception. The shift to credit *murabaha*, or *murabaha* with deferred price, is a first requisite for its transformation into a technique of finance. Credit *murabaha* can be used by non-financial firms to finance the purchase of goods by households and business concerns. Its rise to a fully fledged financial technique used by financial intermediaries, however, requires further amendment of the original contract.

Indeed, banks and other financial institutions which would like to practise credit *murabaha* would need to assume, more or less, a commercial intermediation function, in addition to their original function as financial intermediaries. They would have, in fact, to play the double role of intermediary buyer and seller between the ultimate buyer and seller. However, financial institutions are not specialized in commerce and they are not equipped to perform efficiently the economic functions of traders. Therefore, they would like to depart the least possible from their traditional financial intermediation function and to keep their commercial role to the strict minimum necessary to comply with Islamic principles. More particularly they would like to avoid holding inventories of goods and to market them over a prolonged period of time. This is achieved though the second amendment to the original concept of *murabaha*, that is to say the requirement that the sale contract be preceded by the customer's promise to buy the desired goods, once they are acquired by the financier.

The resulting financing technique may thus be distinguished from the original *murabaha* sale on two grounds: (a) credit is an indispensable feature, and not just a mere possibility, (b) the existence of a prior promise to buy[3] is a prerequisite for the extension of credit. For the sake of clarity, we will refer to this financing technique as 'financial *murabaha*'.[4]

The scope of financial murabaha   Financial *murabaha* may be used, and is actually used, as an alternative to conventional banks' credit, if the latter is tied to the purchase of goods. However, Islamic banks and other financial institutions intervene in this market in a radically different way, as compared to conventional banks. While the latter have the choice between direct lending to the buyers and refinancing the credit originated by the sellers, Islamic financial institutions can only finance the buyers. Refinancing is excluded, as it amounts to the purchase of debts, on which no profit can lawfully be made. On the other hand, while conventional banks assume a purely financial intermediation role, Islamic financial institutions using financial *murabaha* have to further assume some kind of commercial intermediation. It was noted earlier that, by means of the 'promise to buy' device, Islamic financial institutions may avoid building up inventories of goods. Furthermore, they usually mandate the prospective buyer to select the supplier of the demanded goods, to negotiate with him the terms and conditions of the cash sale contract and to check, on delivery, the conformity of the goods with the required specifications. This procedure minimizes for the financier the risk of buying goods that would be later refused by the customer. However, Islamic financial institutions have definitely to assume to some extent a commercial function and cannot act as pure financial intermediaries. They assume the commercial risk attached to their ownership of the demanded goods for the period of time elapsing between their acquisition of the goods from the supplier to their delivery to the customer. This commercial risk is specific to financial *murabaha* and cannot be totally avoided, notwithstanding the abovementioned devices aiming at limiting it. It adds to the credit risk (delayed payment or default) which is common to both Islamic and conventional financial institutions. Furthermore, the commercial risk facing Islamic financial institutions may even be greater, in the case where the promise to buy is considered non-binding.[5] This is because an additional cost may be incurred for marketing goods acquired on the basis of a prior promise to buy, that the customer later refused to honour.

The scope of credit murabaha   Credit *murabaha* provides an alternative to trade credit and retailers' credit extended by business concerns to other business firms or to consumers. They operate in a very similar way, with two exceptions. On the one hand, in the case of a two-part credit offer (discount for early payment or full price for a longer payment period), the choice should be made in advance and the contract should be definite with regard to the selected terms. On the other hand, the deferred price is definite and the contract should make no mention of any additional cost on possible overdues.[6]

The effective use of credit *murabaha* will however be seriously hindered, if the sellers are not efficiently backed by financial institutions. Indeed, the experience of trade credit in interest-based economies shows that refinancing is of vital importance for sellers' credit. Sellers who extend credit to their customers may of course keep the financial claims in their portfolios to maturity. But they frequently sell them for cash before maturity. In any case, sellers need to have the assurance of liquidating their receivables when needed without incurring an excessive cost. Otherwise, the sellers' opportunity cost would be higher and they would not be able to offer competitive credit terms. Business firms financing trade on the basis of credit *murabaha* have the same needs of financial support to enable them to extend credit to their customers. However, once the credit is extended, it becomes a debt that cannot be sold at a discount without violating the *shari'a* rules. Business firms would practically cease to use credit *murabaha*, unless an appropriate alternative was found for the sale of receivables. Is it acceptable to displace credit *murabaha* from the system and to rely completely on financial *murabaha* extended by Islamic banks?

Some Islamic economists advise Islamic banks to become involved in real business,[7] and especially trade. This would be achieved either through merchant departments staffed with adequate commercial skills or through the establishment of merchant subsidiaries (Aspinwall and Eisenbeis, 1985, p. 667). The principal advantage attributed to this way of doing business is that the Islamic banks would assume the business risk implied by the trade activity and thus draw an income which is unambiguously *riba*-free. One cannot underestimate this advantage of the bank–trader method over the *murabaha* method, as currently practised in Islamic banks, in terms of their relative compatibility with *shari'a*. However, this solution is seriously objectionable on macroeconomic and social grounds. Furthermore, it does not solve in all cases the financing problem. For one, Islamic banks raise mostly short-term funds, therefore they cannot use them, beyond certain limits, in long-term investments, like the acquisition of equity capital in trade subsidiaries. Second, the suggested method would lead to the establishment of financial empires controlling and dominating a large part of the economy. At the same time, it would subjugate the traders to powerful financial institutions. It is well known that the ensuing monopoly power is the source of both economic waste and social injustice. As a matter of fact, the subscription of commercial banking institutions to the capital of business concerns is in many countries tightly regulated (Omar, 1992, p. 65). Third, trade credit is indeed intimately linked to trade itself. Traders view it as an indispensable device to promote and expand sales. Fourth, the observed growing importance of trade credit in the developed market economies seems to imply that the provision of credit by business firms is efficient under certain market conditions. The elimination of credit *murabaha* would thus mean a loss of efficiency. Finally, the bank–trader method solves the refinancing problem only if it takes the form of merchant departments. But, when Islamic banks establish trade subsidiaries, these are financially independent of the mother-institutions. Thus, if the subsidiaries need liquidity to refinance the credit they had already extended to their customers, they find themselves in exactly the same situation as any other seller vis-à-vis the resources of the mother-banks. Therefore the establishment of trade subsidiaries does not eliminate the need to design appropriate methods to support financially the credit activity of traders.

Since traders' credit should remain in the system, solutions need to be devised to the impossibility of refinancing sellers' credit. Trade refinancing may be looked at as a financial back-up provided by banks and other financial institutions to sellers subsequent to their extension of credit. The common principle underlying the development of Islamic alternatives to conventional refinancing involves the replacement of the subsequent financial back-up with a prior financial support provided to the sellers. Contrary to conventional refinancing, which is based on the discount of debt instruments, the alternative prior support is based on the profit and loss sharing (PLS) principle. Sellers may obtain the needed support either directly in the financial markets through the issue of PLS certificates or from financial intermediaries. These techniques will be detailed below.

Instalment sale
Instalment sale is a form of credit sale where the deferred price is paid in instalments over a certain period of time. Theoretically, it may be based on *musawamah* (negotiated price) or on *murabaha* (negotiated margin added to a declared cost). Practically, Islamic banks using this technique adopt the *murabaha* type. Instalment sale is appropriate for the medium-term financing of equipment where the size of the financing justifies its splitting up in many instalments.

Producers of capital goods and traders of durables may sell on instalments to their customers, provided they are assured of the support of their banks. Banks may also use this technique for the same purpose. They would however require, as in the case of financial *murabaha*, that the customer undertake to buy the goods beforehand. Banks may not be able to expand much in this type of medium-term financing; their ability to transform short-run resources into longer-term uses is certainly limited.

Ijara-wa-iqtina   This involves the lease of equipment over a certain period of time and the transfer of ownership to the lessee at the end of the period. The transfer may be effected either on grant or on sale basis. Usually, the lease contract is associated with the financier's promise to grant the leased equipment at the end of the period or to sell it at its residual value.

Ijara-wa-iqtina is not known as such in the traditional *fiqh* but appears to be a combination of two lawful contracts: a rent contract on one hand and a grant or a sale contract on the other.[8] This mode of finance is also appropriate for the medium-term financing of equipment. It is therefore a close substitute for *instalment* sale. Its use by sellers or banks is subject to the same conditions and constraints.

Salam
Salam is 'a sale with advance payment for future delivery' (Saleh, 1992, p. 89). *Salam* may have various financial uses (Omar,1992). In the field of trade finance, it may be used as an indirect financing of the purchase of raw materials and intermediate goods. If a producer needed to finance his purchase of inputs, he would agree with a trader, such as a wholesaler or an exporter, to sell him with advance payment finished goods identical to his own.[9] The trader–financier is supposed to specialize in the marketing of the same type of finished goods. Thus he would not require the existence of a warranted demand before financing the producer. This is not the case of a bank providing the same type of finance. Indeed, a bank is not interested in receiving the financed goods at the delivery date. It would therefore require that someone undertake to buy the financed goods from the bank at the delivery date. It seems that *salam* is more appropriate as a trader's finance than as a bank's finance. Of course, here as in other types of traders' credit, banks will have to play a role to support the credit activity of traders on a partnership basis.

The long-term finance of buyer-specific commodities
This is the case of a producer who needs to finance his purchase of capital goods that are not readily available with the supplier because they have to be tailored to meet the specific requirements of the buyer. These customized goods are in general large items necessitating relatively huge investments. The supplier would therefore insist on getting a firm order and partial advance payment.

The financing of these types of commodities may still be provided by the seller, if he is adequately backed up by a bank (Khaleefa, 1993, pp. 41–2), but, since the demanded commodities are not available when ordered, there should be at the start a reciprocal promise to buy and to sell followed by a sale contract when the goods are produced. The supplier would not however invest in producing customized commodities if the buyer's promise is not considered binding. This requirement is much debated among Islamic jurists. Moreover, this solution cannot accommodate the seller's requirement for partial advance payment of the price, because such payment amounts to paying part of the price before the sale contract is concluded.

It seems that the most appropriate techniques to meet the particular requirements of financing the purchase of buyer-specific capital goods are built around the contract of *istisnaa*. Two such techniques will be presented below.

Istisnaa-*cum-instalment sale*
The prospective buyer makes a promise to his bank to buy specified goods, once they are acquired by the bank. The bank and the producer sign an *istisnaa* contract, the purpose of which is to manufacture the goods according to the buyer's specifications. When the goods are manufactured and accepted, they will be sold on an instalment basis to the buyer who made the promise. *Istisnaa* is closely related to *salam* but is more flexible (Dunia, 1990). In particular, the price may be paid at the time of the contract, at the time of delivery or gradually. This flexibility permits meeting the manufacturer's need for down payment.

One weakness of the suggested technique is that *istisnaa* is considered by the majority of Islamic jurists as a non-binding (*ja'iz*) contract. There is however an opinion within the *Hanafi* school which makes it binding for the orderer of manufacture to accept the manufactured goods if they are found to meet the required specifications (Dunia, 1990, p. 35). The other weakness is related to the *shari'a* acceptability of the technical requirement to make the buyer's promise binding.

Two-tier istisnaa
This is the combination of two *istisnaa* contracts. The prospective buyer asks the bank to manufacture certain equipment with well-defined specifications. The price in this first contract is deferred. The bank asks a specialized manufacturer to manufacture the equipment according to the buyer's required specifications. The payment of the price to the manufacturer may be gradual, if he needs to finance the production stage.

Participatory finance of trade operations
Participatory finance involves the participation of the financier in the profits and losses brought in by the means of either reselling the financed goods or incorporating them into an income-generating production process. Participatory finance is normally the preserve of financial intermediaries, because business firms would, in normal circumstances, prefer to provide their customers with the required credit rather than sharing with them the risks inherent in their activities. Financial institutions may provide participatory finance either to the buyers of the goods or to the sellers. In the latter case this is considered as a form of financial support which allows the sellers to extend credit to their customers over and above their own resources; that is, it is viewed as an alternative to conventional refinancing. It was shown earlier in this chapter that this form of finance is practically a necessary condition for the existence of sellers' credit.

The purpose of the partnership
A bank–trader partnership aims here at providing traders with external resources that enable them to extend credit to their customers beyond what is permitted by their own resources. Banks may enter into partnership arrangements with sellers at all levels: producers, wholesalers and retailers. Exporters, extending suppliers' credit to their foreign customers as well as importers reselling on credit to their national customers, may also benefit from this form of financial back-up provided by Islamic banks on a PLS basis.

The subject matter of the partnership
The bank and the seller will contribute, jointly and according to pre-agreed proportions, the capital needed to buy certain well-specified goods and to market them. The funds raised may be assigned for the following uses:

- To buy for cash domestic or foreign goods for subsequent resale on credit.
- To buy for cash domestic or foreign capital goods for subsequent leasing.[10]
- To buy on advance payment finished goods for subsequent resale on a cash basis.
- To buy on advance payment finished goods for subsequent resale on credit.

It should be pointed out that, in the case where the financing is provided to a producer, the subject matter of the partnership is the purchase of already produced goods for subsequent resale on credit. The peculiarity of the case is that the producer will buy for the partnership and on its behalf his own goods. The validity of the transaction requires that the partnership be charged a fair price (*thaman al-mithl*) for the purchased goods.

Types of partnership
Methods of financing based on the idea of partnership between traders and financial institutions may be distinguished according to the form and the scope of the partnership. According to the first criterion, one may distinguish between *mudaraba* and *musharaka* partnerships.

Mudaraba is normally an association whereby one party, the investor, provides the capital and the other party, the agent manager, provides his efforts. In the context of the trader–bank partnership, it is obvious that the trader will be the agent–manager. However, the bank may not like to finance fully the subject matter of the partnership and prefer that the trader obtain a financial stake in the project in addition to his efforts. Similarly, traders may not always require full financing of their transactions. They may prefer using as a priority the available internal resources, and look to the banks only to fill the gap. The *Hanbalis* refer to this particular form of *mudaraba* where the agent–manager is also an investor as *sharika-wa-mudaraba*, but other schools of *fiqh* call it simply *mudaraba*. In this arrangement, the bank as an investor does not intervene in the daily management of the partnership and cannot impose a priori restrictions that would paralyse the trader's liberty of action. The bank may nevertheless impose any other conditions that would preserve its interests. It also has the right to control the faithful implementation of the contract and to check the accuracy of the *mudaraba* accounts.

In a *musharaka* arrangement, the capital is naturally contributed by the two parties, the trader and the bank. Both are also supposed to contribute their efforts. However, one might expect in a trader–bank partnership that the bank would use its intervention right only on an exceptional basis and for control purposes. The trader would, on the contrary, provide most of the managerial work. This kind of arrangement is permissible under the *'inan* type of *sharikat*, according to *Hanafi* and *Hanbali* teachings (Ibn Qudama, n.d., p. 26; Ibn 'Abidin, n.d., p. 312).

The differences between the two arrangements are, in the present context, minimal. In both cases, capital is contributed by the trader and the bank. The trader will provide management exclusively in the case of *mudaraba* and principally in the case of *musharaka*. Entitlement to profits and responsibility for losses are governed by the same principles.

The manager (trader) is entitled to a certain share in the profits for his efforts, but does not bear any losses, except in the cases of negligence, wilful wrongdoing or non-compliance with the terms of the partnership.[11] The remaining part of the profits and all the losses are shared among the partners in proportion to their shares in the capital. Perhaps the most important difference between the two arrangements is that, in a *musharaka*, the bank keeps the right to intervene in the management of the project each time it is deemed necessary, in spite of the delegation of authority initially to the trader. On the contrary, in the case of *mudaraba*, the bank loses its intervention right, as the conditions stipulated.

In addition to this dual classification in *mudaraba* and *musharaka*, trader–bank partnerships may be further classified according to the scope of the association. Accordingly, partnerships may be concluded for one transaction, or for all transactions of a specified nature concluded over a certain period of time. In the first case, the partnership is terminated at the end of the cash-conversion cycle of the goods; that is, once the goods are sold and their proceeds collected. In the other case, the partnership is terminated on the agreed maturity, whether the capital is again converted fully into cash or not. The latter may better suit the operational requirements of the banks, though not without raising some *shari'a* issues. Partnerships of fixed duration are certainly permissible for the *Hanbalis* and the *Hanafis*,[12] but a problem arises when part or all of the capital is not converted into cash on maturity. The problem would be solved if the traders were almost certain of their capacity to market the financed goods and to cash the price before or on maturity, or alternatively if the principle of estimated evaluation (*tandid hukmi*) was admitted. Unfortunately, this principle is not clearly accepted in the traditional *fiqh*, though it is widely practised in Islamic banks, particularly with regard to the yearly determination of the profits attributed to the *mudaraba* accounts. Subject to confirmation of *shari'a* specialists, it will be assumed in the remaining part of the chapter that it is permissible for the banks to back up the credit activity of traders on the basis of fixed-duration PLS methods.

To establish the suitability of PLS modes as an alternative to conventional refinancing of traders, two further issues need to be addressed. On one hand, there is the problem of entitlement to profit of the assets owned by the trader but used by the partnership. On the other hand, one may question the flexibility of PLS finance to meet the variable financial needs of traders.

The relationship between the partnership and the trader's other assets
The capital of the partnership covers the direct costs of purchasing and marketing the financed goods. However, the trader as a manager of the partnership will use his own assets such as transportation vehicles, warehouses and handling equipment. He may also use his own personnel (such as salespersons, accountants, cashiers) to market the merchandise of the partnership. These factors, though external to the partnership, contribute along with the capital to any profits that may be realized from the sale of the financed goods. Such costs should normally be borne by the joint partnership as a business expense or may be indirectly tied to a profit ratio agreed upon between the capital provider and the entrepreneur. Two cases should be differentiated according to whether the trader's assets and personnel are used exclusively by the partnership, or they are concurrently used for other activities of the trader, alone or in association with other financiers.

The case of exclusive use   In this case, variable expenses, such as wages and rent of assets not owned by the trader, are obviously charged to the account of the partnership. As for the assets owned by the trader, they may be rented to the partnership. But as the trader is the decision maker in the partnership, the renting of his own assets would be validated only if the rental was fair (*ujrat-al-mithl*). Alternatively, the assets may be made available to the partnership against a higher share of the trader in the profits. It was pointed out earlier that the trader is entitled by his work to a share in the profit over and above his share as a capital provider. The remuneration of the assets would be included in the share of the work, on the assumption that the assets provided by the trader are considered as his instruments of work.

The case of concurrent uses of the assets   This case raises the issue of apportioning the common costs of the trader's assets among their various users, including the partnership. The apportioning is necessarily arbitrary to one extent or another, therefore it may not be permissible, particularly in the case of *mudaraba*. Three alternative solutions may be suggested for this problem. The first solution considers that the work provided by the trader is not limited to his personal management but also includes all the material and human resources assisting him in performing his work. In return, he would obviously be entitled to a higher share in the profits.

The second suggested solution, valid only for the *musharaka* type of partnership, involves the combination of two contracts. The first contract is a *musharaka* contract between the trader and the bank according to which the two parties will contribute the capital needed to just cover the cost of purchasing the goods and conveying them to the warehouses of the trader. The latter will not perform any additional work under the *musharaka* contract. The profits will therefore be shared proportionately to the capital. Now the partnership, as an independent entity, will enter with the trader in a marketing contract whereby the latter will take all necessary actions to market on the best possible conditions the goods entrusted to him by the partnership. He will bear all the costs entailed by this marketing activity and will be paid, in return, agreed-upon fees. The marketing contract may take the legal form of *ju'alah*.

The third solution is based on the opinion of the *Hanafis* and the *Malikis* (Ibn Qudama, n.d., pp. 7–8; Muaq, n.d., p. 124) validating the contribution to the capital of a partnership with the services rendered by an asset, while the asset itself remains the property of its owner. Applied to our case, the trader will have three different contributions: part of the capital, the services rendered by his assets and his work, while the bank will contribute the remaining part of the capital. The trader will therefore be entitled to a further share in the profits for the services of the assets but will ensure that these services are effectively provided and consequently bear all the related costs.

PLS techniques as alternatives to the refinancing of sellers' credit
In an interest-based system the seller takes two different decisions at two different times. First, he decides at the time of the sale whether to extend credit to the customer or not, and in the affirmative on what terms. This decision is normally taken in the light of a pre-established credit extension policy. Then the seller will have to decide to keep the resulting claim in his portfolio until maturity or to sell it at a discount. Since this refinancing decision may be taken at any moment between the time of the sale and the maturity of the

claim, the seller is able to respond in a flexible manner to any unexpected changes in his liquidity position. If money is suddenly tight, the seller may sell more claims and improve his liquidity position. On the contrary, if the seller is unexpectedly overliquid, he may hold more claims in the portfolio.

In a PLS Islamic system, the timing of the two decisions is reversed. Before buying the goods that will be subsequently sold on credit, the seller should anticipate his sales and the demand for credit, adopt a credit extension policy and estimate the amount of external finance needed to implement that policy. A partnership contract with the bank is therefore concluded prior to the purchase of the goods, while the credit to the customers will be extended at the time of sale. It is clear that, if the expectations regarding the demand for the sellers' goods and/or credit will prove later to be mistaken, the seller may be locked in undesirable positions of either excess or short liquidity.

If the partnership technique was to be adopted by traders as an alternative to bank refinancing, the above rigidity would need to be removed. One way to do it is to consider that the capital subscribed to at the beginning of the partnership would not be paid up in full. Part of it would be callable by the trader when a need arises. Furthermore the trader may at any time use his excess liquidity to pay back part of the capital contributed by the bank, thus increasing his share in the partnership. The profits and losses would be shared on the basis of the amounts contributed and the length of time they remained with the partnership. This suggested solution is also inspired by the current practice of Islamic banks with regard to investment deposits. It should, however, be ensured that it does not violate any established *shari'a* principle.

Participatory finance of standard commodities[13]
The developments of the previous section have shown how participatory finance can be used by Islamic banks to provide the required support to the sellers' credit activity. In the following paragraphs, we will show how Islamic banks can also provide participatory finance directly to the buyers. Banks may enter into partnership arrangements either with traders or with producers for the short to medium term.

Bank–middlemen partnerships
The purpose of this type of partnership is to give the trader the means to buy for cash finished goods for subsequent resale also on a cash basis. The financing is provided to the trader as a buyer and should conceptually be differentiated from the financing provided to him as a seller to enable him to extend credit to his customers. In practice, the two forms of financing may be confused and the bank may enter with a middleman into a partnership, with the purpose of buying goods for cash or on advance payment and selling them on credit.

Bank–trader partnerships are operationally the same, whether the trader is considered as a seller or as a buyer. The classification of the partnerships, according to the legal form and the scope of association, which was undertaken earlier, remains valid here too.

The type of partnership considered here is particularly appropriate for the financing of importers, considered as buyers of foreign goods. It is actually practised in Sudan, particularly by the Sudanese Islamic Bank, for the financing of domestic and foreign trade on a *musharaka* basis (Khaleefa, 1993, pp. 41–2).

Bank–producer partnerships

The objective of this type of partnership is to provide the producer with the funds required to buy raw materials, intermediate goods or capital goods necessary to carry on his productive activity. Contrary to the partnerships presented earlier, the financed goods are not, in the present case, acquired simply for resale but rather to be part of a production process, the outcome of which (profits or losses) will be shared between the bank and the producer.

In the context of trade finance,[14] the financed equipment is seldom used independently. Usually, it is a question of acquiring some equipment for expansion, modernization or replacement purposes. The newly acquired equipment will contribute jointly with existing equipment to the production activity of the beneficiary. Therefore it would not be possible to identify profits that can be separately attributed to the partnership. This inseparability problem is also raised in the case of partnership financing of the purchase of production inputs. Here also, any profits that may accrue are a joint product of the partnership and other factors external to it, such as the equipment owned by the producer.

Assuming that the producer is not willing to include his own equipment in the partnership, the problem may be solved on the basis of the idea of *musharaka* with the services rendered by the fixed asset while the asset itself remains the property of its owner. It was pointed out earlier that this type of *musharaka* is validated by the *Hanafis* and the *Malikis*. The bank–producer partnership will therefore take the form of *sharikat `inan*, the capital of which is composed of (a) the funds provided by the bank for the purpose of buying the equipment and/or the inputs; (b) the funds contributed by the producer for the same purpose; and (c) the services provided by the real assets owned by the producer and utilized by the partnership.

If the partnership contract assigns the management to the producer, the profits will be divided into four parts, one for the management and one for each one of the three components of the capital. The expenses needed to make the real assets render the services expected from them are borne by their owner, the producer.

Market financing of trade operations

Traders may satisfy their financing needs directly on financial markets. They may issue PLS securities, either to buy capital goods or to refinance their credit portfolio. For the latter, the issue of PLS securities plays the same role as the bank–trader partnerships. The main difference is that, in this case, the seller taps a wide range of savers (individual as well as institutional) for the needed finance, instead of relying on his bilateral relationship with a financial intermediary. Islamic banks have an effective role to play on these markets. Through their participation in Islamic investment funds, they can contribute to the indirect long-term financing of capital goods on the one hand and deepen the nascent Islamic financial markets on the other.

Nature of the PLS securities

A PLS security is a title of ownership of a common share in the net worth of a project and, as such, it shares in the profits and losses that may arise from the project's operation. The object of ownership varies according to the nature of the project in which the proceeds of the sale of the issued securities are invested, and also to the stage of investment. A seller issuing PLS securities will invest the raised funds in buying goods for cash or on advance payment and reselling or renting them on a deferred payment basis. The net worth of the project is therefore composed either of cash, commodities and debts or of a mix of them. For instance, if a seller issues certificates to buy *salam* goods that he will resell on credit, the certificates will undergo five stages. When the certificates are sold and not yet invested, they represent common ownership of cash and, when the goods are bought, they represent common ownership of debts. Later, when the goods are delivered but not yet sold, they represent common ownership of commodities. When the goods are sold on credit, they again become common ownership of debts. Finally, when the debts are collected, the certificates return to their original status as representative of common ownership of cash. When the certificates finance a flow of operations of the same type, the stages will be mixed up, and, except for the initial stage, the certificates will represent at any stage an aggregate of cash, commodities and debts.

Types of PLS securities

Similarly to the types of partnerships, the securities issued by the seller to finance his trade credit activity may take one of the following forms: (a) one-transaction *mudaraba* certificates, (b) fixed-term *mudaraba* certificates, (c) one-transaction *musharaka* certificates, and (d) fixed-term *musharaka* certificates.

The maturing of fixed-term certificates should coincide with the dates of publication of audited statements of accounts of the projects in which they are invested. Admitting the principle of evaluation as a substitute for liquidation, the holders of the certificates will, on maturity, share in the profits or losses as they appear in the audited accounts.

Negotiability of the PLS securities

Shari'a rules do not permit the sale of titles representing the common ownership of only debts or money. Furthermore, titles representing a mix of debts, money and real assets are negotiable only if the real assets are dominant.[15]

Negotiability of PLS securities issued by a seller varies according to the type of operations in which they are invested. Certificates issued for the purpose of buying capital goods for subsequent lease are negotiable all the time, except for the very short period separating the sale of the certificates and the purchase of the goods. On the contrary, one-transaction certificates issued for 'refinancing' credit sales start to be negotiable once the goods are possessed by the seller, but lose their negotiability as soon as the accumulating debts become dominant. In the case of certificates issued to 'refinance' the credit sales of a trader during a fixed period of time, the intermingled schedule of purchases and sales makes the negotiability of the certificates unknown a priori. It all depends on the weight of the inventories in the financial aggregate owned by the holders of the certificates.

Negotiability of the certificates is also subject to the general conditions of validity of sales contracts, particularly the condition of knowledge of the subject-matter of the contract. As it is admitted that the certificates are not exchanged per se, but for what they represent, the sale of certificates should only occur when sufficient information is available on the assets and liabilities of the project in which the certificates are invested (Hassan, 1990, p. 39). This is admittedly the case after audited accounts of the project are made public, but could it still be the case if the certificates were exchanged more frequently and even continuously, as is the practice in the financial markets? Would it be possible reasonably to assume that the administration of the stock exchange makes available to the buyers and sellers of the certificates instantaneous relevant information that would avoid an exorbitant lack of knowledge (*jahl fahish*)? The final word is left to the Islamic jurists, but one could not refrain from tentatively replying in the negative.[16]

Obligations of the seller as an issuer of certificates
The issue of PLS certificates creates a partnership between the sellers and the buyers of the certificates. The announcement of the issue is considered as a public offer of intent (*ijab*) and the subscription of investors as an acceptance (*qabul*). The announcement should therefore contain all the terms and conditions required for a partnership contract. The seller should clearly indicate the transaction or activity for which the certificates are issued and the method of determining and distributing the profits and losses. A feasibility study containing in particular the expected return will be attached to the prospectus (Hassan, 1990, p. 36).

The seller should keep separate accounts for the partnership. All the purchase, lease and sale contracts concluded by the seller on behalf of the holders of the certificates should clearly mention that the goods are owned by the partnership and therefore unambiguously separated from other assets owned by the seller. The law regulating the issue of PLS certificates should ensure that the issue of certificates suffices for the legal establishment of the partnership without the need for any specific registration.

The seller should indicate, in the prospectus announcing the issue of the certificates, whether they are deemed negotiable or not. In the case of negotiable certificates, the seller should guarantee that real assets of the project will at no time become less than 50 per cent. If the certificates may become non-negotiable at some future date, the seller will undertake to inform the holders of the certificates of any change in the structure of the net worth which may prevent their negotiability.

The case of different issues financing the same activity
A seller may like to finance his commercial activity by issuing certificates at regular intervals, say quarterly. The proceeds of different issues may be used to finance the same transactions. This may be the case for example when the purchases of a quarter are financed with the proceeds of that quarter's issue in addition to part of the proceeds of previous issues which have completed the cash conversion cycle. This raises the question of the entitlement of different issues' certificates to the end-period result. Two cases may be differentiated according to whether the issues and the publication of audited accounts are synchronized or not.

The synchronization case   It is assumed here that the seller is able to produce and publish audited accounts periodically, say every quarter. The issues are issued at the same periodicity (for example, the quarter) and for maturities which are multiples of the basic period. Certificates of different issues will have the same face value, but newly issued certificates will be subscribed at the book value of old certificates as it appears from the audited accounts or at the market value if they are exchanged in the secondary market. Profits and losses will be shared in the same way by the holders of old and new certificates: proportionately to the face value of their certificates.[17] This method is theoretically equivalent to the dissolution of the partnership at the end of each period and the start of a new one. The new subscribers will therefore share only in the profits and losses generated after they join the common pool.

The diachronic case   In this case, the seller is supposed to need to issue certificates at a frequency which is higher than the periodicity of publishing audited accounts. For instance, he may need to issue certificates every quarter, while he can produce audited accounts only annually.

Sharing in the profits and losses proportionately to the face value of the certificates held by each investor, irrespective of their dates of issue, is of course unjust. The alternative is to consider that each certificate shares in the profits and losses declared at the end of the year proportionately to the product of its duration and its face value.[18] This again is inspired by Islamic banks' practice of sharing the profits among the holders of *mudaraba* accounts in proportion to both the amount invested and the duration of investment. Contrary to the previous case, the holders of new certificates share in the result of the whole year's activities in which they and the old certificates are invested and not solely in the outcome of the operations conducted after their subscription.

Benefits and limitations of PLS securities with respect to trade financing
The attractiveness of financing by the means of issuing securities in general lies in its ability to satisfy the liquidity preference of the savers and the need of the firms for stable investments. Negotiability is, however, of vital importance for the securities to perform their function of transforming short-term savings into medium to long-term investments.

As pointed out earlier, the negotiability of PLS securities issued by the sellers is expected to face serious difficulties, among which the following two may be mentioned: the absence of organized stock markets providing the required information for the negotiability of the certificates; and the variable structure of the financial aggregate owned by the certificates, with the possibility for cash balances and debts to become at some stages dominant, thus preventing the negotiability of the certificates.

Furthermore, the issue of PLS securities by the sellers may itself face difficulties. On the one hand, for an issuer to place his certificates successfully, he should inspire the confidence of savers. This implies a strong financial basis and sound accounting and auditing procedures. Even in developed economies, it was noted that only very strong firms can actually issue commercial paper. On the other hand, PLS certificates are risk sharing and it would be very risky for an individual investor to put his money in a single transaction or even in the activity of a single seller. It is therefore expected that only banks and other institutional investors who can hold a diversified portfolio would subscribe to the sellers' PLS securities.

The role of Islamic banks
Capital goods require medium to long-term financing. Banks may use short-term resources to provide long-term finance, but only to a limited extent. This 'transformation' should be operated with caution, for fear of facing serious liquidity problems.[19]

A more dependable alternative would be to provide medium- and long-term finance indirectly through 'Investment Funds'. The objective of these funds is to raise money for medium- and long-term finance through the issue of negotiable securities,[20] thus reconciling the liquidity preference of the investors and the need of the business firms for stable and longer-term finance. Investment funds may be established as banks' subsidiaries or as independent financial institutions. They are organized alternatively on the lines of *musharaka* or *mudaraba*. They issue shares or *mudaraba* certificates of different maturities.

Investment funds provide medium- and long-term finance to business firms on credit or a participatory basis along the same lines developed earlier with respect to bank finance. Banks would therefore contribute indirectly to meet the medium- and long-term financial needs of traders through holding a portfolio of shares and *mudaraba* certificates issued by investment funds.[21] This indirect method of financing has the decisive advantage of allowing the banks to respect their liquidity constraint. This is achieved by means of two factors: the possibility to form a portfolio that matches the maturity structure of the bank's deposits and the purchased securities; and the ability to liquidate part of the portfolio to meet any net outflow of deposits that may occur unexpectedly.

Conclusion

An Islamic system of trade finance (see Table 12.1) has the following features:

- the system admits both credit and PLS methods of finance;
- business credit needs to be supported by financial institutions and the only way this support can be provided is on a PLS basis;
- banks may provide PLS finance to the buyers for the purpose of covering the cost of the purchased goods or to sellers for the purpose of supporting their credit activity;
- in general, banks provide finance directly to the beneficiaries but, when the maturity is rather long, finance may be provided indirectly through investment funds.

Islamic banks may either confine their role to financial intermediation through partnership arrangements with traders or carry out, in addition, some functions of the trader. Full specialization of Islamic banks in PLS finance is supposed to present some attractive advantages. One of them is that it conforms to an efficient division of labour between traders and financial institutions, each group specializing in the activities where it holds a definite comparative advantage. Financial institutions would not deal in the exchange of goods where they are at a disadvantage compared to traders, and these would deal in credit only as an adjunct to their principal trading activity. The other advantage of full specialization is that the use of *murabaha*-based finance does not require the reliance on a prior promise to buy, whether binding or not.[22] Hence the use of *murabaha*-based techniques becomes unambiguously in line with *shari'a*. However, in a free choice environment, Islamic banks would decide to specialize in PLS finance only if they were motivated to do so. Assuming that a bank is convinced that both credit and PLS finance are legitimate from the *shari'a* point of view,[23] it will choose the alternative which maximizes its profit. A problem may arise if the free choice of a profit-maximizing bank leads to a systematic preference for credit modes. Indeed PLS finance is accredited in the literature (Siddiqi, 1991) as having a positive impact on real macroeconomic aggregates, such as the growth rate, the product mix of the GDP or the income distribution. The preference for the credit modes would be in this case suboptimal. It may be argued that, in such a situation, Islamic banks should accept less than maximum profits in order to come closer to the optimum. However, as long as Islamic banks do not use questionable means, there seems to be no rationale for them not to pursue a profit-maximization objective.[24] They

Table 12.1   A brief account of the methods of financing trade transactions in an Islamic framework

Beneficiary	Purpose of the financing	Sellers' finance		Banks' finance Techniques used
		Financier	Techniques used	
Consumers	purchase of current consumer goods	mostly retailers	credit *murabaha*	financial *murabaha*
	purchase of durables	ditto	credit *murabaha* instalment sale *ijara-wa-iqtina* (I & I)	financial *murabaha* instalment sale I & I on prior promise
Middlemen	build up inventories supporting the beneficiary's credit activity ('refinancing')	producers and wholesalers	credit *murabaha* instalment sale	financial *murabaha* instalment sale on prior promise PLS (bank–buyer partnership) PLS (bank–seller partnership)
Producers	purchase of inputs	upstream producers (producers of the inputs) wholesalers downstream producers (buyers of processed goods) middlemen specialized in marketing the processed goods	credit *murabaha* *salam* (processed goods)	financial *murabaha* PLS (bank–buyer partnership) *salam* (purchase of the processed goods on the basis of a third party's promise to buy the same goods)
	purchase of standard capital goods	equipment producers traders leasing companies	instalment sale I & I	instalment sale I & I on prior promise PLS (bank–buyer partnership)
	purchase of buyer-specific capital goods (down payment required)			*istisnaa*-cum-instalment sale (on a binding prior promise to buy) two-tier *istisnaa*
	supporting the beneficiary's credit activity ('refinancing')			PLS (bank–seller partnership)

may be even more forcefully required to do so, given their status of trustees investing the funds deposited with them by others. It is the responsibility of governments to solve the problem by adopting policies that would prompt banks to take optimum-compatible decisions; that is, to use PLS methods of finance. Such correcting policies include the provision of subsidies to banks and the adoption of cost-reducing measures.

Notes

1. Encyclopedia Britannica defines credit as a 'transaction between two parties, in which one . . . supplies money, goods or securities in return for a promised future payment by the other . . .'. This definition clearly admits as a credit both the sale with a deferred price and the sale with advance payment for future delivery.
2. These and other techniques mentioned in the present study refer to contracts which have their origin in the classical Islamic commercial law. However, being frequently used in contemporary Islamic banking literature, these contracts are introduced here only briefly, assuming that the reader is familiar with the definitions and basic related conditions.
3. It is usually accompanied by a reciprocal promise to sell issued by the financier, though it is not theoretically a necessary condition for the existence of this financing technique.
4. When first introduced (Hamoud, 1985), this financing technique was termed *'Murabaha* Sale for the Orderer of Purchase'. But the usage tended to prefer the much shorter term of *'murabaha'*, thus leading to a blurring of the distinction between the original meaning of the word and its new acceptance. The term 'financial *murabaha'*, suggested here, has the double advantage of shortness and clarity. It evokes the known distinction between 'lease' (operating lease) and 'financial lease'.
5. Contemporary Muslim jurists hold divergent views with regard to the binding or non-binding nature of the promise to buy or to sell. This divergence of views is reflected in the practices of Islamic banks, some of which do not consider the customer's promise binding, while others do.
6. However, the idea of imposing an ex post fine on delinquent debtors is currently debated among *Shari'a* Jurists.
7. As opposed to monetary transactions.
8. The *Fiqh* Academy approved one form of *ijara-wa-iqtina*, in which the lessee will be given the option to buy the leased property at the end of the lease contract and at the market price. See Resolution no. 6 of the fifth session of the Council of the Islamic *Fiqh* Academy.
9. Traditional *fiqh* requires that the subject matter of a *salam* contract should not be the product of a designated field or orchard (or factory) because its availability may be in doubt at the time of delivery.
10. The form of leasing considered here as a trade financing technique involves the sale of usufruct of equipment associated with a promise to sell or to give the equipment to the lessee at the end of the lease period (called in the contemporary literature *ijara-wa-iqtina*); this financing technique is practically very close to an *instalment* sale of the equipment.
11. He of course loses the opportunity cost of his work as a manager.
12. A minority opinion within the *Hanafi* school does not accept the validity of *musharaka* with fixed duration.
13. A priori participatory techniques may also be used to finance buyer-specific goods. However, it was shown earlier that *istisnaa* techniques are more appropriate in this case.
14. As opposed to project finance.
15. See Resolution 5 of the 4th session of the Council of the Islamic Fiqh Academy.
16. The same would also apply to the sale of common shares.
17. Except for the issuer, who is entitled to a higher share for his work.
18. Since all certificates are issued at the same face value, this method amounts to sharing the profits proportionately to the duration.
19. It may be noted in passing that Islamic banks are less inclined than conventional banks to use tier-matched portfolios, because they are less exposed to the 'interest rate risk'.
20. Negotiability of the securities issued by investment funds is subject to the same comments made above with respect to PLS securities issued by traders.
21. Investment funds securities may be subscribed not only by banks, but also by other institutional as well as individual investors.
22. In the context of full specialization, *murabaha* finance is used exclusively by traders.
23. Either because it does not consider the promise as binding or because it is convinced of the correctness of the view held by some Jurists who consider the promise to buy as binding.
24. Islamic economics literature admits that the legitimacy of the pursuit of self-interest should be bounded by the moral values of Islam. See Chapra (1992).

Bibliography

Aspinwall, R.C. and R.A. Eisenbeis (eds) (1985), *Handbook for Banking Strategy*, New York: Wiley Interscience.

Chapra, M. Umer (1992), *Islam and the Economic Challenge*, Leicester & Herndon: The Islamic Foundation & the International Institute of Islamic Thought.

Dunia, Shawqi A. (1990), *Al Ju`ala wal `Istisna': Tahlil fiqhi wa iqtisadi*, Jeddah: IRTI.

Hamoud, Sami H. (1985), *Islamic Banking*, London: Arabian Information.

Hassan, Hussein H. (1990), 'Financial intermediation in the framework of *Shari'a*', in M. Ariff and M.A. Mannan (eds), *Developing a System of Financial Instruments*, Jeddah: IRTI.

Ibn 'Abidin (n.d.), *Radd al-Muhtar*, Beirut: Dar Ihya at-Turath al-Arabi.

Ibn Qudama, Muaffaqud-din (n.d.), *Al-Mughni*, Riyadh: Matba'at Al-Imam.

Islamic Fiqh Academy (n.d.). *Recommendations and Resolutions, 1406H-1409H (1985–1988)*, Jeddah.

Khaleefa, Mohamed O. (1993), 'Islamic banking in Sudan's rural sector', *Islamic Economic Studies*, **1** (Rajab 1414H/December), 37–55.

Muaq (al) (n.d.), *at-Taj wal-Ikleel*, Tripoli: Maktabat an-Najah.

Omar, Mohammed A. (1992), *al-Itar ash-Shar'i wa'l iqtisadi wa'l muhasabi li bay` is-salam*, Jeddah: IRTI.

Saadallah, Ridha M. (1999), *Financing Trade in an Islamic Economy,* Jeddah: IRTI.

Saleh, Nabil A. (1992), *Unlawful Gain and Legitimate Profit in Islamic Law*, 2nd edn, Arab & Islamic Law Series, London: Graham & Trotman.

Siddiqi, Muhammad N. (1991), 'Some economic aspects of mudarabah', *Review of Islamic Economics*, 1–2 (1411H/1991), 21–34.

13 Securitization in Islam
Mohammed Obaidullah

Nature of securitization

Securitization is a process that involves pooling, packaging and transformation of financial assets into securities. It is a way of imparting liquidity to financial assets as securities
are relatively more easily tradeable than the assets. A direct sale of assets, such as housing
loans, auto loans and credit card receivables by one financial institution to another (group
of) financial institution(s) is more difficult and less efficient than a sale of securities to a
large number of investors in an active financial market. Securities naturally enjoy much
greater liquidity in the primary as well as secondary markets.

   Securitization has a short history. It did not develop until the 1970s and 1980s. Since then,
however, the global securitization market has witnessed phenomenal growth with securitization of mortgage loans alone passing the US$4 trillion mark in 2003, up from a level of
US$2 trillion barely five years earlier (Dualeh, 1998). Securitization is a relatively new phe-
nomenon in Muslim economies of the Middle East–North Africa (MENA) and South-East
Asia. As these countries have moved slowly but steadily towards the Islamization of their
financial systems, a question that naturally confronts the policymakers and regulators is: is
securitization, as practised in mainstream developed markets, permissible in Islam? What
are the elements, if any, that would render it illicit? Is it possible to eliminate such elements
from the process and make it *shari'a*-compliant while retaining all the economic benefits of
securitization? In what follows, we focus on these questions. We begin with a closer analysis of securitization as it is practised in the mainstream financial markets. Then we look at
the *shari'a* test. The next section seeks to present the Islamic alternative. Finally, we discuss
a few actual practices of Islamic securitization.

Basic structure of securitization

Securitization of loans and other assets is a simple way of raising additional funds. It
involves a financial institution setting aside a group of income-earning assets, such as
housing loans, car loans and credit card receivables and to sell securities or financial
claims against those assets in the open market. As income from the assets is generated, it
flows to the holders of the securities. In effect, assets are transformed into securities. The
securitizing institution receives the money it originally expended to acquire the assets.
There are several parties involved in the process:

1.   The financial institution from which the assets are pooled is called the originator.
2.   The assets are then sold and passed on to an issuer, called a special purpose entity
     (SPE). The SPE has a distinct legal identity separate from the originator – even while
     the same financial institution creates this entity. This implies that the credit quality of
     the pool of assets is independent of the credit standing of the originator. Even if the
     originator goes bankrupt, this event will not affect the credit status of the assets in
     the pool.

191

3. A trustee is usually appointed to ensure that the issuer fulfils all the requirements of transfer of assets and provides all related services promised earlier. The trustee collects and disburses to investors any cash flows generated by the pooled assets.
4. Credit guarantee or enhancement is provided by independent financial institution(s) as added protection to security holders.
5. A liquidity provider may supply back-up liquidity in the form of liquidity guarantees or enhancement.

A simple process of securitization is presented diagrammatically in Figure 13.1. There are several variants of securities that are structured through this process. The most common types are outlined below. First, a pass-through security represents direct ownership in a portfolio of assets that are usually similar in terms of maturity, yield and quality. The originator services the portfolio, makes collections and passes them on, less a servicing fee, to the investors. Ownership of the assets in the portfolio lies with the investors. Thus pass-throughs are not debt obligations of the originator and do not appear on the originator's financial statement.

Second, another type of securitization results in an asset-backed bond (ABB). Like pass-throughs, an ABB is collateralized by a portfolio of assets, or sometimes by a portfolio of

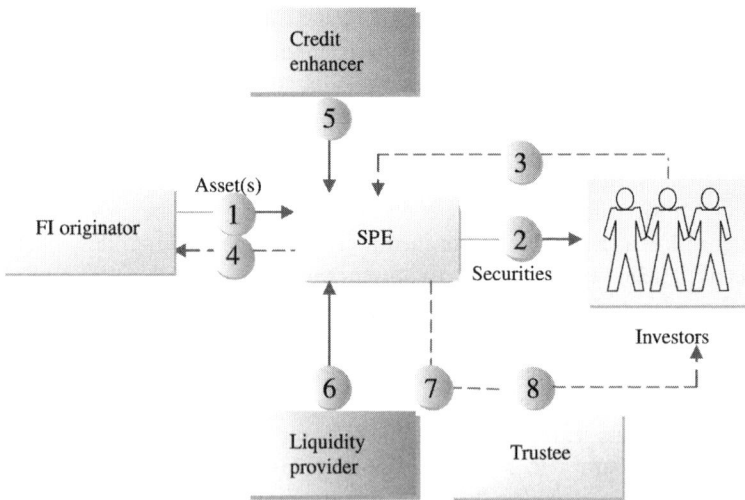

Broken line indicates the flow of funds

Notes
1   Securitizing FI or originator pools and packages assets and sells to SPE;
2   SPE sells securities to investors;
3   SPE collects funds from investors;
4   SPE pays to originator the sale price of assets;
5   Independent FI provides credit enhancement;
6   Independent FI provides liquidity enhancement;
7   SPE passes on incomes from assets to investors in future;
8   Trustee ensures that the issuer fulfils all its commitments relating to transfer of assets, distribution of income and the like.

Figure 13.1   Process of securitization in mainstream markets

pass-throughs. The ABB is a debt obligation of the issuer, so the portfolio of assets used as collateral remains on the issuer's books as assets, and the ABBs are reported as a liability. Also the cash flows from the collateral are not allotted to the investors. They are often reconfigured, with the residual often remaining with the issuer/originator. One important aspect of the ABBs is that they are overcollateralized, that is, the value of the underlying assets is significantly in excess of the total obligation. This is largely done in order to provide some level of comfort to the investors.

A third type of securitization creates what is known as the pay-through bond. A pay-through combines some of the features of the pass-through with those of the ABB. Like an ABB, a pay-through is collateralized by a pool of assets and appears on the issuer's balance sheet as debt. Like a pass-through, the cash flows from the assets are dedicated to servicing the bond.

The process of securitization in some cases also involves the creation of commercial paper and preferred stock.

Islamic evaluation of conventional securitization

The need for liquidity is well recognized in the Islamic framework. Bakar (1996) considers that *al-suyulah* (liquidity) has been an integral part of Islamic commercial law. The study cites various instances of how classical Islamic law provides for *al-suyulah* that is a fundamental requirement for development of an Islamic capital market. It follows, therefore, that the process of securitization that essentially imparts liquidity to financial assets of an Islamic financial institution, such as loans and receivables, has clear economic benefits or *maslaha* in the *fiqhi* sense.

Islamic financial institutions cannot operate in isolated and segregated markets and have to compete with mainstream financial institutions. It is a fact that the mainstream financial sector offers diversified investment and financing products, with access to interbank and capital markets. Whatever may be the requirement, there is always a choice of flexible solutions. In comparison, the modern Islamic financial sector is only 30 years old, and its institutions and infrastructure are relatively much less developed. At the same time, the Islamic institutions have been required to adhere to mainstream regulatory stipulations while meeting *shari'a* requirements. Securitization can play an important role in strengthening these institutions by providing a means to impart liquidity to assets and to raise additional funds.

While the need for liquidity is hardly overemphasized, the process of imparting liquidity through securitization must not violate other, more fundamental, tenets of Islamic finance, such as freedom from *riba* and *gharar*. Mainstream securitization processes as highlighted earlier at times violate these essential norms. Cases where such violation is possible are highlighted below.

First, the underlying asset base in the case of conventional securitization includes loans and other receivables that involve *riba*. Obviously, this is not permissible. The asset base clearly must be free from *riba* and other forbidden elements. Note that the underlying assets may be physical or financial (representing ownership of physical assets). While equity in contrast to interest-bearing bonds appears to be a permissible financial asset that can form part of the pool, such equity must not represent ownership of an institution dealing with interest or manufacture of *haram* items, such as alcohol or pork. Further, where the pool of assets (to be securitized) represents a combination of physical assets (such as equipment, buildings) and financial claims (such as receivables), the former must account for a majority or at least 51 per cent of the total pool. If the condition is not met, then the asset pool cannot be sold at a negotiated or market price. The rationale here is that, since debt or money in Islam cannot be transferred at a premium or discount, the pool of assets (if in the nature of receivables or debt) can only be transferred at its par value. However, if the pool represents a combination of physical assets and debts, its sale will be governed by its dominant component (that is, physical assets). Thus the pool of assets can now be transferred at a negotiated price. By the same token, a security representing part-ownership of the pool of assets can now be transferred at a negotiated price too.

Second, of the above three securitization structures, the pass-through is perhaps the structure closest to satisfying a strict interpretation of Islamic norms. The pay-through, the ABB and the commercial paper involve debt, which makes explicit use of interest. Therefore, only a pass-through with an underlying pool of assets structured as equity or leasing that do not make use of interest either explicitly or implicitly would qualify in the Islamic framework.

Third, credit enhancement is an integral part of the securitization process. When credit enhancement is for a fee that is related to the quantum of facility, this comes dangerously close to *riba* and is rightly frowned upon by *shari'a* scholars. Islamic law provides for credit guarantees through the *kafala* mechanism. However, *kafala* does not allow for a fee in the conventional sense. What is needed, therefore, is to bring in a possibility of profit sharing for the credit enhancer.

Fourth, like credit enhancement, liquidity enhancement too comes under a cloud in the Islamic framework. While this is easily achieved in an interest-based scenario, the Islamic framework provides for short-term *qard hasan* or interest-free loans. Thus, while liquidity enhancement could be provided by independent financial institutions in the conventional framework, this is possible in Islamic securitization only when there is no financial reward for the provider. Liquidity back-up could perhaps be provided by the securitizing financial institution or third-party central monetary authority that is interested in the success of the process of securitization. It may be noted here that short-term liquidity back-up could perhaps be provided by independent financial institutions in a manner similar to some so-called Islamic banking practices through the use of *bai'al-inah* and *tawarruq*. However, these facilities are deemed highly controversial and are best left out of the Islamic framework.

The Islamic alternative
In order to present a securitization structure that is fully *shari'a*-compliant, one may begin with the SPE that is specifically created for the purpose. The SPE in Islamic securitization could take the form of a *mudaraba* comprising investors and the securitizing company as the *mudarib*. The *mudarib* may legitimately claim its share in the surplus. Alternatively, the securitizing company may act as an agent or *wakil* of all the investors (that are organized as a *musharaka* company).

The next issue relates to the nature of assets to be securitized. Islamic financial institutions have an asset structure that is primarily trade-based, such as *murabaha* (cost-plus sale) with deferred payment facility or *bai-bi-thamin ajil* and leasing-based, such as *ijara* (Shabbir, 2002). Equity or partnership-based assets account for a small percentage of the total assets for a variety of reasons. Thus it is natural for Islamic financial institutions to consider securitization of trade receivables as the first choice.

Murabaha or *bai-bi-thamin ajil* (BBA) results in a transfer of ownership of the physical commodity to the buyer and the financial institution's assets now comprise the receivables that are a form of debt. Such assets, therefore, can only be transferred to the SPE at par. The transfer would be in the nature of a *hawalat-al-dayn* and not a sale or *bai*. Where the SPE is a *musharaka* company of investors, the *musharaka* securities would represent part-ownership of this pool of assets. And since each security now represents a debt (*shahadah al-dayn*), it can only be transferred at par. Thus a secondary market in such Islamic debt securities is completely ruled out.

A variation of the *murabaha*–BBA-based securitization involves a process of sale and buy-back. This is done purely as a way to generate additional funds for the securitizing company. The process begins with identifying a pool of physical assets currently owned by the securitizing company. The assets are sold to the SPE organized as a *mudaraba* or *musharaka* and then bought back at a premium on a deferred payment basis. The higher deferred income is then passed on to the investors on a pro rata basis (in proportion to their stake in the SPE). This process is highlighted in Figure 13.2.

What is to be noted in the above process is the use of sale and buy-back (*bai'al-inah*) which effectively amounts to *riba*-based borrowing. Sale and buy-back of assets enables delinking of the financing from the underlying asset. The mechanism, therefore, is not acceptable in the Islamic framework. Nevertheless, it has been widely used by investment bankers in Malaysia. Another forbidden mechanism has also been used by these bankers to impart liquidity to the instruments: sale of debt at a discount or at a negotiated price (*bai-al-dayn*). The *sukuk-al-murabaha* created through the aforesaid mechanism can be traded freely at any mutually negotiated price only if sale of debt at a discount is permissible. However, it is not.

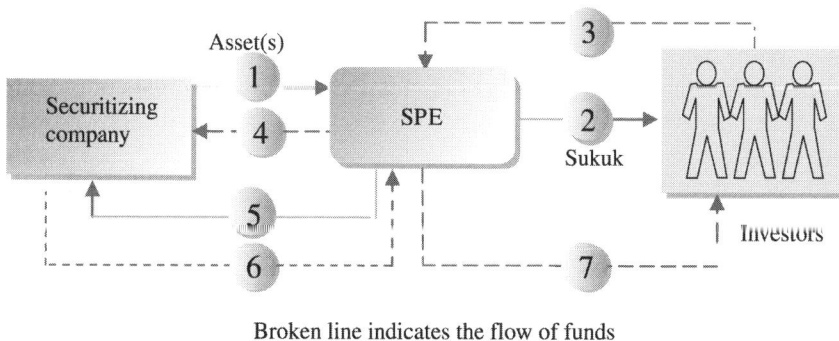

Broken line indicates the flow of funds

Notes:
1   Company identifies, pools physical assets and sells them to SPE (*musharaka* or *mudaraba*);
2   SPE issues securities to investors against these assets;
3   SPE collects funds from investors;
4   SPE pays to company the sale price of assets;
5   Company buys back assets on deferred payment basis;
6   SPE receives payments by company in future;
7   SPE passes on payments by company to investors after deducting *mudarib* share or *wakala* fee.

Figure 13.2   Murabaha-*based securitization*

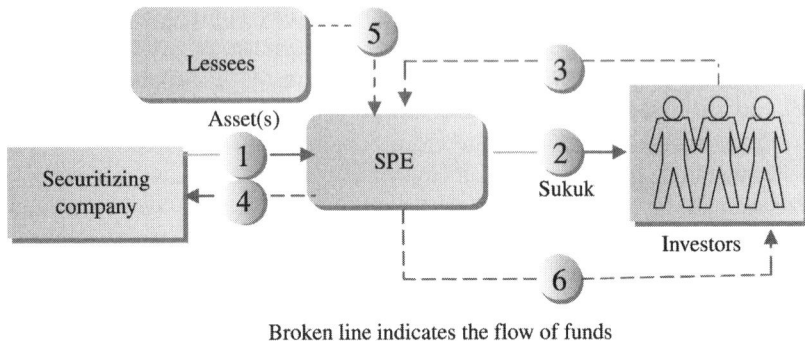

Broken line indicates the flow of funds

Notes:
1   Company identifies, pools physical assets and sells them to SPE (structured as a *musharaka* or *mudaraba*);
2   SPE issues securities to investors against these assets;
3   SPE collects funds from investors;
4   SPE pays to company the sale price of assets;
5   SPE receives *ijara* rentals from lessees in future;
6   SPE passes on *ijara* rentals to investors after deducting *mudarib* share or *wakala* fee.

Figure 13.3   Ijara-*based securitization*

The above problems are taken care of in *ijara*-based securitization. *Ijara* or Islamic leasing, though less popular as an asset than *murabaha*, offers much greater flexibility. *Ijara*-based securitization involves securitization of physical assets and not of financial claims. It involves transfer of ownership of physical assets and, consequently, all risks and rewards of ownership of existing assets of the company to the SPE representing investors. Ownership of SPE is now made equivalent to ownership of the physical assets that are given on lease against rental income. Each investor shares in the rental income on a pro rata basis. Each security called *sukuk-al-ijara* represents a pro rata ownership of physical assets as against a pro rata share in financial claim or debt in the case of *sukuk-al-murabaha*. While debt can only be transferred at par, ownership in physical assets can always be transferred at a mutually negotiated price. Thus *sukuk-al-ijara* allows for creation of a vibrant secondary market. The process of *ijara*-based securitization is presented in Figure 13.3.

In *ijara*-based securitization each investor becomes a part-owner of the group of physical assets. The assets are then given on *ijara* against future rental payments. What makes this mechanism unique is that the investors as owners of the assets are exposed to risk associated with ownership of assets and also to default risks associated with rental payments. At times, a third party is willing to bear or share in such risks, as is the case with the *sukuk-al-ijara* issued by the Bahrain Monetary Agency. We take up some such cases in the next section.

As discussed earlier, credit enhancement is an important component of the securitization process. Since the classical mechanism of *kafala* does not permit any reward for the guarantor or *kafeel*, there is a need to bring in the possibility of profit sharing. It is perhaps possible to use the *musharaka* mechanism to introduce a credit enhancer in a profit-sharing and *takaful* role. The SPE now would be a *musharaka* with a credit enhancer as one of the partners or *musharik*, and the partners would mutually guarantee one another (*takaful*). An alternative structure could be to introduce the credit enhancer as the master lessee who, in turn, subleases to the ultimate lessees. This would, of course, be possible when the securitized assets were 100 per cent *ijara*. The full *shari'a* implications of these two alternatives need to be explored further.

Islamic securitization in practice

Islamic securitization has witnessed two important phases in its short history. The first phase occurred in the 1990s with the popularization of Islamic Private Debt Securities (PDS) in Malaysia. The PDS were primarily based on securitization of *murabaha* receivables. The market for such PDS witnessed a lot of activity because of a more liberal interpretation of *fiqh* by Malaysian jurists permitting sale of debt (*bai-al-dayn*) at a negotiated price. Called *murabaha* notes issuance facility (MuNif) and *al-bai-bithamin ajil* Islamic debt securities (ABBA) these so-called Islamic securities effectively blurred the distinction between *murabaha* instruments and conventional debt instruments. For example, each one of the above *murabaha* instruments was tradeable before maturity at a discounted price. The Malaysian investment bankers went several steps further and disaggregated the instrument into zero-coupon bonds, separating the principal amount from the profit component (coupon). In both MuNif and ABBA, primary notes representing capital component and secondary notes representing profit portions were issued.

The practice, however, was found to be totally unacceptable in the Middle East and other parts of the globe. It was rightly asserted that sale of debt at a negotiated price (price that is different from the face value of debt) or at a discount opens the floodgates of *riba*-based transactions. Only if investors hold on to the instruments until maturity will the yield on the instrument constitute legitimate profit and not *riba*. The impermissibility of secondary market trading, however, severely restricted the liquidity and, therefore, attractiveness of the instrument from an investor's standpoint.

Ijara-based securitization was then seen as an ideal alternative for structuring debt securities. Such securitization took off in a big way with the issue of *ijara* certificates by the Bahrain Monetary Agency (BMA). The BMA issued, in 2001, Islamic Leasing Certificates with a five-year maturity to the value of $100 million. This issue, with bond-like characteristics, is the first of its kind by a Central Bank in the world. The securities matured in 2006 with a rental return of 5.25 per cent per annum. The *ijara* securities were issued in the capital markets to mobilize short-term deposits for the development of long-term infrastructure projects. This mobilization was effected through the securitization of government tangible assets, such as airports, roads, buildings, factories, schools, hospitals, power stations, refineries or a pool of such assets. Once these tangible assets were identified and specified, securities were issued and sold to the public. The unique feature of these securities or *sukuk* is that rental payments are guaranteed by the government, providing security and returns. Because the yield is predetermined (rental income) and the underlying assets are tangible and secured, the *ijara* certificates are also tradeable in the secondary market like any other conventional debt security.

It may be noted that, while a valid *ijara* requires that the owner of the physical assets (investors in this case) must bear the risk related to ownership and rental payments, the same is borne in this case by the government on a voluntary basis. While the *shari'a* scholars associated with BMA have found such innovative and creative financial engineering to be *shari'a*-compliant, the product is certainly deemed controversial.[1] Notwithstanding the controversies, the notion of *ijara*-based securitization, especially when issued and guaranteed by government, seems to have caught on with multiple mega issues in the offing by several governments across the Islamic world.

Another feature of the BMA securitization is that it uses a sale-and-lease-back structure. Advocates point out that, while sale-and-buy-back (*bai'al-inah*) is adjudged equivalent to *riba*-based borrowing and lending, sale-and-lease-back is not. While the former frees the financing from any linkage with the underlying assets, the latter does not and, hence, is permissible. Some recent scholars, however, have strongly asserted that sale-and-lease-back is indeed problematic. Some problem areas highlighted are as follows. One, the sale contract is supposed to be a full sale of property and usufruct. A sale conditional on leasing back or selling back includes a restriction on the buyers' ownership rights, and would invalidate sales. Two, sale of the physical asset involves sale of the object itself (*bai-al-raqabah*) as well as its usufruct (*bai-al-manfah*). The sale-and-lease-back as stipulated in securitization structures is only another form of prohibited *bai'al-inah* (same object sale–resale).[2]

Conclusion
Securitization is a means to provide liquidity to financial assets and the need for liquidity is recognized by *shari'a*. A review of the theory and practice of Islamic securitization reveals that the Islamic framework indeed provides for securitization to be undertaken in a *shari'a*-compliant manner. Conventional securitization involves *riba*. The problem of *riba* may be taken care of in several ways. The foremost requirement is that the underlying asset pool must not comprise interest-based assets, such as conventional loans or receivables. Even when underlying assets are in the nature of Islamic debt, such as *murabaha* receivables, the need to eliminate *riba* rules out sale of debt at a negotiated price. *Murabaha*-based securitization, therefore, is not an attractive proposition.

Of the three commonly found securitization structures, the pass-through structure is closest to satisfying a strict interpretation of Islamic norms. The pay-through, the ABB and the commercial paper involve debt, and make explicit use of interest. Therefore, only a pass-through with underlying pool of assets structured as equity, or *ijara* that do not make use of interest either explicitly or implicitly, would qualify in the Islamic framework.

Ijara-based securitization involves securitization of physical assets and not of financial claims. It involves transfer of ownership of physical assets and, consequently, all risks and rewards of ownership of existing assets of the company to the investors. Each security called *sukuk-al-ijara* represents a pro rata ownership of physical assets as against a pro rata share in a financial claim or debt. While debt can only be transferred at par, ownership in physical assets can always be transferred at a mutually negotiated price. Thus *sukuk-al-ijara* allows for creation of a vibrant secondary market.

Notwithstanding the fact that there are Islamically sound and economically efficient securitization structures, financial institutions in practice have often attempted to bring in further innovations and to include elements that are deemed un-Islamic or, at the very least, highly controversial. Such attempts have included, in the past, use of *bai'al-dayn* to sell debt at a negotiated price, use of *bai'al-inah* or its variant sale-and-lease-back and sovereign guarantees on returns. This does not augur well for the future of Islamic securitization. In the long run, only the pure forms of securitization would be acceptable to the market.

Notes

1. Suggestions have been made in the past in favour of similar sovereign guarantees for bank deposits too. These were, however, rejected overwhelmingly by Islamic scholars and economists on the ground that the return on deposits would amount to *riba* once the possibility of loss was eliminated through sovereign guarantee. The impact of sovereign guarantee on *sukuk* returns is perhaps less clear and, hence, tolerated. In effect, such a guarantee transforms Islamic debt securities into conventional ones.
2. The arguments of Dr Mahmoud El-Gamal on IBF Net Discussion Forum (http://islamic-finance.net) while discussing the Tabreed Sukuk Structure are particularly interesting.

References

Bakar, Mohd. Daud (1996), 'Al-Suyulah: The Islamic Concept of Liquidity', paper presented at the Second Islamic Capital Markets Conference organized by Securities Commission Malaysia at Kuala Lumpur.

Dualeh, Suleiman Abdi (1998), 'Islamic securitisation: practical aspects', paper presented at World Conference on Islamic Banking, Geneva, 8–9 July.

Shabbir, Muhammad (2002), 'Securitising Islamic financing receivables: a rating agency's perspective', paper presented at the Second International Islamic Banking & Finance Conference on 'Securitisation & Capital Markets: Challenges and Opportunities for Islamic Financial Institutions', Beirut, Lebanon, 12–13 March.

14 Islamic project finance
Michael J. T. McMillen[1]

14.1 Project finance: an overview

Large, capital-intensive projects present unique financing challenges. Their size, complexity and cost necessitate the involvement of many participant entities. The participants include developers, sponsors, other equity participants, financiers, construction contractors, specialized operators, suppliers, off-takers, insurers and, sometimes, host countries and rating agencies. The capital requirements exceed the capabilities and exposure limits of any single institution and thus require financing groups. The financiers may include international, regional and local financial institutions, development banks, export credit banks and multilateral lending and support institutions. These transactions are frequently international in scope and involve compliance with multiple legal systems as well as commerce among participants in several nations.

The required risk analysis and subsequent risk allocation among the participants is detailed and complex. Each of the participants will engage in (a) a risk analysis, to determine whether all risks associated with the construction, operation, ownership and financing of the project have been adequately covered, (b) an economic analysis, to determine whether the project will provide, ultimately, acceptable rates of return to the equity investors, (c) a financial analysis, to assess the adequacy of cash flows for operation of the project and servicing of the associated debt and (d) a legal analysis, to determine the viability of the project and the contemplated financing structure under existing applicable legal frameworks and to identify needed changes and accommodations. For example, consideration of project environment risks will focus on product market risks, political and country risks, the established and predictable legal and regulatory structure, and the necessity or desirability of recourse to international courts or arbitral bodies. Similarly, construction risk considerations include those pertaining to cost overruns, delays in completion, performance deficiencies, increased financing costs and political interference. Operating risk considerations will include a detailed examination of operating cost overruns, feedstock or raw materials availability, off-taker performance, transportation methods and costs, foreign exchange availability and convertibility, project performance deficiencies, political interference and long-term market movements, to name just a few.

The body of principles and structures that has evolved to address the panoply of issues and allocations relating to the financing of the construction and operation of any of these projects is generally subsumed within the concept of 'project finance'. Commonly used conventional definitions of 'project financing' are focused on the productive capabilities of an economic unit (that is, the project) and the needs and preferences of the debt participants in financing the construction and operation of such units, with the impact on the equity participants being implied by the debt structure. In general terms, a 'project financing' is the financing of an economic unit in which the lenders look initially to the cash flows from operation of that economic unit for repayment of the project debt and to those cash flows and the other assets comprising the economic unit as collateral security for the loans. Often it is an 'off-balance sheet' method of financing from the vantage of the operator and sponsors of the project.

Project financing techniques have become a primary means of financing a broad range of economic units throughout the world. The application of these techniques has been refined in most industrial categories and with respect to most types of assets. For example, they are used for the financing of power generation, transmission and distribution assets, for upstream, midstream and downstream assets in the oil and gas industries, for petrochemical, paper, mining, manufacturing and transportation projects, for telecommunications systems and satellites, for the complete range of real estate projects and for all types of infrastructure projects, including roads, airports, public buildings, stadiums and desalination plants. These same techniques have been used for the financing of tankers and other vessels, aircraft, rail carriages, trucks and virtually every type of manufacturing, transportation, computer and telecommunications equipment.

There is a pressing need for industrial, infrastructure and real estate development in all Islamic jurisdictions. The desire is to broaden the capital base within each country, draw upon funds from a worldwide financing base, and reduce reliance on local capital for financing needs. Project financing techniques will help facilitate achievement of those goals, as well as the off-balance sheet treatment desired by sponsors. And, being a type of cash flow financing, they will help ensure economic efficiency in achieving these ends.

Project financing techniques have evolved to allow for precise risk allocation among the various project participants in accordance with their transactional roles. With few exceptions, those risk allocations have been based upon the perceived roles of the participants within the context of a Western financial system: that is, an interest-based (*riba*-based) system as used in countries such as the United States of America, Europe, Australia and Japan.[2] As a result, those risk allocations have not accommodated role modifications that are necessary to achieve compliance with the principles and precepts of Islamic law (the *shari'a*),[3] even in those transactions that have included a *shari'a*-compliant financing tranche. They take no cognizance of the conflict of certain Islamic principles with the fundamental debt-leverage principle of Western project financing, namely *shari'a* prohibitions on the payment or receipt of interest and other aspects of the doctrines of *riba* and *gharar*.[4] In considering and implementing *shari'a*-compliant project financing structures, one of the challenges relates to adjustment of risk allocations among the participants in conformity with both the *shari'a* and the developed expectations of those participants that are not constrained by the *shari'a*.

Another implementation challenge relates to the current state of development and use of *shari'a*-compliant project-financing structures. To date, most of the *shari'a*-compliant transactions have been effected as a separate tranche in an otherwise conventional, interest-based project financing. That approach requires structuring collateral sharing and inter-creditor arrangements with the conventional lenders, and these arrangements themselves raise significant *shari'a* issues. Beyond those single-tranche arrangements, there is a pronounced dearth of available financing structures that bridge Western financial systems and Islamic systems. And there is a continuing, if gradually receding, perception that Western legal systems and principles and the Islamic legal systems and principles are so fundamentally divergent as to be unbridgeable.

14.2 Scope of the analysis

As noted, most large project financings will involve multiple and diverse parties and jurisdictions, and the application of multiple legal systems. Each of the participant parties will desire to maximize predictability and stability and to minimize uncertainty with respect to all elements of the project financing transaction. Of course, predictability, stability and uncertainty are matters of individual perception based upon the past experience of the individual participants. For a range of reasons, the perceptions of most participants will be based upon project-financing techniques and structures that have been developed in the Western interest-based economic and legal system. Some of those reasons include (a) the dominance of the Western interest-based economic system over the last few centuries, (b) the predominance of United States and European financial institutions, lawyers and accountants in the development and refinement of the most widely used project-financing techniques, (c) the refinement and exportation of Anglo-American law, (d) the relative infancy of modern Islamic finance, (e) the lack of familiarity with the operation of legal systems in the Middle East, North Africa and Southeast Asia, and (f) the general lack of knowledge of, and familiarity with, the *shari'a*. Those perceptions are also influenced by the existence of 'standardized' practices and structures, including 'standardized' contracts, applicable to many of the activities that comprise a project financing. Those standardized practices, structures and contracts have evolved, have become 'standardized', because of the economic efficiencies that they facilitate, particularly with respect to risk allocation, risk coverage and minimization of transactional costs. Of course, most of those standardized practices, structures and contracts were developed in, and have evolved within, a Western interest-based paradigm and reflect little, if any, sensitivity to the principles and precepts of *shari'a*.

Each of the participant parties will come to the project-financing transaction bound by their existing institutional perceptions and practices with respect to such matters as risk allocation, risk coverage, underwriting criteria and accounting treatment. Each must continue to operate within an existing regulatory framework, and that framework has probably shaped many of the embedded institutional practices. Each participant party will have strong expectations, based upon past 'best practices' within its realm of experience, as to the enforceability of the many contracts that comprise the project financing. Frequently that means that parties will desire to have the contracts governed by either English or New York law, rather than the law of the host country.

Participants in *shari'a*-compliant transactions will continue to include parties that proceed from, and are focused on, structures, methodologies and documents that proceed from a Western interest-based perspective. However, almost by definition, these transactions will also include participants that proceed from a different set of principles and precepts: those embodied in the *shari'a*. Thus, in many cases, *shari'a*-compliant project financings will utilize structures, methodologies and documents that allow both Muslim and non-Muslim (particularly Western) parties to operate within a sphere of predictability, stability and certainty that is acceptable to those parties.

This chapter thus focuses on two types of *shari'a*-compliant transactions. One type of transaction involves a 'coexistence' or 'melding' of traditional Western interest-based structures, methodologies and documents with *shari'a*-compliant structures, methodologies and documents: both are present and harmonized in the single integrated transaction, but are separated so as to allow segregated differential analysis under the *shari'a* and

Western practices. Another type of transaction is purely *shari'a*-compliant, and participation by a Western interest-based participant will require that participant to consider risk allocation from the perspective of the *shari'a*-compliant participant. Examples of each type of transactional structure are presented and discussed in this chapter.

Most of the examples set forth in this chapter proceed from the vantage of the *shari'a*-compliant investor. They assume, as has historically been the case, that the *shari'a*-compliant investor is initiating the use of *shari'a*-compliant techniques and structures, and that many of the other participants are unfamiliar with such techniques and structures.[5] This allows for exploration of how the transaction is structured and implemented from its inception.

For reasons of simplicity, and to retain the focus on the primary financing parties, this chapter ignores certain parties that participate in international project financings of the types being discussed. Thus, for example, there is no discussion of participation by host governments, raw materials suppliers and off-takers. Guarantors and their roles in the various *shari'a*-compliant structures are not discussed.[6] Also ignored are the contributions of multilateral agencies and export credit agencies; with apologies, each is treated as 'just another financier' for purposes of this chapter.

14.3 Conventional project-financing structures

This chapter focuses on *shari'a*-compliant project financing structures. There are many different non-compliant or 'conventional' project-financing structures, and none of them is discussed here. Given the inevitability and desirability of participation by Western parties in *shari'a*-compliant transactions, and given that they will bring their preconceptions, methodologies and risk allocation requirements to the table (however flexible and willing to adapt to the *shari'a*-compliant structures they might be), it is worthwhile to outline the general concepts of these conventional structures as a base for considering how the conventional structures and the *shari'a*-compliant structures can be adapted one to another.

In a conventional interest-based financing, a developer or sponsor (the 'Developer') will desire to undertake the construction and operation of a real estate, petrochemical, electricity, mining, desalination, manufacturing, infrastructure or other project (the 'Project').[7] The Developer will arrange for a group of banks and other financial institutions (the 'Banks') to make an interest-bearing loan to a project company (the 'Project Company') that will own and operate the Project. That loan will be made pursuant to a conventional loan agreement and related documents and will be evidenced by a promissory note (such documents and instruments, collectively, the 'Loan Agreement'). The Developer will execute a construction contract (the 'Construction Contract') with a general contractor (the 'General Contractor') and the General Contractor will cause the construction of the Project. The Project Company will operate the Project on a continuing basis. The Project Company will be structured as a limited partnership or limited liability company. The Developer will serve as the general partner or managing member of the Project Company and a group of investors, as limited partners or members, will infuse equity into the Project Company.[8]

Money will be advanced by the Banks to the Project Company on a periodic basis (say, monthly) upon submission of a draw request by the Developer. There will be conditions precedent to the making of each draw. Those conditions will include (a) performance of work in accordance with agreed plans and specifications and an agreed-upon timetable and evidence of payment for such work, (b) continuing satisfaction of a wide range of financial, construction and operational covenants, and (c) evidence of the continuing economic viability of the Project.

The terms of the loan, as embodied in the Loan Agreement, will provide for a construction period and an operating period. During the construction period, the Project Company will be obliged to pay only interest on the loan (and that interest will likely be capitalized and paid through borrowings on the loan itself). The interest will be determined using either variable rates or a fixed rate. During the operating period, the Project Company will likely make both interest and principal amortization payments, although this will vary considerably from industry to industry. For example, there may be significant periodic amortization of the principal amount of the loan in a petrochemical project, while a real estate project may have little or no amortization during the operating period and a bullet repayment in full of the principal at the maturity of the loan. The tenor of the loan will also vary considerably, based upon a wide range of factors, including the industry. For example, a loan for a petrochemical project may have a long operating term (say, ten to 15 years), while a construction and mini-term loan in the real estate industry may have an operating period of only two or three years after completion of construction.[9]

The loan will be secured by a collateral security structure that usually includes (a) a mortgage or deed of trust on the Project assets constituting real property, (b) a series of security agreements (pledges) on the personal property of the Project Company, including the Construction Contract, the input agreements, the off-take agreements, all accounts and reserves, and all cash and receivables, (c) environmental indemnity agreements running to the benefit of the Banks, (d) completion guarantees, and (e) technology guarantees.

Frequently, the Banks will require the establishment of a system of bank accounts, and each account will be subject to a security interest in favour of the Banks. A 'cashcade' or 'waterfall' will then be constructed which will provide for the flow of funds, and the timing of those flows, from one account to another. For example, the proceeds from operation of the Project (that is, from off-take and sales agreements) will be deposited directly in one account. A specified amount will then flow into an operating account to allow the Project Company to continue to operate the Project. A second amount will flow into a debt service account to accumulate for payment of debt service payments as they become due. Other amounts will flow into insurance and tax reserve accounts, capital improvement accounts, the operating account (again) and other required accounts. The order in which money moves into different accounts, and the types of different accounts, is specifically dependent upon the type of project, the comfort level of the Banks with the nature of the project, and the risk analysis with respect to the Project. In all cases, the account structure and the 'cashcade' are heavily negotiated.

14.4 The single *shari'a*-compliant tranche

To date, with the exception of real estate financings, very few project financings have incorporated *shari'a*-compliant elements and even fewer have been structured entirely on a *shari'a*-compliant basis.[10] In almost every such case involving *shari'a* compliance, the *shari'a*-compliant portion has been limited to a single tranche of the financing, with conventional interest-based financing providing the remainder of the funds for the construction and operation of the Project.[11] Two primary structures have been used to effect these *shari'a*-compliant tranches: the *istisnaa* (asset construction contract) structure,[12] and the *ijara* (asset lease) structure. Each of these structures is discussed in detail in succeeding sections of this chapter.[13] The use of a single *shari'a*-compliant tranche raises significant issues, some of which engender spirited debate as to whether the tranches are in fact *shari'a*-compliant. Without entering upon that debate, a review of some of these issues is instructive.

In each of the single-tranche transactions, a portion of the assets comprising the overall Project were isolated. In the cases of the tranches using an *istisnaa*-based structure, the construction of those assets was financed by the use of *istisnaa* contracts applicable to those designated assets, and the remainder of the Project was financed using conventional interest-bearing debt. In the case of the *ijara* tranches, construction of those assets was usually financed with conventional interest-bearing debt and the assets were then leased to the Project Company pursuant to a *shari'a*-compliant *ijara*.

The degree of identity or divergence of triggers, rights and remedies under the conventional Loan Agreement and the *istisnaa* or *ijara* documents presents difficult issues for the body of financiers (the Banks and the providers of the *shari'a*-compliant debt equivalent). For example, in most project financings it will not be acceptable to have one set of documents in default but not the other set of documents. The events of default generally need to be identical in each set of papers lest a part of the Project be subject to remedies or strictures while another group of assets is not subject to remedial action. Similarly, it is generally unacceptable to have one set of financiers (say, those under the conventional Loan Agreement) not being paid while the other set of financiers is being paid from revenues of what is for all practical purposes one integrated Project, or to have a portion of the overall assets sold pursuant to the exercise of remedies while the remainder of the assets cannot be sold as an integrated whole. Other examples relate to the sharing of proceeds upon the exercise of remedies. Even in the instance where there is absolute harmony with respect to events of default and the exercise of remedies and where all of the assets are sold as an integrated whole, it is unlikely that the assets allocated to one portion of the financing (say, the *ijara*) will have a collateral value equal to the amounts secured under that portion of the transaction (here, the *ijara*). Given the strong position of both groups of financiers to participate on a pro rata basis, there is likely to be collateral sharing to achieve rateability. Thus some of the assets subject to the *ijara* are in essence pledged to secure a *riba*-based financing, and vice versa. Given the low probability that realization can be other than on the basis of the Project as an integrated whole, the compliant and noncompliant portions of the transaction inevitably end up securing one another. Further, there are significant issues of which group of financiers will control the exercise of remedies, and related issues of priority of the respective interests in any remedy proceeding. Complicated inter-creditor arrangements will be structured to address these and similar issues, and those inter-creditor arrangements will themselves stress *shari'a* compliance (and have given rise to extensive debate among Islamic scholars, financiers and investors).

14.5   *Istisnaa–ijara* structures
14.5.1   Istisnaa–ijara *structures*
A project financing structure that has found widespread use in the United States and some Middle Eastern countries combines a construction (*istisnaa*) contractual arrangement

with a lease (*ijara*) arrangement to effect a construction and development financing involving conventional Western financiers and 'Shari'a-Compliant Investors'. United States banks and construction contractors, in particular, have achieved a high degree of comfort with this *istisnaa–ijara* structure and have participated in many such transactions since the end of 2000. The structure has evolved, and been simplified, since its first use in the United States.[14] This structure is amenable for use with most type of projects, including those in the electricity, petrochemical, mining, real estate, manufacturing, industrial and infrastructure industries as well as those pertaining to construction and operation of vessels and aircraft. The example chosen is for a cross-border real estate project (because it allows illustration of some of the *shari'a* considerations regarding use of the constructed asset, in this case by tenants).[15] However, with only slight modifications, the structure can be used for any other type of project or equipment.

An *istisnaa* is a type of contract in which a *mustasne'* (a client requiring the manufacturing or construction of an asset) orders from a *sane'* (manufacturer or constructor) an asset meeting certain specifications (the *masnou'*), with asset delivery to be within a specified period of time.[16] The *mustasne'* will be required to pay the purchase price of that asset if the asset is manufactured or constructed within the specified time period and meets the agreed-upon specifications.[17] The *sane'* need not manufacture or construct the asset itself; it may locate the asset in the market and purchase it for delivery to the *mustasne'* or it may cause another party to manufacture or construct the asset. If the original *sane'* causes another *sane'* to manufacture or construct, the original *sane'* remains liable to the original *mustasne'* for the delivery of the *masnou'*. In a financial transaction, the Banks or a special purpose Funding Company would be the original *sane'* and would contract with another *sane'* (the end *sane'*) for the manufacture or construction of the asset.[18]

Among the *shari'a* principles applicable to an *istisnaa* contract is the requirement that the amount to be paid for the *masnou'* be fixed. That price may not be altered unless the specifications of the *masnou'* are altered.[19] While there can be no contractual privity between the original or end *mustasne'* and the end *sane'* (in the circumstance where there are multiple *sane'*), the end *mustasne'* is permitted to supervise the manufacture or construction by the end-*sane'* to ensure compliance with specifications.[20] Warranties from the end-*sane'* to the financing banks as original *sane'* may be transferred to the end *mustasne'*. Such warranties may pertain to defects, including latent defects, continuing maintenance, defect-free delivery (if the end-*sane'* takes responsibility for damage during shipment) and similar matters.[21] Finally, note should be made of the *shari'a* principle that allows the *mustasne'* to sell the *masnou'* to a third party.[22]

It is also helpful to review a summary of certain relevant *shari'a* principles relating to *ijara* (lease or hire) arrangements (*Majelle*, articles 404–11; Al-Zuhayli, 2003, pp. 381–434). The *ijara* is a lease of an object or services involving the transfer of the usufruct or *manfa'a* (the use of an object or the services of a person) for a rent consideration.[23] The nature of the *manfa'a* must be precisely defined, the rental consideration must be for a fixed value, whether payable in a lump sum or instalments (*Majelle,* articles 466–79; Al-Zuhayli, 2003, pp. 289–409) and the term of the *ijara* must be precisely determined. The lease arrangements may be such that the lessee acquires ownership upon the termination of the lease. Both the rent and the term must be clearly ascertained and designated in the *ijara* (*Majelle*, articles 450, 454, 464, 484–96). The rent will commence immediately upon execution of the *ijara* if the *manfa'a* has sufficient economic value and substance at that time, meaning that it can be, and is, put to the use for which it is intended.[24] If it does not then have such economic value and substance, the rent will commence when such value and substance do exist. If the rent is reviewed during the term of the *ijara*, each such review and any agreement (if reached) changing the rent results in the creation of a new lease. The rent must be specified as a fixed sum for each *ijara* and the related rental term. However the rent may escalate or diminish during the rental term so long as the amounts of such escalation and/or decrease are specified and known to both parties.[25]

The lessor of assets is permitted to claim compensation from the lessee for misuse of the leased assets, but may not make claims in respect of ordinary wear and tear of the assets. The lessor is responsible for structural maintenance of the assets and this obligation may not be passed to the lessee pursuant to the *ijara*.[26] The lessor is entitled to rent as long as the lessee has the enjoyment of the leased assets as specified in the *ijara*. If the lessee does not have such enjoyment, as upon destruction or condemnation of the *manfa'a* or a breach by the lessor of the quiet enjoyment provision, the lessee may rescind the *ijara* and any contrary provision will be invalid.

For purposes of illustration, assume the construction and operation of a real estate Project in which the Developer acts as the general partner or managing member of the Project Company and *Shari'a*-Compliant Investors act as limited partners or non-managing members of the Project Company. The debt component of the Project will be provided by a group of international Banks. Pursuant to the Loan Agreement, the debt component of the financing will be structured as a 'construction and mini-term loan' with a tenor of five years and variable rate financing. The Project will be constructed pursuant to the Construction Contract with the General Contractor and will be operated by the Developer on behalf of the Project Company. Upon completion of construction, the Project will be (sub)leased to end user tenants (the 'End User Tenants').

By way of background and context, and considering the assumptions previously set forth, it is useful to note some of the primary transactional constraints. Real estate transactions have relatively thin margins; the margins in large-scale industrial projects are greater.[27] In most project financings, there is considerable structural standardization, often industry-specific, and documentary standardization. These types of standardization, and others, exist because they provide for economic efficiency and significant predictability, stability and certainty as to risk allocations and coverages. Often large portions of the existing structures and documentation cannot be modified, at least without unacceptable transaction cost incurrences. Similarly, legal, regulatory, tax accounting and other systemic constraints and characterizations cannot be modified.

14.5.2   *Basic structural considerations*

In effecting a *shari'a*-compliant transaction, sensitivity must be had to the existing positions and predispositions of the non-Muslim participants and to convincing those participants not only that they will end up in the same risk-allocated position as in a conventional Western financing, but also that the *shari'a*-compliant structure will achieve the same economic efficiencies, although likely with somewhat increased transactional costs until there is more widespread knowledge and acceptance of the *shari'a*-compliant structures and documentation.

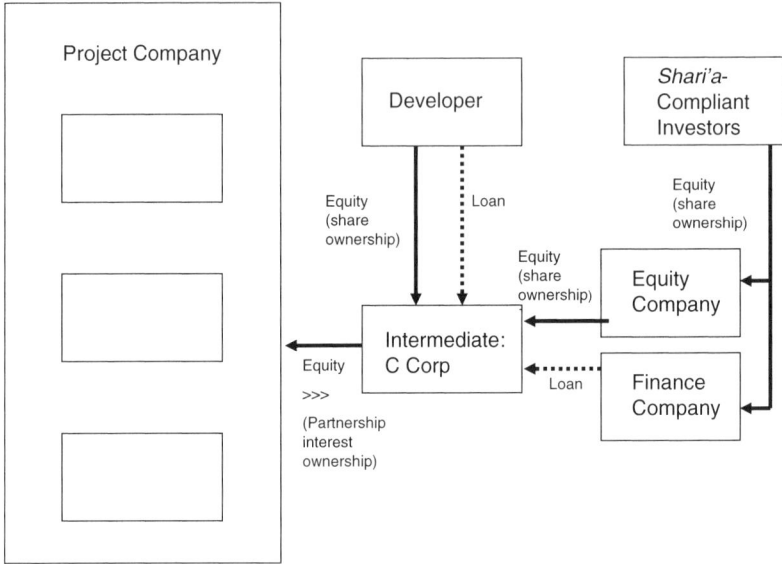

Figure 14.1   Investment structure

In most transactions of this type, one of the first considerations from the vantage of the *Shari'a*-Compliant Investor is determination of a tax-efficient investment structure that will also accommodate existing non-Islamic constraints. This usually does not involve transactional participants other than the *Shari'a*-Compliant Investors and the developer (the latter because of its joint venture relationship with the *Shari'a*-Compliant Investors by virtue of the participation in the Project Company). Often this involves considerable offshore as well as onshore tax and legal structuring. In many jurisdictions, multiple entities are used. As set forth in Figure 14.1, the *Shari'a*-Compliant Investors frequently invest through a 'fund' or 'general offshore investment vehicle' that invests in an 'intermediate' vehicle that in turn invests in the Project Company. As a generalized statement, and using the United States as an example: the 'fund' is often sited in a tax-efficient jurisdiction (such as the British Virgin Islands, the Cayman Islands, Ireland or Luxembourg) and comprises two or more companies (an 'Equity Company' and a 'Finance Company');[28] the 'intermediate' entity is a 'C corporation' (the 'Intermediate C Corp'); and the project company is a general partnership or limited liability company.

The *Shari'a*-Compliant Investors will make their equity contribution by purchasing shares in each of Equity Company and Finance Company. In United States transactions, this investment is usually made in a 3:1 ratio between Finance Company and Equity Company, respectively.[29] Equity Company, in turn, will purchase shares in the Intermediate C Corp, in an amount equal to its entire capital contribution from the *Shari'a*-Compliant Investors (which is one-quarter of the total amount invested by the *Shari'a*-Compliant Investors). Finance Company will make a loan to the Intermediate C Corp in an amount equal to its entire capital contribution from the *Shari'a*-Compliant Investors (which equals three-quarters of the total amount invested by the *Shari'a*-Compliant Investors). Similarly, the Developer will purchase shares in the Intermediate C Corp[30] and make a loan to the

Intermediate C Corp in a 1:3 ratio that mirrors the ratio by the Equity Company and the Finance Company, respectively.[31] The respective loans will begin accruing and compounding interest from the inception of the investment in the Project and will be at then-current market rates and tenors for loans of this type.

The 3:1 equity-to-debt ratio is driven by tax laws and regulations in the United States, in particular the portfolio interest exemption considerations. From a *shari'a* vantage, the loan from the Finance Company to the Intermediate C Corp is 'self-lending' because the Intermediate C Corp is owned by the Equity Company (and the Developer) and the Equity Company interest is, in turn, owned by the *Shari'a*-Compliant Investors.

As distributions are made out of the transaction, money will move from the End User Tenant into the Project Company and then out to the Intermediate C Corp.[32] The Intermediate C Corp will first make debt service payments on the loans from the Finance Company and the Developer. After payment of all such debt service, cash (usually from the sale of the real estate Project) will be trapped in the Intermediate C Corp and then the Intermediate C Corp will be liquidated, with any trapped cash being distributed as a liquidating distribution at lower tax rates.[33]

14.5.3 *Presentation of the structure*

After determination of the viability of the Project, determination of appropriate tax structures, identification of the participant parties, determination of the economic structure and terms for the project, negotiation of the relevant term sheets, and structuring to satisfy other regulatory (particularly bank regulatory), tax, legal and accounting considerations, one of the first steps is to review the transactional structure with the Banks and their counsel. Frequently, two methods of presentation are made to the Banks, both at commencement of the transaction and throughout its implementation: first, slide shows are used to demonstrate structural and documentary relationships; and, second, the 'risk grid' is prepared and updated. The slide show focuses on relationships between the parties and documentary relationships. The risk grid focuses on underwriting factors and risk coverage.

The slide show begins with an explanation of some of the basic principles of the *shari'a* that are applicable in the structure. For example, the concepts of *riba* and *gharar* are briefly addressed, noting that the *Shari'a*-Compliant Investors and entities in which they participate can neither pay nor receive interest. Some of the *shari'a* leasing principles are discussed, such as the requirements that the lessor retain obligations pertaining to the provision of a rentable property and the correlative principles that the lessor must maintain structural maintenance obligations and the obligation to provide casualty insurance on the Project (thus precluding triple-net leases). Some general structural principles are also explored, such as the rule that, as a general matter, there can be no privity of contract or relationship between the Project Company (in which the *Shari'a*-Compliant Investors make and hold an investment) and the Banks providing conventional financing. And some general 'useful guidelines' are explored, such as the principle that one should follow the money from the End User Tenant to the Project Company and out to the *Shari'a*-Compliant Investor to get a feeling for whether a given flow is compliant with the *shari'a*; if the money passes through an entity that is not compliant with the *shari'a*, the structure or flow is probably not compliant.

Similarly, the manner in which the *shari'a*-compliant documents are constructed is examined. The *shari'a*-compliant documents are 'modularized' for each Bank, and the

Disbursement Side	Repayment Side
• Commitment to lend	• Rate calculations
• Disbursement mechanics	• Amortization
• Conditions precedent	• Mandatory prepayment
• Representations and warranties	• Voluntary prepayment
	• Covenants
	• Events of default
	• Remedies
	• Indemnities

Figure 14.2   Conventional loan agreement

modules are then attached to backbone or skeleton documents. The backbone documents are *shari'a*-compliant, having been reviewed and approved by the relevant *Shari'a* Supervisory Boards. There are a number of modules for each transaction, including one for each of (a) the representations and warranties, (b) the covenants, (c) the events of default, (d) the insurance provisions, and (e) other relevant sections of the financing contracts. Each module is a mirror image of the corresponding provisions of the conventional Loan Agreement for the transaction,[34] although each module is redrafted in terms of lease (*ijara*) or undertaking (put and call option) concepts. Figures 14.2 and 14.3 provide a demonstration of the technique that is used.[35] Figure 14.2 shows a conventional loan agreement, with distribution provisions (money out from the Banks to the borrower) summarized in the left column, and repayment concepts summarized in the right column. After dividing the loan agreement in half down the middle, Figure 14.3 illustrates how these provisions are reallocated into the *shari'a*-compliant documents.

Additionally, the impact of tax, legal and accounting considerations, and their implementation in the overall *shari'a*-compliant structure, is discussed. For example, it is usually critical that the Project Company be the 'tax owner' for purposes of local tax laws, such as the federal income tax laws of the United States.[36] This allows effective use of the tax benefits (such as depreciation) by the Project Company as the only party that can make use of those benefits (because it has taxable income from operations and the eventual sale of the Project). To achieve such a result, it is imperative that the Funding Company, in particular, and the Construction Arranger be treated as 'disregarded entities' for federal tax purposes.[37] Exact matching of the obligations and liabilities that the Project Company has to the Funding Company under the *shari'a* documents with those that the Funding Company has to the Banks under the loan documents is advisable to ensure 'disregarded entity' status for the Funding Company. In addition, to support the tax ownership and disregarded entity positions that will be taken by the Funding Company, the Construction Arranger and the Project Company, care must be taken (a) in developing and implementing the appropriate relationship and documentary structure, (b) in structuring cash flows, and implementing that structure in the documents, so that neither the Funding Company nor

CONSTRUCTION
(*Istisnaa*)

- Commitment for construction
- Disbursement mechanisms
- Conditions precedent
- Representations and warranties
- Covenants

LEASE
(*Ijara*)

- Rent rate calculations
- Periodic rent
- Covenants
- Representations and warranties
- Events of default
- Remedies
- Indemnities

PUT OPTION
CALL OPTION

- Mandatory prepayments
- Voluntary prepayments

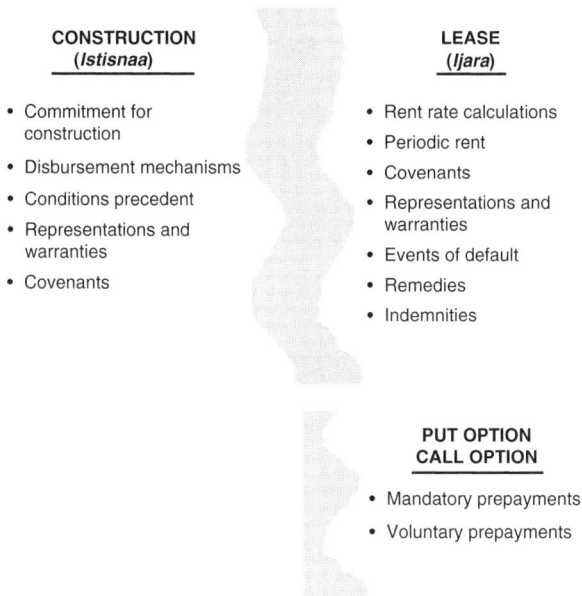

Figure 14.3   Reallocation of provisions in shari'a-*compliant structures*

the Construction Arranger has taxable income,[38] and (c) in crafting the substantive terms of both the loan documents and the *shari'a* documents.

Before proceeding to a discussion of the structure (and the remainder of the slide show), it is worthwhile to describe the risk grid. The risk grid is essentially a spreadsheet that lists each provision of each conventional Loan Agreement and other loan documents, including loan agreements, indemnity agreements, completion agreements, guarantees and collateral security documents on one axis and then lists each provision of the various *shari'a*-compliant documents: the lease (*ijara*), understanding to purchase (put option), understanding to sell (call option), managing contractor agreement, and collateral security documents on the other axis. The cell opposite any loan document provision will indicate exactly where that provision is addressed in the *shari'a* documents. This allows the Banks, and particularly their credit and underwriting committees, to determine exactly where and how each risk addressed in their conventional and customary forms of documents is addressed in the *shari'a*-compliant structure. Usually, the risk grid is only prepared for the first transaction with a Bank or counsel to a Bank because the preparation process is tedious and expensive.

14.5.4   General documentary definitions
Before examining the structure, the general categories of documents should be defined. The 'Loan Documents' consist of the Loan Agreement and such other loan and Project support documents as are customary for the Banks providing the financing. Those other documents include promissory notes, environmental indemnity agreements, completion guarantees in respect of construction, technology guarantees in respect of the operating technology, loan guarantees, often for a specified duration (such as until completion of

construction) and the Owner Security Documents. The 'Owner Security Documents' include all documents providing collateral security to the Banks in respect of the loan pursuant to the Loan Agreement, and include a first mortgage on the Improvements (and, if the Funding Company owns the land, the land), a security agreement covering all accounts, cash flows and personal property of the Funding Company, an assignment of the Construction Arranger's rights under the Construction Contract with the General Contractor, an assignment of the Lease (*ijara*), the Understanding to Purchase, the Understanding to Sell, and, if present in the particular transaction, the Site Lease,[39] an assignment of all leases and rents payable to the Funding Company, and an assignment of the Funding Company's rights in, to and under the Lessee Security Documents.

The '*Shari'a* Documents' include (a) the Construction (*istisnaa*) Agreement, (b) the Site Lease (if title to the land is retained in the Project Company), (c) the Agreement to Lease, (d) the Lease (*ijara*), (e) the Understanding to Purchase, (f) the Understanding to Sell, (g) the Managing Contractor Agreement, (h) the Contractor Consents, (i) the Tax Matters Agreement, if there is one for the specific transaction, and (j) the Lessee Security Agreements.[40] The 'Lessee Security Agreements' include all collateral security agreements and assignments provided by the Project Company to the Funding Company to secure the obligations of the Project Company under (i) the Lease (*ijara*), (ii) the Understanding to Purchase, and (iii) the Understanding to Sell, and may include a lessee mortgage, a first mortgage on the land (if ownership of the land is retained in the Project Company), a security agreement covering all accounts, cash flows and personal property of the Project Company, an assignment of leases and rents for subtenants of the Project Company (that is, End User Tenants), an assignment of raw materials contracts, suppliers contracts and off-take contracts in those transactions having such elements, and an assignment of the Construction Contract and the rights of the Construction Arranger thereunder.

14.5.5 Equity and debt funding and construction documents

Figure 14.4 provides an overview of three different aspects of the transaction. The first aspect focuses on the fact that, in real estate construction financings, the Developer has often acquired the land for the transaction well in advance of locating the equity participants (that is, the *Shari'a*-Compliant Investors) and before approaching the Banks in respect of construction and operations financing.[41] The Developer will often have done permitting and development work in advance of obtaining other equity and the debt. The Developer will frequently desire to contribute the land as an in-kind equity contribution. This allows the Developer to receive the benefit of previously expended cash and of market value appreciation of the land as part of its capital contribution. This method also allows the avoidance of a separate taxable transfer of the land in certain circumstances, which is significant because of the size of transfer taxes in many jurisdictions. If the land is transferred into the Project Company, or the Developer's special purpose entity holding title to the land becomes the Project Company, a Site Lease must be put into place to allow for the *shari'a*-compliant financing. The Site Lease will be between the Project Company, as the site lessor, and the Funding Company, as the site lessee.

The 'Funding Company' (or 'Owner') is a special-purpose vehicle that is established for the transaction. It is frequently owned by a corporate service provider, such as Global Securitization Services, to avoid *shari'a* issues pertaining to common ownership by the *Shari'a*-Compliant Investors (and their affiliates) of interests in both the lessor and the

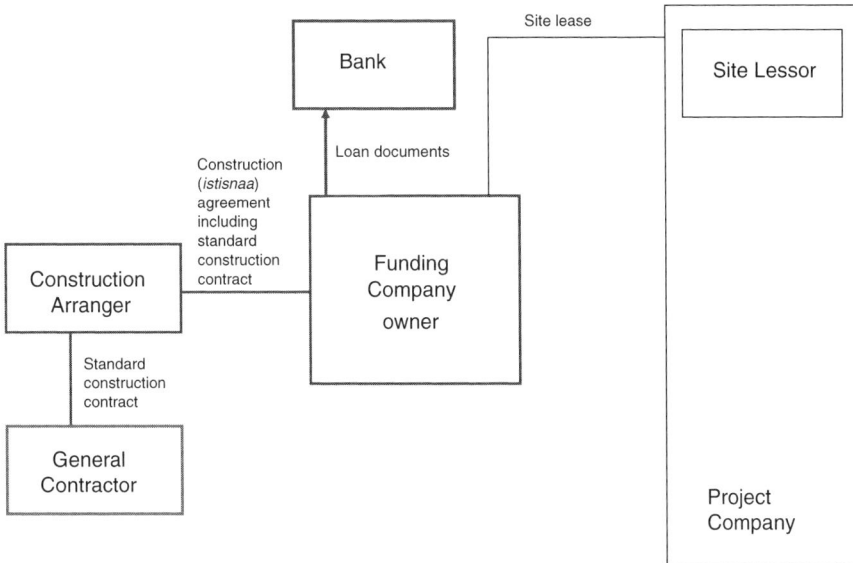

Figure 14.4   Site lease, equity and debt funding: construction arrangements

lessee under the *shari'a*-compliant lease (*ijara*) (discussed below). The Funding Company will, at a minimum, own the improvements to be constructed on the land (the 'Improvements'). If the Developer has previously acquired the land, the Funding Company will be the site lessee under the Site Lease, and thus have rights to build, operate and maintain the Improvements on the land.[42]

The second aspect of focus in Figure 14.4 pertains to the construction arrangements. In addition to the Funding Company, there is a second special-purpose entity: the 'Construction Arranger'. The Construction Arranger is frequently owned by the same corporate service company that owns the Funding Company. The purpose of having the Construction Arranger is primarily to allow the structuring of the Construction (*istisnaa*) Agreement (discussed below) between two agreeable parties. This is essential because the Construction (*istisnaa*) Agreement contains the provisions that mirror the disbursement half of the Loan Agreement, a capitalization mechanism for disbursements during construction and, in some cases, a range of other *shari'a*-compliant provisions. In the first *istisnaa–ijara* transactions, there was no Construction Arranger and provision had to be made with a General Contractor to include the foregoing provisions in an otherwise standard construction contract. While that particular General Contractor agreed to inclusion of those provisions, the cost of considering and negotiating the included provisions was enormous. Most General Contractors will not tolerate inclusion in their standard form of construction contract of provisions such as are included in the Construction (*istisnaa*) Agreement, at any price. From the standpoint of *shari'a*-compliant structuring, it is far preferable, and much less expensive, to create the Construction Arranger and allow two sister entities (the Construction Arranger and the Funding Company) to enter into the Construction (*istisnaa*) Agreement. This will allow the Construction Arranger to enter into an absolutely standard Construction Contract with the General Contractor, and the General Contractor need not be made aware of the intervening *shari'a* structure at all.

The final aspect of Figure 14.4 pertains to the infusion of funds for the construction and operation of the Project. The Project Company will contribute equity to the Project, usually amounting to approximately 20 per cent of the total project costs. The exact nature of the contribution will vary with each transaction and will be determined by, among other things, the proclivities and desires of the Banks and their legal counsel, tax laws, legal and regulatory considerations, and accounting desires and standards. In all cases, whether the equity is retained in the Project Company (the in-kind land contribution, for example), or contributed in cash to construction payments or otherwise, the Funding Company will obtain the benefit of this equity investment.

The Banks will fund continuing construction costs, usually on a monthly basis, in an aggregate amount equal to approximately 80 per cent of the total project costs. The funding by the Banks will be pursuant to a conventional Loan Agreement, with the Funding Company as the borrower. As noted above, the basic 'modular' provisions of the Loan Agreement will be mirrored in the *shari'a*-compliant documents, and the economic terms of the transaction will be mirrored in both the conventional Loan Documents and the *shari'a*-compliant documents. The disbursement provisions will be mirrored primarily in the Construction (*istisnaa*) Agreement. This is a 'mirroring' rather than a 'duplication' because the loan agreement treats of a conventional debt financing while the Construction (*istisnaa*) Agreement treats of a construction arrangement. Thus, for example, the Construction (*istisnaa*) Agreement will contain a monthly milestone payment mechanism that mirrors the loan disbursement request and payment mechanism in terms of deliverables and conditions precedent.

In terms of the movement of cash flow in connection with the financing provided by the Banks, money will be lent, on a monthly basis, in an amount equal to the requested disbursement and milestone completion payment, by the Banks to the Funding Company. The Funding Company will make payment on the milestone completion certificate and payment request provided by the Construction Arranger. The milestone completion certificate and request is duplicative of the disbursement request with respect to evidence of completion and amount requested, thus leaving no residual cash in the Funding Company. The Construction Arranger, in turn, will make monthly payments to the General Contractor and its subcontractors, as well as any payments in respect of construction that are outside the General Contractor's Construction Contract. Again, the disbursement request mechanism will be structured to include all elements of the General Contractor milestone completion request and payment structure. No residual cash will be left in the Construction Arranger.[43]

14.5.6   Primary shari'a *documents for operation and repayment*
Figure 14.5 shows the addition of the main *shari'a*-compliant documents pertaining to the repayment of the financing and the day-to-day operation of the Project. The additional *shari'a*-compliant documents are (a) the 'Agreement to Lease', (b) the 'Lease (*ijara*)', (c) the 'Understanding to Purchase' (put option), (d) the 'Understanding to Sell' (call option), (e) the 'Managing Contractor Agreement', (f) the various 'Consents', comprising (i) the 'General Contractor Consent' and (ii) the 'Construction Arranger Consent', and (g) in some jurisdictions, the 'Tax Matters Agreement'.

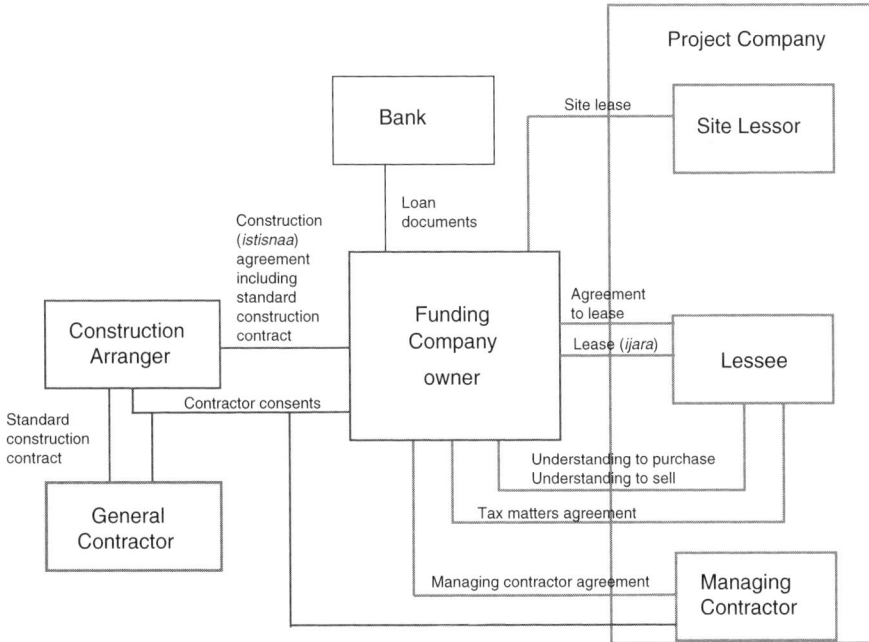

Figure 14.5   Overall transaction (without collateral security documents)

The Agreement to Lease modifies one section of the Lease (*ijara*) requiring the payment of Basic Rent to the Funding Company, rendering it inactive until such time as the Project has attained 'economic sufficiency' under applicable *shari'a* interpretations. Under the *shari'a*, a property may not be leased until such time as it has sufficient economic substance and worth as to be useable and rentable. The determination of when such economic sufficiency is obtained is very fact-dependent and the *Shari'a* Supervisory Boards debate this topic at length. In virtually all construction projects, *shari'a* determinations on this matter do not affect the financing arrangements because debt service is not payable during the construction period in any event: interest is capitalized and paid from loan proceeds. Thus no Basic Rent would be payable to allow payment of amounts due under the Loan Agreement in any case. However, most *Shari'a* Supervisory Boards do require that the documentary structure address this structural element, and that is done in the Agreement to Lease.

The primary repayment documents are the Lease (*ijara*), the Understanding to Purchase and the Understanding to Sell. The Lease (*ijara*) provides for the payment of Basic Rent and the expenses of operating the Project. Basic Rent is established as an amount equal to the amount necessary to service current Bank debt to the Funding Company. The Lease (*ijara*) is structured to mirror, by module inclusion, the major sections of the Loan Agreement, as shown in Figures 14.2 and 14.3. The primary modules relate to representations and warranties, covenants, insurance provisions and events of default. The backbone of the Lease (*ijara*) is *shari'a*-compliant and, at the behest of different *Shari'a* Supervisory Boards, addresses some of the fundamental *shari'a* issues that arise in project financings. These matters include (a) inspection and delivery precepts under the *shari'a*, including liability in respect of such matters, (b) retention by the Funding Company, as the lessor, of structural maintenance and casualty insurance obligations in respect of the Project, and (c) casualty and condemnation, including events of loss, and payments in respect of such events. The different modules are mirrors, not duplicates, of the corresponding Loan Agreement provisions, modified for insertion in a lease and the understandings to purchase and sell. The modules are included as exhibits to the backbone of the Lease (*ijara*).

Under a *shari'a*-compliant lease, the obligation to pay rent ceases upon termination of the Lease (*ijara*) or an event of loss constituting total destruction. It is not permissible to collect future rents in such circumstances, which means that it is not possible, under the Lease (*ijara*), to accelerate the amounts necessary to pay, through the Funding Company, outstanding principal amounts under the Loan Agreement. If the Lease (*ijara*) were terminated in respect of a Lease Event of Default, it would similarly be impossible to collect future Basic Rent amounts to enable the Funding Company to pay outstanding principal under the Loan Agreement.

The customary method of addressing these issues, and of implementing other mandatory prepayment concepts, is set forth in the Understanding to Purchase. Pursuant to the Understanding to Purchase, the Project Company undertakes, in certain circumstances (such as a Lease Event of Default or a Loss and Condemnation),[44] and at the election of the Funding Company, to purchase the Project (or a portion of the Project) from the Funding Company. The purchase price in such a circumstance and for a complete purchase of the Project is fixed at an amount equal to the then-outstanding principal amount of the loan. As noted, in certain circumstances, or at the election of the Funding Company, the purchase may be of less than the totality of the Project; it will be a purchase of a specified fractional undivided interest, for example. In certain circumstances, the Funding Company may be restricted to such a partial purchase, as where the partial purchase has the effect of curing the onerous circumstance that allowed the Funding Company to exercise the option to compel the purchase in the first instance.[45]

The Undertaking to Sell focuses on permissible prepayment concepts and sale of asset concepts. Pursuant to the Understanding to Sell, the Project Company may elect to purchase from the Funding Company all or a portion of the Project. Partial purchases may be of specified assets or units (such as individual condominiums or houses) or fractional undivided interest payments. If the entirety of the Project is to be sold to a third party, for example, the Project Company will call the entire Project and the purchase price will be a fixed amount equal to the then-outstanding principal amount of the loan. If the Project Company desires to sell one or more, but less than all, of the condominiums, homes, buildings, treatment facilities or generating stations that have been constructed, it will call the specified assets and pay a previously negotiated price (say, 80 per cent of the proceeds of the sale of those assets or another fixed amount). If the Project Company desires to decrease the amount of the financing without purchasing specified assets, it will make payment of a portion of the overall purchase price in the equivalent of a fractional undivided interest purchase.

As noted above, various obligations (such as structural maintenance and the purchase of casualty insurance) must remain with a lessor. Under an established *shari'a* principle, a lessor may hire another party to undertake obligations that the lessor has with respect to property, even where that property is subject to a lease. In the structure used in many project financings, the Funding Company hires the Project Company to perform some of the obligations that the Funding Company has retained under the Lease (*ijara*). The relationship established in respect of this arrangement is embodied in the Managing Contractor Agreement. This is a services agreement that establishes those activities to be performed by the Project Company as the managing contractor and the fee arrangements in respect of that relationship.

The second set of provisions in the Managing Contractor Agreement address structural matters pertaining to the making of decisions and determinations in respect of a wide range of matters. In summary, and except as limited by the *shari'a*, the Project Company will make all decisions for and on behalf of the Construction Arranger in respect of construction and the Construction Contract with the General Contractor and will otherwise make decisions and determinations in respect of the operation of the Project.[46] The making of decisions and determinations in the Lease (*ijara*) that correspond to, and mirror, the rights of the Funding Company under the Loan Documents will be binding upon the Banks as decisions and determinations of the Funding Company under the Loan Documents. Certain of the rights of the Project Company in the Managing Contractor Agreement are self-limiting. For example, they may terminate upon the exercise of remedies in respect of a Lease Event of Default. Other rights of the Project Company are unlimited. Those rights mirror the non-terminable rights that the Project Company would have under the Loan Documents if the Project Company were the direct borrower in the conventional loan financing. The principle, as in other aspects of the structure, is to place the parties as closely as possible, given *shari'a* restrictions, in the same position (including in respect of risk allocation and legal rights) as the parties would occupy if this were a conventional financing.

The General Contractor Consent is a standard form of consent used in project financings. Basically, the General Contractor consents to the assignment of the Construction Contract to secure the financing arrangements and agrees to complete the construction of the Project in accordance with the Construction Contract subsequent to the exercise of remedies in respect of defaults if the General Contractor is paid and the construction arrangements are otherwise relatively undisturbed. The Construction Arranger Consent also contains provisions effecting the structure and mechanics of the transaction, particularly in respect of collateral security matters. In addition, the Construction Arranger Consent contains certain provisions that give effect to the allocation of cash flows and the making, by the Project Company, of decisions and determinations in respect of the construction of the Project.

In certain jurisdictions, such as the United States, it is advisable to have a Tax Matters Agreement. The Tax Matters Agreement serves two primary functions: the signatory parties are bound, first, to take specified tax positions (for example, that the Project Company is the 'tax owner' of the Project and is solely entitled to take related tax benefits) and, second, to provide a roadmap of the transaction to the applicable tax authorities (understanding that such an agreement cannot bind those authorities). In many jurisdictions, there is no need for a Tax Matters Agreement.

14.5.7 *Collateral security*
Most jurisdictions have laws governing mortgages, security interests, assignments of contracts and similar elements of the collateral security package that is provided to a secured creditor. The discussion in this chapter focuses on such jurisdictions and assumes the

existence of recording systems that provide for some or all of the elements of perfection and priority of security interests. There are some jurisdictions where such laws do not exist, or the record systems are not utilized, and resort must be had to the structuring of a *rahn* (mortgage or pledge) under pure *shari'a* principles. Collateral security structures in these latter jurisdictions are addressed in other articles.[47]

In a conventional project financing, the secured creditor is an agent on behalf of a group of banks, insurance companies or other financial institutions providing one or more loans to the Project Company. However, the secured creditor could also be a lessor under a lease (*ijara*) in a *shari'a*-compliant financing. Or the secured creditor could be the original *sane'* in an *istisnaa* transaction, the *rabb al-mal* in a *mudaraba* transaction, the silent partners in a *sharikat mahassa–murabaha* transaction, or the *sukuk* holders in a *sukuk* issuance transaction.[48] Alternatively, the secured creditor could be any other person to whom an obligation is owed under either a conventional or *shari'a*-compliant project financing: the laws governing collateral security instruments will not take cognizance of, or vary according to the nature of the transaction.

A generalized collateral security structure is described in Figure 14.6. In the collateral security structure illustrated in the figure, one of the Banks will act as agent for all of the Banks as secured party and the enforcement agent.

There are three sets of collateral security documents in the basic *istisnaa–ijara* structure. The precise configuration of collateral security documents will vary considerably from jurisdiction to jurisdiction, from bank to bank, and from transaction to transaction, depending upon numerous factors, including the types of assets that are essential to the construction and operation of the Project. What follows is a generalized discussion.

The first set of collateral security documents comprises the General Contractor Consent (previously discussed) and the assignment by the Construction Arranger to the

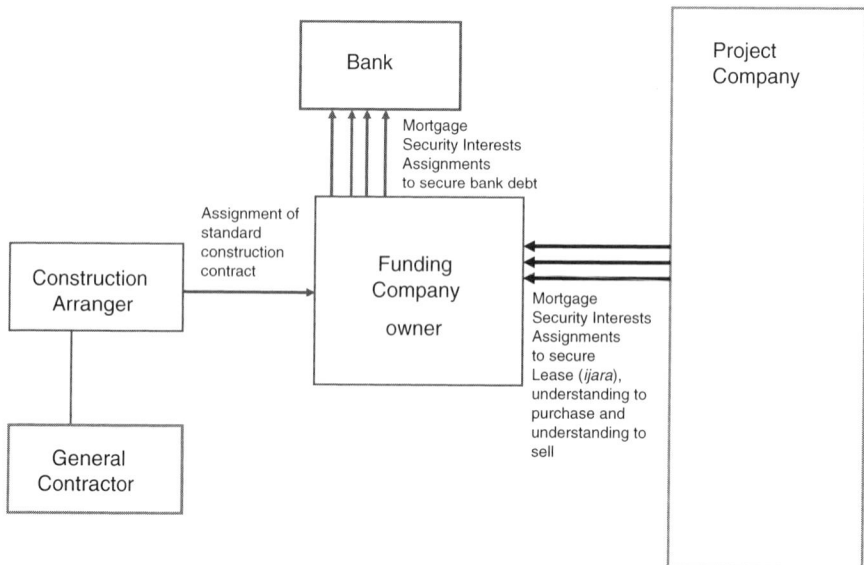

Figure 14.6   Collateral security

Funding Company of the Construction Arranger's interest in, to and under the Construction Contract between the Construction Arranger and the General Contractor. The assignment is further assigned (in the third set of documents) by the Funding Company to the Bank to secure the obligations of the Funding Company to the Bank under the Loan Documents. This collateral security package is generally provided to secure the obligations of the Project Company under the Lease (*ijara*), the Understanding to Purchase and the Understanding to Sell. However, as it is on the non-compliant side of the transaction, some *Shari'a* Supervisory Boards have permitted this set of documents to secure the loan directly.

The second set of collateral security documents is the remainder of the Lessee Security Documents and is provided by the Project Company to the Funding Company to secure the Project Company's obligations under the Lease (*ijara*), the Understanding to Purchase and the Understanding to Sell. This second set comprises a first mortgage on the land (if the Project Company retains title to the land), a leasehold mortgage (in some jurisdictions, although this is not frequently used), a security interest covering all cash, accounts and personal property of the Project Company, an assignment of leases and rents payable to the Project Company pursuant to any End User Lease, an assignment of supplier agreements, raw materials agreements and off-take agreements (in transactions where those concepts are applicable), and such other customary collateral security agreements as the Banks obtain in transactions of this type.[49] Rights under the first two sets of collateral security documents (that is, the Lessee Security Documents) may be exercised in connection with a 'Lease Event of Default' under the Lease (*ijara*), but not a 'Loan Event of Default' under the Loan Agreement.

The third set of collateral security documents is provided by the Funding Company to the Bank to secure directly the obligations of the Funding Company under the Loan Documents. It comprises a first mortgage on the Improvements (and on the land if title to the land is held in the Funding Company), a security interest in all the cash, accounts and other personal property of the Funding Company, an assignment of the Funding Company's interest in, to and under the Lease (*ijara*), the Understanding to Purchase, the Understanding to Sell and, if title to the land is held in the Project Company, the Site Lease, an assignment of leases and rents payable to the Funding Company pursuant to any lease to which it is a party – including the Lease (*ijara*) – and a further assignment of the Lessee Security Documents. Rights under these Owner Security Documents may be exercised in connection with a 'Loan Event of Default' under the Loan Agreement.

The distinction between the Lessee Security Documents, and the ability to exercise rights thereunder in connection with a Lease Event of Default, and the Owner Security Documents, and the ability to exercise rights thereunder in connection with a Loan Event of Default, focuses again on the care that must be taken in structuring and documenting these *shari'a*-compliant transactions. The Loan Events of Default may include any Lease Event of Default. However, the Lease Events of Default may not include a Loan Event of Default. Thus the mirroring of representations and warranties and covenants (which play into the events of default) and the remainder of the events of default in the Loan Documents and the *Shari'a* Documents must be precise. Otherwise, there will be mismatch, with an event of default under one set of documents, but not the other, which may interfere with the exercise of remedies as a coherent structural whole.

14.6   *Istisnaa* and parallel *istisnaa* structures

A project-financing structure that is frequently used in Middle Eastern jurisdictions involves the use of two *istisnaa* contracts. The original (or end) *mustasne'* (the Developer) will ask the Banks, as the original *sane'*, to finance the construction of the Project pursuant to an *istisnaa* agreement. In accordance with accepted *Shari'a* principles, the Banks will act as *sane'* in a parallel *istisnaa* agreement with a construction contractor, the end *sane'*. The terms of the *istisnaa* and parallel *istisnaa* agreements will be identical except as regards payment. Pursuant to the parallel *istisnaa* agreement, the Banks will make payment to the construction contractor on a current basis (which may be an instalment basis itself based upon completion of work)[50] while the obligation of the Developer to pay the Banks for construction will be on a deferred instalment basis and will include a profit amount for the Banks. Of course, all required elements for a valid *istisnaa* agreement must be satisfied with respect to both the *istisnaa* and the parallel *istisnaa* agreement.[51]

It is important to note that the Banks will be obliged to the Developer on the *istisnaa* agreement regardless of whether the construction contractor performs on the parallel *istisnaa* agreement. The *istisnaa* and the parallel *istisnaa* agreements are entirely separate agreements and there will be no privity between the Developer, as the original or end *mustasne'*, and the construction contractor, as the end-*sane'*. Great care must be taken in structuring the transaction and drafting the documentation to address the liability exposure of the Banks, and this aspect of the transaction has been an impediment to widespread acceptance of the structure by many banks and financial institutions. *Shari'a* Supervisory Boards have generally allowed contractual provisions to be used to address this structural feature. For example, damage limitation provisions in the *istisnaa* agreement may limit the damages payable by the Banks to the Developer in circumstances where there was a default on the parallel *istisnaa* agreement (although the damage limitation provisions usually do not make direct reference to the parallel *istisnaa* agreement). As another example, a provision may be included in the *istisnaa* agreement that allows for extensions of time for performance where the parallel *istisnaa* is not performed in a timely manner (again, usually without direct reference to the parallel *istisnaa* agreement).[52]

Given the necessity of conformity to the agreed specifications, the options of inspection, the *shari'a* principles applicable to delivery and the *shari'a* principles applicable to defects, particularly latent and nondiscoverable defects, are of particular importance in structuring the *istisnaa* and parallel *istisnaa* agreements.[53] The drafting should incorporate inspection rights and appropriate waivers of liability to address these *shari'a* principles and should be precise as to the time and liabilities associated with delivery of the *masnou'*. For example, and in light of the fact that current payment on the parallel *mustasne'* is frequently made on an instalment payment as work is completed over relatively short intervals (such as a month), it is prudent to require the original *mustasne'* (the Developer) to inspect construction on a continuing basis. Failure to so inspect, or negligence in conducting such an inspection, will result in liability for discoverable defects being placed with the Developer. Similarly, with the guidance and instruction of the relevant *Shari'a* Supervisory Boards (whose positions vary), delivery may be structured so that discrete portions of the *masnou'* are delivered sequentially with completion of the work on the respective portions. This will have the effect of transferring certain liabilities in respect of that work to the Developer.

The collateral security structure for an *istisnaa*–parallel *istisnaa* structure is relatively simple, and not significantly different from that provided in any other *shari'a*-compliant or conventional interest-based financing (although it will secure a different type of obligation).[54] The banks will have direct rights to the construction arrangements by virtue of being a party signatory to the parallel *istisnaa*. The banks will take a mortgage and security interest over the Project and over the cash flows, accounts and personal property of the Project Company. The Banks may also obtain environmental indemnities, construction and completion guarantees and other similar collateral security as is customary in project financings. The collateral security package will secure the obligations of the original *mustasne'* (the Developer) to make payments and perform its obligations under the *istisnaa* agreement.

14.7 *Mudaraba* structures

A preferred method of project financing under the *shari'a* involves the use of the *mudaraba* agreement (consider the discussions in the *Majelle*, articles 1404–48, and Al-Zuhayli, 2003, pp. 497–521). A *mudaraba* is a profit-sharing partnership under which one party (the Banks) acts as the *rabb al-mal* (the capital provider) and the other party (the Developer) acts as the *mudarib* (the entity investing the capital and performing the work). The Developer will then construct and operate the Project using the capital provided by the Banks.[55] Guarantees may not be taken for the purpose of securing the *mudaraba* capital. Guarantees may be taken by the *rabb al-mal* to secure the ultimate repayment of the capital, minus losses plus profits, and/or to secure the *rabb al-mal* against infringement, default, negligence or breach by the *mudarib*. Obligations of the *mudarib* may also be secured by a mortgage or pledge (*rahn*).[56]

Profit, in a *mudaraba*, is that amount which exceeds the *mudaraba* capital provided by the *rabb al-mal*. Profit is determined by *tandeed,* or actual or construction conversion of assets into cash. Loss (*wadee'ah*) is the amount by which the *mudaraba* capital is decreased or diminished and is also determined by *tandeed*. *Mudaraba* expenses are deducted from the *mudaraba* funds prior to distribution of profits. The profit and loss allocations are the critical difference between a conventional interest-based project financing and one using a *mudaraba* structure. The remainder of the conventional financing structure and documentation can be incorporated in the *mudaraba* structure and documentation with thoughtful structuring and drafting.

Under the *shari'a*, a *mudaraba* may be established by contract, and that contract may specify in detail the terms under which the partnership will operate. The *mudaraba* may be free or limited, with the vast percentage of *mudaraba* undertakings being strictly limited. A *mudaraba* may be limited as to scope, time, activities and other factors, and may (and should, in the project financing context) be very strictly limited. The *mudaraba* agreement may specify a wide range of matters that require the consent of the *rabb al-mal* Banks. For example, a *mudarib* may not mix its money with that of the *rabb al-mal* without the express permission of the *rabb al-mal*. These principles allow considerable comfort to participating Western Banks because they permit inclusion of most of the positive and negative covenants and time restrictions[57] that would be included in a conventional interest-based Loan Agreement and allow the Banks to utilize much of the credit and underwriting criteria and analyses that would be used in an interest-based financing. Various matters may be conditioned upon the consent of the Banks. And the

Banks may grant (and will probably require that) the Developer mix its funds in the undertaking.[58]

A wide range of covenants, in both a conventional Loan Agreement and a limited *mudaraba*, specify how the Developer is to conduct the agreed-upon business. For example, the *mudarib* must cause the Project to be constructed in accordance with agreed-upon plans and specifications, in accordance with an agreed-upon budget, so as to produce a specified product or line of products in a specified manner. The *mudarib* is permitted to engage only in a defined range of activities and is subject to limitations on its activities. Such limitations will likely include conducting business so that it is in compliance with applicable law and so that other persons and entities do not have rights in, or liens on, the project. The *mudarib* will not be permitted to incur indebtedness except as specifically permitted.[59] The activities that the *mudarib* may undertake or may not undertake may be tied to the financial condition from time to time of the *mudaraba*, which would allow, for example, for the inclusion of different 'financial covenants', including what are conventionally styled as 'coverage ratios' (although, in a *mudaraba*, those ratios would not be structured around interest-bearing debt).

Similarly, the *shari'a* contemplates that the *mudaraba* agreement may specify that the expenses of the *mudaraba* will be borne by the *mudarib* and the activities that the *mudarib* conducts. The *mudarib* is responsible for operational expenses, including the purchase, transportation, storage, sale and collection activities of a business. For example, the *mudarib* is responsible for collecting the debts owed to the *mudaraba*, whether the *mudarib* realizes a profit or loss as a result of such collection efforts. These principles allow for many of the same risk allocations that would be found in a conventional interest-based Loan Agreement. The *mudaraba* agreement may also specify required reserves, which may be treated as expenses of the *mudaraba*. Thus, as in any interest-based financing, reserves may be structured for taxes, insurance and bad debts. The *mudarib* will be responsible for collecting the debts owed to the *mudaraba*, whether the *mudarib* realizes a profit or loss as a result of its activities.[60] This principle is also consistent with similar risk allocations in an interest-based project financing, if drafted properly.

Each of the foregoing, and similar *shari'a* principles, allow for the construction of a *mudaraba* agreement incorporating much of the covenant (and representation and warranty) structure that is found in a conventional Loan Agreement. These matters, properly presented and considered, do not usually give rise to differences between Western financiers and the *Shari'a*-Compliant Investors.

The *mudaraba* capital must be known and designated in a definite currency, although it may include debt for which a *mudarib* or another person is liable.[61] The Banks and the Developer may agree that the capital will be made available upon demand, or satisfaction of certain conditions, up to a specified ceiling amount.[62] These principles allow the infusion of the *mudaraba* capital to be structured almost identically to the infusion of loan moneys under a conventional Loan Agreement. A loan is made upon demand by submission of a draw request and satisfaction of relevant conditions precedent up to an amount equal to the available commitment or facility amount; and the *mudaraba* capital infusion may be similarly structured and conditioned. Carefully considered, even the failure to complete construction in accordance with the budget or available commitment (capital) raises identical issues under each of the conventional loan and *mudaraba* structures. The critical difference, of course, is in how profits and losses are allocated, and preferences of allocation, if there is a failure to agree on a resolution or an insufficiency in performance.

The most troubling aspects of the *mudaraba* financing structure for interest-based financial institutions relate to the *shari'a* concepts with respect to profits and losses and the principle that the *mudarib* Developer is not liable for failure to return the capital (except in specified situations). Accommodation has been found with respect to some of the *shari'a* principles, but, at base, there is a fundamental divergence of the *shari'a* from the practices in interest-based financing.

Profit is the excess over contributed *mudaraba* capital (capital being the equivalent of principal in the conventional loan arrangement). Profits may only be paid after the *rabb al-mal* has received a return of its capital (including a retrieval of previous losses). Thus any periodic distributions of profit during the period of the *mudaraba* are considered tentative and are subject to the final accounting upon liquidation of the *mudaraba* (see, for example, Fadeel, 2002, pp. 90–108). While the percentage distributions of profit must be specified at the inception of the contract, it is permissible to provide for different percentages of profit distribution when the profit exceeds certain levels, thresholds or amounts.[63] These principles have been used to enhance repayments to the Banks as *rabb al-mal* in *shari'a*-compliant project financings, although lack of precision and care in drafting may result in the payment provisions being determined to be impermissible. In some transactions, timing of payment, with accrual of liability for amounts then unpaid to the *mudarib*, have been used as further enhancements. It is not permissible to assign one of the participants in a *mudaraba* a predetermined profit; there must be a sharing in accordance with agreed percentages. Interest, under a conventional interest-based loan, would constitute a predetermined profit and is not permissible.

Losses from the operation of the *mudaraba* must be borne by the *rabb al-mal* in the absence of infringement, default, negligence or breach of contract provisions by the *mudarib* Developer. The *rabb al-mal* suffers the loss of its capital, and the *mudarib* suffers the loss of its work and efforts. This allocation of losses is a particularly difficult point for conventional interest-based financiers in a project financing. The primary means of addressing this consternation in transactions involving interest-based financiers has focused on the contractual provisions pertaining to infringement, default, negligence and breach.

Under the *shari'a*, the Banks and the Developer may agree upon methodologies for determinations as to the occurrence of infringement, default, negligence or breach. Should any of those categories of behaviour or status occur, the *mudarib* may be held liable for the return of the *mudaraba* capital. Clearly, defaulting under the *mudaraba* agreement or breaching its terms will result in liability for the *mudarib* Developer. So also will exceeding of contractual authority by the *mudarib*. And, under the *shari'a*, failure of the *mudarib* to carry out activities or exercise care that it is supposed to carry out or exercise under usage and practice will result in liability to the *mudarib*.

Careful drafting of the *mudaraba* agreement can significantly narrow the area of consternation and controversy. The first step in the drafting exercise is to provide a detailed description of the scope of the *mudarib*'s authority, responsibilities, obligations, liabilities and ability to act in a wide range of situations. Most conventional loan agreements already provide the necessary detail, without further modification as to authority, responsibilities and ability or inability to act. This is done primarily through the positive and negative covenants[64] and through the representations and warranties. Conventional loan agreements also adequately address defaults, particularly through the 'event of default' sections of the agreements. To move toward a risk allocation acceptable to Western financiers, it is advisable to focus on the drafting of those sections of the *mudaraba* agreement that address the concepts of infringement, default and breach that do not, in each case, constitute an event of default. For example, an infringement, default or breach that does not give rise to an immediate event of default may be structured so that it does give rise to monetary liability to the *rabb al-mal* Banks, and thus addresses many of the disconnections perceived by those Banks. It is also prudent to specify clearly, if only by reference to applicable law and industry standards, the principles and paradigm to be used in determining usage and practice. Legal standards of negligence provide a useful base of reference and have been incorporated in *mudaraba* agreements as liability triggers.

Upon the termination of the *mudaraba*, the Developer *mudarib* is obliged to return the *mudaraba* capital, plus profit and minus loss, to the Banks as *rabb al-mal*. Failure to do so results in liability on the *mudarib*, including as a usurper. Any profits made by the *mudarib* through the use of assets after the capital should have been returned to the *rabb al-mal* will be payable over to the *rabb al-mal*.

A collateral security package will be provided by the *mudarib* (the Developer) and by the *mudaraba* as a separate entity.[65] The collateral security package will secure the obligations of the *mudarib* to the Banks as *rabb al-mal*. For example, it will secure the obligations to pay profit and, to the extent not diminished by losses, the capital to the Banks. It will also secure the obligations of the *mudarib* in respect of possible infringement, default, negligence or breach. The package will be similar to that in any other project financing: it will likely include a mortgage and security interest covering the Project and cash flows, accounts and personal property used in the operation of the Project. It may also include environmental indemnities, completion guarantees and other guarantees.

14.8   *Sharikat mahassa–murabaha* structures

Another structure in which there is no interest-bearing loan, and the entire transaction is *shari'a*-compliant, entails the formation of a joint venture (*sharikat mahassa*) among the Banks providing the financing and the project sponsor that will operate the Project and a *murabaha* (deferred payment sale) in respect of the shares or joint venture interests (*hissas*).[66] The structure allows for participation by both Islamic banks and conventional Western banks.[67] One of the benefits of the *sharikat mahassa–murabaha* structure is the simplicity of the structure and documentation (there are only three primary agreements: (a) the *sharikat mahassa* agreement, (b) the *murabaha* agreement, and (c) the Nondisclosure Undertaking and Indemnity Agreement).[68] However, unanimity among the *Shari'a* Supervisory Boards is lacking with respect to some critical *shari'a* issues pertaining to matters such as (i) the breadth of the indemnity provided by the Electric Utility (as hereinafter defined) in respect of the operation of the Project, (ii) permissible segmentation of the overall transaction to facilitate *hissa* purchases by the Banks, (iii) profit and loss allocations among the members of the *sharikat mahassa*, (iv) the times at which the *murabaha* agreement or agreements pertaining to the sale of the *hissas* by the Banks to the Electric Utility may occur, and (v) the valuation of the *hissas* in connection with the *murabaha* sales. These issues are discussed in this section.

As an illustrative example of a project financing using the *sharikat mahassa–murabaha* structure, an electric utility (the 'Electric Utility') desires to construct and operate electric generation and transmission assets. Three banks desire to provide the financing necessary for construction and operation of these assets (referred to, individually, as 'Bank 1', 'Bank 2' and 'Bank 3' and, collectively, as the 'Banks'). As discussed in this section, collateral security will be provided to secure the obligations of the Electric Utility under the *murabaha* agreements.

In this example, the financing is to be structured as a combined fixed and floating rate financing: Bank 1 providing fixed rate financing; and Bank 2 and Bank 3 providing floating rate financing. The tenor of the financing is to be seven years, to include a two-year construction period and a five-year repayment period. Repayment will be made in 60 equal monthly instalments commencing upon the 'handover' date of the Project.

The Electric Utility will negotiate and enter into the Construction Contract for the Project. In connection with the capitalization of the *sharikat mahassa*, the Electric Utility will contribute the Construction Contract to the *sharikat mahassa*.

14.8.1 *Formation of the* sharikat mahassa

The *sharikat mahassa* will be formed by four parties: the Electric Utility and the three Banks. Each of such parties will hold *hissas* in the *sharikat mahassa*. The Electric Utility will be designated the 'Technical Manager' for the *sharikat mahassa* and Bank 1 will be designated as the 'Administrative and Finance Manager' of the *sharikat mahassa*. As the Technical Manager, the Electric Utility will have responsibility for all liabilities in respect of unforeseen and technical matters.

The laws of most jurisdictions provide for the formation and operative existence of joint ventures. In certain instances, the existence of the joint venture need not be disclosed (an undisclosed joint venture). In the example being discussed, the *sharikat mahassa* and the participation of the Banks in that venture will be undisclosed and third parties, such as the General Contractor, will deal only with the Electric Utility. In some jurisdictions, if the joint venture is disclosed, the participants in the joint venture (here the Banks and the Electric Utility) will be liable for the actions of the joint venture in respect of the construction and operation of the Project.[69] To address this disclosure liability issue, and protect the Banks from liability exposure in respect of the construction and operation of the Project, the Electric Utility and the Banks will enter into a 'Nondisclosure Undertaking and Indemnity Agreement'.[70] Pursuant to the Nondisclosure Undertaking and Indemnity Agreement, the parties agree not to disclose the existence of the *sharikat mahassa* and each party agrees to indemnify the other parties from liabilities resulting from any such disclosure by such party. The extent of the allowable indemnity is a matter that will be considered by the relevant *Shari'a* Supervisory Boards, and not all *Shari'a* Supervisory Boards are in agreement as to the breadth of available coverage.

The *sharikat mahassa* will own the Project. The *sharikat mahassa* will be capitalized by nominal initial cash contributions from the Electric Utility and each of the Banks. In addition, the Electric Utility, as part of its initial capital contribution, will assign the Construction Contract to the *sharikat mahassa*. In order to effect this capital structure, care must be taken in the drafting of the Construction Contract to allow such an assignment to the *sharikat mahassa* without disclosure of the existence of the *sharikat mahassa* to the General Contractor: no small accomplishment. Further capital contributions will be made by each of the Banks on a periodic basis. That is, each time a construction milestone is completed, upon notice from Bank 1 as the Administrative and Finance Manager, each of the Banks will purchase *hissas* from the *sharikat mahassa* in proportion to such Banks' percentage participation in the financing. The proceeds of such *hissa* purchases will then be used to make payments to the General Contractor. As with an *istisnaa–ijara* structure, the milestone completion certificate and request require the presentation of various deliverables and is quite similar to a conventional loan disbursement request in terms of substantive coverage.

Each *Shari'a* Supervisory Board will likely have a different position on exactly what constitutes a 'milestone completion' that gives rise to a purchase of *hissas*. At one end of the spectrum is the position that no *hissa* purchase is permissible until construction of the entire Project is completed. At the other end of the spectrum is the position that a *hissa* purchase is permissible for any work that is completed at any time. Most *Shari'a* Supervisory Boards seem to take a position that is closer to the later end of the spectrum, although they do focus on the completion of discrete and definable work segments or components. Because of the nature of construction scheduling, careful structuring will allow for regularity and periodicity in the making of construction payments. In any case, this aspect of the structuring should be clarified with the *Shari'a* Supervisory Board early in the process of structuring the transaction.

In the period prior to completion of construction, *hissas* may be transferred from one Bank to another without the consent of the Electric Utility.[71] Any other transfers of *hissas* require the consent of the Electric Utility.

The agreement governing the operation of the *sharikat mahassa* will have to address allocations of profits and losses among the members of the *sharikat mahassa*. Local laws governing such allocations will play a significant role in the structuring of the transaction. The principle that the parties try to effect in a project financing structure using the *sharikat mahassa–murabaha* structure is that the Banks are not allocated any profits and are not liable for any losses, at least prior to the completion of construction. This is another instance in which *Shari'a* Supervisory Boards have varying positions, and the positions of the relevant *Shari'a* Supervisory Boards should be sought early in the structuring process. In many cases, because of the economics of a Project during construction and start-up and commissioning, the allocations of profits and losses will be of little consequence prior to the completion of construction (assuming completion occurs: the issues pertaining to failure to complete become complex). In other cases, those allocations may themselves cause a recalculation of, or be included in the calculation of, the sale price of the *hissas* in the *murabaha* phase of the transaction. In most transactions there is segmentation of the Project to allow achievement of the profit and loss allocation principles set forth above. For example, at a minimum, most transactions have been segmented into completion and commissioning phases, but greater segmentation has also been used: in some cases the segmentation has been to the level of work done on a monthly basis. The determination of the degree of segmentation will be dependent upon local legal requirements, the position of the *Shari'a* Supervisory Board with respect to profit and loss allocation, and the position of the *Shari'a* Supervisory Board with respect to the time at which the *murabaha* agreement or agreements may be executed and delivered.

14.8.2   Murabaha *phase*

The *murabaha* phase of the transaction involves the sale to the Electric Utility by each of the Banks of the *hissas* owned by that Bank. Payments in respect of the *murabaha* sale are made by the Electric Utility on a monthly instalment basis over a period of 60 consecutive months. The pricing for the *hissas* sold by each Bank varies according to the type of financing provided by that Bank (fixed or floating rate and, if floating, the reference rates used for that sale).

An important issue, upon which the positions of different *Shari'a* Supervisory Boards vary, pertains to the timing of execution of the *murabaha* agreements. Some *Shari'a* Supervisory Boards allow execution of the *murabaha* agreement relating to all the *hissas* to be sold by the Banks to be executed at the inception of the transaction (that is, at the time of formation of the *sharikat mahassa*). Other *Shari'a* Supervisory Boards have taken the position that the *murabaha* agreement relating to all of such *hissas* must be executed at the time of completion of construction. Yet another *Shari'a* Supervisory Board position is that a *murabaha* agreement with respect to each group of *hissas* may be executed at the time the related milestone completion certificate is submitted and accepted by the Administrative and Financial Manager and that group of *hissas* is purchased by the Banks (essentially, the execution and delivery of the *murabaha* agreement becomes a condition precedent to the purchase of the related group of *hissas*). Some *Shari'a* Supervisory Board opinions essentially mandate multiple *murabaha* agreements. Any position that does not allow for execution of the *murabaha* agreement or agreements at the inception of the *sharikat mahassa* that covers all *hissas* purchased during the course of the financing transaction raises concerns that the Electric Utility might decline to execute a *murabaha* agreement after the Banks have funded part of the construction but prior to completion of construction. This is a difficult circumstance for the Banks, and one that they generally will not accept. Again, it is important to clarify the positions of the relevant *Shari'a* Supervisory Boards early in the structuring process.

The purchase price for the *hissas* being sold pursuant to the *murabaha* transaction is another element of the transaction that generates considerable discussion with the relevant *Shari'a* Supervisory Boards. Some take the position that the *hissas* should be valued at the net asset value at the time of handover of the Project, while others focus on fair market value measurements at the time of handover. In practice, most *Shari'a* Supervisory Boards have allowed establishment of the *hissa* purchase price to be structured so that the price is equal to the principal amount paid by the Banks for the *hissas* at the time of their purchase from the *sharikat mahassa*, plus the agreed-upon profit amount (whether determined at a fixed or a variable rate).

14.9   *Sukuk* structures

The recent (re)emergence of the *sukuk* as a financing technique holds great promise for the future of *shari'a*-compliant project financing. A *sukuk* is usually referred to as an 'Islamic bond'. *Sukuk* are actually more akin to 'pass-through certificates',[72] 'equipment trust certificates' or 'investment certificates' (Wilson, 2004, p. 3) because of ownership attributes. Thus a *sukuk* represents a proportional or undivided ownership interest in an asset or pool of assets.[73]

The Accounting and Auditing Organization for Islamic Financial Institutions ('AAOIFI') has issued a Standard for Investment *Sukuk* (AAOFI, 2003), which defines investment *sukuk* as certificates of equal value representing receipt of the value of the certificates, which value is applied to a planned and designated use, common title to shares and rights in tangible assets, usufructs and services, equity of a given project, or equity of a special investment activity (Adam and Thomas, 2004a, pp. 42–3; Adam and Thomas, 2004b, pp. 73–5). The AAOIFI *Sukuk* Standard provides for 14 eligible assets classes, some of which are applicable in the project finance context (Adam and Thomas, 2004a, pp. 36–7):

1. securitization of an existing tangible asset through a *sukuk* issuance, whereby the investor owns, through the *sukuk al-ijarah*, a share of the asset and related income;
2. obtaining acquisition funds through a *sukuk* issuance where a person seeks to acquired a tangible asset that will be leased and whereby the investors will own, by virtue of a *sukuk ijarah mowsufa bithima*, a divisible share in that asset and any related gain or income;
3. securitization of the beneficial interest in a leasehold estate by the owner of that lease-hold estate through the use of a *sukuk manfa'at al-ijarah*;
4. securitization of the beneficial interest in the underlying assets and related leasehold estate to be acquired and leased by way of a *sukuk manfa'at al-ijarah mowsufa bithima*;
5. presale of goods to be manufactured at a future date through issuance of a *sukuk al-salam*;
6. funding of the cost of construction or manufacture of projects or goods to be con-structed or manufactured in the future through the issuance of a *sukuk al-istisnaa*;
7. capital participation in a business, including a project, through the issuance of a *sukuk al-musharakah* in which the *sukuk* holders participate in the risk and rewards of the *musharaqah*; and
8. capital participation in a *mudaraba*, as the capital provider, through the issuance of a *sukuk al-mudaraba* in which the *sukuk* holders share in the risks and rewards of a *mudaraba* as capital providers.

A review of the foregoing indicates that they may be divided into *sukuk* that bear prede-termined returns and *sukuk* that allow for sharing of profit and, in some instances, loss. To date, most issued *sukuk* have borne predetermined returns, and most such *sukuk* have been *sukuk al-ijara*, frequently at a predetermined rate of return. The *sukuk al-musharaka* and the *sukuk al-mudaraba* are examples of profit and loss-sharing *sukuk*.

14.9.1 *Generic* sukuk al-ijara *structures*
A generic model of a *sukuk al-ijara* is illustrated in Figure 14.7. The transaction comprises three basic stages. In the first stage, the Project Company agrees, pursuant to the 'Asset Sale Agreement', to sell a pool of assets to the Funding Company for a specified amount. The Funding Company issues *sukuk al-ijara* to the '*Sukuk* Holders' for an amount equal to the purchase price (in the diagram, the amount of the 'Asset Sale Payment') of the assets being acquired by the Funding Company pursuant to the Asset Sale Agreement. The Funding Company makes the Asset Sale Payment to the Project Company against delivery by the Project Company to the Funding Company of the assets.[74] At the incep-tion of the transaction, the Project Company will also agree, pursuant to the 'Asset Repurchase Agreement', to purchase the assets from the Funding Company at a specified date and for a specified amount.

In the second stage, the Funding Company, as the lessor, and the Project Company, as the lessee, enter into the Lease (*ijara*) with respect to those assets.[75] The rental payments

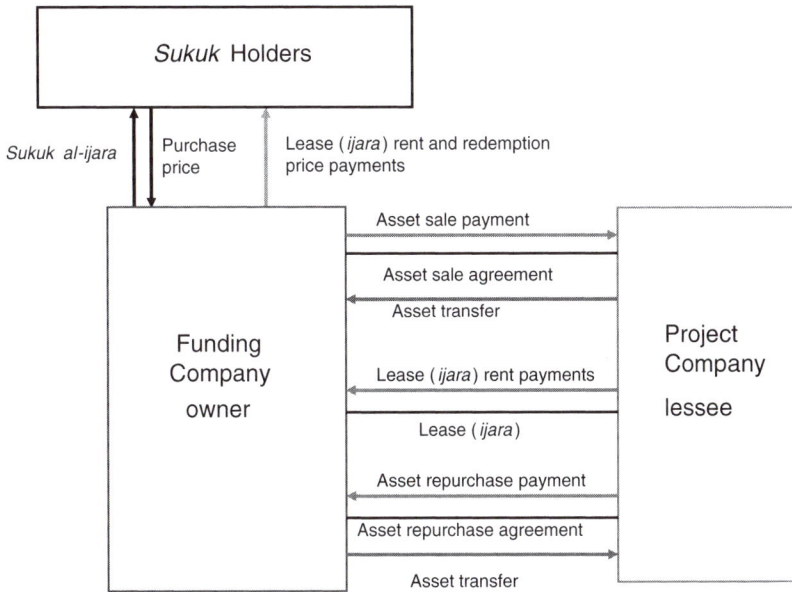

Figure 14.7   Generic model of a sukuk al-ijara

will be structured to (a) provide the desired returns on the *sukuk* and, in certain cases, to the investors in the Funding Company,[76] and (b) to provide funds for periodic redemptions, whether at maturity of the *sukuk* or periodically.[77] The Project Company, as the lessee, pays periodic lease rentals to the Funding Company. In the example set out in Figure 14.7, all of such lease rentals are then paid by the Funding Company to the *Sukuk* Holders. Alternatively, and depending upon the structuring of ownership of the Funding Company, a portion of the rentals under the Lease (*ijara*) may be paid to the *Sukuk* Holders, with the remainder paid to the investors in the Funding Company.

In the final stage of the transaction, the *Sukuk* Holders will submit the *sukuk* for redemption (upon maturity and, depending upon the liquidity features of the transaction, periodically prior to maturity). At the time of redemption, the Project Company will purchase the assets from the Funding Company, and the assets will be transferred by the Funding Company to the Project Company against payment by the Project Company of the agreed amount of the 'Asset Repurchase Payment'.

14.9.2   Generic sukuk al-mudaraba *structures*
The *mudaraba* structure may also be incorporated into a *sukuk* offering in a number of different variants of the *sukuk al-mudaraba*. A generalized generic form of a *sukuk al-mudaraba* for a project financing is set forth in Figure 14.8.

For the purposes of discussion, this example assumes that both the equity portion and the debt-equivalent portion of the financing of the construction and operation of the Project will be *shari'a*-compliant and that different investors will participate in the equity and the debt-equivalent. Thus it is assumed that the Project Company is formed by the Developer and the *Shari'a*-Compliant Investors (who provide the equity).

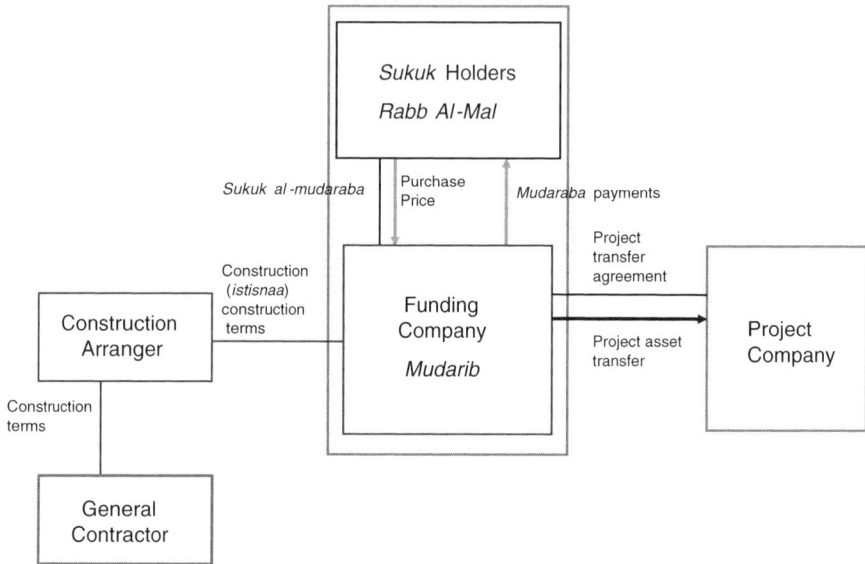

Figure 14.8   Sukuk al-mudaraba *structure*

The Funding Company is established as a restricted, single-purpose, special-purpose vehicle to act as the *mudarib* for the construction of the Project. The Funding Company will act as the issuer of the *sukuk al-mudaraba*. The *mudaraba* agreement for the transaction will be included in the subscription agreement for the purchase of the *sukuk al-mudaraba*, and thus includes the terms set forth in the private placement memorandum or prospectus relating to the offering. The financing for the construction of the Project will be provided by the *Sukuk* Holders in the simplest structure of this type. In more complex structures, a portion of the financing (say, 80 per cent) will be provided by the *Sukuk* Holders, with the remainder being provided by the Project Company.[78]

The Funding Company will enter into a Construction (*istisnaa*) Agreement for the construction of the Project. The example shown in Figure 14.8 utilizes a Construction Arranger that, in turn, enters into a standard construction contract (labelled 'Construction Terms'). That formulation allows the General Contractor to use its customary construction agreement, which may not be *shari'a*-compliant, while preserving the ability of the Funding Company to enter into a *shari'a*-compliant *istisnaa* agreement. Many General Contractors use a standardized form of construction agreement, and will not use any other form. Even if the General Contractor were willing to use a *shari'a*-compliant form, the transactional costs of negotiating such a modified construction contract would be prohibitive. The use of the Construction Arranger allows avoidance of *shari'a* compliance issues in negotiating with the General Contractor and implementing the construction of the Project.

At the time of issuance of the *sukuk al-mudaraba*, the Project Company will enter into a 'Project Transfer Agreement' with the Funding Company. This agreement provides significant structural flexibility. For example, a construction *mudaraba*, such as that formed between the Funding Company and the *Sukuk* Holders, must extend into the operational period in order for any returns, whether of capital or profit, to be provided to the *Sukuk* Holders or the Funding Company; there is no income to the *mudaraba* during the construction period. That precludes a pure construction financing using the *sukuk al-mudaraba* structure unless another means of income generation exists for the *mudaraba*. The Project Transfer Agreement provides a number of possible solutions. In the simplest case, the transfer price payable under the Project Transfer Agreement can be structured to provide for payment of an amount equal to (a) the capital contributed by the *Sukuk* Holders plus (b) a calculated return to the *Sukuk* Holders. For all practical purposes, this allows for the creation of a 'fixed income *sukuk al-mudaraba*' because the capital and profit amount will be known and the date of transfer of the Project will be established in the Project Transfer Agreement.

Interesting structural issues arise with respect to the timing of the receipt of funds from the *Sukuk* Holders and, possibly, the Project Company. For example, it is economically inefficient to take down all of the funds that will ultimately be required through the issuance of the *sukuk al-mudaraba* at the inception of construction. Greater efficiency is obtained if those funds are taken down on an as-needed basis, that is, as payments must be made on the Construction (*istisnaa*) Agreement for the Project. Serial issuances of the *sukuk al-mudaraba* are one possibility. However, serial issuances do not provide the pre-existing *Sukuk* Holders, the Developer, and the *Shari'a*-Compliant Investors with completion comfort. Another approach is to provide in the subscription agreement that the subscriber is irrevocably committed to fund a specified amount through the purchase of *sukuk al-mudaraba* on a periodic basis that coincides with construction payment schedules and realities. This, of course, presents an issue of the creditworthiness of the *Sukuk* Holders with respect to further payments for the future *sukuk* issuances as well as disjunctions in funding if the estimate of the construction schedule is not exact. However, contractual provisions in the subscription agreement may be constructed to provide significant incentives for such *Sukuk* Holders not to default on future payment obligations. Yet another alternative is to take down the full amount that will ultimately be required from issuance of the *sukuk al-mudaraba* (or a larger portion) at inception, and take none (or relatively little) of the portion of the construction cost to be contributed by the Project Company. In the late stages of construction, the Project Company contribution can be infused. This last element can be structured to provide the *Sukuk* Holders with comfort that the Project Company portion will be infused by having the Project Company contribute its entire amount to a reserve account at the inception of construction. This reserve account would then be pledged as collateral security for the obligations of the Project Company to make the contribution. The early contribution by the Project Company puts the Developer and *Shari'a*-Compliant Investors in no worse a position than they would otherwise occupy as pure equity and, thus, does not disadvantage their internal rate of return calculations.

14.10 Conclusion
The focus of this chapter is on the financing of major economic undertakings of great complexity involving multiple and diverse parties from multiple international jurisdictions and subject to multiple legal regimes. One of the critical assumptions is that the size, complexity and scope of these economic undertakings will require cooperative, knowledgeable participation by both Western and *shari'a*-compliant participants. It will require just and fair allocation of risks among the participants. Each participant will have preconceptions,

primarily based upon its past experience within the economic, institutional, political, legal and financial systems in which it operates. Each participant will be subject to a wide range of constraints, based upon those same systems. And each participant will need to be satisfied that the financing structure used to effect the endeavour allocates risk in accordance with its needs, and that those allocations will be fairly and justly enforced.

In this chapter, the focus is on project financings involving groups of participants that have fundamentally different conceptions of the justifications for economic reward based upon fundamentally different conceptions of risk participation in any such economic undertaking. In the Western interest-based system, financiers are preferentially provided with their economic reward (interest and principal). Under the *shari'a*, a preference of this type is impermissible *riba*; the risks of the transaction or undertaking are not adequately shared by the participants. The challenge is to develop and implement structures that permit involvement of both types of participants without violation of the *shari'a* and in a manner that satisfies the competing economic, institutional, political, legal, regulatory and accounting constraints upon each of the participants.

This chapter presents an overview of two categories of *shari'a*-compliant project financing structures. One category includes those in which Western interest-based structures 'coexist' with or 'meld' with *shari'a*-compliant structures, both being present and harmonized in the single integrated transaction. However, the Western and *shari'a*-compliant structures are segregated within the overall structure so as to allow each of the Western participants and the *shari'a*-compliant participants to achieve the requisite level of comfort and determination of compliance based upon their differing perspectives. The other category of structures is purely *shari'a*-compliant, and participation by a Western interest-based participant will require that participant to consider risk allocation from the perspective of the *Shari'a*-Compliant Investor. In each case, issues are raised, and suggestions are made, with respect to the way each of these groups of participants can work within the structure to achieve the requisite degree of predictability, stability and certainty for all participants, each from their own perceptual state, and satisfy the economic, institutional, legal, regulatory and accounting constraints that are imposed upon the participants.

These structural discussions are general and, as is so often the case, the difficulties are in the details. The process of implementing and refining these structures, of adapting them to the business needs of the participants, of exploring the details, should be viewed as a rare opportunity at the threshold of greater understanding, cooperation and mutual benefit. That process will increase awareness of, and knowledge concerning, the fundamental principles, including economic principles, underlying both the Western interest-based system and the Islamic economic system. The process will increase awareness and understanding of the fundamental cultural, moral and religious principles that guide the existence of people. If the recent past is any indication, *shari'a*-compliant structures can be implemented, and can be continually refined, in a manner that allows cross-systemic participation with a high level of comfort for all participants and in a process that promotes a continual process of greater knowledge, awareness and comfort.

Notes

1. Views expressed in this chapter are those of the author and not those of Dechert LLP. Part of this chapter, including discussions of certain of the structures discussed here and variants on those structures, have appeared in McMillen (2000a, 2001, 2003, 2004a, 2004b).

2. However imprecise and inelegant, this chapter adopts the convention of referring to such interest-based financings as 'Western' or 'conventional'.
3. *Shari'a* means, literally, 'the Way'. While the *shari'a* includes principles and precepts of a religious and ethical nature, in addition to matters of a 'legal' nature, this chapter will use the term as a reference to Islamic legal precepts and principles only (without regard to whether such precepts and principles have been incorporated in applicable secular law). The notes of this chapter cite various sources with respect to the nature of applicable *shari'a* principles and precepts. Those are not the only sources used for descriptions of those principles and precepts. Since 1996, many Islamic scholars have graciously given of their time and learning in assisting the author in understanding those principles and precepts, and the fruit of their efforts is also reflected in this chapter (with any mistakes being solely attributable to the author). The author expresses his gratitude to some of the scholars that have made the most significant direct contribution to his understanding of the *shari'a*: Mohammad Taqi Usmani, Mohamed Ali Elgari and Abdul Sattar Abu Guddah (who comprised the first *Shari'a* Supervisory Board to review structures developed by the author), Nizam Yaquby and Yusuf Talal DeLorenzo, and many others. Each of these gentlemen has been forthright in his critical analysis, while also exhibiting imperturbable patience, support and encouragement. The author also expresses his gratitude to Hafedh Maamouri, who initiated, and skilfully guided, a collaboration with the author on a wide range of *shari'a*-compliant products and introduced the author to many *shari'a* scholars, including those mentioned above; few individuals are as generous with their time and learning.
4. *Riba* is traditionally translated as 'usury'. However, jurists have a more expansive concept in Islamic jurisprudence addressing not only prevention of the exploitation of those in a weak bargaining position, but also 'the illegality of all forms of gain or profit which were unearned in the sense that they resulted from speculative or risky transactions and could not be precisely calculated in advance by the contracting parties' (Coulson, 1984, p. 11). This broad definition encompasses, generally, both *riba al-nasia* (where there is insufficient financial risk) and *riba al-fadl* (which addresses duress, market exclusion and subterfuge transactions). See also Vogel and Hayes (1998, pp. 71–95), Saleh (1992, pp. 11–43), Comair-Obeid (1996, pp. 43–57) and El-Gamal (2000, pp. 29–40). A history of usury in medieval Europe, including the Canon Law positions at different periods, is Noonan (1957); this work provides an interesting perspective on the Islamic concept of *riba*.
   Gharar focuses on the concept of risk and is traditionally defined as uncertainty in a contract with respect to the subject matter of the contract and matters such as the deliverability, quantity or quality of such subject matter. It also frequently encompasses ambiguity with respect to consideration or the terms of the contract. Consider, in particular, Vogel and Hayes (1998, pp. 87–93). See also the discussion of risk (and not, specifically, *gharar*) in Mohammad Fadel (2000, pp. 81–8).
5. The historical trend is shifting. Increasingly, conventional Western banks, fund managers, developers and other project participants are initiating the use of *shari'a*-compliant structures. Many conventional Western banks, particularly large international banks, have a significant base of Muslim clients and desire to introduce *shari'a*-compliant products to serve this client base. In other cases, fund managers and developers desire access to investment capital from *Shari'a*-Compliant Investors. In some cases, government mandates (such as a mandate that at least part of a project financing be *shari'a*-compliant) induce participants to be both responsive and proactive in developing *shari'a*-compliant alternatives.
6. With respect to some of the types of broad range of credit enhancement devices, including guarantee concepts, see Toan and Barakat (2001, pp. 115–20). The focus is on *ijara* transactions, but the principles extend to other *shari'a*-compliant structures as well.
7. Terms defined in this section will be used throughout this chapter with reference to all structures.
8. Local tax considerations will be one of the primary determinants of the type of investment vehicle (limited partnership, limited liability company, corporation) that is used for a specific transaction.
9. There are as many permutations as the creativity of businessmen and financiers will allow. As an example, and one that should be borne in mind as the reader considers the structures presented in this chapter, in a condominium or residential housing project, individual condominiums or houses will be sold to third parties as they are completed. The Project Company and the Banks will negotiate the principal repayment schedule based upon the unit sale schedule. A percentage of the sale price for each condominium or house will be applied to principal repayment, and that percentage may decrease after predetermined numbers of condominiums or houses are sold. The Project Company will pay all or a portion of the difference between the sale price and the principal amortization amount to its investors. This is particularly true if the investors are participating through a fund structure because the fund will desire to achieve a continuing internal rate of return and a cash flow distribution stream. The Project Company may also desire to retain some of that differential for reinvestment in the Project. Such a case would be where the Project Company desires to use some of the return from the early condominium or house sales as equity for a later expansion stage of the Project or otherwise desires to reduce the leverage in the financing structure.
10. The exception of the real estate realm is significant. There have been many real estate financing transactions that have been structured on a *shari'a*-compliant basis, particularly in the United States and Europe.

This section of this chapter is focused on non-real estate project financings. To date, real estate project financings have primarily used an *istisnaa–ijara* structure and are discussed in section 14.5 of this chapter. Some of the reasons that there have been so few *shari'a*-compliant project financings are set forth in Husain (2002, p. 143). This article also provides short summaries of some of the *shari'a*-compliant transactions that have been done to date.

11. A project financing that was structured and implemented entirely as a *shari'a*-compliant transaction is described in section 14.8 of this chapter. That transaction was a *sharikat mahassa–murabaha* transaction for the financing of electric generation and transmission assets in the Kingdom of Saudi Arabia.

12. In this chapter, and bowing to common Western convention at the time of writing, the term '*istisnaa*' (rather than, for example, '*bina*') is used for construction contracts, although a more literal usage of the term '*istisnaa*' would be limited to manufacturing contracts.

13. Section 14.5 of this chapter addresses an *ijara* structure and sections 14.5 and 14.6 discuss *istisnaa* structures, although none of such sections focuses on single tranche transactions.

14. To the author's knowledge, the first use of this structure in the United States was in the year 2000, with immediate implementation in a series of transactions. The structure was modified in the early transactions in order to reduce transactional costs substantially, and some of those modifications are discussed later in this section. As banks and financial institutions have become more familiar with the structure, the documentation has been greatly simplified. The development and structure of the initial United States transactions are discussed in detail in McMillen (2000a, pp. 1237–60, 2004a, pp. 214–23, 2003). A general description of the financing of the Maconda Park *istisnaa–ijara* financing, the first such financing in the United States, appeared in McMillen (2000b, pp. 28–9).

15. A range of legal and tax issues pertaining to cross-border Islamic transactions, particularly those implemented in the United States, are discussed in Salah and Knight (1998, pp. 155–8). Tax aspects of a cross-border lease (*ijara*) structure with structural aspects in common with the *istisnaa–ijara* discussed in this chapter are discussed in Toan (2000, pp. 191–7).

16. See Al-Adliyah – the *Majelle* ([1933] 1968, articles 338–92). See also wa-Adillatuh (1997), al-Zuhayli (2003, pp. 165–231). Of course, the type of asset must itself be permissible under the *shari'a*. Thus, for example, *shari'a*-compliant project financing could not be undertaken with respect to, among others, plants used for the production of alcohol for human consumption or houses of prostitution. While rarely applicable in a project financing, natural products should be financed through the use of *salam* contracts rather than *istisnaa* contracts, unless the natural product is to undergo treatment or processing.

17. There are a variety of *shari'a* principles applicable to the specification of type, quality and quantity. The purpose of these principles is to avoid unknown elements (*jahala*) and deceit (*gharar*). See, for example, the *Majelle* (article 390).

18. Such a back-to-back arrangement is customarily referred to as 'an *istisnaa–parallel istisnaa*' transaction. That structure is discussed in section 14.6 of this chapter. The terms of the *istisnaa* and the parallel *istisnaa* are identical, except for the amount and timing of payment. The Banks (the 'original *sane*') are the *mustasne*' in the parallel *istisnaa* and the actual manufacturer or constructor is the *sane*' (sometimes referred to as the 'end-*sane*').

19. The application of this principle, and its specifics, become important in considering how to structure the change order process.

20. It is good practice in compliance with the *shari'a* to incorporate these supervision provisions, and correlative waivers, in the Managing Contractor Agreement and the Lease (*ijara*) (each as hereinafter defined and discussed). See *Majelle* (articles 300–360) and Al-Zuhayli (2003, pp. 165–231).

21. Good practice in compliance with the *shari'a* would suggest incorporation of these assignments, and correlative waivers, in the Managing Contractor Agreement and the Lease (*ijara*).

22. This principle, in its specifics, is one of the bases for the use of the Understanding to Sell (as hereinafter defined). There are other bases as well.

23. Al-Zuhayli (2003, pp. 386–8) summarizes the positions of some of the different schools of Islamic jurisprudence.

24. See *Majelle*, articles 443, 470–72, 477, 478. As noted in the text of this chapter, this is a difficult structural and documentary issue in any project financing involving construction of an asset and is the subject of considerable debate among *shari'a* scholars. See McMillen (2000a, pp. 1249–52, and footnotes 92–4 and 2003, pp. 96–7, and footnotes 23–6).

25. There is substantial discussion of variable rate rental arrangements in *shari'a*-compliant leases of equipment and real property. Many such leases make reference to the London Interbank Offered Rate ('LIBOR') as a base from which to compute periodic rentals. Given the absence of reference rates based on Islamic financial instruments, most *shari'a* scholars allow the use of LIBOR as a reference rate. However, most *shari'a* scholars object to the direct determination of rental rates by reference solely to variable or floating rates in the body of a current *ijara* (Elgari, 1999, p. 153). See McMillen (2000a, p. 1254 and footnote 100)

with respect to a methodology by which periodic rate adjustments are incorporated in a *shari'a*-compliant *ijara*. See also Al-Zuhayli (2003, pp. 386–7).

26. *Majelle*, articles 513–21 (pertaining to the concept of an option for defect). See also, above, note 10 and accompanying text, and Al-Zuhayli (2003, pp. 416–17). These provisions, and the *shari'a* precepts implementing these principles, are a major factor in structuring financing leases, particularly in the United States and Europe where financing parties rely heavily on triple-net leasing concepts. This chapter refers to 'structural maintenance' and similar concepts. These references are a shorthand, and one often used by *Shari'a* Boards as well, to those elements of structure, maintenance and integrity of the project that pertain directly to the benefits sought to be obtained through leasing of the leased assets, and thus include items beyond pure structural maintenance, including related and derivative concepts such as casualty insurance. Those items will be determined on a case-by-case factual analysis of the leased assets and the purposes of the *ijara*.

27. A real estate project was chosen as the illustrative example in part because of thin margins; it is useful to examine the types of accommodations and structural and documentary modifications that must be made to ensure that a *shari'a*-compliant real estate transaction is competitive with conventional Western transactions, which are highly standardized and economically efficient. Fewer such accommodations need to be made in a large-scale industrial project because of the thicker margins, although the sensitivities of the participants are no less than in a thin-margin transaction.

28. The number of companies varies from transaction to transaction and is significantly influenced by the identities of the *Shari'a*-Compliant Investors and the application of the tax 'attribution' rules in respect of the relationships between and among the investors.

29. Most tax counsel will agree that the 3:1 ratio is conservative. Some counsel take a more aggressive position on these ratios. The precise ratio will also vary with the total amount of debt in the overall structure, among other things.

30. In certain structures, the equity and loan investments by the developer are made directly into the project company. In other structures, the equity and loan investments by the developer are split between the intermediate C Corp and the project company. Tax planning considerations will affect the choice of structure.

31. Maintenance of consistency of the debt-to-equity ratio for all participants is important to ensure compliance with applicable *shari'a* principles pertaining to pro rata payments.

32. Often, and perhaps more frequently than in the example used as illustration, the partnership agreement or limited liability company operating agreement will address distributions to, respectively, the developer and the intermediate C Corp, particularly where the developer has invested in the project company rather than the intermediate C Corp. Country-specific and entity-specific tax considerations will influence the structure to be used and the priority and locus of distributions. Funds will also move from the project company out to service a lease (*ijara*) and the conventional debt financing, and this movement will precede the movement of cash to the intermediate C Corp. The lease (*ijara*) and debt service payments are discussed later in this section.

33. The tax considerations, and thus the structuring, for operating industrial (non-real estate) projects are significantly different from those noted in the textual example. They have considerable operating income in excess of the debt service on the loans from the finance company and the developer and the liquidation profile is quite different from that for real estate investments. Careful tax planning must be done to maximize efficiencies in each type of transaction.

34. See section 14.5.5 of this chapter for a discussion of the Loan Agreement in the *Shari'a*-compliant structure.

35. The collateral security documents are ignored for the moment.

36. Concepts of tax ownership and the allocation of capital allowances in the United Kingdom, France and other European countries are more complex and tied to form than in the United States. Thus, in various transactions in the United Kingdom and France, the funding company has been the tax owner and careful structuring is necessary to ensure effective use of all available tax benefits.

37. *See* Figure 14.4 and sections 14.5.4 and 14.5.5 of this chapter for a description of the role of these entities in the transaction. In structuring any *shari'a*-compliant transaction, it is critical that there be a thorough understanding of the concept of 'ownership' under the *shari'a* and under applicable tax laws (as well as other laws). If the bundle comprising ownership is properly allocated in the structure, ownership may be in one entity (the funding company) for *shari'a* purposes and simultaneously be in another entity (the project company) for tax purposes.

38. Or, in the case of a transaction in a jurisdiction such as the United Kingdom where the funding company is the tax owner of the project, that any excess income to the funding company or the construction arranger is offset by available capital allowances and expense items or refundable deposits.

39. The rights of the funding company under the managing contractor agreement are not assigned to the banks because these provisions are self-operative rules as to the making of decisions and determinations rather than substantive rights, and the rules are self-limited (that is, by their express terms they disappear in certain circumstances) or unlimited (those rights that the project company would have under conventional loan agreements in a direct conventional borrowing by the project company from the bank). The

40.   Capitalized terms used in this definition are defined in subsequent subsections of this section.

rules set forth in the managing contractor agreement are intended to put the parties in the same risk-allocated position that they would occupy in a conventional financing. Similarly, the tax matters agreement is not assigned because its purpose is to fix the tax-filing position of the funding company and the project company, and conform to the positions that would be occupied by such parties in a conventional financing arrangement; those matters will not change under any circumstances, including events of default.

40.   Capitalized terms used in this definition are defined in subsequent subsections of this section.

41.   This is a peculiarity of real estate transactions. In an industrial project financing, it is much less common and the discussion of the site lease and in-kind contribution of land as equity can be ignored.

42.   If the developer has not previously acquired the land, the initial acquisition will be by the funding company (owner), and there will be no site lease. In such a case, the funding company will own both the land and the improvements, which is almost always the situation in a *shari'a*-compliant acquisition financing or private equity financing.

43.   In many transactions, there is direct payment by the bank to the general contractor, although the legal obligations are structured as set forth in this paragraph.

44.   In some transactions, other circumstances will give rise to a right to purchase upon election of the funding company. Examples include illegality events and regulatory adjustment events where the funding company is unable to effect the transaction.

45.   Additional examples include situations in which a financial test is violated; for example, a rent-to-value ratio or other credit test is violated. In such a case, the only remedy available to the funding company may be a partial purchase and the funding company may not be permitted to effect a complete purchase.

46.   Where permissible, and to the extent that rights in respect thereof do not end upon the exercise of remedies in respect of a lease event of default, various decision-making rights are included in the lease (*ijara*), particularly as covenant matters. Other similar decisions are established pursuant to rules set forth in the lease (*ijara*), and mirroring similar rights in the loan agreement and other loan documents.

47.   A comprehensive *rahn-adl* collateral security structure for a large-scale petrochemical project financing in the Kingdom of Saudi Arabia is discussed in McMillen (2000a, pp. 1184–1232, 2004b, pp. 208–14).

48.   See sections 14.6, 14.7, 14.8 and 14.9, respectively, of this chapter.

49.   Each bank will vary in what it requires for collateral security at this level, and there will be variances with the type of transaction and the type of assets involved. For example, there may be a separate environmental indemnity agreement from the project company. In some transactions, there may be assignments of permits and licences, to the extent the same can be assigned.

50.   The drafting of these provisions of the parallel *istisnaa* will then take cognizance of, and be harmonious with, the types of terms and conditions that the banks would include as part of the 'draw request' in a conventional financing. These focus primarily upon satisfaction of certain conditions precedent, particularly evidence of completion or payment of specified work milestones in a given period.

51.   See the summary provided in section 14.5.1 of this chapter.

52.   These provisions are often harmonious with the positions of Abu Hanifa and the Hanafi school with respect to whether an *istisnaa* agreement becomes binding upon execution of the agreement or after inspection and acceptance of the *masnou'*.

53.   See the summary provided in section 14.5.1 of this chapter, including the sources cited in that section.

54.   See sections 14.3, 14.5.4 and 14.5.7 of this chapter for discussions of the collateral security package, which will be similarly constituted for this type of transaction.

55.   A *mudaraba* is a particularly flexible structure because it focuses on any defined set of productive assets as distinct from the legal form of organization of a business. Thus, for example, the *mudaraba* may focus on a single production line rather than the entirety of the business (all production lines within the same company). Allocation of expenses and revenues will then be determined with respect to the single production line.

56.   See sections 14.3, 14.5.4 and 14.5.7 of this chapter for discussions of the collateral security package, which will be similarly constituted for this type of transaction.

57.   Note, however, that a *mudaraba* agreement would not be able to require return of capital or a specified return or amount of profit within a specified period, which is significantly at odds with the base concept of interest-based lending. Interesting discussions have been had with *shari'a* scholars as to whether the *mudarib* developer's representation and warranty that it would return an amount equal to the capital plus a specified property amount in a specified time frame, when breached, would constitute a default giving rise to *mudarib* liability for return of capital. Even if it would give rise to that liability, it would probably not give rise to any liability in respect of a profit amount.

58.   The right of the developer *mudarib* to a proportionate profit, as agreed, then comes into play. As noted in the text, contractual modifications of percentage rates and timing of payment, among other similar concepts, will then become of even greater import.

59.   There are numerous *shari'a* principles prohibiting the incurrence of additional indebtedness by the *mudarib* and addressing loss allocation to the *rabb al-mal* in connection with the incurrence of any such indebted-

ness (or guarantees in respect of such indebtedness). In summary, a *mudareb* may not effect purchases or incur liabilities in excess of the *mudareb* capital. The banks and the developers will certainly negotiate a limited concept of 'permitted indebtedness' in most project financings. The existence of such permitted indebtedness under a *mudaraba* structure will have a greater adverse impact on the banks than it would under a conventional interest-based structure and therefore will be more heavily negotiated in a *mudaraba* arrangement.

60. The *shari'a* principles applicable to bad debts, valuation of debts, write-offs of bad debts, allocation of surplus upon collection of a debt formerly written off, and ultimate attribution of bad debts (to the *rabb al-mal*) are not discussed in this chapter but will be a significant factor in drafting project financing agreements using the *mudaraba* structure.

61. The debt might include, for example, debt owed by a third party to the *rabb al-mal* banks, or it might be debt owed by the *mudarib* developer to the banks. Use of debt capital is not discussed in this chapter, although it is sometimes a useful structural element, particularly in refinancings.

62. The text focuses on involvement of conventional interest-based banks. However, these *shari'a* principles and precepts are of particular importance where the financing banks are Islamic banks or financial institutions that are investing funds that have been deposited with the Islamic bank or institution by its clients.

63. These principles find application in many *shari'a*-compliant financings with non-Muslim Western investors where partnership and operating agreements include 'hurdles' and preferences with varying rates and allocations between and among the joint ventures.

64. The report of the *mudaraba* agreements of Abbas Bin Abdul Muttaleb serves as an example: his agreements stipulated, with respect to travel, that the *mudarib* would not be permitted to 'travel by sea, nor through valleys, nor by a riding animal' and violation would make the *mudarib* liable for repayment of the entire capital.

65. See sections 14.3, 14.5.4 and 14.5.7 of this chapter for discussions of the collateral security package, which will be similarly constituted for this type of transaction.

66. One of the project financings in which this structure was implemented was for electric generation and transmission assets of Saudi Consolidated Electric Company in the Central Region (now a part of Saudi Electric Company) in the Kingdom of Saudi Arabia in the late 1990s. The illustrative example set forth in this section is based upon that financing. As a general matter, the applicable *shari'a* principles with respect to a *sharikat* are set forth in the *Majelle* (articles 1045–1403), and in Al-Zuhayli (2003, pp. 447–81).

67. In the Saudi Arabian transaction, one of the banks was an Islamic financial institution and the other two banks were conventional interest-based banking institutions.

68. Some *Shari'a* Supervisory Boards allow the Nondisclosure Undertaking and Indemnity Agreement to be incorporated into the *sharikat mahassa* agreement, others do not.

69. See, for example, Chapter 46 of the Regulations for Companies of the Kingdom of Saudi Arabia (the 'Regulations for Companies').

70. Alternatively, if permitted by the *Shari'a* Supervisory Board, the substance of the Nondisclosure Undertaking and Indemnity Agreement may be incorporated in the *sharikat mahassa* agreement itself.

71. Various issues arise with respect to transferability among the Banks during the pre-completion period, particularly where, as in the Saudi Arabian electric example, one of the Banks is providing fixed-rate financing while the others are providing floating-rate financing.

72. Descriptions of various securitization structures are contained in Fabozzi (2001). For an interesting comparison of the earliest securitizations with more recent securitization trends, compare the foregoing revised edition with Fabozzi (1985).

73. *Sukuk*: Adam and Thomas (2004a, p. 54, Exhibit 2) and related text, provide a useful summary orientation to the differences between *sukuk*, bonds and equity shares.

74. The issuance of the *sukuk al-ijara* may be simultaneous with or follow the asset transfer, or a *sukuk ijara mowsufa bithima* may be issued in anticipation of the asset transfer.

75. Some or all of the elements of the *ijara* portion of the *istisnaa–ijara* structure may be incorporated into the various *sukuk al-ijara* structures. For example, if the Funding Company is a special-purpose entity, the relevant *sukuk* structure may include a Managing Contractor Agreement. See section 14.5.6 of this chapter.

76. Structural examples in this chapter assume that the Funding Company is a special-purpose entity owned by a corporate service company and that it is a 'disregarded entity' for tax purposes. However, it is possible to structure the transaction so that the Funding Company is owned by investors with an economic interest and is not a disregarded entity for tax purposes. In such a case, the tax structuring will be significantly different than described in section 14.5 of this chapter. Of course, the *shari'a* rules as to disparate ownership of the interests in the Funding Company and the Project Company will remain applicable.

77. Structuring for periodic redemptions requires considerable care in light of the applicable *shari'a* precepts pertaining to rent payments and those pertaining to payment of the repurchase price, on the one hand, and the uncertainty of periodic redemptions, on the other hand. In such a structure, the Asset Repurchase

Agreement will be structured to allow the Project Company to purchase some of the assets, either as identifiable assets or through fractional undivided interest payments, at the time of the redemptions and in such amount as will allow for payment to the redeeming *Sukuk* Holders.

78. The more complex structures often have some distinct advantages under applicable tax laws. For example, if the Project Company is intended to be the owner of the Project for tax purposes from the inception of the undertaking, it may be appropriate for the Project Company to infuse a portion of the needed construction funds. For *shari'a* purposes, the contribution by the Project Company may be a prepayment of a portion (or all) of the amount payable under the Project Transfer Agreement (hereinafter defined).

References

AAOFI (2003), *Shari'a* Standard No. (17), ISBN 999-01-23-06-03.

Adam, Nathif J. and Abdulkader Thomas (eds) (2004a), *Islamic Bonds: Your Guide to Issuing, Structuring and Investing in Sukuk*, London: Euromoney Books.

Adam, Nathif J. and Abdulkader Thomas (eds) (2004b), 'Islamic fixed income securities: *sukuk*', in Sohail Jaffer (ed.), *Islamic Asset Management: Forming the Future for Shari'a-Compliant Investment Strategies*, London: Euromoney Books.

Al-Adliyah, Majalat Al-Ahkam, trans. Judge C.A. Hooper ([1933] 1968), *The Civil Law of Palestine and Trans-Jordan*, vols I and II, reprinted in various issues of *Arab Law Quarterly* (the *Majelle*).

Al-Zuhayli, Wahbah (2003), *Financial Transactions in Islamic Jurisprudence*, trans. Mahmud al-Jamal, Damascus: Dar al Fikr.

Comair-Obeid, Nayla (1996), *The Law of Business Contracts in the Arab Middle East,* The Hague: Kluwer Law International.

Coulson, Noel J. (1984), *Commercial Law in the Gulf States: The Islamic Legal Tradition*, London: Graham & Trotman.

El-Gamal, Mahmoud A. (2000), 'An economic explication of the prohibitions of riba in classical Islamic jurisprudence', *The Proceedings of the Third Harvard University Forum on Islamic Finance*, Cambridge, MA: Harvard University Press.

Elgari, M.A. (1999), 'Some recurring shari'ah violations in Islamic investment agreements used by international banking institutions', *The Proceedings of the Second Harvard University Forum on Islamic Finance*, Cambridge, MA: Harvard University Press.

Fabozzi, Frank J. (ed.) (1985), *The Handbook of Mortgage-Backed Securities*, New York: McGraw-Hill.

Fabozzi, Frank J. (ed.) (2001), *The Handbook of Mortgage-Backed Securities*, 5th edn, New York: McGraw-Hill.

Fadeel, Mahmoud Nasreldin Ahmed (2002), 'Legal aspects of Islamic finance', in Simon Archer and Rifaat Ahmed Abdul Karim (eds), *Islamic Finance: Innovation and Growth*, London: Euromoney Books and Accounting and Auditing Association for Islamic Finance Institutions.

Fadel, Mohammad (2000), 'The regulation of risk in Islamic law, common law and federal regulatory law', *The Proceedings of the Third Harvard University Forum on Islamic Finance: The Task Ahead*, Cambridge, MA: Harvard University Press.

Husain, Syed Tariq (2002), 'Project finance', in Simon Archer and Rifaat Ahmed Abdul Karim (eds), *Islamic Finance: Innovation and Growth*, London: Euromoney Books and Accounting and Auditing Association for Islamic Finance Institutions.

McMillen, Michael J.T. (2000a), 'Islamic shari'ah-compliant project finance: collateral security and financing structure case studies', *The Proceedings of the Third Harvard University Forum on Islamic Finance: Local Challenges, Global Opportunities*, Harvard Islamic Finance Information Program, Center for Middle Eastern Studies, Cambridge, MA: Harvard University Press, pp. 111–31.

McMillen, Michael J.T. (2000b), 'Special report US, briefing: Islamic finance: breaking the mould', *Middle East Economic Digest*, **44** (38).

McMillen, Michael J.T. (2001), 'Islamic shari'ah-compliant project finance: collateral security and financing structure case studies', *Fordham International Law Journal*, **24** (4), 1184–1263.

McMillen, Michael J.T. (2003), 'Shari'ah-compliant finance structures and the development of an Islamic economy', *The Proceedings of the Fifth Harvard University Forum on Islamic Finance: Islamic Finance: Dynamics and Development*, Harvard Islamic Finance Information Program, Center for Middle Eastern Studies, Cambridge, MA: Harvard University Press, pp. 89–102.

McMillen, Michael J.T. (2004a), 'Structuring the shari'ah-compliant transaction involving non-compliant elements', in Sohail Jaffer (ed.), *Islamic Asset Management: Forming the Future for Shari'a-Compliant Investment Strategies*, London: Euromoney Books.

McMillen, Michael J.T. (2004b), 'Structuring shari'ah-compliant transactions involving non-compliant elements: use of the nominate contracts', paper presented at the Islamic Financial Services Board Conference, Islamic Financial Services Industry and the Global Regulatory Environment Summit, London, 18–19 May.

Noonan, J.T. (1957), *Scholastic Analysis of Usury*, Cambridge, MA: Harvard University Press.

Salah, Isam and W. Donald Knight, Jr. (1998), 'Practical legal and tax issues in Islamic finance and investment in the United States', *The Proceedings of the Second Harvard University Forum on Islamic Finance: Islamic Finance Into The 21st Century*, Cambridge, MA: Harvard University Press.

Saleh, Nabil A. (1992), *Unlawful Gain and Legitimate Profit in Islamic Law*, London: Graham & Trotman.

Toan, Robert W. (2000), 'Cross-border Ijarah: a case study in the U.S. taxation of Islamic finance', *The Proceedings of the Third Harvard University Forum on Islamic Finance: Local Challenges, Global Opportunities*, Harvard Islamic Finance Information Program, Center for Middle Eastern Studies, Cambridge, MA: Harvard University Press.

Toan, Robert W. and Monir Barakat (2001), 'Credit enhancement in Ijarah transactions', Fourth Harvard Islamic Forum on Islamic Finance, Cambridge, MA: University of Harvard Press.

Vogel, Frank E. and Samuel L. Hayes (1998), *Islamic Law and Finance: Religion, Risk and Return*, The Hague: Kluwer Law International.

wa-Adillatuh, Al-Fiqh Al-Islami (1997), *Islamic Jurisprudence and its Proofs 1–11*, Damascus: Dar Al-Fikr.

Wilson, Rodney (2004), 'Overview of the *sukuk* market', in Nathif J. Adam and Abdulkader Thomas (eds), *Islamic Bonds: Your Guide to Issuing, Structuring and Investing in Sukuk*, London: Euromoney Books.

15 Islam and speculation in the stock exchange
Seif El-Din Tag El-Din and M. Kabir Hassan

Introduction

One major property of the stock exchange upheld by most economists is the capacity to ensure a liquid investment market. The strong appeal of a liquid investment market cannot be exaggerated, but excessive speculation is viewed as a harmful and non-productive use of a society's scarce resources. Keynes' dismissal of the liquidity rationale in secondary financial markets stands out as an extreme position which, nonetheless, voices macroeconomic concerns about the allocation of economic resources.[1] The need for a liquid financial market is accepted within the efficient market hypothesis (EMH), but speculation is viewed within the same hypothesis as an empty box. The EMH underpins the proposition that no privately 'informed' player in the modern financial markets can outwit the market. Efficient financial markets, it is believed, are capable of absorbing relevant economic information more quickly than any single player at a point of time, which implies the common belief that speculative dealings are pure gambling activities. This theory, however, is challenged in actual practice by the existence of market makers, professional analysts and stock brokers who claim specialized skills in the art of optimal portfolio selection paid for by individuals and institutional investors. Yet, among the findings which equate professional analyst services with pure gambling and, therefore, confirm the efficient market hypothesis, is Cowles' theory of 'dartboard' stock selection (Samuelson and Nordhaus, 1992, p. 520). This theory advances the hypothesis that any randomly selected portfolio of stocks formed by throwing a dart at the *Wall Street Journal* is as good as any alternative portfolio selected through professional expertise.

On the other hand, speculation is taken in the current literature as a pivotal force in the pricing of modern financial markets, though it is defined differently by different writers. Harrison and Kreps define speculation as follows: 'An investor may buy the stock now, so as to sell it later for more than he thinks it is actually worth, thereby reaping capital gains' (Biais and Pagano, 2001, p. xix). This situation is believed possible because different investors are assumed to hold different beliefs about the stochastic processes that generate equity dividends. In effect, speculation creates buyers and sellers with different views. Yet, over the last few years, other models of speculation have been developed, as in Dow and Gordon (1994), Balduzzi, Bertola and Foresi (1995), Biais and Bossaert (1998), and Morris and Song (1998). The problem addressed in the literature is to explain how it could be possible for the initial buyer of the stock to find somebody who is willing to buy the same stock at a price much in excess of its worth. Some of these findings are briefly mentioned here, but from the Islamic perspective there are different issues involved. Speculation is mostly an issue about jurist legitimacy because of the equating of stock market speculation with gambling. Accordingly, this chapter starts with a brief background of how the stock exchange is viewed from the Islamic perspective. The objective, which will be more formally stated in a subsequent section, is to offer an Islamic assessment of stock market speculation, given two principles: first, that gambling is strictly prohibited in Islamic jurisprudence and, second, that economic waste violates the principles of Islamic economics.

The Islamic stock exchange in theory and practice

The paramount importance of economic information in the Islamic jurist theory of contracts underpins the strict prohibition of gambling, and justifies why the issue of stock market speculation is a major theme in the writings of Islamic economists. The Islamic characterization of financial markets, or the concept of Normative Islamic Stock Exchange (NISE), has been discussed by Tag el-Din (1985, 1996) and Kia (2001). In a nutshell, NISE is characterized as a purely equity-based market, free from interest rate financing and carefully guarded against *gharar*. The interest-free property is the core feature of Islamic finance, whereas guarding against *gharar* makes up for NISE's informational efficiency. *Gharar* is the jurist term for inadequate market information or uncertainty about exchange objects, particularly when no practical obstacles stand in the way of furnishing full information to the contracting parties about the objects of exchange. Some *gharar* is, therefore, tolerable because it often proves impracticable to eliminate uncertainty totally from exchange contracts. But when deliberately embodied in the contract, *gharar* becomes sufficiently serious to warrant strict prohibition, as exemplified by the classical jurist cases of selling birds in the sky or fish in the sea (Al-Dharir, 1967; Saati, 2003). Gambling is a special case of serious *gharar*.

Indeed, the issue of *gharar* prevention, or adequate market information, is the more sensitive in the stock exchange because of the very nature of the objects being exchanged. No real goods are traded except for information-loaded documents (that is, securities) and the flow of external market information which constitutes the basis of a financial market. It is little surprise that failures and occasional crises in financial markets are largely attributable to failures in the flow of economic information. A financial security is an information document reducible to a set of terms and conditions between investor and investee. On top of it, market information (movements in stock prices, tax policy, corporate dividend policy, risk rating and so on) is often the initial trigger that invites investors to decide on which security to buy and what security to sell. Hence interest rate elimination and *gharar* minimization are the two primary features of an information-efficient NISE. Apart from the interest-free property and concerns with information efficiency, in the sense of *gharar* control, the legitimacy of trade in corporate shares has been taken for granted in the above characterization of NISE.

It is noteworthy, however, that the very acquisition of company shares was open to question by many *shari'a* scholars during the greater part of the twentieth century. Early jurist controversy about the legitimacy of the modern corporation is reflected in the 1980s writings on the theory of an Islamic stock exchange when this concept was at an infant stage (e.g. Tag el-Din, 1985). Al-Khayyat (1971) provides a detailed background of different jurist viewpoints about the legitimacy or otherwise of the modern corporation. The modern corporation differs from the received jurist concept of a company (*sharika*) or partnership in terms of two main features: limited liability of shareholders and the company's assumed perpetuity which, at any point of time, makes its legal existence independent of any particular group of shareholders. Limited liability absolves shareholders from any obligation towards the company's debts beyond the amount of their shares. It also provides for the possibility that a corporation continues indefinitely to survive while shares may constantly change hands. By contrast, the jurist form of company cannot exist independently of its originating partners, who must also bear total liability towards the company's debt.

This controversy had ultimately been resolved, or more accurately outmoded, by the early 1990s when an upsurge in internationally geared equity funds, carrying *shari'a* certification, entered Islamic financial markets. The late 1990s saw the creation of *shari'a*-audited international indices, namely Islamic Dow Jones and Islamic FTSE. Simply defined, international *shari'a* audit is a screening process aimed at the formation of investment portfolios from common stocks of listed international companies which ideally satisfy three basic criteria: legitimate field of economic activity, interest-free dealings in both assets and liabilities, and the dominance of real assets. Thus a company must not be engaged in the production of illegitimate goods like pork and alcoholic drinks; it must not deal with interest rate financing as a means to leverage its capital structure through fixed debt liabilities, or generate interest income from investment securities; and since a company's shares represent equity rights in its assets, the latter should be real assets, not liquid money or receivable debt as they cannot be sold freely at a profit like real goods, real estate and machinery. But because interest-rate dealings are unavoidable in the usual practice of international companies,[2] the strict criterion of interest-free finance has been relaxed to tolerate reasonably small percentages of debt/equity ratios (such as 30 per cent) and still smaller percentages of interest income in the companies' income statements (such as 5 per cent). Liquid cash and receivable debt are tolerable so long as they constitute only a small percentage of a company's assets (less than 50 per cent can do).

Shari'a audits have been concerned, not only with the formation of corporate equity portfolios, but also with the structuring of variable-rate or fixed-rate securities, in the form of the so-called *sukuk*. Variable-rate *sukuk* are based on profit-sharing *mudaraba* or *musharaka*, while fixed-rate *sukuk* are bond-like securities mostly based on *ijara* (lease finance). The term 'Islamic bond' often refers to the *ijara*-based *sukuk* as they also enjoy the facility of being marketable and negotiable. Properties similar to conventional bonds, like alternative coupon structures, can be satisfied by Islamic bonds, except that an Islamic bond cannot be structured so as to be sold at par value. This follows from the fact that repayment of the principal cannot be promised in an Islamic bond. More recently, in 2002, the Bahrain-based International Financial Market has been launched with appropriately structured Islamic *ijara*-based bonds. A year later, the Bahrain International Islamic Rating Agency was established to provide rating services for Islamic bonds.

The problem of speculation
Joining the World Trade Organization (WTO) has made it imperative for countries to open up their financial markets to foreign funds, which raises fears of exposure to destabilizing forces from international stock market speculation. For example, worries about the potential destabilizing effect of international investment speculation on the Saudi Stock Market and the Riyal exchange rate have recently been voiced in the first national Riyadh Symposium on the prospects of entry into the WTO. Al-Mubarak calls for a gradual market liberalization of the Saudi economy.[3] A policy of constraining the outflow of foreign funds for at least two years has been proposed. As it stands, this is a means to constrain international speculation, but within the national boundaries. Speculation may still be practised using the Saudi Riyal unless further measures are introduced to constrain local speculation.

The destabilizing effects of excessive speculation and measures to guard against it are covered in the literature, and are not addressed here. Rather, our concern is the more fundamental question of the legitimacy of stock market speculation within an Islamic stock exchange. There are two main questions. One is whether or not stock market speculation is pure gambling, as is most commonly believed. The other is whether or not stock market speculation should be regarded as pure economic wastage.

As mentioned above, informational efficiency is more of a jurist norm affecting the legitimacy of the NISE than an hypothesis in the current controversy about the nature of modern markets. Apart from the well-known economic damage of excessive speculation, this phenomenon falls in the category of serious *gharar*. However, Islamic equity funds are managed along the same lines of conventional equity funds, apart from the *shari'a* audit-screening criteria considered earlier. No special guidelines are prescribed by *shari'a* audits to guard against speculation which might amount to serious *gharar*. To assume away completely the problem in the daily management of 'Islamic portfolios' should render the legitimacy conferred by *shari'a* audits open to question. Short sales are obvious speculative practices which violate the Islamic theory of contracts as they involve the selling of stocks through a broker before they are bought by the investor.

Selling what one does not own is sufficient to invalidate short sales, but, as we have seen in the discussion about NISE, excessive speculation invokes concerns about serious *gharar* even if it obeys the formal condition of selling what is owned. If the object of sale is a documentary title to an unknown prospect, like a gambling ticket, the formal juristic structure of the sale contract could be valid, but the objects of sale are clearly illegitimate. Hence, even if short sales are prohibited, the fundamental question is how prudent is the use of economic information by the appointed portfolio manager in the stock exchange. Admittedly, it is not an easy question to decide on the critical level of 'ill-informed' or 'excessive' speculation that makes it illegitimate. Speculation per se is a normal trade practice in real goods when reliable information is lacking, but it is a problem in financial securities where trading on reliable economic information is what the stock exchange is meant to be about.

Why the gambling charge?
Apparently there is more than one reason to label speculators as 'gamblers' in the common parlance. On the one hand, if the efficient market hypothesis in the modern financial markets is empirically true, no player should ever be able to capitalize on a special informed position to make a capital gain. Information is already absorbed by the market, and all that speculators can do is to take pure chances of capital gains or losses. The 'dartboard theory' is one such argument to confirm the 'gambling' label on stock exchange speculators. On the other hand, even within the practitioners' classification of stock exchange dealers, speculators are defined as pure chance players as opposed to hedgers and arbitrageurs. Hedgers are seeking to protect current positions against unpredictable future movements in prices. Typically they are insurers against future risks. In general, hedging is acceptable, but *shari'a* audits are particularly keen on the scrutiny of conventional hedging techniques, which often violate the formal structure of Islamic contracts. The basic concerns expressed by *shari'a* scholars as regards hedging tools involve the use of interest rate, futures and options.[4] Arbitrageurs, on the other hand, are genuine users in the sense of 'believing' in the market's efficiency and not attempting to 'outwit' it.

Yet, when the movement of stock prices is seen to outstrip certain upper and lower bound-aries of the random walk which represents daily price movements around true stock prices, it is believed possible beyond those boundaries to buy or sell stocks at expected profit margins. In this sense, arbitrageurs perform a commendable service in the stock exchange whereby wild swings in price movements are checked. Arbitrageurs may share the same market information, but differ drastically about cost considerations which affect the decision 'whether and when' to invest. At least in principle, the decision whether and when to engage in an arbitrage transaction depends on the viability of transaction costs as perceived by different arbitrageurs and the expected duration of a complete arbitrage transaction, not on different beliefs about market information (Blake, 2002).

The last category, speculators, are therefore left to play with unpredictable residual pat-terns within the random walks of stock price movements through the adoption of different 'gambling' positions. A random walk by definition is a pure chance process, as there is hardly any definitive market information to explain the continuous volatility of stock prices. In fact the best safeguard against a stock exchange crash is the adoption of different 'gambling' positions by speculators, for otherwise a single position means a unanimous agreement among speculators to all sell at once. This is the same phenome-non addressed by Keynes in his deep scepticism about the nature of information used by stock exchange professionals. Rather than basing their investment decisions on real eco-nomic information about expected movements in stock market prices, Keynes argues, these professionals try to predict what other players believe is the right decision. They are trained in mass psychology to guess better than the crowd how the crowd behaves, in the same manner as judges in a beauty contest would base their valuations on what they expect other judges to do (Keynes, 1936 [1970], p. 157).

All said about speculative dealers, it still remains to be seen whether their characteri-zation as 'gamblers' in the common parlance conforms to the Islamic jurist position. It is noteworthy that jurist qualifications on any perceivable matter must draw upon the primary Islamic sources, namely, the Qur'an, the Prophet's traditions (*hadith*), analogy (*qiyas*) and consensus (*ijma*), which need not match automatically commonly held judg-ments. The first two are the original scriptures of Islam. The third source (analogy) is the logical vehicle which enables *shari'a* scholars to reach sound judgments on all newly arising matters that are not originally covered by the first two sources, provided that the new judgments are logically consistent with the original scriptures. The fourth source refers to the prevalent or mainstream opinion on any certain issue held by the majority of scholars at any point of time. Stock market speculation is a newly arising phenomenon since no consensus, as yet, has been formed about it. Therefore this inquiry must be handled through analogy.

Analogy in the received jurisprudence is more than a pragmatic formulation of Aristotelian logical syllogism. It is for this reason that the early founders of analogy have distinguished between 'meaning analogy' (*qiyas al-ma'na*) and 'similarity analogy' (*qiyas al-shabah*). The former is the righteous course of action while the latter is not. The idea, therefore, is to see whether the commonly held description of stock market speculators as gamblers follows a meaning analogy or one of similarity analogy. On the other hand, the labelling of stock market speculation in the common parlance as 'gambling' is based on the following logical syllogism. Gambling is the making of money out of pure chance. Speculators take pure chances in their stock exchange dealings. Therefore, speculators are gamblers. The basic premise which justifies the qualification of speculative activity as gambling is the definition of 'gambling' as the making of money out of pure chance. Indeed, the same gambling label should follow from the Islamic jurist perspective if the above definition is adopted.

The above syllogism has, thus, simplified the question about the legitimacy of speculative dealings by reducing it to the way gambling is defined in the Islamic jurist perspective. To address this question, this chapter provides a formal definition of gambling from the Islamic perspective by reference to the original sources. The objective is not to issue a *fatwa* on the legitimacy or otherwise of the current schemes of portfolio management, but to call for a more careful scrutiny of Islamic portfolio management against possibilities of serious *gharar*.

Gambling in terms of 'meaning analogy'
Analogy is the means to manifest meaningful intents of *shari'a* in all newly arising situations, if not explicitly covered by the Qur'an and the Prophet traditions. The general consensus among the different schools of jurisprudence, with the exception of a few (such as Zahirites), uphold the proposition that *shari'a* rulings in all social, economic and family matters (*fiqh al-mu'amalat*) obey meaningful intents (Al-Shatibi, n.d. vol. 2, p. 233). But because it is highly sensitive to judge on newly arising matters in the authority of the Qur'an and the traditions, recourse to analogy has been had with great care and governed by highly refined criteria developed by early scholars of jurisprudence. It is beyond the scope of this chapter to discuss these criteria, but a few examples below may help illustrate the fundamental basis of distinguishing between meaning and similarity analogy. The former is the jurist ideal, but the latter is a source of misguidance. A clear example is the physical similarity between 'sea-pig' and 'land-pig' as they are both called 'pig' (*khinzir*) in Arabic. The meat of land-pigs is strictly forbidden by the Qur'an, whereas sea-pig meat belongs to the wider class of sea-meat which is generally permissible. Thus the legitimacy of sea-pig is based on meaning analogy, as the apparent similarity between the two animals and the fact both are called 'pigs' in Arabic is meaningless.

A more relevant example from economics is the Qur'anic permissibility of trade and the prohibition of usury (which means money lending at interest). This prohibition was ill-received by pre-Islamic Arabs (Jahilites) who claimed that sale and usury are similar, and hence failed to appreciate the reason why sale should be permitted while usury is prohibited. This is a typical argument, as in the above example of 'pigs', which does not stand the test of meaning analogy since sale and usury are two different, though similar, 'animals'. On the one hand, trade is the primary source of people's sustenance, making it easy for them to exchange real goods and services and, thereby, satisfy their economic wants. Usury, on the other hand, favours only a small minority of wealth owners to the deprivation of the needy, apart from the contractual structure of usury which involves no exchange of real utilities. The lending/borrowing structure is not tenable to commercial exchange, which explains why money lending is restricted in Islamic jurisprudence to benevolence dealings. In other words, it is not the money value of time per se which stigmatizes usury; it is, rather, the failure of a usury transaction to cater for a socially commendable utility. Incidentally, the same similarity analogy tends to reiterate in the contemporary dialogue when Islamic banks' modes of finance like *salam* and *murabaha* are seen, like the interest rate, to command a definite time value of money. Again, similarity in terms of time value should not mistake traders for usurers. The fact that sale is permitted entails the provision for all reasonable factors which might affect the prices of goods, including the time factor.

At the same time, trade can easily be confused with gambling through a similarity analogy. In this case, the taking of pure chance is the gamblers' key activity which, incidentally, could be shared by traders. But a trader who supplies goods to society cannot be called a 'gambler' even if he takes pure chance in his selling decisions. A trader who depends on pure chance is irrational. He is susceptible to loss, but there is more to gambling than the taking of pure chance. Gambling is more formally defined as a two or multiperson game of chance which ends up in redistributing total stakes committed by the game's players among only one or a few of them. It is a purely competitive zero-sum game among its individual parties, or groups of parties. There is no seller or buyer of a utility within the game, except, perhaps, for the person or persons who hire gambling halls or gambling equipment. Players enjoy the gamble for many reasons, most particularly with a view to lucrative pay-off expectations, thrilling suspense while the game proceeds and a dramatic excitement when expectations are realized. Although it is a game of chance, it has one sure outcome: excitement for one party and displeasure and vexation for another. Gambling, consequently, shares with warfare the iron rule that the winner's pleasure is the loser's displeasure. No matter what ethics of self-restraint might be sustained or assumed as professional ethics, experience has shown that gambling fosters family disintegration, profound social tension and deep vindictive feelings which could frequently lead to bloodshed. For this reason, the prohibition of gambling in the Qur'an is combined with the prohibition of alcoholic drinks as they share the evil of irresponsible excitement and unpredictable consequences.

It is stated in the Qur'an: 'Oh believers, intoxicants, and gambling, and reverence of stones, and (divination by) arrows are abomination of Satan's handwork; so eschew these things in order to prosper. Satan's plan is to excite enmity and hatred between you with intoxicants and gambling and hinder you from the remembrance of God and the prayer. Will you then abstain?' (al-Ma'ida, S5:90, 91). Gambling in pre-Islamic Arabia was used primarily for distributing camel meat (*jazur*) among the contestants through a game of chance which consisted of ten short arrows, each one bearing a particular number or value. The game involved shuffling the ten arrows in a specially designed bag, then an appointed neutral party would eject arrows at random from a small opening in the bag to decide on who wins or loses (Ibn 'Ashur, 1997, vol. 2, pp. 345–50; vol. 4, pp. 69–99). The rationale of the gambling prohibition is clearly stated in this verse as one of exciting enmity and hatred among people and thereby hindering God's remembrance. As mentioned above, this is due to a zero-sum property of the game, not simply the element of pure chance.

The concept of gambling, therefore, cannot be mixed up with trade even though 'pure chance' has a vital role in trade practices. Trade is a means to raise the welfare of all parties involved, whereas gambling is a strict win–lose game. Reference to the theory of profit by Frank Knight will help illuminate the nature of speculation in trade. In Knight's interpretation, risk refers to situations where the decision maker can assign mathematical probabilities to the randomness with which he is faced, while uncertainty refers to situations of randomness which cannot be expressed in terms of specific mathematical probabilities. Risk is, hence, measurable and insurable but uncertainty is purely speculative and non-insurable. On this basis, Knight interprets entrepreneurial trade profit as an 'uncertain' quantity depending more on subjective speculation than on measurable probabilities (Knight, 1921). However, many economists dispute this distinction, arguing that risk and uncertainty are indeed one and the same thing. One of the arguments is that probability can be defined as a subjective belief rather than an objective measure of relative frequency, and therefore any situation of uncertainty can also be formulated, like risk, in terms of mathematical probabilities. But obviously this argument does not refute Knight's theory, for if probabilities are subjective, in the sense of being speculative hunches, they cannot act as a basis for commercial insurance, which is exactly what 'uncertainty' means.

On the other hand, the modelling of speculation in the current literature reflects the standpoint that speculators are indeed stock traders acting within an 'uncertain' environment, as defined above. Harrison and Kreps define speculation as a situation where sellers and buyers have different beliefs about the real worth of stocks (Biais and Pagano (2001, p. xix). However, as a simplifying assumption in the Harrison–Kreps model, parties are assumed to stick to their original beliefs even though they can observe new data. This assumption has been relaxed by Biais and Bossaert (1998) through a model which allows for updating the original beliefs on the basis of market information. In their analysis of currency speculation, Morris and Song (1998) adopt the same definition of speculation as above. One interesting exception from the pure uncertainty hypothesis is provided by Dow and Gordon (1994) who assume that speculation starts off from 'informed' investors. Investors are assumed to act under the constraint that they ought to sell their stock holdings before a given date at favourable prices. In this case speculation takes place, not because of different subjective beliefs about the real worth of the stock, but owing to a deliberate policy adopted by the initial buyers of stocks. In a nutshell, the policy is to use the information privately and not to publicize it before buying the stock, but, once the stock is bought, the policy is to publicize the information so that the price will rise and the stock will be sold at a higher price. As it seems, this theory of speculative behaviour does not believe in the EMH.

To sum up, the above background alludes to the conclusion that, far from being stigmatized as 'gamblers', speculators in the stock exchange work on 'uncertainty' like any normal market traders. Yet as we have seen financial markets differ drastically from real goods markets in terms of information discipline. Real goods are vulnerable to unpredictable changes in consumer taste, emergence of new competitive products, and shifts in costs and productivity due to technological development, which account for a wider margin of 'uncertainty' than in financial markets. Yet all financial securities are reducible to three variables, cash flow, time and risk, all of which are measurable quantities, making for a solid quantitative database. Unlike real goods which can directly be sensed by buyers, financial securities are pure information-loaded documents perceived in the context of contractual terms and conditions as well as external market information. These two considerations make financial securities more *gharar*-prone than real goods. Therefore the jurist issue is more about ensuring a *gharar*-free stock exchange than one of resolving a gambling evil. And since *gharar* is only a matter of degree, the question boils down to the same issues in relation to NISE (Tag el-Din, 1985, 1996). The need for a liquid investment market makes it imperative to accommodate speculative activity, but NISE calls for the placement of appropriate measures to curb excessive speculation and, thereby, a closer matching between financial and real markets.

Towards a definition of excessive speculation

To define excessive speculation, a cost–benefit method is used similar to the one implied in the definition of serious *gharar*. The general rule is that *gharar* is tolerable if its benefits outweigh its damages. One clear example is where the Prophet (pbuh) allowed the sale of fresh dates on palm tress against an agreed quantity of dry dates (called *bai' al-'araya*), though the deal meets the formal criterion of serious *gharar*. The rationale, as explained by many jurists, is to cater for needy people who benefit from this kind of transaction to secure their food (al-Zuhaili, 1984, pp. 3408–15).

To adopt a similar cost–benefit approach on speculation, the latter is best perceived as a wastage of scarce economic resources. In this sense, restriction on speculative behaviour is viewed as a resource reallocation policy encouraging economic resources to move away from wasteful speculation in secondary investment assets to a productive engagement in primary investment markets. Yet, as mentioned in the characterization of NISE, some speculation is imperative to maintain a liquid investment market. Appeal to the observed behaviour of investors establishes that they are more willing to commit their funds to productive projects when an opportunity of a liquid secondary investment market is available. Regulatory policy must, therefore, weigh the benefit of a liquid secondary investment market against the opportunity cost of keeping resources away from primary investment markets. Unless a reasonable balance is maintained, undue restrictions on speculation may backfire on the incentive to commit investment funds in productive activities. Considering the close complementarity of the two markets, the ideal policy is to maintain an optimal level of secondary market liquidity just sufficient to provide the necessary incentive for an active primary investment market. In this sense, excessive speculation can be defined as the level of stock market speculation in excess of the level just needed for the attainment of an optimal liquidity in the secondary investment market.

Understandably the above definition of excessive speculation is irrelevant to international Islamic equity funds originating in Western markets which abide by given macroeconomic policies and regulations. This environment may provide a justification for the current *shari'a* audits on international equity funds which focus exclusively on the screening rule. But a broader vision to accommodate both microeconomic and macroeconomic dimensions of equity funds' management is needed by Muslim countries which seek to establish suitable regulatory systems for secondary stock markets, with a view to a positive role for the financial market in the achievement of real socioeconomic targets. In this case the question arises as to how excessive speculation can be guarded against, and hence, a reasonable balance struck between secondary market liquidity and primary investment market activity.

Admittedly, the key concept in the above definition, optimal liquidity, is not easy to assess objectively since it needs a thorough empirical analysis to formulate and test the relationship between observed levels of secondary market liquidity and levels of primary market activity. In the absence of reliable empirical evidence to assess the extent of complementarity between the two markets, the matter would fall back on pure discretionary judgment. At one end, soft-liners may argue that money making through stock market speculation is legitimate trade if it observes a minimal set of jurist restraints as provided by the *shari'a*-audit screening rules. But relentless pursuit of profit would run foul of Islamic economics, which is about caring for the social good and imparting an ethical role to trade in this vital pursuit. When jurist scholars focus primarily on the scrutiny of individual contracts to ensure microeconomic legitimacy, almost oblivious to the macroeconomic repercussions, justice will not be done to the Islamic vision of a more equitable socioeconomic order. At the other end, hard-liners, best exemplified by the Keynesian disapprobation of speculative secondary market investment, may call for the allocation of all investment resources to finance primary investment activity, leaving too little scope for secondary market liquidity. In other words, on this conception, all speculation is excessive and, therefore, pure economic wastage.

The above standpoint raises an important question on how to view the hard-liners' outlook from an Islamic perspective. If money-making activity is pure wastage, unless it embodies a real investment value, stock market speculation cannot be sustained in Islamic economics even though it makes real investors better off. As it seems, apart from the gambling issue, stock market speculation is viewed as pure money-making activity adding no real value to the economy. This leads us to the Islamic vision on money making in the next section.

Money making and monetary stability
Although juristically vindicated from the gambling label, stock exchange speculation is a non-productive money-making activity which threatens monetary stability when practised in excess. The middle course policy prescribed above involves the maintenance of a liquid capital market through the placement of suitable regulations against excessive speculation, yet this conclusion fails to satisfy hard-line ideologists in the Muslim world who warn against all forms of stock market speculation and against the very principle of a Muslim country's integration with world financial markets. This attitude underlies the argument that, if speculation is a pure money-making activity, contributing no real value in trade, then total abolition must be the right Islamic policy. Incidentally, this is the Aristotelian philosophy on money and trade, as opposed to the Islamic philosophy.

Although money is fundamental to Aristotle's thinking, he holds a negative attitude towards trade as a means of money making. He does not consider trade for the sake of money a useful or 'natural' practice (Backhouse, 2002, pp. 22–4). This philosophy rests on the postulate that economic goods have three possible uses: to be used in consumption, exchanged for consumption with another party, or exchanged for money. The first and second options, Aristotle believes, are the proper and natural procedures since people can satisfy their consumer needs, either directly from their own production, or indirectly by exchanging with others. However, exchange for the simple purpose of making money is considered unnatural, since goods would not have been used for their proper purpose. This standpoint is justified by Backhouse on the historical grounds of the structure of Greek economy which consisted of internally self-sufficient polis or cities and, therefore, with limited needs for external trade. An important part of the polis was that citizens had limited economic wants, which meant accumulation of wealth was not a socially acceptable practice. Wealth accumulation, however, was the usual practice of traders who occasionally procured goods to the cities, but traders were not citizens. This historical background explains the model of self-sufficient cities as the ideal, Aristotle's just economic order. At the same time, this philosophy underlies Aristotle's most popular theory, the so-called 'money sterility' view, which is often cited as an argument against usury. The theory of economic justice implied by Aristotle's sterility theory of money condemns not only usury but trade profits also. In this sense it might have a closer affinity to Marxism than to Islamic thought.

It may be suggested, however, that Aristotle failed to appreciate the economic consequence of the monetization process which, eventually, leads to a complete separation between producer (that is, trader) and consumer decisions. When the economy is fully monetized, traders' behaviour becomes in no way related to their consumption behaviour. Behaving as market agents, traders work for pure money, but as heads of households they dispose of money to satisfy consumption needs. Therefore, the fact that traders are 'money makers' does not in its own right invoke a negative attitude towards trade from an Islamic perspective. Understandably, there exists a wide range of jurist checks and balances to regulate trading behaviour and redirect it towards the fulfilment of society's needs. Otherwise, the Prophet's own tradition has been to avoid interference with free market operations, even at a time when his Companions complained about soaring market prices.

Returning to the question of how stock market speculation can be controlled, one of the major preoccupations is how to guard against its destabilizing impact on the economy's exchange rate. Excessive stock exchange speculation, in particular, threatens monetary stability in Muslim countries in two ways. At the international level, any sudden massive outflow of foreign funds can seriously depress the exchange rate and fuel domestic inflation. At the local level, the risks of excessive speculation can lead to a collapse in the stock exchange with serious repercussions for the stability of the financial system. Again, a comparison with Aristotle will reveal the fact that 'stability of money' has a genuine Islamic context. Money in the Aristotelian philosophy is assigned three functions: a medium of exchange, measure of value and a store of value for future transactions. But Aristotle makes no reference to the uniqueness of money as a store of purchasing power (Backhouse, 2002, pp. 36–7). This additional function was introduced by the Muslim scholar, Ibn Rush (Averroës) (1126–1198), who noted that any commodity can act as a store of value by its being sold for money in the future, but money is a unique store of purchasing power that need not first be sold. Ibn Rush draws from this additional function the important implication that the value of money has to be unchangeable since it is the yardstick to value goods and services.

Stability of money is perceived from the Islamic perspective as inherently inseparable from the basic functions of money. In his analysis of the rationale of why *riba al-fadl* is prohibited in money (gold and silver in those days), Ibn al-Qayyim argues that it is all about ensuring the stability of the function of money as a means to value other goods (Ibn al-Qayyim, 1996, vol.2, pp. 103–4). Money making commands an ethical Islamic value only to the extent that it originates in useful trade as cherished in the Qur'anic verse: 'God permits sale (trade) and forbids usury (interest income)' (al-Baqara, S2:276). In the context of trade, money is the means to create real utility to help promote people's welfare, but, in the context of usury, money is both the means and the end. Seen as a liquid lubricant to facilitate economic exchange, money has paved the way for economic specialization, technological innovation and, thereby, has widened the scope of economic interdependence among the world economies. Yet, when money making becomes a business in its own right, it retards the smooth flow of trade, and sustains an idle class of money lenders who live upon interest income. Nonetheless, trade is open to the same evil of usury, typically in terms of monopoly and wealth concentration into a few hands, unless properly regulated and ethically restrained. Trade circulation has, thus, been prudently governed in the Islamic jurist experience through appropriate ethical and legalist measures to ensure its merits and avert its demerits. Speculation to excess in financial and commodity markets is, therefore, not an exception to these rulings.

Empirical literature on speculation

Many researchers have been interested in the relationship between efficient market hypothesis and speculative bubbles, especially involving Islamic stock markets. Beechey et al. (2000) survey influential articles on the efficient market hypothesis (EMH), which contends that asset prices in financial markets should reflect all available information. This paper also examines the implications of speculative bubbles on efficient financial markets and the issue of whether prices should always be consistent with 'fundamentals'.

In the Islamic literature, Obaidullah (2001) identifies related concepts on allocational efficiency, pricing efficiency, operational efficiency and informational efficiency to explain the relationship between ethics and efficiency in Islamic stock markets. There is a high degree of commonality between Islamic ethics and the secular notions of ethics and efficiency underlying existing regulations in conventional markets. However, what makes an Islamic market distinct is its emphasis on the prohibition of *riba* and curbs on speculation. Regulation is a dynamic process and the *shari'a* jurist should be part of a process of continuous monitoring and surveillance of the market in order to develop regulatory rules based on the realities in a given market. Islamization of the stock market ought not to hamper market efficiency within Islamic ethics. Rather, a clear focus on Islamic ethics as a goal would aid stability and allocational efficiency by reducing disparity between prices and stock values.

Amir Kia (2001) focuses on factors such as excess speculative bubbles and non-ethical practices, which result in the inefficiency and resource misallocation of modern financial markets. To achieve efficient Islamic financial markets, he emphasizes the role of high-level regulation to make financial markets more competitive.

Jo (2002) reviews theoretical analyses on speculative bubbles involving rational bubbles, contagion bubbles and irrational bubbles. Rational bubbles theory can explain the frequent divergence of market prices from fundamental value without violating efficient market conditions. Furthermore, a rational bubble framework can explain the existence of multiple equilibria of assets if fundamentals are fragile and self-fulfilling expectations prevail among market participants.

Financial researchers have developed a number of econometric procedures to detect rational speculative bubbles in various asset returns. Gürkaynak (2005) surveys traditional asset bubble tests including variance bounds tests, West's two-step tests, and integration/cointegration based tests. He concludes that it is very difficult to distinguish bubbles from time-varying or regime-switching fundamentals.

Hassan (2002) examines issues of market efficiency and the time-varying risk–return relationship for the Dow Jones Islamic Index (DJIM) over the period 1996–2000, employing serial correlation, variance ratio and Dickey–Fuller tests. The results show that DJIM returns are normally distributed. The returns show that DJIM index returns are efficient. The paper also examines calendar anomalies of the DJIM and the results show that there is no turn-of-calendar-year, turn-of-financial-year, month effect of DJIM index (DJIMI) returns. Utilizing a GARCH econometric framework, the volatility of the DJIM index returns are studied showing a significant positive relationship between conditional volatility and DJIM equity index returns.

Hakim and Rashidian (2002) consider the relationship between DJIMI, the Wilshire 5000 index and the risk-free rate, proxied by the three-month Treasury bill rate over the time period 1999–2002 by employing cointegration and causality analysis. They find that the DJIMI is not correlated with either the Wilshire 5000 index or the three-month Treasury bill rate. Also changes in the DJIMI are not caused by the Wilshire 5000 or the three-month Treasury bill rate. The authors conclude that the filtering criteria adopted to eliminate non-compliant firms (see below) lead to an Islamic index with unique risk–return characteristics that are not affected by the broad equity market. Hakim and Rashidian (2004) use the capital asset pricing model (CAPM) to examine to what extent the *shari'a*-compliant index is correlated to the Dow Jones World Index (DJW) and Dow Jones Sustainability World Index (DJS) or green index. Overall, their results show that DJIMI performs well compared with the DJW, but underperforms in relation to the DJS.

Hussein (2004) examines whether the performance of the FTSE Global Islamic index is significantly different from that of the FTSE All-World index during the sample period (1996–2003). A comparison of the raw and risk-adjusted performance shows that the Islamic index performs as well as the FTSE All-World index over the entire period. There is evidence that the Islamic index yields abnormal returns in the bull market period, though it underperforms the FTSE All-World index in the bear market period. In general, the results suggest that the application of ethical screens does not have an adverse impact on the FTSE Global Islamic index performance.

Hussein and Omran (2005) study the performance of each Islamic index by capturing the effects of industry, size and economic conditions on DJIMI returns. Covering the period 1996–2003, they examine the hypothesis that returns earned by investors who purchase each share in Islamic indices for an equal amount of money are significantly different from their index counterparts, in the entire, bull and bear periods. Like the previous study, they also find that Islamic indices provide investors with positive abnormal returns over the entire and bull periods, but underperform their index counterparts over the bear market period. The positive abnormal returns generated by Islamic indices are not due to the technology sector, but are driven by investing in small size, basic material, consumer cyclical, industrial and telecommunication firms.

The Dow Jones Islamic Market Index (DJIMI), a subset of Dow Jones Global Indexes (DJGI), was launched in December 1995. The DJIMI excludes from the index universe any industry group that represents a line of business incompatible with Islamic principles. Such activities include tobacco, alcoholic beverages, pork, gambling, arms, pornography, hotel and leisure industry, and conventional financial services (banking, insurance and so on). Other companies classified in other industry groups may also be excluded if they are deemed to have a material ownership in or revenues from prohibited business activities. Once companies with unacceptable primary business activities have been eliminated, the remaining stocks are tested according to three financial filters: first, excluding companies if total debt divided by total assets is equal to or greater than 33 per cent; second, excluding companies if accounts receivable divided by total assets is equal to or greater than 45 per cent; and third, excluding companies if non-operating interest income is equal to or greater than 5 per cent. Companies that pass these criteria are included in the DJIMI investable world. This allows the DJIMI to invest in profitable companies that make positive contributions to society (Hassan, 2002; Hussein, 2004).

The DJIMI indices are calculated and disseminated to major market data vendors in real time. Index calculation is based on Laspeyres' formula; it does not include reinvested dividends. The composition of the index is monitored by a supervisory board of Islamic scholars who advise Dow Jones on matters pertaining to the *shari'a* compliance of the indices' twin screening criteria based on ethical investing and financial ratio compliance. Dow Jones Islamic Market Indices are reviewed quarterly, with component changes implemented on the third Friday of March, June, September and December. This frequency ensures that the indices reflect the latest trends and developments in the global stock market. In addition to the quarterly and annual composition reviews, the DJIMI is reviewed on a continual basis. A change in the index is necessary if an extraordinary event such as bankruptcy, merger and take-over affects the index component. Furthermore, when there is a new issue and it is added to the Dow Jones Global Indices, it is also evaluated according to the DJIMI criteria to determine whether it will be included in the DJIMI. The twin screen of ethical and financial ratio filters allows the DJIMI to take highly leveraged firms out of the DJIMI world before they go out of business. DJIMI was able to detect the corporate troubles of Enron and Worldcom and remove these companies from the DJIMI indices a year before these companies' stocks became worthless (Hassan, 2002; Hussein, 2004)

Like DJIMI indices, the Amana funds also invest according to Islamic principles, following the twin *shari'a* criteria of ethical investing and financial ratio compliance. The funds seek protection against inflation by making long-term equity investments. There are two types of Amana mutual funds. The primary objective of the Growth Fund is long-term capital growth. It favours companies expected to grow earnings and stock prices faster than the economy. Growth investing offers greater opportunity for long-term gain, with a related increase in price volatility. The Income Fund seeks current income and preservation of capital. It invests only in dividend-paying common stocks, which are expected to have more stable stock prices (Amana Mutual Funds website, www.amanafunds.com).

None of the above studies deals directly with the speculative behaviour of Islamic stock markets which is, however, studied by Hassan and Tag El-Din (2005), who adapt duration dependence tests to analyse the Dow Jones Islamic Index and Islamic Mutual Funds. The fundamental idea of the tests comes from survival analysis, frequently used by engineers and biostatisticians. According to the rational speculative bubbles model, if bubbles do not exist, runs of positive excess returns should not display duration dependence. To make this implication testable, the authors transform the returns into series of positive and negative observed excess returns. Then they examine whether the probability that a run – a sequence of observations of the same sign – of positive excess returns have positive dependence or negative hazard function with the length of the run. This approach is reliable and robust since duration dependence is not affected by fundamental price movements and is unique to bubbles, unlike the traditional measures of detecting bubbles such as autocorrelation, skewness or kurtosis (see McQueen and Thorley, 1994). The authors use both weekly and monthly data of DJIMI and AMANX and AMAGX to test for speculative bubbles in these markets. Their results show that none of the weekly and monthly returns of AMANX, AMAGX and DJIMI shows evidence of speculative bubbles during the sample periods. Kia (2001) found similar results for Canadian general stock markets.

Concluding remarks

Despite the obvious relevance to the topic in Islam, there is only a limited literature to date on the relationship between the efficient market hypothesis (that asset prices in financial markets reflect all available information) and speculative bubbles. One exception is Hassan and Tag El-Din (2005) discussed above. Tag El-Din (1996) and Kia (2001) argue against the inefficiency created by growing speculative activities in the stock markets, and they both discuss the need for an optimal level of speculation required for liquidity and efficiency of the stock market. Tag El-Din suggests a publicly traded company must hire professional portfolio managers who will determine the fundamental value of the company's stock on a daily basis, and the investors will determine the equilibrium prices in exchange using this fundamental value as a benchmark. There must be restrictions on the trading activities of large and small investors, and small investors should be allowed to trade in open-ended funds. Kia also suggests that the government policy should ensure that investors have complete knowledge of the stock market mechanism through training. He also recommends a tax on short-term stock-trading activities.

While generally in agreement with these views, Hassan and Tag El-Din (2005) argue that the information collection and dissemination could be done by independent investment banks to reduce agency costs. There may be trading rules to curb short-term speculation in the market because taxing short-term trading may create other unwanted stock market inefficiency.

Notes

1. Keynes (1936 [1970]), questions the soundness of 'liquidity' as the sole reason for trading in secondary investment markets (p. 155). He remarks: 'The spectacle of modern investment markets has sometimes moved me towards the conclusion that to make the purchase of an investment permanent and indissoluble, like marriage, except by reason of death or other grave cause, might be the useful remedy for our contemporary evils' (p. 160).
2. The provision by *shari'a* scholars for small percentages of interest rate assets or liabilities in international equity markets is justified by reference to basic jurist postulates like 'pressing necessity' or *al-hajatu tuqaddaru bi qadariha.*
3. Riyadh's First National Symposium on the regulation of the stock market was held on 21 April 2005. One of the participants, Fahd al-Mubarak, is a member of the Saudi Consultative Assembly.
4. Tag el-Din (2004) discusses the possibility of adapting the Islamic financing mode, *istisnaa*, to perform a similar hedging role like futures.

References

Al-Dharir, Siddiq (1967), *Al-Gharar wa Atharuhu fil Uqud* [*Gharar* and its effect on contracts], Cairo: Thaqafa Press.
Al-Khayyat, Izzat Abdulazziz (1971), *Al-Shari'akt fil Shari'a al-Islamiyyah*; Amman: Ministry of Awqaf.
Al-Shatibi, Abu Ishaq (n.d.), *Al-Muafaqt Fi al-Usal al-Shariyya*, vol. 2, Beirut: Dar al-Kutub al-Arabiyyah.
Al-Zuhaili, Wahaba (1984), *al-Fiqh al-Islami wa Adillatuhu*, vol. 5, Beirut: Dar al-Fikr al-Mu'asir.
Backhouse, Roger E. (2002), *The Penguin History of Economics*, London: Penguin Books
Balduzzi, Pierluigi, Ginseppe Bertola and Silverio Foresi (1995), 'Asset price dynamics and infrequent feedback trades', *Journal of Finance*, **50** (5), republished in Bruno Biais and Marco Pagano (2001), *New Research in Financial Markets*, Oxford: Oxford University Press.
Beechey, Meredith, David Gruen and James Vickery (2000), 'The efficient market hypothesis: a survey', discussion paper RDP2000–05, Economic Research Department, Reserve Bank of Australia, Sydney.
Biais, Bruno and Peter Bossaert (1998), 'Asset prices and trading volume in a beauty contest', *Journal of Economic Studies*, **65**, republished in Bruno Biais and Marco Pagano (2001), *New Research in Financial Markets*, Oxford: Oxford University Press.
Biais, Bruno and Marco Pagano (2001), *New Research in Financial Markets*, Oxford: Oxford University Press.
Blake, David (2002), *Financial Markets Analysis*, New York: John Wiley & Sons.
Dow, James and Garry Gordon (1994), 'Arbitrage chains', *Journal of Finance*, **49** (3), republished in Bruno Biais and Marco Pagano (2001), *New Research in Financial Markets*, Oxford: Oxford University Press.

Gürkaynak, Refet S. (2005), 'Econometric tests of asset price bubbles: taking stock', FEDS working paper no. 2005–04, Board of Governors of the Federal Reserve System, Washington, DC (http://ssrn.com/ abstract= 658244).

Hakim, S. and M. Rashidian (2002), 'Risk and return of Islamic stock market indexes', paper presented at the 9th Economic Research Forum Annual Conference in Sharjah, U.A.E., 26–28 October.

Hakim, S. and M. Rashidian (2004), 'How costly is investors' compliance to *Shari'a*?', paper presented at the 11th Economic Research Forum Annual Conference in Sharjah, U.A.E., 14–16 December, Beirut, Lebanon.

Hassan, M. Kabir (2002), 'Risk, return and volatility of faith-based investing: the case of Dow Jones Islamic Index', *Proceedings of the Fifth Harvard University Forum on Islamic Finance*, Cambridge, MA: Harvard University Press.

Hassan, M. Kabir and Seif I. Tag El-Din (2005), 'Speculative bubbles in Islamic stock market-empirical assessment', MIHE working paper, Leicester, UK.

Hussein, Khaled (2004), 'Ethical investment: empirical evidence from FTSE Islamic index', *Islamic Economic Studies*, **12** (1), 21–40.

Hussein, Khaled and Mohammed Omran (2005), 'Ethical investment revisited: evidence from Dow Jones Islamic indexes', *Journal of Investing*, **14** (3), 105–26.

Ibn al-Qayyim, Shamsuddin (1996), *'Ilam al-Muwaq'in 'an Rab al-'Alamin*, vol.2, Beirut: Dar al-Kutub al-'Imiyyah.

Ibn 'Ashur, Mohammed al-Tahir (1997), *Tafsir al-Tahrir wa al-Tanwir*, vols 2 and 4, Tunis: s.d.

Jo, Tae-Hee (2002), 'A survey of literature on speculative bubbles and speculative attacks', working paper, Department of Economics, Texas A&M University.

Keynes, J.M (1936 [1970]), *The General Theory of Employment, Interest, and Money,* London: St Martin's Press.

Kia, Amir (2001), 'Speculative activity, efficiency and normative stock exchange', *JKAU: Islamic Economics*, **13**, 31–52.

Knight, Frank (1921), *Risk, Uncertainty and Profit*, Boston and New York: Houghton Miffin Co.

McQueen, Grant, and Steven Thorley (1994), 'Bubbles, stock returns, and duration dependence', *Journal of Financial and Quantitative Analysis*. **29**, 379–401.

Morris, Stephen Shin and Hyun Song (1998), 'Unique equilibrium in a model of self-fulfilling currency attacks', *American Economic Review*, **88** (3), republished in Bruno Biais and Marco Pagano (2001), *New Research in Financial Markets*, Oxford: Oxford University Press.

Obaidullah, Mohammed (2001), 'Ethics and efficiency in Islamic stock markets', *International Journal of Islamic Financial Services*. **3**, 1–10.

Saati, Abdel Rahim (2003), 'The permissible gharar in classical jurisprudence', *JKAU: Islamic Economics*, **16** (2), 1–39.

Samuelson, P. and William Nordaus (1992), *Economics*, New York: McGraw-Hill.

Tag el-Din, Seif I. (1985), 'Towards an Islamic model of stock exchange', first published in the Arabic section of *JKAU*, **3**, 31–52, and republished in English (2002), *JKAU*, **14**, 3–39.

Tag el-Din, Seif I. (1996), 'Characterizing the stock exchange from an Islamic perspective', *JKAU: Islamic Economics*, **8**, 29–49.

Tag el-Din, Seif I. (2004), 'The question of an Islamic futures market', *IIUM Journal of Economics and Management*, **12** (1), 1–19.

16 Islamic mutual funds
Said M. Elfakhani, M. Kabir Hassan and Yusuf M. Sidani

Introduction

Islam is a religion that unites both spiritual and temporal aspects of life. It regulates not only an individual's relationship with God, but also human relationships in social and financial settings. Thus the *shari'a*, or the Islamic Law, is part of every Muslim's cultural, social and behavioural identity. The application of *shari'a* to investment choices and management is not a new phenomenon. Earlier Muslims were able to establish an interest-free financial system for mobilizing resources to finance productive activities and consumer needs, which had worked effectively for centuries. As Muslim societies became more sophisticated, and their financing needs more complex, coupled with stagnating Islamic thought evolution, the Islamic-based financial system was gradually replaced by the interest-based system in recent times. The current increasing desire of Muslims to bring their modern economic and financial activity to conform again with their cherished religious values and beliefs, has led to a growing interest in Islamic-approved investment vehicles.

The wider acceptance of equity investments by *shari'a* scholars in the early 1990s paved the way to launch mutual funds that operate in compliance with the ethical guidelines of the Islamic Law (hereafter in this chapter to be called 'Islamic mutual funds'). In the early 1990s, many *shari'a*-compliant mutual funds started to appear. There are now about 126 funds with approximately US$4 billion in assets under management. Other than being a *halal* (approved) investment alternative available for Muslim investors, the funds also respond to the specific need for more liquid investment tools.

Further, the launch of reliable equity benchmarks by the Dow Jones Islamic Market Index (DJMI) and FTSE Global Islamic Index Series, followed by the the Malaysian Kuala Lumpur Syariah Index, has been a turning point for the industry, giving both Islamic and conventional investors something with which to compare. The Dow Jones Islamic Market Index, for example, started with 600 companies in 30 countries, down from 3000 before the religious screening process. One finds reputable companies included in the index, including Microsoft, Intel, Kimberly-Clark, Gillette and Hewlett-Packard (Hassan, 2002). The Dow Jones now has more than 50 Islamic indices that track industries which are compliant with Islamic laws (Hussein and Omran, 2005).

Despite the escalating interest in Islamic mutual funds, there has not yet been, to the authors' knowledge, any research concerning the performance of these funds and how they fare in comparison with conventional funds. This study aims at assessing the performance of the Islamic mutual funds, examining whether there exists any significant reward or penalty for investing in them.

A primer on Islamic mutual funds

Muslims represent around one-fifth of the world population with more than $800 billion to invest. This amount is growing by 15 per cent annually. Only a small portion of the available funds are invested in Islamic products, which is indicative that this market is, for the most part, unexploited (Hassan, 2002). The Islamic mutual funds market is one of the fastest rising segments within the Islamic financial system, yet, when compared to the mutual fund industry at large, Islamic mutual funds are still in their infancy stage of growth and development, most being around for less than a decade. Islamic funds are fairly diverse for a young industry. While the majority of the funds are equity funds (84 per cent of the total 126 funds), balanced (or secured) funds (14 per cent) as well as Islamic bond *(sukuk)* funds (2 per cent) have recently been launched. Moreover, among the equity funds, several sectors and geographical investment areas are featured. Out of the total 126 available Islamic funds, 35 are global equity funds (28 per cent), 10 are American equity funds (8 per cent), 5 are European equity funds (4 per cent), 5 are Asian equity funds (4 per cent), 29 are Malaysian equity funds (23 per cent), 13 are country funds – mostly Saudi Arabian, Egyptian and South African (10 per cent) – and 8 are technology and small capitalization equity funds (6 per cent). Most Islamic funds do not aim at high net-worth people; minimum investment subscription ranges from $2000 to $5000 (Hussein and Omran, 2005).

Islamic equity funds witnessed strong expansion during the late 1990s as they benefited from the technology boom, most of them demonstrating high positive returns, even higher than their benchmarks. Their number increased from eight funds prior to 1992, to 95 funds with about US$5 billion in assets in 2000, then dropped to about US$4 billion by the end of 2001. Nevertheless, more funds have been launched since 2002, on the back of rising market expectations and with more lessons having being learned.

The drop in the industry's total assets that occurred in 2000–2001 is related to the downslide of world equity markets generally and investors' inclination to move funds into safer instruments. Islamic-based equity fund managers reacted consequently by reshuffling the makeup of their portfolios, with those overweight in technology shifted to the healthcare and energy sectors. In addition, the new funds had a propensity to be more capital-protected or balanced funds. Of the 23 funds initiated in 2000, nine were global equity funds and five were capital protected or balanced funds; whereas, of the 20 funds initiated in 2001, five were capital protected or balanced and only three were global equity funds (Failaka International, 2002).

Usmani (2002) explored the principles of *shari'a* governing Islamic funds. He explained several types of investment funds which may be accommodated – with some conditions – under Islamic precepts. For that matter he explained the principles underlying equity, *ijara*, commodity, *murabaha* and mixed funds, as follows.

Equity fund
Usmani explained the differences in opinion among Muslim scholars pertaining to the permissibility of investment in companies which are involved in a *halal* business but nevertheless have a portion of their transactions involving incidental *haram (shari'a*-non-compliant) activities such as interest. He concluded that a large number of present-day scholars argue that such incidental business activities do not render the whole business unlawful. Nevertheless a list of conditions has to be met before investment in such funds can be ruled as *shari'a*-compliant. Accordingly Muslims can invest their funds in such businesses that meet some specific conditions, as follows:

1. The investment has to be made in businesses that do not violate *shari'a*. In that respect no investment can be made in companies that engage in unlawful activities such as liquor, gambling and pornography.
2. In the case where the main line of business is lawful but the company is involved in interest-related activities, shareholders have to express their disapproval for such dealings wherever possible.
3. The income generated from dividends has consequently to be purified from such activities by allocating a percentage of that dividend to designated charities in proportion to the income generated from interest-related activities.
4. The shares of the company can only be negotiable if the business owns some illiquid assets. Shares for companies whose assets are all in liquid form can only be traded at par value.

The above conditions require a strict filtering process to determine which companies might be included in the fund and which companies should be excluded. The filtering process will first exclude all companies involving forbidden items. The second filtering mechanism involves a set of financial ratios which have to be met by any company before it can be included. These ratios are used in order to safeguard against earning profits resulting from interest. El-Gamal (2000) indicated that most Islamic funds have reached similar compromises pertaining to the ratios acceptable in companies that could belong to the fund. For example, the Dow Jones Islamic Market Turkey Index (DJI, 2005) indicates that the stocks excluded represent companies involved in any of the following activities: alcohol, tobacco, pork-related products, financial services, defence/weapons, entertainment. In addition the financial ratio screens exclude all companies for which any of the following ratios are 33 per cent or more:

1. 'Total debt divided by trailing 12-month average market capitalization
2. The sum of a company's cash and interest-bearing securities divided by trailing 12-month average market capitalization
3. Accounts receivables divided by trailing 12-month average market capitalization.' (DJI, 2005)

Ijara *fund*

Ijara means leasing whereby funds are used to purchase assets and lease them out to third-party users. *Ijara* is increasing in popularity and is the most popular method of Islamic house finance in the United Kingdom (Matthews et al., 2002). Leasing is an increasingly acceptable instrument from the perspective of many Muslims scholars (Warde, 2000). Rentals are collected from the users and the investors in the fund own a proportionate share of the leased assets. Ownership is authenticated in certificates or *sukuk* which are negotiable in the secondary markets. *Ijara* is permissible according to *shari'a* but also subject to certain conditions (Usmani, 2002). The assets themselves have to be *halal*; that is assets used in gambling casinos or manufacturing alcoholic products do not qualify. The rental charges should be set at the outset and known to the parties involved in the transaction and should cover the whole period of the lease. The lessor assumes all the responsibilities subsequent to ownership so that the lessor has the duty to manage the assets including repairing the assets in case of malfunction (Warde, 2000; Usmani, 2002).

In addition, the leasing agency must own the leased object for the duration of the lease (El-Gamal, 2000). *Ijara* is considered a useful tool leading to economic development and is increasingly used in retail finance such as home mortgages and cars (Warde, 2000). In the *ijara* fund, the fund management acts as an agent of the subscribers and thus can charge a fee for the service it renders. Such fees can be fixed or a percentage of the rentals received (Usmani, 2002).

Commodity fund

Islamic jurisprudence also allows commodity funds which entail the purchase and subsequent sale, by the fund, of commodities for a profit. These profits are distributed among the investors in the fund in proportion to their investment. Some conditions also apply in this case. The commodities themselves have to be *halal*. In addition, the price of the commodities has to be known to the parties at the time of the transaction. If the price is unknown or attached to another eventuality, this is not allowed. Moreover the seller has to have physical or constructive control over the commodity to be sold. Constructive possession refers to any activity which indicates that the risk of the commodity is transferred to the purchaser (Usmani, 2002). Accordingly forward sales are not allowed in most cases as they involve dealing in commodities which a person does not own or possess at the time of the transaction. Two exceptions are *istisnaa* and *salam* (Usmani, 2002). *Istisnaa* means commissioning a manufacturer to manufacture commodities for later delivery to the purchaser. *Salam* refers to a sale contract in which the purchaser pays fully against the deferred delivery of the goods involved. These two types of forward contracts can be used lawfully by Islamic investment funds.

As an example of the increasing interest in commodities funds, Sedco, a company that pursues public and private equity Islamic investment opportunities, collaborated with Goldman Sachs to establish the AlFanar Goldman Sachs Commodity Fund. Company officials asserted that there will be an extensive array of commodities in the fund, with a particular stress on energy and precious metals (The International Islamic Finance Forum, 2005a).

Murabaha *fund*

This is a specific case of a commodity sale in which the buyer knows the price and agrees to pay a premium over the initial price (El-Gamal, 2000). Such commodities are said to be sold on a cost-plus basis. While *murabaha* is essentially a sale agreement and not a financing agreement, it can be used as a financing vehicle through adopting specified procedures (Usmani, 2002). *Murabaha* typically involves a client approaching an institution and they together come to an agreement that the institution makes the purchase from a third party. The transaction could also be realized through the client purchasing the commodity as an agent of the institution and then the institution sells the commodity to the client for a deferred price. It is important to note that the institution immediately sells the items purchased to the clients after their purchase. Accordingly, the portfolio of *murabaha* – and the units of a *murabaha* fund – would not include any commodities; it would just include cash and receivables that would be paid by the client at a later date. The fund has to be a closed-end fund and its units cannot be negotiated in a secondary market (Usmani, 2002). Despite its wide acceptance and popularity, *murabaha* is sometimes controversial as it seems to emulate the features of a traditional financing arrangement. *Murabaha* represents the most popular scheme of Islamic financing, accounting for over 70 per cent of Islamic financing transactions (Curtis Davis Garrard, 2000). The National Commercial Bank located in Saudi Arabia manages the largest *murabaha* fund in the world, over $3billion (Banker Middle East, 2005).

Mixed funds
These funds represent cases where the transactions are made in different types of investments including equities, leasing, commodities and so on. Usmani (2002) indicates that, if the tangible assets of the fund are more than 51 per cent, then the units of the fund become negotiable. If the liquid assets and debts exceed 50 per cent then the units of the fund cannot be traded and the fund must be a closed-end fund.

The fundamentals of Islamic investing
Islamic alternatives to traditional investment tools have been driven by the fact that such tools do not conform to the Islamic standards (Usmani, 2002). There has been a growing desire to have funds in which profits are not based on *riba* or interest which is rejected in Islam. Muslims deem that profit should come as a result of efforts; this is not the case in interest-dominated investments. In addition, there is a desire to have investment portfolios which are morally purified. Thus investments in companies that are not in compliance with Muslims' moral orientations are not permitted and are eliminated from the portfolio. To ensure compliance with the foregoing condition, Islamic mutual funds are governed by *shari'a* advisory boards whose role is mainly to give assurance that money is managed within the framework of Islamic laws (Hassan, 2001, 2002).

An Islamic mutual fund is similar to a 'conventional' mutual fund in many ways. However, unlike its 'conventional' counterpart, an Islamic mutual fund must conform to *shari'a* investment precepts. The *shari'a* encourages the use of profit sharing and partnership schemes, and forbids *riba* (interest), *maysir* (gambling and pure games of chance) and *gharar* (selling something that is not owned or that cannot be described in accurate detail in terms of type, size, and amount) (El-Gamal, 2000). The *shari'a* guidelines and principles govern several aspects of an Islamic mutual fund, including its asset allocation (portfolio screening), investment and trading practices, and income distribution (purification).

When selecting investments for their portfolio (asset allocation), conventional mutual funds can freely choose between debt-bearing investments and profit-bearing investments, and invest across the spectrum of all available industries. An Islamic mutual fund, however, must set up screens in order to select those companies that meet its qualitative and quantitative criteria set by *shari'a* guidelines. Qualitative screens are used to filter out companies according to the nature of their business (for example, firms producing or selling alcohol, and biotechnology firms using aborted embryos and human cloning), or securities that contain one of the *shari'a* prohibited elements (for example, involving *riba, maysir* or *gharar*) as explained earlier, or companies that conduct unethical business practices as per *shari'a*, such as companies that are engaged in biotechnology using aborted embryos and human cloning. Thus, excluded from Islamic-approved securities are fixed income instruments such as corporate bonds, treasury bonds and bills, certificates of deposit (CDs), preferred stocks, warrants and some derivatives (such as options), and so on. Moreover, Islamic mutual funds cannot trade on margin; in other words, they cannot use interest-paying debt to finance their investments. Nor is it permissible to engage in sale and repurchase agreements (that is, repos or buy-backs). These transactions are considered akin to indirect interest charges.

The basis upon which an Islamic mutual fund operates must also be *shari'a*-compliant: its invested funds must be liberated from interest-based debt or speculation. Traditional funds that rely heavily on interest-based debt to finance their activities are not compliant with Islamic law. In addition, Islamic fund managers are not allowed to speculate. An Islamic economic unit is expected to assume risk after making a proper assessment of such risk with the help of information. Only in the absence of information or under conditions of uncertainty is speculation akin to a game of chance and therefore reprehensible.

On another front, most scholars allow partially 'contaminated' earning income to be cleansed or purified. This means that investment in stocks of companies with a tolerable amount of interest income (that is, kept at a minimum proportion) or with tolerable revenues from unacceptable business activities can be made if all 'impure' earnings are 'cleansed' by giving them away to designated charities. If, for example, the company has 8 per cent interest-related income, then 8 per cent of every dividend payment must be given away to 'purify' the fund earnings. Cleansing capital gains, however, remains debatable as some scholars argue that this is not necessary since the change in the stock price does not really reflect interest, while others suggest that it is safer and more equitable to purify earnings made from selling shares as well (Usmani, 2002). This purification process is done either by the fund manager before any distribution of income, or by reporting the necessary financial ratios for investors to purify their earnings on their own. Some researchers affirm that the fund ought to encompass a clear procedure and techniques of sorting out interest-based income and other sources of contaminated profits from the portfolio (Valpey, 2001).

Another form of purification is *zakat*. *Zakat* is a form of charity paid on personal wealth (exceeding a minimum amount called *nisab*) held idle for one lunar year. The rate of *zakat* differs with the type of the asset, 2.5 per cent being the rate on most forms of monetary wealth and earned income (Al-Qaradawi, 1999). *Zakat* calculation on investment profits, however, is still controversial (DeLorenzo, 2000). In addition, such calculation is complicated, given the intricacies of the timing of the portfolio incomes and capital gains (Hassan, 2001). Recipients of *zakat* are clearly identified in Islamic jurisprudence and include charities and other bodies identified by the funds' supervisory boards.

In addition to the above principles, Valpey (2001) identifies other pillars that help in promoting socially responsible business practices. Shareholder advocacy refers to the mechanism of involving shareholders in positively influencing corporate behaviour. Shareholders in the Islamic environment are not merely concerned with higher returns on their investment, but have a proactive role, given their position as corporate owners. Constant monitoring and timely reporting are also needed to make sure that the companies included in the portfolio continuously meet the guidelines for Islamic investing. Often company shares are dropped from a certain fund after information about a violation is reported.

The governance and control of Islamic mutual funds

The *shari'a* also provides guidance regarding governance and management structure of Islamic mutual funds. An Islamic mutual fund is subjected to continuous monitoring by its *Shari'a* Supervisory Board. The existence of such boards represents the salient features that distinguish Islamic mutual funds from their conventional counterparts. The Board assumes the responsibility for auditing the *shari'a* compliance of a fund, including its components and management. It effectively functions as a customer advocate representing the religious interest of the investor (DeLorenzo, 2000). The Board usually comprises a group of well-known Islamic legal scholars, who are well-educated about the intricacies of financial transactions on the one hand, and religious knowledge on the other. The Board should be autonomous and assume an advisory and supervisory function in overseeing the fund's activities. In general, the Board is responsible for the following:

- advocating the rights of the investors through assuring them that the money is invested within the scope of Islamic *shari'a*. This includes the screening process and setting the investment guidelines. In addition, the board monitors the fund fee structure to ensure that it is reasonable and clearly transmitted to investors;
- monitoring the fund's activities to ensure continuous adherence to the above guidelines. This includes continuous evaluation of the stocks and gathering information about the different stocks composing the fund to ensure continued compliance;
- reporting on the status of the fund, addressing concerns that are of importance to investors. Such reporting could be done on a quarterly basis;
- overseeing the fund's portfolio purification and advising on, or selecting, the appropriate charities;
- assisting the fund management with issues of concern to the Muslim community through shareholder resolutions and other tools of corporate governance;
- advising on *zakat* (charity) and identifying the procedures for its calculation. It is best if those guidelines are published and distributed to investors although the final computation of *zakat* varies according to each investor's financial situation;
- keeping itself always abreast of issues relevant to the industry in which they operate. This includes understanding developments in the products in the marketplace and making decisions on the degree of their compatibility with the set guidelines.

As an example, the *Shari'a* Supervisory Board for the Dow Jones Islamic Market Indexes, in an effort to make sure that all securities selected are acceptable under *shari'a*, included notable prominent scholars such as Abdul Sattar Abu Ghuddah (Syria), Justice Muhammad Taqi Usmani (Pakistan), Nizam Yaquby (Bahrain), Dr Mohamed A. Elgari (Saudi Arabia), Yusuf Talal DeLorenzo (United States) and Dr Mohd Daud Bakar (Malaysia).

An assessment of Islamic mutual funds
General description of ethical funds
Because of recurring incidents of grave corporate misconduct, more organizations in general have been incorporating ethics into their decision-making processes. This move has been augmented by increased consumer pressure stemming from religious considerations, or concerns about the environment, community involvement, social responsibility, safety matters, advertising policies and other similar issues. Some investor groups have been increasingly concerned about the type of companies in which they invest and look beyond mere returns when they make investment decisions. Hence we find ethical investment,

sometimes called 'socially responsible investing', going beyond the small slot it used to occupy several years ago. The funds reached a size of over \$2 trillion in the US in the past few years. According to a report by the Social Investment Forum, more than one out of every nine dollars invested and professionally managed in the United States involves an ethical or socially responsible investment. The report also indicates that assets involved in social investing have grown 40 per cent faster than all professionally managed assets in the United States. Socially responsible investing is also growing on a global basis with related instruments now available in more than 21 countries (Social Investment Forum, 2003).

Nevertheless, it is difficult to assess the proportion of investments that meet the rubric 'ethical investment' because of a lack of agreement as to what exactly comes under such investments. Ethical investment includes those investments that are made in harmony with personal values and principles. Consequently, the selection could be made by the investor alone, or through a fund. Such an investment may stem from environmental or social concerns, religious beliefs, or other concerns. Langbein and Posner (1980, p. 73) define ethical investment as 'excluding the securities of certain otherwise attractive companies from an investor's portfolio because the companies are judged to be socially irresponsible and including the securities of certain otherwise unattractive companies because they are judged to be behaving in a socially laudable way'.

Several studies have assessed the performance of ethical funds, with no conclusive results. Mixed results were found in Cooper and Schlegelmilch's (1993) study depending on the funds involved and the time periods assessed. Langbein and Posner (1980) suggest that ethical investments seem to be riskier but indicate that they should not lead to inferior returns. On the other hand, Orlitzky, Schmidt and Reynes (2003) conclude, using a meta-analysis of 52 studies, that there is a positive association between corporate social performance and corporate financial performance across industries. The link between the two was found to be significant, varying from highly positive to moderately positive. Kurtz (1997) found no relationship between the ethics or social responsiveness of an investment portfolio and its performance. Additional indications suggest that the performance of the average socially screened mutual fund fared better than 58 per cent of all mutual funds for the 12-month period that ended in September 1994 (Melton, 1995).

Luther, Matatko and Corner (1992) provide weak evidence that the UK ethical funds outperform two market indexes. Since the ethical funds tend to invest a larger part of the funds in smaller companies with lower dividend yields, Luther and Matatko (1994) deem it appropriate to introduce a small company index as the market proxy. Their reported findings demonstrate that ethical funds perform much better when evaluated against a small company benchmark than when only the Financial Times All Share index (FTSA) is used. Kreander et al. (2002) broaden his investigation to consider European funds from a small number of countries. They find that European ethical funds perform at least as well as the Morgan Stanley Capital International (MSCI) World Index. When Swedish ethical funds are evaluated against a Swedish benchmark, their performance is outstanding, while it is much more modest when compared to a global index.

The study of Mallin, Saadouni and Briston (1995) overcame the benchmark problem of the early studies by using a matched-pair analysis. They studied the returns earned by 29 UK ethical funds and 29 UK non-ethical funds, matched on the basis of age and size, between 1986 and 1993, using the Jensen, Sharpe and Treynor performance measures. A small majority of funds from both groups underperform the market as measured by the FTSA index. In addition, ethical funds were more likely to fare better compared to their corresponding non-ethical pairs despite the fact that such an effect was not strong.

Girard *et al.* (2005) report that, among 97 socially responsible mutual funds, only one out of five has a total return greater than its inherent benchmark over different time periods (one, three and five years). The ratio decreases even further for ten-year periods. They report the results of several studies that agree that socially responsible mutual funds tend to under-perform broad benchmarks (for example, Sauer, 1997; Goldreyer and Diltz, 1999; Plantinga and Scholtens, 2001; Bauer, Koedijk and Otten, 2002; Geczym, Stambaugh and Levin, 2003). Girard *et al.* (2005) report the results of their own investigation pertaining to the per-formance of socially responsible mutual funds and conclude that 'our findings suggest that socially responsible mutual funds (SRMF) entails costs associated with poor selection skills in direct relation with the ethical screening process, as well as a higher cost for (a lack of) diversification unwarranted by social screens' (pp. 15–16).

A study of UK ethical fund performance by Gregory, Matatko and Luther (1997) adopts a matched-pair approach, and employs a size-adjusted measure of performance. Their study concludes that there is no noteworthy variation between the returns generated by the ethical and non-ethical funds, and that both groups underperform the FTSA benchmark index. However, the age of a fund appears to be an important factor influ-encing each fund's alpha measure, whereas the size of a fund and its ethical status are found insignificant.

The UK results mirror the findings of studies that analyse the performance of US ethical funds. For example, using monthly data from 1994 to 1997, M'Zali and Turcotte (1998) compare the performance of 18 American and Canadian ethical funds with ten non-ethical funds, where both groups are managed by the same investment groups. They employ the Sharpe and Treynor measures to assess fund performance and find that four of the ethical funds outperform the market index. However, the majority of funds under-perform the Standard & Poor's S&P 500 Index and the Toronto Stock Exchange TSE 300 Index. Hamilton, Jo and Statman (1993) compare the performance of a sample of 32 American ethical funds to that of 170 ordinary funds over a ten-year period (1981–1990). The average return for the ethical funds is found to be higher than the average returns for the 'ordinary', suggesting that investors do not lose by investing in similar ethical funds. The same finding is later confirmed by Reyes and Grieb (1998).

Based on the above, it is clear that much disagreement surrounds the performance of ethical or socially responsible mutual funds, although it appears that there is no signifi-cant negative consequence for investing in such funds compared to conventional funds.

Islamic funds – an empirical assessment
Muslim involvement in stock markets has been very scant during the past few decades owing to the religious ruling that discouraged such activities, if not prohibiting them out-right. Most Islamic investing revolved around low-risk, modest-return financial products (Siddiqi, 2000). The 1990s witnessed a major change due to developments in Islamic jurisprudence which resulted in the appearance of several Islamic equity funds (Hussein and Omran, 2005). Recent estimates put Islamic financial markets at around $230 billion, with 15 per cent annual growth (Hakim and Rashidian, 2004). Islamic funds can be thought of as being a special case of ethical funds where, in addition to the keeping out

of certain sectors, such funds do not do business in fixed-income markets, and transactions involving interest are not allowed (Hussein and Omran, 2005).

Sources of data about Islamic mutual funds are still very limited compared to their ethical or conventional counterparts. Failaka International Inc. (www.failaka.com), established in Chicago in 1996, is the first specialized organization to monitor and publish performance data on Islamic equity funds. In addition to customized research and consulting services offered by Failaka, the company publishes on its website periodic lists of all known Islamic mutual funds, yearly performance reports on nearly half of the existing funds, periodic analysis of the industry and information about each fund, and performance graphs showing the percentage change of the fund's monthly net asset value (NAVs) and its relative market proxy over a given year. Failaka, however, has no historical data or rating on these funds.

We report here the results of three studies (Elfakhani, Sidani and Fahel, 2004; Elfakhani, Hassan and Sidani, 2005; Girard and Hassan, 2005) conducted to assess the performance of Islamic mutual funds. Failaka's list of August 2002 included the names of 106 Islamic mutual funds. Those funds were directly contacted for historical NAVs or returns since their fund's inception date, of which 37 responded. On a parallel track, Standard & Poor's (www.sp-funds.com) provided historical data on 48 Islamic mutual funds, ten of which are also available through Failaka; thus 75 was the total number of funds for which monthly data were available. Next, one filter used in funds selection was the availability of the fund's monthly returns over a period of no less than two years, resulting in a final sample of 46 Islamic mutual funds. The median age of the whole sample was only 2.5 years for the 75 gathered funds and 3.25 years for the whole Islamic mutual funds population.

Using a sample of 46 Islamic mutual funds classified into eight sector-based categories, the performance of each fund and fund category was measured and compared to the performance of two market benchmarks, an Islamic index and a conventional one. Funds were then classified into eight categories according to their regional or sector investment exposure: global equity funds, American equity funds, European equity funds, Asian equity funds, Malaysian equity funds, emerging markets equity funds, emerging markets (South Africa and Small Cap/Technology) funds. This classification gave further insights about sector performance.

The period covered in the study extended from 1 January 1997 and ended on 31 August 2002. The 1 January 1997 date was chosen since a relatively good number of funds became available in the market around that time. One feature of this period is that it covered a booming phase extending from 1997 to early 2000, and a recessionary phase starting in 2000. Hence the total 68-month sampling period was further divided into two equal sub-periods, the first 34 months ending on 31 October 1999, and the remaining 34 months to reflect the booming–slowing sub-periods.

Two stock market indices were used as benchmarks in the study to evaluate the performance of the Islamic funds and the funds' categories: an Islamic market index (representing region or sector specific index) and a conventional broad market index. With regard to the general market index, the Standard & Poor's S&P 500 Composite Price Index was used as an acceptable proxy. With regard to Islamic-based indices, we considered the FTSE Islamic Index Series and the Dow Jones Islamic market index. Both FTSE and Dow Jones screen out stocks, the core of which activities are not permitted by *shari'a*. The FTSE has five indices, the global Islamic index and four regional (the Americas,

Europe, the Pacific Basin and South Africa) with data available starting in 1994. The Dow Jones has regional Islamic market indices covering the United States, Europe, Asia/Pacific, Canada and the United Kingdom. In addition to its geographical indices the Dow Jones has Islamic indices for technology stocks and extra liquid securities. The FTSE series does not have any sector index.

Arguably it is appropriate to use the FTSE and Dow Jones indices to compare the performance of dollar-denominated Islamic global equity funds, but they may not be as relevant when evaluating the performance of equity markets in Muslim countries, where country-specific indices can be more relevant, if available. Yet not all Muslim countries provide such indices, thus we used a list of the Islamic indices that correspond to each fund category as closely as possible. For instance, we used five FTSE indices (Global, America, Europe, Pacific Basin and South Africa) as benchmarks to match their corresponding regional categories in our sample of Islamic mutual funds categories (Global, America, Europe, Asian and Emerging markets–South Africa, respectively). The Dow Jones technology index was used as the benchmark for our sample of small capitalization fund. The Kuala Lumpur Stock Exchange Syariah Index from April 1999, and the FTSE Pacific Basin Islamic Index were used for the period before that as the benchmark for the Malaysian funds. Finally, since the emerging markets category had no specific country Islamic index, the FTSE Global Islamic Index was used as the benchmark for funds in this category.

Several performance measures were used to assess the performance of Islamic mutual funds, including Sharpe, Treynor, Jensen, Fama and Transformed Sharpe measures. Sharpe measure results indicated that the performance of the Emerging markets funds was the highest, followed by the Emerging markets–South Africa funds and the American funds. Then came, respectively, the European, the Technology, the Malaysian, the Global and the Asian fund categories. When comparing each fund to its relevant Islamic indices, four of the eight categories performed better than the market; these were, respectively, from the best performing, the Emerging markets, European, American and the Malaysian fund categories. Compared to the S&P 500, also four categories performed better than the index. Treynor measure results revealed that the Emerging markets category was the best performer compared to its two benchmarks, and the Asian and Malaysian categories were the worst performers. Using the Jensen measure, it was found that the Emerging markets category was the best performing compared to its two benchmarks, and the Asian category was the worst performing. Fama results indicated that the emerging markets–South Africa category was the best performer given its highest return on overall performance, followed by the emerging markets fund and the American fund.

Considering the results of the first half of the overall study period, from 1 January 1997 to 31 October 1999, it may be noted that, compared to their relevant Islamic index, only one (the Emerging markets–South Africa category) out of the eight categories outperformed the benchmark with positive and statistically significant Transformed Sharpe difference. When compared to the S&P 500, the Technology fund category was the only one out of the eight categories that outperformed the benchmark and the difference was significant. As for the results of the Transformed Sharpe measures for the second half of the overall study period, from 1 November 1999 to 31 August 2002, it may be noted that, compared to their relevant Islamic index, six out of the eight categories outperformed their benchmark with positive Transformed Sharpe difference that was significant at the

5 per cent level, except for the Emerging markets, the results of which were not significant. When compared to the S&P 500, seven out of the eight categories outperformed their benchmark with positive Transformed Sharpe difference, all statistically significant except for the Emerging markets, whose results were not significant. In general, it appears that Islamic mutual funds have shown strong performance during the recessionary sub-period. The one-way ANOVA test of means revealed that there was not any statistically significant difference among the performance of any of the eight Islamic fund categories against all six Islamic indices as well as the S&P 500 Index, at both the 5 per cent and 10 per cent levels of significance.

Elfakhani, Hassan and Sidani (2005) use the Treynor-Mazury (TM) model to measure security-selection ability and market-timing ability of Islamic mutual fund managers. Their results show that the American Equity Fund, the European Equity Fund, the combined Emerging Fund, and the Technology Fund all had positive security selection, but only the Emerging Equity Fund had positive selectivity that is statistically significant. The remaining three funds (Global, Asian and Malaysian funds) had negative selectivity performance during the same period. This is not so surprising as the results could be dominated by the Asian crisis, while Western funds were less affected during the same sampling period. In particular, the Asian Equity Fund performed very badly as the intercept was statistically and significantly negative at the 1 per cent level. However, other results show that the Asian Equity Fund had a significant positive market timing performance; all remaining funds had negative market timing performance particularly the European and the combined Emerging Funds that are statistically significant at the 5 per cent level. This observation was confirmed by the negative correlations reported, except for the Asian fund.

Girard and Hassan (2005) examine the comparative performance of the Dow Jones Islamic Indices and its seven indices vis-à-vis their non-Islamic counterparts using a variety of measures such as Sharpe, Treynor, Jensen and Fama's selectivity, net selectivity and diversification. They also investigate the persistence of performance using Carhart's (1997) four-factor pricing models. Moreover, they also use cointegration to examine how the Islamic indices are related to their non-Islamic counterparts. The sample period starts from January 1996 and ends in November 2005 (118 data points). It is further broken down into two periods: January 1996 to November 2000 (59 data points) and December 2000 to November 2005 (59 data points). They find that there is no great difference between the Islamic and non-Islamic indices. The Dow Islamic indices outperform from 1996 to 2000 and underperform from 2001 to 2005 their conventional counterparts. Overall, similar reward to risk and diversification benefits exist for the two indices.

Nevertheless, for traditional performance measures and for the full period, Islamic indices return on average 7.04 per cent per annum as compared to 5.34 per cent for MSCI indices. Also Islamic series are less risky than MSCI indices (average of 17.52 per cent standard deviation per annum versus 18 per cent per annum). Islamic indices are somewhat correlated with their peers (0.78), but less correlated with the MSCI AC World (average correlation of 0.69 with MSCI AC World) than MSCI indices (average correlation of 0.87 with MSCI AC World). This result translates into a lower beta with the world (0.78) as compared to MSCI indices (1.028). Overall, the Sharpe and Treynor ratios indicate that Islamic indices outperform their non-Islamic peers. More specifically, the Islamic indices offer an average of 206 basis points of excess performance as compared to MSCI indices.

Interestingly, Islamic indices are less diversified as compared to their peers: the cost of diversification is 31 basis points above the average MSCI index. On a diversification-adjusted basis, all Islamic indices outperform MSCI indices by 175 basis points over the last 118 months (Girard and Hassan, 2005).

Controlling performance for style and time variability (Carhart multi-factor model), and for the full period, Islamic indices exhibit more global and local factors exposure as compared to conventional indices. (In 12 out of 14 cases the hypothesis of constant betas can be rejected at least at the 10 per cent level as indicated by the Wald test statistics indicating strong time-variation in betas.) The difference in conditional alphas between MSCI and Islamic indices, however, decreases from those observed with the unconditional models. Islamic indices are more exposed to small caps (capitalization), while non-Islamic indices on the other hand are relatively more invested in value stocks. In sum, Islamic indices are more growth and small-capitalization-oriented than value and large cap oriented, when compared to conventional indices. A reason for the high proportion of growth stocks may lie in the exclusion of traditional value sectors like chemical, energy and basic industries. As these represent a higher environmental risk, ethical portfolios are often underweighted in them, which leads to a growth focus. Finally, after controlling for market risk, size, book-to-market, momentum, local and global factors, the difference in return between Islamic and conventional funds remains negligible: none of the alphas is significantly different from zero, and we cannot distinguish between the two. Also the multivariate cointegration analysis suggests that both groups (Islamic and conventional) are poorly integrated for the overall period. However, there seem to be some strong common stochastic trends in both groups during the first period (at most two significant cointegrating equations). For the second period, the Islamic group remains somewhat cointegrated while the non-Islamic group shows little evidence of common stochastic trends (Girard and Hassan, 2005).

Overall, the statistical findings suggest that the behaviour of Islamic mutual funds does not differ substantially from that of other conventional funds, with some *shari'a*-compliant mutual funds overperforming their benchmarks and others underperforming them. However, some recent evidence indicates that the Islamic indices may generate higher returns at lower risk over the full period. Another major observation is the strong performance of Islamic mutual funds compared to both benchmarks during the recession period. One possible explanation of this pattern is that these funds' performance is improving with time, as fund managers are gaining more experience and a better sense of the market.

Marketing and distribution of Islamic mutual funds
Islamic-based mutual funds offer Muslim investors the double advantage of mutual fund investment and compliance with Islamic guidelines. The tolerability of common stock screening guidelines by an overwhelming majority of *shari'a* scholars has not been deciphered into more demand for such investing mechanisms. One reason behind this phenomenon could be the fact that Islamic funds have not fared well in marketing and differentiating themselves from their conventional counterparts. Moreover, some Muslim investors fear that there remain some *haram* elements in them. They prefer to place their money in Islamic banks and institutions that 'truly' invest in acceptable products offered by Islamic companies in Muslim countries. Such products include *ijara*, *istisnaa*, *murabaha* and *mudaraba*.

According to an analysis made by Failaka International (2002), the 15 most successful funds were those that have strong retail distribution channels. The National Commercial Bank and Al-Rajhi Bank in Saudi Arabia are given as prime examples of such funds. These funds charge small or no up-front sales charge (load). They command minimum investment thresholds that are attractive for the retail investor. The average fund size of this group is US\$108.2 million. Conversely, three of the bottom 15 funds in terms of assets have relatively higher minimum investment thresholds (over US\$25 000). Nine of those funds charge an up-front load, six of which are 5 per cent or more. Six of these funds have annual management fees of 2 per cent or more. The average funds size of this group is US\$4.4 million (Failaka International, 2002).

Some fund managers acknowledge the fact that Islamic funds have been facing severe marketing problems. Bashar Qasem, President of Azzad Asset Management, contends that carefully orchestrated marketing campaigns should aim at educating Muslims about investing in mutual funds. He suggests that a grassroots campaign in mosques and Islamic cultural centres would raise awareness about the industry and increase potential interest in financial instruments that are compliant with Islamic laws (Fund Marketing Alert, 2002). Given the size of funds that are available for possible investments in such venues, it is clear that much of the potential for this market is yet to be realized.

It appears that marketing Islamic mutual funds share some of the problems faced by other Islamic financial instruments (see Chapter 8). They face competition from regular funds, doubts about the legitimacy of their affairs from the perspective of many observing Muslims, supervision challenges and regulatory impediments, in addition to the scarcity of a well-informed human resource work base. In order to face these challenges, the points in the following paragraphs are worthy of investigation.

It would not be far-fetched to say that, judging by the political events of the past few years leading to a negative image about Islam in general, an extra effort has to be exerted in terms of clarifying the role of Islamic investment alternatives in the betterment of lives. The role of the media cannot be ignored. Accordingly, an aggressive media campaign needs to be undertaken in explaining the Islamic opportunities available in the world of investment. Farhan Bokhari, a journalist addressing the International Islamic Forum held in Dubai in March 2005, suggested that efforts should be undertaken to translate and clarify the 'alien terminology' used by the experts when explaining products based on traditional Islamic structures that non-Muslims (and indeed many Muslims) simply do not understand (The International Islamic Finance Forum, 2005b). Islamic financial institutions use terms such *sukuk, murabaha, gharar* and *mudaraba* which are poorly understood by the vast majority of Muslims, let alone non-Muslims. This applies to both Arab-speaking and non-Arab-speaking individuals because many of these terms do not feature in the daily lexicon of the average individual. The challenges ahead can be realized when one sees the effort expended by traditional non-Islamic banks and financial institutions in establishing rapport with their customers and using terminology that their clients can follow.

Islamic financial institutions should also realize the benefit of appealing to a broader target market that includes Muslims and non-Muslims alike. At the same Dubai forum mentioned above, Hajj Abdalhamid Evans, Director of Research and Intelligence for the Malaysia-based *Halal Journal*, indicated that in Malaysia 80 per cent of the customers of the country's Islamic banks are non-Muslim Chinese attracted by the profit and loss sharing mechanisms and ethical standards. Islamic institutions should do a better job at promoting, to both Muslims and non-Muslims, the benefits that, although primarily driven by religious concerns, do not neglect the ethical and social aspects of investing in Islamic instruments. 'Islamic mutual funds are socially responsible funds' is the message that should be given to the public at large. This will make such instruments appealing to many individuals irrespective of their religious backgrounds. Given the fact that the vast majority of Muslims live in religiously diverse environments, this message becomes even more significant.

Islamic institutions should also do a better job at training their employees on Islamic instruments and developing their skills in dealing with enquiring customers who are attracted to Islamic investment alternatives. The ranks of those graduating from universities with knowledge of Islamic finance and Islamic instruments are small. In addition, some customers may fear that the institution they are dealing with may not be doing a careful job in screening out unlawful activities. Well-trained employees will make customers more confident about the legitimacy of the transactions conducted if they are able to explain comfortably to their clients the intricacies of the transactions involving the different investment options.

Finally, there is the role of the *shari'a* boards in boosting confidence and trust in Islamic investment funds. In an environment where people attach great importance to the ideas of the *'alim* (Muslim scholar), no marketing campaign could parallel the addition of a prominent *'alim* to the supervisory board overseeing investment activities. Many investment fund managers have been increasingly aware of this phenomenon and are placing famous *'alims* in such boards. But with the increase of Islamic mutual funds, shortage of qualified informed scholars is bound to happen. Sheikh Nizam Yaquby, a prominent scholar on Islamic finance, indicated that there is indeed a lack of qualified scholars who can fill the void. He urged financial institutions to fund the training of scholars in order to build a think-tank of scholars who do not only give opinions about the legitimacy of products but also are able to come up with *shari'a*-sanctioned innovative financial products (The International Islamic Finance Forum, 2005c).

Summary and conclusions

This study has examined Islamic mutual funds and the fundamentals of investing in such venues. In doing so, it has explored the dynamics of Islamic mutual funds, their governance and control, and marketing and distribution. We have presented the results of a study verifying whether the application of the Islamic investment guidelines in asset allocation and portfolio selection has had a downside effect on investors' wealth in terms of risk-adjusted returns relative to the market benchmark. Considering the overall sample of 46 Islamic mutual funds, the total number of overperforming funds ranges between 29 (63 per cent of the sample) and 11 (24 per cent), depending on the performance measure and market benchmark used. In terms of fund category, four of the eight fund categories outperform their benchmarks regardless of what performance measure was used. Moreover the ANOVA statistical test showed that no statistically significant disparity existed for the performance of the funds compared to all indices used. Therefore a conclusion of this study is that the behaviour of Islamic mutual funds does not differ from that of other conventional funds, with some *shari'a*-compliant mutual funds overperforming their benchmarks and others underperforming them.

Another interesting finding is observed when studying the performance of the funds over two successive periods within the overall study period. The first witnessed a booming equity market, while the second was a declining market. The results of the Transformed Sharpe measure showed that the performance of the Islamic mutual funds compared to both benchmarks during the second period dominated by recession is better than that during the first (booming) sub-period. This might imply that the performance of these funds is improving with time, as fund managers are gaining more experience and sense of the market. Another implication from this result is that Islamic mutual funds might be a good hedging investment for any equity investor, if used to hedge against market downturns and recessions.

Despite some limitations noted earlier, in general the results suggest that there is not any statistically significant risk-adjusted abnormal reward or penalty associated with investing in *shari'a*-compliant mutual funds, and thus with following one's belief in financial investment. Therefore conventional investors can consider Islamic mutual funds in their portfolio collection, especially during slow market periods. However, the onus remains on the investor always to screen out various candidate mutual funds according to performance, regardless of whether the fund is a conventional one, Islamic or other type of ethical or socially responsible fund.

In order for an Islamic mutual fund to succeed, it must be successfully promoted. Retail bank employees are insufficiently knowledgeable of investments to sell mutual funds. Their jobs are focused on selling banking products. A qualified investment advisor may be capable of selling mutual funds, but they must also be versed in Islamic practices to promote Islamic funds. Investment firms must avoid customer confusion at all costs. The input of the *shari'a* board is useful in this situation, providing recommendations on how to promote the Islamic mutual fund. Another key to growth in the Islamic mutual fund industry is patience. The concept of equity investing is new to Muslims, who are typically accustomed to real estate or leasing investments. Therefore time must also be spent in educating the investor.

Distribution is also important. The fund must be easily accessed through multiple distribution channels. These channels include automated telephone systems, communication with a broker, or the Internet. A key ingredient in today's financial market is the ability to access investment accounts via the Internet. A fund itself can be marketed through a distributor such as Al-Rajhi, a national organization operating in the field of finance, or a financial investment firm (such as Fidelity) may create its own fund. Either way the company should have a solid reputation for successful investments and customer service. At this point, the reputation of the *Shari'a* Advisory Board must also be considered. In order for a fund to obtain widespread Muslim approval, the *shari'a* members must be well-respected members of the community. In many ways the success of the fund rests on the Board's reputation.

Bibliography

Al-Qaradawi, Y. (1999), *Fiqh az-Zakat, A Comparative Study*, London: Dar al-Taqwa Ltd.
Banker Middle East (2005), http://www.bankerme.com/bme/2004/jan/local_news_inbrief.asp, accesssed 11 November.
Bauer, C. John and Richard P. Keigher (2001), 'Islamic equity funds: challenges and opportunities for fund managers', paper presented at the 4th Annual Harvard Forum on Islamic Finance, 30 September to 1 October, Boston, MA.

Bauer, R., K. Koedijk and R. Otten (2002), 'International evidence on ethical mutual fund performance and investment style', working paper, Maastricht University.

Carhart, M. (1997), 'On persistence in mutual fund performance', *Journal of Finance*, **52**, 57–82.

Cooper, C and B. Schlegelmilch (1993), 'Key issues in ethical investment', *Business Ethics: A European Review*, **2** (4), 213–27.

Curtis Davis Garrard (2000), 'Islamic banking and finance' (http://www.cdg.co.uk/), accessed 11 November 2005.

DeLorenzo, Y.T. (2000), 'Shari'a supervision of Islamic mutual funds', (http://www.failaka.com), accessed November 2005.

DJI (2005), http://djindexes.com/mdsidx/downloads/meth_info/DJIM_Turkey_Method.pdf, accessed 11 November.

Elfakhani, Said, Yusuf Sidani and M. Fahel (2004), 'An assessment of performance of Islamic mutual funds', *European Journal of Management and Public Policy*, **3** (1), 41–64.

Elfakhani, Said, M. Kabir Hassan and Yusuf Sidani (2005), 'Comparative performance of Islamic versus secular mutual funds', paper presented at the 12th Economic Research Forum Conference in Cairo, Egypt, 19–21 December.

El-Gamal, M.A. (2000), 'A basic guide to contemporary Islamic banking and finance' (http://www.ruf.rice.edu/~elgamal/files/primer.pdf), accessed November 2005.

Failaka International (2002), 'Islamic equity funds: analysis and observations on the current state of the industry' (http://www.failaka.com), accessed November 2005.

Fama, E.F. (1972), 'Components of investment performance', *Journal of Finance*, **27** (3), 551–67.

Fund Marketing Alert (2002), 'Va. Firm plans five Islamic fund launches within three years', **7** (38), 3.

Geczym C., R. Stambaugh and D. Levin (2003), 'Investing in socially responsible mutual funds', working paper, University of Pennsylvania.

Girard, E. and M. Kabir Hassan (2005), 'Faith-based investing – The case of Dow Jones Islamic Indices reexamined,' University of New Orleans working paper, New Orleans, LA.

Girard, E., H. Rahman and B. Stone (2005), 'Socially responsible investments: Goody-two-Shoes or Bad to the Bone', FMA Annual Meeting Program Academic Sessions, The Financial Management Association International, Chicago, USA.

Goldreyer, E. and D. Diltz (1999), 'The performance of socially responsible mutual funds: incorporating sociopolitical information in portfolio selection', *Managerial Finance*, **25** (1), 23–36.

Gregory, A., J. Matatko and R. Luther (1997), 'Ethical unit trust financial performance: small company effects and fund size effects', *Journal of Business Finance and Accounting*, **24** (5), 705–25.

Hakim, S. and M. Rashidian (2004), 'Risk and return of Islamic stock market indexes', paper presented at the International Seminar of Non-bank Financial Institutions: Islamic Alternatives, Kuala Lumpur, Malaysia.

Hamilton, S., H. Jo and M. Statman (1993), 'Doing well while doing Good? The investment performance of socially responsible mutual funds', *Financial Analysts Journal*, **49** (6), 62–6.

Hassan, M. Kabir (2001), 'Nuances of Islamic mutual funds', *Islamic Horizons*, **30** (3), 16–18.

Hassan, M. Kabir (2002), 'Risk, return and volatility of faith-based investing: the case of Dow Jones Islamic Index', paper in Proceedings of 5th Harvard University Forum on Islamic Finance, Harvard University.

Hussein, K. and M. Omran (2005), 'Ethical investment revisited: evidence from Dow Jones Islamic indices', *Journal of Investing*, Fall.

The International Islamic Finance Forum (2005a), 'Commodities – the next big asset class' (www.ifii.com) accessed 11 November.

The International Islamic Finance Forum (2005b), 'Is how good you appear as important as how good you are?' (www.ifii.com), accessed 11 November.

The International Islamic Finance Forum (2005c), 'Scholars cannot be grown like mushrooms', (www.ifii.com), accessed 11 November.

Kreander, N., R. Gray, D. Power and C. Sinclair (2002), 'The financial performance of European ethical funds 1996–1998', *Journal of Accounting and Finance*, **1**, 3–22.

Kurtz, L. (1997), 'No effects, or no net effects? Studies on socially responsible investing', *The Journal of Investing*, **6** (4), 37–49.

Langbein, J. and R. Posner (1980), 'Social investing and the law of trusts', *Michigan Law Review*, **97** (72), 72–111.

Luther, R. and J. Matatko (1994), 'The performance of ethical unit trusts: choosing an appropriate benchmark', *British Accounting Review*, **26**, 77–89.

Luther, R., J. Matatko and D. Corner (1992), 'The investment performance of UK "ethical" Unit Trusts', *Accounting Auditing and Accountability Journal*, **5** (4), 57–70.

Mallin, C., B. Saadouni and R. Briston (1995), 'The financial performance of ethical investment trusts', *Journal of Business Finance and Accounting*, **22** (4), 483–96.

Matthews, R., I. Tlemsani and A. Siddiqui (2002), 'Islamic finance', working paper, Centre for International Business Policy, Kingston Business School.

Melton, J. (1995), 'Can you really do well by doing good?', *Your Money and the World: Financial Planning for a Better Tomorrow*, Washington: Co-op America, pp. 18–19.

M'Zali, B. and M.F. Turcotte (1998), 'The financial performance of Canadian and American environmental and social mutual funds', Proceedings of 7th International Meeting of The Greening of Industry Network Research and Policy for a Sustainable Future.

Orlitzky, M., F.L. Schmidt and S.L. Reynes (2003), 'Corporate social performance and financial performance: a meta-analysis', *Organization Studies*, **24** (3), 403–41.

Plantinga, A. and B. Scholtens (2001), 'Socially responsible investing and management style of mutual funds in the Euronext stock markets', working paper, University of Groningen.

Reyes, M. and T. Grieb (1998), 'The external performance of socially-responsible mutual funds', *American Business Review*, **16** (1), 1–7.

Sauer, D. (1997), 'The impact of social-responsibility screens on investment performance: evidence from the Domini 400 Social Index and Domini Equity Mutual Fund', *Review of Financial Economics*, **6** (2), 137–49.

Siddiqi, M. (2000), 'Islamic mutual funds: equity culture among Muslim investors', *The Middle East*, April, 37–9.

Social Investment Forum (2003), '2003 report on socially responsible investing trends in the United States' (http://www.socialinvest.org/areas/research/trends/sri_trendsreport2003.pdf), accessed October 2005.

Usmani, Mufti T. (2002), *An Introduction to Islamic Finance*, The Hague: Kluwer Law International.

Valpey, F.S. (2001), 'Structuring Islamic equity funds: *Shari'a* portfolio management and performance', paper presented at the 4th Annual Harvard Forum on Islamic Finance, Harvard University.

Warde, I. (2000), *Islamic Finance in the Global Economy*, Edinburgh: Edinburgh University Press.

PART IV

ISLAMIC SYSTEMS

17 Islamic banks and economic development
Monzer Kahf

Introduction
The objective of this chapter is to give an overview of the developmental nature and characteristics of Islamic banking as a concept and how this mandate is implemented. Islamic financing itself is intrinsically interlinked with transactions in the physical goods market and is socially and morally committed. Therefore, to understand the developmental role of Islamic banking, we first look at the foundations of Islamic financing and the operations of Islamic banks in both fund mobilization and fund utilization. In the next section it is argued that Islamic banking has three major intrinsic characteristics that are developmental in nature. These three characteristics are: a direct and undetachable link to the real economy or physical transactions; integration of ethical and moral values in financing so that financing is directed to useful products only; and the building of a relationship with depositors on the basis of sharing instead of lending. The last section will discuss how the Islamic model of banking would serve as an alternative banking system.

Foundations of Islamic financing
What is Islamic financing?
The basic principles of Islamic banking are derived from the axioms of justice and harmony with reality on one hand and human nature on the other (Kahf, 1992, 2004; Kahf and Khan, 1992). The most genuine and plain definition of financing, in general, is that it is the provision of factors of production, means of payment and even goods and services without requiring an immediate counterpart to be paid by the receiver. For instance, a labourer finances the employer by waiting until the end of the month for getting compensation for the working hours given throughout the month; a physical capital owner finances the entrepreneur by waiting until the sale of production to get the rent of his/her machine; also a shopkeeper finances his/her customers by waiting until their pay day for the payments of consumer goods they purchased during the week; and a bank finances its customers when it provides money for them to use in their buying of goods and services.

Islamic financing is no more than that, in its full, plain and direct sense. Islamic financing is a name for providing factors of production, goods and services for which payment is deferred. So simple and so straightforward! Real-life exchange and production processes have, as part of their components or forms, the provision of goods to consumers as well as machines and equipment, materials and other input goods used in production to producers. The essence of Islamic banking practices is the provision of such goods and services while payments for them are delayed to later dates. Islamic banking also provides means of payment in the form of producers' principal in projects on the basis of sharing the actual, real-life outcome of a production process.

The guiding principle in Islamic financing

The principle of justice is essential in all forms of Islamic financing. In profit sharing, when an Islamic bank provides means of payment to the producers, both parties share in the actual outcome or net profit/loss of a productive project. It is not just throwing the risk burden on one party, the entrepreneur, by guaranteeing a given return to the provider of money regardless of whether the project makes or loses money. The fair play of market forces determines the rates of distribution of profit of the operation between the financier and beneficiary.

When financing is done on the basis of sale or lease principles, the Islamic bank carries the kind of risk associated with buying and owning a good and then providing it for its user. In both cases, the fair play of market forces determines the profit/rent of the goods provided by the financier to the beneficiary.

Since Islamic law assigns to private property a cornerstone role, the owner should have a full right to the increase, growth, benefit and profit that is attributed to one's property. By the same token the owner carries the liability of any loss or destruction that may happen to its property. This is not only fair and consistent with human nature, but it is the only rational thing to be done.

If a property is entrusted, by its owner, to someone else (through financing), the user's efforts that contribute to growth and profit creating must also be recognized. That is also humanly natural and the rational thing that should be done. The principle of justice and fairness requires that the actual result or profit of such cooperation should be fairly distributed between the two parties and nothing else. In other words, any distribution that is based on giving either party a predetermined fixed amount regardless of the actual profit may not be fair or just.

Interest-based lending, instead of entrusting a productive property to an entrepreneur, sees money or real goods (be it life-time savings or any other loanable goods/funds) lent to the borrower against a notional right, that we call debt. This process changes the nature of what is owned from real balances that have claims on goods and services in the society to a legal commitment, which is purely an interpersonal abstract concept. A debt is, by definition and by its nature, incapable of growing or increasing because it is purely conceptual; it is a relationship between a person and another person. How can a debt grow? How can it increase, except by arbitration, artificialities and pure contrivance?

In contrast, the same savings and/or real goods may be given on a sharing basis. The owner holds on to the right of ownership and the user exerts efforts for making the goods grow and increase, like a peasant who plants seeds in the soil and tends them, or like a trader who buys merchandise and finds a good market for it. Ownership remains in the hands of the finance provider and the work is applied by the finance receiver. Both contributions are recognized as they participate in creating an increment, increase or growth. Therefore the parties deserve to share the real outcome of that exercise.

Why should one have a claim on a part of the output of a project while bearing no part of its pain and risks? Fairness and justice require that losses should be carried in proportion to financing advanced. If a financier wants to have a claim on a part of the return of a project, she/he must also carry a proportional share of the risks and burdens of the same. This is what we call the rule that 'gains should always be linked to risk exposure'.

Finance on the basis of profit/loss sharing opens the way to direct investment, where the utmost attention of the Islamic bank is directed to the profitability of investment. In this case, close working relations between the bank and the fund user (project manager) is required to monitor performance and to solve unexpected problems. As long as returns are commensurate with risk, direct investment would not shy away from high-risk projects, or from financing small and micro enterprises.

In contrast, direct investment does not seem to be favoured by conventional banks. We quote an article in the *World Bank Research Observer* :

> In the absence of full information, banks tend to allocate credit to firms with reliable track records or available internal funds, even if other firms present better investment opportunities. . . . They are generally also reluctant to finance small firms that lack adequate collateral, even though such firms may be more innovative and promising than others. (Vittas and Cho, 1996)

Financial intermediation in Islamic banking
Financial intermediation is the major function of a modern banking system. Financial intermediation means taking funds from people who have more than they need at this juncture in time and providing those funds to persons who need them for their economic transactions and activities. This is done in conventional banks on the basis of loan contracts.

Islamic banks are also financial intermediaries. They collect savings from income earners who have surplus and distribute them to entrepreneurs and consumers who need them to finance their purchases of goods and services. But Islamic banks make their financial intermediation on the basis of several contracts that do not include lending and borrowing because interest in prohibited in the Islamic law (Siddiqi, 2004). Instead of the loan contract, Islamic banks rely on a combination of three principles: sharing, leasing and sale. What is essential in their function of financial intermediation is that Islamic banks leave the initiative of investment and use of funds to the entrepreneurs and other users of funds. In other words, while the provision of funds in Islamic financing is channelled through sale, sharing and lease contracts, the decision making of getting goods that are purchased for sale or lease and of establishing projects is left to the users of funds, and the Islamic bank acts upon orders from the users of funds.

Operations of Islamic banks
Modern Islamic banks have been founded on the banking model that existed in Europe and North America, with regard to their main layout, departmental structure and their basic functions of mobilizing financial resources and using them to finance those who are in need of investable funds (Kahf, 1999). Obviously, the difference lies in the area of modes of financing that are, in the case of Islamic banks, derived from the Islamic system and structured within the Islamic legal framework.

Fund mobilization
Resources are mobilized from shareholders and savings owners. Shareholders own the bank's net equities while savers participate in the ownership of the bank's investments. In other words, savings are mobilized on the basis of sharing rather than interest-based lending except, of course, for demand deposits that are based on *wadia* and guaranteed by the bank. In Islamic banks, there are two kinds of depositors: those who are investors or in a sense a special category of shareholders and those who want their money intact and guaranteed by the bank.

Fund utilization

Islamic banks use available funds by means of three major categories of financing modes: sharing modes, sale modes and leasing modes. None of them has any interest component. Under the principle of sharing, the Islamic banks provide financing to projects on the expectation of a share in the return. Obviously, if a project loses, all capital providers and financing contributors lose together and proportionately. There are two forms of application of this principle: full partnership financing and non-voting partnership financing.

The idea of sale modes of financing is also straightforward. The bank would be asked to buy goods and supply them to users (producers and/or consumers) against future repayment. Sale modes may take several forms. The simplest of them is where the bank sells real goods, equipment and machinery to their users at an agreed-upon marked-up price. Two other forms of sale-based placement of funds are also practised by Islamic banks: construction/manufacturing contract and deferred delivery contract. Sale-based modes can end up in one lump sum deferred payment or in instalments spread over a certain period of time.

Finally, as practised in leasing companies and recently in many conventional banks, leasing modes can have a variety of forms with fixed or variable rents, declining or fixed ownership, operational or financial, along with different conditions regarding the status of leased assets at the end of the lease period.

Developmental characteristics of Islamic financing

The essential characteristic of Islamic modes of financing is their direct and undetachable link to the real economy or physical transactions. Sharing modes are only possible for productive enterprises that involve real-life businesses that increase quantity or improve quality or enhance usability of real goods and services. By doing this, such businesses generate a return that can be distributed between the entrepreneur and the financier.

Sale-based modes are those that involve actual, physical exchange of commodities or provision of services from one to another whereby financing is measured only by the real sale of commodities and can only be provided to the extent of the real value of goods exchanged. The same thing also applies to leasing where leased assets are the pivotal element around which financing is built. In other words, Islamic financing is purely a real-life, real-goods/services financing. No financing can find its way to the Islamic system without passing through the production and/or exchange of real goods and services.

In contrast to conventional finance methods, Islamic financing is not centred only on creditworthiness and ability to repay loans and their return. The key in Islamic financing is the worth and profitability of a project and the exchange of goods, merchandise and services. On the other hand, the ability to recover the financing principal becomes a by-product of profitability and value of the project itself. It is a necessary condition in Islamic financing, but it is not sufficient.

Consequently, the nature of Islamic financing makes it exclusively restricted to the construction, establishment and expansion of productive projects and to the exchange and trade of commodities and services. In other words, Islamic financing is intrinsically integrated with the goods and commodities market and is limited to the needed amount of finance that is required by actual transactions taking place in the market.

Whether it is done by means of sharing, sale or lease contracts, Islamic financing is bound by the extent of transactions in the real goods and services market. The Islamic modes of financing, by virtue of their very nature, are incompatible and unsuitable for debt rescheduling, debt swap, financing of speculative cash balances, inter-bank liquidity, speculative transfers and other purely monetary/financial activities that make up a substantial part of current activities of conventional banks. This is, in fact, the first and foremost characteristic of the Islamic approach to financing.

Additionally, the second characteristic of Islamic banking is the integration of ethical and moral values with Islamic finance so that banking complements economic development. Islamic banks cannot detach themselves from ethical/moral considerations even if they try, especially since their own environment, including both staff and clientele, expects from them a pattern of behaviour that is consistent with their commitment to moral and ethical standards as laid down by the Islamic religion and measured according to those values and standards.

The immediate and most important outcome of the moral and ethical commitment of Islamic banks is developmental in nature. Islamic banks restrict their financing to goods and services that are useful and abstain from financing harmful goods such as alcoholic beverages and tobacco or morally unacceptable services such as casinos and pornography, regardless of whether or not such goods and services are legal in a given country. Thus, unlike conventional banks that take the creditworthiness and rate of interest as standards in judging their provision of financing, the Islamic banks have to apply the Islamic moral/ethical criteria in screening their financing. They do not extend their help to activities that are, in the final analysis, harmful to society and consequently antidevelopmental even when such activities are allowed by the law of the land. This adds another dimension to the developmental role of Islamic banks that has a long-term effect on the productivity in the economy as it reduces the social and economic cost of such harmful products and activities.

There are other forms in which the ethical/moral commitment of Islamic banks is manifested. For instance, many Islamic banks have established a practice of providing goodly (interest-free) loans to their clientele in cases of dire need, overdrafts or unexpected circumstances.

Many Islamic banks also establish social funds especially designed for relieving the economic hardship of the poor and needy. These funds are usually financed by the yearly *zakat* dues on shareholders' equity as well as many investment depositors who give their consent to the bank's management for the deduction and distribution of *zakat* annually. These charitable activities of Islamic banks are also financed by interest that may accrue to the bank from its deposits in conventional banks and from certain transactions that the *shari'a* boards may find doubtful/suspicious from a *shari'a* point of view. This is on the ground that such earned interest cannot be taken by the bank and must be distributed to charity. Charitable funds of Islamic banks are usually also open to receiving donations from the public.

In this regard, the experience of two Islamic banks may be used as examples. The Islamic Development Bank in Jeddah, Saudi Arabia is an Islamic intergovernmental bank with 57 Muslim countries in its membership. It accumulated about one billion US dollars in earned interest by the end of the last century and established the largest ever Islamic charitable endowment fund (*waqf*) for charitable services throughout the Muslim countries and communities. This *waqf* was established in 1999 with one billion US dollars as an initial endowment. This is in addition to money spent for research, training, development studies, research scholarships, technical assistance programmes and disaster relief, servicing the Muslim countries, peoples and communities in Muslim-minority countries.

The Jordan Islamic Bank is the other example. It established a special fund for interest-free loans to needy persons. In the three years 2001 to 2003, the fund provided US$ 22 million to more than 40 000 beneficiaries, an amount that is approximately 230 per cent of the total net profits realized by the bank during these three years (Jordan Islamic Bank, 2003).

When we look at financial reports and statements of individual Islamic banks we will find each of them has a list of contributions to community, environment and social welfare. Interestingly, the employee health insurance programmes of most Islamic banks cover not only the immediate family members of the employee (spouse and children) but also parents and unmarried or divorced daughters, without any age limit. Such practices are motivated by the Islamic concepts of extended family and financial responsibilities of the income earner for parents and all adult females in the family.

Additionally, since most Islamic banks operate within an interest-based environment and have working relationships with conventional banks, they often accumulate interest balances as a result of such deals and transactions. According to the *shari'a*, earned interest cannot be taken as income. It is considered unlawful for the earner and must be disposed of to the poor and needy in a way that does not directly benefit the Islamic bank. Hence those Islamic banks that happen to earn interest spend it on benevolent social activities. In other words, although profit growth is essential to Islamic banks as to other businesses, the underlying philosophy of these institutions is conducive toward social commitment and activities that usually cannot be interpreted by the profit motive.

The third developmental characteristic of Islamic banks is found in the nature of their relationship with depositors. While conventional banks receive current and time deposits against fixed interest, Islamic banks deal with their depositors on investment grounds. They, in turn, receive deposits on the basis of sharing in the result of the bank's activities. The application of sharing in fund mobilization makes the bank's performance the criterion of its ability to raise deposits, which means that each bank will keep attempting to outperform other banks if it wants to attract funds from investors. This outperformance will have a clear and strict measure that is expressed in the bank's profitability. The result will be that the management of the Islamic bank will have to appease not only the shareholders but also the depositors, both of whom will be looking for profitability. Consequently, competition among banks drives profitability in both the short run that concerns depositors and the long run that concerns shareholders. This is in contrast to using advertisements and other means to attract deposits.

Additionally, making the profitability criterion the measure of performance for depositors makes them more aware and attached to the real market. This helps create an entrepreneurial spirit in the depositors because it keeps them alert to profit making. This applies to their selection of the bank of choice and to profit making as a means of earning, in contrast to relying on fixed incomes that are provided by conventional banking. Furthermore, involving the masses of depositors in the profitability of banks brings them closer to the real market instead of keeping a firewall between those who save and those who invest. It also changes the nature of financial intermediation of the banking system, making it more in harmony with the real market and developmental changes in it. This can be seen by noticing that in good times the banks will be able to distribute higher profits to depositors while they can lean on them in bad times by distributing lower profits, instead of going into bankruptcy if they have to pay depositors pre-fixed rates of interest.

In the world of today and with prevailing cultural intermingling, having Islamic banking services available to every person, Muslim and non-Muslim alike, in all countries is a very important achievement, because the Islamic banking methodology provides customers with expanded options of banking services from which they can choose. Moreover, Muslim communities in the West need to have Islamic banking institutions, as they represent, for Muslims, an approach for development that is compatible with their faith and it is in this sense an essential element of their religious fulfilment.

Islamic banking as an alternative approach
One might wonder whether Islamic banking and finance is an alternative approach to conventional banking or may be the most modern generation of banking. In an attempt to answer this question we have to observe that the banking business is no more than a possible means to satisfy the needs of society according to the prevailing conditions and circumstances. Those needs should always govern the means, not be their subject.

The most important function of modern banking is the art of mobilizing funds for investment. Islamic banking is a system that mobilizes savings on the basis of profit/loss sharing that is considered to be fairer and more conducive to investment and development, although it is for Muslims a matter of faith.

The ultimate test of such an alternative is whether it is successful or not. It can be safely said that the idea of Islamic banking has been successful. It has been expanding at an annual rate of more than 11 per cent for the last three decades. It is, therefore, not surprising to find several international banking institutions establishing their own Islamic units, windows, branches or fully-fledged Islamic banks to better serve their customers and capture the opportunity. Islamic banking has been partially practised by several of the international giant banks and financial institutions in Switzerland, Britain and the United States (Archer and Karim, 2002; Siddiqi, 2000; Iqbal et al., 1998).

Economists have argued that the wider the freedom of choice, the higher is the level of social welfare. A wider choice implies greater respect for human rights. When an alternative concept such as Islamic banking is introduced, a new choice is open to the market, with obvious economic and social benefits. Introducing Islamic banking as a new choice also has further benefits related to the advantages it provides to many fund users. Commodity and service producers would certainly appreciate equal opportunities for obtaining capital based on the merits of their businesses rather than on their personal creditworthiness alone. Those entrepreneurs who prefer to be self-employed need ways to obtain financing other than by borrowing. Islamic banking gives those pioneers such an opportunity on the basis of profit/loss sharing.

In general, Islamic banking/finance places more weight on the merits of the business to be financed than on the wealth of the fund user. As a result, under this new banking alternative, a better distribution of credit may be achieved.

A concluding note
This chapter must end with a note that the innovation of Islamic banking in restructuring the financing relationships between the bank and its depositors on the one hand, and the bank and funds users on the other, is religion-neutral in the sense that, although it

originates from the Islamic attitude to finance and business, its application is not religion-based. Hence it fits and can be applied alongside any culture and religion.

However, one has to keep in mind that there may always be certain differences between theory and practice. The basic shortcoming of today's Islamic banking is from two sources: inability of management and staff to cope with the principles and approaches of Islamic banking, and negative effects of the interest-ridden financial environment within which Islamic banks operate. Both factors cause the actual practice to fall short of the ideals on which Islamic banks are established and lead these institutions to copy and imitate their interest-based counterparts in a number of directions. The final upshot of this is known only to God.

References

Archer, Simon and Abdel Karim (2002), *Islamic Finance: Innovation and Growth*, London: Euromoney.
Iqbal, Munawar, Ausaf Ahmad and Tariqullah Khan (1998), *Challenges Facing Islamic Banking*, Jeddah: IRTI.
Jordan Islamic Bank for Finance and Investment (2003), *Annual Report,* Jordan.
Kahf, Monzer (1992), *The Concept of Finance in Islamic Economics* [Arabic], Jeddah: Islamic Research and Training Institute.
Kahf, Monzer (1999), 'Islamic banking at the threshold of the third millennium', *Thunderbird International Business Review*, **41** (4/5), 445–60.
Kahf, Monzer (2004), 'Islamic banks: the rise of a new power alliance of wealth and shari'ah scholarship', in Clement Henry and Rodney Wilson (eds), *Politics of Islamic Finance*, Edinburgh: Edinburgh University Press.
Kahf, Monzer and Tariqullah Khan (1992), 'Principles of Islamic Financing: A Survey' in M.A.Mannan, Monzer Kahf and Ausaf Ahmad, *International Economic Relations From Islamic Perspective*, Jeddah: IRTI.
Siddiqi, Muhammad Nejatullah (2000), 'Islamic banks, precept and prospects', *Review of Islamic Economics,* **9**, 21–35.
Siddiqi, Muhammad Nejatullah (2004), *Riba, Bank Interest and the Rationale of its Prohibition*, Jeddah: IRTI.
Vittas, Dimitri and Yoon Je Cho (1996), 'Credit policies: lessons from Japan and Korea', *World Bank Research Observer*, **II** (2), 277–98.

18 Islamic methods for government borrowing and monetary management

M. Fahim Khan

Government borrowing

Governments often make two types of borrowing: short-term borrowing from the money market and longer-term borrowing from capital markets. Conventionally these borrowings are made simply by issuing debt-based instruments that carry a certain rate of interest. Being interest-based, these instruments are not compatible with Islamic law. Those governments which would like to mobilize resources from the public or from the banking system to meet the budget deficit have found *shari'a*-compatible ways to do so.

Why would any government like to seek *shari'a*-compatible ways to mobilize resources? There may be two main reasons. First, there is a growing popular demand in some countries to convert the financial system to conform to *shari'a*. Democratic countries with dominant Muslim populations are more likely to face such pressures. For such countries a primary question is this: if a policy decision is made to adopt an interest-free financial system, what will be the instruments for money market and capital market that will not only enable governments to mobilize funds to meet their budget deficit but also help them in the macroeconomic monetary management of their economy? Without such instruments, the transformation of the financial system in an economy cannot even be thought of.

A government needs funds for development of the economy. The absence of suitable Islamic instruments will force the government to continue to borrow on interest from the public to meet the development needs. Without finding Islamic alternatives to the government borrowing and government debt, it will be a futile exercise to transform the rest of the financial sector in the economy to conform to *shari'a*, as a substantial part of banks' income and the public's income from their financial assets will be coming from holding interest-based government securities. Thus any country intending to transform its financial system to conform to *shari'a* will be seeking possible alternative Islamic instruments for replacing interest-based government borrowing.

These instruments will be required to have the ability not only to mobilize desired funds annually but also to serve as effective tools for monetary management in the economy. In other words, these instruments should have effective secondary markets allowing the public and businesses to have full confidence in purchasing and selling them whenever they need to do so.

Second, irrespective of whether there is a demand for changing the entire financial system to conform to *shari'a*, governments in Muslim countries often may like to tap extra resources from that part of the population that remains excluded from the financial markets because of their faith and belief in the prohibition of interest. Inclusion of such classes of population by providing them with Islamic alternatives to utilize productively their fund will not only provide the government with extra channels for mobilizing resources but will also help strengthen the financial system of the economy. Islamic instruments to mobilize resources thus may be sought by governments even if there is no pressure on them to Islamize the financial system. They may be sought even in non-Muslim countries, if a large Muslim community exists there.[1]

Consequently, we need to discuss Islamic instruments for both the money market and the capital market. The concept of a money market and a capital market have nothing, at least in principle, to bar their existence from an Islamic point of view. It is the *modus operandi* of these markets that is required to be quite different in an Islamic framework, compared to that of the conventional system. The differences lie in the nature of financial instruments being traded in the market. The instruments traded in conventional markets are essentially debt instruments. Since debt, in principle, cannot be traded according to Islamic law, the instruments traded in an Islamic market cannot be debt instruments.[2] They will essentially be investment-based instruments linked to real assets. However, in order to be competitive and efficient in the market, these instruments are required to have risk–return profiles that are comparable to those of conventional debt-based instruments.

Government money market instruments
Money market operations for government are more challenging than operations in the capital market. This is because the money market is needed by the individuals and businesses to 'park' their short-term liquidity until they find proper investment opportunities to deploy their funds. They would like, therefore, to have risk-free opportunities to place their money for short periods. While it is easy to engineer short-term debt instruments that will offer a risk-free return, it is a challenge to engineer investment instruments that would yield risk-free returns in the short run. The short-term investment instruments as alternatives to debt instruments or securities of government are required to have two features: (a) the risk-free return and (b) their ability to be sold quickly if liquidity is needed urgently. Such short-term government securities play a major role in the development of a money market.

The economy needs a money market for two main purposes, first as a means for liquidity management for businesses, banks and households and, second, as a means for macro monetary management for the government. Business, banks and households often have money in hand that they do not need immediately. It lies idle temporarily. They look for a suitable place where they can put this money in the sense that it remains safe, it earns them some return and they can retrieve it as soon as they need it. Government instruments for short-term borrowing provide one such opportunity. This opportunity provides: (a) means for short-term investments, that (b) yield reasonable returns, and (c) are risk-free.

Macroeconomic management of an economy requires policy makers to keep watch on the money demand in the country and manage it to achieve various macroeconomic objectives, such as growth in the economy, control of inflation, reduction of unemployment and so on. For achievement of such objectives, the macroeconomic managers of a country may need to conduct open market operations, purchasing the government securities from the money market to inject money into the economy and selling government securities in the money market to reduce holdings of money. The most popular instrument for such purposes is a Treasury bill. Treasury bills, the most commonly used short-term debt instruments issued by the government, are also used to finance its budget deficit. They may be issued in three, six or 12 months maturities and pay a set amount at maturity. They are sold at a discount, which effectively means borrowing at interest.

Treasury bills are the most liquid of all the money market instruments because they can be easily sold and bought. The backing of the government provides the confidence which makes the bill attractive for the people buying them. They are the safest of all money market instruments because there is little possibility of default. These instruments are particularly useful for banks as they can be used for liquidity management. Banks may need liquidity to meet demands from the public for withdrawal of deposits. These instruments give liquidity while providing income as well. Finding an Islamic alternative to Treasury bills for the money market is a big challenge.

Mobilizing resources from the capital market
Mobilizing funds from the capital market for government is less of a challenge as mobilization of such funds can always be linked to specific projects. The funds can be mobilized on the basis of known Islamic modes of financing, such as those based on trading, leasing and hire-purchase.

A government can divide the financing needs for development activities into the need to finance purchases of materials (such as construction material or machinery) or the need to lease fixed assets (such as manufacturing plants, aeroplanes or buildings). The government can then get the financing from the banking system for each of these purposes on the basis of an appropriate method of financing such as mark-up, leasing, rent-sharing or *istisnaa*-based modes of financing. Alternatively, the government can invite investments from the banking system as well as from the public on the basis of the sharing of profit of any income-generating projects like airports or bridges. It is always possible for the government to securitize a portfolio of its investments or assets where the securities will carry a return linked to the income generated by the underlying investments or assets. Such securities will be *shari'a*-compatible.

In principle, the return on such securities cannot be predetermined and may fluctuate from year to year. This would be in contrast to the risk-free fixed return that interest-based securities conventionally offer. Government securities, however, are mostly demanded for the guaranteed predetermined fixed return on them, not only because of the convenience of holding such instruments but also because of the various benefits of such instruments for the individuals that help them in economic decision making at a micro level. This poses a challenge for the government in the capital market of how to develop fixed-return capital market instruments that would be compatible with Islamic law. Before discussing how to develop *shari'a*-compatible fixed-return government instruments, it may be instructive to see the reasons why such fixed-return instruments are needed. Seeking *shari'a* alternatives would make sense only if there is a good reason to do so because one basic objective of *shari'a* is to facilitate, not to complicate or create hardship (Masud, 1995; Hassan, 1994; Nadwi, 2005).

The case for fixed-income securities
In conventional capital markets, instruments such as equity or leasing are often preferred over fixed-income securities because of the higher returns. An Islamic financial system is thus, in principle, not necessarily at a disadvantage if it does not explicitly offer fixed-income securities. But when it is a question of mobilizing resources for government, then it cannot be denied that fixed-income securities are needed to play an important economic role not only in the portfolio management and investment decision making but also in the

smooth operation of capital markets. This is true not only for countries that would like to transform their entire financial system to conform to *shari'a* but also for countries which would like to have a dual system (parallel operation of Islamic and conventional financial systems).

As economies develop, the interest-based institutional framework may make capital mobilization through debt finance easier (though, in the later stages of development, the equity markets take over and play a more effective role in capital mobilization). The economic growth in the developing economies, therefore, may face problems, if debt finance is absent or is restricted. Islamic finance is emerging from countries which are mostly in the initial stages of development. The significance of *shari'a*-acceptable fixed-income securities as an alternative to interest-based debt securities, therefore, cannot be underestimated and they are needed to contribute positively to economic development and to facilitate operations of the firms willing to work on Islamic principles. However, the firms that opt to operate according to the Islamic principles face a serious dilemma in accessing the conventional capital markets where they cannot benefit from the use of the interest-based fixed-income securities. Some reasons for this are discussed below.

First, in the presence of income tax, it is always beneficial for the firms to raise capital through borrowing on interest than to raise capital through equity.[3] The more a firm borrows via debt the more profitable it becomes. (This is the famous M&M Proposition No. I: see Modigliani and Miller, 1958, 1963.) If there is no fear of bankruptcy or risk of getting the firm acquired by the creditors, the firm will like to have all its capital in the form of funds borrowed on interest. If an Islamic firm does not raise funds through risk-free fixed-return based bonds, it stays at a disadvantage relative to the firms that can do so. The Islamic firm will be forced to operate with a suboptimal capital structure in the conventional capital market. If the Islamic firm is operating in recession, so that it has a rate of return on equity less than the rate of interest on bonds, there will not be as much supply of capital as there will be for the firms that can raise capital through fixed-return bonds. If the firm is operating in high profit conditions, the cost of equity capital for it will be high and it will be disadvantaged in raising capital from the market. The competitive operation of an Islamic firm within the conventional market requires Islamic firms to have an ability to benefit from fixed-income securities, bonds and so on. These firms will feel more comfortable if fixed-income securities bonds and so on developed on Islamic principles are available for their use.

Second, the absence of *shari'a*-compatible fixed-income securities not only limits the leverage capabilities of an Islamic firm (and therefore limiting their ability for capital budgeting and financial management) but also inhibits the Islamic firm with respect to hedging and risk management. With the choice of utilizing *shari'a*-based fixed-income securities, the Islamic firm will have the ability to get some of its financial risks hedged and more effectively compete with the firms that are using interest-based instruments as tools for hedging.

'Fixed-return' instruments in an Islamic framework

Not long ago, it was unthinkable to talk about an Islamic financial instrument that would guarantee a fixed return. In the last five years or so, this has not only become a reality to specifically engineer financial instruments offering *shari'a*-compatible fixed returns but also the supply and demand of such instruments is growing fast in Muslim countries as well as at a global level and are becoming popular not only with Muslims but with non-Muslims as well. It will be instructive to have an overview of what makes it possible to design fixed-income instruments that are *shari'a*-compatible too. A fixed-return financial instrument implies two things: the principal amount is guaranteed, and the return is known ex ante.

These two features were supposed to be present only in an interest-bearing loan contract which is prohibited by Islamic law. Islamic methods of financing were generally thought of as offering risk-bearing returns only. Although some Islamic modes of financing, such as those based on trading and leasing, did require the party receiving the finance to make a fixed payment periodically or in lump-sum on the principal amount obtained, the return for the provider of finances was considered to be risk-bearing (Khan, 1992). Some explanation is given below.

Trading-based financing
The trading-based mode of financing works as follows. If a party needs financing to purchase a commodity, it will approach a financial institution to provide the required financing. The financial institution will purchase the required commodity and will resell it to the client with a fixed mark-up on the cost price. The client will agree to pay back the principal amount along with a predetermined mark-up at a predetermined future date or may agree to pay in predetermined instalments. The client would sign a loan contract for an amount which includes the price of the commodity plus a mark-up charged by the financial institution. The mark-up can vary with the length of the duration within which the client agrees to pay back (the price of the commodity and the mark-up). For the client, it is obvious that he ends up paying a predetermined fixed amount on the principal (the cash price of the commodity). This is permissible in Islamic law because the contract between the client and the financial institution is a real transaction reflected in a sale–purchase contract, and not merely a financial or monetary transaction in the form of a borrowing–lending contract. The mark-up, therefore, is not in the nature of an additional amount paid on the principal amount of a loan but is in the nature of a profit charged in a trade transaction.

This, however, does not mean a predetermined fixed return for the financial institution on the financing that it provided to the client. The financial institution undertook to conduct a trading transaction and in the process took certain risks related to acquiring and owning the goods before reselling them to the client. This risk bearing, associated with the assumption of ownership of the goods (even if it is for a short period), implies the possibility of loss on various accounts to financial institutions. The financial institution cannot be certain about the exact return on its investment (even though the mark-up is predetermined) until the goods have been delivered to the client and a sale agreement has been concluded with the client.

Leasing financing
A similar situation is witnessed in the case of leasing-based financing. For a client that needs financing to acquire equipment or a building or any other fixed asset, the financial institution can acquire it and lease it on rent to the client. The payment of rent by the client is fixed and predetermined. This means that the client ends up making a fixed payment on the principal amount (the cost price of the asset). In the case of the financial institution,

it does not mean that it will end up receiving a predetermined fixed return on the financing it provided. Again it is a real transaction and not merely a financial transaction. Acquiring the asset, owning it and bearing the risks associated with the ownership during the lease period and the uncertainty of the market price with respect to scrap value of the asset at the end of the lease period, would not allow the financial institution to know its actual return on its investment until the lease ends and the asset has been disposed of.

These were the features that underlay the earlier notion that earning a fixed predetermined return on financing was not possible. The continued and growing practice of Islamic finance, however, soon made the Islamic finance industry realize that its growth will be severely constrained if it is unable to provide Islamic alternatives to fixed-return lending–borrowing of funds. The fixity of the payment of mark-up in a trading contract and of rent in a leasing contract led the financial engineers to find means to minimize the risk and the uncertainties for finance providers and financial institutions in the use of these two modes of financing so that their return becomes fixed and predetermined.

Trading-based securities
In the case of trading-based modes of financing, the following has been found possible within the premises of Islamic law: (a) the financial institution may appoint the client himself to purchase on behalf of the financial institution the commodities that the client wants the financial institution to finance so that there is no risk of purchasing something that the client may not like; (b) arrangements can be made that, as soon as the goods are purchased on behalf of the bank, they are immediately sold to the client on an agreed cost-plus mark-up basis so that the period of ownership of physical goods by the financial institutions and risks associated with the ownership are reduced to a minimum.

These two elements allow the risks in the transaction to become almost negligible for the financial institutions and the return on the financing provided by the financial institution becomes almost fixed and predetermined.

These receivables resulting from the sale deal with the client of the financial institution can be securitized to mobilize resources from the market for this deal. The securities can carry a fixed return based on the fixed return already contracted in the deal. These financial instruments can be of long-term duration as well as short-term duration and hence can be used in the capital market as well as in the money market. This provides an opportunity to the government of the Islamic country also to mobilize resources to meet its budget deficit, without violating *shari'a* rules. The government requires a very large part of its budget to be used for the purchase of commodities. Instead of borrowing on interest to make such purchases, the government could use such purchases financed by banks or through its own subsidiaries in mark-up-based sale–purchase deals which in turn can mobilize resources from the public on the basis of securities described above.

The problem is that these instruments result from securitizing receivables and, according to the opinion of the majority of schools of Islamic law, cannot be traded in secondary markets. According to the rulings of the majority of schools of Islamic law, debt cannot be sold or exchanged at a price other than face value, nor can it be discounted. Most of the Muslim economies follow this opinion. Hence such securities cannot have secondary markets and thus will not provide liquidity to the holders, if they need it before the maturity of these instruments.[4] They are not a good alternative to replace conventional government borrowing through interest-based bonds and Treasury bills.

Leasing-based securities
Leasing-based modes of financing have also been found to have the potential to generate fixed-income securities. There are two elements that make the return from a leasing contract uncertain for a financial institution: (a) the cost of maintaining the asset which remains in the ownership of the financial institution during the lease period, and also the risks associated with ownership of the asset; (b) uncertainty about the market value of the asset at the end of the lease period.

The uncertainty with respect to the first element can be taken care of by taking out an appropriate insurance policy. The uncertainty with respect to the scrap value of an asset can be taken care of if the contract can be made for a period during which the financial institution will recover the principal amount as well as an appropriately benchmarked rate of return. The asset at the end of the lease period can then be transferred to the lessee. This makes the contract generate a fixed return for the financial institution on its investment. This contract can be securitized, accordingly, carrying a predetermined fixed return linked to the rental income from the asset. More importantly, these securities can be traded in the secondary market because they represent a share in the ownership of the underlying physical asset, and unlike the trading-based mark-up securities, do not represent a share in any debt or financial asset. This mode of financing thus provides the most suitable basis to develop fixed-income securities for mobilizing funds for government. A large part of the government budget is meant for acquiring fixed assets: machinery, industrial plants, buildings, roads, bridges and so on. All expenditure meant to acquire such assets could be financed through resources mobilized on the basis of leasing-based securities.

Before going into specific cases and how this mode has actually been utilized, it will be useful to have an overview of other methods of financing that can also be utilized to mobilize resources for government.

Variable-return securities
While fixed-return government securities have their own merit for the economy as well as for individual investors, the variable-return securities also have their own attractions. Such securities provide opportunities to investors to build up their investment portfolio with a risk-return profile to match their own risk-return preferences.

Some early attempts
Governments of several Muslim countries have been in search of variable-return instruments for mobilization of resources as well as for monetary management which will not be based on a promise of paying predetermined risk-free rates of return. In the 1970s, when the concept of Islamic finance came into practice and popular demand in a country like Pakistan forced the government to find an alternative financial system that could operate without interest, the biggest worry was Islamic alternatives to government borrowing. Loans, according to *shari'a*, could be returned only on the nominal face value of the loan. Any additional payment over the nominal value of the loan for any reason, fixed or variable, was commonly considered as interest and hence was not acceptable.

An alternative, strongly proposed by the government economic planners and policy makers to *shari'a* scholars in such countries, was to index government borrowing to GDP growth. The return would not be predetermined and fixed. It would depend on the performance of the economy. Government bonds linked with growth in the economy were supposed to help the government to better manage its debt because returns on debt would be paid in proportion to economic performance in the country. This was a proposal that had been under consideration with the multilateral foreign donor agencies as well. This proposal, however, could not pass the *shari'a* test. The return on instruments, according to *shari'a* rule, should relate to the return of the assets on which the securities are actually based.

Another strong proposal initiated by government economic policy makers was to index the borrowing to the inflation rate. This was meant to protect the real value of loans. This, too, failed to get *shari'a* approval. Several workshops were held to allow an exchange of views between economists and *shari'a* scholars to discuss the need to index loans to the inflation rate as an alternative to interest-based borrowing. The last one was held in 1988 under the auspices of the Islamic Research and Training Institute of the Islamic Development Bank. This was attended by renowned scholars of *shari'a*, economics and Islamic economics of the Muslim world. All arguments, legal and economic, in favour of indexation were exhaustively discussed. The final conclusion, however, remained that loan contracts, in Islamic law, cannot be indexed to the inflation rate. No *shari'a*-acceptable solution could be found.

A special methodology for indexing loans which is claimed to have been given *shari'a* acceptance in Iran was to link the rate of return on government borrowing with the rate of return in the private sector after making certain adjustments (see Haq and Mirakhor, 1999). The methodology suggested to link the return on government instruments to the observed rate of return in the private sector revolved around adjustment for risk premiums. This methodology did not get *shari'a* acceptance in any other country and even in Iran, where it is claimed to have received, in principle, *shari'a* acceptance, no government securities have yet been issued on this basis. The Central Bank of Iran, however, modified the proposed methodology and issued instruments called Central Bank Participation Paper. The idea of issuing National Participation Paper, the return on which is linked to an index of the return on capital in the private sector, is, however, still under consideration in Iran.

Participation securities
The only *shari'a*-acceptable way to issue government securities is to develop them on the concept of equity participation or profit (and loss) sharing, utilizing the Islamic legal concepts of *mudaraba* and *musharaka*. The *musharaka*-based securities offer a share in the ownership of the project/enterprise for which the resources are to be mobilized. It has been mentioned earlier that it is not difficult for the government to raise resources from the capital market by securitizing a portfolio of its investments in development projects and linking the return on the securities to income generated by these projects. Such securities have been used to mobilize funds for various public enterprises, particularly in such sectors as telecommunication, energy and transport. This method of mobilizing resources can be used for new as well as old enterprises in the public sector and can also be used to shed debt in these enterprises. The debt too can be replaced by equity shares.

Such securities are not difficult to structure as they do not pose any complications arising out of *shari'a* considerations. What the government has to do is simply define a portfolio of its investments and securitize the portfolio linking the return on these securities to the income generated from the underlying portfolio of investments. The funds mobilized by the sale of securities can be used by the government to meet its current budget deficit or to carry out its development activities. Sudan and Iran have used the *musharaka* principle to finance government operations.

Such instruments can be used for mobilizing short-term as well as long-term investment. Generally it is considered more feasible to create an intermediary institution for the issuance and management of these instruments. The intermediary, on the one hand, will issue securities to mobilize resources for government enterprises/projects and, on the other hand, allocate these funds to the income-generating enterprises/projects for which the funds have been mobilized. The return on these securities is linked to the return on the specified enterprises and projects, or they may be linked to a pool of income from different enterprises or a group of enterprises. Sudan, for example, has used *musharaka*-based securities to link the return to a pool of income of specific government enterprise. These securities are variable-return securities and the return cannot be fixed in advance. However, since the investment is made in a pool of enterprises, it is possible to develop a pool of enterprises the incomes of which are not interdependent so as to get the benefit of diversified risk and hence reduce volatility in the total income to be shared with the securities holders. Since these securities represent ownership in the specific projects, their trading in the secondary market is permissible in Islamic law. But their volume may not be sufficient to conduct effective open market operations. This method, however, would be of limited use to governments, owing to a number of factors.

First, governments, through borrowing, raise large amounts of resources every year for meeting the resources needed for socioeconomic development and the expenditures needed to meet growing administrative responsibilities. The governments' portfolio of income-generating investment may not provide a definite and continuous source of mobilizing resources by issuing securities on these investments.

Second, governments often need funds to carry out projects which may not generate income. These may be the projects relating to sectors like health, education, social security, defence and so on, and government may need funds to meet the development and/or administrative expenses for such projects. It may not be possible to securitize investments in such projects in order to mobilize resources for the market.

Third, governments often need flexibility in the use of the funds that they mobilize from the market. A government's priorities can change. But if the funds have been mobilized by securitizing the government's portfolio of investment, these funds cannot be shifted to a different portfolio if changed priorities arise. If a government prefers to issue variable return (Islamic) securities, it will be seeking flexibility too in the mobilization as well as in the use of funds. Also governments would like such instruments to be capable of being effectively used for monetary management of the economy, particularly for use in conducting open market operations. *Shari'a*-acceptable variable-return securities may not be sufficient to do so.

Other instruments for raising funds
There are two other forms of financing contracts that are linked to real assets and can be securitized. These contracts are called *salam* and *istisnaa*. Both contracts involve the financing of projects that produce assets or output at a specified date in the future. A contract to provide funds, for example, for a bridge or building to be constructed and delivered at a future date is called an *istisnaa* contract. A contract to deliver certain specified

goods normally available in the market at a future date is called a *salam* contract (see Khan, 1992).

Istisnaa
Istisnaa contracts can be securitized to raise funds on the basis of the rental income that the asset (for example, a building or bridge) will generate. In that case it will generate fixed-return securities, or it can be securitized on the basis of variable income (such as a toll tax on the bridge), generating variable-return securities.

Salam
The *salam* contract also can be used. While an *istisnaa* contract generally refers to the construction of a physical asset at a future date, the *salam* contract refers to the delivery of specific commodities at a future date. A government may need funds to produce or purchase a certain commodity on a certain date in the future. These goods will be sold to the public or to different departments or government bodies on mark-up. The deal, thus, will generate profit which can be shared with those who provided the funds. The transaction can be securitized and they will be fixed-return securities, representing ownership of goods to come into existence at a future date. Their tradeability in the secondary market, however, is not permissible among a majority of the *shari'a* opinions on this subject because of the rule in *shari'a* that a good cannot be sold before coming into its possession. Some *shari'a* opinion, however, would consider it permissible because of the government guarantee to provide these goods and hence removing uncertainty about the existence of the goods being sold. In any case, an instrument based on the *salam* contract will be a valid instrument to park liquid funds for a short period as these types of securities can be constructed for very short durations as well, like three-month securities or one-month securities or even two-week securities, as governments often have to do all sorts of commodity operations in the course of carrying out its business.

Zero-return instrument
Still another type of instrument that can be mentioned under the category of other forms of instruments for mobilizing funds for government is what we may refer to as zero-return instruments. Government can always borrow money from the public without promising any return and simply guaranteeing the repayment of principal. This is always a strong possibility for an Islamic government in a Muslim country when governments want to raise funds for a defined cause linked to social activities that have religious significance, particularly projects that relate to reducing poverty or the treatment of sick persons or taking care of orphans, widows and so on. These are called *qard hasan* or 'good loans', and supporting such activities carries a 'big' reward in the hereafter.[5] Since the government is guaranteeing paying back the amount at a specific date, the willingness to make such an 'investment' will always be available in Muslim societies. These instruments will always be very liquid at their face value as there will always be people who would like to seek rewards in the hereafter by temporarily depositing their excess liquidity in such instruments. Some institutional arrangements, of course, will be needed to facilitate exchange at face value and confidence will have to be built that money raised for defined causes will actually be spent judiciously on these causes and will not be squandered through corruption, inefficiency and the like.

Pricing of government instruments

The pricing mechanism of Islamic financial instruments, including those of government securities, would, basically, be similar to that for conventional financial instruments. The time value of money in economic and financial transactions is recognized in Islam. The only difference is that the time value of money cannot be realized as a part of the loan contract. It can be realized only as an integral part of a real transaction. Thus, in a trade transaction, if the payment of price is deferred, the time value of money will be included in the price of the commodity. Similarly, in a leasing contract, time value is an integral part of the rent that parties agree upon. But a pure loan contract cannot include any compensation for the time value of money (Khan, 1991).

A premium for risk in investment activities is also recognized in Islamic law. An Islamic adage which reads in Arabic as *Al-Ghunmu bil Ghurmin* (profit making is by risk bearing) implies that, if there is higher risk in an investment activity, the demand for a higher premium would be justified. Thus the pricing mechanism of an Islamic financial instrument would not, in principle, differ from the conventional mechanism. The only condition would be that a financial instrument should be based on real assets or should be a result of real transactions. An issue in the pricing mechanism, however, would be in the nature of the benchmark for a risk-free return.

In conventional markets, the interest rate of Treasury bills is a convenient benchmark for a risk-free return. In the Islamic framework, an alternative benchmark would be needed. When developed, the return on Islamic short-term government securities will serve as a benchmark for the risk-free return. But, until this Islamic alternative to Treasury bills is developed, some other measure will be needed as an indicator of the risk-free return. In the literature, the following has been proposed (Khan, 1991).

If the entire financial system in an economy is working on an Islamic basis, the mark-up on short-term trading-based financing charged by banks will provide a proxy of the risk-free return. This is because the banks have worked out a model of trading-based financing in a way in which banks bear almost no risk associated with trading. The bank appoints the client (who needs financing to purchase some material) as agent to make the desired purchase on behalf of the bank. The client is then required to purchase it back as soon as the purchase has been made on behalf of the bank. The purchasing from the bank will be at cost price plus mark-up agreed upon between the client and the bank. The client would owe the bank the price and nothing else. The mark-up in this case includes a payment for two things, not separable from each other: the risks associated with trade transactions and risk associated with ownership of the goods until they are sold to the client, and the time value of money for deferring the payment price.

However, we know that, in practice, it is possible for the banks to minimize, to an almost negligible level, the risk associated with trading and owning the goods. So the mark-up for a short-term deal with a client would approximate very closely to the time value of money. If commodity and financial markets are competitive, the mark-up is expected to be uniform across all the banks in the economy and this mark-up would serve as a benchmark for the risk-free return which can be used for pricing the financial instruments, including government instruments.

The government may like to use this mark-up as a policy variable for monetary management in the economy. Also, if the government issues short-term securities based on its commodity operations (as an alternative to the Treasury bills) to meet the budget deficit, the mark-up rate on its commodity operations can be fixed. The return on these government securities will better reflect the time value of money (and hence better indicate the benchmark) than the mark-up rate charged by the banks.

If there is a dual system in the economy with the parallel existence of Islamic and conventional finance, the mark-up will be determined by the interest rate on government Treasury bills. This rate will be the benchmark for the risk-free rate of return for conventional as well as Islamic financial instruments. There is nothing in Islamic law against using an interest rate as a reference point or benchmark for pricing the Islamic financial instruments as long as the instruments are not loan contracts and are asset-based or based on real transactions.

Examples of government Islamic financial instruments
While the Islamic banking and finance industry has grown at an unprecedented rate over the last 30 years, there has not been much in the area of developing instruments for government to mobilize resources in the Islamic way. Efforts in this direction have started only over the last five years. They are, however, gaining momentum. Below are some examples of the instruments that have been fashioned for mobilizing resources for government, developed both for long-term needs to raise capital and for short-term needs for liquidity management and dealings in the money market. Some instruments are designed to be traded in the secondary market and some are designed to be held until maturity.

Malaysia and Bahrain are two countries that have been active in issuing such instruments. The Malaysian government has been offering Islamic bonds for more than a decade, both long-term and short-term instruments, tradeable in secondary markets. Bahrain has been issuing, in the past, mostly the instruments which are not tradeable in secondary markets because they have been based on trading-based modes of financing and hence represent debt obligations which cannot be bought and sold in the market. For this reason, Bahraini instruments had limited application for raising public funds. Lately, Bahrain has developed instruments which can be traded in secondary markets as well. Pakistan, Indonesia and Qatar are other countries whose governments are actively involved in issuing Islamic bonds for mobilizing resources for government activities.

All these instruments experienced an overwhelming response from the public. Even the *salam* certificate, which made no reference to market rates, received strong support. All issues have generally been substantially oversubscribed. The success of these instruments encouraged the establishment of institutions in Malaysia and Gulf countries to provide institutional support for the standardized development of instruments for the money market and to provide opportunities for liquidity management. The Liquidity Management Centre (LMC) and International Islamic Financial Market (IIFM) have already been established as a part of a financial infrastructure to provide institutional support for systematic development and growth of the Islamic financial market. IIFM was established in April 2002 as a result of a joint effort between central banks of Bahrain, Brunei, Dar es Salaam, Indonesia, Malaysia, Sudan and the Saudi Arabian-based Islamic Development Bank with the objective to promote a suitable environment for the development of *shari'a*-compatible instruments and to facilitate their trading.

Labuan International Financial Exchange is a similar institution developed in Malaysia as an international offshore financial exchange to facilitate the secondary markets of Islamic financial securities. Malaysia established in August 2002 the Malaysian Global

Sukuk Inc (MGS) as a Special Purpose Vehicle (SPV) which issues certificates to tap resources for the government from the Islamic financial markets. MGS is owned by the Ministry of Finance. All instruments issued by MGS are listed for secondary market trading. The instruments are leasing-based and are internationally rated by Moody as Baa2 (positive) and by Standard and Poor as BBB (positive). These instruments are called *sukuks*. The construction of these instruments is now explained.

The MGS issued US$600 million *sukuk at-ijara* Trust Certificates in 2002. The proceeds were used to finance the purchase of beneficial title to specified parcels of land located in and around Kuala Lumpur. MGS then leased the land to the government of Malaysia under a lease (*ijara*) agreement with semi-annual rental payments for a period of five years. The rental payments are used to meet the periodic distribution due on the certificates. The lease agreement commenced on 3 July 2002 for dissolution scheduled in July 2007. The government of Malaysia undertakes to re-acquire the land at the end of the tenure.

HSBC was the sole lead manager and sole book runner for the issue of these certificates while HSBC Ammanah Finance, Dubai, was the transaction adviser for the issue. The *Shari'a* Supervisory Committee of HSBC as well as the *Shari'a* Supervisory Committee of the Bahrain-based International Islamic Financial Market (IIFM) certified the *shari'a* compatibility of these *sukuk* certificates.

With an almost similar arrangement, the government of Pakistan has issued $600 million *shari'a*-compatible *sukuk* (or Islamic Bonds). These *sukuk* are aimed not only at Muslim investors in the country but also at non-Muslim investors abroad. The *sukuk* are *ijara*-based with a segment of a major motorway of the country as the underlying asset. The *sukuk* were oversubscribed to the tune of $4.2 billion on the order book.

Some examples of short-term government securities are given below. The Malaysian Parliament passed the Government Investment Act in 1983 to enable the government of Malaysia to issue non-interest-bearing certificates known as Government Investment Certificates (GICs). This was the first attempt to introduce alternatives to government Treasury bills for institutions and individuals who did not like to hold interest-bearing short-term securities. These GICs represented beneficial loans *qard hasan* (zero interest-bearing) and promised no return. However, the government had the discretion to pay some return on them at the time of maturity. Since this was at the absolute discretion of the government and nothing was committed in advance, the return therefore was not considered as in the nature of interest but was considered a gift from the government. These certificates were later replaced by Government Investment Issues (GII). These instruments also used the concept of *qard hasan*. Being loan-based, these issues could not be traded in the secondary market.

On 15 June 2001, the government of Malaysia issued a three-year GII of RM 2.0 billion on the basis of *bai' al-inah* (a modified version of the popularly know *murabaha*-based financing) which allowed the GII to be tradeable on the secondary market.[6] Financial institutions in Malaysia hold these GIIs to make short-term investments from excess liquidity and they can also sell these documents to the Central Bank of Malaysia in case they need liquidity.

The Bahrain Monetary Agency has issued short-term government securities in the form of Treasury bills, having a maturity of 91 days. These securities have been based on the concept of *salam*, with aluminium being the underlying asset. The government of Bahrain sells a specified quantity of defined quality of aluminium to be delivered on a future date, in exchange for advance payment to be made by the Islamic banks. Simultaneously, the Islamic banks (that purchased the aluminium for future delivery with advance payment) appoint the government of Bahrain as their agent to market, at the time of delivery, the contracted aluminium through its channels of distribution. The proceeds from the sale go to the Islamic banks in exchange for financing they provided. The documents that the government issues as an agent of the banks to deliver the specified aluminium, however, cannot be sold in the market, because of the *shari'a* ruling that goods cannot be sold until they have been delivered to the seller. Since the documents mature in 91 days, these securities still remain in demand for liquidity management purposes. The cumulative value of these *salam sukuk* is expected to reach US$1billion.

The Bank of Sudan (the country's Central Bank) issued *musharaka* certificates in 1998 against the Bank of Sudan's ownership in commercial banks. The return on these certificates is linked to the profits of the Bank of Sudan that it earns on its equity in the commercial banks. The Bank of Sudan is issuing these certificates to regulate and manage liquidity within the banking system. The Ministry of Finance of Sudan also issued similar certificates in 1999. There are also *musharaka* certificates against the government ownership in some specific, commercially profitable, public enterprises and joint ventures in the public sector. These certificates are used to regulate and manage liquidity within the economy as a whole. Both the certificates are being successfully traded in the market.

Iran initiated in 1994 the issuance of Islamic instruments for mobilizing funds for government. They were *musharaka*-based certificates issued to finance government projects. Holders of these certificates were owners of the project to the extent of the proportion of value of their certificates to the total capital of the projects. The certificates carried a 20 per cent nominal annual rate of return (the inflation rate being 17 per cent). This return was based on minimum productivity/profitability of the projects where these funds mobilized from the certificates were invested. Any profit realized over and above the minimum expected was distributed upon maturity. This was done specifically to be in line with the opinion of *shari'a* scholars of Iran that considered a fixed return equivalent to interest.

Rating of government Islamic financial instruments
The rating of such instruments will have two elements, the financial element of rating and the Islamic rating element. As far as the financial element of the rating is concerned, the instruments will be distinguished with respect to whether they are fixed-return instruments or variable-return instruments. The fixed-return instruments, such as those structured on the mark-up trading-based modes of financing or the leasing-based mode of financing, would carry the financial rating of the institution that is creating the payment stream. Thus the financial rating of instruments structured on mark-up trading will be the same as the financial rating of the institutions that purchased the commodity on mark-up, while the financial rating of instruments structured on a leasing basis will be the same as the rating of the lessee.

The financial rating of fixed-return instruments of the government will be the financial rating for the government itself which will matter only when the instruments address both national and international investors. Such rating can be done by any rating agency using their own criteria for the financial rating of the country. For example, the Malaysian Global *Sukuk*, issued through the Malaysian Global *Sukuk*, Inc. as an SPV (described earlier) is rated by S&P as A- and the Pakistan *sukuk* issued by the SPV Pakistan

International *Sukuk* Co. is rated as B+ reflecting the respective rating of the country issuing the instrument.

These ratings do not refer to the Islamic element in their rating. An Islamic International Rating Agency has been incorporated in Bahrain with an initial capital of US$ 2.0 million. This agency will carry out the rating of sovereigns and entities and Islamic instruments. It will also provide an assessment of compliance with the principles of *shari'a*.

A word of caution
The rapid emergence of *sukuks* and financial instruments in national and global markets is also creating wide differences in terms of *shari'a* and *fiqh* rules underlying them. The issue of the standardizing of *shari'a* application in the development of Islamic financial instruments, including *sukuks* issued by governments, is something that is yet to take place. Unless this standardization takes place such instruments as *sukuks* will continue to face controversies about their *shari'a* compatibility. When the Islamic International Rating Agency mentioned above becomes operational, it may take up this issue as well.[7]

Pricing of sukuks *in practice*
There is no independent Islamic benchmark available to be used for pricing Islamic financial instruments, particularly for pricing the *sukuks*. For the fixed-return *sukuks* issued by the government which carry a risk-free return, LIBOR is being mostly used as a reference point for pricing these instruments. This is so because most of the government *sukuks* issued so far have been aimed at the international market. Where national bonds or *sukuks* have been issued, they have been issued in countries where interest-based government securities are also being issued, and the interest rate on those conventional securities serves as a benchmark for the government's Islamic securities issued at the national level.

It may seem an anomaly from a *shari'a* point of view that Islamic securities are being priced with reference to an interest rate. There is, however, undisputed *shari'a* opinion from scholars of all schools, that it is permissible to use an interest rate as a reference point for determining the price of an Islamic security, Islamic-based or *sukuk*. Once a country decides to Islamize the entire financial system in the domestic economy, the government will be able to fix a mark-up-based rate of return in its trading operations or trading-based *sukuks* which will serve as an independent Islamic reference point for any *sukuks* issued for the domestic economy.

Growth of government sukuks
The history of *sukuks* is very recent. Government *sukuks* began in 2001, with the issuance of five-year *sukuks* of $100 million by the government of Bahrain, carrying a fixed return of 5.25 per cent. Since then, government *sukuks* have gained momentum. In 2004, four countries issued government *sukuks*. This included the $100 million five-year *sukuks* issued by a local government (Saxony-Anhalt) in Germany carrying a return of EURIBOR plus 1 per cent. In 2005, the government of Pakistan issued $600 million five-year international *sukuks* carrying a return of a six-month LIBOR plus 2.2 per cent. The *sukuks* were oversubscribed by 233 per cent.

With the interest of multilateral organizations like the IFC, the Asian Development Bank and the World Bank, who have already issued or are in the process of issuing Islamic bonds, the national governments in all Muslim countries will be tempted to issue their own Islamic bonds to mobilize resources from that part of their population that was unwilling to invest in government interest-based securities. A high growth rate in the issuance of government Islamic bonds and certificates over the next five to ten years is very likely in the national as well as in global financial markets.

Economics of government Islamic instruments
There is a question whether the economy will be paying a 'cost' for replacing interest-based borrowing by Islamic methods of government financing or whether it would be desirable on its own merit. This requires an assessment of the economic features of the Islamic instruments described above within a general equilibrium macroeconomic mode. This is yet to be done.

   It may, however, be instructive to identify some economic features of using Islamic methods instead of the current methods of mobilizing resources for government.

1.   The variety of the instruments described above suggests that governments will not be short of tools to get the resources to meet their genuine needs. Those providing a whole spectrum of risk–return profiles will always have appeal to different risk–return preferences of different sections of society. Since governments always have a large stock of assets, including land, buildings, roads, bridges, railways, airways, machinery, equipment and so on, there will not be a shortage of assets to issue *ijara*-based instruments to raise needed funds. The absence of interest-based borrowing is not likely to pose any resource constraint on the government to carry out its functions, activities and plans.
2.   Despite this potential, there would still be pressure to discipline the government with respect to its spending. The mobilization of resources requires defining assets worthy of renting and conducting commodity operations. With interest-based borrowing, the government only has to justify the expenditure to be met from borrowing. In the absence of interest-based borrowing, the method of financing will also have to be justified. Each method has its own costs and benefits and its own features with its specific impact on society and economy. The choice of method of financing will require appropriate prioritizing of the government spending.

   Spending has to be linked to a specific method of financing, each with its different costs of raising funds. Without prioritizing the spending, the government may find itself constrained in raising funding for more important spending if it was not judicious in the selection of the method of financing. This choice will act as a discipline on government expenditure, particularly in view of the fact that the option to borrow to repay previous debts will no longer be available and the possibilities of rescheduling government obligations will be less.
3.   The difficulties in rescheduling debt and the absence of the option of borrowing to repay previous debt puts pressures on the government to enhance its productive capacity. In *ijara*-based instruments, for example, if the return is not paid in time, the government's ability to raise funds for such instruments will be severely constrained.
4.   The option of cost-free borrowing (*qard hasan*) is an additional and useful source of mobilizing resources for government. Financing a cause cherished by Islam provides a new source of borrowing, not available if the government is borrowing at interest.
5.   The underlying financial contracts that can be used to develop instruments for resource mobilization for government differ in nature and in economic features (Khan,

1992). Unlike an interest-based economy where the interest rate is the only policy variable, the Islamic alternatives offer a variety of policy variables that can be used for macro monetary management and the management of aggregate demand in the economy. The economy will have a policy variable in the form of mark-up in trade-based instruments, rental return in *ijara*-based instruments and profit–loss sharing ratios in *mudaraba* and *musharaka*-based instruments that can be used independently to manage aggregate demand in different sectors of macroeconomic activity.

Notes

1. A local government in Germany (Saxony-Anhalt) issued Islamic bonds in 2004 (see p. 299).
2. Some schools of Islamic law allow certain kinds of debt instruments to be traded in money markets. The majority of Islamic jurists, however, do not approve this practice as conforming to Islamic law.
3. A wealth tax, rather than an income tax, is more compatible in the economic financial system. *Zakat*, one of the five pillars of Islam, is also closer to a wealth tax than an income tax. The above discussion will not be valid if firms are operating in economies that follow wealth tax regimes rather than income tax regimes.
4. Some schools of law, however, make a distinction between a debt arising out of monetary or financial transaction and debt arising out of a real activity such as trade of goods and services. These schools of law apply the prohibition of sale of debt only to the former category of debt and not to the latter category.
5. The reward mentioned in the Qur'an (2:265) is 700 times or more.
6. Many schools of Islamic law, however, do not approve *bai' al-inah* as a *shari'a*-compatible mode of financing. For details of *bai' al-inah*, see Nadwi (2005).
7. For the discussion on issues relating to the standardization of *shari'a* applications in the Islamic finance industry, see Khan (2005).

Bibliography

Ahmed, Ausaf and Tariqullah Khan (eds) (1997), *Islamic Financial Instruments for Public Sector Resource Mobilization*, Jeddah: Islamic Research and Training Institute, IDB.
Haq, Nadeemul and Abbas Mirakhor (1999), 'The design of instruments for government finance in an Islamic economy', *Islamic Economic Studies*, **6** (2), 27–43.
Hassan, Hussein Hamed (1994), *Jurisprudence of Maslaha and Its Contemporary Applications*, Jeddah: Islamic Research and Training Institute, Islamic Development Bank.
Kahf, Monzer (1992), 'Financing public sector in Islamic perspective', in Zaid Sattar (ed.), *Resource Mobilization and Investment in an Islamic Economic Framework*, Washington, DC: Association of Muslim Social Scientists.
Khan, M. Fahim (1991), 'Time value of money and discounting in Islamic perspective', *Review of Islamic Economics*, **1** (2), 25–45.
Khan, M. Fahim (1992), *Comparative Economics of Some Islamic Financing Techniques*, Jeddah: Islamic Research and Training Institute, Islamic Development Bank.
Khan, M. Fahim (1999), 'Islamic capital markets: need for institutional development', in Imtiaz Ahmed (ed.), *Islamic Banking and Finance: The Concept, The Practice and the Challenge*, Plainfiled: Islamic Society of North America.
Khan, M. Fahim (2005), 'Setting standards for *Shari'ah* application in Islamic finance industry', Islamic Research and Training Institute, Islamic Development Bank, Jeddah mimeograph.
Masud, Muhammad Khalid (1995), *Shatibi's Philosophy of Islamic Law*, Islamabad: Islamic Research Institute, International Islamic University.
Modigliani, F. and M.H. Miller (1958), 'The cost of capital, corporate finance and theory of investment', *American Economic Review*, **48** (3), 261–97.
Modigliani, F. and M.H. Miller (1963), 'Corporation income taxes and the cost of capital: a correction', *American Economic Review*, **53** (5), 433–43.
Nadwi, Ali Ahmed (2005), '*Al-Qawaid al-Fiqhi al-Muamalaat*' (Arabic), Jeddah: Islamic Research and Training Institute, Islamic Development Bank.
Sundarajan, V., David Marston and Ghiath Shabsigh (1998), 'Monetary operations and government debt management under Islamic banking', IMF working paper 144, Washington, DC (http://www.imf.org/external/pubs/cat/longres.cfm?sk &sk=2761.0).

19 Accounting standards for Islamic financial services[1]

Simon Archer and Rifaat Ahmed Abdel Karim

Introduction

In this chapter, we use the phrase 'Islamic financial services' in preference to the commonly used phrase 'Islamic financial institutions'. We do so because, in our view, the term 'Islamic financial services' is much broader and bypasses the debate of whether the definition of financial institutions includes banks, investment funds and insurance. Hence the newly established Islamic Financial Services Board, the primary objective of which is to set prudential and supervisory standards for the full spectrum of Islamic financial services, namely, banking, capital markets and insurance services.

This chapter will focus on some fundamental issues which we have found to be of concern to those who have an interest in accounting for Islamic financial services. In particular, we will attempt to address the following questions: (a) Do Islamic financial services (IFS) need financial reporting standards and guidelines other than those issued by the International Accounting Standards Board (IASB)? (b) If there is a genuine need for such standards, to what extent would such standards benefit/disadvantage the institutions that offer such services internationally, given the current efforts toward the convergence of national accounting standards and International Accounting Standards (IAS), which are now known as International Financial Reporting Standards (IFRS)?

The remainder of this chapter is structured as follows. The next two sections relate to question (a) above. The first issue addressed is whether IFS need financial reporting standards other than those issued by IASB. Put another way, are IFRS adequate to cater for the specificities of Islamic financial services which, as claimed by students of Islamic finance, require accounting treatments which are not specifically spelled out in IFRS? If these requirements are overlooked, this will render the financial statements of the providers of these services both non-comparable and opaque.

This question relates to a wider issue concerning the regulation of IFS, extending beyond financial reporting to capital adequacy, for example. Given the specificities of IFS, do they require (a) separate regulatory structures and rules, (b) complementary regulatory structures and rules, (c) neither separate nor complementary structures and rules?

Following this, we will argue that, in respect of financial reporting, the requirement is for complementary (not separate) accounting rules. (A similar argument could be applied to capital adequacy, for example, but that is not our concern.) Then the chapter considers the issues raised in question (b) above, namely to what extent such financial reporting standards would benefit or disadvantage the institutions that offer such services internationally, given the current efforts being made to promote convergence between national accounting standards in the USA and the European Union, for example, and International Financial Reporting Standards (IFRS). Finally, some concluding remarks are provided.

IFS financial reporting standards

This section examines the following question: Do IFS need financial reporting standards other than those issued by IASB? One of the salient features of IFS is that they are governed by *shari'a*-approved contracts. Since Islam does not recognize the separation between spiritual and temporal affairs, and considers commerce as a matter of morality and subject to the precepts of the *shari'a*, such an approach to business has implications for the financial reporting standards that are meant to give a faithful representation of the transactions that are governed by these contracts.

According to Gambling and Karim (1991, p. 103), 'the conceptual framework of accounting currently applied in the West finds its justification in a dichotomy between business morality and private morality. As such, it cannot be (unquestioningly) implemented in other societies which have revealed doctrines and morals that govern all social, economic and political aspects of life'. Indeed, Western accounting rules are presented as technical, not ethical rules (Karim, 1996). Hence, in the context of institutions that offer IFS, if accounting information is to give a faithful representation of the economic transactions or events that it purports to represent, it is necessary that they be accounted for and presented in accordance with the substance as well as the form of the *shari'a* contracts that govern these transactions or events. For example, a *murabaha* deferred-payment sale transaction, while providing a *shari'a*-compliant credit facility, is not an 'in-substance' purchase financed by a loan, and an *ijara muntahia bittamleek* is a *shari'a*-compliant form of leasing whereby the lessor normally ends up by owning the asset, but because of certain *shari'a* requirements regarding the lessor's responsibilities it should not be considered as an 'in-substance' capital lease (the reasons for this are discussed further below).

In fact, although each of the *shari'a* contracts used by institutions that offer IFS has some characteristics that match those of financial instruments used by conventional business organizations, each of the *shari'a* contracts has specific rules that have no parallels in the financial instruments currently available in the West. For example, a *murabaha* contract may be used for a type of instalment sale, as noted above, but it involves an option of a binding (irrevocable) purchase order or a non-binding one. In addition, there are cases where the bank is likely to obtain a discount or rebate on the price of the asset to be sold after its acquisition. The *shari'a* precepts that govern this contract do not permit the splitting of deferred *murabaha* profits into financing and trading profits.

It is the specificities in many *shari'a* contracts that have no parallels in the conventional financial instruments, and which have significant financial reporting implications that, if ignored or not standardized, could lead to the financial statements not fairly representing the financial health of the institutions that offer these services. For example, should we measure the assets in the bank's ownership (pending delivery to a customer) that are governed by a *murabaha* contract which has a binding purchase order on the basis of historical cost, while the assets that do not have a binding order are measured at their cash equivalent value (that is, their market or fair value), or alternatively at the lower of cost and market value? Do we recognize the profit of a *murabaha* transaction which offers a deferred payment facility beyond one financial period on a front-end loading basis or allocate them proportionately over the period of the contract, knowing that we cannot make a split between financial income and trading profit as is recommended in International Accounting Standard (IAS)18? Should we report profit-sharing investment accounts, which are mobilized on the basis of the *mudaraba* contract, on or off balance sheet and, if on balance sheet, should we treat them as a liability or as an equity item?

We could cite numerous other examples where IFRS are silent and which need to be addressed if users of the financial statements of these institutions are to be provided with relevant and reliable information which they can use in their decision making. The inadequacy of IFRS has resulted in a vacuum of sufficient international accounting guidelines that help to render the financial statements of institutions that offer IFS comparable. Accordingly, what seems to have happened (and still appears to take place) is that institutions which offer IFS tended to choose subjectively from the available IFRS those standards or part of standards that in their opinion matched the contracts that govern the underlying transaction.

Another important aspect which is not adequately catered for by IFRS is the necessary disclosures that should be made by the institutions which offer IFS. We know that the majority of banks that offer IFS perform a hybrid mix of services of both commercial and investment banking. The latter is mainly carried out by mobilizing funds in investment accounts which are commingled in the majority of banks with the shareholders' funds. In addition, both funds are invested by the bank's management in the same investment portfolio, and these investments and their results are reported in the bank's balance sheet and income statement. Logically, holders of these accounts should be entitled to a number of rights, including receiving a regular flow of information on the investment objectives and policies relating to their funds, operational guidelines that govern the relationship between the bank and holders of these accounts, and the basis of allocation of profits between the two parties. More importantly, full disclosure of information, whereby holders of these accounts are better able to assess the potential risks and rewards of their investments and, thus, take decisions to protect their own interests, should be a requirement.

Given that, until recently, almost all institutions that offer IFS were required by their relevant authorities in the countries in which they operate to implement IFRS and/or their national accounting standards which tend to be largely based on IFRS, what seems to have happened was (and still is happening) is that these institutions and their external auditors ended up in a process of interpreting IFRS/national accounting standards because these standards do not cater for the specificities of IFS's transactions. This has resulted in a lack of (a) adequate transparency and comparability of the financial statements, and (b) proper presentation and adequate disclosure to reflect the universal banking nature of Islamic banks. These considerations lead us to the matters to be discussed in the next section.

Appropriate accounting rules for IFS
Do IFS require separate or complementary accounting rules, or neither? We believe that an answer to this question can be provided by considering the historical development discussed below.

The perception of a lack of comparable and transparent financial statements led a number of institutions that offer IFS, together with other interested parties, to take an initiative in 1991 to self-regulate their financial reporting by establishing the Accounting and Auditing Organization for Islamic Financial Institutions (AAOIFI) with a mandate to set international financial reporting standards based on the *shari'a* precepts.

The development of such standards raised two fundamental issues which AAOIFI had to address. The first issue had to do with the approach that should be used in developing the standards. This involved examining the relevant available IFRS (at that time it was IAS) to identify (a) the extent to which they were *shari'a*-compliant; and (b) whether they catered for the specific requirements of the *shari'a* contracts, and the practices that emanated from the universal banking model of Islamic banks (Karim, 2001).

A principles-based approach was adopted whereby the same recognition and measurement rules were used as in IAS/IFRS, provided they were *shari'a*-compliant (for example, net present value was not acceptable as a measurement attribute). In addition, the same presentation and disclosure requirements were adopted provided they were consistent with the nature of operations undertaken by the institutions that offer IFS.

However, the added value of AAOIFI's standards was to use the identified recognition, measurement, presentation and disclosure requirements to develop guidelines that catered for the specificities of the *shari'a* contracts that govern the transactions carried out by the institutions that offer IFS, as well as some of the unique business practices developed by these institutions, for example the formation of profit equalization reserves and investment risk reserves. This is how AAOIFI complemented IFRS by using the principles recommended in those standards to promulgate the required accounting standards for the *shari'a* contracts. Nevertheless, there were situations in which the latter required a treatment that differed from what was advocated in IFRS. For example, unlike the accounting treatment for instalment sales, it is not *shari'a*-acceptable in a *murabaha* to the purchase orderer to split the financial income, which is recognized on a time-proportion basis in IAS/IFRS, from the trading profit, which is recognized under IAS/IFRS at the date of sale. Hence AAOIFI recommends that the profit earned in a *murabaha* to the purchase orderer transaction should be recognized on an accrual basis and allocated proportionately over the period of the contract, a treatment which was not universally practised by institutions that offer IFS.

On the other hand, in certain cases, AAOIFI had to take the lead where there were no available IFRSs that catered for the financial reporting issues that called for the development of accounting standards. For example, AAOIFI spearheaded the development of four accounting standards for Islamic insurance companies, or what is known in Malaysia as *Takaful* insurance, before IASB issued its first exposure draft for insurance contracts. In addition, AAOIFI is the only standard-setting body that has so far issued a standard on investment funds.

The second fundamental issue in the development of AAOIFI accounting standards was the *shari'a* contracts which governed the transactions of institutions that offer IFS. The point has already been made that the *raison d'être* for the establishment of AAOIFI was to cater for the accounting treatments of these contracts. However, the big challenge that had to be addressed was the lack of standardization of the *shari'a* provisions in these contracts.

It is an established fact that almost every institution that offers IFS appoints a *shari'a* supervisory board (SSB) to assure the institution's clients (mainly those who are keen to have their funds managed in accordance with *shari'a* rules and principles) that it has rendered its financial services in a *shari'a*-compliant manner. Each SSB issues the *shari'a* rulings that it considers appropriate, based on its interpretation of the underlying *shari'a* principles. However, the variations in the *shari'a* rulings for the same transaction seem to have resulted in a lack of standardization and in many cases rendered the financial statements of these institutions non-comparable. For example, an SSB may allow the Islamic bank to charge a financial penalty on the clients that default in the payment of their debt and to treat such a penalty as revenue in the bank's income statement, while another SSB may rule that such a penalty should be disposed of to charitable causes. Yet a third alternative is not to allow the bank to charge any penalty.

In addition to the above functions, some SSBs tend to influence the accounting treatment of some of the contracts that govern the bank's transactions. For example, the SSB in one Islamic bank rules that the profit generated from *murabaha* transactions should be recognized after all instalments have been received, while in another Islamic bank the SSB has ruled that the profit should be recognized when each instalment is received. Both accounting methods depart from the basic accrual method of revenue recognition which was practised by other Islamic banks.

This meant that, in order for the accounting standards issued by AAOIFI for *shari'a* contracts to be effective, the contracts themselves needed to be well specified; in other words, the interpretations of the provisions of the contracts needed to be tightened up and codified in a generally accepted manner. AAOIFI tackled this situation in two steps. In the first step, to each standard were appended AAOIFI's presuppositions, in the form of the juristic basis for the standard, as provided by AAOIFI's own committee of *shari'a* experts. These appendices were the precursors of, and set the terms of reference for, what was to follow. In the second step, AAOIFI issued a set of *shari'a* standards for the *shari'a* contracts in question. These were developed following the same due process as that used for the accounting standards, which involved, among other things, the issuance of exposure drafts and the holding of public hearings.

AAOIFI's *shari'a* standards have provided a unified basis with which its accounting standards should comply. An example is the *shari'a* standard on *ijara muntahia bittamleek*, in which it is spelled out that in an *ijara muntahia bittamleek* contract the lessor cannot transfer all significant risks and rewards to the lessee. Hence, unlike what was (and still is) practised by many institutions that offer IFS, the *ijara muntahia bittamleek* does not qualify to be treated as a finance lease.

One important theme that emerges from the experience of AAOIFI in setting accounting standards for *shari'a*-compliant transactions is the necessity to address three significant interrelated processes. The first is to identify the relevant details of the *shari'a* provisions in each contract that govern a transaction and to understand their accounting implications. The second is to identify the relevant corresponding IFRS and to ascertain the proposed recognition, measurement, disclosure and reporting requirements which do not contravene *shari'a* precepts and are compatible with the nature of the practices of the institutions that offer IFS. It is worth noting that, in this process, there may be more than one relevant IFRS, as in the case of AAOIFI's Financial Accounting Standard (FAS) 17, which addresses accounting treatments for investments that relate to those in IFRS 32, 39 and 40. The third process is to develop a standard that combines the first two.

It is the ability of AAOIFI to address these three interrelated processes in a competent manner that would determine both the quality of the promulgated standards and their acceptance by the preparers and users of the financial statements of institutions that offer IFS. Furthermore, given the growing importance of financial stability in today's global financial architecture, AAOIFI's financial reporting standards should be consistent with sound risk management and control practices in institutions that offer IFS and should facilitate market discipline. With regard to such issues, the IFSB is currently preparing two sets of guidelines, on risk management and capital adequacy. These guidelines are intended to be complementary to those issued by bodies such as the Basel Committee on Banking Supervision, just as AAOIFI's standards are complementary to those issued by the IASB.

Impact of the standards on financial institutions

We now turn to the issue of the extent to which such standards would benefit or disadvantage, at the international level, the institutions that offer IFS, given the current efforts to make national accounting standards converge with IFRS. Some critics say that although AAOIFI's standards would render the financial statements of institutions that offer IFS comparable and enhance their transparency, they would disadvantage these institutions at the international level. They argue that IFRS is becoming the *lingua franca* of financial reporting, and hence institutions that offer IFS which adopt AAOIFI's standards would also have to prepare their financial statements using IFRS, a process which will be costly for these institutions.

The critics argue the following points:

- the use of IFRS would be necessary when institutions that offer IFS send their accounts to their international counterparts with whom they conduct business or to regulatory agencies in countries in which they wish to open branches because their counterparts or regulatory agencies would not be familiar with AAOIFI's standards, and it would be costly for them to engage the service of firms to perform the necessary financial services;
- preparation of financial statements according to IFRS is consistent with the efforts of the International Organization of Securities Commissions to bring about the possibility that companies with stock market listings in many countries can satisfy all the regulatory requirements with one set of accounting standards; and
- even in stock markets that allow the use of AAOIFI's standards, users of financial statements who are not familiar with AAOIFI's standards are more likely to discount the shares or profit-sharing investment account *sukuks* of institutions that offer IFS, thereby depressing the values of these instruments and disadvantaging their institutions.

At issue here are two conflicting objectives. One of the objectives of the International Accounting Standards Committee (IASC) Foundation, among others, is as follows:

> to develop, in the public interest, a single set of high quality, understandable and enforceable global accounting standards that require high quality, transparent and comparable information in financial statements and other financial reporting to help participants in the world's capital markets and other users make economic decisions. (IASC Foundation Constitution, Part A, 2(a))

However, from what we have argued above, it is unlikely that the use of IFRS by institutions that offer IFS would render the information in their financial statements transparent and comparable. This would defeat the purposes of using IFRS which are cited by the critics who argue against the use of AAOIFI's standards.

The critics should also note that, in an unpublished study conducted by AAOIFI in which its Financial Accounting Standards (FAS) are compared to those of IFRS, it was found that, in most cases, compliance with an applicable FAS is compatible with IFRSs, but the FAS involves some additional recognition, measurement or disclosure requirements in order to cater for the specificities of the contracts governing the transactions. Only in one or two cases (such as revenue recognition on *murabaha* sales, mentioned above), is the treatment required by the applicable FAS not entirely compatible with IFRS.

However, the caveat here is that IASB requires, in IAS 1, that 'Financial statements should not be described as complying with International Accounting Standards unless they comply with all the requirements of each applicable Standard and *each* applicable Interpretation of the Standing Interpretation Committee' (para. 11). Nevertheless, in IAS 1, IASB also states: 'In the extremely rare circumstances when management concludes that compliance with a requirement in a Standard would be misleading, and therefore that departure from a requirement is necessary to achieve a fair presentation, an enterprise should disclose' certain information specified in the Standard. We believe that the very few cases to which we alluded earlier would qualify for such a departure.

Preparers of the financial statements of institutions that offer IFS should not be penalized for adhering to AAOIFI's standards, given that IASB has preferred not to address the specificities of the *shari'a* contracts that govern the transactions of institutions that offer IFS. Rather, it has opted to appoint a representative from the industry, who is the current Secretary-General of the IFSB, to sit on its Standards Advisory Council (SAC). This indicates that the IASB recognizes that the views of the Islamic financial services industry should be given an opportunity to be heard when the SAC meets to inform the IASB, among others, of the implications of proposed standards for users and preparers of financial statements.

This situation results in something of a dilemma, and those who stand behind the idea of promulgating financial reporting standards that produce relevant and reliable information in the financial statements of institutions that offer IFS must face up to its implications. In other words, they should accept that the improved financial reporting using AAOIFI standards involves a cost that may not be fully balanced by the benefits until the use of AAOIFI's standards by preparers and users of the financial statements reaches a critical mass. However, we should remember that such an imbalance would remain at a minimum as long as AAOIFI adheres to a principles-based convergence process with IFRS, provided the latter do not contravene the *shari'a* precepts and cater for the specificities of the institutions that offer IFS.

Concluding remarks

In this chapter, we have sought to raise some important issues in international financial reporting for certain types of entity that do not altogether fit the template used by the IASB, a template that the Board cannot currently modify in order to cater for such entities, given its other pressing (and to some extent conflicting) preoccupations with achieving convergence with US GAAP (generally agreed accounting principles) as well as acceptance by the European Union's 'endorsement mechanism' (the stresses involved may be seen, for example, in the well-documented problems over IAS 39, *Financial Instruments: Recognition and Measurement*). More generally, the whole field of financial reporting for Islamic financial services suffers from a severe dearth of published research in reputable journals. We hope that our discussion of these issues in this chapter may help to trigger further research in the field.

Note

1. The views expressed in the chapter are those of the authors and do not represent a position held by the Islamic Financial Services Board.

References

Gambling, T. and R.A.A. Karim (1991), *Business and Accounting Ethics in Islam*, London: Mansell Publishing Co.

Karim, R.A.A. (1996), 'Economic consequences of accounting standards and Islamic banks', *Research in Accounting Regulation*, **10**, 111–38.

Karim, R.A.A. (2001), 'International accounting harmonization, banking regulation and Islamic banks', *The International Journal of Accounting*, **36** (2), 169–93.

20 Mutualization of Islamic banks
Mahmoud A. El-Gamal

Sheikh Kamel does not fancy the word customer or depositor and prefers to use the term 'partner'. 'Those people who place their money in Al-Baraka bank or any other Islamic bank are considered shareholders of these banks. This means if these banks prosper so will they. (*The Daily Star*, Monday, 15 August 2005, Osama Habib, 'Saudi businessman tackles task of polishing Islam's image')

Historical background

In the opening quotation about Sheikh Saleh Kamel, he suggested that Islamic banks are in fact mutual banks (or credit unions or other mutually owned thrift institutions), where depositors are shareholders. In fact, had Islamic banks adopted this style of mutual banking, they might have simultaneously approached the Islamic ideal intended by the prohibition of *riba*, and allowed regulators in various countries to adopt the regulatory standards applied to such mutual financial institutions in the West. Moreover, they would have been able to create a niche market that serves an important social function, a niche wherein they would be protected from competition by large multinational banks that are the primary beneficiaries today of Islamic banking. Alas, Islamic banks did not adopt the mutuality structure suggested in the opening quotation, and consequently the treatment of investment account holders (IAHs) has continued to raise a number of regulatory concerns for Islamic banks and their regulators worldwide.

Most Islamic economists attribute the vision of the Islamic bank structure to the work of Mohammad Uzair in the mid-twentieth century.[1] With very few exceptions, Islamic jurists of the nineteenth and twentieth centuries have equated 'interest' (or its Arabic counterpart, *fa'ida*) with the forbidden *riba*.[2] The rise of Islamism under the influence of the Muslim Brotherhood in Arab countries and the *Jamat-i-Islami* in the South Asian subcontinent did not stop at condemnation of interest-based banking. The movement also called for replacing existing banking systems, which they characterized as an alien Western intrusion into the Islamic world, with an Islamic alternative. The model envisioned by Uzair, Siddiqi and others was one of a two-tier silent partnership or *mudaraba*.

Banks operating under this principle would only guarantee fiduciary deposits, on which depositors receive no guaranteed rate of return.[3] Other deposit alternatives on the liabilities side of Islamic banks would take the form of investment accounts, for which investors' principal sums were not guaranteed, as they were envisioned to share in the bank's profits and losses from various pools of investments. Those investments comprising the assets of Islamic banks were envisioned also to be silent partnerships, wherein the bank acts as principal, with each of its customers (would-be borrowers of conventional banks) acting as an investment agent (*mudarib*). It is important for understanding Islamic banking today, and for developing an appropriate regulatory framework thereof, to understand how Islamic banking behaviour has emerged in fact, both on the assets and on the liabilities side.

On the assets side, Islamic banks quickly abandoned the *mudaraba* model, because of its forms of moral hazard and adverse selection problems that are unfamiliar to conventional bankers. Islamic bank officers are mostly ex-bankers, who are proficient at credit risk analysis for their customers, but not particularly skilled in monitoring customer behaviour. Consequently, to capitalize on their comparative advantage, and to minimize losses driven by customer incompetence and/or dishonesty, Islamic banks adopted debt-financing modes that were proposed by the late Dr Sami Humud. Dr Humud's vision was to find the closest approximation to conventional banking practice that does not violate the precepts of Islamic Law.[4] The instruments of choice for Islamic banks thus became cost-plus credit sales (*murabaha*) and lease financing (*ijara*), where the mark-up profit component and the rent component, respectively, are commonly benchmarked to market interest rates. In recent years, sovereign governments in the Islamic world, as well as a number of corporations, have issued Islamic bond alternatives (known by the Arabic name *sukuk*, or debt certificates) for which the primary buyers are Islamic banks. Rates of return on those *sukuk* are also benchmarked to the appropriate interest rate, and based on the issuer's credit rating. Thus Islamic banks have come to replicate the asset structures of conventional banks almost perfectly, replacing loan receivables on the balance sheet with credit–sale price receivables and rents, and replacing bonds with *sukuk*.

On the liabilities side, the envisioned model of silent partnership has been more difficult to abandon. Some economists and jurists mounted early resistance to replacing banks (which are fundamentally financial intermediaries, restricted by prudential regulators to intermediation practices) with what are essentially investment companies or collective investment schemes.[5] In fact, one can easily envisage how Islamic bank financial intermediation could have taken place in parallel with conventional banking practice, with principal plus interest being guaranteed for depositors. Since Islamic banks guarantee for themselves principal plus interest from borrowers (in the form of credit buyers, lessees and issuers of sukuk), the only issue in passing similar fixed-interest instruments through to its creditors would be replacing the bank debtors' credit risk with the bank's own. However, this would require combining the bank's agency for its depositors – investing in fixed return securities, credit sales and leases – with a guarantee of the bank's debtors and issuers of debt securities. Unfortunately, while some earlier jurists had allowed the combination of agency and guarantee (*wakala* and *kafala*), Islamic finance jurists forbade such combinations.[6]

Problematic investment account structure

Thus Islamic banks have not been allowed to act directly – through agency and guarantee – as financial intermediaries that insulate their investment account holders from the credit risk associated with the bank's own debtors. Saeed sympathized with arguments by Sami Humud, Baqir al-Sadr and others, who aimed to find alternatives within the *mudaraba* context to allow the Islamic bank to guarantee investment account holders' principal. He justified that position based on the view, reported by ibn Rushd in *Bidayat al-Mujtahid wa Nihayat al-Muqtasid*, that an entrepreneur (*mudarib*) who forwards an investor's funds to another entrepreneur thus guarantees the invested principal for that original investor. However, he notes correctly that most Islamic economists and bankers feared that this approach would remove any substantive distinction between Islamic and conventional banking. In particular, he argued that the Hanafi view that depositors can be entitled to a return based on provision of money, rather than liability for risk, 'could shatter the foundations of *riba* theory as it is accepted in Islamic banking' (Saeed, 1999, pp. 104–5).

Besides, he points out correctly, Islamic banks benefited from the provision that investment account holders (as investors) bear the financial risk. Thus the Accounting and Auditing Standards, and the Shari'a Standards of the Accounting and Auditing Organization for Islamic Financial Institutions (AAOIFI) stipulated the following:

> One of the basic characteristics that distinguish Islamic banks from conventional banks is that the contractual relationship of Islamic banks with investment account holders does not specify that holders of these account [*sic*] are entitled to a predetermined return in the form of a percentage of their investment as this is strictly prohibited by *Shari'a*. Rather, the contractual relationship is based on the mudaraba contract which stipulates that profit realized from investing the mudaraba fund is shared between investment account holders – as rab-al-mal – and the Islamic bank – as a mudarib (AAOIFI, 2004, p. 215).
>
> The basis for considering the mudarib as a trustee with respect to the mudaraba funds is that the mudarib is using another person's money with his consent and the mudarib and the owner of the funds share the benefits from the use of the funds. In principle, a trustee should not be held liable for losses sustained by the funds. Rather, the risks of such losses must be borne by the Mudaraba funds. (AAOIFI, 2004, p. 241)

Needless to say, this structure greatly exacerbates the moral hazard problem between depositors and banks, which is the primary focus of regulators' efforts to protect depositors from excessive risk taking by bank managers. That fundamental moral hazard problem is further increased by the fact that, contrary to the assertion attributed to Sheikh Saleh Kamel in the opening quotation, the interests of bank-owners or shareholders of the bank on the one hand, and investment account holders on the other, are actually in conflict, at least in the short term. Islamic bank managers answer primarily to the shareholders, rather than the investment account holders, and they choose how to allocate various profits and losses from the bank's investments between the two groups. This prompted the issuance of an AAOIFI standard on reporting the basis and procedure for profit allocation:

> The accounting treatments of the equity or profits of investment account holders differ greatly from one Islamic bank to another. This has prompted AAOIFI, as a first step, to promulgate Financial Accounting Standard No.5: Disclosure of Bases for Profit Allocation Between Owners' Equity and Investment Account Holders in order to provide users of the financial statements of Islamic banks with information on the bases which Islamic banks adopted in allocation profit [*sic*] between owners' equity and investment account holders. (AAOIFI, 2004, p. 215)

Thus AAOIFI has restricted its role in protecting investment account holders to maximizing transparency and uniformity of reporting standards. The only recourse for investment account holders, assuming that the Islamic bank does not engage in negligence or fraudulent activities, is to withdraw their funds from that bank. This gives rise to what AAOIFI research and later analysts called 'displaced commercial risk'. That threat of fund withdrawal drives Islamic banks to use their loan-loss reserve accounts to smooth rates of return paid to investment account holders, ensuring their competitiveness against rates paid by other Islamic and conventional financial service providers. This complex set of competing incentives has made the issue of corporate governance of Islamic banks one of the most difficult.

As of the writing of this chapter (May 2005), the publication of a consultation paper on the subject in early 2006 was promised by the Islamic Financial Services Board. All indications at the present time are of maintaining the 'mutual fund' model, whereby investment account holders continue to lack the protection of board representation as equity holders, or the protection of principal guarantee as depositors. Under the mutual fund model, all that is required of Islamic banks – as de facto collective investment schemes, even if not labelled as such – is to provide consistent and transparent distribution rules for profits and losses between the competing interest groups (equity-holding owners and quasi-equity investment account holders). In the remainder of this chapter, it will be argued that this solution is vastly inferior to the solution in mutuality that is implicitly assumed in Sheikh Saleh Kamel's reference to investment account holders as 'partners' who would prosper when the Islamic bank prospers; that is, whose incentives are aligned with those of shareholders and the managers they appoint and oversee.

Possibility of debt-structured Islamic deposits
Before proceeding to discuss the specific financial areas wherein Islamic banking may be required, and how it should be structured, one should point out that Islamic bank liabilities can easily be made to mimic conventional bank liabilities, in a manner similar to Islamic banks' use of synthetic debt assets. However, the bulk of thinking on Islamic bank regulation and governance has maintained the assumption that investment or savings accounts offered to Islamic bank customers must be based on *mudaraba* or profit and loss sharing. This maintained assumption is patently false.

Clearly, since jurists have allowed Islamic banks to synthesize debt-finance instruments on their asset side through sales and leases, the same can be done on the liabilities side. An Islamic bank obviously owns physical assets, which can be sold to depositors and leased back (perhaps through a Special Purpose Vehicle – SPV), thus guaranteeing those depositors' principal plus interest in the form of rent. An Islamic bank can also engage with customers in commodity sale contracts based on [reverse] *murabaha* or *salam*, where depositors provide the immediate 'price' and collect the higher deferred price (in *murabaha*) or spot resale price (in *salam*), in the same manner that Islamic banks and *sukuk* buyers collect interest synthesized from price differentials in multiple sales. In the case of rent-based debt instruments, liquidity (withdrawal rights) can be provided for depositors through a unilaterally binding option to resell the property to the bank. For sale-based debt instruments, Islamic banks can provide resale facilities similar to the ones developed by the Bahrain Monetary Agency to facilitate Islamic banks' liquidity management with its *sukuk al-salam*.

In other words, miniature variations on the debt instruments that allow banks and *sukuk* buyers to collect a guaranteed principal plus interest (characterized as price differential, profit or rent, depending on the contract) may be utilized equally successfully to synthesize Islamic bank deposit structures. Moreover, Islamic deposit contracts may use the same legal covenants used in structuring *sukuk*, which allow those instruments to pay a rate of return that is benchmarked to the London Interbank Offered Rate (LIBOR), and based solely on the credit rating of the issuer. In this regard, the fundamental non-tradeability of bank deposits (discussed in the following section) makes it possible extensively to use cheaper sale-based structures for Islamic bank savings deposits, which would be practically mirror-images of those banks' assets.

This approach has the added advantage of aligning the structures of Islamic bank assets and liabilities, which helps Islamic banks in their management of liquidity, credit and interest rate risks. Indeed, this author had argued in an earlier paper that 'Islamic bonds', which can be used in open market operations, should be optimally structured through sale and lease-based contracts, to mimic Islamic banks' other assets, thus making involvement in open market operations a natural component of asset and liability management.[7] In fact, the current structures of *sukuk* have precisely mimicked the structures of other Islamic bank assets along the 'reverse financial engineering' approach suggested in that paper. The same can be accomplished with equal ease for Islamic bank liabilities.

Of course, this approach would have some drawbacks, including the two issues raised by Abdullah Saeed: that passing some of the risk of loss to depositors is financially advantageous for Islamic banks, and allows them to have a distinguishing feature from their conventional counterparts (Saeed, 1999, pp. 104–5). However, there are more substantive economic issues that suggest altering the structure of Islamic banks along the mutuality dimension suggested in the Sheikh Saleh Kamel opening quote. In the following two sections, it will be argued that, given the recent advances in securitization and structured finance, the bulk of financial activities need not be intermediated through any type of bank, Islamic or otherwise. For the remaining areas where banking continues to play an important role, the spirit of Islamic law strongly suggests favouring a mutuality structure, rather than the current commercial structure utilized by Islamic banks.

Debt and equity in Islamic banking
In this section, we investigate the need for Islamic 'banks' (as differentiated from other financial institutions), and the specific financial areas wherein Islamic banks can play a useful role. The answers to these questions revolve around the general nature of banks and the financial services and products that banks provide. Consequently, we begin by briefly reviewing the informational asymmetry, specialization and scale economy justifications for financial intermediation in general, and banking in particular. We then focus on the financial areas wherein conventional banks continue to play an important role. For those specific areas, we finally turn to the role that a distinctive Islamic banking sector can play, and the corporate structure that can allow them to fulfil their religious mission.

Banks as financial intermediaries exist generally to solve a number of market failures due to information asymmetry, economies of scale and liquidity mismatches. Providers of funds may find it prohibitively expensive to collect information on investors seeking funds, thus adverse selection and moral hazard problems prevent those investors from acquiring funds directly through financial markets. Banks solve this market failure due to information asymmetry by specializing in rating the creditworthiness of various investors. The cost of hiring and retaining skilled loan officers can be significantly reduced thanks to economies of scale. Banks also help to convert the funds of savers who demand high degrees of liquidity into longer-term investments with entrepreneurs who need the funds for extended periods of time. Of course, while banks solve the adverse selection and moral hazard problems between savers and investors, they create multiple other moral hazard problems. There is a moral hazard problem between the bank and the entities that it helps finance, another moral hazard problem between banks and the providers of funds, and a third potential moral hazard problem between banks and any deposit insurance scheme that might be put in place. The liquidity transformation function of banking interacts with those information asymmetries to magnify the risk of bank failure.

On both sides of financial intermediation, banks can use either equity or debt instruments. In the early literature on Islamic economics and finance, Islamic banks were envisioned to use equity or quasi-equity instruments on both the asset and the liability side. In that regard, they would have become the polar opposite of commercial banking practice (wherein debt instruments dominate both the asset and liability sides) in most countries that do not allow German-style universal banking. In general, it is well known that debt contracts are superior in dealing with information asymmetries of the type discussed above, especially when monitoring is costly.[8] It is not surprising, therefore, that Islamic bankers have discovered at an early stage that the moral hazard problem made equity investment on the assets side of Islamic banking prohibitively risky. Thus Islamic banks have switched the bulk of their assets to debt instruments, as discussed above. On the other hand, Islamic banks chose a peculiar structure on the liabilities side: with some equity holders and some quasi-equity holders. Before turning to that particular structure, we should consider the two natural mixed combinations of debt and equity on the assets and liabilities sides.

The first would be using debt instruments on the liabilities side, guaranteeing principal and interest for depositors, while investing the funds using equity contracts. This appears to be the model underlying the [in]famous *fatwa* issued by Al-Azhar's *Majma' al-Buhuth al-Islamiyyah* (Islamic Research Institute), wherein the characterization of interest on deposits was justified as fixed profit rates on funds forwarded to banks to 'invest in permissible ventures'.[9] This closely approximates the model of universal banking, wherein savers deposit their funds with the bank on a debt basis, usually with an added deposit insurance scheme, while banks can take equity positions in various companies. Under this structure, Boyd, Chang and Smith (1998) have shown that moral hazard problems between the bank and the deposit insurance company have increased substantially, especially when banks can benefit from diversion of funds ostensibly being invested (a very real threat in the developing Islamic world where similar abuses exist even within a debt-based bank asset structure). Thus the model implicitly envisioned by Al-Azhar's *fatwa* – with equity-based bank investments being funded by guaranteed bank deposits – seems to be a very poor candidate for further examination.

Thus, to recap, we have eliminated three of the four possible combinations of debt and equity structures on the asset and liability sides:

1. Debt assets and debt liabilities is the classical commercial banking model, which can be replicated, as I have argued in the previous section, by mimicking Islamic bank asset structures on the liabilities side. This structure has the advantage that all corporate governance and regulatory issues will be handled in the same manner as for conventional banking. However, as Saeed (1999) has argued convincingly, adopting this structure may undercut the very rationale for the existence of Islamic banks.
2. Equity assets and equity liabilities give rise to a very meaningful and successful model of mutual funds, private equity and venture capital, which have gained substantial market shares worldwide. However, this is not a model of banking, as Islamic banks quickly discovered from practice. This class of models plays an important financial intermediation role, through aggregation of savings on the liabilities side, and diversification of investments, with various levels of risk, on the assets side. It must thus play an important part in any financial system, Islamic or otherwise. However, it does not provide the appropriate solution for information asymmetries that require financial intermediation in the form of banking, wherein loan officers can specialize in

credit risk analysis, and utilize economies of scale to reduce moral hazard and adverse selection problems economically.
3.   Equity assets and debt liabilities give rise to a universal banking system, which some of the jurists at Al-Azhar appear to find plausible. However, this model does not seem to be appropriate for reducing moral hazard and adverse selection problems on the investor side, especially in developing Islamic countries where those information problems have been extreme even when debt instruments are used to extend bank credit.

This leaves us with the fourth potential combination of debt and equity structures on the asset and liability sides, which simultaneously resembles the model envisioned in Sheikh Saleh Kamel's attributed remarks, as well as the structures of thrift institutions such as mutual savings banks, credit unions and so on. Under this model, Islamic banks would (as they do currently) build the bulk of their assets in the form of debt-based instruments, through *murabaha*, *ijara* and various *sukuk* structures. The finance (loan) officers at those Islamic banks would, as they do currently, utilize the same criteria used by their conventional bank counterparts (prospective debtors' earnings before interest, taxes and depreciation, credit risk scores and so on). In the meantime, the liabilities side of the bank will consist mainly of shares (after excluding various owed debts, such as for leased bank buildings), whereby shareholders and investment account holders will be put on par. As we shall see in the following section, while this does not eliminate information asymmetry problems, it does eliminate the substantial short-term conflict of interest that currently exists between Islamic bank shareholders and investment account holders, which is addressed by the AAOIFI standard quotations in previous sections. In other words, this would reduce the corporate governance and regulatory issues for Islamic banks to their well-studied counterparts for mutual thrift institutions such as mutual savings banks and credit unions.

Mutual banking: secular considerations of corporate governance and regulation
While there are a number of different secular models of corporate governance in the world, the Anglo-American model is the one of greatest relevance for Islamic finance, since most countries with fast-growing Islamic financial sectors (excluding Iran and Sudan) were previously under various types of British control, and continue to have strong links with English and US banks and law firms. In this regard, it is important to note that the bulk of academic and practical advances in corporate governance in the Anglo-American world have the objective of aligning manager interests with those of shareholders. This is accomplished through a variety of mechanisms ranging from shareholder representation on the board of directors to external market discipline and manager compensation schemes.[10]

As Allen and Gale (2000) have argued persuasively, the emphasis in theory and practice of corporate governance on making managers pursue exclusively the interests of shareholders is too restrictive. However, the focus in countries where other stakeholders of the firm are considered in corporate governance is often restricted to firm employees (especially in the traditional Japanese context). Within the context of the banking firm, the interests of depositors are not included within the scope of corporate governance, since depositors are considered creditors and first claimants on the banks' assets. Thus the interests of depositors in the commercial banking set-up are guarded by regulators, including deposit insurance corporations, who impose restrictions such as reserve ratios and capital adequacy to reduce the probability of bank failure, and potential depositor losses in case of such failure.

If Islamic banks adopt either of the two debt-based deposit structures discussed in the previous section, corporate governance and regulatory recommendations would be no different from their best-practice counterparts in the Anglo-American system. Boards of directors and external market discipline will ensure that managers pursue the best interests of shareholders, while capital adequacy and other risk management regulatory requirements protect the interests of depositors. However, as we have noted previously, this solution is likely to appeal only to customers who are currently satisfied with conventional banking, and thus may undercut the very rationale for having Islamic banking.

The mutual fund solution, with equity Islamic bank investments and quasi-equity investment account shares, has its own conventional corporate governance and regulatory requirements in the Anglo-American financial system. For such a collective investment scheme, transparency and information dissemination are paramount for protecting the rights of investors. Of particular interest for Islamic countries with underdeveloped regulatory structures are the conflict of interest-driven abuses of universal banking prior to the Glass–Steagall Act in the US, and more recent conflicts of interest caused by conflation of securities research and marketing, partially addressed by the Sarbanes Oxley Act of 2002 (Pari, 1996; Micaela and Womack, 1999). Owing to the general low degree of investor sophistication in the Islamic world, and the higher riskiness of mutual funds, even under the best regulatory oversight imaginable, it seems compelling that the mutual-fund model should best be kept as a tool of collective investment, separate from banking. Unfortunately, all indications to date suggest that the Islamic Financial Services Board (IFSB) will continue pursuing this model for Islamic banking, focusing its corporate governance recommendations on transparency of investment vehicles and profit distribution rules.

Meanwhile, the solution to the fundamental corporate governance problems of Islamic banks as they exist today, which revolve around the status of investment account holders, and the protection of their interests, can be easily found in the quotation attributed to Sheikh Saleh Kamel: the rhetoric of Islamic banking suggests that investment account holders are in fact shareholders, whose interests are aligned with the Islamic banks' owners. The solution is to align the corporate structure of Islamic banks with that rhetoric, through a process of mutualization which puts those investment account holders on a par with shareholders, and affords them the same corporate governance protections, through internal representation on the board of directors and external market discipline. In fact, it is interesting to note that early Islamic banking experiments in Pakistan, Malaysia and Egypt were inspired by European mutual forms of banking, and many utilized mutual forms to varying degrees (Warde, 2000, p. 73; Saeed, 1999, pp. 119–28).

The phenomenal growth of Islamic finance at the hands of large multinational banks, such as HSBC, Citibank and so on; will no doubt continue in various areas of investment banking and fund management. Needless to say, those activities do not fall within the scope of banking proper, where assets are financed primarily by deposits. Those non-banking segments of Islamic finance can continue to grow – as they have to date – within the same corporate governance and regulatory frameworks for conventional financial markets and institutions. In the meantime, mutualization can help to bring Islamic banking proper (focusing on the depositary function of banks) within the familiar governance and regulatory framework of thrift institutions. In the remainder of this section, we shall review the performance of thrift institutions in comparison to commercial banks.[11]

In mutually owned banks, shareholders and depositors are one and the same, which resolves the fundamental corporate governance problem in Islamic banking. However, since mutual bank shares are non-tradeable, one of the main mechanisms of corporate governance through external market discipline – linking managers' compensation to stock prices – is missing. Of course, tying manager compensation to internal accounting entries (profits, volume of transactions, risk adjusted rates of return and so on) is possible, but it lacks the external discipline and objectivity commonly associated with capital market pricing of stocks. This concern is somewhat ameliorated by the likely high concentration of shareholdings by current owners of Islamic banks, who will continue to have a strong incentive for internal monitoring of bank manager performance and risk taking (Allen and Gale, 2000, pp. 95–110).

In fact, the very lack of linkage of mutual bank managers' compensations to profitability appears to align their interests with those of the mutual bank shareholders, who generally do not buy mutual bank shares seeking a high-risk high-return profile. This is in contrast to investors in commercial banks, whose stocks may in fact be bought as part of the riskier components of their shareholders' portfolios. Consequently, mutual bank managers recognize that their potential gains from taking higher risk are limited, while their potential losses are substantial, since they may lose their jobs (Fama, 1980; Fama and Jensen, 1983a, 1983b).

As long as managers of mutuals avoid excessively risky investment opportunities, managers of mutual banks tend to keep their positions for long periods of time, receiving higher compensations in non-pecuniary forms, including more leisure, better office furniture and company automobiles and so on (O'Hara, 1988). The advantage of longer and more comfortable job tenure increases the mutual bank manager's incentive to shun risks, thus providing shareholder–depositors with the types of low-risk, low-return investments that they desire. Research has shown that mutual banks have in fact chosen less risky investment portfolios, thus providing excellent low-risk investment opportunities to uninformed depositor–shareholders who have no resources for monitoring bank manager performance (Rasmusen, 1988). In addition, empirical research has shown that mutual banks are no less efficient in their operations than their stockholder-owned counterparts, even though there is no theoretical reason to think that mutual bank managers would be interested in cost minimization (Altunbas, Evans and Molyneux, 2001).

Thus there appears to be no secular reason to question the economic merits of mutualization. Indeed, there is evidence that mutual banking institutions played a very important role in the development of the US financial system during the nineteenth century, when they were every bit as competitive as stockholder-owned banks (Hansmann, 1996). Many, if not most, mutuals are also structured as non-profit organizations, which ensures that customers who obtain financing from such mutual organizations have access to credit at lower rates than those generally offered by profit-oriented banks. In the following section, the argument is made that this non-profit approach to credit extension may bring financial practice closer to the Islamic ideal enshrined in the prohibition of *riba*. Indeed, it is not surprising that early credit unions and mutual savings banks in Europe and North America were closely associated with churches and other religious institutions that sought to avoid usury by providing credit at affordable rates to community members, and to avoid profiting from the extension of such credit.

Religious considerations of *riba* and profiting from extension of credit

In his main work on comparative jurisprudence, *Bidayat al-Mujtahid wa Nihayat al-Muqtasid*, the jurist, judge, philosopher and physician ibn Rushd (Averroës) provided what has perhaps remained – to this day – the best Islamic juristic analysis of the reason for forbidding *riba*. Ibn Rushd sought an argument to justify his agreement with the Hanafi view, which broadened the scope of the prohibition of *riba* from the six commodities mentioned in the Prophetic tradition (gold, silver, wheat, barley, salt and dates) to all fungibles measured by weight or volume. His own Maliki school of jurisprudence had limited the application of rules of *riba* only to monies (gold and silver) and storeable foodstuffs (by inference from the other four commodities). In contrast, the Hanafi school had viewed gold and silver as examples of fungibles measured by weight, and the listed four foodstuffs as examples of fungibles measured by volume. The Shafi'i and Hanbali schools accepted the narrower Maliki scope of *riba*, with slight modifications. Ironically, this restriction has allowed for *fatwas* that permitted essentially *ribawi* loans, provided that the commodity that is used is not gold or silver. For instance, jurists in pre-modern times excluded copper coins (*fulus*) from the rules of currency exchange and *riba*, and Al-Rajhi's Shari'a advisory board ruled in its *fatwa* 101 that platinum is excluded from those rules (reasoning that only gold and silver constituted 'universal monies' – http://fatawa.al-Islam.com – in Arabic, search for 'Platin').

To justify his adoption of the more general Hanafi rule, ibn Rushd reasoned as follows:

> It is thus apparent from the Law that what is targeted by the prohibition of *riba* is the excessive inequity (*ghubn fashish*) that it entails. In this regard, equity in transactions is achieved through equality. Since the attainment of such equality in trading different products is difficult, property values are determined in monetary terms (with the *dirham* and the *dinar*). For non-fungibles (properties not measured by weight and volume), justice can be determined by means of proportionality. What I mean is this: the ratio of one item's value to its kind should be equal to the ratio of the other item's value to its kind. For example, if a person sells a horse in exchange for clothes, justice is attained by making the ratio of the price of the horse to other horses the same as the ratio of the value of the clothes to other clothes. Thus, if the [monetary] value of the horse is fifty, the value of the clothes [for which it is exchanged] should be fifty. [If each piece of clothing has a monetary value of five], then the horse should be exchanged for 10 pieces of clothing. (Ibn Rushd, 1997, vol. 3, p. 184)

Ibn Rushd thus made the argument implicitly that equity is attained through equating the ratio of benefits to the ratio of prices. Written five centuries prior to the invention of differential calculus, ibn Rushd could not be expected to state the Pareto-efficiency criterion that the ratio of prices should be equated to the ratio of marginal utilities. However, the argument and the context suggest that he had something very similar in mind: *riba* was forbidden to ensure equity in exchange, and an easy criterion for equity in trading fungibles of the same genus is equality – hence the examples given, wherein equity is established through equality in same-genus trading:

> As for [fungible] goods measured by volume or weight, they are relatively homogenous, and thus have similar benefits [utilities]. Since it is not necessary for a person owning one type of those

goods to exchange it for the exact same type, justice in this case is achieved by equating volume or weight since the benefits [utilities] are very similar. (Ibn Rushd, 1997, vol. 3, p. 184)

In a previous article by the present author, this analysis was combined with a well-known Prophetic tradition, wherein exchanging high-quality for low-quality dates in different quantities was forbidden, in preference for selling one and using the proceeds to buy the other. In other words, if equity is known to be impossible through equality, then we should refer to market values, to ensure the Pareto-efficiency condition of equality of the ratio of prices to the ratio of [marginal] utilities. In turn, the latter is ensured through competitive markets, where the seller will seek the highest possible price he can get for his goods, and the buyer will seek the lowest possible price, thus marking trading ratios to market.[12]

In this chapter, we are mainly concerned with institutions that facilitate credit extension, which is the primary business of Islamic and conventional banks alike. Although Islamic banks may conduct their credit operations through multiple trades or leases, it is clear in most cases that the objective is to extend credit and earn a return thereof, rather than trading in homes, automobiles and other properties the purchase of which they finance. In this regard, Islamic banks rely on the fact that credit sales in Islamic jurisprudence are allowed at prices that exceed the cash prices of the same properties.[13] Likewise, time value can be recognized in a lease setting by charging the customer 'rent' in place of interest. What we need at this point is to link ibn Rushd's view of prohibition of *riba* (to ensure equity in exchange) to the practice of Islamic banking as it exists today. Then, we can proceed to consider the advantages of a model of mutuality in avoiding *riba*.

We begin by considering loan-based finance, since this is the classical commercial banking model that Islamic banks aim simultaneously to emulate and to replace. It is important in this regard to recognize that classical Islamic jurists viewed loans as contracts of exchange. Hanafi jurists viewed a loan as exchange of the lent amount in exchange for an equal amount in the future, and jurists of the other major Sunni schools viewed it as exchange of the lent amount in exchange for an established liability to deliver an equal amount in the future.[14]

Thus, when lending fungibles, the rules of *riba* ensure equity in exchange (as explained by ibn Rushd) through equality of amounts. Any added benefit to the lender is thus tantamount to a surcharge for the very act of extending credit, which can lead to excessive injustice, as lenders exploit people's need for credit.[15] Islamic banks manage to avoid the formalistic prohibition in a money-for-money transaction by turning it into a money-for-property transaction (in cost-plus credit sale or *murabaha* financing) or money-for-usufruct transaction (in lease or *ijara* financing). Of course, the very substance of forbidden *riba* (including its most inequitable usurious forms) can easily be realized in those types of transactions. For instance, one can charge a needy person an implicit 200 per cent overnight interest by selling him an amount of aluminium worth $10 in exchange for a monetary debt equal to $30, payable the next day. Technically, this would be viewed as a legitimate sale, since there are no legal ceilings on profits in sales. However the net result is usury of the worst form, which is ironically easy to prevent in loans under current usury laws, that impose interest rate ceilings.[16] In other words, using sales and leases does not ensure avoidance of the substance of usury, which is inequity in exchange – in the case of finance, charging a debtor more or less than the equitable interest rate.[17]

Of course, one cannot make a general claim that all for-profit financial intermediaries would engage in usurious lending if they could, although the cited *Business Week* and *Wall Street Journal* articles in April 2005 suggest that line may be easily crossed in pursuit of profits (Hibbard, 2005; Hagerty and Hallinan, 2005). More generally, though, a profit-oriented financial intermediary is more likely to charge its borrowers the highest interest rates it can, and to pay its depositors the lowest interest rates that it can, subject only to regulations and market pressure stemming from competition. Needless to say, the level of competition in Islamic finance continues to lag behind its counterpart in conventional banking. Thus, for-profit Islamic financial intermediaries have a distinct incentive to charge their debtors higher interest rates, and to pay lower profit rates to its investment account holders, subject only to the limited commercial risk of losing customers on either side of the balance sheet to conventional or Islamic competitors. The incentive structure in those institutions is such that managers would serve the interests of shareholders (that is, maximize profits) at the expense of customers on both sides of the balance sheet, subject only to market pressures. Indeed, the lack of competition among mortgage providers was cited in Hagerty and Hallinan (2005) as one of the primary culprits in excessive sub-prime mortgage lending to black people at exorbitant interest rates. When debtors of Islamic financial intermediaries are charged higher interest rates (in the form of profit or rent), and when depositor-like investment account holders receive lower interest rates (in the form of profit shares) than they would otherwise, the shareholders of those intermediaries are thus profiting from the very act of extending financial intermediation (including credit) to a captive market. Lack of competition exacerbates this problem, thus resulting in the types of inequity for which the rules of *riba* were established – according to the analysis of ibn Rushd.

Concluding remarks

Interestingly, the mutual banking movement in Europe and North America was initiated by religious-minded groups who also feared that commercial banks did not face sufficient competition, and hence charged them exorbitant interest rates.[18] The mutuality structure has been shown to solve some of the secular corporate governance issues raised in the previous section. In this regard, Allen and Gale (2000) listed a number of industries in which mutual corporate forms compete successfully with stock-ownership corporate forms, despite the absence of external market discipline that plays such an important role in the corporate governance theoretical literature. Moreover, this success appears to take place despite mutuals often having unchanging boards of directors, implying that the internal discipline focus in the mainstream corporate governance literature is also misplaced. Instead, mutuals appear to adopt a model akin to the traditional Japanese managers' focus on serving the interests of all stakeholders. In conventional banks, the debt–equity structure of depositors and shareholders, respectively, creates a conflict of interests between those two sets of stakeholders.

Regulators mainly focus on protecting the interests of depositors through reserve ratios, capital adequacy requirements and the like, while managers focus on serving the interests of shareholders, who are the only remaining stakeholders, subject to regulatory constraints. Since the majority of Islamic bank managers built their careers originally in conventional banking, they naturally bring this frame of mind to their Islamic financial institutions. Consequently, it is highly unlikely that those managers would serve the interests of the other stakeholders: mainly the investment account holders and the bank debtors (who receive credit through *murabaha* and *ijara*). This results in a regulatory dilemma for protection of the rights of those two groups, in the absence of loan-based structures of deposits and financing (where reserve ratios and capital adequacy protect the depositors, and usury and predatory lending rules protect borrowers). Thus, while Islamic bankers aim to avoid *riba* in form, their mode of operation may encourage the substance of *riba*, as argued earlier in this section. Mutuality, especially in its credit union form, appears to address simultaneously religious as well as secular regulatory and corporate governance concerns.

Notes

1. For instance, see Siddiqi (1983). The most widely cited publication of the initial vision of two-tier *mudaraba* was Uzair (1955).
2. Most influential in this regard have been the writings of Abu al-A'la al-Mawdudi of Jamat-i-Islami, including Mawdudi (1977), and Sayyid Qutb of the Muslim Brotherhood, including Qutb (n.d.).
3. Although unpromised gifts were allowed; see for instance fatwa 12/1 in Abu Ghuddah and Khujah (1997b). The idea of offering unpromised gifts on guaranteed principal instruments was offered by Egyptian National Bank in the form of certificates of deposit (type C, with gifts) and utilized in Malaysian Government Investment Certificates, which also guaranteed the principal, but not the rate of return.
4. Dr Humud's main publication was Humud (1976).
5. For instance, Saeed (1999, pp. 102–3) cites arguments by Rafiq Yunus al-Misri and Mahmoud Abu el-Saud against the use of *mudaraba* or *qirad* in banking.
6. See, for instance, fatwa 13/1 in Abu Ghuddah and Khujah (1997a, p. 219), and fatwa 11/3 in Abu Ghuddah and Khujah (1997b, p. 167).
7. See El-Gamal (1999). This paper was originally presented at a seminar on 'Design and Regulation of Islamic Financial Instruments', organized and hosted by the Central Bank of Kuwait in Kuwait City on 25–26 October 1997.
8. See, for instance Townsend (1979), and Hart and Moore (1991). Similar analysis for Islamic finance was conducted by Humayun Dar and John Presley (2000), who suggested that equity financing is only optimal for sufficiently small-scale operations, wherein the cost of monitoring is minimal.
9. For a detailed analysis of this *fatwa*, including suggestions of its incoherence since bank assets in Egypt are restricted to interest-bearing loans, see El-Gamal (2003).
10. This literature arose as a response to the realization that managers may pursue their own interests, rather than those of shareholders, following the publication of Berle and Means (1932). For major advances in this field, see Schleifer and Vishny (1997).
11. For discussions of the uniqueness of deposit-based banking, see Wood (1970) and Hodgman (1961).
12. See El-Gamal (2000) for extension of the 'mark to market' setting, as well as discussion of dynamic inconsistencies leading to uncontrollable debt cycles.
13. See Al-Misri (1997, pp. 39–48) for multiple quotations from all major schools of jurisprudence establishing that 'time has a share in the price'.
14. The vast majority of jurists from all schools also reasoned that ownership of the lent property is transferred to the lessor (upon receipt for the majority of Hanafis, Shafi'is and Hanbalis, and upon conclusion of the contract for the Malikis); c.f. Al-Zuhayli (El-Gamal, trans., 2003, vol.1, pp. 373–4).
15. Interestingly, in his famous fatwa in Detroit permitting the use of home mortgage financing in America, Dr Yusuf Al-Qaradawi reasoned that the beneficiary in this case is the borrower, who gets to live in a better house, and to build home equity. Since Muslims in a non-Muslim land are not required to establish social aspects of the religion, according to the opinion of Abu-Hanifa that was accepted by Al-Qaradawi in this fatwa, they are only required to adhere to personal aspects of the religion. In this regard, the rules of *riba* would make sense as a social custom, for example providing a form of implicit social insurance, as argued by Glaeser and Scheinkman (1998). Otherwise, that is, in the absence of this social function of the prohibition, Al-Qaradawi seemed to reason, as long as the Muslim was not a victim of extreme inequity, the prohibition does not play any useful role.
16. This argument was articulated in Al-Misri (2004).
17. Of course, Western legal and regulatory systems have built-in provisions against predatory lending, especially to minority groups. However, there are difficulties in quantifying the appropriate interest rate to charge debtors with very high levels of credit risk; c.f. Hibbard (2005). See also Hagerty and Hallinan (2005).

18. See, for example, MacPherson (1999), for a history of the global credit union movement. See also El-Gamal (2005) on the role of mutuality in combating rent-seeking Shari'a arbitrage behaviour in Islamic finance.

References

AAOIFI (Accounting & Auditing Organization for Islamic Financial Institution) (2004), *Accounting, Auditing and Governance Standards for Islamic Financial Institutions 2003–4*, Manama: AAOIFI.

Abu Ghuddah, A. and E. Khujah (eds) (1997a), *Fatawa Nadawat al-Baraka*, Jeddah: Dalla Al-Baraka.

Abu Ghuddah, A. and E. Khujah (eds) (1997b), *Fatawa al-Hay'ah al-Shar'iyyah lil-Barakah*, Jeddah: Dalla Al-Baraka.

Allen, F. and D. Gale (2000), *Comparing Financial Systems*, Cambridge, MA: MIT Press.

Al-Misri, R. (1997), *Bay' al-Taqsit: Tahlil Fiqhi wa Iqtisadi*, Damascus: Dar al-Qalam.

Al-Misri, R. (2004), 'Hal al-Fa'idah Haram bi-Jami' Ashkaliha?' (Are all forms of interest prohibited?), *Majallat Jami'at al-Malik 'Abdulaziz lil-Iqtisad al-Islami*, **17** (1), 87–92.

Altunbas, Y., L. Evans and P. Molyneux (2001), 'Bank ownership and efficiency', *Journal of Money, Credit and Banking*, **33** (4), 926–54.

Al-Zuhayli, W. (2003), *Financial Transactions in Islamic Jurisprudence*, (trans. M. El-Gamal) Damascus: Dar al-Fikr.

Berle, A. and G. Means (1932), *The Modern Corporation and Private Property*, New York: Commerce Clearing House.

Boyd, J., C. Chang and B. Smith (1998), 'Moral hazard under commercial and universal banking', *Journal of Money, Credit and Banking*, **30** (3), 426–68.

Dar, H. and J. Presley (2000), 'Lack of profit–loss sharing in Islamic banking: management and control imbalances', *International Journal of Islamic Financial Services*, **2** (2).

El-Gamal, M. (1999), 'Involving Islamic banks in central bank open market operations', *Thunderbird International Business Review*, **41** (4/5), 501–21.

El-Gamal, M. (2000), 'An economic explication of the prohibition of Riba in classical Islamic jurisprudence', *Proceedings of the Third Harvard University Islamic Finance Forum*, Center for Middle Eastern Studies, Cambridge, MA: Harvard University Press.

El-Gamal, M. (2003), 'Interest and the paradox of contemporary Islamic law and finance', *Fordham International Law Journal*, **27** (1), 108–49.

El-Gamal, M. (2005), 'Mutuality as an antidote to rent-seeking shari'a-arbitrage in Islamic finance', *mimeograph* (http://www.ruf.rice.edu/~elgamalfiles/ Mutu-ality.pdf).

Fama, E. (1980), 'Agency problems and the theory of the firm', *Journal of Political Economy*, **88** (2), 288–307.

Fama, E. and M. Jensen (1983a), 'Agency problems and residual claims', *Journal of Law and Economics*, **26** (2), 327–49.

Fama, E. and M. Jensen (1983b), 'Separation of ownership and control', *Journal of Law and Economics*, **26** (2), 301–25.

Glaeser, E. and J. Scheinkman (1998), 'Neither a borrower nor a lender be: an economic analysis of interest restrictions and usury laws', *Journal of Law and Economics*, **41** (1), 1–36.

Hagerty, J. and J. Hallinan (2005), 'Blacks are much more likely to get subprime mortgages: weaker lender competition in some low-income areas is cited as part of the problem', *Wall Street Journal*, 11 April, p. A2.

Hansmann, H. (1996), *The Ownership of Enterprise*, Cambridge, MA: Harvard University Press.

Hart, O. and J. Moore (1991), 'A theory of debt based on the inalienability of human capital', *Quarterly Journal of Economics*, **109** (4), 841–79.

Hibbard, J. (2005), 'The Fed eyes sub-prime loans: new disclosure rules aim to flush out discriminatory rates' (cover story), *Business Week*, 11 April.

Hodgman, D. (1961), 'The deposit relationship and commercial bank investment behavior', *The Review of Economics and Statistics*, **43** (3), 257–68.

Humud, S. (1976), *Tatwir al-A'mal al-Masrifiyya bima Yattafiqu wa al-Sari'ah al-Islamiyyah*, Cairo: Dar al-Ittihad al-'Arabi lil-Tiba'a.

Ibn Rushd, M. (1997), *Bidayat al-Mujtahid wa Nihayat al-Muqtasid*, Beirut: Dar al-Ma'rifah.

MacPherson, I. (1999), *Hands Around the Globe*, Madison, WI: World Council of Credit Unions.

Mawdudi, A. (1977), *Interest (Sood)*, Lahore: Islamic Publications.

Micaela, R. and K. Womack (1999), 'Conflict of interest and the credibility of underwriter analyst recommendations', *Review of Financial Studies*, **12** (4), 653–86.

O'Hara, M. (1988), 'Property rights and the financial firm', *Journal of Law and Economics*, **24** (2), 317–32.

Pari, M. (1996), 'Commercial banks in investment banking: conflict of interest or certification role?', *Journal of Financial Economics*, **40**, 373–401.

Qutb, S. (n.d.), *Tafsir Ayat al-Riba*, Cairo: Dar al-Buhuth al-'Ilmiyyah.

Rasmusen, E. (1988), 'Mutual banks and stock banks', *Journal of Law and Economics*, **31** (2), 395–421.
Saeed, A. (1999), *Islamic Banking and Interest*, Leiden: Brill.
Schleifer, A. and R. Vishny (1997), 'A survey of corporate governance', *Journal of Finance*, **52** (2), 727–83.
Siddiqi, M.N. (1983), *Banking without Interest*, Leicester: Islamic Foundation.
Townsend, R. (1979), 'Optimal contracts and competitive markets with costly state verification', *Journal of Economic Theory*, **21**, 265–93.
Uzair, M. (1955), *An Outline of Interestless Banking*, Karachi: Raihan Publications.
Warde, I. (2000), *Islamic Finance and the Global Economy*, Edinburgh: Edinburgh University Press.
Wood, J. (1970), 'Two notes on the uniqueness of commercial banks', *Journal of Finance,* **25** (1), 99–108.

21 Challenges facing the Islamic financial industry
M. Umer Chapra[1]

Introduction

The prohibition of interest in Islam, as in some other major religions, and the aspiration of Muslims to make this prohibition a practical reality in their economies, has led to the establishment of the Islamic financial services industry (IFSI). The industry has made substantial progress over the last three decades after the establishment of the first Islamic bank (Dubai Islamic Bank) in 1975. The number of institutions offering *shari'a*-compliant services has risen, as has the number of conventional banks that have opened Islamic windows and branches. The total volume of assets that all these institutions manage has risen rapidly and so has the international acceptance of Islamic finance. Nevertheless, the industry is still in its formative stage and faces a number of challenges that need to be addressed to enable it to continue its rapid expansion without facing any serious crisis and, thereby, acquire greater respectability and a much greater share of the international financial market. This raises the question of what these challenges are and how they can be faced.

The challenges

Challenges arise essentially from the disparity that exists between the vision of a system (where it wishes to go) and its present position (the progress that it has made so far). The greater the disparity, the more serious may be the challenges faced. The most crucial challenge that all financial systems, including the Islamic, face at present is to be sound and efficient and free from crises and instability. All the guidelines laid down by the Basle Committee for Banking Supervision (BCBS) need to be carefully considered and implemented to meet this challenge satisfactorily. However, even if the Islamic financial system meets this challenge successfully, it may still not be able to be a genuine reflection of Islamic teachings if it fails to realize the vision of Islam by actualizing justice, which is one of the primary objectives of Islam (*maqasid al- shari'a*) (al-Qur'an, 57:25). It may not be possible to realize this vision unless all human institutions, including the financial system, contribute positively towards this end. The financial system may be able to promote justice if, in addition to being strong and stable, it satisfies at least two conditions. One of these is risk sharing by the financier so as not to shift the entire burden of losses on the entrepreneur, and the other is equitable distribution of the benefit of deposits provided by a wide spectrum of depositors to a similarly wide spectrum of the population by helping eliminate poverty, expand employment and self-employment opportunities, and reduce inequalities of income and wealth.

The first condition of justice

The first condition would be satisfied if the profit as well as loss is shared equitably by both the financier and the entrepreneur. It is against the principles of justice that, in the event of a loss, the entrepreneur bears the entire loss in spite of his hard work and entrepreneurship, while the financier gets a positive rate of return without doing anything. The sharing of risks will lead to an increase in the reliance on equity and profit-and-loss-sharing (PLS) modes of financing (*mudaraba* and *musharaka*)[2] and reduce that on debt. This will help introduce greater discipline into the financial system. If investment depositors share in the risk to get a return, they will be motivated to take more interest in the affairs of their banks and demand greater transparency and more effective management. Similarly, if the bankers also participate in the risk, they will also be motivated to evaluate loan applications more rigorously.

The introduction of such a discipline in the financial system should help reduce funds available for speculation and unproductive spending and, thereby, control excessive expansion of credit and living beyond means by both the public and the private sectors. Moreover, since the rate of profit is only known ex post, it cannot change daily like the rate of interest. This, along with the check on excessive credit expansion, should help reduce volatility in the movement of funds and, thereby, inject greater stability into the financial markets (see Chapra, 2002, for details). No wonder Mills and Presley have stated: 'There are sufficient grounds to wish that, in hindsight, the prohibition of usury had not been undermined in Europe in the sixteenth century. More practical wisdom was embodied in the moral stand against usury than was then realized' (1999, p. 120).

However, since it is not possible for the *mudaraba* and *musharaka* modes to accommodate all different types of financial needs, Islam has also allowed some other modes of financing (*murabaha, ijara* (leasing), *salam* and *istisnaa*),[3] which create debt rather than equity and in which the rate of return gets fixed in advance. *Sukuk* (asset-based Islamic bonds) have also now gained prominence as instruments for raising large amounts of finance by governments and corporations. These are based primarily on the *ijara* mode and have the advantage of converting leasing assets into *shari'a*-compatible financial assets which are tradeable in the market (for details see Ali, 2005). There is hardly any significant need for financing that all the different modes of Islamic finance cannot together help satisfy. Nevertheless, it should be possible to create more *shari'a*-compatible modes in the future in response to need.

It may be argued that the above-specified debt-creating modes with a predetermined rate of return are not different from the interest-based modes. This is not so because the debt that arises in the case of these modes does not arise as a result of lending and borrowing on interest. It rather arises as a result of the sale or lease of goods and services on a deferred payment basis. The rate of return becomes a part of the price of the goods or services sold or leased. The debt, therefore, gets linked with the growth of the economy. There is, however, a danger that these modes may degenerate into purely financing devices. The *shari'a* has therefore laid down certain conditions for their validity. The most important of these conditions is the requirement that the seller or the lessor cannot sell or lease what he/she does not own and possess. When the financer purchases an asset for the purpose of sale or lease, he converts cash into real assets and, thereby, takes risk. The return he gets is a reward for the risk that he has taken.

The second condition of justice
Fulfilment of the second condition of justice about the equitable distribution of credit is imperative because it would help realize the vision of Islam which is not only to improve the condition of the oppressed but also to make them leaders and heirs and to establish

them firmly on earth (al-Qur'an, 28:5–6). One of the ways of actualizing this vision would be to spread the benefit of resources that become available to banks from a wide spectrum of depositors to a similarly large spectrum of the society rather than to just a few rich individuals, as the banking systems generally end up doing at present. Islamic finance will not be able to fulfil this criterion of justice if increased financing does not become available to the poor and the middle-class entrepreneurs. A number of these people have the talent, drive and innovative ability to establish a successful business enterprise, but do not have the resources they need to make use of their talents. Availability of finance would perform the function of pump priming in enabling such talented individuals not only to advance themselves economically but also to make a positive contribution to their economy.

The dream and the reality
The way the Islamic financial system has progressed so far is not in accordance with this vision. It has not been able to come out of the straitjacket of conventional finance. The use of equity and PLS modes has been scant, while that of the debt-creating sales-based modes has been predominant. Moreover, even in the case of debt-creating modes, all Islamic banks and branches or windows of conventional banks do not necessarily fulfil the conditions laid down by the *shari'a*. They try to adopt different legal stratagems (*hiyal*) to transfer the entire risk to the purchasers or the lessees, in violation of the first condition of justice stated above. Significant progress does not seem to have been made even towards fulfilment of the second condition of justice, which is realization of equitable distribution of credit. The result is that the Islamic financial system, as it is being practised, does not appear to a number of its critics to be a genuine reflection of Islamic finance.

How to be genuine (1): greater reliance on equity and PLS modes
The most important challenge facing the Islamic financial industry is to be as genuine and authentic a reflection of Islamic teachings as is possible within the present-day environment. This would happen not only when interest was removed definitively from the economy but also when the two conditions for realizing justice specified in the introduction were genuinely fulfilled. The system would lose its *raison d'être* if it did not make significant progress in promoting greater reliance on equity and PLS financing in the financial system and bringing about a more equitable distribution of credit with the objective of eliminating poverty, expanding employment and self-employment opportunities and reducing inequalities of income and wealth. It is only this which will enable the Islamic financial system to gain credibility in the eyes of the Muslim masses.

This raises the question of why the system has failed to make significant headway in using the equity and PLS modes and to bring about a relatively more equitable distribution of credit. It may not be possible to answer this question without answering some other questions, such as the following. Did the system ever operate successfully in Islamic history? What were the factors that contributed to its success? Can the system operate in a changed environment? If it can, then what are the different institutions that need to be established to enable it to operate in the modern environment when the favourable conditions that existed during the Classical period do not exist any more?

Financial intermediation in Islamic history
From a very early stage in Islamic history, Muslims were able to establish a financial system without interest for mobilizing resources to finance productive activities and consumer needs. The system to finance productive activities was based largely on the profit-and-loss-sharing (PLS) modes of *mudaraba* and *musharaka*. Other modes, including interest-free loans (*qard hasan*), were also used to help finance purchases on credit by consumers as well as businesses and to help the needy.

There are no empirical data available about the operation of the Islamic system in the past. However, whatever historical evidence is available seems to indicate that the system worked quite effectively during the heyday of Muslim civilization and for centuries thereafter. According to Udovitch, the Islamic modes of financing *(mudaraba* and *musharaka)* were able to mobilize the 'entire reservoir of monetary resources of the medieval Islamic world' for financing agriculture, crafts, manufacturing and long-distance trade. They were used not only by Muslims but also by Jews and Christians (Udovitch, 1970, pp. 180, 261) to the extent that interest-bearing loans and other overly usurious practices were not in common use (Udovitch, 1981, p. 257; see also p. 268). According to Goitein, breach of the Jewish, Christian and Islamic law against interest was found in the Geniza documents 'only once in the record of a judgment', even though 'an unusually large amount of Geniza documents deal with credit' (Goitein, 1967, pp. 255 and 250, respectively. See also Goitein, 1966, pp. 271–4). Schatzmiller has also concluded that 'financial capital was developed during the early period by a considerable number of owners of monetary funds and precious metals, without the supposed interdiction of *riba*, usury, hampering it in any way' (Schatzmiller, 1994, p. 102).

Financiers were known in the early Muslim history as *sarrafs*.[4] By the time of the Abbasid Caliph al-Muqtadir (908–932), they had started performing most of the basic functions of modern banks (Fischel, 1992). They had their own markets, something akin to Wall Street in New York and Lombard Street in London, and fulfilled all the banking needs of commerce, industry and agriculture (Duri, 1986, p. 898) within the constraints of the then-prevailing technological environment. However, since the *sarrafs* were not banks in the strictly technical modern sense, Udovitch has preferred to call them 'bankers without banks' (Udovitch, 1981).

The legal instruments necessary for the extensive use of financing through *mudaraba* and *musharaka* were already available in the earliest Islamic period (Udovitch, 1970, p. 77). These instruments, which constituted an important feature of both trade and industry and provided a framework for investment, are found in a developed form in some of the earliest Islamic legal works (ibid., pp. 77–8). Some of the institutions, practices and concepts already fully developed in the Islamic legal sources of the late eighth century did not appear in the West, according to Udovitch, until several centuries later (ibid., p. 261).

The ability to mobilize the financial resources, along with a combination of several economic and political factors (for a discussion of some of these, see Chapra, 2000, pp. 173–85), provided a great boost to trade which flourished from Morocco and Spain in the West, to India and China in the East, Central Asia in the North, and Africa in the South. The extension of Islamic trade influence is indicated not only by the available historical documents but also by the Muslim coins of the seventh to the eleventh centuries found through excavations in countries like Russia, Finland, Sweden, Norway and the British Isles which were on the outskirts of the then-Muslim world (Kramers, 1952,

p. 100; see also pp. 101–6). The expansion of trade generated prosperity, which, in turn, 'made possible a development of industrial skill which brought the artistic value of the products to an unequalled height' (Udovitch, 1970, p. 104). Since businesses were in general small, even the poor and middle-class entrepreneurs seem to have flourished. This takes us to the second question of what were the factors that led to the success of primary modes in the classical period.

Factors that contributed to past success
All the functions that the *sarrafs* performed demanded minimization of the principal/agent conflict of interest so as to ensure the total confidence of all the stakeholders (*sarrafs*, and providers and users of funds) in each other. This leads us to the questions of what were the factors that made it possible to minimize the principal/agent conflict of interest in the Classical period and what can be done in modern times to create the same trust and confidence of the stakeholders in each other when the conditions have changed.

The answer lies in the support that the system received from an enabling environment. First, the market mechanism worked effectively and induced all participants in the market to do their jobs honestly and efficiently in their own long-term self-interest. This received further support from Islamic values which were generally observed by the market participants.

Second, the *sarrafs* operated in communities which were far smaller compared with the communities in which modern banks operate. Accordingly, the providers and users of funds as well as the *sarrafs* were all well-known to each other. This was further reinforced by membership of nearly all participants in tribes, guilds, fraternities or sufi orders. This established a 'moral community' with social solidarity and mutual trust and cooperation. This acted as an 'informal contact enforcement mechanism' and served as a deterrent against cheating and fraud. Anyone who tried to cheat or procrastinate unduly became ostracized. The entire community would refrain from doing business with the guilty party. This, along with the effective operation of market forces, was further reinforced by the then-prevailing religious environment which helped create self-enforcement of religious values. This climate of mutual trust and cooperation, according to Udovitch, was not based on 'a casual or occasional favour', but rather 'a recognized commercial practice looming large in the discussion of partnership [*mudaraba* and *musharaka*] on the same level as deposit, pledge and similar contracts' (Udovitch, 1970, p. 102; see also Grief, 1997; Rauch, 2001).

Third, the economic environment was also less complex and, in general, there seems to have been less volatility in economic variables, particularly prices and exchange rates, than what prevails in modern times.

Fourth, the *sarrafs* were individual proprietors or partnership firms and the separation of ownership and control was not a problem. The self-interest of the *sarrafs* themselves as well as the users of funds reinforced mutual trust and confidence in a system in which *mudaraba* and *musharaka* were the primary methods available for mobilizing financial resources. They brought to the disposal of commerce and industry the 'entire reservoir of monetary resources of the medieval Islamic world' and served as a 'means of financing, and to some extent, insuring commercial ventures, as well as providing the combination of skills and services for their satisfactory execution' (Udovitch, 1970, pp. 180, 261). The absence of a predetermined positive rate of return made everyone (rich and poor) a prospective candidate for financing by the *sarrafs*, provided that he had the necessary skill and experience for doing business successfully along with a reputation for honesty. The poor were not, therefore, necessarily at a disadvantage.

Fifth, the legal instruments necessary for the extensive use of financing through *mudaraba* and *musharaka* were also already available in the earliest Islamic period (Udovitch, 1970, p. 77). These instruments, which are found in a developed form in some of the earliest Islamic legal works (ibid., 1970, pp. 77–8), were inspired by the Qur'anic requirement that all loan transactions must be consummated in writing with witnesses (al-Qur'an, 2.282). Written instruments thus became an important feature of financial intermediation.

Last, but not least, what helped further was the strength and independence of the judicial system (*mahkamah al-qada*). The courts helped ensure the honest fulfilment of contractual obligations. It was also possible to get justice promptly at a low cost in terms of time, trouble and money. The office of the *qadi* (judge) 'proved to be', according to Schacht, 'one of the most rigorous institutions evolved by Islamic society'. The *qadis*, along with the *ulama* (religious scholars), 'played an important part in maintaining Islamic civilization, and in times of disorder they constituted an element of stability' (Schacht, 1970, p. 558).

Consequently, a climate of trust prevailed, conflict of interest was minimized and the transactions costs of enforcing contracts were reduced. The system worked effectively. This led to an expansion of trade and helped boost commerce, industry and agriculture to an optimum level, as indicated earlier.

Institutions needed to enable the system to work
This takes us to the next question of whether the revival of the *mudaraba* and *musharaka* modes of Islamic finance can operate successfully in the modern world when the enabling environment prevailing in the Classical period does not exist. Banks operate in relatively larger communities where all the different stakeholders (shareholders, depositors, directors, management and users of funds) do not necessarily know each other very well. In a situation of anonymity that now prevails, depositors may hesitate to entrust their savings to banks, and the banks may also be reluctant to provide financing to users on a PLS basis unless the moral hazard is reduced and a climate of trust is created between the principals and agents.

The question that, therefore, needs to be addressed is how to recreate the climate of trust that prevailed in the past. Without effectively addressing this question the primary modes of *mudaraba* and *musharaka* financing may not be able to gain ground and the banks may even try to avoid the risks associated with the secondary modes by adopting different stratagems *(hiyal)*. Consequently, the claimed benefits of the Islamic system resulting from the greater reliance on equity and PLS modes may also fail to be realized. It is therefore necessary to create a new environment compatible with modern conditions to help minimize the risks and to create a climate of trust and confidence among all the participants in the Islamic financial market.

Risks are not a peculiarity of only the Islamic financial system. They are present in all financial systems: risks associated with fiduciary money, interest rate and exchange rate fluctuations, loan default, operational failures, natural calamities and a range of other human, managerial and environmental weaknesses. The Islamic financial system is equally exposed to all these risks. The only risk that gets added to the Islamic financial system is that which arises from the greater reliance on equity and PLS modes. Here also the Islamic financial system is not unique. Corporations as well as universal banks have long been exposed to similar risks and their experience in handling them can provide valuable insights to Islamic banks.

Of course it is not possible to replicate the environment that prevailed during the Classical period. It is possible, however, to create institutions that may help minimize the risks associated with anonymity, moral hazard, principal/agent conflict of interest, and late settlement of financial obligations. These institutions should be able to help the banks in different ways. They should enable them to obtain reliable information about their clients and to ensure that the funds lent by them to their clients are employed efficiently according to agreement and that the profit declared by them reflects the true picture of the business. They should also help them receive repayments on schedule, and get justice promptly in case of dispute with, or wilful procrastination by, their clients. They should also enable banks to gain liquidity when it is needed by them owing to unforeseen circumstances. The establishment of such institutions should go a long way to providing the favourable environment that was available to the *sarrafs* in the Classical period. If such institutions are not available, then even banks with the best corporate governance may face difficulties and the movement of the Islamic financial system in the desired direction may not be able to gain momentum. Some of the institutions that need to be created are briefly indicated below.

Credit-rating agencies, chambers of commerce, and trade associations   One of these shared institutions is credit-rating agencies which rate banks themselves as well as their counterparties. In the relatively smaller communities of the Classical period, such rating was available informally without the help of any formal credit-rating agency through the operation of market discipline and the intimate personal contacts of the parties concerned. This was further reinforced by the built-in discipline of the socioeconomic structure of tribes, guilds, fraternities and sufi circles. Now it is the credit-rating agencies and chambers of commerce and trade associations which can perform this task. Most Muslim countries do not at present have private credit-rating agencies. Moreover the chambers of commerce and trade associations are perhaps not concerned with enforcement of the necessary discipline.

The International Islamic Rating Agency (IIRA), which has been established in Bahrain, is a step in the right direction. It will perform a number of functions including the rating of all public and private issuers of credit instruments with respect to their financial strength, fiduciary risk and creditworthiness. It will also assess the compliance with the *shari'a* of financial instruments as well as their issuers. It will have a *shari'a* board of its own to advise it on *shari'a* issues. It will, thus, complement the work of the Islamic Financial Services Board (IFSB) and the Accounting and Auditing Organization for Islamic Financial Institutions (AAOIFI) in setting standards for adequate disclosure. This will help promote an international capital market for Islamic financial instruments.

Even though the IIRA will rate private non-bank organizations, it will not be possible for it to rate the thousands of counterparties with whom banks deal. It would therefore be desirable to have private credit-rating agencies in all Muslim countries to facilitate the task of Islamic banks in choosing their counterparties. In fact the establishment of such institutions would also facilitate the task of the IIRA itself in getting the information that is necessary to know the financial strength, fiduciary risk and creditworthiness of even those private issuers of financial instruments whose rating the IIRA wishes to provide.

Centralized shari'a board   It is also necessary to standardize the *shari'a* modes of financing to the extent to which this is possible. Some differences of opinion are bound to remain and this may be healthy for the financial system because it will provide different alternatives for doing business instead of imposing a rigid conformity. The establishment of a centralized *shari'a board* should help create the needed harmony. In the absence of such a centralized board every bank is under an obligation to have its own *shari'a* board. This is very costly, particularly for smaller banks. Moreover, the existence of a large number of *shari'a* boards leads to conflicting opinions, which creates inconsistency and uncertainty. It may be expected that, with the passage of time and the free discussion of all controversial issues, the conflicts may tend to be gradually resolved. However, in the initial phase of evolution, such a centralized board seems to be necessary to minimize the differences and to standardize the instruments of Islamic finance. Such standardization will also help pave the way for the creation of an Islamic financial market. While some Muslim countries have already standardized their instruments, it may be desirable for other countries to do the same. It is also necessary that the standardization should take place, even at the level of all Muslim countries. The *Shari'a* Board of the Islamic Development Bank should be able to complement and accelerate the work of the OIC (Organization of the Islamic Conference) *Fiqh* Committee in the pursuit of this goal.

Shari'a *clearance and audit*   Among the most crucial challenges before an Islamic bank is to create confidence in its depositors as well as all the other operators in the market about the harmony of its operations with the *shari'a*. For this purpose two important steps need to be taken. The first step is to get clearance from a *shari'a* board about the *shari'a* compatibility of all its products. The second step is to provide an assurance that all its transactions are actually in conformity with the verdicts of the *shari'a* board. The first step is like going to a legal expert to ascertain whether a specific action of the bank is in conformity with the country's laws and, if not, what changes need to be introduced in it to make it so. The second is what auditors and banking supervisors do: ensuring that none of the bank's transactions violates the country's laws.

The *shari'a* boards are like legal experts. They can only perform the first task. It is difficult for them to perform the second task, which demands a review of all, or at least a random sample of, the different transactions that have taken place in different branches of the bank to ensure that they are in conformity with the verdict of the *shari'a* board. This demands a visit to the bank's premises to examine its operations in the same way as auditors and supervisors do. It is generally assumed that the *shari'a* boards do perform this task. However, members of the *shari'a* board do not have either the time or the staff to perform such a task effectively. The question that therefore arises is how to ensure the implementation of *shari'a* board decisions by the bank management. If this is not ensured the existence of the *shari'a* board loses its meaning. There are three alternatives which may be considered for this purpose.

One of these is for the supervisory authority itself to undertake the *shari'a* audit in the course of its normal supervisory visits. This may not be considered desirable by Islamic banks in countries where the government and supervisory authorities are not favourably inclined towards Islamic banking. However it has the advantage that, if the supervisory authorities perform the *shari'a* audit, they will also try to standardize the *fiqhi* decisions.

The second, more preferable, alternative is to establish independent *shari'a* audit firms in the private sector. These firms would have to hire and train sufficient staff to examine the transactions of banks with a view to determining whether they are in conformity with the *shari'a*. This alternative has the disadvantage that it would involve a proliferation of institutions. Inspectors from three different institutions would knock at the doors of banks at different times. The first of these inspectors would be from the supervisory authority which sends examiners to banks to determine the conformity of their operations with the country's laws and the principles of safe and sound banking. Others would be the *shari'a* auditors who go to the bank to determine the conformity of its operations with the *shari'a*. The third group would be the chartered auditors who would go to ensure that the bank's financial statements had been prepared in conformity with the generally accepted accounting standards. This might not be convenient for banks because it would keep a number of their staff engaged in assisting three inspectors at different times, and thus add to their costs.

A third, and even more preferable, alternative is for the existing chartered audit firms to acquire the necessary expertise in the *shari'a* to enable them to undertake the *shari'a* audit. This will help avoid the proliferation of institutions with which Islamic banks have to deal. The banks would probably prefer this alternative because it will be more convenient for them to have the *shari'a* audit at the same time as the accounts audit.

External audit   The growing complexity of the banking business as well as the crises that the international financial system has witnessed have raised the function of external audit to a position of critical importance in all financial systems. It is, however, even more demanding and challenging in the Islamic financial system. It would be necessary for the external auditor to ensure not only that the bank's financial statements are prepared in all material respects in conformity with the professionally accepted financial reporting standards but also that the profit or loss declared by the bank truly reflects the bank's condition and that its profit has been derived without violating the teachings of the *shari'a*.

It is conventionally not considered to be the task of auditors to perform *shari'a* audit. They are not even equipped at present to do so. However, if this task is assigned to them in the light of what has been discussed above under the subject of *shari'a* audit, then the external auditors will have to create the necessary expertise to perform this task. This would demand that the training of auditors also include necessary training in the financial aspects of the *shari'a*, just as it includes training in auditing and law. If such training proves to be too cumbersome for the auditors, it may also be possible for the auditing firm to hire *shari'a* scholars and provide them with some necessary background in auditing.

For the external auditor to be able to do an effective job of auditing, he must have independence and objectivity. The experience of the auditing firm Arthur Andersen has clearly revealed that there should not be anything that indicates the auditor's vested interest in protecting the bank's management. It is only such impartial auditing that would create trust in the auditor's report and promote confidence in the bank. Even though it is the job of the internal controls system to prevent, or detect and correct, material misstatements arising from fraud and error, the external auditor cannot be exonerated from the responsibility of ensuring that this has been done conscientiously. He will have to design and carry out audit procedures in a way that would help reduce to an acceptably low level the risk of giving an inappropriate audit opinion. The shareholders, the Board of Directors, the management and the depositors all depend on his report and it would be a pity if he failed them. The auditor's success in his job would, however, depend greatly on the work of internal auditing. If internal auditing is weak, the external auditor may find it very difficult to do his job effectively. The strength of the internal auditor is greatly influenced by the competence, conscientiousness and integrity of the Board of Directors and management.

Shari'a courts or banking tribunals   Another indispensable requirement of the Islamic financial system is availability of some judicial facility that would help the banks recover their loans promptly from clients who are unjustifiably procrastinating about repayment and also help bank clients get prompt justice at a low cost when the bank is itself acting unjustly. The establishment of *shari'a* courts or banking tribunals would be very helpful in getting prompt verdicts on the disputes of banks with their clients, and vice versa. Normal civil court verdicts usually take several years in most Muslim countries.

The *shari'a* courts or banking tribunals would have a greater deterrent effect if the names of banks or their clients whom these courts have found to be guilty were also published in newspapers. The fear of getting bad publicity would help minimize contractual violations. Furthermore, the names of parties who violate habitually may also be sent to the chambers of commerce and trade associations for blacklisting to create the same effect that social ostracism had in the Classical period.

Audit organization   It may also be desirable to have an audit organization jointly owned by banks to evaluate the profit-and-loss accounts of those of their clients who the banks feel have tried to cheat them in a PLS arrangement. The fear of being exposed to a thorough check of their accounts by such an organization would complement the market forces in helping minimize the effort made by users of funds on a PLS basis to shortchange the banks.

The creation of such an audit organization would save the individual financial institution the need to hire a large staff of auditors. It would thus create a substantial economy in expenses for all financial institutions. It would also give assurance to investors who provide their funds directly to businesses that, in case of need, they will be able to have the accounts properly examined by a qualified, impartial institution.

The whole concept of 'audit' may have to undergo a transformation in the case of primary modes of Islamic finance.[5] Conventional auditing is 'not expressly designed to uncover management frauds' (Elliot and Willingham, 1980, p. viii). If the auditor performs a diligent audit and evaluates the financial statements according to 'the generally accepted accounting principles', the professional obligations of the auditor have been fulfilled. The auditor has no responsibility to detect management malpractices or to determine the 'real' profit. He does not have the responsibility to check and to question (Lechner, 1998, p. 143). Accounting firms generally tend to accommodate their clients, particularly the big clients, who hire them. The auditor would fail in discharging his responsibility in a PLS system if he did not try to detect and disclose dishonest and questionable acts of the management and to determine the real amount of profit so as to ensure a 'fair' return to the shareholders and *mudaraba* depositors.

Qualified pool of talent   To enable the Islamic system to fulfil the requirements of the *shari'a* as well as the BCBS, it is necessary to train both the staff and clients of banks, as well as the general public, in the principles of Islamic banking. This will not be enough, however. It is also necessary to create a large pool of experts and highly qualified professionals with in-depth knowledge of not only the *shari'a* and its objectives, but also Islamic and conventional finance and financial engineering. This would be possible if first-rate institutions were created for this purpose with the collaboration of financial institutions, central banks, universities and the governments. Directors and senior management of Islamic banks as well as *shari'a* advisers should also be required to take such courses. If the central banks as well as universities could make arrangements for this purpose, as is done in the case of conventional banking, the task of Islamic banks would become relatively easier.

Islamic financial market   It is also necessary to create an Islamic financial market. The absence of a secondary market for Islamic financial instruments makes it extremely difficult for Islamic banks to manage their liquidity. Consequently, they end up maintaining a relatively higher ratio of liquidity than that which is generally maintained by conventional banks. This affects their profitability and competitiveness. The establishment of the Islamic Financial Services Board (IFSB), International Islamic Financial Market (IIFM) and the Liquidity Management Centre (LMC) will help provide the institutional infrastructure needed for an Islamic financial market.

The IFSB will help promote uniform regulatory and supervisory practices and prudential standards for Islamic financial institutions in the same way as is done by the BCBS. The IIFM will enhance cooperation in the field of finance among Muslim countries and financial institutions by promoting product development and harmonizing trading practices. This will serve as a catalyst for the development and promotion of a larger supply of *shari'a*-compatible financial instruments. The LMC will serve as an operating arm of the IIFM in the effort to facilitate the creation of an inter-bank money market that will enable Islamic financial institutions to manage their assets and liabilities effectively. It will create short-term *shari'a*-compatible investment opportunities by providing liquid, tradeable, asset-backed treasury instruments (*sukuks*) in which these institutions can invest their surplus liquidity. It will also facilitate the sourcing and securitization of assets and trade actively in *sukuks* by offering buy/sell quotations. The three institutions will together help establish an Islamic financial market by removing the drawback experienced by Islamic banks of the lack of standardization of terms and instruments and the non-availability of quality *shari'a*-compatible assets for trading in the secondary markets. This should help the Islamic financial system to expand at a faster rate in the future and create for itself a larger niche in the financial markets of Muslim countries.

Lender of last resort   Islamic banks also need some facility akin to the lender-of-last resort which is available to conventional banks to overcome liquidity crises when they occur suddenly as the result of unforeseen circumstances. Such a facility is available to Islamic banks at present on the basis of interest and is, therefore, unacceptable because of its incompatibility with the *shari'a*. Its use exposes Islamic banks to a great deal of criticism. It may be worth considering the creation of a common pool at the central banks to provide mutual accommodation to banks in case of need. All banks may be required to contribute a certain mutually agreed percentage of their deposits to this common pool, just as they do in the case of statutory reserve requirements. They would then have the right to borrow interest-free from this pool with the condition that the net use of this facility is zero (that is, drawings do not exceed contributions) over a given period of time.[6] In a crisis, the central banks may allow a bank to exceed the limit, with appropriate penalties, warning and a suitable corrective programme. This will in a way be a more organized means of replacing the framework for mutual cooperation that prevailed among the *sarrafs* during the Classical period.

Reform of the stock market   Reform of the stock market is also necessary in the light of Islamic teachings to ensure that share prices reflect underlying business conditions and do not fluctuate erratically as a result of speculative forces. The discipline that the *shari'a* helps introduce through the prohibition of short sales, or the sale of what one does not own and possess, should greatly help in realizing this goal (See Chapra, 2002). In addition, rules and procedures need to be streamlined and enforced to protect investors and ensure stability and sanity in the stock market. This will help raise the confidence of savers and investors in the system and enable them to buy or sell shares in response to their circumstances or their perceptions of future market developments. Such a reform would constitute one of the most important pillars for supporting the edifice of an interest-free and equity-based economy.[7]

How to be genuine (2): equitable distribution of credit
Finance has always been a powerful political, social and economic weapon in the world. It plays a prominent role, not only in the allocation and distribution of scarce resources, but also in the stability and growth of an economy. It also determines the power base, social status and economic condition of an individual in the economy. Hence no socio-economic reform in Muslim societies can be meaningful unless the financial system is also restructured in conformity with the socioeconomic goals of Islam in which justice occupies a prominent place.

Since the resources of financial institutions come from deposits placed by a wide cross-section of the population, it is only rational to regard them as a national resource in the same way as water supply coming out of a public reservoir. They must be utilized for the well-being of all sectors of the population and not for the further enrichment of the wealthy and the powerful. However, as Arne Bigsten has rightly observed, 'the distribution of capital is even more unequal than that of land' and 'the banking system tends to reinforce the unequal distribution of capital' (1987, p. 156). This bodes ominously for society because it leads to the recruitment of entrepreneurs from only one social class and to the failure to utilize its entire resource of entrepreneurial talent (Leadbearer, 1986, p. 5).

Hence it is necessary to correct the tendency of the financial system to contribute to concentration of wealth by promoting an equitable distribution of credit in the economy. Micro enterprises have generally proved to be not only viable institutions with respectable rates of return and low default rates but also a successful tool in the fight against poverty and unemployment. The experience of the International Fund for Agricultural Development (IFAD) is that credit provided to the most enterprising of the poor is quickly repaid by them from their higher earnings (*The Economist*, 16 February 1985,

p. 15). Testimony from the Grameen Bank in Bangladesh indicates a constant repayment rate of 99 per cent since the Bank's inception (Yunus, 1984, p. 12). The Select Committee on Hunger established by the US House of Representatives concluded in its Report that 'the provision of small amounts of credit to micro enterprises in the informal sector of developing countries can significantly raise the living standards of the poor, increase food security and bring about sustainable improvements in local economies' (1986, p.v). Dr Muhammad Yunus, founder of the Grameen Bank, has aptly emphasized that financing for self-employment should be recognized as a right that plays a critical role in attaining all other rights (1987, p. 31).

No wonder a number of countries have established special institutions to grant credit to the poor and lower-middle-class entrepreneurs. Even though these have been extremely useful, they have proved not to be adequate and, therefore, unable to make significant headway in realizing the goal of equitable distribution of credit. This goal may be difficult to realize unless the microfinance sector is scaled up by integrating it with the commercial banks to enable the use of a significant proportion of their vast financial resources on a commercial basis for actualizing a crucial socioeconomic goal. Commercial banks do not at present fulfil this need and the Select Committee on Hunger is right in observing that 'formal financial institutions in these countries do not recognize the viability of income generating enterprises owned by the poor' (1986, p. v).

Commercial banks need not get directly involved in the business of financing micro enterprises if they find this to be too cumbersome. They can operate through their own subsidiaries or through the institutions that already exist for this purpose, like the agricultural banks, cooperative banks, development banks and leasing and finance companies. To enable the commercial banks to be integrated into the micro finance business, it is necessary to make it profitable for them to do so. This requires significant improvement in the environment for micro business through better access to markets and the provision of the needed physical and social infrastructure. Such an infrastructure, including vocational training institutions, roads, electricity and water supply, will help increase the efficiency of micro enterprises and reduce their costs, thereby enabling them to compete successfully in the market.

The reason normally given by commercial banks for diverting a very small proportion of their funds to micro enterprises is the greater risk and expense involved in financing a large number of small firms instead of a few large ones. Hence small enterprises are generally unable to get financing from banks and have to go to the informal sector where they are able to borrow only at prohibitive rates of interest. Thus the growth and survival of these firms is jeopardized even though they carry a great potential for increased employment and output and improved income distribution.

It is therefore necessary to reduce the risk and expense of such financing for commercial banks. The risk is great because micro enterprises are unable to provide acceptable collateral to the banks. The risk would be reduced to a substantial extent if the group solidarity method used by the Grameen Bank was employed and the financing was not provided in the form of cash loans but rather in the form of tools and equipment through the *ijara* mode of Islamic finance. The raw materials and merchandise as well as the working capital they need may be provided on the basis of *murabaha, salam* and *istisnaa*. These would involve greater risk than the *ijara* mode. To handle the risks involved in all such financing, it is imperative to establish the now-familiar loan guarantee scheme which has been introduced in a number of countries. It may also be possible to cover from the *zakat* fund the losses arising from the default of very small micro enterprises.

The additional expense incurred by commercial banks in evaluating and financing micro enterprises also needs to be reduced. In the case of financing provided to the very poor, the expense may also be covered from the *zakat* fund, one of the primary purposes of which is to enable the poor to stand on their own feet. For those who are not eligible for *zakat* but still deserve some help, it would be worthwhile for the governments to consider subsidizing a part of the cost, at least in the initial phase, in the interest of helping realize an important socioeconomic goal of Islam. As the system matures, the dependence on *zakat* as well as the government subsidy may tend to decline.

Effective corporate governance
What has been discussed so far in the sections above has been related primarily to the challenge of gradually raising the share of equity and PLS financing in the financial system and bringing about a more equitable distribution of credit by removing the obstacles that prevent this from happening. This, however, is only one of the challenges faced. An equally important challenge is to ensure the soundness, stability and accelerated development of the system, without which it will be difficult not only to meet successfully the first challenge, but also to ensure the system's survival. This necessitates effective corporate governance, prudent regulation and supervision, protection of depositors, and resolution of unresolved *fiqhi* disputes. This is what will be discussed in this and the following sections.

Corporate governance has gained great prominence over the last two decades even in the conventional financial system because of continued financial instability. It would be of even greater importance in the Islamic system because of the additional risk to which the depositors would become exposed when the banks really started moving into the risk-sharing modes. This poses an important challenge before Islamic banks to improve all crucial aspects of corporate governance. The challenge will become more serious as these institutions expand and their problems become more complex. This challenge could be successfully met if the Board of Directors and senior management become more effective in the performance of their responsibilities.

For this purpose, it is important to sharpen the tools of corporate governance, the most important of which are internal controls, risk management, transparency, loan accounting and disclosure, *shari'a* clearance and audit, external audit, and prudential regulation and supervision. Total reliance on these would, however, not be sufficient. Moral commitment on the part of all market operators is indispensable. Without such commitment, market operators will find different ways of violating the law without being detected and punished. This will create the need for more and more legal checks and controls, which will raise transactions costs to an unbearably high level. Making them truly accountable before shareholders and depositors by the adoption of measures discussed in this chapter should also be of great help. What is also needed is the establishment of a number of shared institutions, as discussed above. Without such institutions even banks with the best corporate governance may not be able to avoid crises.

However, corporate governance is generally weak in all countries and particularly so in developing countries, in which category nearly all Muslim countries fall at present. This is because all the institutions that play a crucial role in disciplining markets and ensuring efficiency and integrity are not well-developed in these countries. Information asymmetries are more severe, market participants less experienced, and regulations, even if they exist, are not always enforced effectively and impartially because of political corruption and the general weakness of judicial systems. Disclosures are also not adequate and accounting practices are not well developed (see Prowse, 1998, p. 16). The adverse effects of ineffective corporate governance can be more serious in the case of financial institutions because their leverage is much higher, the number of their stakeholders is more extensive and the systemic risks of their failure are far more serious. There is no reason to assume that, even though the Islamic financial institutions have done fairly well so far, they have necessarily been able to escape the trappings of the prevailing weak corporate governance in developing countries. It is therefore not possible to avoid the taking of all those measures that would help improve the functioning of these institutions. The role of the Board of Directors and senior management is of crucial importance in this respect. It is gratifying to note that almost all Muslim countries are currently in the process of implementing the BCBS guidelines.

The Board of Directors
The Board of Directors cannot, however, play this role effectively if its members do not have a high degree of moral integrity as well as professional competence in banking business. They must be adequately aware of the risks and complexities involved in the banking business. In an Islamic system, they must have the additional qualification of being well-versed in the *shari'a* and its objectives and in particular the rationale behind the prohibition of interest. They should ensure adequate transparency in keeping with the standards laid down by the BCBS, the IFSB and the supervisory authority of their own country through a smooth flow of relevant information to directors, senior management, auditors, supervisors, shareholders, depositors and the public according to the needs of each with a view to ensure a proper check on the affairs of the bank. They must establish a strong internal control system, proper accounting procedures, effective internal and external audit, efficient risk management and all necessary checks and balances, rules, regulations and procedures (for some of these, see Iqbal, Khan and Ahmad, 1998; Chapra and Khan, 2000; Khan and Ahmed, 2001; and Al-Jarhi and Iqbal, 2001).

Experience has shown that directors do not necessarily perform their roles effectively (Mace, 1996). There are a number of reasons for this. One of these is that the Board members may not necessarily have the professional competence and the moral integrity that are needed to manage the bank efficiently. Another reason is that Board members are not always genuinely elected by shareholders and are not necessarily accountable before them. Elections do not take place regularly at defined intervals and, even if they do, evidence indicates that shareholders are not actively involved in the election or removal of directors (Prentice, 1993, p. 31). This enables board members to perpetuate themselves and it is generally difficult to dislodge them except through takeovers. These are, however, expensive and potentially disruptive and may not, therefore, be a possible remedy except in extreme cases (Morck, Schleifer and Vishny, 1990). To correct this situation, it is necessary to have a transparent procedure for elections and to adopt measures that would enable minority shareholders and investment depositors to have a say in Board decisions. It is also necessary to enable shareholders to remove Board members in the event of their performance falling far short of what they expect. It is, therefore, imperative to institute reforms in election procedures as well as proxy rules to enable shareholders to elect competent and conscientious persons to the Board of Directors and to prevent them perpetuating themselves in spite of their poor performance.

It is also necessary to develop a legal and regulatory infrastructure to protect the rights of not only minority shareholders but also depositors (both being outsiders). In a number of countries companies are allowed to ask registered shareholders, who are unable to attend general meetings, to transfer their votes to the Board of Directors. This further strengthens the hands of the Board and enables it to control decisions at shareholder meetings. Since the transfer of voting rights often leads to far-reaching consequences, which may not always be in the interest of all stakeholders, it would be desirable to transfer voting rights to shareholder associations, if they exist. If such associations do not exist, then voting rights may be transferred to supervisory authorities or to specialized chartered firms established in the private sector to protect the interest of stakeholders, against a fee, as discussed below. All three of these institutions would perhaps be better qualified to protect the interests of stakeholders.[8]

It would also be helpful if there were an adequate number of non-executive directors on the Board. Empirical evidence in the conventional system indicates that non-executive directors influence positively a Board's capabilities to evaluate and discipline managers (Alvarez et al., 1998, p. 2). This is perhaps because such directors do not have any management responsibility and may not, therefore, have a vested interest in protecting the management. They may, therefore, be expected to attach greater weight to the interests of minority shareholders and depositors and, thereby, help inject equity into the company. If they do not come up to this expectation, they would hurt their own reputation in the directors' labour market. Removal of the Chief Executive Officer (CEO) caused by poor performance is more likely in outsider-dominated Boards than in insider-dominated ones. However, here too there are problems. If the non-executive directors have not been elected by shareholders but rather handpicked by the dominant shareholder or the CEO, they would owe their careers to him and would, therefore, 'lack the information and incentives required to provide consistent effective corporate governance' (Herzel, 1994, p. 472). There will thus be conflict of interest, which will create a lack of willingness on their part to discipline senior management (Sykes, 1994, p. 118). Moreover, Board meetings may not be frequent and non-executive directors may not, therefore, be able to monitor the activities of the company effectively and ensure correction, particularly if overt criticism of management policies in Board meetings is considered to be rude (Morck, 1994, p. 476).

Since Islamic banks are generally small compared to their conventional counterparts even in Muslim countries, leave alone the rest of the world, the amount of capital held by them is also very small. This enables concentration of shares in the hands of a few executive directors.[9] The number of non-executive directors who can serve as a check on the executive directors is also accordingly small. Since the small size as well as the concentration of shareholdings carries the potential of leading to undesired consequences for protecting the interests of all stakeholders, it is desirable to enlarge the size of banks and to institute legal reforms with the objective of reducing concentration, diversifying risks and increasing the ability of these banks to absorb losses.

It would also be desirable to introduce some other reforms to make the Board of Directors more effective in its functions. One of these, which needs to be considered seriously, is to relate the remuneration of Board members to their performance in the same way as is required in *mudaraba* contracts.[10] The directors in their capacity as *mudaribs* (managing entrepreneurs) should be compensated only for their actual expenses and not be entitled to a fixed management fee or remuneration as they do in modern corporations. Their remuneration should be a certain percentage of the profit earned by the bank, if the bank makes a profit. This must be in addition to their normal share in profit like other shareholders on the basis of their shareholdings. The percentage share of profits to be allocated to the directors for their management services must be clearly specified in the Articles of Agreement so that it is well known to the shareholders. If the corporation makes a profit, the directors receive the specified percentage of profit for their services. But if the corporation makes a loss, the directors do not, like the *mudarib*, receive a 'fee' for their management services, and should share in the losses in proportion to their stockholdings. The directors would thus have a reward for their services only if they had contributed to profits: the higher the profit, the greater their reward. This should prove to be an incentive to them for better performance.

Senior management

While the Board of Directors refers to persons who are generally not only shareholders themselves but also participate in the governance of the bank, senior management refers to the CEO and other senior members of the staff who perform management functions but are not necessarily shareholders. Modern corporations are in general not managed by their owners (shareholders) (Berle and Means, 1932; Jensen and Meckling, 1976). Instead, professional managers are hired to run the business. They are 'fiduciaries'.[11] This creates the principal/agent problem and leads to a conflict of interests. It is therefore necessary to impose restrictions on self-dealing, fraud, excessive compensation in different hidden forms, and other malpractices.

One of the most important constraints on management is that key positions should not be held by one person ('four eyes principle'). Since the CEO and the Chairman of the Board perform two distinct functions in the bank, it would be preferable to have two different persons holding these positions so that there is a clear division of responsibilities at the top of the bank to ensure independence and balance of power and authority. Neither the directors nor the management should be allowed to stay in the job if they are no longer competent or qualified to run the bank. As argued by Jensen and Ruback, poor managers who resist being replaced might be the costliest manifestation of the agency problem (cited from Jensen and Ruback, 1963, by Schleifer and Vishny, 1997, p. 743). A survey conducted by IRTI has revealed that, in all the banks covered by the survey, the positions of CEO and Chairman were held by different persons (Chapra and Ahmed, 2002). This is gratifying. However, it need not necessarily be true for banks not covered by the survey, and it is necessary to ensure that this is the case.

It is the responsibility of the Board of Directors and senior management to ensure proper internal controls, and effective management of all risks, including credit risk, liquidity risk, interest-rate risk and operational risks. Even though the exposure of most Islamic banks to these risks seems to be relatively high, they have been able to manage them fairly well so far. Nevertheless, this may not necessarily continue in the future. It is, therefore, extremely important to cultivate an effective risk management culture in these banks to ensure their competitiveness and survival in a world full of uncertainties and crises. This cannot be done, however, without the active collaboration of the Board of Directors, senior management, the *shari'a* scholars and bank supervisors.

Prudential regulation and supervision
A survey conducted by IRTI has revealed that, while the overall regulatory environment for conventional banks seems to be relatively good and the variation among them is also relatively less in Muslim countries, the regulatory and institutional environment for Islamic banks does not appear to be adequate and the variation is also relatively greater (see Chapra and Ahmed, 2002, Tables 1.2, 1.3 and 1.5). This indicates that there are a number of issues confronted by the authorities with respect to the regulation and supervision of Islamic financial institutions. The first of these issues relates to the removal of all the legal obstacles that hinder the rapid expansion of Islamic financial institutions. The second issue is about the clarification and harmonization and codification of standards of Islamic finance as much as is possible and about ensuring the compliance of these institutions with these standards; and the third issue relates to implementation of the guidelines provided by the BCBS.

The removal of legal obstacles does not seem to have received due attention so far from regulatory authorities in most Muslim countries. The laws with respect to financial institutions were formulated in these countries in the image of conventional banking before the initiation of Islamic finance. These have in general remained unchanged, with some cosmetic changes introduced here and there. For example, while interest payments continue to be tax-deductible, dividend payments do not get the same treatment in most jurisdictions. This puts firms using the Islamic modes of finance as well as Islamic banks at a disadvantage. What is needed is a thorough review of the whole legal structure so as to bring it into harmony with the needs of Islamic finance.

The harmonization of standards is a difficult task because of the differences of opinion among the jurists. While the existence of some differences is natural and healthy, an effort needs to be made to bring about as much harmony as possible. This is happening as a result of the continuing dialogue among the jurists and the role that the IDB and the IFSB are playing. Where there are differences of opinion, the differences should appear as alternative ways of conducting Islamic finance. In this case, the law should require transparency in contacts about the alternative that is being used so as to avoid misunderstanding. It also needs to be clearly stated that the liability of the financers in a *mudaraba* contract is limited to the extent of finance provided by him/her. This is generally understood to be the case. It would nevertheless be desirable to have a clear *fiqhi* verdict on this issue and the reflection of this in the laws so that no ambiguity remains. All this would help introduce greater clarity and harmony in Islamic finance and make the job of *shari'a* courts or banking tribunals relatively easier in the resolution of disputes.

While the successful resolution of the first two issues will enable the Islamic financial industry to grow rapidly and gain credibility in Muslim countries, the third, which is in the process of being fulfilled, will help it gain respectability in the international financial markets. All these will together help in not only promoting accelerated development of an Islamically compliant safe and sound financial system but also protecting the payments system from instability and ensuring efficient operation of the capital market and its institutions.

The regulatory authorities should not, however, make the regulations so tight and comprehensive that they may raise compliance costs unbearably and also strangulate innovation and creativity. They should, nevertheless, ensure the following:

- that the banks are preferably joint stock companies and that all the members of their Board of Directors and senior management do not belong to a single family or business group;
- that the major shareholders, and members of the Board of Directors and senior management not only enjoy a reputation for integrity and fairness as well as financial strength but also possess adequate knowledge of the *shari'a* and the skills and experience necessary to operate an Islamic bank in a safe and sound manner;
- that the banks have adequate risk-weighted capital in conformity with the requirements of the BCBS;
- that the banks have appropriate checks and balances, and their internal controls and risk management systems are effective to ensure not only efficient operation but also freedom from fraud, overlending, credit concentration, exploitation and mismanagement; and their non-executive directors and external auditors are independent and do not have a vested interest in supporting the banks' board or management;
- that the banks disclose adequate qualitative and quantitative information about their operations, particularly their capital, reserves, liquidity and risk profile to enable all market participants and particularly the shareholders and depositors to monitor the banks effectively.

Regulation cannot, however, be effective if it is not enforced. It should therefore be accompanied by effective supervision. The objective of supervision must be to ensure that, first, the financial system is safe and sound in accordance with the guidelines laid down by the BCBS, and, second, that it is also in conformity with the teachings of *shari'a*. This is what will help it gain credibility in the domestic as well as international financial markets and enable it to compete successfully and achieve an accelerated rate of growth. For this purpose the supervisory authorities will have to develop effective mechanisms to monitor and limit (and if possible, also measure) all the different types of risks to which banks are exposed. They will also have to assess the quality of the banks' loans and investments, and in particular the risk of default of a debtor, which is crucial in the case of Islamic banks. It is this assessment which may turn out to be the most critical determinant of an Islamic bank's financial condition and ability to survive. It is also important for the supervisor to ensure that the bank has in place an effective internal controls system in conformity with the nature and scale of its business and that its management has the necessary training and experience to manage the risks and to handle the challenges that it faces.

It is also important for the supervisors to develop and institute a set of indicators of financial soundness to help assess and monitor the strengths and vulnerabilities of the financial system at both micro and macro levels. At the micro level, the indicators should show the condition of individual institutions while at the macro level they should help assess and monitor the soundness and vulnerabilities of the financial system as well as the economy. The International Monetary Fund (IMF) has suggested a set of these indicators, called 'macro-prudential indicators', which include a core set as well as an enlarged set of financial soundness indicators (see Sundararajan, et al., 2002, for details of these indicators, especially pp. 3 and 8).

Asymmetric information from which banks suffer makes supervision a difficult task. This difficulty is accentuated if accounting, auditing and information systems are less developed, as they are in most developing (including Muslim) countries. These difficulties make the role of shareholders and depositors absolutely crucial in monitoring the banks and strengthening the safety and soundness of the banking system. It may be hoped that the risks to which investment depositors are exposed would motivate them to monitor the banks more carefully and thereby help strengthen them. Risk-based adequacy of capital also has an important role to play. However, it cannot be relied upon fully because the problem with capital is that, while supervision can ensure its quantity, it cannot ensure its quality. Excessive reliance on capital may not, therefore, be prudent.

This call for regulation and supervision of Islamic banks is not something new. It has always been considered to be a challenge for the Islamic financial system, as is evident from the attention drawn towards it more than two decades ago by the governors of central banks and monetary authorities of the member countries of the OIC in their detailed report on 'Promotion, Regulation and Supervision of Islamic Banks', approved by them in their Fourth Meeting held in Khartoum on 7–8 March 1981. This was done at a time when Islamic banking was still in its infancy. The first fully-fledged Islamic bank had been established in Dubai in March 1975, just six years before this report. Now that Islamic banking has spread and is expected to continue to spread, regulation and supervision are even more crucial. The more conscientiously this challenge is met, the better it will be for the development of a sound and healthy Islamic financial system.

However it is not just the soundness of the financial system at both the micro and the macro levels that the supervision of an Islamic financial system should be concerned about. It is also necessary to ensure that the Islamic goal of justice is also being realized. This cannot be done by means of regulation. What needs to be done is to remove the obstacles that prevent banks from being integrated with the microfinance network to be able to provide credit to a larger spectrum of society. This will necessitate the establishment of institutions that help banks overcome their difficulties in the realization of this goal, as discussed earlier.

Protecting the depositors
The financial crises faced by almost three-quarters of the member countries of the IMF over the last two decades have brought into focus the question of protecting the depositors. Although effective corporate governance along with prudential regulation and supervision can greatly help protect the depositors, they cannot be considered to be sufficient and there is a need to find other ways.

Deposit insurance
Deposit insurance has received maximum attention as a way of protecting the depositors from losses, and many countries have adopted this (Laeven, 2002). Even countries which do not have deposit insurance have rescued the depositors in the case of bank failures because of the fear that refusal to do so may lead to the collapse of the financial system. If this is the case in countries where the conventional financial system prevails and the depositors do not participate in the risks of banking business, then the imperative of PLS brings into even sharper focus the challenge of protecting the depositors. While this has the hazard of making depositors complacent and, thereby, less motivated towards the monitoring of their banks' affairs, it has the advantage of making the insurance provider complement the regulatory and supervisory authorities in their task of ensuring the health of financial institutions. This raises the question of whether all

deposits should be insured, as in the conventional financial system, or only the demand deposits.

Since demand depositors do not participate in the risks of banking business and do not, therefore, get a return, their deposits need to be fully protected. However, deposit insurance systems do not normally insure demand deposits beyond a certain limit. This raises the question of whether demand deposits should, or should not, be fully insured in the Islamic system. The knowledge that their deposits are protected will inspire the depositors' confidence in the Islamic financial system as a whole and prevent panics. It is of particular importance to fully protect small depositors. Large depositors may or may not be fully protected because they have the resources to monitor the condition of their banks, and giving them full protection may tend to reduce market discipline by lowering the motivation to assess the soundness of their banks.

Protecting investment depositors may, however, be in conflict with the spirit of Islamic finance. Nevertheless a case has been made by some *shari'a* scholars in favour of protecting small investment depositors from losses (see Al-Misri, 1998). This proposal is worth considering seriously because it would remove the criticism levelled against Islamic finance that it does not protect small depositors who need income but are not able to risk the loss of their principal. Even if it is not possible to do this because of a lack of consensus on this issue, it should always be possible for banks to invest such deposits in relatively safe ventures so as to minimize the risk of loss. There also arises the question of whether large investment deposits can be insured against fraud, mismanagement and violation of the *mudaraba* contract. The answer would depend on the willingness of insurance providers to provide such insurance. However, if it is possible to have medical malpractice insurance, it should also be possible to provide insurance against fraud and mismanagement in the case of investment deposits. This would help introduce greater discipline in the financial system by also making the insurance provider assess more carefully the quality and practices of bank management and requiring greater transparency.

Keeping in view the nature of Islamic finance, it would be desirable to have an explicit insurance scheme specifying the kind and extent of coverage available to different categories of depositors. This would be better for building the depositors' confidence in the Islamic financial system. They would be aware of the extent of protection they have. In the absence of such an explicit coverage, the depositors may tend to assume a full implicit coverage, particularly in the case of large banks, because of the 'too big to fail' doctrine. This will be more costly for the financial authorities because they will have to bail out all depositors, irrespective of the size and nature of their deposits. It will also introduce a moral hazard and reduce depositor watchfulness of large banks which is necessary for greater market discipline and systemic stability.

Other ways of protecting depositors
Another way of protecting the depositors would be to allow them to have a representative on the bank's Board of Directors and also a voice in the shareholders' meetings. The ease with which shareholders as well as depositors can participate in meetings and use their votes to influence important bank decisions or to remove directors and senior management from office, can play an important role in improving corporate governance in Islamic banks. However, when even shareholders do not necessarily attend shareholders' meetings, it may not be possible for depositors, being far greater in number than shareholders, to do

so, particularly if the banks are large and have several branches, not only within the country but also abroad. Moreover, if shareholders and depositors can exercise voting rights only by attending the meetings, this will virtually guarantee non-voting and the voting rights will be almost meaningless. One way of solving the problem of non-voting would be to transfer voting rights to the regulatory authorities who may appoint a representative on behalf of depositors on the banks' Board of Directors. The banks may perhaps resent this. It is, however, important not only for safeguarding the interests of depositors but also for systemic stability.

If such representation is ruled out, it may be desirable to encourage the formation of depositors' associations to protect the depositor's interests. If this also happens to be practically difficult, it would be worth considering the establishment of specialized chartered firms in the private sector to protect the interests of depositors, just as it is the job of external auditors to protect the interests of shareholders. Their fee could be paid by the banks out of the dividends distributed to the investment depositors. An important objection to this suggestion may be that it would lead to an unnecessary proliferation of institutions. To avoid such proliferation, external auditors may be assigned the task. It will be cheaper and more convenient if the external auditors are required to act as guardians not only of the rights of shareholders but also those of of the depositors. It is also necessary to ensure that adequate transparency prevails so that the depositors know what is going on in the bank and are thus able to play a greater role in safeguarding their own interests.

There is also another aspect of safeguarding the interest of depositors in Islamic banks. The depositors would like to ensure that what they are getting is not wine with the label of honey. Compliance of Islamic banks with the *shari'a* in the acquisition as well as the use of funds is, therefore, an important challenge. This has already been discussed.

Some unresolved *fiqhi* issues[12]

Fiqhi verdicts related to the financial system have remained dormant for a long period and, in particular, over the last two centuries, during which time the conventional financial system has made tremendous advances. However, a great deal of progress has been made over the last three decades in facing the new challenges, although a number of crucial issues still remain unresolved. It is not possible to encompass all of these in this brief chapter. Some of these, however, are discussed below for the consideration of jurists. In case it is found that the prevalent *fiqhi* opinion cannot be changed, it will be necessary for the jurists and financial experts to join hands to find practical *shari'a*-compatible solutions for the problems faced by Islamic financial institutions. In the absence of such solutions, the risks faced by Islamic banks may be higher and the need for capital greater. Capital standards which are significantly higher than those for conventional banks may reduce the profitability of these banks and make them less competitive.

Late settlement of financial obligations

One of the most important of these issues relates to the failure of the purchaser of goods and services under the *murabaha* mode of financing to settle payment on time even when he is capable of doing so. If this failure were due to strained circumstances, then Islam recommends not just rescheduling but even remission, if necessary. However, if it is due to unscrupulousness, then the question is whether a penalty can be imposed on the defaulter and whether the financier or the bank can be compensated for the damage as well as the loss of income caused by such default. If the late payment does not lead to any penalty, there is a danger that default may tend to become a widespread phenomenon through the long-run operation of path dependence and self-reinforcing mechanisms. This may lead to a breakdown of the payments system if the amounts involved are significantly large.

Scholars have expressed a number of opinions on the subject, but so far there is no consensus.[13] The conservative view allows blacklisting of the defaulter's name and also his imprisonment if the delay is unjustified, but prohibits the imposition of any monetary penalty on the defaulter or the payment of any compensation to the aggrieved party for fear that this may become a disguise for charging interest.

The possibility of blacklisting and imprisonment of the defaulter can serve as a strong deterrent and help minimize default cases provided that this can be enacted promptly. However, if the lender and police highhandedness are to be eschewed, imprisonment should not be allowed except on the basis of a court decree issued after a due process of law. This may be difficult because, given the present-day inefficient judicial system of many Muslim countries, court decisions usually take several years and involve substantial litigation costs. It is therefore imperative that special *shari'a* courts or banking tribunals be established, as discussed earlier, to penalize promptly the unjustifiably defaulting party and thereby help minimize default cases. Although blacklisting and imprisonment may serve as deterrents to the unjustified delaying of payments, it does not provide any relief to the aggrieved party, which has suffered damage and loss of income.

The relatively liberal view, therefore, allows the imposition of a financial penalty on the debtor who delays payment without any justification, but allows it to be made available to the aggrieved party as compensation only if the penalty is imposed by a court. However, even in the case of a court decision, there are two different views. One view permits the court to determine compensation for the damage caused by late payment as well as the loss of income suffered by the aggrieved party. The other view allows the court to determine compensation for only the actual damage but not for the loss of income. If the penalty is not determined by a court, the proceeds must be utilized for charitable objectives only and cannot be made available as compensation to the aggrieved party.

If the concept of compensation for loss becomes accepted by the jurists, there will arise the question of how to determine the compensation in a way that reduces subjectivity as well as the possibility of injustice to either the defaulting or the aggrieved party. The answer may lie in developing an index of 'loss-given-default' (LGD). It should be possible to develop and maintain such an LGD index using internationally recognized standards. The LGD will, for example, provide a schedule of the loss incurred by a bank if $100 is defaulted in payment for a given number of days. The LGD will capture all costs related to the administration of the default until its settlement, the litigation cost and the loss of income. The ultimate decision will, of course, have to be made by a special banking tribunal in keeping with the LGD schedule with adjustments for individual circumstances.

Some issues about leasing

The jurists are unanimously agreed on the need for the lessor to bear at least a part of the risk of lease financing to make the lease contract lawful. Nevertheless there are differences of opinion among them on the permissibility of different types of lease contacts.

The kind of leasing which the jurists have generally discussed in the classical *fiqh* literature, and about the permissibility of which there is no difference of opinion, is what is now called the operating lease. This form of lease distinguishes itself from the other forms in a number of ways. First, the lessor is himself the real owner of the leased asset and, therefore, bears all the risks and costs of ownership. All defects, which prevent the use of the equipment by the lessee, are his responsibility, even though it is possible to make the lessee responsible for the day-to-day maintenance and normal repairs of the leased asset. Second, the lease is not for the entire useful life of the leased asset, but rather for a specified short-term period, and ends at the end of the agreed period unless renewed by the mutual consent of both the lessor and the lessee. The entire risk is thus borne by the lessor. This has, however, the potential of introducing a moral hazard through the misuse of the leased asset by the lessee.

The financial lease helps take care of the moral hazard problem by making the lease period long enough (usually the entire useful life of the leased asset) to enable the lessor to amortize the cost of the asset with profit. At the end of the lease period the lessee has the option to purchase the asset from the lessor at a price specified in advance or at its market value at that time. The lease is not cancellable before the expiry of the lease period without the consent of both the parties. There is, therefore, little danger of misuse of the asset.

A financial lease has other advantages too. The leased asset serves as security and, in the case of default on the part of the lessee, the lessor can take possession of the equipment without court order. It also helps reduce the lessor's tax liability owing to the high depreciation allowances generally allowed by tax laws in many countries. The lessor can also sell the equipment during the lease period so that the lease payments accrue to the new buyer. This enables the lessor to get cash when he needs liquidity. This is not possible in the case of a debt because, while the prevailing *fiqhi* position allows the sale of physical assets, it does not allow the sale of financial debt instruments except at their nominal value.

Some of the jurists have expressed doubts about the permissibility of a financial lease. The rationale they give is that the long-term and non-cancellable nature of the lease contract shifts the entire risk to the lessee, particularly if the 'residual' value of the asset is also fixed in advance. The end result for the lessee may turn out to be worse than the outright purchase of the asset through an interest-bearing loan. A financial lease thus has the potential of becoming more exploitative than outright purchase. Supposing the lease contract is for five years, the lessee would have to continue making lease payments even if he does not need the asset, say, after two years. In the case of a purchase through an interest-bearing loan, the purchaser can sell the asset in the market and repay the loan, thus reducing his loss. This he cannot do in a financial lease. If he is unable to make lease payments, he may lose his stake in the asset even though he has paid a part of the asset price beyond the rental charge he would normally pay in an operating lease.

There are, however, jurists who consider a financial lease to be permissible if certain conditions are satisfied. First, the lessor must bear the risks of leasing by being the real owner of the leased asset. He cannot lease what he does not own and possess, and should be responsible for all the risks and expenses related to ownership.[14] Therefore a lease contract where the lessor acts only as an intermediary between the supplier and the lessee and plays the role of only a financier, with ownership of the asset being nothing more than a legal device to provide security for repayment of the loan and legal protection in case of default, is not allowed. In this case the lessor leases an asset before buying it and taking possession of it, and gets a reward without bearing any risk. Second, obligation of the lessee to make lease payments does not start until he has received possession of the leased asset and can continue only as long as it remains useable by him.[15] Third, all manufacturing defects and related problems should be the lessor's responsibility. The lessee can, however, be made responsible for the proper upkeep and maintenance of the leased asset. Fourth, the lease contract should be separate from, and independent of, the contract for the purchase of the residual asset. The residual value has to be market-related and cannot be fixed in advance. The purchase contract has, therefore, to be optional and not a condition for the lease contract because the quality of the asset at the end of the lease period as well as its market-related price, two of the essential requirements for a valid contract, are unknown when the lease contract is signed.

Almost all Islamic banks use the financial lease by fulfilling, or at least making an effort to fulfil, the *shari'a* conditions. The residual value remains a problem, but the banks have tried to overcome it by setting a small nominal value for the residual asset or transferring it as a gift from the lessor to the lessee. This does not satisfy the jurists who are opposed to the financial lease because, according to them, it does not fulfil the *shari'a* requirements. The residual value is automatically predetermined and becomes built into the lease payments, and thereby leads to injustice. The lessee loses the asset as well as the extra payments made by him in the case where he dies or is unable to continue lease payments. The alternative suggested by them is that the lessor should sell the asset to the 'lessee' on an instalment basis and then get it hypothecated to ensure full payment. However, once the asset is owned by the 'lessee', it is very cumbersome for the bank to get it back from him in a number of Muslim countries even if he is unable to make payments. Moreover, the ownership of the asset enables him to sell the asset and use the money, leaving the bank with nothing to fall back upon.

The jurists are agreed that the security lease (also referred to as 'financing' lease) is not acceptable from the point of view of the *shari'a* because it is not a lease contract in the traditional sense. It is just a financing transaction, and nothing more than a disguised security agreement. It involves the effective transfer to the lessee of all the risks and rewards associated with ownership. The security lease has therefore been ruled out from the modes of Islamic finance.

Securitization and sale of debts
There is a general agreement among the jurists that the sale of debts is not allowed except at their face value. The rationale usually given for this position is that the sale of debts involves *riba* (interest) as well as *gharar* (excessive uncertainty),[16] both of which are prohibited by the *shari'a*. Such a position is undoubtedly true with respect to the sale of debts incurred by borrowing money. Since it is normally not possible to sell a debt except at a discount, such a sale would be nothing but a disguised way of receiving and paying interest. It is also argued that, as a result of what is now called 'asymmetric information', the buyer of the debt may be unaware of the true financial position of the debtor and of his willingness and ability to honour the debt. Consequently there is *gharar* in the transaction. Hence the jurists have a strong rationale in not allowing the sale of debts.

The rationale does not, however, apply to debts sold by Islamic banks in modern times, for two main reasons. First, the debt is created by the sale of goods and services through the sales-based modes of Islamic finance, particularly *murabaha*. If, say, an aeroplane or a ship is sold by a bank or a consortium of banks to a government or a corporation, the debt is not incurred by borrowing money. The debt is created by the *murabaha* mode of financing permitted by the *shari'a* and the price, according to the jurists themselves, includes profit on the transaction and not interest. Therefore, when the bank sells such a debt instrument at a discount, what it is selling is a part of an asset and the return that the buyer is getting is not interest but rather a share of the profit that the bank has earned in the *murabaha* transaction.

Second, in the present-day sale of debts by banks, we are not talking of a debt owed by an unknown *(majhul)* person with an unknown credit rating, such that the buyer of the debt instrument does not know whether the debt will be honoured or not. The debt instruments intended to be sold are generated by the financing provided through the sales-based modes to governments and well-known corporations and firms having a high credit rating. The buyer of the debt instrument can know about the rating as much as the bank. Moreover, the debt is not unsecured. It is rather asset-based and well-secured. Its payment is therefore almost certain and there is no question of any *gharar*. The past ruling of the jurists, given in entirely different circumstances, does not, therefore, seem to fit the changed realities of modern times.

The jurists may therefore wish to reconsider their verdict, not because the earlier verdict was wrong, but because circumstances have changed. They should definitely retain the ban on sale of debts in the form of treasury bills, bonds and other such interest-based instruments which involve pure lending and borrowing against interest. However, their ruling with regard to the sale of asset-based debt instruments, which originate in the sale of real goods and services and which transfer a part of the profit, and not interest, from the original financier to the new financier, needs to be reviewed. The development of a general agreement on this important issue would help create a secondary market for such debt instruments and thereby lead to the accelerated development of an Islamic money market.

The absence of such a secondary market for debt instruments creates two major problems for banks and thereby serves as a hindrance to the further development and expansion of Islamic banking. First, the banks are stuck with the debt instrument until its maturity. There are so many uncertainties facing banks in the modern volatile financial system that, even without being guilty of overlending, it is possible for them to get into a tight liquidity situation. This may be the result of an excessive net outflow of funds from the banks for some unexpected reason. It may also be due to the failure of a major client of the bank to settle payment on time because of some unexpected developments. There may be a number of other unforeseen reasons for the liquidity crisis of an individual bank. If the bank cannot sell some of its debts to acquire the badly needed liquidity before the maturity date of those debts, it may not be able to meet its obligations or to fund more profitable opportunities for investment.

Second, it is difficult for banks to play their role of financial intermediation effectively without being able to securitize their receivables. When banks grant a big sales-based credit for an expensive item (say, an aeroplane, a ship or a building), they would like to package it into small portions and sell these to small financiers. In this way they would be able to provide a large amount of credit without straining their own resources excessively and would simultaneously be able to provide investment opportunities to small investors. If they are unable to play this role effectively, the economy may suffer from the hesitation on the part of banks to finance the purchase of costly items. Companies will have to sign loan agreements separately with numerous investors to raise a large amount. This would undoubtedly be a cumbersome task. Syndicated loans may not be a substitute for the sale of debts because, in addition to the lead bank, there are generally only a few big lenders participating in such loans. Therefore, while a large purchase may be facilitated for a major borrower, the packaging of the amount into small portions would not be possible and small financiers would not be able to benefit from the investment opportunity.

Hedging and financial engineering
Hedging has become an important instrument for the management of risks in the present-day international economic and financial environment where there is a great deal of instability in exchange rates as well as other market prices. If individuals, businesses and financial institutions do not resort to this instrument for the management of their risks, there is a strong likelihood that they may suffer substantial losses with knock-on effects for the whole economy.

Exchange rate risks do not seem to have been common during the days of the Prophet, peace and blessings of God be on him, and the *Khilafah al-Rashidah*. The rates of exchange between gold and silver coins in the then-prevailing bimetallic monetary system were relatively stable at around ten. Such stability did not, however, persist later on. The two metals faced different supply and demand conditions, which destabilized their relative prices. The ratios sometimes moved to as low as 20, 30 and even 50 (Al-Qaradawi, 1969, vol. 1, p. 264; Miles, 1992, p. 320). This instability enabled bad coins, according to al-Maqrizi (d.1442) and his contemporary al-Asadi (d.1450), to drive good coins out of circulation (Al-Misri, 1990, pp. 54, 66), a phenomenon which has become known since the sixteenth century as Gresham's Law. Such instability created difficulties for everyone, but there was no solution at that time to protect individuals and economies from its adverse effects.

To solve this problem the world abandoned the bimetallic standard and moved to the gold standard and then to the dollar exchange standard, both of which helped stabilize exchange rates because of the fixed parities. These two standards, however, created other difficult problems and had to be abandoned in favour of floating exchange rates. The farewell to fixed parities has introduced a great deal of instability in the foreign exchange markets and the risks involved in foreign trade and finance have become unduly intensified. In such an unstable climate, hedging has proved to be a boon. It has made it possible for banks and businessmen to manage the exchange rate and price risks by passing them on to those who are willing to bear them at a certain cost.

To understand the problem, let us assume that a Saudi businessman places an order for Japanese goods worth a million dollars (Rls 3.75 million) to be delivered three months from now. If the rate of exchange is 117 Yen per dollar, and if the exchange rate remains stable, ¥117 million will become due at the time of delivery of the goods. Since exchange rates are not stable and, consequently, if the Yen appreciates over these three months by, say, 5 per cent, the Saudi importer will have to pay Rls 3.94 million for the goods instead of Rls 3.75 million. The Saudi businessman will therefore incur an unforeseen loss of Rls 190 000.

One way of protecting himself against such loss would be to purchase now the Yen that will be payable three months later. This will freeze his financial resources unnecessarily and create a liquidity crisis for him. To avoid such liquidity tightness, the alternative solution available in the conventional financial system is to purchase ¥117 million in the forward market at the current exchange rate of ¥117 per dollar plus or minus a premium or discount. All that the importer has to do is to pay a small percentage of the total amount as deposit for this purpose. Such a transaction is called hedging.

The question that therefore arises is whether the mechanism of hedging to protect the importer from exchange rate fluctuations is permissible. The verdict of the jurists so far is that hedging is not permissible. This opinion is based on three objections: hedging involves *gharar* (excessive uncertainty), interest (*riba*) payment and receipt, and forward sale of currencies. All three of these are prohibited by the *shari'a*.

As far as *gharar* is concerned, the objection is not valid because hedging in fact helps eliminate *gharar* by enabling the importer to buy the needed foreign exchange at the current exchange rate. The bank, which sells forward Yen, also does not get involved in *gharar*, because it purchases the Yen spot and invests them until the time of delivery. The bank therefore earns a return on the Yen that it invests for three months but also loses the return that it would have earned on the Riyals or the dollars that were used to purchase the Yen. The differential in the two rates of return determines the premium or the discount on the forward transaction.

The second objection with regard to interest can be handled by requiring the Islamic banks to invest the Yen or other foreign currencies purchased by them in an Islamically permissible manner to the extent to which it is possible for them to do so. There would not then be any interest, but rather profit earned on the investments.

The third objection is, of course, very serious. The Prophet, peace and blessings of God be on him, has clearly prohibited forward transactions in currencies. However, we live in a world where instability in the foreign exchange markets has become an unavoidable reality. It is not possible for businessmen as well as Islamic banks to reduce their exposure to this risk. How are they going to manage it? It is very risky for them to carry unhedged foreign exchange liabilities or assets on their balance sheets, particularly in crisis situations when exchange rates are volatile. If they do not resort to hedging, they actually get involved in *gharar* more intensively. In addition, one of the important objectives of the *shari'a*, which is the protection of wealth *(hifz al-mal)*,[17] is compromised unnecessarily.

Institutions, which provide the needed protection through hedging, are well-qualified for this service because of their greater financial resources and better knowledge of market conditions. The fee that they charge can be 'Islamized' by resort to Islamic instruments. The question, therefore, is about whether hedging could be accepted in an unstable exchange rate environment. Here we need to look at the reason (*illah*) for the prohibition of forward transactions. If the *illah* is to prevent speculation in the foreign exchange markets, which is a source of great volatility in the flow of funds and exchange rates, this could be overcome by confining hedging to only foreign exchange receivables and payables related to real goods and services.

Concluding remarks

The Islamic financial industry has made commendable progress over the last three decades since the establishment of the first Islamic bank in Dubai in 1975. Nevertheless, the industry has a long way to go before it can hope to realize the vision for which it was established.

The vision consists of two indispensable parts. The first part relates to the removal of interest from the financial systems of Muslim countries in such an orderly manner that all their financial needs are satisfied in conformity with Islamic teachings without creating any setback for their economies. It is hoped that, with the gradual coming of age of Islamic finance, reliance on equity and the PLS modes of financing will steadily rise in Muslim countries and that on the debt-creating modes will decline until a suitable mix of the two has been achieved in accordance with the needs of accelerated development of their economies within the framework of financial health and stability. The second part of the vision is to bring about a more equitable distribution of credit so that the financial system helps reduce poverty, unemployment and concentration of income and wealth instead of continuing its existing tendency of making the rich richer at the expense of the poor.

As far as the quantitative aspect of the vision is concerned, there has been an unexpectedly rapid progress in the expansion of the industry in terms of the number of banks and the volume of deposits and assets. What has helped greatly is the recent emergence of *sukuk*, which have made it possible for governments and corporations to have access to a relatively large volume of financing. Experience so far leads to the hope that *shari'a*-compatible products will continue to respond to the increasing demand for these in the future to satisfy the rising financial needs of all countries until a respectable niche has been achieved in the international financial markets.

The movement into equity and PLS financing, however, has not been significant. This is because the kind of institutional infrastructure that is needed to make progress in this direction does not exist to a satisfactory level. This indicates the urgency of establishing shared institutions that would enable banks to minimize the principle–agent conflict of interest through appropriate incentives and deterrents and the prompt settlement of disputes. It is also necessary to strengthen corporate governance through well-enforced internal controls, risk management, transparency, loan accounting and disclosure, *shari'a* clearance and audit, external audit and prudential regulation. Total reliance on these may not, however, be sufficient. Moral commitment on the part of all market operators is indispensable. Without such commitment, market operators will be able to find clandestine ways of violating the law without being detected and punished. This will blunt the system of incentives and deterrents and accentuate the need for more and more legal checks and controls which will raise transactions costs to an unbearably high level. It may not be an exaggeration to say that no human institution can work effectively without the injection of a moral dimension in human society.

Progress in the realization of the second part of the vision – equitable distribution of credit – has not been significant. It may be difficult to realize this part of the vision without integrating the microfinance sector with the mainstream financial system. This will make available a significantly larger volume of funds for financing micro enterprises in urban and rural areas to reduce poverty, unemployment and income inequalities. Commercial banks need not enter directly into microfinance if they find this to be cumbersome. They may do it through their subsidiaries and the institutions that already exist for this purpose. If a relatively greater share of the resources of the financial system does not become available to the poor and lower middle classes, then Islamic finance will not be able to contribute positively to the realization of the *maqasid* (objectives) of *shari'a* and, thereby, fail to come up to the expectations of the people.

In conclusion, one may say that, even though a substantial degree of progress has been made in quantitative terms, progress toward the realization of the Islamic vision has lagged behind. This is because the Islamic system has so far been unable to escape the trappings of conventional finance. A part of the explanation lies in the difficulties faced in the successful establishment of a new system in place of the well-entrenched interest-oriented conventional system when even the necessary shared institutions do not exist to support its operations.

However, a number of things have happened that will help reduce the difficulties in the future and enable the industry to meet successfully the challenges that it faces. The most important of these is the establishment of some needed infrastructure institutions. One of these is the Islamic Development Bank, which was established in the very initial phase of Islamic finance, and is in the nature of a World Bank for Muslim countries operating on Islamic principles. It has also played a catalytic role in the accelerated development of the Islamic financial industry. Another is the IFSB, which is in the process of setting standards and guidelines for the industry. Once these guidelines are set, their implementation by the regulatory and supervisory authorities will begin. This will bring about greater harmony in the operations of the industry and help not only remove some of its weaknesses but also strengthen and expand it significantly. The establishment of the IIRA, AAOIFI, IIFM and LMC will also bring positive results. Other infrastructure institutions, particularly academic institutions for training highly qualified expertise in Islamic finance, will add further strength to the industry. The central banks have also become more active and are trying to help remove the difficulties that lie in the path of ensuring Islamization of the industry in the real sense. On the whole the future looks bright for the industry.

Notes

1. This chapter draws heavily on the author's previous writings, especially Chapra (1985, 1992, 2000), Chapra and Khan (2000) and Chapra and Ahmed (2002). He is grateful to the co-authors of the latter two occasional papers for their permission to adapt some of the material here. The views expressed in this chapter do not necessarily reflect the views of IRTI or IDB. The author is also grateful to Abdel-Hameed Bashir for his valuable comments on an earlier draft and to Shaikh M. Rashid and M. Rasuil Hoque for the efficient secretarial assistance provided by them.
2. *Mudaraba* (commenda) refers to an agreement between two or more persons whereby one or more of them provide finance, while the others provide management. The purpose is to undertake trade, industry or service with the objective of earning profit. The profit may be shared by the financiers and the managers in any agreed proportion. The loss must, however, be borne only by the financiers in proportion to their share in total capital. The loss of the manager lies in having no return for his /her effort.
    Musharaka (partnership) is also an agreement between two or more persons. However, unlike *mudaraba*, all of the partners contribute finance as well as entrepreneurship and management, though not necessarily equally. Their share in profits can be in accordance with the agreement but the share in losses must be in proportion to their share in capital.
3. *Murabaha* (also called *bai' muajjal*) refers to a sales agreement whereby the seller purchases the goods desired by the buyer and sells them at an agreed marked-up price, the payment being settled within a specified time frame, either in instalments or a lump sum. The seller bears the risk for the goods until they have been delivered to the buyer.
    Salam refers to a sales agreement whereby full payment is made in advance against an obligation to deliver the specified fungible goods at an agreed future date. This is not the same as speculative forward sale because full, and not margin, payment is required. Under this arrangement the seller, say a farmer, may be able to secure the needed financing by making an advance sale of only a part of his expected output. This may not get him into delivery problems in case of a fall in output due to unforeseen circumstances.
    Istisnaa refers to a sales agreement whereby a manufacturer (contractor) agrees to produce (build) and deliver a certain good (or premise) at a given price on a given date in the future. This, like *salam*, is an exception to the general *shari'a* ruling which does not allow a person to sell what he does not own and possess. However, unlike *salam*, the price need not be paid in advance. It may be paid in instalments in step with the preferences of the parties, or partly at the front end and the balance later on as agreed.
4. These were also called *sayarifah* (sing., *sayrafi*) (see the word *sarf* in Ibn Manzur, *Lisan al-'Arab*). Another less popular word used for *sarrafs* was *jahabidhah* (sing., *jahbadh*). The *sarrafs* were more widespread

because they provided banking facilities to the public sector as well as an extensive private sector. The *jahabidhah* were less prevalent because they served mainly the public sector (cf., Duri, 1986, p. 898).

5. Abdul Jabbar Khan, ex-President, Habib Bank of Pakistan, has emphasized that the 'auditing system presently in vogue suffers from a number of weaknesses. There is, therefore, an urgent need for a thorough reappraisal of the existing laws and practices governing the role of auditors and for evolving a really independent auditing system'. (See his privately circulated paper, 'Commercial Banking Operations in the Interest-Free Framework', p. 39). See also al-Qabbani (n.d.) and Khan (1981).

6. Some of the jurists do not find this to be acceptable because it appears to them as a form of reciprocal lending *(qurud mutabadalah)* which is like deriving benefit from a loan, and hence equivalent to interest. However, some other highly respectable jurists have allowed this, provided that it does not involve the taking and giving of interest (see Ahmad and Abu Ghuddah, 1998, p. 236). Mutual help of this kind is a form of cooperative insurance, whereby the banks provide themselves with protection in case of need. Such cooperation had prevailed in Muslim history between businesses in the form of what was then called *ibda'* or *bida'ah* (see Chapra, 1985, pp. 75, 250).

7. The detailed discussion that this subject requires is beyond the scope of this chapter. For some relevant discussion on the reform of the stock market, see Chapra (1985, pp. 95–100) and Chapra (2002).

8. In Germany it is customary for individual shareholders to transfer their voting rights to banks or to shareholder associations who send their representatives to the meeting (Balling et. al., 1998, p. xxii).

9. See Tables 2.3 and 2.4 in Chapra and Ahmed (2002) for the results of a sample survey conducted by IRTI. Figures have not been given above because of the small size of this sample.

10. The *mudaraba* form of business allows only normal expenses of the *mudarib* to be charged to the *mudaraba* account. The *mudarib* is not entitled to a fixed remuneration or an absolute amount of profit specified in advance. His only entitlement beyond the normal expenses of business is a mutually agreed share in profit as a reward for his management services.

11. A fiduciary is 'a person who is entrusted to act as a substitute for another person for the sole purpose of serving that person' (Iwai, 2001).

12. This section has been adapted from Chapra and Khan (2000, pp. 71–83).

13. For a range of opinions expressed on the subject, see M.A. Zarqa and M.A. El-Gari (1991, pp. 25–27) as well as the comments by M. Zaki 'Abd al-Barr, and Habib al-Kaf, on pp. 61–4 of the same issue, and by Rabi' al-Rabi on pp. 67–9 of the 1992 issue of the same journal. See also al-Misri (1997, pp. 131–54; al-Zu'ayr, 1997, pp. 50–57; Abu Ghuddah and Khoja, 1997, pp. 55 and 91).

14. The jurists, however, allow the sub-lease of a leased asset even though the sub-lessor is not the owner of the asset. The sub-lessor then bears the risk, but can pass it on to the original lessor.

15. This does not mean that the lessee cannot make lease payments in advance of the lease period. However, his liability cannot start until he has received the leased asset.

16. For a detailed meaning and explanation of *gharar*, see Saleh (1986, pp. 49–52).

17. According to al-Ghazali (d.1111): 'The objective of the *Shari'a* is to promote the well-being of the people, which lies in protecting their faith, their life, their intellect, their posterity, and their wealth. Whatever ensures the protection of these five serves public interest and is desirable' (1937, pp. 139–40). The same objectives have been upheld in the same, or a somewhat different, order by a number of other jurists. (For a discussion of these *maqasid*, see Chapra, 2000, pp. 118–123.)

Bibliography

Abu Ghuddah, Abd al-Fattah and Izz al-Din Khoja (1997), *Fatawa Nadwah al-Barakah, 1981–1997*, Jeddah: Shirkah al-Barakah li al-Istithmar wa al-Tanmiyah.

Ahmad, Muhay al-Din Ahmad and Abd al-Sattar Abu Ghuddah (1998), *Fatawa al-Khidmat al-Masrafiyyah*, Jeddah: Majmu 'ah Dallah al-Barakah.

Ali, Salman Syed (2005), *Islamic Capital Market Products: Development and Challenges*, occasional paper no.9, Jeddah: IRTI/IDB.

Al-Qaradawi, Yusuf al- (1969), *Fiqh al-Zakat*, Beirut: Dar al-Irshad.

Alvarez, Ana, Silvia Anson and Carolos Mendez (1998), 'The effect of board size and composition on corporate governance', in Morten Balling, Elizabeth Hennessey and Richard O'Brien (eds), *Corporate Governance, Financial Markets and Global Convergence*, The Hague: Kluwer Academic Publishers.

Balling, Morten, Elizabeth Hennessey and Richard O'Brien (eds) (1998), *Corporate Governance, Financial Markets and Global Convergence*, The Hague: Kluwer Academic Publishers.

Berle A. and G. Means (1932), *The Modern Corporation and Private Property*, New York: Macmillan.

Bigsten, Arne (1987), 'Poverty, inequality and development', in Norman Gemmell (ed.), *Surveys in Development Economics*, Oxford: Basil Blackwell.

Chapra, M. Umer (1985), *Towards A Just Monetary System*, Leicester: The Islamic Foundation.

Chapra, M. Umer (1992), *Islam and the Economic Challenge*, Leicester: The Islamic Foundation.

Chapra, M. Umer (2000), *The Future of Economics: an Islamic Perspective*, Leicester: The Islamic Foundation.
Chapra, M. Umer (2002), 'Alternative visions of international monetary reform', in Munawar Iqbal and David Llewellyn (eds), *Islamic Banking and Finance: New Perspectives on Profit-Sharing and Risk*, Cheltenham, UK and Northampton, MA, USA: Edward Elgar.
Chapra, M.U. and Tariqullah Khan (2000), *Regulation and Supervision of Islamic Banks*, occasional paper no. 3, Jeddah: IRTI/IDB.
Chapra, M. Umer and Habib Ahmed (2002), *Corporate Governance in Islamic Financial Institutions*, occasional paper no.6, Jeddah: IRTI/IDB.
Dinsdale, Nicholas, and Martha Prevezer (1994, reprinted 2001), *Capital Markets and Corporate Governance*, Oxford: Clarendon Press.
Duri A.A. (1986), 'Baghdad', *The Encyclopaedia of Islam*, vol. 1, Leiden: Brill, pp. 894–909.
Elliot, R.K. and J.J. Willingham (1980), *Management Fraud: Detection and Deterrence*, New York: Princeton.
Fischel, W.J. (1992), 'Djahbadh', *The Encyclopaedia of Islam*, vol. 2, Leiden: Brill, pp. 382–3.
Gemmell, Norman (ed.) (1987), *Surveys in Development Economics*, Oxford: Basil Blackwell.
Ghazali, Abu Hamid al- (d.1111) (1937), *al-Mustasfa*, Cairo: al-Maktabah al-Tijariyyah al-Kubra.
Goitein, S.D. (1966), *Studies in Islamic History and Institutions*, Leiden: Brill.
Goitein, S.D. (1967), *A Mediterranean Society*, Berkeley and Los Angeles: University of California Press.
Grief, Avner (1997), 'Informal contract enforcement: lessons from medieval trade', *The New Palgrave Dictionary of Economics and the Law*, vol. 2, London: Palgrave, pp. 287–95.
Herzel, Leo (1994), 'Corporate governance', *The New Palgrave Dictionary of Money and Finance*, vol. 1, London: Palgrave, pp. 472–5.
Iqbal, Munawar and David Llewellyn (eds) (2002), *Islamic Banking and Finance: New Perspectives on Profit-Sharing and Risk*, Cheltenham, UK, and Northampton, MA, USA: Edward Elgar.
Iqbal, Munawar, Tariqullah Khan and Ausaf Ahmad (1998), *Challenges Facing Islamic Banking*, occasional paper no. 2, Jeddah: IRTI/IDB.
Iwai, Katsuhito (2001), 'What is corporation: the corporate personality controversy and comparative corporate governance', in F. Cafaggi, A. Nicita and V. Pagano (eds), *Legal Orderings and Economic Institutions*, London: Routledge.
Jarhi, Ma'bid al- and Munawar Iqbal (2001), *Islamic Banking: Answers to Some Frequently Asked Questions*, occasional paper no. 4, Jeddah: IRTI/IDB.
Jensen M. and W. Meckling (1976), 'Theory of the firm: managerial behaviour, agency costs and ownership structure', *Journal of Financial Economics*, **3**, 305–60.
Khan, M. Akram (1981), 'Auditing in an Islamic framework', unpublished paper.
Khan, Tariqullah and Habib Ahmed (2001), 'Risk Management: an analysis of issues in Islamic financial industry', Occasional Paper No. 5, IRTI, IDB, Jeddah.
Kramers, J.H. (1952), 'Geography and commerce', in T. Arnold and A. Guillaume (eds), *The Legacy of Islam*, London: Oxford University Press.
Laeven, Luc (2002), 'Bank risk and deposit insurance', *The World Bank Economic Review*, **16** (1), 109–37.
Leadbearer, Charles (1986), 'Rags to riches: fact or fiction', *Financial Times*, 30 December, 5.
Lechner, Alan (1998), *Street Games: Inside Stories of the Wall Street Hustle*, New York: Harper & Row.
Mace, Myles (1996), *Directors: Myth and Reality*, Boston: Harvard Business School Press.
Miles, G.C. (1992), 'Dinar' and 'Dirham', *The Encyclopaedia of Islam*, vol. 2, Leiden: Brill, pp. 297–9 and 319–20.
Mills, Paul and John Presley (1999), *Islamic Finance: Theory and Practice*, London: Macmillan.
Misri, Rafiq Yunus al- (1st edn 1990, 2nd edn 1997), *Bay' al-Taqsīt: Tahlīl Fiqhī wa Iqtisādī*, Damascus: Dār al-Qalam.
Misri, Rafiq al (1998), 'Hal Yajuz Istithmar Amwal al-Yatama bi al-Riba?' (Is it permissible to invest the wealth of orphans on interest?), *Majallah al-Amwal*, Jeddah, **6**, 1419.
Morck, Randall (1994), 'Corporate ownership and management', *New Palgrave Dictionary of Money and Finance*, vol. 1, London: Macmillan, pp. 475–7.
Morck, R.K., A. Schleifer and R.W. Vishny (1990), 'Do managerial objectives drive bad acquisitions?', *Journal of Finance*, **45** (1), 31–48.
Organization of the Islamic Conference (1981), 'Promotion, regulation and supervision of Islamic banks', report prepared by a Committee of the Governors of Central Bank and Monetary Authorities of the Organization and adopted by the Governors at their fourth meeting held in Khartoum, 7–8 March.
Prentice, D.D. (1993), 'Some aspects of the corporate governance debate', in D.D. Prentice and P. Holland (eds), *Contemporary Issues in Corporate Governance*, Oxford: Clarendon Press.
Prentice, D.D. and P. Holland (eds) (1993), *Contemporary Issues in Corporate Governance*, Oxford: Clarendon Press.
Prowse, Stephen (1998), 'Corporate governance: emerging issues and lessons for East Asia' (World Bank) (www.worldbank org/html/extdr/pos 981).
Qabbani, Thana 'Ali al- (n.d.), *Ba'd Khasa'is Tatawwur al-Fikr al-Muhasabi al-Mu'asir wa al-Muhasabah al-Islamiyyah*, Cairo: *Matabi' al-Ittihad al-Dawiī li al- Bunuk al Islamiyyah*.

Rauch, James E. (2001), 'Business and social networks in international trade', *Journal of Economic Literature*, December, 1177–1203.

Saleh, Nabil A. (1986), *Unlawful Gain and Legitimate Profit in Islamic Law: Riba, Gharar and Islamic Banking*, Cambridge: Cambridge University Press.

Schacht, J. (1970), 'Law and justice', in P.M. Holt, Ann Lambton and Bernard Lewis (eds), *The Cambridge History of Islam*, vol. 2, Cambridge: Cambridge University Press, pp. 539–68.

Schatzmiller, Maya (1994), *Labour in the Medieval Islamic World*, Leiden: Brill.

Schleifer, A. and R. Vishny (1997), 'A survey of corporate governance', *Journal of Finance*, **52**, 737–83.

Sundararajan, V., C.A. Enoch, A. San Jose, Paul L. Hilbers, Russell C. Kruger, Marina Moretti and Graham L. Slack (2002), *Financial Soundness Indicators: Analytical Aspects and Country Practices*, Washington, DC: IMF.

Sykes, Allen (1994), 'Proposals for a reformed system of corporate governance to achieve internationally competitive long-term performance', in N. Dinsdale and M. Prevezer (eds), *Capital Markets and Corporate Governance*, Oxford: Clarendon Press, pp. 111–27.

Udovitch, Abraham L. (1970), *Partnership and Profit in Medieval Islam*, Princeton, NJ: Princeton University Press.

Udovitch, Abraham L. (1981), *Bankers without banks: commerce, banking and society in the Islamic world of Middle Ages*, Princeton Near East Paper no. 30, Princeton, NJ: Princeton University Press.

United States House of Representatives (1986), *Banking for the Poor: Alleviating Poverty Through Credit Assistance in Developing Countries, Report of the Select Committee on Hunger*.

Yunus, Muhammad (1984), *Group-Based Savings and Credit for the Rural Poor*, Dhaka: Grameen Bank.

Yunus, Muhammad (1987), 'The poor as the engine of growth', *The Washington Quarterly*, **10** (4), 05309.

Zarqa, M. Anas and M. Ali El-Gari (1991), 'Al-Ta'wid 'an Darar al Mumamatalah fi al-Dayn bayn al-Fiqh wa al-Iqtisad', *Journal of King Abdulaziz University: Islamic Economics*, 25–57.

Zu'ayr, M. Abd al-Hakim (1997), '*Fatwa* and *Shari'a* supervision at Islamic banks', *The American Journal of Islamic Finance*, Rancho Polos Verdes, CA, **3**, 4–6.

PART V

GLOBALIZATION OF ISLAMIC BANKING

22 International Islamic financial institutions[1]
Munawar Iqbal

Introduction
Every system has its institutional requirements. Islamic banks are no exception. They need a number of supporting institutions/arrangements to perform various functions. In the last 30 years, Islamic banking institutions all over the world have tried to benefit from the institutional framework that supports conventional banking which is not generally geared to meet their specific needs. Building a proper institutional set-up is perhaps the most serious challenge for Islamic finance in the coming years. Iqbal et al. (1998) and Jarhi al- and Iqbal (2001) have identified some of the requirements for proper institutional arrangements. The process of institution building for the Islamic financial industry is already under way and has gained momentum in the last few years, yet a lot of ground still needs to be covered. In this chapter we provide a brief review of the emerging international financial architecture for the industry.

Major international infrastructure institutions established so far that support the Islamic financial industry include the following:

1. Islamic Development Bank Group (IDB Group),
2. Accounting and Auditing Organization for Islamic Financial Institutions (AAOIFI),
3. Islamic Financial Services Board (IFSB),
4. International Islamic Financial Market (IIFM),
5. International Islamic Rating Agency (IIRA),
6. International Islamic Centre for Reconciliation and Commercial Arbitration,
7. General Council of Islamic Banks and Financial Institutions (GCIBFI).

A brief overview of each of these is provided below.

Islamic Development Bank Group
The Islamic Development Bank Group (IDB Group) is a multilateral development finance institution comprising four entities: the Islamic Development Bank (IDB), the Islamic Corporation for the Insurance of Investment and Export Credit (ICIEC), the Islamic Corporation for the Development of the Private Sector (ICD), and the Islamic Research and Training Institute (IRTI). These entities, with IDB as the flagship, were established at different times in the history of the Group, each with its objectives and operational modalities but sharing common vision and mission. Headquartered in Jeddah (Saudi Arabia), the IDB Group has three regional offices in member countries: Almaty (Kazakhstan), Kuala Lumpur (Malaysia) and Rabat (Morocco). It also has eight field representatives in ten member countries: Bangladesh, Guinea, Guinea Bissau, Indonesia, Libya, Mauritania, Pakistan, Sierra Leone, Senegal and Sudan. Of the four members of the Group, IRTI is not a financial institution and as such falls outside the scope of this chapter. The other three institutions are reviewed in the following sections.

Islamic Development Bank (IDB)
It was the establishment of the Islamic Development Bank (IDB) in 1975 that heralded the emergence of the Islamic financial industry. The IDB was established in pursuance of the Declaration of Intent issued at the Conference of Finance Ministers of Muslim Countries held in Jeddah in Dhul Qaadah 1393H (December 1973). Following the inaugural meeting of the Board of Governors of the IDB in Rajab 1395H (July 1975), the IDB formally commenced operations on 15 Shawwal 1395H (20 October 1975).

Objectives   The main objective of the IDB is to foster the economic development and social progress of its member countries as well as Muslim communities in non-member countries either individually or jointly in accordance with the principles of *shari'a*. In pursuit of this aim, the IDB provides support to member countries in the form of project finance. It also establishes and operates special funds for specific purposes, including a fund for assistance to the Muslim communities in non-member countries.

Structure   The apex body of the IDB is the Board of Governors. Each member nominates one governor and one alternative governor to this Board (usually a finance/economic minister or the Central Bank governor of the country concerned). The Board meets once every year in a member country, by rotation. Among other things, the Board of Governors elects the president (chief executive) of the bank for a five-year term which is renewable.

The operational policies of the IDB are set by a Board of Executive Directors (BED) which comprises 14 members. Seven are permanent members nominated by the countries with the largest shares, as shown in Figure 22.1. The other seven members are elected for a three-year term on a rotation basis from the members grouped into seven groups. The BED is chaired by the president.

All member countries of the OIC are eligible for membership of the IDB. However, to become a member, a country has to make a specified contribution to the capital of the IDB and undertake to accept terms and conditions to be decided upon by its Board of Governors.

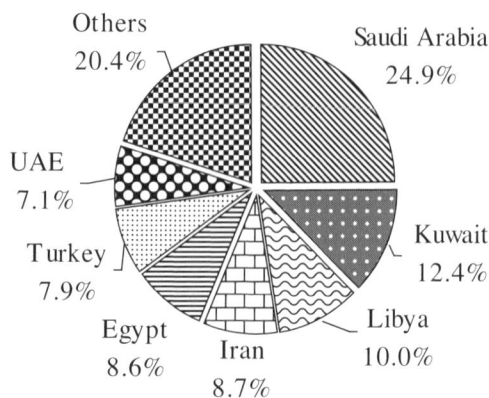

Figure 22.1   Major shareholders of IDB

The membership of the bank has increased steadily over time, from 22 founding member countries in 1395H (1975) to 55 countries by the end of 1425H (9 February 2005).

Resources   The main source of its financial resources is the member country funds. Unlike other financial institutions, the bank does not receive interest-based deposits, nor does it augment its financial resources by borrowing funds from conventional world financial markets because this would involve payment of interest, which is not compatible with *shari'a*. Instead, the bank has developed new schemes and financial instruments which are in conformity with the principles of *shari'a*, with a view to supplementing its ordinary financial resources.

The capital base of the bank has witnessed significant expansion over the years. The authorized capital of IDB has increased over time from Islamic Dinar (ID)2 billion to ID15 billion (US $22.56 billion).[2] Similarly, the issued capital has increased to ID8.1 billion ($12.18 billion). At the end of 1425H (2005),[3] the paid-in capital of the bank stood at ID2.73 billion ($5.42 billion) and the ordinary capital resources consisting of the member countries' funds (that is, the paid-in capital, reserves and retained earnings) stood at ID4.27 billion ($6.42 billion) (Islamic Development Bank, 2005).

In order to supplement its capital resources the bank has launched several *shari'a*-compatible schemes at different times. The first such scheme, the Investment Deposit Scheme, was introduced in 1400H (1980). It provides investors with an option for making investments through participation in the financing operations of the bank. Under the scheme, the bank accepts deposits from investors and uses them to make short-term investment through participation in foreign trade financing operations. The Islamic Banks Portfolio (IBP) is another window through which the bank mobilizes liquidity available with the Islamic banks, financial institutions and individual investors, and channels it to finance beneficiaries in its member countries. The Unit Investment Fund (UIF) is a private sector window that raises additional resources for the bank from the market and, at the same time, provides investors with a profitable channel of investment in conformity with *shari'a*. The Export Financing Scheme (EFS) mobilizes funds to be used exclusively for promoting exports from the member countries. As of the end of 1425H, the funds raised through these schemes were $138.96 million through the Investment Deposit Scheme, $100 million through the IBP, $325 million through the UIF and $201.53 million through the EFS.

Recently IDB has started mobilizing resources from the international capital markets on competitive rates through *sukuk*. The bank issued its first *sukuk* bond in 1424H, which generated $400 million. In order to meet the growing needs for additional resources, the bank has recently launched (second quarter 2005) the second *sukuk* issue under the Euro Medium Term Note (EMTN) Programme for $1billion with a 'benchmark issue'/first tranche of $500 million. The remaining tranche of a smaller amount will be offered later, depending on the liquidity requirements of the bank.

Activities   IDB conducts its development assistance mainly through three types of financing operations, namely (i) ordinary operations comprising project financing and technical assistance operations; (ii) trade financing operations; and (iii) Waqf Fund operations. The extent of the efforts made over the years is indicated by the assistance given by the bank to its member countries during the past 31 years. Up to the end of 1425H,

Table 22.1   IDB financing operations

IDB financing operations	Total cumulative approval
Project financing	ID 10.7 billion ($14.5 bn)
Trade financing	ID 17.6 billion ($23.3 bn)
Special assistance operations	ID 0.47 billion ($0.6 bn)
Total	ID 29.0 billion ($38.4 bn)

financing approved by the bank for different operations amounted to ID28.8 billion ($38.3 billion).[4] The break-up of net financing of IDB for the period 1396–1425H is given in Table 22.1. All financing is provided through Islamic modes of finance. These modes of finance include interest-free loans, equity participation, leasing, instalment sale and *istisnaa*. Among these modes of financing loan, instalment sale and leasing are the most important. Between 1396H (1976) and 1425H (2005), 84 per cent of the project financing was done through these modes. Over one-third (35 per cent) of the financing was provided in the form of loans – a concessionary mode of IDB financing. The shares of leasing and instalment sale were 26.4 and 22.7 per cent, respectively.

A brief description and salient features of these modes as used by IDB are given below.

Loans

1. Loans provide long-term financing for the implementation of development projects, mainly in agriculture (canals, rural water supply, etc.) and infrastructure (roads, social facilities such as schools, hospitals, etc.).
2. Currently loans are limited to a maximum of ID7 million per project. They are given interest-free and bear only a service fee to cover related administrative expenses incurred by IDB when formulating and processing the project. Repayment is made in equal semi-annual instalments and extends over a period varying between 15 and 25 years, with a grace period of three to five years, depending on the country and the project.
3. IDB financing usually covers (fully or partially) the foreign cost of specific components. In certain cases, particularly for least-developed countries, it may also cover part of the local cost.
4. The beneficiary is expected to contribute to the project financing. Co-financing with other institutions is also possible under certain conditions (usually parallel financing or, if procedures are similar to those of IDB, joint financing).
5. Loans are normally extended to governments or public institutions having the government guarantee. The private sector may benefit from loans only in special cases.
6. While loans are mainly for least developed countries, they may also be extended to other member countries, particularly in combination with other modes (leasing or instalment sale) when possible.
7. Regional operations as well as projects which promote complementarity between the economies of the member countries are given special consideration.

Instalment sale

1. Instalment sale is a medium-term mode of financing introduced by the Islamic Development Bank in 1405H (October 1984).
2. A request for financing by a government agency or a private entrepreneur under this mode has to be made to the IDB through the office of the governor, IDB of the relevant member country. The official request must be accompanied by a feasibility study or an appropriate project document.
3. This mode of financing calls for a contract between the IDB and the beneficiary entity for whom the bank procures tangible asset(s) and sells it at a mark-up allowing him to make the payment on a deferred basis.
4. The bank finances both locally fabricated as well as imported items of capital assets. Under special circumstances, however, IDB also finances special services associated with a project/operation and supervision during the construction. The minimum limit of financing provided directly by the bank under instalment sale is ID2.0 million and the upper limit is about ID20 million. Total IDB financing could be higher if combined with its other windows of financing such as IBP, UIF and so on.
5. The items eligible for financing under this mode generally include equipment under various economic sectors, such as infrastructure, industry, agriculture, education and health, and covers construction equipment and machinery, industrial equipment, transport equipment and so on. The main criterion for determining the eligibility of an equipment for financing under this mode is that its useful life should not be less than the period proposed for repayment of the IDB financing.
6. Payment is usually made by the beneficiary in semi-annual instalments. The maximum period allowed for instalment sale operations is generally ten years, including the gestation period. However, it could be extended to 12 years for infrastructure projects with a ceiling of ID10 million per project. IDB may also consider extending the period up to 12 years for countries with a Structural Adjustment Programme of the IMF and having no scope to obtain financing from other institutions for repayment in less than 12 years. On delivery of the asset(s) to the beneficiary, the ownership of the asset(s) is transferred from the IDB to the beneficiary.
7. The mark-up currently ranges between 7.5 and 8.5 per cent, depending on the nature of the project and the economic standing of the concerned member country. There is, however, a 15 per cent rebate on the mark-up if the payment is made on time by the beneficiary in accordance with the agreed schedule of payment.
8. For all projects/operations financed by the IDB under this mode, the beneficiary has to provide a guarantee. If it is a project sponsored by the government or its agencies, guarantee by the government is sufficient. In the case where it is a private sector project, it is necessary to provide a guarantee from a first-class commercial bank acceptable to IDB.
9. All purchases are to be undertaken by the beneficiary as an agent of the bank and in close coordination with and concurrence of the bank. The equipment is to be procured in conformity with the bank's procurement procedures, that is, by international competitive bidding. Procurement through local competitive bidding or restricted tendering may, however, be permitted only under special circumstances.
10. The IDB generally disburses funds only after the costs have been incurred. After the finalization of contract and award of bids, the bank asks the beneficiary to open a

letter of credit in favour of a supplier and the payment is made directly to the supplier. The standard disbursement procedure is as follows: (i) down-payment of 10 per cent to the supplier on signature of contract and against an acceptable bank guarantee; (ii) disbursement of 80 per cent against shipping documents; (iii) disbursement of the balance on satisfactory completion of the supply of goods and services.

Leasing

1. As introduced and practised by IDB, leasing is a source of medium-term financing to meet the financing requirements of income-generating projects in industry and other important sectors for which the rental payment and lease period are determined in the light of the projected profitability and cash flow of the project.
2. Under leasing, IDB finances various items such as plant, machinery and equipment for industrial, agroindustrial, infrastructural, transport and other projects, normally of an income-generating nature in both public and private sectors. Lease financing is also provided for ships, oil tankers, trawlers and other specialized cargo vessels either new or second-hand, up to five years old.
3. IDB normally finances the total cost of machinery and equipment which comprises the cost including freight (CIF) price, inland transportation, erection and installation.
4. The bank retains the ownership of the leased assets throughout the entire lease period which may extend up to 12 years, including a period of gestation that ranges between six and 36 months, depending on the envisaged implementation period of the project. The prevailing return to IDB is 7.5–8.5 per cent if calculated on a yearly basis.
5. After the end of the lease period and full payment of the rentals by the lessee, the IDB transfers the ownership of the equipment to the lessee as a gift.
6. The lessee should provide the bank (the lessor) with an irrevocable and unconditional guarantee from the government or a first-class commercial bank acceptable to IDB to cover all obligations of the lessee under the lease agreement to be signed between IDB and the lessee.

Lines of financing   In addition to financing projects directly, IDB also extends lines of financing to the National Development Financing Institutions (NDFIs) in member countries especially to promote the growth and development of small and medium enterprises (SMEs) mainly in the private sector. The lines extended comprise, and under a line the IDB approves, a certain amount of financing for a national development financing institution which can use the line to finance industrial/commercial projects identified and appraised by it. Under the line of equity, the IDB participates in the share capital of a company sponsoring technically and financially viable projects up to a maximum of one-third of its equity capital while, under the lines of leasing and instalment sale, IDB finances the procurement of machinery, equipment and other capital assets for new or expansion projects. Under the line of leasing, the asset is acquired by the IDB and leased to the company until the lease period expires. The ownership of the leased asset is transferred to the lessee by the lessor (IDB) following the payment of the last instalment by the beneficiary. Under the line of instalment sale, the ownership of the asset which is procured by the IDB is transferred to the beneficiary on its delivery. The maximum repayment period allowed for projects under the line of instalment sale and leasing is generally

12 years, including a gestation period of up to a maximum of three years, depending mainly on the anticipated implementation and commissioning period. Under a line of leasing the maximum period may be extended to 15 years. The gestation period may be extended to 48 months or more, depending on the merits of each case.

For each project financed under the line of leasing/instalment sale, a bank guarantee is required for repayment of IDB dues. However, the NDFIs concerned generally provide the required guarantee. In some countries where the development banks are not authorized or are not willing to give guarantees, a commercial bank or a government guarantee is acceptable.

Priority areas   Two areas have always been high on the agenda of the IDB: trade promotion among member countries and poverty alleviation. Its activities in these areas are summarized below.

Trade promotion activities   IDB accords high priority to the promotion of trade amongst member countries, recognizing that trade contributes immensely to the development process. To this end, IDB has evolved several modes of financing to support and encourage trade.

An Import Trade Financing Operations (ITFO) scheme was launched in 1397H (1977) to finance the import of raw materials, intermediate and finished goods of member countries. The scheme received an overwhelming response as it enabled the member countries to benefit from ITFO financing for imports of developmental raw materials and inputs. The scheme also served as a vehicle for utilization of the bank's liquid funds in a *shari'a*-compatible way.

The bank launched another scheme, the Export Financing Scheme (EFS), in 1408H. As a suppliers' credit scheme, it aims to promote exports from the member countries through provision of short- and long-term financing for the exports destined for both the member and non-member countries. The mark-up charged on the EFS operations is generally kept below the market levels. The EFS has its own membership, capital, budget and resources, and its accounts are maintained separately. Currently, the scheme has 26 participating countries as its members, with a total contribution of ID170 million. This amount, together with the IDB's contribution of ID150 million, brings the total subscribed capital to ID320 million. The paid-up capital of the scheme is ID134 million, of which ID75 million was paid by the bank.

In addition to these two major schemes, trade financing is also conducted through the bank's other windows, namely the Islamic Banks' Portfolio (IBP), the Unit Investment Fund (UIF), the Islamic Corporation for Private Sector Development (ICD) and the Awqaf Properties Investment Fund (APIF). The IDB also manages a special programme on behalf of the Arab Bank for Economic Development in Africa (BADEA) based in Khartoum, which is designed to finance exports originating from Arab member countries to non-Arab league member countries of the African Union.

The total net financing approved by the IDB under its trade financing schemes since its inception until the end of 1425H (2005) amounted to ID17.6 billion ($23.3 billion).

Poverty alleviation programmes   Among the 55 member countries of the IDB, 26 are 'least developed', while four other member countries are treated as such. These countries are given priority in respect of concessionary (loan and technical assistance) financing of the bank. Loans are provided free of interest and the bank charges a modest service fee to enable it to recover only the administrative costs incurred in its financing. In addition, loans provided by the bank include a grace period of three to seven years and the repayment is spread over a period of 15–25 years. LDMCs are usually given the maximum grace and repayment periods. Loans are provided for projects with a significant socioeconomic developmental impact.

As a demonstration of the bank's concern for poverty alleviation, in 1413H (1992) the Board of Executive Directors established a special window called 'Special Account for the LDMCs'. The objective of the window is to increase the total financial resources available to these countries to meet the basic and urgent needs. This account is used to finance projects or components of projects that would not, normally, be financed by the bank under its regular programmes. Loans from this account are granted for a maximum period of 30 years, including a grace period of ten years, with a service fee not exceeding 0.75 per cent per year. Special consideration is given to the needs of poor segments of the population. The areas of support include primary services, such as basic schooling and health care, provision of adequate and safe drinking water, and micro projects in remote locations. Following the full utilization of the initial amount of $100 million, the LDMC Account was replenished in 1420H and was supplemented with a second tranche of $150 million. An aggregate amount of ID13.29 million ($19.04 million) was approved from this account until the end of 1425H.

The total amount of project and TA financing approved for the LDMCs so far has reached ID2.15 billion ($2.83 billion), representing 41 per cent of the aggregate financing approved for all type of operations in LDMCs and 26 per cent of total ordinary resources approved by IDB. LDMCs share in cumulative loan approvals of the bank has reached 83.8 per cent (ID2.28 billion).

IDB also established a Special Assistance Account in 1399H (1979). The account is kept separate from its ordinary resources and is used, among others, for the following purposes: (a) provision of relief in the form of appropriate goods and services to member countries and Islamic communities afflicted by natural disasters and calamities, (b) provision of financial assistance to Muslim communities in non-member countries to improve their socioeconomic conditions, (c) provision of financial assistance to member countries for the promotion and furtherance of Islamic causes, and (d) training and research aimed at helping and guiding member countries to reorient their economies, financial and banking activities in conformity with *shari'a*.

Islamic Corporation for the Insurance of Investment and Export Credit (ICIEC)
As mentioned above, trade promotion among member countries is high on the agenda of the Islamic Development Bank. It was realized that provision of export insurance services could contribute significantly towards the achievement of that objective. Therefore, the Board of the bank decided to establish a specialized institution for that purpose. Accordingly, ICIEC was established on 24 Safar 1415H (1 August 1994).

Membership of ICIEC is open to the Islamic Development Bank and countries which are members of the Organization of the Islamic Conference (OIC). At the end of 1425H, there were 35 shareholders of ICIEC, comprising the IDB and 34 countries. Several other countries are in the process of completing the membership requirements.

The authorized capital of ICIEC is ID100 million (US$150 million). The subscribed capital of the Corporation is ID96.99 million (US$145.87 million). IDB contributed ID50 million (US$75.20 million), which represents 50 per cent of authorized capital. Member countries subscribed ID46.99 million (US$70.67 million) (Islamic Corporation for the Insurance of Investment and Export Credit, 2005).

Objectives The objectives of ICIEC are (a) to increase the scope of trade transactions from the member countries of the OIC, (b) to facilitate foreign direct investments into OIC member countries, and (c) to provide reinsurance facilities to Export Credit Agencies (ECAs) in member countries.

Activities ICIEC fulfils these objectives by providing appropriate Islamic *shari'a*-compatible insurance instruments. It provides *shari'a*-compliant export credit insurance and reinsurance to cover the non-payment of export receivables resulting from commercial (buyer) and non-commercial (country) risks. It also provides investment insurance and reinsurance against country risk, emanating mainly from foreign exchange transfer restrictions, expropriation, war and civil disturbance and breach of contract by the host government. ICIEC commenced its business operations with three types of insurance policies. Since then, it has introduced new products, services and facilities. A brief description of these is given below.

Export Credit Insurance Programme The Export Credit Insurance Programme is the most active and readily recognized element of ICIEC's operations. It was launched in 1995 in tandem with the official start of ICIEC operations. The programme's main focus is to facilitate trade and project finance flows strictly between member countries. ICIEC provides different insurance instruments to address specific customer needs. It offers three types of insurance policies, viz. a Comprehensive Short Term Policy (CSTP), a Supplemental Medium Term Policy (SMTP) and a Bank Master Policy (BMP).

   Recently, ICIEC has launched two new insurance products. The first is the Documentary Credit Insurance Policy (DCIP) which is an instrument available to commercial banks. The policyholder – the commercial bank – is protected against the risk of non-payment of an Import Letter of Credit issued by an importer's bank and confirmed by the policyholder on behalf of its exporting customer. The second new instrument launched is the Specific Transaction Policy (STP). The STP is designed to insure single short and medium export transactions, usually associated with project finance. It covers the same risks as the existing Supplemental Medium Term Policy (SMTP) which caters for medium-term whole-turnover business. The Export Credit Insurance Products, including the new ICIEC products, are summarized in Table 22.2.

Foreign investment insurance services ICIEC introduced the Foreign Investment Insurance Policy (FIIP) in 1419H (1998). The FIIP provides insurance cover against country risks to investors from member countries who intend to invest in other member countries. Such risks include war, civil disturbance, foreign exchange convertibility and transfer restrictions, nationalization and other forms of host country government interference which may deny the investor his rights to repatriate his investments and profits. The policy cover can be for up to 20 years.

Table 22.2   ICIEC insurance products

Segment	Instrument/product	Maximum term	Purpose	Risk covered
Exporters	Comprehensive Short Term Policy (CSTP)	1 year	To protect exporters and banks against the risk of non-payment of an export receivable	Commercial and country risks
	Supplemental Medium Term Policy (SMTP)	7 years		
	Specific Transaction Policy (STP)	7 years		
Banks	Bank Master Policy (BMP)	7 years		
	Documentary Credit Insurance Policy (DCIP)	7 years	To protect the confirming bank of a Letter of Credit against the risk of non-payment by the issuing bank	

Reinsurance facility   In 1425H, ICIEC developed and launched a new reinsurance product named a Reinsurance Facility Agreement (RFA). This agreement is a facultative reinsurance arrangement that could be developed into a quota share treaty. The Corporation can also participate in existing reinsurance treaties of the ECAs in member countries.

Investment promotion   ICIEC is mandated to facilitate the flow of investments to its member countries. Many of the ICIEC member countries have not been successful in attracting investment flows because of an unfavourable investment environment, lack of investment promotion capacity/capabilities, inability to articulate their competitive sectors and investment projects and the lack of a centralized investment information database.

In order to address these critical issues, an IDB Technical Cooperation Programme in the field of investment promotion has been designed and is ready to be launched. The objective of the programme is to assist member countries in identifying and promoting promising investment opportunities which would encourage foreign investment flows in the member countries. This activity will be undertaken in partnership with relevant specialized multilateral agencies such as the Multilateral Investment Guarantee Agency (MIGA), the United Nations Industrial Development Organization (UNIDO) and more importantly by leveraging IDB's own knowledge base and expertise in project development and finance in member countries.

Since inception, the Corporation has shown a robust growth in its operations. It has underwritten more than 1700 transactions, with an aggregate insurance commitment in excess of US$1.2 billion. It has supported an aggregate of US$650 million in insured business.

Islamic Corporation for the Development of the Private Sector (ICD)
The private sector is one of the most important engines of growth. A vibrant private sector enhances both savings and investment, which in turn lead to higher rates of growth. The

private sector is also more dynamic as decision making is quicker. Unfortunately, in most member countries of the IDB, the public sector has dominated in the last four decades. However, in the 1990s, active privatization programmes were initiated in many countries. In the same period, financial sector reforms were also introduced in these countries. In order to support this process and help member countries build strong private sectors, the Islamic Development Bank decided to establish the Islamic Corporation for the Development of the Private Sector (ICD), which became operational in November 1999.

ICD has an authorized capital of US$1 billion, of which US$500 million are currently open for subscription in the following proportions: 50 per cent for the IDB, 30 per cent for IDB's member countries, and 20 per cent for public financial institutions of ICD's member countries. By the end of 1425H, 44 member countries had joined ICD (Islamic Corporation for the Development of the Private Sector, 2005). In addition, five public financial institutions (three from Iran, one from Saudi Arabia, and one from Algeria) have subscribed to the ICD. Other member countries of IDB are also in the process of ratifying ICD's Articles of Agreement and will soon enjoy full membership. ICD is supervised by an independent Board of Directors.

Objectives   The purpose of ICD is to promote, in accordance with the principles of the *shari'a*, the economic development of its member countries by encouraging the establishment, expansion and modernization of private enterprises producing goods and services in such a way as to supplement the activities of the IDB. The objectives of ICD are (a) to identify opportunities in the private sector that could function as engines of growth, (b) to provide a wide range of productive financial products and services, (c) to mobilize additional resources for the private sector in member countries, and (d) to encourage the development of Islamic financial and capital markets.

Activities   ICD finances private sector projects (projects in which the majority of the voting stock is held by private entities). Only projects that have a majority of the voting stock held by citizens of ICD member countries are eligible. The minimum investment required for a project to be considered by the ICD is US$2 million and the ICD financing cannot exceed 50 per cent of the project's cost. The terms and conditions of ICD's financial products are determined according to the market conditions. Profit margins are set as a sum of the London Interbank Offered Rate (LIBOR) plus a spread. The latter is determined by the country and project-specific risks. Repayment periods are, in general, around five to eight years although, in exceptional cases, tenures can be up to 12 years. These tenures are inclusive of grace periods, the duration of which is determined according to the nature of the project (usually around one year).

ICD provides a wide variety of financial products and services. This enables ICD to offer a mix of financing that is tailored to meet the needs of each project. Some of these products are discussed below.

Direct financing   ICD provides direct financing through equity participation, the purchase of assignable bonds or provision of term financing in productive and viable projects in member countries. As a general policy, ICD will not be the single largest shareholder in any project, nor will it acquire a majority or controlling interest in the share capital of a project or enterprise except when such acquisition is necessary to protect its interest.

Lines of financing   ICD extends lines of financing to commercial banks and national development financing institutions. These lines represent a means to contribute in a cost-effective manner to the financing of small and medium enterprises (SMEs). The modes of financing used within the framework of the lines are usually leasing and instalment sale. Equity and quasi-equity may also be used in certain cases.

Corporate finance   ICD extends short-term corporate finance to cover working capital or raw materials requirements of private sector entities through *murabaha* or purchase and lease-back for a period of (up to) 24 months.

Asset management   ICD can act as a manager (*mudarib*) or sponsor for funds created by other institutional investors. It can create venture capital or sector funds for the financing of projects.

Structured finance   ICD structures, arranges and manages syndications, underwrites and manages shares and securities issues, makes private placements and also carries out securitizations for its clients.

Advisory services   ICD provides advisory services to governments, public and private companies on economic, financial, institutional and legal aspects relating inter alia, to creating a suitable environment for private sector development, project financing, restructuring/rehabilitation of companies, privatization, securitization, Islamic finance and development of Islamic capital markets.

Priority sectors and project types   All sectors other than tourism and recreation are eligible for ICD financing. However the priority sectors for ICD are telecommunications, power, technology and health. Furthermore special attention is given to the export potential of the project. In deciding to finance a project, ICD considers the project's developmental impact on the concerned country, in addition to its financial and technical merits.

Projects eligible for financing by ICD are the following.

Greenfield projects   This refers to investment/financing of start-up companies/projects which will have some impact on the economy as a whole.

Expansion projects   This refers to financing/investment in plant expansion or capacity enhancement.

Existing projects under restructuring/rehabilitation   As most countries are restructuring their industries to reduce dependence on a particular sector, ICD has the opportunity to finance companies that are being restructured or rehabilitated.

Privatization operations   ICD can finance state-owned enterprises which are being privatized as long as the remaining investment by the government in the company does not exceed 49 per cent. ICD will also structure and finance projects implemented through concession agreements (build-operate-transfer (BUT), build-own-operate-transfer (BOOT), build-own-operate (BOO) and so on) and finance the modernization of privatized companies to enhance their productivity and competitiveness.

The total value of approved projects by the ICD from its inception to the end of 1425H reached US$298.8 million, while the total disbursed amount during the same period amounted to US$146.4 million. Of the total approved amount leasing had the largest share (46 per cent), followed by instalment sale (20 per cent), equity (18 per cent), *murabaha* (7 per cent), line of finance (7 per cent) and *istisnaa* (2 per cent).

Accounting and Auditing Organization for Islamic Financial Institutions
Transparency and corporate governance issues are very important for financial institutions to gain the confidence of the clients. In this respect, preparation of financial statements in a way that provides sufficient and comparable information assumes critical importance. The shareholders, depositors, investors and regulators utilize the information provided in the financial statements to assess the health of the institution. Usually it is the central banks that lay down the rules and procedures of disclosure, but several specificities of the operations of Islamic financial institutions warrant some special treatment. If financial statements of these institutions were prepared on the basis of uniform standards, it would facilitate objective comparison between different financial institutions. It would also ensure better market discipline. Industry leaders realized this need and responded with the establishment of the Accounting and Auditing Organization for Islamic Financial Institutions (AAOIFI). AAOIFI was established in accordance with the Agreement of Association which was signed by Islamic financial institutions on 26 February 1990 in Algiers. It was registered on 27 March 1991 in the Kingdom of Bahrain. AAOIFI is an international autonomous non-profit corporate body that prepares accounting, auditing, governance, ethics and *shari'a* standards for Islamic financial institutions.

Objectives
AAOIFI has the following objectives:

- Develop accounting, auditing, governance and ethical standards relating to the activities of Islamic financial institutions which comply with Islamic *shari'a* taking into consideration the international standards and practices.
- Disseminate the accounting, auditing, governance and ethical thoughts relating to the activities of Islamic financial institutions and their application through training seminars, publication of newsletters, preparation of reports, research and any other means.
- Harmonize the accounting policies and procedures adopted by Islamic financial institutions through the preparation and issuance of accounting standards and the interpretations of the same to the said institutions.
- Improve the quality and uniformity of auditing and governance practices relating to Islamic financial institutions through the preparation and issuance of auditing and governance standards and the interpretation of the same to the said institutions.
- Promote good ethical practices relating to Islamic financial institutions through the preparation and issuance of codes of ethics to these institutions.
- Achieve conformity or similarity (to the extent possible) in concepts and applications among the *shari'a* supervisory boards of Islamic financial institutions to avoid

contradiction and inconsistency between the fatwas and the applications by these institutions, with a view to activating the role of the *shari'a* supervisory boards of Islamic financial institutions and central banks through the preparation, issuance and interpretations of *shari'a* standards and *shari'a* rules for investment, financing and insurance.

● Approach the concerned regulatory bodies, Islamic financial institutions, other financial institutions that offer Islamic financial services, and accounting and auditing firms in order to implement the standards, as well as the statements and guidelines that are published by AAOIFI.

Structure
The structure of the AAOIFI comprises the following.

General Assembly   The supreme body of all the members of AAOIFI which consists of founding members, associate members, regulatory and supervisory authorities, observer members and supporting members. The total membership of AAOIFI under various categories stands at 115. Observer members and supporting members have the right to participate in the meetings of the General Assembly without a right to vote.

The founding members of AAOIFI include the Islamic Development Bank, Dar Al-Mal Al-Islami (represented by Shamil Bank of Bahrain), Al-Rajhi Banking and Investment Corporation, Dallah Albaraka Group, Kuwait Finance House, and Bukhary Capital (Malaysia).

Board of Trustees   The Board of Trustees of AAOIFI is composed of 15 part-time members appointed by the General Assembly every three years. The members of the Board of Trustees are elected from among the following categories, taking into account their geographical distribution:

● regulatory and supervisory authorities,
● Islamic financial institutions,
● accounting and auditing firms whose professional work relates to Islamic financial institutions,
● *shari'a (fiqh)* scholars,
● users of financial statements of Islamic financial institutions.

Accounting and Auditing Standards Board   The Standards Board is one of the two technical boards, the most important functional bodies of AAOIFI. It is composed of 15[5] part-time members who are appointed by the Board of Trustees for a four-year term. Members of the Standards Board represent the following categories:

● regulatory and supervisory authorities,
● Islamic financial institutions,
● *shari'a (fiqh)* scholars,
● the accounting and auditing profession that relates to the work of Islamic financial institutions,
● users of financial statements of Islamic financial institutions,
● university professors in accounting and financial studies.

Shari'a board The *Shari'a* Board is the second technical body of the organization. It is composed of (up to) 15 members appointed by the Board of Trustees for a four-year term from among *fiqh* scholars who represent *shari'a* supervisory boards in the Islamic financial institutions which are members of AAOIFI, and *shari'a* supervisory boards in central banks.

Activities
AAOIFI started producing standards in 1993. To date, it has issued 56 standards on accounting, auditing, governance, ethical and *shari'a* issues. A list of these standards is given in Table 22.3.

AAOIFI standards are not automatically mandatory. They are basically advisory in nature. However, over the years, AAOIFI has taken significant steps to encourage the application and enforcement of its standards throughout the world. These efforts have helped to increase the remit of AAOIFI standards. Now they are either mandatory or used as a guideline by the regulators in jurisdictions such as Bahrain, Sudan, Jordan, Malaysia, Qatar, Saudi Arabia, Dubai and Lebanon. Most recently, Syria has signed an agreement to mandate and adopt AAOIFI's standards.

Islamic Financial Services Board
Proper regulation and supervision of banks and financial institutions is also important for financial efficiency and stability. Some of the risks faced by the Islamic financial industry are unique because of the requirement of *shari'a* compliance. Bank supervisors utilizing the traditional standards cannot assess such risks. The need for special guidelines for the regulation and supervision of Islamic banks has long been felt.

With an active involvement of the International Monetary Fund (IMF), the IDB and support of the Bahrain Monetary Agency (BMA), Bank Negara Malaysia (BNM) and some other central banks, an Islamic Financial Services Board was established in Malaysia in November 2002 and has been in operation since March 2003. Its mandate is to serve as an international standard-setting body of the regulatory and supervisory agencies that have an interest in ensuring the soundness and stability of the Islamic financial services industry (defined broadly to include banking, capital market and insurance). In advancing this mission, the IFSB will promote the development of a prudent and transparent Islamic financial services industry through introducing new, or adapting existing, international standards consistent with Islamic principles, and recommend them for adoption. To this end the work of the IFSB complements that of the Basel Committee on Banking Supervision, International Organisation of Securities Commissions and the International Association of Insurance Supervisors.

Objectives
The objectives of the IFSB include:

- To promote the development of a prudent and transparent Islamic financial services industry through introducing new, or adapting existing, international standards consistent with *shari'a* principles, and recommending these for adoption.
- To provide guidance on the effective supervision and regulation of institutions offering Islamic financial products and developing for the Islamic financial services industry the criteria for identifying, measuring, managing and disclosing risks,

Table 22.3   AAOIFI standards

Accounting	Auditing and corporate governance	*Shari'a*
Financial Accounting Statements 1. Objective of financial accounting of Islamic banks and financial institutions 2. Concepts of financial accounting for Islamic banks and financial institutions Financial Accounting Standards 3. General presentation and disclosure in the financial statements of Islamic banks and financial institutions 4. *Murabaha* to the purchase orderer 5. *Mudaraba* financing 6. *Musharaka* financing 7. Disclosure of bases for profit allocation between owners' equity and investment account holders and their equivalent 8. *Salam* and Parallel *Salam* 9. *Ijara* and *Ijara Muntahia Bittamleek* 10. *Istisnaa'* and Parallel *Istisnaa'* 11. *Zakah* 12. Provisions and reserves 13. General presentation and disclosure in financial statements of Islamic insurance companies 14. Disclosure of bases for determining and allocating surplus or deficit in Islamic insurance companies 15. Investment funds 16. Provisions and reserves in Islamic insurance companies	Auditing 1. Objective and principles of auditing 2. The auditor's report 3. Terms of audit engagement 4. Testing by an external auditor for compliance with *Shari'a* rules and principles 5. The auditor's responsibility to consider fraud and error in an audit to financial statements Governance 6. *Shari'a* Supervisory Board: appointment, composition and report 7. *Shari'a* review 8. Internal *Shari'a* review 9. Audit and governance Committee for Islamic financial institutions Ethics 10. Code of ethics for accounting and auditors of Islamic financial institutions 11. Code of ethics for the employees of Islamic financial institutions	1. Dealing in currencies 2. Debit card, charge card and credit card 3. Default in payment by debtor 4. Settlement of debts by set-off 5. Guarantees 6. *Murabaha* to the purchase orderer (reclassified) 7. *Ijara* and *Ijara Muntahia Bittamleek* (reclassified) 8. *Salam* and Parallel *Salam* (reclassified) 9. *Istisnaa'* and Parallel *Istisnaa'* (reclassified) 10. Transfer of debts 11. Conversion of a conventional bank to an Islamic bank 12. *Mudaraba* 13. *Sharika* (*musharaka*) and modern corporations 14. *Mudaraba* 15. Documentary credit 16. *Jua'lah* 17. Commercial papers 18. Investment *Sukuk* 19. Possession (*Qabd*) 20. *Qard* (Loan) 21. Sale of commodities in organized markets 22. Financial paper (shares and bonds)

Table 22.3   (continued)

Accounting	Auditing and corporate governance	*Shari'a*
17. Foreign currency transactions and foreign operations		
18. Investments		
19. Islamic financial services offered by conventional financial institutions		
20. Contributions in Islamic insurance companies		
21. Deferred payment sale		
22. Disclosure on transfer of assets		
23. Segment reporting		

> taking into account international standards for valuation, income and expense calculation and disclosure.
>
> - To liaise and cooperate with relevant organizations currently setting standards for the stability and the soundness of the international monetary and financial systems and those of the member countries.
> - To enhance and coordinate initiatives to develop instruments and procedures for efficient operations and risk management.
> - To encourage cooperation amongst member countries in developing the Islamic financial services industry.
> - To facilitate training and personnel development in skills in areas relevant to the effective regulation of the Islamic financial services industry and related markets.
> - To undertake research into, and publish studies and surveys on, the Islamic financial services industry.
> - To establish a database of Islamic banks, financial institutions and industry experts.

Structure
The structure of the IFSB consists of the following elements.

General Assembly   The representative body of all the members of the IFSB, including full members, associate members and observer members. Full membership is available to the leading financial supervisory authority of each sovereign country that recognizes Islamic financial services, whether by legislation or regulation or by established practice, and to intergovernmental international organizations that have an explicit mandate for promoting Islamic finance and markets upon application for membership by that authority or organization. No country is permitted to have more than one full member. Associate membership is available to any central bank, monetary authority or financial supervisory or regulatory organization or international organization involved in setting or promoting standards for the stability and soundness of international and national monetary and financial systems, which does not qualify for full member status or which does not seek to become a full member upon application for membership by that central bank, authority or organization. Associate members can participate in the deliberations of the General Assembly, but do not have voting rights. Observer status can be granted to any national, regional or international professional or industry association, any institution that offers Islamic financial services or any firm or organization that provides professional services, including accounting, legal, rating, research or training services.

Council   This is the highest executive and policy-making body of the IFSB. It consists of one representative for each full member who shall be the senior executive officer of that full member or such other senior person nominated to represent him from time to time.

Technical Committee   This is the body responsible for advising the Council on technical issues within its terms of reference (as determined by the Council). It consists of ten persons selected by the Council and has a term of office of three years.

Working groups   A working group is a committee that is established to be responsible for drafting standards and guidelines. It reports to the Technical Committee.

Secretariat   The permanent administrative body of the IFSB. It is headed by a full-time secretary-general appointed by the Council.

Activities

The IFSB has begun the development of prudential standards for the Islamic financial services industry. The standards being prepared by the IFSB follow a lengthy process which involves, among other things, the issuance of an exposure draft and, where necessary, the holding of a public hearing. Through this process the IFSB expects to contribute to the development of a robust and resilient Islamic financial system that can effectively preserve financial stability and contribute to balanced growth and development. It is also expected to facilitate integration of the Islamic financial system as a viable component of the global financial system.

Work on two standards, namely, Capital Adequacy and Risk Management standards, was initiated in July 2003. Exposure drafts of these two standards were issued on 15 March 2005. These standards were expected to be issued by the end of 2005. Preparation of a standard on Corporate Governance started in 2004. An exposure draft on this standard was issued in late 2005. In April 2005, the preparation started for two more standards, Supervisory Review Process and Transparency and Market Discipline.

In addition to developing prudential standards for the industry, the IFSB is also actively involved in promoting awareness and educating interested parties on issues that have an impact on or relevance to the regulation and supervision of the Islamic financial services industry. This mainly takes the form of international conferences, workshops, training, meetings and dialogues staged in many countries.

International Islamic Financial Market

Despite its remarkable growth and recognition, the Islamic banking industry is still in its infancy. Key challenges faced by it are product innovation, to meet the varying demands of investors in a fast-changing market environment; support infrastructure, which will address the critical need for liquidity management among Islamic financial institutions; and standardization and codification of laws and market practices. Financial authorities from several Islamic countries recognized the critical need for an organization to fill this gap and came together to create the International Islamic Financial Market (IIFM). Its founding members include the Islamic Development Bank, Bahrain Monetary Agency, Labuan Offshore Financial Services Authority, Central Bank of Sudan, Central Bank of Indonesia and Ministry of Finance Brunei Darussalam. IIFM is an independent, non-profit organization headquartered in the Kingdom of Bahrain. The IIFM became operational on 1 April 2002.

Objectives
The chief objective of the IIFM is to facilitate international secondary market trading of Islamic financial instruments. This would considerably enhance cross-border acceptance of Islamic financial instruments and strengthen cooperation among Muslim countries.

Activities
IIFM faced some logistical problems after its establishment and did not have an active operational programme for some time. It has now become more active and is expected to increase its activities in the near future. It intends to achieve its objectives through the following:

- developing a market for independent *shari'a* enhancement of existing or new Islamic financial instruments through increasing the number of issuance and participants;
- providing guidelines for the issuance of new Islamic financial instruments;
- enhancing cooperation amongst market participants by encouraging product development and trading of instruments in the secondary market;
- undertaking research for the development of Islamic financial markets.

International Islamic Rating Agency
Market discipline is important for an efficient and stable financial system. In this regard, external rating systems and accounting standards play a vital role in improving the availability of information to investors, bankers and regulators. Obtaining a good rating is very important for any institution to attract funds from other institutions and investors. Islamic financial institutions mobilize funds on a profit-and-loss sharing basis. Funds are invested in these institutions with an expectation that all risks and rewards will be equitably shared between the investor and the IFI. Islamic financial institutions are no longer confined to the boundaries of Muslim countries. They are rapidly expanding into other countries and dealing with institutions and regulatory authorities which may not fully comprehend the specific characteristics or the risk profile of Islamic financial institutions. Further, the development of a secondary market in Islamic products such as *sukuk* has increased the importance of credit assessment. In such a market, both issuers and their instruments need to be rated in terms of their inherent risks. This is a prerequisite if the market's products are to be accurately priced and actively traded. In order for Islamic financial institutions to compete in the global financial arena, it is critical that these institutions obtain a

good rating. An institution/instrument whose creditworthiness has been positively rated will enhance the investors' confidence.

Existing conventional rating systems are primarily concerned with the financial strength of counterparties and ignore compliance with the *shari'a* requirements. Since non-compliance of even a financially sound Islamic bank with the *shari'a* requirements can be a serious cause of systemic instability, the need for an Islamic rating agency has always been felt. Keeping this need in mind, an International Islamic Rating Agency (IIRA) was incorporated in Bahrain in October 2002 with an authorized share capital of US$10 million and a paid-up capital of US$2 million. The main activities of the IIRA are to undertake research, analysis, rating of the obligations, dues, commitments, and other securities and to give an independent assessment of compliance by the concerned entity, or the financial instrument with the principles of *shari'a*. Although similar to conventional rating agencies, IIRA aims at developing a distinct market niche whereby it will, among other things, rate funds being raised for the Islamic market/investors as well as banks and insurance companies incorporated or operating in the IDB member countries. The IIRA will scrutinize *shari'a* aspects of financial institutions and products, which will be of major importance to the Islamic financial industry, bearing in mind the global character/appeal of the new international agency. An internationally recognized rating will give these institutions the credibility and the transparency they need to deal with the international market. As a specialized rating agency, the IIRA will be complementary to the existing agencies, adding value to the market. By assessing fiduciary relationships and credit risk inherent in any instrument or issuer, the IIRA will help create a higher degree of confidence and acceptability of products among the players in the industry.

International Islamic Centre for Reconciliation and Commercial Arbitration for Islamic Finance Industry
Islamic financial institutions work under different legal jurisdictions and, sometimes, because of their special nature, the legal basis in the ordinary laws of the country may not be very clear. This may result in disputes among contracting parties which may be difficult to resolve in courts. It is estimated that litigation, on average, costs nearly 20 per cent of the value of the disputed amount and, even if the decision of the court is in favour of the financial institution, only 80 per cent of the value of the disputed amount is recovered. The cost of an out-of-court settlement is nearly 17 per cent of the disputed amount. The absence of institutions providing alternative dispute services to Islamic financial institutions had been seriously felt for the past several years. In order to solve this problem, the Islamic Development Bank and the General Council of Islamic Banks and Financial Institutions took a joint initiative to establish an Arbitration Centre to resolve any possible disputes. The government of the United Arab Emirates welcomed the initiative and agreed to host such an institution. Accordingly, the International Islamic Centre for Reconciliation and Commercial Arbitration for Islamic Finance Industry was established on 19 April 2005. The centre is headquartered in Dubai, UAE.

Objective
The objective of the centre is to settle financial and commercial disputes between financial or commercial institutions that have chosen to accept the *shari'a* law to settle their

disputes. It will also attempt to settle disputes between these institutions and third parties through reconciliation and arbitration.

Structure
The structure of the Centre comprises the following.

General body Central banks, Islamic financial institutions and conventional financial institutions offering Islamic financial services wishing to subscribe to the centre.

Board of Trustees Up to 15 members chosen by the general body for a period of three years, renewable once. The first Board of Trustees comprises Islamic Development Bank, General Council of Islamic Banks and Financial Institutions, Abu Dhabi Islamic Bank (UAE), Dubai Islamic Bank (UAE), Bahrain Islamic Bank (Bahrain), Al Jazeera Bank (Saudi Arabia), Kuwait Financial House (Kuwait), Qatar Islamic Bank (Qatar), EN Bank (Iran), Family Finance Institution (Turkey), Bank Islam Malaysia (Malaysia), Saudi-Tunisian Finance House (Tunisia), Association of Sudanese Banks (Sudan), Jordan Islamic Bank (Jordan) and Bangladesh Islamic Bank (Bangladesh).

Executive Committee The Board of Trustees will select a seven-member Executive Committee for a period of three years. The members of the Executive Committee will be from amongst the members of the Board of Trustees or experts from outside.

Technical (Investigation) Committee The Technical or Investigation Committee will comprise five members appointed by the Board of Trustees from amongst the members of the Board of Trustees or experts from outside.

General Secretariat The General Secretariat will comprise a secretary general and such other staff as may be needed.

General Council of Islamic Banks and Financial Institutions
The General Council of Islamic Banks and Financial Institutions (GCIBFI) is an international autonomous non-profit corporate body that represents Islamic banks and financial institutions and the Islamic financial industry globally. It was incorporated into the Kingdom of Bahrain on 16 May 2001. Its mission is to support and promote the Islamic financial services industry by being the organizational umbrella for the Islamic Financial Institutions (IFIs). It serves the industry through information, media, research and development, consultancy, and human resources development.

Objectives
The objectives of GCIBFI include the following:

- to provide the IFIs with the information needed for their development and growth;
- to promote the Islamic Financial Services Industry (IFSI) and enhance its image;
- to contribute to the growth of the IFSI by providing research and development services;
- to improve and enforce the growth of the IFIs by providing them with the needed advisory and consultancy services;

- to contribute to the human resources development required to face global challenges and meet growth opportunities.

Activities
The activities of GCIBFI are centred around four major areas, which are summarized below:

1   Media and awareness
   — Internet website and the e-newsletter,
   — conferences and seminars,
   — global awareness programmes,
   — local public awareness campaigns;
2.   Information and research
   — administrative and financial directory for Islamic financial institutions,
   — series of Islamic banking applications,
   — monthly educational bulletin;
3.   Policies and strategic planning
   — model law for Islamic banking,
   — International Islamic Bank;
4.   Islamic financial products
   — Islamic QMS Certification for Islamic financial products.

Conclusion
In recent years a number of initiatives have been taken to strengthen the Islamic financial architecture. Under the leadership of the Islamic Development Bank and with active support from international institutions such as the World Bank, IMF and the Basle Committee, several international Islamic financial institutions have been established. In addition, though many of the traditional infrastructure arrangements for conventional finance, such as payment systems, trading arrangements and information systems, are also available to IFIs, in most cases the operational modalities need to be adjusted in varying degrees to accommodate the specific requirements of IFIs. To make these adjustments, a 'functional approach' towards building the infrastructure of the Islamic financial industry is needed. The functions being performed by various institutions in the conventional framework should be examined and attempts should be made to modify the existing institutions in a way that enables them to provide better support, or establish new ones as needed.

While there is no doubt that the emerging Islamic financial architecture requires further strengthening, two other requirements are also urgent. One is the need to consolidate the emerging set-up and to coordinate the activities of the newly established institutions so as to avoid duplication. The other is the need to integrate the Islamic financial architecture into the global institutional framework without losing its specificities. In this respect the impact of the current trend towards globalization as well as the technological developments which are changing the shape of financial firms need to be seriously considered and responded to. The Islamic financial industry has a bright future, but it will be achieved only if the past achievement on the one hand and the floodlight of imminent changes on the other do not blind its active players.

Notes

1. The views/information contained in this chapter are the personal responsibility of the author and not of the institution he is affiliated with.
2. The accounting unit of the bank is the Islamic Dinar, which is equal to 1SDR.
3. The bank uses the Islamic (Hijrah) calendar as its accounting year.
4. All figures cited are net of cancelled operations.
5. Recently, the General Assembly has approved increasing membership of technical boards to 20.

Bibliography

Iqbal, Munawar, Ausaf Ahmad and Tariqullah Khan (1998), *Challenges Facing Islamic Banking*, occasional paper no. 2, Jeddah: Islamic Research and Training Institute, Islamic Development Bank.

Islamic Corporation for the Development of the Private Sector (2005), *Annual Report 1425H*, Jeddah: Islamic Corporation for the Development of the Private Sector.

Islamic Corporation for the Insurance of Investment and Export Credit (2005), *Annual Report 1425H*, Jeddah: Islamic Corporation for the Insurance of Investment and Export Credit.

Islamic Development Bank (2005), *Annual Report 1425H*, Jeddah: Islamic Development Bank.

Jarhi, Mabid Ali al- and Iqbal, Munawar (2001), *Islamic Banking: Answers to Some Frequently Asked Questions*, occasional paper no. 4, Jeddah: Islamic Research and Training Institute.

23 Islamic financial centres
Ricardo Baba

Introduction
The expansion of Islamic finance has been phenomenal since the mid-1970s, with growth rates of around 10–15 per cent per annum (Hassan and Ahmed, 2002; Lewis and Algaoud, 2001). The latest figures from the General Council for Islamic Banks and Financial Institutions (GCFBFI) show that the global Islamic banking industry has grown by almost 23.5 per cent since 2001. The worldwide consolidated assets stand at over US$260 billion, while the number of Islamic banks has increased from 176 in 1997 to 267 at present (Bahrain Monetary Agency, 2005).

An Islamic financial centre is characterized by compliance with *shari'a* – the Islamic law of human conduct, which prohibits *riba* (interest), payment over and above what is lent. Besides the *shari'a* requirement, an Islamic financial centre should have the ability to attract both the Islamic investment money and the international financing activities which would qualify as being *shari'a*-compatible (Lewis and Algaoud, 2001). Currently Bahrain and London are two major centres for Islamic finance, while Malaysia has grown in importance in recent years, with Kuala Lumpur already established as a domestic Islamic financial centre, and Labuan is aspiring to be an offshore Islamic financial centre.

Bahrain as a global centre for Islamic finance
The pre-eminence of Bahrain in the Middle East
Since the establishment of its offshore banking sector in October 1975, when international banks set up offshore operations, Bahrain has become the pre-eminent financial centre for the Middle East. Today, there are 52 offshore banks, and their consolidated assets stand at US$83.4 (Bahrain Monetary Agency, 2003). With a population of only 650 600, Bahrain plays host to 357 financial institutions, 24 full commercial banks, and ten locally incorporated and 14 branches of foreign banks. There are 35 investment banks, 30 representatives, two specialized banks, 21 money changers/brokers and 157 insurance companies (Bahrain Monetary Agency, 2005). In 2004, the financial sector employed 7406 people, 5521 Bahraini nationals and 1885 foreign nationals. Bahrain is in Islamic finance in much the same way as London is in the international market (Lewis and Algaoud, 2001).

According to Lewis and Algaoud (2001), Bahrain's emergence as a pre-eminent Islamic financial centre in the Middle East may be attributed to some strategic factors. They identified seven of these factors, as follows.

Position Nature has endowed Bahrain with a strategic location in the Middle East and the Gulf region. There is a high concentration of specialized Islamic financial institutions, and high net worth individuals, both of them ready investors for Islamic financial products. The 14 commercial banks, five investment banks, and three offshore banking units operating in Bahrain have all the necessary expertise in Islamic financing.

Trading   There are 187 banks operating in Bahrain, of which 23 are Islamic banks (Bahrain Monetary Agency, 2005). As an Islamic financial centre it would need to create a secondary, as well as a primary, market in equity and real asset-based instruments, which are seen as *shari'a*-compliant to investors. Conventional banks' expertise in securitization would be very useful, and Bahrain should benefit from the critical mass of both Islamic and conventional banks. The head offices, branches and associated companies of these financial institutions are well versed in secondary market trading. Bahrain's and other Arab financial institutions are very familiar with property trading in international capital markets (Lewis and Algaoud, 2001).

Attraction   Conventional banks in Muslim countries, as well as those from Western countries like Dresdner Kleinwort Benson, Citibank, UBS and HSBC, increasingly are participating in Islamic banking. They offer Islamic banking products, which provide Islamic banks with *murabaha*, *ijara* and *mudaraba* investment opportunities, a range of managed investment funds, and *shari'a*-compliant liquidity facilities. Bahrain offers a regulatory and cultural environment conducive to their continued participation in this market, as evidenced by the establishment of Citi Islamic Investment Bank (Lewis and Algaoud, 2001).

Innovation   Financial institutions in Bahrain have almost two decades of proven record of accomplishment in financial innovations. In the late 1990s, Bahrain Islamic investment banks and investment companies started to manage special types of Islamic securities or Islamic financial instruments, which are similar to unit trusts (Lewis and Algaoud, 2001). Such securities are normally shares in issues or funds that represent contributions to an investment or a collection of investments for specific periods, with unit values determined weekly and negotiable at the market price. Bahrain Islamic investment banks also pioneered the issuance of *sukuks* (Islamic bonds) and some of these instruments are listed on the Bahrain Stock Exchange (BSE), the Luxembourg Stock Exchange (LX) and Labuan International Financial Exchange (LFX) (Bahrain Monetary Agency, 2004).

Infrastructure   An international financial centre requires a wide range of supporting facilities in the areas of specialized staffing, information and communication technology, legal advice, accounting and auditing needs, office space and facilities, and so on. Bahrain offers a full range of facilities and has a well-educated and trained labour force, and advanced training in Islamic banking is provided by the Bahrain Institute of Banking and Finance.

Regulation   A number of regulatory issues are posed by the growth of Islamic banking, particularly in the light of new capital adequacy standards related to market risk, which would seem to be central to the profit-and-loss sharing activities of Islamic banks. This is the main reason why it is difficult to get Islamic banking products off the ground in centres of conventional banking such as in UK and Australia (Lewis and Algaoud, 2001). Being at the centre of Islamic wealth, Bahrain offers a supportive environment. The Bahrain Monetary Agency has a strong interest in Islamic financing, and its excellent reputation has been acknowledged internationally.

Prime mover   It is relatively easier to capture a big market share as 'prime movers' in a new
business than in duplicating conventional financial products from the more advanced financial centres (Lewis and Algaoud, 2001). As a prerequisite to attract other reputable players
a financial centre has to be recognized as a truly international financial centre and, with the
highest concentration of Islamic financial institutions among international financial centres
(Bahrain Monetary Agency, 2005), Bahrain possesses a highly beneficial starting point.

Growth of Islamic banking
Bahrain has a dual banking system, where Islamic banks operate side-by-side with their
conventional counterparts. The first Islamic bank, Bahrain Islamic Bank, was established
in 1978 to provide commercial banking services and, after more than two decades of
growth, Bahrain has emerged as the leading centre for Islamic finance in the Middle East
(Bahrain Monetary Agency, 2002; Lewis and Algaoud, 2001). The emergence of Bahrain
as an international Islamic financial centre has added another dimension to the diversity
of the financial activities and products available in the market. Bahrain has a higher concentration of Islamic financial institutions than any other country. It is home to five
Islamic commercial banks, 14 Islamic investment banks, three offshore Islamic banking
units, one Islamic representative office, two Islamic investment advisors and 16 *takaful*
firms, along with several banks with Islamic 'windows' (Bahrain Monetary Agency, 2002).
Table 23.1 shows the Islamic financial institutions operating in Bahrain in 2005.

The Islamic banking and finance industry in Bahrain consists of institutions of different
categories. Some are dedicated fully to Islamic banking services, such as the Bahrain
Islamic Bank, Shamil Bank of Bahrain and Al Baraka Islamic Bank. Other Islamic banks
are resident banks with originally conventional banking activities that saw potentially
profitable opportunities in diversifying their services to Islamic banking. Arab Banking
Corporation is a notable example of this. The final category of Islamic banks operating in
Bahrain is represented by major multinational banks, such as the Citi Islamic Investment
Bank, a subsidiary of CitiGroup. The consolidated balance sheet of Islamic banking operating in Bahrain showed total assets of US$5.9 billion in February 2005. Islamic banks
employed 834 staff in 2001, of which 91 per cent were Bahraini (Bahrain Monetary
Agency, 2005). Bahrain now hosts 41 Islamic financial institutions dealing in diversified
activities including commercial banking, investment banking, offshore banking, funds
management and Islamic insurance.

Table 23.1   Islamic banks and financial institutions in Bahrain (30 March 2005)

Type of financial institution	No.
Full commercial banks	5
Offshore banking units	3
Investment banks	14
Representative office	1
Investment advisory and other financial services	2
Takaful companies	16
Total Islamic financial institutions in Bahrain	41

Source: Bahrain Monetary Agency (2005).

An important feature of the Islamic banks' operations is their use of Bahrain as a base for some of their global activities in terms of leasing and commodity financing, especially for syndication (Algaoud and Lewis, 1997). Islamic syndication was introduced by Faisal Islamic Bank of Bahrain (now the Shamil Bank of Bahrain) in 1987 (Bahrain Monetary Agency, 2002) and, since then, Shamil Bank of Bahrain has been active in Islamic syndications. It has managed more than 20 deals totalling over US$2 billion in which 56 leading Islamic financial institutions, regional banks and other conventional financial institutions participated. Other Islamic financial institutions in Bahrain such as the Al-Baraka Group are also active in Islamic syndication.

There is a trend among Bahrain Islamic banks of increasing internationalization of their operations. This is evidenced by the total amount of assets and liabilities held outside the region. By year-end 2003, more than US$1.2 billion of Islamic banks' assets and US$780 million of liabilities were held in Asia, the Americas and Western Europe (Bahrain Monetary Agency, 2003, p. 27). Bahrain has 14 Islamic investment banks, and these have been active in designing Islamic securities, which are similar to unit trusts representing shares in an investment or collection of investments for specific periods of time (Algaoud and Lewis, 1997). Since 1993, a wide range of *shari'a*-compliant investment banking products have been developed, with a focus beyond the retail market in terms of emerging market equity funds, equipment leasing funds, initial public offerings and project financing (Khalili, 1997).

Bahrain has been able to attract a relatively large number of banks with such international operations to its shores thanks to its strategic geographic position in the heart of the Gulf region. Besides this, Bahrain has a well-developed infrastructure, excellent telecommunication facilities and support services, a skilled workforce and professional capabilities that provide the centre with a conducive banking environment (Algaoud and Lewis, 1997). These attributes make Bahrain well qualified to become a convenient base for Islamic banks as it can put at their disposal a wide range of resources and facilities.

Bahrain hosts a number of international Islamic financial infrastructures and supporting organizations, such as the Liquidity Management Centre (LMC), International Islamic Financial Market (IIFM), Accounting and Auditing Organization for Islamic Financial Institutions (AAOIFI), International Islamic Rating Agency (IIRA), General Council for Islamic Banks and Financial Institutions (GCIBFI) and Bahrain Institute of Banking and Finance (BIBF). With the backing of such infrastructures and support organizations, Bahrain has been very active in promoting innovations to broaden the depth and liquidity of Islamic financial markets through the issuance of new Islamic financial instruments and other financial innovations.

Islamic financial instruments

The Bahrain Monetary Agency (BMA) has been very active in promoting the liquidity of the Islamic financial market. Since June 2001, and on a monthly basis, the BMA has launched an Islamically structured short-term government bills programme of US$25 million. This marks the beginning of a programme with the issuance of three-month bills, rolling forward, to the value of US$25 million per month. According to the BMA, these issues are going to be a permanent feature of the Bahrain Islamic financial market. Allowing for redemptions, the government bill issues raise US$75 million per year and a short-term investment opportunity for Islamic financial institutions. The bills are tendered for each month and, in the case of oversubscription, the bills are sold on a pro rata basis.

In August 2001, the BMA issued a US$100 million Islamic leasing (*ijara*) security, the first of its kind in the world by a central bank, and it was fully subscribed. This issue was followed by a second US$70 million government leasing *sukuk* in February 2002, which was oversubscribed by 60 per cent. The *sukuk* was issued for three years, with maturity in February 2005, with the average annual lease return of 4.52 per cent paid semi-annually. The securities are based on the Islamic concept of *Al Salam* and accordingly are referred to as *Al Salam Sukuk* securities. Parallel with its *Sukuk Al Salam* programme the BMA issued, in September 2001, Islamic Leasing Certificates with a five-year maturity to the value of US$100 million. This bond-like security was also the first of its kind issued in the world by a central bank. The securities with maturity in September 2006 had a rental return of 5.25 per cent per annum (BMA, 2002).

Islamic financial infrastructure
Bahrain is not only the host to a considerable number of Islamic banks and financial institutions, but it is a location for two major components of the Islamic financial infrastructure, the Liquidity Management Centre and the International Islamic Financial Market (IIFM).

The Liquidity Management Centre (LMC)
The establishment of the Bahrain-based Liquidity Management Centre (LMC) in February 2002 was a historical landmark for the Islamic banking industry. The LMC enables Islamic financial institutions to manage an asset–liquidity mismatch, creates a pool of quality assets for Islamic financial institutions, creates liquidity for conventional players, enhances *shari'a* credibility, and achieves higher returns for investors and shareholders. The LMC facilitates the pooling of assets acquired from government, financial institutions and corporations. This asset pool will be securitized through the issuance of tradeable instruments (*sukuk*) where Islamic Financial Services Institutions (IFSIs) will invest their surplus liquidity. By creating a secondary market for the trading of these instruments, the LMC is able to provide competitive returns on short-term, liquid investment opportunities for IFSIs.

The establishment of the LMC addresses two critical constraints currently afflicting the Islamic banking industry: the lack of both quality assets and secondary markets. By securitizing pools of tangible long-term assets acquired from a variety of sources, the LMC presents IFSIs with access to investment in quality assets. The *sukuks* issued to securitize this pool offer enhanced *shari'a* credibility in comparison to the current short-term investment opportunity to channel their excess liquidity to the benefit of regional economies. The LMC enables IFSIs to maintain maturity and other mismatches between the assets and liabilities, which is fundamental to the business of banking and imperative if the industry is to maintain its current growth.

The LMC also creates secondary markets for its products by establishing a consortium of liquidity providers. These provide impetus to the active trading of *sukuks* in over-the-counter deals or through the LMC as IFSIs gain access to competitively priced, liquid instruments. No individual bank or product currently offers this combination of quality instruments with diversified risk together with a ready market for trading. Asset and liquidity risks for *sukuk* holders will be diversified across multiple assets and institutions. No single issuer of instruments or provider of products offers such an investment opportunity (BMA, 2002).

The International Islamic Financial Market (IIFM)
As the Islamic financial and business activities become more global, the need for Islamic financial institutions to be increasingly involved in cross-border financial transactions gains greater prominence. The IIFM facilitates a cooperative framework among the financial institutions involved in Islamic finance. It is expected to boost the creation of Islamic financial products and to address the liquidity requirements of the industry.

The establishment of the International Islamic Financial Market (IIFM) in 2002 constitutes part of the overall efforts to strengthen the efficacy of the Islamic financial system as a component of the global financial system in achieving balanced growth and development. The IIFM provides the infrastructure to facilitate the mobilization of foreign capital according to *shari'a* principles, stimulate the creation and trading of Islamic financial instruments, enhance investment opportunities for global investors and facilitate efficient liquidity management by Islamic financial institutions. Malaysia spearheaded the issuance of the first sovereign global Islamic *sukuk* to give impetus to the development of the IIFM. The global Islamic bond served as a benchmark and catalyst that spurred the issuance of subsequent global Islamic bonds.

Currently a considerable amount of funds from Islamic financial institutions are invested in conventional markets through a synthetic product of the commodity *murabaha*. This is unavoidable given that a viable global Islamic financial system as an alternative to the conventional system has yet to be established. The IIFM is designed to broaden the coverage and to ensure continuous growth of the Islamic financial system. Bahrain was among the first countries that recognized this need and has worked hard for its achievement.

With the endorsement of the first global corporate *sukuk* issued by UAE's National Central Cooling Company, Tabreed in April 2004, the IIFM had endorsed five global *Sukuk* issues totalling US$2.05 billion. Previous endorsements have been for the US$600 million Malaysian Global *Sukuk*, the US$400 million Islamic Development Bank Trust Certificate, the US$700 million Qatar Global *Sukuk* and the US$250 million Bahrain International *Sukuk* (Bahrain Monetary Agency, 2004). The endorsement from IIFM's *Shari'a* Supervisory Committee ensures the harmonization and standardization of Islamic financial products to achieve global appeal and acceptance.

Supporting organizations for Islamic banking in Bahrain
In addition to the Islamic financial infrastructure, Bahrain also hosts a range of institutions supporting the Islamic banking and finance industry. Support takes various forms, including standard setting, training and development, credit rating and information services. Bahrain has four supporting organizations for Islamic banking:

- The Accounting and Auditing Organization for Islamic Financial Institutions (AAOIFI);
- The International Islamic Rating Agency (IIRA);
- The General Council for Islamic Banks and Financial Institutions (GCIBFI);
- Bahrain Institute of Banking and Finance (BIBF).

The Accounting and Auditing Organization for Islamic Financial Institutions (AAOIFI)
The AAOIFI was established in 1991 as an international autonomous non-profit-making corporate body and based in Bahrain. By 2001, the organization had released 16 financial accounting standards, four auditing standards, four governance standards, one code of ethics, and one Statement on the Purpose and Calculation of the Capital Adequacy Ratio for Islamic banks. AAOIFI has also been working hard in persuading regulatory authorities to adopt its standards. To date Bahrain, Sudan, Jordan and Saudi Arabia have adopted the AAOIFI standards (BMA, 2002).

AAOIFI has also been continuously working with international bodies involved in the development of standards and regulation of banks in order to create international recognition for its standards. Close links have been maintained with numerous regulatory bodies, including the International Monetary Fund, International Accounting Standards Board, and the Basel Committee. AAOIFI has also been very active in disseminating knowledge relating to Islamic banking and finance through the organization of international conferences, seminars and training courses. The latest initiative undertaken by the AAOIFI is the development of the first-ever global qualification, the Certified Islamic Public Accounting (CIPA). The programme is modelled on the Certified Public Accountant (CPA), which is specifically aimed at the Islamic banking and finance industry (Bahrain Monetary Agency, 2005).

The International Islamic Rating Agency (IIRA)   The Bahrain-based International Islamic Rating Agency (IIRA) was incorporated in 2002, and started operation in 2005. The shareholders include the Islamic Development Bank (IDB) and its affiliates, with a 42 per cent stake, Malaysian Rating Corporation, JCR-VIS Credit Rating Company from Pakistan and leading industry players from different geographic regions. The agency is the first of its kind to cater for the need of the Islamic banking industry worldwide. The establishment of the IIRA helps increase transparency and gives more confidence to investors, regulators and the public of the Islamic banking industry.

The IIRA is aimed at rating and evaluating Islamic banks and instruments, as well as providing an independent assessment and opinion on the future of the rated entity or financial instrument. It also provides an independent assessment of compliance by the entity or instrument with *shari'a* principles and plays a critical role in promoting transparency and enhancing investors' confidence in Islamic financial institutions and financial instruments.

When it started operations in early 2005, the IIRA announced that it would start with *shari'a* rating and would only look into credit rating at a later stage. This raised a debate among those in the industry who believe that investors as well as the Islamic financial institutions (IFIs) are more in need of credit rating (Ahmed, 2005). Their arguments are, first, that IFIs need international recognition as they now deal more with international business counterparties in Europe, America and Asia, and, second, that *sukuk* issues are increasing and increasingly more Western institutional investors are buying them. For the distribution of *sukuk* in Western markets a credit rating is essential.

General Council for Islamic Banks and Financial Institutions (GCIBFI)   The General Council for Islamic Banks and Financial Institutions (GCIBFI) was established in 2001 as a non-profit organization based in Bahrain to work for the support of the Islamic banking industry with a view to promoting it through the dissemination of appropriate information and accurate data. The council has been active in preparing and publishing information bulletins, brochures, magazines, newsletters and books. It also organizes conferences, seminars and workshops. This is in addition to establishing a database for Islamic banking and finance.

Bahrain Institute of Banking and Finance (BIBF) The Bahrain Institute of Banking and Finance (BIBF) was established in 1981 in order to provide up-to-date training and education in the areas of management and leadership, banking, Islamic banking, insurance, accounting and finance and information technology. The BIBF continues to deliver a diverse programme of short courses on specific aspects of Islamic banking and finance, such as Islamic Structured Finance Securitization, Risk Management and Islamic Banking. The institute is seeing a significant growth in demand for Islamic financial training, both in and outside Bahrain. In April 2004, it conducted a four-day introductory course in Islamic financial instruments for Bosnia International Islamic Bank (BIIB) in Sarajevo (Bahrain Monetary Agency, 2004, p. 7).

Threats to Bahrain's pre-eminence
Bahrain's status as the leading financial centre in the Gulf region is not unchallenged. Dubai aspires to become a major centre for product innovations for Islamic investors and borrowers (DIFC, 2005; Algaoud and Lewis, 1997; Lewis and Algaoud, 2001). In a survey conducted by Algaoud and Lewis (1997) among bankers in Bahrain, respondents viewed Dubai as a major threat to Bahrain. Part of the plan to enhance Dubai's position as a financial centre was the establishment of the Dubai International Financial Centre (DIFC) in 2002, a fully-fledged 'onshore' capital market comparable to Hong Kong, London and New York (DIFC, 2005). In September 2004, the DIFC issued its first three licences, marking the launch of a free zone that Dubai officials hope will bring their city into the major league of global financial hubs (*The Banker*, 2004).

However, the threat has yet to materialize. The Dubai banking industry comprises 15 banks of which only two, the Dubai Islamic Bank and Emirates Islamic Bank, are Islamic banks (CBUAE, 2005). These figures are far too small compared with 187 conventional and 23 Islamic banks in Bahrain (Bahrain Monetary Agency, 2005, p. 8). With very few players, it is hard to imagine how Dubai might be able to compete with Bahrain in Islamic financing, at least in the short term.

Malaysia as a regional centre for Islamic finance
Growth of Islamic banking
Islamic finance in Malaysia has made a significant growth since the launching of the first Islamic bank in 1983 and the establishment of the first *takaful* company in 1984. The strategy adopted by Malaysia has been to develop a comprehensive Islamic financial system. It started with the establishment of one Islamic bank to spearhead the introduction of Islamic banking products and services and, at the same time, identified the relevant financial segments that were required to support the expansion of Islamic banking activities. The Islamic financial system operates in parallel with the conventional system, similar to that of Bahrain's dual banking system. Malaysia expanded its implementation approach by allowing the conventional banks to offer Islamic banking products through the

'Islamic windows'. By year-end 2004, total assets of the Islamic banking sector had increased to RM94.6 billion or 10.5 per cent of the total assets of the banking industry. The market shares of Islamic deposits increased to 11.2 per cent, and financing increased by 11.3 per cent (Bank Negara, 2004).

Malaysia's experience in the development of its financial system is outlined in Bank Negara Malaysia's ten-year Financial Sector Masterplan (FSMP) (2001). The master plan represents a blueprint that provides the strategic direction for the development of the financial industry beyond the short term and takes a long-term perspective on the needs of the future (Aziz, 2004). In the development of Islamic finance, a comprehensive approach has been adopted. Malaysia has given emphasis to the development of a comprehensive financial infrastructure that includes the Islamic financial markets, Islamic financial instruments, contract law and law enforcement procedures, a *shari'a* governance framework, Islamic accounting practices and valuation standards, and appropriate disclosure requirements as well as an efficient and secure payment and settlement system. Attention has also been given to developing the prudential regulatory and supervisory framework that underpins the stability of the Islamic financial industry.

The development of Islamic finance in Malaysia consists of both the domestic and the offshore markets. The Malaysian government objective is for Islamic finance to constitute 20 per cent of the domestic financial market by 2010, and Islamic finance is identified as a niche activity for the Labuan International Offshore Financial Center (IOFC) to complement the development of the domestic Islamic financial market (BNM, 2001).

The Islamic banking system
In Malaysia's dual banking environment, the Islamic financial system operates in parallel with the conventional financial system. The Islamic financial system comprises the Islamic banking system, Islamic money market, Islamic insurance, Islamic capital market and the specialized financial institutions, which provide alternative sources of financing (Table 23.2). The Islamic banking system, which forms the backbone of the Islamic financial system, plays an important role in mobilizing deposits and providing financing to facilitate growth.

The Islamic banking system is currently represented by 42 Islamic financial institutions, comprising four domestic Islamic banks, three foreign Islamic banks, four offshore

Table 23.2   Islamic banking system in Malaysia (31 May 2005)

Type of financial institution	No.
Full Islamic commercial banks	4
Offshore Islamic banks	4
Foreign Islamic banks	3
Commercial banks with Islamic windows	12
Finance companies with Islamic windows	3
Merchant banks with Islamic windows	4
Discount houses with Islamic windows	7
Development financial institutions offering Islamic banking facilities	5
Total of financial institutions	42

Source: BNM, LOFSA and some interviews.

Islamic banks and 31 conventional banking institutions offering Islamic banking products and services under the Islamic 'windows'. Table 23.2 shows the list of financial institutions offering Islamic banking facilities in Malaysia.

The Islamic banking market in Malaysia was liberalized in 2004, three years ahead of the liberalization date for the country's banking industry aimed at 2007 (Bank Negara, 2004). In 2004, Bank Negara Malaysia issued new Islamic banking licences to three leading foreign Islamic financial institutions from the Middle East, namely, Kuwait Finance House, Al-Rajhi Banking and Investment Corporation, and a consortium of Islamic financial institutions represented by Qatar Islamic Bank, RUSD Investment Bank Inc, and Global Investment House (Bank Negara, 2004; Nathan, 2004). With the issuance of the Islamic banking licences to foreign players, Bank Negara Malaysia hopes to enhance the diversity and depth of players in the Islamic financial landscape. The presence of fully-fledged foreign Islamic banks would increase the potential to tap new growth opportunities as well as to raise the performance and development of the overall Islamic banking industry. In 2004, several of the conventional banking groups participating in the Islamic Banking Scheme transformed their 'Islamic window' into an 'Islamic subsidiary', and Bank Negara Malaysia gave approval to five domestic banking groups to establish Islamic banking subsidiaries. To date two new Islamic banking subsidiaries have commenced operations, namely, the RHB Islamic Bank Berhad, and Commerce Tijari Bank Berhad (Aziz, 2005a, 2005b; Nathan, 2004).

The Islamic banking institutions offer a comprehensive and broad range of Islamic financial products and services, from savings, current and investment deposit products to financing products such as property financing, working capital financing, project financing, plant and machinery financing, hire purchase, education financing and other financing products including trade finance products. The ability of the Islamic banking institutions to arrange and offer products with attractive and innovative features at prices that are competitive with conventional banking products has appealed to both Muslim and non-Muslim customers, reflecting the capacity of the Islamic banking system as an effective means of financial intermediation. By year-end 2003, the distribution network of Islamic banking institutions comprised 152 fully-fledged Islamic banking branches and 2065 Islamic banking 'windows' (Bank Negara, 2003).

The Islamic inter-bank money market
The existence of an active Islamic inter-bank money market is another important component of the Islamic financial system. Under the *mudaraba* (profit-sharing) inter-bank investment (MII) mechanism, Islamic banking institutions are able to raise funds to meet their short-term funding requirement based on a profit-sharing arrangement. Since its inception in 1994, the volume of MII increased from only RM0.5 billion in 1994 to RM2583.8 billion in 2003. The availability of a broad spectrum of short- and long-term Islamic financial instruments such as Government Investment Issues (GII), Bank Negara Negotiable Notes (BNNN) and Islamic private debt securities as well as the active trading of these instruments allow Islamic banking institutions to meet their investment and liquidity needs. The GII and BNNN are also among the instruments used by Bank Negara Malaysia to manage liquidity in the Islamic banking system.

The Islamic capital market
In the Islamic capital market, funds are raised to finance long-term infrastructure and development projects through the issuance of Islamic private debt securities. The Islamic capital market reduces overdependence on the Islamic banking system for long-term financing and allows Islamic banking institutions to diversify part of the risk due to assets and liabilities mismatches. The Islamic capital market plays an important role in reducing potential sources of financial vulnerabilities and contributes to enhancing the robustness and resilience of the Islamic financial system, leading to greater financial stability. The issuance of diverse Islamic financial instruments ranging from short-term commercial paper and medium-term notes to long-term Islamic bonds helps Islamic banking institutions to meet their investment liquidity needs. The different financial structures of the Islamic instruments also provide flexibility to issuers in managing their distinct financing needs. Moreover the Islamic financial instruments attract a wider investor base, encompassing both Islamic and conventional institutional investors, and thereby the funds raised can be tapped at competitive cost. In addition, the active participation of Islamic banking institutions in deal origination, underwriting and corporate advisory services expands the breadth and depth of the Islamic capital market, contributing to the increased effectiveness and efficiency of the Islamic financial system.

Islamic equity market
In the Islamic equity market, the Islamic institutional investors participate in capital-raising exercises to finance business expansion of corporations. The Islamic unit trusts provide investors with access to professional management of funds to maximize returns on different risk profiles. The comprehensiveness of the Islamic financial system creates significant investment opportunities for both Islamic and conventional investors in managing their portfolios to meet financial needs.

Takaful *industry*
The *takaful* industry adds significant synergies to the overall Islamic financial system. *Takaful* operators, particularly in general *takaful* business, contribute to mitigate part of the risks of the banking system resulting from financing transactions and to strengthen the resilience of the Islamic financial system. In the family *takaful* business, *takaful* operators assume an important role as economic agents that motivate long-term savings for long-term investments and economic growth. The role of *takaful* operators as institutional investors has contributed to stimulate the development of Islamic financial instruments and consequently adds depth to the Islamic financial markets.

Specialized non-bank institutions
Specialized non-bank institutions offering Islamic financial products and services such as the development financial institutions (DFIs) and Pilgrims Fund Board complement the Islamic banking system in expanding its reach to specific strategic economic sectors, thereby enhancing the capacity of the Islamic financial system in its overall contribution to economic growth and development. Meanwhile the existence of ancillary institutions such as the National Mortgage Corporation (Cagamas Berhad) contributes to enhancing resilience of the Islamic financial system through securitization of the Islamic house financing and Islamic hire purchase receivables in the portfolios of Islamic banking institutions.

Islamic Financial Services Board (IFSB)
The Islamic Financial Services Board (IFSB) was established in Kuala Lumpur in 2002 to develop international prudential regulatory standards in accordance with the distinct features and risks of Islamic financial institutions. Since its establishment, it has contributed towards ensuring the soundness and stability of the Islamic financial system and attracted wide participation. By year-end 2003, the number of IFSB members had increased to 13 full members, three associate members and 20 observer members. The IFSB has made progress in developing prudential standards on capital adequacy and risk management and will commence preparation of an additional standard on corporate governance.

Islamic Banking and Finance Institute Malaysia (IBFIM)
The Islamic Banking and Finance Institute Malaysia (IBFIM) was established in 2001 as an industry-owned private company to spearhead greater collaborative efforts with universities to undertake research in areas that are vital for the progressive development of the Islamic financial industry. The IBFIM provides consultancy, training and education as well as research and development in all aspects of Islamic finance. The establishment of the institute is a positive step towards the enhancement of skills and expertise of managers and other staff members working in the Islamic financial industry. In 2005, IBFIM introduced the IBFIM i-series programme, a four-series course on Islamic finance, *takaful* and the Islamic capital market that runs for the whole year (IBFIM, 2005).

Internationalization of the Malaysian Islamic financial industry
Malaysia may not be a global centre for Islamic finance, as Bahrain is, but it is increasingly gaining prominence in the region. Both Indonesia and the Philippines have enlisted the expertise of Bank Islamic Malaysia to set up their own Islamic banks and, more recently, Singapore has indicated its interest in developing its own Islamic financial services with the help of Malaysia (Hamid, 2005; Ibrahim, 2005). Malaysia is located in a region that has the highest population of Muslims and, with more than two decades of experience in Islamic finance, it has the potential to be a regional centre. About 60 per cent of its 24 million people are Muslims, and there are 180 million Muslims in Indonesia, 6.8 million Muslims in Thailand, 7.6 million Muslims in the Philippines, 50 million Muslims in China (Lewis and Algaoud, 2001), 350000 Muslims in Singapore (Gerrard and Cunningham, 1997) and 250000 Muslims in Brunei (Borneo Bulletin Brunei Yearbook, 1998).

The significant progress achieved by the domestic Islamic financial system has set the stage for its integration into the global marketplace. The presence of foreign players will also accelerate the global integration of the domestic Islamic banking industry. To date, three foreign Islamic banks are operating in the domestic market, and there is increasing participation by international financial institutions in the ringgit bond market. In September 2004, under the gradual liberalization policy, the Malaysian government allowed multilateral development banks, multilateral financial institutions and corporations to raise ringgit-denominated bonds in the domestic capital market. The market responded positively to these changes, and three multilateral development agencies have taken advantage of this initiative. The Asian Development Bank became the first foreign entity to issue ringgit bonds (RM400 million) in November, followed by the International Finance Corporation, which became the first foreign entity to raise ringgit Islamic bonds (RM500 million). More recently, in April 2005, the International Bank for Reconstruction and Development (World Bank) issued RM2.66 Islamic bonds (Ibrahim, 2005), and announced its intention to sell at least RM1 billion five-year Islamic bonds (Bloomberg, 2005).

The Malaysian Islamic offshore market
In the Financial Sector Masterplan (FSMP) Islamic banking has been identified as a niche activity for the Labuan International Offshore Financial Centre (IOFC). The Labuan IOFC complements the International Islamic Financial Market in the issuance, listing and trading of foreign currency-denominated Islamic financial instruments as well as in forging linkages with other Islamic financial centres to further expand the global reach of Islamic banking and finance. By year-end 2004, total Islamic assets of the Labuan IOFC stood at US$678.7 million and Islamic deposits at US$304.1 million (LOFSA, 2004). At present, the centre is host to four Islamic banks. Three of these are Malaysian banks (Bank Islam (L) Ltd., Al-Hidayah Investment Bank (L) Ltd., and an offshore branch of Bank Muamalat Malaysia Bhd.), the other is a Saudi bank, RUSD Investment Bank Inc. Labuan's recent notable transactions include (a) First Global *Sukuk* by Guthries Group – US$150 million, 2003; (b) First Sovereign Malaysian Global Islamic *Sukuk Ijarah* – US$600 million, 2003; (c) Islamic Development Bank *Sukuk Ijarah* – US$300 million, 2003; and (d) Qatar *Sukuk Ijarah* – US$700 million, 2003. In terms of geographic distribution of Labuan Global Islamic *Sukuk*, 51 per cent were bought by investors in the Middle East, 30 per cent were taken up by investors in Asia, 15 per cent were bought by investors in Europe, and the remaining 4 per cent were taken up by Islamic investors in the US (Alam Shah, 2004). Labuan is playing a very important role in the development and promotion of Islamic banking and finance globally. Although there are only four Islamic banks in Labuan, these institutions offer various Islamic financial products that include foreign currency financing facilities under schemes such as *murabaha* (cost plus), *wakala* (agency), *istisnaa* (order sale), *ijara* (leasing) and *musharaka* (joint-venture) (LOFSA, 2002, p. 41).

Some empirical evidence
In a survey conducted in 2004, 86 per cent of the offshore banks believed that Islamic banking instruments have a considerable potential to be marketed in the Labuan IOFC (Baba, 2004). The conventional offshore banks are willing to train their officers in Islamic banking skills, and to participate in future Islamic deals. The offshore banks also acknowledge that they do not have competitive advantages over Bahrain and London, currently the leading Islamic finance centres in the world, but that their strengths in political stability, low taxes and a reliable legal system would make this an attractive centre.

In the area of tax incentives, Islamic banks have been given an income tax rebate equivalent to the amount of *zakat* paid to the religious authority (LOFSA, 2003). This incentive is aimed at attracting banks from Islamic countries where *zakat*, and not income tax, is paid on business income. A creative tax regime should have a substantial impact in terms of increased profit margin or reduced cost on the part of the offshore banks. This may convince more conventional offshore banks to participate in Islamic transactions.

The survey finding above concurs with the result of an earlier study conducted by Algaoud and Lewis in 1997, where they asked the Islamic banks in Bahrain to rate locations they see as the main competitors to Bahrain as a centre of Islamic finance. Malaysia was seen as a major threat, with 67 per cent of the respondents agreeing that it is an important centre for Islamic finance (Algaoud and Lewis, 1997). However, Malaysia does not intend to compete head-on with Bahrain. In fact, it is more interested in working closely with Bahrain, as close relations would benefit Labuan by tapping Bahrain's strength to develop new products and services, and marketing them in the Middle East. The exchange of knowledge and expertise would promote greater economic and financial linkages between Malaysia and the Middle Eastern region, and foster greater harmonization in terms of *shari'a* interpretation and understanding.

Malaysia's intention to work closely with Bahrain was evidenced when it strongly supported the establishment of the International Islamic Financial Market to be based in Bahrain, and recommended a Malaysian banker, Abdul Rais Abdul Majid, as its first CEO. Labuan is determined to overcome all barriers by working closely with the Islamic Development Bank, and other financial institutions from the Middle East. Labuan has introduced *Amanah Dar al-maal al-Islami* Labuan (ADIL) or *Dar al-maal al-Islami* Trust Labuan – an Islamic growth fund, which is supported by the internationally recognized *Dar al-maal al-Islami* (DMI) Trust Group. ADIL operates on the concept of profit sharing and is designed to attract investors from the Middle East, and those from other Muslim countries in Asia. The strength of ADIL is the monitoring of its activities by the International *Shari'a* Council (Ahmad and Kefeli, 2002).

London as the Western centre for Islamic finance
The attractions of London
London has earned itself a status as the major Islamic financial centre in the West (Wilson, 1999). London has been able to attract the major Islamic banks because of the breadth of specialist financial services offered, the depth of the markets and the reputation of the major banks, which include all the leading international financial institutions (Lewis and Algaoud, 2001). London is nearer to the Middle East than to New York, and in a convenient time zone. Thanks to long historical connections with the United Kingdom, most Arab businessmen and bankers speak English (Wilson, 1999). Some of London's conventional banks provide an extensive range of Islamic financing services, including investment banking, project finance, Islamic trade finance, leasing, private banking and mortgages (Lewis and Algaoud, 2001). Islamic banks and businesses can rely on the expertise, experience and contacts of these banks. In addition, London law firms provide legal advice on leasing and other Islamic financing techniques. London has actually become a global ancillary centre for Islamic financing (Lewis and Algaoud, 2001).

Much of Islamic financing business that is booked in London comes from Muslim countries, mainly from the Middle East, and most of the services cater for the international clients rather than the local Muslims. Although there are more than two million Muslims residing in the UK, the potential domestic market is not fully tapped. The services offered by the Islamic banks in Britain are mainly related to investment banking, corporate finance and trade finance, and retail banking is still in its infancy (Cox, 2000; Wilson, 1999). Despite the breadth and depth of London financial services, very few banks are offering Islamic financing. Out of the hundreds of banks in the City of London only seven are active in Islamic financing, and only three (ANZ International, Citibank and Dresdner Kleinwort Benson) are Western owned. Although the United Bank of

Kuwait and the Islamic Bank of Britain are London-based, they are of Middle Eastern ownership (Wilson, 1999, 2005).

Development of Islamic banking in Britain
The history of Islamic finance in Britain began in 1982, when the Jeddah-based Al Baraka Investment Company set up the Al Baraka International Bank in London. The bank's major customers were the high net worth individuals from the Middle East who spent the summer months in London, and to a limited extent it also catered for the needs of the local Muslims (Wilson, 1999). Al Baraka offered current accounts, investment deposits, housing finance and investment management until it decided to surrender its banking licence in 1993 to focus on investment management. The United Bank of Kuwait set up its specialist Islamic Banking Unit in 1991 to cater for the needs of its Middle Eastern clients for Islamic trade-based investment. In 1995, the unit was renamed Islamic Investment Banking Unit, and later merged with Al Ahli Bank to form a new entity, Al Ahli United Bank.

An interesting development in Islamic finance in the United Kingdom was the establishment of the Islamic Bank of Britain. The bank started operations in September 2004, catering to the needs of Britain's Muslims in the retail Islamic banking market, offering current, savings, and treasury accounts, and personal finance through the *tawarruq* arrangements. It entered the Islamic mortgage market in late 2005. Other banks entering Islamic home finance were HSBC Amanah in 2004 and Lloyds TSB in March 2005 (Wilson, 2005).

Citibank, Dresdner Kleinwort Benson and ANZ Grindlays are active in arranging the short-term Islamic trade finance for Western blue-chip end-users (Cox, 2000, p. 272). What is apparent is that the three institutions were all, because of their own business orientation and established Middle Eastern investor relationships, well placed to deliver the specific services sought by Islamic institutions and investors during the initial phase of accelerated growth within the Islamic financial system. During the late 1970s and early 1980s, Islamic banks and finance houses were actively seeking outlets for the growing volume of liquidity under management.

A number of factors determine the suitability of specific, conventional bank appointments as agents or arrangers, including location. Those residing in London were particularly favoured because of their relative proximity to the Middle East, and their business focus and ability to deliver the investment opportunities matched Islamic bank requirements at a time when trade and commodity investment were at a premium. They provided acceptable, short-term outlets that involved the physical transfer of tangible assets and represented the main source of international investment for most of the market liquidity.

The London-based trading or merchant banks had the added advantage of direct involvement and penetration of a very mature trade finance market. Their existing exposure to large corporate and industrial end-users enabled them to act as a conduit for introductions, to reassure the Islamic bank by sharing in the risk of the credit or, even perhaps more controversially, to provide support by guaranteeing the obligations of the names that they promoted. They also had the scale of in-house resources to handle all the necessary aspects of negotiation, documentation and administration, including the legal and taxation issues relating to individual structures.

For the above reasons, conventional banks, with developed trading credentials, were not only able to act as agents for their Islamic principals, they actually became regular end-users of Islamic finance to support their own in-house and subsidiary trade requirements. The additional benefit for them was their being well positioned to offer a greater, more diversified, range of options to corporate clients and this was to take on greater significance as the system matured (Cox, 2000).

Concluding remarks
Bahrain is undoubtedly the global centre for Islamic finance, and it has the highest concentration of Islamic financial institutions. Bahrain has a strategic geographic position in the heart of the Gulf region, and a well-developed infrastructure, excellent telecommunication facilities and support services, a skilled workforce and professional capabilities that provide the centre with a conducive banking environment. These attributes make Bahrain well qualified to become a convenient base for Islamic banks as it can put at their disposal a wide range of resources and facilities.

In addition, Bahrain hosts a number of international Islamic financial infrastructure and supporting organizations, such as the Liquidity Management Centre (LMC), International Islamic Financial Market (IIFM), Accounting and Auditing Organization for Islamic Financial Institutions (AAOIFI), International Islamic Rating Agency (IIRA), General Council for Islamic Banks and Financial Institutions (GCIBFI), and the Bahrain Institute of Banking and Finance (BIBF). With the backing of these organizations Bahrain has been very active in promoting innovations to broaden the depth and liquidity of Islamic financial markets through the issuance of new Islamic financial instruments and other financial innovations.

On the other hand, though not yet a regional centre Malaysia certainly has the potential to be one. Both its domestic and offshore Islamic banking industries are enjoying international recognition. Islamic banks from the Middle East are setting up operations in both Kuala Lumpur and Labuan. In addition, increased interest is shown by both international and regional development banks in the ringgit Islamic bond market. Recently, Singapore has expressed its interest in developing an Islamic financial services industry. Having more than two decades of experience in Islamic finance, Malaysia has the head start in the region, which has more than 260 million Muslims with growing economic influence. Malaysia can be a regional centre for Islamic finance in Asia, much as Singapore is the centre of conventional international financing in the region.

London's attractions to the major Islamic banks are mainly due to the breadth of specialist financial services offered, the depth of the markets and the reputation of the major banks, which include all the leading international financial institutions. London is closer to the Middle East than to New York, and is in a convenient time zone. Besides, many Arab businessmen and bankers have a long historical connection with the United Kingdom. Some of London's conventional banks provide an extensive range of Islamic financing services, including investment banking, project finance, Islamic trade finance, leasing, private banking and mortgages. London law firms provide legal advice on leasing and other Islamic financing techniques. London has actually become a global ancillary centre for Islamic financing business booked in London, which comes from Muslim countries, mainly from the Middle East. Most of the services are for international clients rather than for the local Muslims.

References

Ahmad, N. and Z. Kefeli (2002), 'Labuan International Offshore Financial Centre: performance, challenges and prospects', *Ulum Islamiyyah*, **1** (1), 73–88.

Ahmed, T. (2005), 'The challenges of rating Islamic financial institutions', *Islamic Finance Review*, April, **9**, 5.

Alam Shah, R.Z. (2004), 'Islamic banking products: a niche for developing an international Islamic financial centre', lecture given to University of Malaysia Sabah, Labuan, 5 February.

Algaoud, L.M. and M.K. Lewis (1997), 'The Bahrain Financial Centre: its present and future role in Islamic financing', *Accounting, Commerce* and *Finance: The Islamic Perspective*, **1** (2), 43–66.

Aziz, Z. (2004), 'Ensuring stability in the Islamic financial system', speech given at the 3rd Annual Islamic Finance Summit, London, 13 January.

Aziz, Z. (2005a), Speech given at the Launch of Commerce RHB Islamic Bank Berhad, Kuala Lumpur, 1 March.

Aziz, Z. (2005b), Speech given at the Launch of Commerce Tijari Bank Berhad, Kuala Lumpur, 15 April.

Baba, R. (2004), 'Labuan as an international offshore financial center', DBA thesis, University of South Australia, Adelaide.

Bahrain Monetary Agency (2002), *Islamic Banking* and *Finance in the Kingdom of Bahrain*, Manama: Bahrain Monetary Agency.

Bahrain Monetary Agency (2003), *Annual Report*, Manama.

Bahrain Monetary Agency (2004), 'Bahrain financial sector factfile', *Islamic Finance Review*, April, **5**, 7.

Bahrain Monetary Agency (2005), 'Bahrain financial sector factfile', *Islamic Finance Review*, April, **9**, 8.

Bank Negara Malaysia (2001), 'Financial sector stability – the masterplan: building a secure future', Kuala Lumpur, 1 March.

Bank Negara Malaysia (2003), *Annual Report*, Kuala Lumpur.

Bank Negara Malaysia (2004), *Annual Report*, Kuala Lumpur.

Bloomberg (2005), 'World Bank to sell RM1 billion Islamic bonds, bankers say', *Business Times*, 26 April, p. 24.

Borneo Bulletin Brunei Yearbook (1998), *Key Information on Brunei*, Bandar Seri Begawan: Brunei Press Sdn Bhd.

Central Bank of UAE (2005), 'Banks in the UAE: locally incorporated and foreign banks' (online, accessed 9 November 2005) http://www.cbuae.gov.ae/banks.html.

Cox, S. (2000), 'Islamic finance: marketing and investment', in A. Siddiqi (ed.), *Anthology of Islamic Banking*, London: Institute of Islamic Banking and Insurance.

Dubai International Financial Centre Authority (2005), About DIFC: the gateway to the region (online, accessed 6 November 2005) http://www.difc.ae/about_us/index.html.

Gerrard, P. and J. Cunningham (1997), 'Islamic banking: a study in Singapore', *International Journal of Bank Marketing*, **15**, 204–16.

Hamid, H. (2005), 'Singapore keen to learn from Malaysia on Islamic financial services', *Business Times*, 19 May, p. 24.

Hassan, M. Kabir and Mahmood Ahmed (2002), 'Islamic banking versus conventional banking: a questionnaire survey of their apparent similarities and differences', seminar proceedings, The 1st International Conference on Islamic Banking, Finance and Insurance, Labuan, 30–31 January.

Ibrahim, M. (2005), 'Malaysian foreign exchange and financial markets – recent developments', Keynote Address given at The Malaysian Finance Association 7th Annual Conference 2005, Kuala Terengganu, 9–10 May.

Islamic Banking and Finance Institute Malaysia (online, accessed 3 June 2005), http://www.ibfim.com.

Khalili, S. (1997), 'Unlocking Islamic finance', *Infrastructure Finance*, April, 19–25.

Labuan Offshore Financial Services Authority (LOFSA) (2002), *Annual Report*, Labuan.

Labuan Offshore Financial Services Authority (LOFSA) (2003), *Annual Report*, Labuan.

Labuan Offshore Financial Services Authority (LOFSA) (2004), *Annual Report*, Labuan.

Lewis, M.K. and L.M. Algaoud (2001), *Islamic Banking*, Cheltenham, UK and Northampton, MA, USA: Edward Elgar.

Nathan, D. (2004), 'Islamic banking – licensed to grow', *Star Bizweek*, 24 July, p. 3.

The Banker (2004), *High hopes as Dubai financial centre issues its first licences, 4 October, 15* (online, accessed 6 November 2005), http://www.thebanker.com/news/printpage.php/aid/2156.

Wilson, R. (1999), 'Challenges and opportunities for Islamic banking and finance in the west: the United Kingdom experience', Islamic Research and Training Institute of the Islamic Development Bank, Jeddah.

Wilson, R. (2005), 'Islamic banking in the United Kingdom', Universita Degli Studi Di Napoli Federico II, Dipartimento Di Diritto Comune Patrimoniale Convegno Internazionale Di Studi, 8–9 April, Rome.

24 Islamic banking and the growth of *takaful*
Mohd Ma'sum Billah

Development of Islamic banking practices

An Islamic banking system which combines the practices of Islamic banking and finance with a commercial return has been successfully developed, with the Islamic Development Bank (IDB), established in 1974 in Jeddah, as the role model. A significant stimulus came from the development in the Muslim world in the 1970s and 1980s of the pan-Islamic movement. This movement aimed to restore Islamic values and began to demand the application of *shari'a* in all aspects of life. The formation of Islamic banks and financial institutions was one signal of the back-to-religion movement and the starting point of a new era of the Muslim world.

Islamic banking operations have been appreciated widely in Muslim and in non-Muslim countries for giving a different perspective to banking and financial practices. Muslims need banking services for a variety of purposes, such as to finance new businesses, to buy a house, to facilitate capital investment, to undertake trading activities or to offer a safe place for savings. The central idea of an Islamic Bank, as approved by the General Secretariat of the Organization of the Islamic Conference (OIC), is as follows:

> An Islamic Bank is a financial institution, which applies statutes, rules and procedures that expressly state its commitment to the principles of Islamic *Shari'a* and prohibit the receiving and paying of interest (*riba*) on any of its operations. (Mannan, 1982)

Islam is strongly prohibitive of *riba* or usury transactions as adopted in conventional bank transactions on the grounds that they would lead to injustice. The *shari'a* disallows *riba*, and there is now a general consensus among Muslim economists that *riba* encompasses all, not just excessive, interest.

The emergence of Islamic banks

The fundamental basis of modern Islamic banking had been discussed in the mid-1940s. Later, the model of Islamic banking appeared in the mid-1950s, but comprehensive and detailed concepts for interest-free banking only appeared in the late 1960s. The first experiment in Islamic banking was set up under cover in Mit Ghamr, Egypt, in 1963. The model for the experiment was the German savings bank, modified to comply with Islamic principles, that is, the prohibition of *riba*.

In the 1970s, Islamic banking emerged after the Islamic Development Bank (IDB) was established in 1974. It was followed by the Dubai Islamic Bank in 1975, the Faisal Islamic Bank of Sudan in 1977, the Faisal Islamic Egyptian Bank and the Islamic Bank of Jordan in 1978, the Islamic Bank of Bahrain in 1979, the International Islamic Bank of Investment and Development, Luxembourg, in 1980 and Bank Islam Malaysia Bhd (BIMB) in 1983.

Islamic banking and insurance (*takaful*) has developed rapidly in Malaysia since 1983. This is a manifestation of the Islamization policy of the Mahathir administration in Malaysia, with separate Islamic legislation and banking regulations existing side-by-side with conventional banking. Islamic banking in Malaysia is governed by the Islamic Banking Act (IBA), which came into force on 7 April 1983. IBA provides Bank Negara Malaysia (BNM) with powers to supervise and regulate Islamic banking operations.

BIMB was the first Islamic bank developed in Malaysia. All banking operations and activities are based on *shari'a* principles. After more than a decade in operation, BIMB has proved to be a viable banking institution with its activity expanding rapidly throughout the country via a network of 80 branches and 1200 employees. The bank was listed on the Main Board of Kuala Lumpur Stock Exchange on 17 January 1992.

A second Islamic bank, Bank Muamalat Malaysia Berhad (BMMB), commenced operations in 1999. The establishment of BMMB was the effect of the spin-off following the merger between Bank Bumiputra Malaysia Berhad and the Bank of Commerce Berhad. Under the merger arrangement, the assets and liabilities of these two banks were combined to form two banks – the Islamic bank, BMMB, and the conventional bank, Bumiputra-Commerce Berhad (BOCB). BMMB has 40 branches in various locations in Malaysia as a result of this merger process. A dual banking system was also introduced. Most of the banks and financial institutions in Malaysia have opened Islamic windows to provide banking services.

Rational outlook
Application of Islamic principles to banking and finance has promoted Islamic communities. A large portion of the Muslim world had been dominated culturally, economically and politically by the European colonial powers and Western principles are still deeply rooted in the social, economic, political and cultural life of Muslim communities. Islamic banks are part of the process of liberating Muslims from Western thought, values and institutions, and remodelling their socioeconomic life in accordance with *shari'a*.

While Islam strictly prohibits the paying and receiving of interest, it recognizes the productivity of capital. Therefore providing capital for an economic activity and sharing profit or loss is allowed, as well as charging higher prices for deferred payments in trade. These two concepts, profit-and-loss sharing schemes and financing techniques based on permissible profits from trade, underpin Islamic banking practices.

Commercial banks try to plan and formulate policies to earn profit and not just provide services for economic and social development. On the other hand, the objective of an Islamic bank is not purely to make profit, but also to create a balanced economic society. An Islamic bank can earn profit, but not by profiteering. Maximization of profit does not create welfare for society at large.

As illustrated in Figure 24.1, Islam places economic activities including banking and financing activities within the same framework of societal interrelationships. Islam may be perceived as comprising three basic elements. The first element is *aqidah*, which concerns all forms of faith and belief by a Muslim in Allah and His Will, from the fundamental faith and belief. Second, there is *ibadat* (worship) and third, *akhlaq*, which relates to behaviour, attitude and work ethics.

Shari'a should be practised in all aspects of a Muslim's daily life. It can be divided into two, *ibadat* and *muamalat*. *Ibadat* is concerned with the practicalities of worship to Allah, in the context of a man-to-Allah relationship, whereas *muamalat* is concerned with the practicalities of daily life, in the context of various forms of man-to-man relationships. An important component of *muamalat* is the conduct of economic activities within the

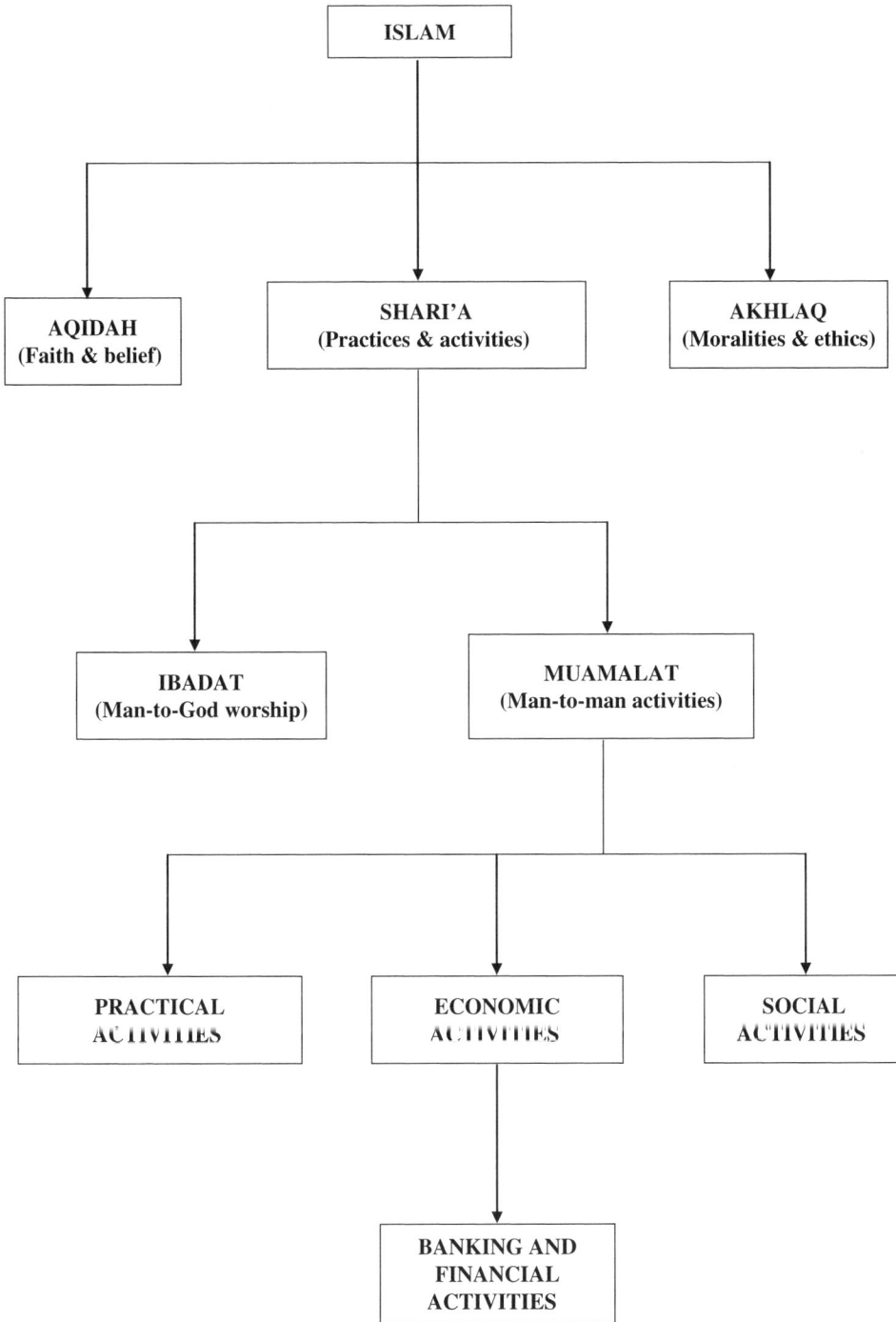

Figure 24.1   Islam, shari'a, *banking and finance*

economic system and also within the banking and financial system. Within this schema, banking and financial activities can be traced through economic activities, to *muamalat*, to *shari'a*, to Islam and finally to Allah. This is the root of Islamic banking and finance.

Legal approaches
There are two different legal approaches amongst Islamic jurists. Traditionalists (*ahl al-hadith*) rely solely on Qur'an and *sunna* (traditions) of the Prophet as the only valid sources for jurisprudence. The non-traditional approach (*ah al-ray'*) relies on the free use of reasoning and opinion in the absence of reliable *hadith*. Non-traditional approaches are proclaimed in Iraq, whereas the traditional approach is heralded in Medina. Differences arose between these two schools owing to the abundance of reliable *hadith* that scholars could depend on when forming legislation in Medina. On the other hand, in Iraq, the sources that were available were not as reliable as in Medina. This is the main reason why jurists had to turn to analogy (*qiyas*). As a consequence of these differences among Muslim scholars, a *hadith* may have been accepted by Malik (from Medina) and not by Abu Hanifa (from Iraq) who had used analogy in the absence of reliable *hadith*. Therefore the sources of Islamic law in Islamic banking could be discussed from these two approaches.

Basically there are four sources of Islamic law: the Qur'an, the *sunna* or tradition of the Prophet, *qiyas* or analogies, and *ijma* or unanimous agreement. Throughout history, Muslim jurists would determine the legality of an issue of these sources in descending order. If the legality was not based on an explicit command in the Qur'an, then the jurists turned for explicit commands in the *hadith*, *qiyas* and *ijma* (consensus). Unfortunately not all aspects of the methodology were agreed upon unanimously, the Qur'an could be interpreted differently, some traditions of the Prophet were questioned for their authenticity and the extent to which they were religiously imperative, the use of analogies was greatly debated and there was little unanimous agreement among scholars in Islamic history about unclear issues (www.aibim.com.my).

Riba and investments in shares
Regarding shares and stock market investments, *ulama'* have classified this issue under the category of *awraq al-naqdiyyah*. Basically this is something which is allowed, with certain conditions, and it is also subject to *zakat* payment, provided that it fulfils the *nisab* and *hawl* and its *nisbah* is 2.5 per cent of its value. Consider Al-Fiqh Al-Islami wa 'Adillatuh, p. 774: 'Shares [are] defined as one of the equal parts into which the capital of a company is divided, entitling the holder of the share to a proportion of the profits. [. . .] Dealing in shares is permissible in the *shari'a*' (Al-Zuhayli, 1997).

Shaykh Syed Mutawalli ad-Darsh declared:

> Money in Islam has a role to play. It should not be kept away, hoarded in a vault or safe but should circulate to allow people to make use of its benefits. That is why the books of *Fiqh* say that the guardian of an orphan must invest that inheritance in a good manner so that *Zakah* would not deplete the wealth of the child.

Muslims can buy shares in any company which offers good services to the community, and companies which do not pursue unlawful trade. For example, it is not allowable to buy into the conventional banking sector because it is ridden with interest. It is forbidden to buy shares in breweries because they are producing something which is *haram*. Also it is not permissible to buy shares in chemical companies, because they produce products which damage people and the environment. But companies which are good pose no problem.

General principles
It is necessary for all Muslim communities not to practise *riba* or any kinds of transactions contrary to the teaching of Allah and His messenger Prophet Muhammad (p.b.u.h.). In such matters Islamic states have established certain legal laws regarding the prohibition of *riba* according to the Qur'an, and there are certain organizations, such as the Council of Islamic World League, established to give some decisions regarding *riba* for the people who are dealing in this area, and setting out the legal opinion on taking interest. This form of unlawfulness is condemned by the book, the *sunna* and the consensus of Muslims and all these sources have explained clearly why it was prohibited and what is the punishment from Allah for involvement in this. The Holy Qur'an threatens usurers with war from Allah and his messenger (surah Baqarah 278–9). It has been verified that the Prophet and Allah condemned those who take, give, write about and witness usury. Furthermore, Islamic banking needs to be considered as performing socioeconomic functions in line with the Prophet's social justice agenda.

All Islamic banks need to be seen to be following *shari'a* rulings. For this reason, Islamic banks establish a *Shari'a* Supervisory Board. This Board should comprise trustworthy scholars who are highly qualified to issue *fatawa* (a religious ruling) on financial transactions. Such a Board should be formed from the moment the financial institution is incorporated, and is needed to provide continued supervision and permanent checks on contracts, transactions and procedures.

Growth of *takaful* business
The *shari'a* alternative to conventional insurance is *al-takaful*. The word *al-takaful* is derived from a verb, *kafala*, which means to help or to take care of one's needs. *Takaful* is operated on the basis of shared responsibility, brotherhood, solidarity and mutual cooperation or assistance, which provides for mutual financial security and assistance to safeguard participants against a defined risk. Its operation should be within the *shari'a* spirit, and there may not be any justification to involve herewith any element which is against *shari'a* principles. Allah (s.w.t.) says to this effect:

> . . . And co-operate ye with one another in righteousness and piety, and do not co-operate in sin and rancour. . . . (al- Qur'an: 5:2)

> . . . Allah s.w.t. permitted trade and transaction while prohibited in involving usury. . . . (al-Qur'an 2:275)

The basic notion of *takaful* is to bring equity to all the parties involved. Profit earning is not the prime objective, but rather the aim is to help others who face risks and share misfortunes.

In *takaful*, there are four parties involved, namely, the participant, the operator, the insured and the beneficiary. The contribution or premium made by the participant is put into two accounts. One of them is an investment account that follows the principles of *mudaraba* (profit and loss sharing). The other account is treated as charity or a donation according to the principles of *tabarru*. There are three operational models of *takaful*: *tijari* in Malaysia, *ta'awuni* in Sudan and *wakala* in Bahrain. Each of these models will be examined below.

Shari'a *rulings on* takaful
Takaful does not protect, but if there is any loss or damage in the future, for example on the property insured, it ensures financial security, based on shared responsibility. *Takaful* policyholders cooperate among themselves for their common goal of mutual security against risk. The payment of a premium made by policyholders is to assist those of them who need financial security and it is regarded as a donation contract. A *takaful* transaction is free from the element of uncertainty, unjust enrichment, and *riba*. The Holy Prophet (p.b.u.h.) said to this effect: 'Reported by Said Ibn al-Musayyib r.a verily the Holy Prophet (s.a.w.) forbade an uncertain transaction' (Muwatta Imam Malik).

Nor does *takaful* aim to take advantage at the cost of other individuals. In all of its aspects of operation, *takaful* shall abide by the absolute *shari'a* principles. Therefore, *takaful* falls under a condition which makes it permissible in the Islamic transaction: 'Muslims are bound by their conditions except the condition which prohibits the lawful one or the one which permits the unlawful one. . .' (al- Tirmizi).

General structure of a takaful *company*
The organizational structure of a *takaful* company as applied in Malaysia, Bahrain and Saudi Arabia is one in which the general manager is the chief manager of a *takaful* company, and a company has four departments under his supervision, each covering a specific area.

General manager   Generally in a *takaful* company, the general manager has a duty to control four departments, that is, family *takaful*, general *takaful*, finance and administration, and marketing. He has the overall responsibility to implement organizational plans, and to achieve organizational goals. He also has full authority to make decisions for all the departments under his control.

Family takaful *division*   Family *takaful* schemes have been grouped into two classes, an individual *takaful* and a group *takaful*. In an individual *takaful*, the participant has a policy to protect himself/herself for security against defined risk. A legal operator will manage the premium paid by the participants. The operator has responsibilities to gain collective rights over contributions and benefits. All these activities will be treated according to the principles of *mudaraba*, that is, profit-and-loss sharing in a participant's account (PA), while in the participant's special account (PSA) it will be treated in line with the principles of *al-tabarru'* (charity). For example, Syarikat Takaful Malaysia Berhad provides many products for individual plans. There are Family *Takaful* Plans, Family *Takaful* Plans for Education, *Takaful Rawat*, *Takaful* Mortgage, *Takaful Keyman*, *Takaful Ma'asyi*, *Takaful Siswa*, *Takaful Waqaf*, *Takaful Dana Pekerja*, *Takaful Ziarah* and *Takaful Hawa*.

In a group *takaful*, a participant will have the policy for a group, that is, his own and also his family, as a protection for them from any defined risk. Similar to an individual *takaful*, a legal operator will manage the fund. As an example, in group plans in Syarikat Takaful Malaysia Berhad, it provides Group Family Takaful Plan (credit) and Group Medical Takaful Plan.

General takaful *division*   In this division, all operations are managed by functions and usually grouped into three: underwriting, claim and re-*takaful*. The underwriter has a responsibility to arrange the terms and conditions of the cover and its price, at levels which reflect the degree of risk which the case brings to the general *takaful* fund by way of potential frequency and potential security and loss. The *takaful* underwriter must also ensure that the one who proposes has the capacity to contract and is in compliance with *shari'a* law.

The various underwriting plans have been grouped into several main classes: fire *takaful* schemes such as basic fire and business interruption, motor *takaful* schemes such as private motor car and motor cycle, miscellaneous or accident *takaful* schemes such as personal accident and personal accident for pilgrims, and engineering *takaful* schemes such as machinery breakdown and construction risks. Meanwhile, for policy claims there is a division into two parts, motor and non-motor.

Finance and administration   Finance and administration is very important for any company, for it to be able to manage the business successfully. For that reason, the *takaful* company has these two departments to make management easily controllable, and to trace the problems quickly.

Finance   The Finance department itself is divided into two parts, investment and account. Under the account division, the first is a shareholder fund where all the premiums paid by participants will be collected and managed by a legal operator for a legitimate consideration for the services given. Secondly, the Family *Takaful* Fund, which is collected through the contribution made by the participants, is put into two accounts – participant's account (PA), where the fund is invested according to the principles of *mudaraba* (profit-and-loss sharing), and participant's special account (PSA), which is treated as a charity according to the principles of *al-tabarru'*. Lastly, there is the General *Takaful* Fund, which is treated on the basis of *al-tabarru'* in a PSA account. For example, A has a Family *Takaful* policy for the right to claim from the operator the total amount of paid contribution together with a share of the profits made over the contribution. In addition, he will also get a bonus and dividend according to the company's policy. But if A dies before the maturity of the certificate, the trustee/nominee shall have the right to claim the total paid contribution and share of the profit made, bonus and dividend which he will receive based on the company's policy and also a donation from the company's *al-tabarru'* fund. Then nominee (X) will give all that money to A's legal heirs.

Furthermore, the other part of the finance division, which is investment, is responsible for investing all the contributions paid by participants to gain profits. These profits will be distributed to participants and also operators based on the principle of *mudaraba*. But, if it incurs a loss, only participants will bear the losses.

Administration   This is the part of a company where all matters to do with employees and business transactions, and other matters concerning a *takaful* company must be reported and recorded. The Administration Department is also known as the Human Resources Department, where it is classified into three specific areas: branch operation, general administration and personnel and training.

Branch operation highlights any matter or problems of a *takaful* company's branch/outlet. All managers at every outlet must refer to headquarters about any problems arising, especially management problems, before making any changes or decisions. General administration acts as the main management office where all information, problems and any matters to do with business are discussed and kept. For example, information is kept about participants' personal details.

A *takaful* company needs good trust *(amanah)* and well-trained people as operators who will manage the entire funds paid in by participants. Therefore a *takaful* company has a special division which provides training and takes care of employees' welfare; this division, called the Personnel and Training Division, will provide, for example, special training for a new operator to work effectively and efficiently.

Marketing   A *takaful* company needs a marketing department to plan and promote all the products and services it provides. To make it more effective and efficient, the Marketing Department is divided into two areas, using an agency to help them promote their product, and corporate marketing for the company itself. Nowadays, the marketing department of a *takaful* company promotes the company and its product through the internet. For example, Syarikat *Takaful* Malaysia Berhad has its own website, www.takaful-malaysia.com.my, where all information about the company and products provided by the company is given.

Different models of *takaful*

Ta'awuni *model (cooperative insurance)*
The concept of *ta'awuni* originated in Sudan and Saudi Arabia. It was first established in 1979, when scholars realized that there is a need for cooperation in insurance. From this came the idea that members should donate their contribution to the fund. Both the operators and the contributors acknowledge their rights and responsibilities to the fund. The profit surplus is to be distributed entirely to the participants.

Under the *mudaraba* principle employed, the *takaful* company and the participants share the direct investment income, in which participants are entitled to all of the surplus with no deduction made prior to distribution. This model is applicable to life family *takaful* as the fund is entirely distributed to the participants.

Consider the following example. An individual lends his money to a *takaful* operator who manages the fund on behalf of the participant. Islam tells us to help one another so long as it does not violate the rulings of *shari'a*: 'And co-operate ye with one another in righteousness and piety . . .' (5:3).

The contribution paid is based on the principles of *tabarru*. A *tabarru* concept is a one-way transaction in which, once the contribution is made, the contributor has no right to take any benefits out of it. The fund is used for any participant who faces difficulties within the time period as agreed upon in the insurance policy. When the participant contributes to the fund, he is indirectly applying the golden principle of 'bear ye one another's burden'.

Not all companies, including insurance companies in Sudan itself, comply with the recommendation to accept *ta'awun* as a basis for Islamic insurance. When people contribute their money, they are actually expecting something in return, that is, financial reward or profit sharing. There is an argument regarding the true nature of *ta'awun*. Is it really cooperative? Insurers/*takaful* operators are often described as 'custodian or treasurer of the common fund'. Unfortunately, the practitioners believe that the above notion is rather inaccurate in terms of what has been practised by most of the insurance companies today. With the exception of the mutual insurance companies, most of them are more than treasurers, as they believe that they are the owners of the fund.

Dr. Qaradawi (1989, p. 275) mentioned that none of those who buy insurance are aware that the premium is for mutual help: 'The insured individuals do not pay the premium as donations; such a thought never occurs to them. . .'. Afzalur Rahman (1979, vol. 4, p. 224) has said that it is incorrect to imply the principle of 'mutuality' in all insurance. He asks:

> How can all forms of insurance be mutual when this mutual character is actually unknown to the insurer and insured? What is the value of an economic interdependence between all the insured and between the insured and the insurer, of which neither of them is aware?

Such a question urges us to think more critically regarding the issue of true mutual co-operation.

Each contributor in *ta'awun* practice will share the profit, liability, indemnity and surplus, and parties in the same group will receive equal benefit and advantages. For instance, suppose a member of a *takaful* fund meets with an accident and claims for indemnity to repair his car that costs him RM1000. In this case, he will be entitled to receive his compensation. The purpose of the *takaful* company is to help and assist the participants in reducing the losses due to unexpected misfortune or disaster.

Figure 24.2 shows the accounting flow in a *ta'awuni* concept. The *ta'awuni* model produces no issue pertaining to the PA and PSA, because the proportion is equally divided: 50:50. The fund in PA will be used for long-term investment and profit gained from the investment will be shared among the family members. Meanwhile, in PSA, the fund is viewed as a donation or *sadaqah*, intended to help the needy and the suffering. Suppose the premium paid by the participant is RM200, and it will be divided into two, for PSA and PA. For PSA, the RM100 attributed to PSA will be deducted as business expenses. On the other hand, for PA, the RM100 will be used for underwriting surplus. Underwriting is best described as an insurable risk. The role of the underwriter is to decide whether to accept or reject the application for insurance. This is important in order to maintain a safe and profitable distribution of business for the company. The money will be invested in the project in conformity with *shari'a* and the gains will be distributed between the participant and the *takaful* operator, 50:50.

For the RM40 in the participant's part, the money is reserved for those participants who did not make any claim during the period. For the operator's part, the RM40 will be subtracted for management expenses, for example staff cost, maintenance, establishment expenses and administration general expenses. The remainder will then be subtracted from the *zakat* family fund. In the end, the balance is actually the net profit for the operator or the shareholder.

General *Takaful* :

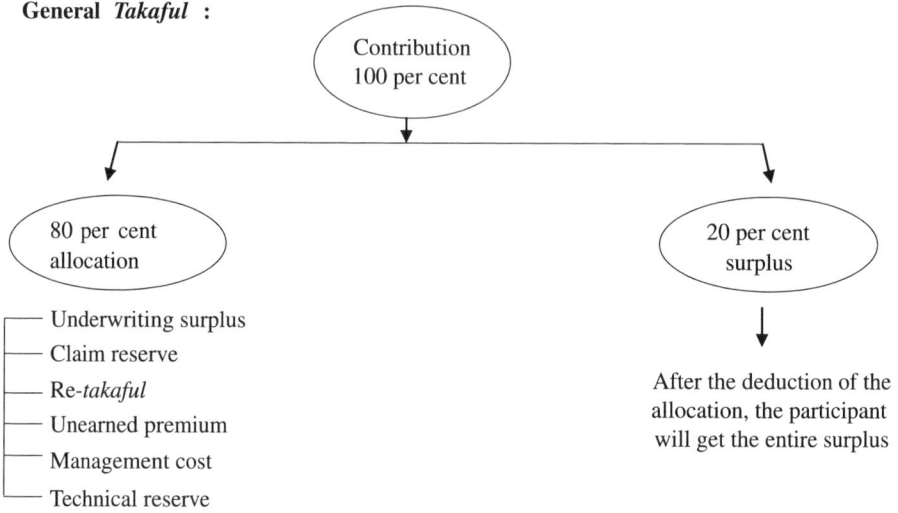

Contribution
100 per cent

80 per cent
allocation

20 per cent
surplus

- Underwriting surplus
- Claim reserve
- Re-*takaful*
- Unearned premium
- Management cost
- Technical reserve

After the deduction of the
allocation, the participant
will get the entire surplus

Family *Takaful* :

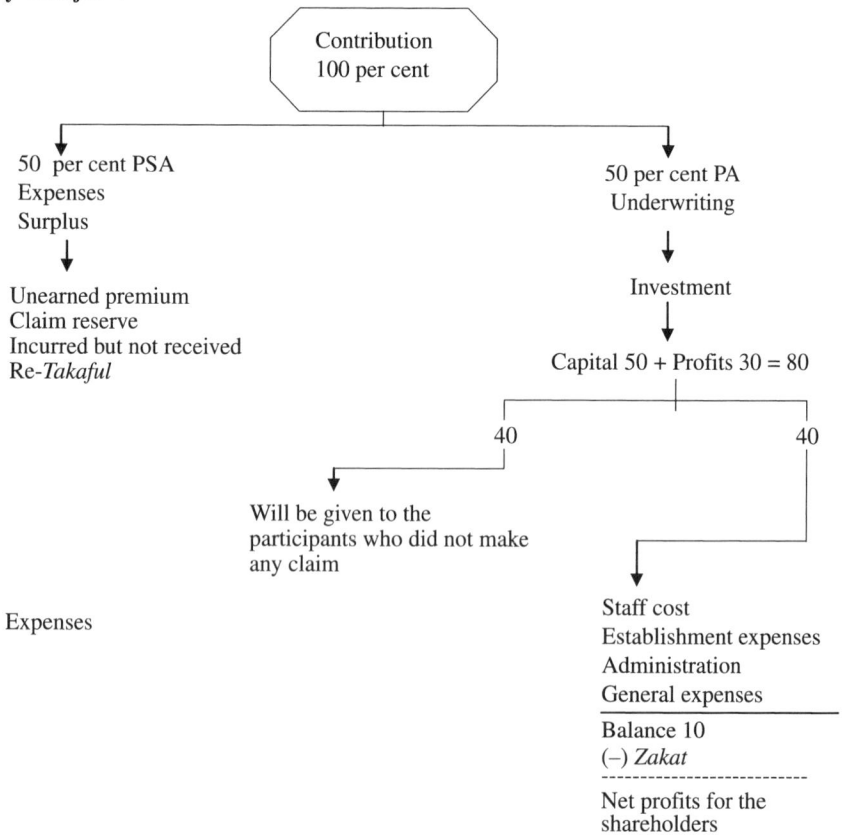

Contribution
100 per cent

50 per cent PSA
Expenses
Surplus

50 per cent PA
Underwriting

Unearned premium
Claim reserve
Incurred but not received
Re-*Takaful*

Investment

Capital 50 + Profits 30 = 80

40   40

Will be given to the
participants who did not make
any claim

Expenses

Staff cost
Establishment expenses
Administration
General expenses
_____
Balance 10
(–) *Zakat*
- - - - - - - - - - - - - -
Net profits for the
shareholders

Figure 24.2   Illustration of the Ta'awuni *concept*

Wakala *model (agency)*

Wakala is a contract of agency. According to this principle, a person will delegate his right or business to other people to act as his agent or *wakil*. The agent is responsible for contributing his/her knowledge, skills and ability in performing the task assigned to them. In a *takaful* operation, a *takaful* company as the insurer/operator has the right to employ the agent on either a full-time or a part-time basis. The agents employed by the insurance company are bound by the contract of *wakala* to market and distribute the company's products.

The *takaful* operation is still new in the market compared to conventional insurance companies. Thus strategies must be taken into consideration in order to increase the awareness of its existence, as an alternative and substitute for the existing conventional insurance system. It is within the agent's responsibility to identify the potential participants and disseminate information regarding the concept and policy practice in *takaful* business. They need to explain thoroughly to these people so that they will gain a comprehensive understanding and avoid misconceptions. Furthermore, the agent is obliged to convince people of the operation's advantages compared to the conventional alternatives in order to gain competitive edge and good credibility. An agent may also assist the *takaful* company by collecting the fund. Since they are representing their company, it is very important for them to produce a good image and build a strong relationship to maintain the credibility and integrity of *takaful* business.

An increasing number of companies have embarked on implementing the concept of *wakala* in their *takaful* operation. Most of the companies are operating in Bahrain and Saudi Arabia: for example, the Bahrain Islamic Insurance Co., Sharikat Takaful Al-Islamiyah, Global Islamic Insurance Co. and Takaful Islamic Insurance Co. Bahrain.

If we compare the modes of payment applied between Islamic and conventional insurance, we can see that they are basically different in several ways. In the conventional insurance system, the agent will receive their commission by deducting some percentage contributed by the participants. For instance, Mr X is appointed as an agent by one of the insurance companies. Under the agreement, Mr X would get his commission, say of 20 per cent, from each participant.

However, the Islamic insurance system believes that the above transaction is unfair. An agent is representing and working for the company, therefore, they should be treated as an employee and the *takaful* operator as the employer, who is obliged to pay a sum of money in terms of salary to the appointed agent.

Figure 24.3 illustrates how the *wakala* model is applied in a *takaful* fund: General *Takaful* and Family *Takaful*. For example, A is the *takaful* operator, B works as an agent or *wakil* and represents A and C as participants or policyholders of the *takaful* business.

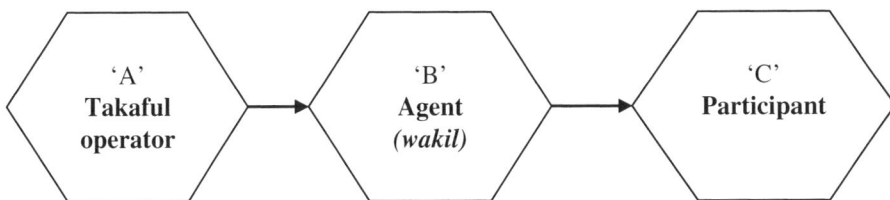

Figure 24.3   The wakala *model*

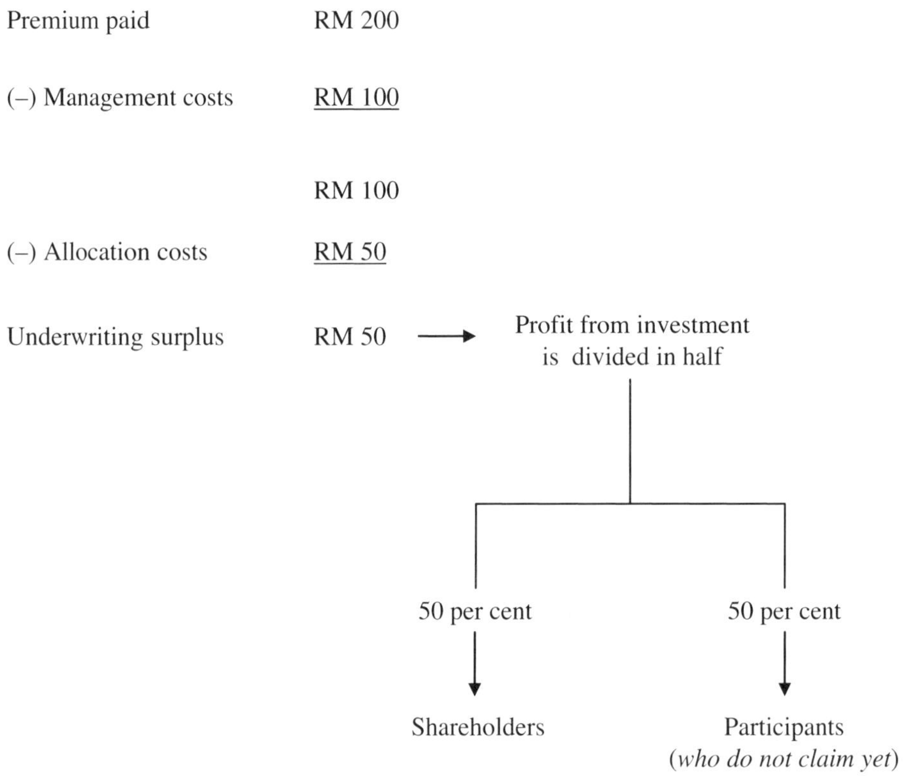

Premium paid	RM 200
(–) Management costs	RM 100
	RM 100
(–) Allocation costs	RM 50
Underwriting surplus	RM 50

Premium paid   RM 200

(–) Management costs   RM 100

                                          RM 100

(–) Allocation costs   RM 50

Underwriting surplus   RM 50 ⟶ Profit from investment
                                                            is divided in half

                              50 per cent   50 per cent

                              Shareholders   Participants
                                                                      (*who do not claim yet*)

Figure 24.4   Example of calculation of general takaful *fund (* wakala *)*

Note that C is obliged to pay his contribution (premium) to A. However, C could give his contribution to B as B has been authorized to collect the contributions from C as well as other participants. The contribution collected will then be pooled into the *takaful* fund. The fund will be managed by A, according to the principles of *mudaraba* and *tabarru'*. Thus it can be concluded that all participants are actual owners of the fund.

The general takaful *fund*   Before A wants to start managing the fund, A will first deduct some amount from the PSA account on a basis of *tabarru'* for management and services expenses. The remaining balance will be deducted to allocate costs: unearned contributions, claim reserves, technical reserves, re-*takaful* cost and incurred but not reported (IBNR). The balance is called 'underwriting surplus'. This surplus will be used for investment that is not violating the rulings of *shari'a*. Profits obtained will be distributed between the shareholder and participants who have not made any claim during the time period. Normally it will be allocated equally, 50:50. Figure 24.4 illustrates the arrangement.

Contribution paid   RM 200

(−) Management costs   RM 100
                              _____

                 RM 100 ⟶ PA (investment account) – 95 per cent
                              (accumulated contribution + profit)

                          ⟶ PSA (Risk mgt. account) – 5 per cent
                              (for allocation costs)

                                 –   Re-*takaful*
                                 –   Unearned contribution
                                 –   Technical reserves
                                 –   Incurred but not reported
                                 –   Claim reserves

Figure 24.5   Example of calculation of family takaful *fund (*wakala*)*

The life / family takaful   Two types of accounts are involved in this fund, PA and PSA. It is up to the operator, A, to manage both accounts according to the principles of *mudaraba* and *tabarru'*, respectively. The fund pooled from the contributors will then have management costs deducted. The balance from this amount is separated into PA and PSA.

For PA, when no claim is made by B, he/she is entitled to receive an accumulated contribution paid together with profits. However, participants are not entitled to any benefits from PSA accounts as they are earmarked for various business expenses. Figure 24.5 provides an illustration.

Tijari *model (business / commercial)*
The practice of *takaful* operation in Malaysia is based on the Malaysian *Tijari* Model, divided, like the others, into general *takaful* and family *takaful*. Two concepts have been applied. One is known as the pure *mudaraba* and the other is the modified *mudaraba*. The pure *mudaraba* approach is applied when the *takaful* and the participant are entitled to all of the surplus. No deduction is required for the operational expenses. This model is only applicable for the family *takaful* business because it is basically life insurance coverage provided to the participants.

The modified *mudaraba* model includes the investment income that is put back into the *takaful* fund. The surplus that is developed from the *takaful* fund is shared between the *takaful* company and its participants. This second model is applicable to general *takaful* business in which the deduction of expenses is taken into consideration. The rationale is due to a short-term contract, inherent risk and competition. Using the first model would lessen competition, but the *takaful* company would have to charge higher premiums and obtain larger contributions just to cover its expenses. Operational expenses can always be deducted, but the whole contribution charge would remain at a high rate.

There are issues involving the reasons for deducting operational expenses among scholars in different schools of thought. Some claim that this practice is not parallel to *shari'a's* rulings, and suggestions have been made to solve this issue by adopting the principles of *talfiq* (that is, combining the doctrines of more than one school). These scholars feel that the prohibiting of deduction expenses is not similar to the current practice of the *mudaraba* model. Also, the *takaful* contribution will benefit from the deduction of operational expenses, according to the current tax laws of Malaysia. There are two different approaches taken by the *takaful* companies with regard to the eligibility of participants in the sharing of the surplus. Some companies feel that only some of the *takaful* participants are entitled to actually participate in the distribution of surplus provided. These are those who have not yet made any claims, or received any *takaful* benefits that were offered by the *takaful* companies.

Claims   Briefly, two steps are involved in the settlement of a claim. The first step is either payable or not payable, but it is divided into four different parts. The first part is where the policy and certificate are enforced, either expired or not. Obviously, knowing that the certificate has expired, the participant cannot make any claim whatsoever. The second part depends on whether the risk is covered or not covered. The third party is involved in this particular situation. This person, who is chosen as a trustee, would be the one to distribute the claimed benefits among the legal heirs of the deceased participants. This event would be in accordance with the principles of *faraidh* (inheritance). The cause of death, being natural, accidental or even lawful is not important because it is the will of *Allah s.w.t.*, as the only one that determines the death of all His creatures. The following verse from the Holy Qur'an provides proof of such a statement: 'Nor can a soul die except by Allah's leave, the term being fixed as by writing' (3: 145). The third part is warranty, which means that there are limitations on claims based on *takaful* companies' regulations. The last part is excess. The objective of excess is to avoid the small claims that are made by the participants. For example, if the amount of excess is fixed at RM 200 in the case of an accident and the participant loses RM 1000, the company will only pay RM 800. The second step is known as quantum. The main purpose of this step is to avoid excess claims. The two steps are depicted in Figure 24.6.

Accounting treatment   The insurance industry has its own accounting standards. In Malaysia, income has been acknowledged on an accrual basis. However, for *takaful* operators in Malaysia, namely Syarikat *Takaful* and MNI *Takaful*, income is accounted and recognized on a cash only basis. Syarikat *Takaful* and Bank Islam Malaysia Berhad (BIMB) will only accept shared and distributed profits if the income is actually realized. MNI *Takaful* argued that an accrual basis could also be used. This is based on the *hadith* regarding estimates on the quantum, that is, *zakat* on dates.

1ˢᵗ Step

```
                          ┌─────────────┐
                          │   Claims    │
                          └─────────────┘
                   ┌─────────────┴─────────────┐
            ┌────────────┐              ┌──────────────┐
            │  Payable   │              │ Not payable  │
            └────────────┘              └──────────────┘
```

On policy certificate	Risk coverage	Warranty	Excess

2ⁿᵈ Step

```
                  ┌──────────────┐
                  │   Quantum    │
                  └──────────────┘
            ┌────────────┴────────────┐
      ┌──────────────┐          ┌──────────────┐
      │ Not adequate │          │   Adequate   │
      └──────────────┘          └──────────────┘
```

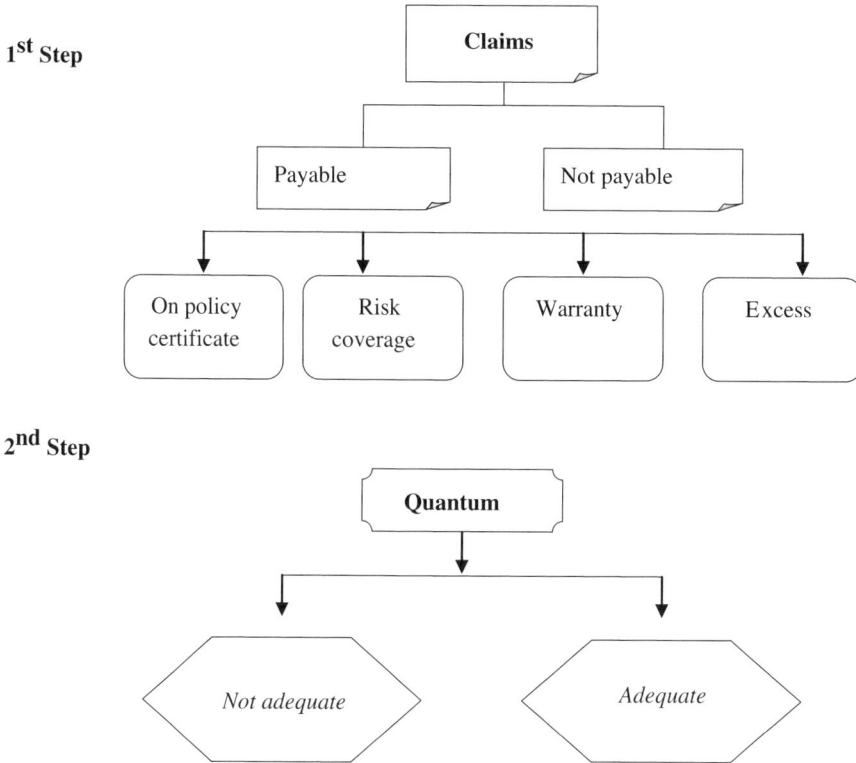

Figure 24.6   Steps in the settlement of a claim

Agency (marketing executive)   *Takaful* operators rarely use agents because they believe that the current practice is unfair. They feel it is not right to deduct expenses from certain *takaful* funds. Participants also feel it is unfair if the companies deduct management expenses. It has been said that using agents would keep the commission from being part of the contribution. Consequently, *mudaraba* is paid upon the basis of net contributions. The Malaysian *Takaful* Act of 1984 provides for the use of agents but not brokers because they must be separately licensed.

The *tijari* model also acknowledges the concept of *wakala*. Agents are authorized representatives of their *takaful* company, or work on behalf of their company. Thus the salary should be allocated to them as a return for completing the task assigned to them. Another term for them is 'marketing officers' and the roles and responsibilities are similar to those of an agency relationship (*wakala*).

The *tijari* model conceives that the main operator of the company acts as an entrepreneur, or *dharib*. Participants for the *takaful* policy are called *shahibul maal*. Participants who are holders of the *takaful* policy have to pay a certain agreed amount of contribution (*maal*), which should be declared in their contract. The *dharib* has the authority to manage this *maal* according to *shari'a* rules.

The general takaful *fund*   The contributions paid are regarded as *al-tabarru'*. Therefore the participant has no right to claim the fund since it is already treated as a donation. However, if they are based on defined risk of the subject matter, the participants can claim their rights. The deduction made is for allocation costs, that is, re-*takaful*, claim reserves, technical reserves, IBNR and unearned contributions. Note also that the *tijari* model is based on a business instead of a service charge.

All contributions paid by participants are directly deducted for allocation. The balance left is the operator's responsibility and the term given is the amount of underwriting surplus. The underwriting surplus is invested in lawful investment projects if there is no claim made by donors under the principles of *mudaraba* financing technique. The profit from the investment will then be distributed accordingly between the *dharib* (*takaful* operator) and the *sahibul maal* (donor). Figure 24.7 gives an example.

The life / family takaful *fund*   There are two different accounts involved, the PA and the PSA. The PA is managed according to the principles of *mudaraba* financing under the profit-and-loss sharing technique. It means that any profit gained from the lawful investment will be shared according to an agreed ratio between the shareholder and the participant. The scenario will be slightly different in term of loss in which only the participants bear the incurred loss and shareholders will receive nothing from the services rendered.

For the PSA account, the *tabarru'* principles are applied and, for that reason also, the participants are not allowed to make any claim if there is no risk incurred within the maturity period of the *takaful* policy. After deducting the allocation costs, the remaining (underwriting surplus) will be invested in business in conformity with *shari'a*. The amount left is allocated between the shareholder and *tabarru'* fund. Figure 24.8 shows the workings.

Diversified models of takaful
As has been made apparent, there are three different operational models of *takaful*, namely *tijari, ta'awuni* and *wakala*, and each of these models has its own strong and weak points. In general, all three have several problems. Such problems include the confusion among scholars and practitioners. Many of the *shari'a* experts do not really understand the *takaful* system, while many *takaful* practitioners lack knowledge and information about *shari'a* principles. This dissonance creates differences of opinion between scholars, academics and professionals, accentuated as the practitioners and *shari'a* experts seldom meet and sit together to have a discussion on *takaful* issues. Sometimes they just give their own opinions, based only on what they know and think.

Another problem is that the practitioners in the *takaful* industry are often not well versed in the subject of *takaful*. Many *takaful* practitioners lack the knowledge and practical experience of conventional insurance operations. In terms of *mudaraba*, they are yet to appreciate the implications of the calculation formulas. There are also problems with the accountants, who are usually just concerned about financial accounting, without having any comprehensive knowledge and information about the *takaful* system.

One solution would be to educate *takaful* practitioners and the general public about the Islamic financial laws and other related matters involving *takaful* through seminars, conferences, lectures and the internet. Practitioners need comprehensive training on how to

Contribution paid	RM 200	
(−) Management costs	RM 100	– Re-*Takaful*
		– Unearned contribution
		– Technical reserves
		– Incurred but not reported
		– Claim reserves
Underwriting surplus	RM 100 ⟶	Belongs to company

No claim? – invested

Balance
+
Mudaraba profit/bonus

Distributed

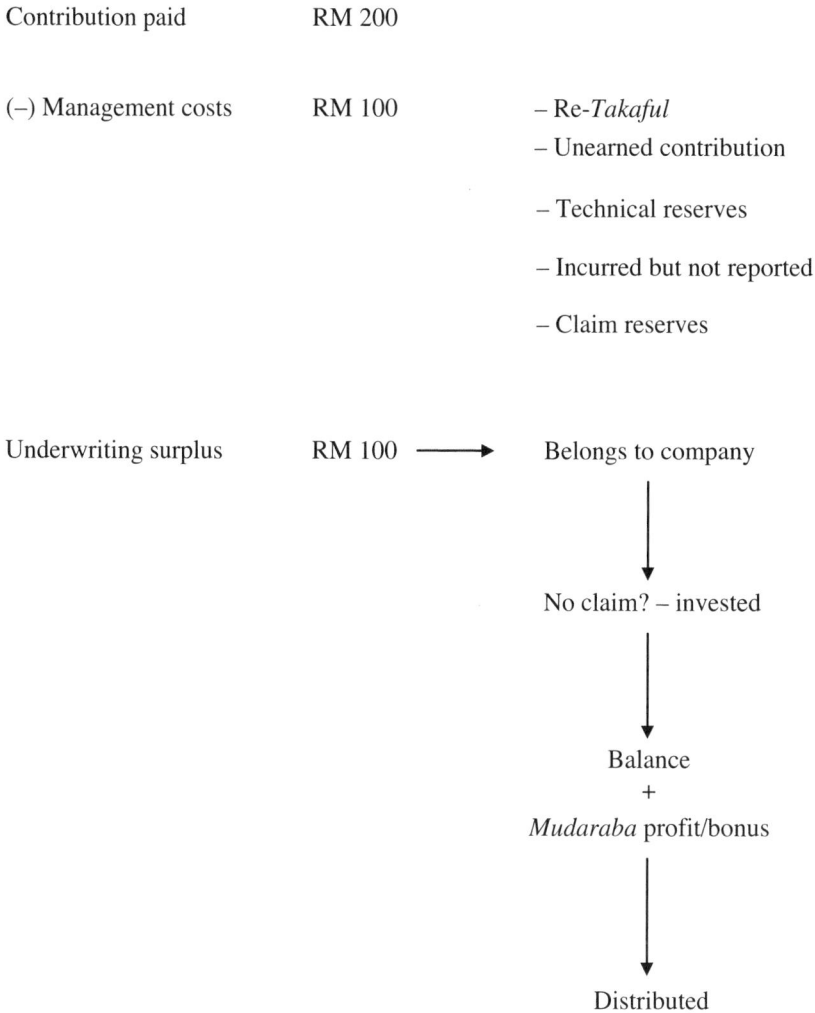

Figure 24.7   Example of calculation of general takaful *fund (*tijari*)*

operate the system effectively, according to the principles of *shari'a*. Some governments give support to the *takaful* industry by issuing licences, providing business and issuing loans for housing and other purposes.

Even though the *takaful* system has three different operational models, this fact should not prevent operators from maintaining a close relationship and cooperating by sharing information among themselves for the success of *takaful* business and to protect the interest of the Muslim *umma* in general. Such differences should be a source of inspiration, research, debate and *ijtihad* to make *takaful* operations more meaningful.

Contribution paid   RM 200   ⟶   95 per cent (PA)

                                                            –   Shared by shareholder
                                                                and participants

                                                            Who do not make a claim

                                                       ⟶   5 per cent (PSA)
                                                            –   (–) Allocation costs
                                                            –   Underwriting surplus
                                                            –   Balance shared by
                                                                – shareholder
                                                                – *Tabarru'* fund

Figure 24.8   Example of calculation of family takaful *fund (*tijari*)*

Final remarks

Takaful is the Islamic alternative to conventional insurance. However, unlike conventional insurance which is relatively standardized, *takaful* operates under three different models. These three models bring the principles of cooperation, solidarity and brotherhood that underlie *takaful*.

The *ta'awun* model which is being practised by Sudan and Saudi Arabia applies the concept of participants lending their money to the operator and the operator managing their fund without seeking any benefit. The *wakala* model, practised by Bahrain, contributes to the same principles by building a good relationship between the company and participants, which is arranged by an agent or representative. The mutual cooperation concept can be explained by the *tijari* model which is being practised by Malaysian *takaful* companies, using the *mudaraba* (profit-and-loss sharing) technique.

These three alternatives are all in line with the principles of *shari'a*. Nevertheless the system as a whole would benefit at the global level if *takaful* practitioners, *shari'a* experts and government authorities employed mutual cooperation and understanding to reconcile some of the differences that have arisen.

References

Al-Qaradawi, Yusuf (1989), *The Lawful and the Prohibited in Islam,* Kuwait: International Islamic Federation of Student Organisations.
Al-Zuhayli, W. (1997), *Al-Fiqh Al-'Islami wa 'Adillatuh*, 4th rev. edn, Damascus: Dar Al-Fikr.
Mannan, M.A. (1982), *Islamic Perspectives on Market Prices and Allocation*, Jeddah: CRIE.
Rahman, Afzalur (1979), *Economic Doctrine of Islam*, London: Muslim Schools Trust.

25 Islamic banking in the West
Rodney Wilson

Scope

This chapter examines the experience of Islamic banking in the West, mainly focusing on the developments in the United Kingdom since 1980 and the more recent experience in the United States. The major Islamic finance activities comprise wholesale operations, the provision of retail saving and investment products and home finance. Regulatory and legal issues are discussed, as well as institutional developments and the challenges of serving the British Muslim community of over 1.8 million people and the American Muslim community of over 6 million people.

The operations of exclusively Islamic banks are examined, notably in the case of the United Kingdom, the Al Baraka International Bank during the 1980s and early 1990s and the Islamic Bank of Britain from 2004. The activities of conventional banks offering Islamic facilities in London are also analysed, the focus being on the United Bank of Kuwait and its successor the Al Ahli United Bank, and more recently HSBC through its Amanah Islamic finance subsidiary and Lloyds TSB. In the United States, the institutions surveyed include LARIBA, the American Finance House of California, the Devon Bank of Chicago, the Shape Financial Group and the Guidance Financial Group of Virginia.

Islamic banking in the United Kingdom

Initially the major Islamic finance activity involved wholesale operations, with banks in London providing overnight deposit facilities for the newly established Islamic banks in the Gulf. In other words the business was *shari'a*-compliant liquidity management. The Islamic banks could not hold liquid assets such as treasury bills, which paid interest, but the joint-venture Arab banks in London, such as Saudi International Bank and the United Bank of Kuwait, accepted deposits on a *murabaha* mark-up basis, with the associated short-term trading transaction being conducted on the London Metal Exchange (Maroun, 2002).

Although the staff of the joint-venture banks were mainly British and non-Muslims, they became increasingly well informed about *shari'a* requirements regarding finance, and were able to respond to the demands of their Muslim clients in an imaginative manner. There was considerable interaction between British bankers involved with Gulf clients, *shari'a* scholars and the British Pakistani community, notably through the Institute of Islamic Banking and Insurance (IIBI) (www.islamic-banking.com), that had been established in 1976 by Muzzam Ali, a former journalist and head of the Press Association of Pakistan. Muzzam Ali worked closely with Prince Mohammed Bin Faisal of Saudi Arabia, a leading advocate of Islamic finance, and became Vice Chairman of Dar Al Maal Al Islami in Geneva, the international Islamic finance organization established by Prince Mohammed in 1982. The IIBI was initially located in the King's Cross area, near to the City of London where the Arab joint-venture banks operated, and in 1990 moved to more prestigious premises in Grosvenor Crescent in the West End of London.

The Al Baraka International Bank

The next milestone in 1982 was when the Jeddah-based Al Baraka Investment Company bought Hargrave Securities, a licensed deposit taker, and converted it into an Islamic bank. This served the British Muslim community to a limited extent, but its main client base was Arab visitors of high net worth who spent the summer months in London. Its business expanded from 1987 when it opened a branch on the Whitechapel Road in London, followed by a further branch on the Edgware Road in 1989, and a branch in Birmingham in 1991 (Wilson, 1994), as by then the bank had between 11 000 and 12 000 clients (Al-Omar and Haq, 1996, p. 45). It offered current accounts to its customers, the minimum deposit being £150, but a balance of £500 had to be maintained to use cheque facilities, a much higher requirement than that of other United Kingdom banks. These conventional banks usually allow current accounts to be overdrawn, although then clients are liable for interest charges, which Al Baraka, being an Islamic institution, did not levy.

Al Baraka also offered investment deposits on a *mudaraba* profit sharing basis for sums exceeding £5000, with 75 per cent of the annually declared rate of profit paid to those deposits subject to three months' notice, and 90 per cent paid for time deposits of over one year. Deposits rose from £23 million in 1983 to £154 million by 1991. Initially much of Al Baraka's assets consisted of cash and deposits with other banks, which were placed on an Islamic basis, as the institution did not have the staff or resources to monitor client funding adequately. Some funds were used to finance commodity trading through an affiliate company, as Al Baraka was not a specialist in this area.

Al Baraka's major initiative was in housing finance, as it started to provide long-term Islamic mortgages to its clients from 1988 onwards. Al Baraka and its clients would sign a contract to purchase the house or flat jointly, the ownership share being determined by the financial contribution of each of the parties. Al Baraka would expect a fixed pre-determined profit for the period of the mortgage, the client making either monthly or quarterly repayments over a 10 to 20 year period, which covered the advance plus the profit share. There was some debate about whether the profit share could be calculated in relation to the market rental value of the property, but this was rejected, as frequent revaluation of the property would be expensive and administratively complicated, and, given the fluctuating prices in the London property market, there would be considerable risk for the bank.

Although Al Baraka provided banking services in London, its most profitable area was investment management, and in many respects it functioned more like an investment company than a bank. It lacked the critical mass to achieve a competitive cost base in an industry dominated by large institutions, and the possibility of expanding through organic growth was limited. In these circumstances, when the Bank of England tightened its regulatory requirements after the demise of the Bank of Credit and Commerce International (BCCI), the bank decided that it was not worth continuing to hold its banking licence, as it would have meant a costly restructuring of the ownership and a greater injection of shareholder capital.[1] Consequently, in June 1993, Al Baraka surrendered its banking licence and closed its branches, but continued operating as an investment company from Upper Brook Street in the West End of London.[2] Depositors received a full refund, and many simply transferred their money to the investment company. This offered greater flexibility, as it was no longer regulated under the 1987 Banking Act but under financial services and company legislation.

The United Bank of Kuwait

By the late 1980s, there was an increasing demand from the United Bank of Kuwait's Gulf clients for Islamic trade-based investment, and the decision was taken in 1991 to open a specialist Islamic Banking Unit within the bank. Employees with considerable experience of Islamic finance were recruited to manage the unit, which enjoyed considerable decision-making autonomy. In addition to being a separate unit, accounts were segregated from the main bank, with Islamic liabilities on the deposit side matched by Islamic assets, mainly trade financing instruments. The unit had its own *shari'a* advisors, and functioned like an Islamic bank, but was able to draw on the resources and expertise of the United Bank of Kuwait as required. In 1995, the renamed Islamic Investment Banking Unit (IIBU) moved to new premises in Baker Street, and introduced its own logo and brand image to stress its distinct Islamic identity.[3] Its staff of 16 in London included asset and leasing managers and portfolio traders and administrators, and by the late 1990s investment business was generated from throughout the Islamic world, including South East Asia, although the Gulf remained the major focus of interest.[4] Assets under management exceeded $750 million by the late 1990s, just prior to the merger with Al Ahli Bank, which resulted in the bank being renamed the Al Ahli United Bank (www.ubk-plc.com).

After Al Baraka pulled out of the Islamic housing market the United Bank of Kuwait entered the market in 1997, with its Manzil home ownership plan based on a *murabaha* instalment structure (www.iibu.com). A double stamp duty was incurred on *murabaha* transactions, firstly when the bank purchased the property on behalf of the client, and secondly when it resold the house to the client at a mark-up. This was felt by many in the Muslim community to be discriminatory and, following effective lobbying by the Muslim Council of Britain, and a report by a committee charged with investigating the issues, the double stamp duty was abolished in the 2003 budget (Paracha, 2004), with the change taking effect from December of that year.[5] The double stamp duty also applied to the *ijara* mortgages introduced under the Manzil plan in 1999 (Jarvis and Whitfield-Jones, 2003).

The Islamic Bank of Britain

The development that has attracted the greatest interest in recent years has been the establishment of the Islamic Bank of Britain (www.islamic-bank.com). It had long been felt by many in Britain's Muslim community, especially since the withdrawal of Al Baraka from the retail Islamic banking market, that the United Kingdom should have its own exclusively Islamic bank. A group of Gulf businessmen, with its core investors based in Bahrain but with extensive business interests in the United Kingdom, indicated that they were prepared to subscribe to the initial capital of £50 million. A business plan was formulated in 2002, and a formal application made to the Financial Services Authority (FSA) for the award of a banking licence (Hanlon, 2005).

The FSA was well disposed towards the application; indeed, its staff charged with regulating the London operations of banks from the Muslim world were knowledgable about Islamic banking and believed that, in a multicultural and multi-faith society such as that of Britain in the twenty-first century, Islamic banking was highly desirable – to extend the choice of financial product available to the Muslim community (Fiennes, 2002). There was no objection to the new bank being designated as Islamic, as this was not felt to be a sensitive issue in the UK, unlike the case in some countries where there are large Christian populations, such as Nigeria, where the terms 'Muslim' and 'Islamic' cannot be used to designate banks. In Saudi Arabia, a wholly Muslim country, the term 'Islamic bank' also cannot be used, as the major commercial banks and many *shari'a* scholars object to religion being used as a marketing tool.

The major concern of the FSA was that the new Islamic bank should be financially secure by being adequately capitalized, and that the management had the capability to adhere to the same reporting requirements as any other British bank. The emphasis was on robustness of the accounting and financial reporting systems, and on proper auditing procedures being put in place. Systems of corporate governance were also scrutinized, including the responsibilities of the *shari'a* advisory committee, and their role in relation to the management and the shareholders of the Islamic Bank of Britain. The FSA cannot of course provide assurance of *shari'a* compliance, as that is deemed to be a matter for the Islamic Bank of Britain and its *shari'a* committee. However the FSA wishes to satisfy itself that the products offered are clearly explained to the clients, and that full information on their characteristics is provided in the interest of consumer protection.

The Islamic Bank of Britain opened its first branch on the Edgware Road in London in September 2004, less than one month after regulatory approval was given. Its operational headquarters are in Birmingham, where costs are lower, and it has already opened other branches in Birmingham and Leicester. Five further branches opened in late 2005, including Bradford in the north of England and Glasgow. The size of the Muslim population in the immediate locality is one factor determining the choice of branch location, the socioeconomic status of the potential clients being another factor, as middle-class Muslims in professional occupations with regular monthly salaries are obviously more profitable to service than poorer groups. The bank stresses the Islamic values of faith and trust, as these are fundamental, but it also emphasizes value and convenience, the aim being to have standards of service and pricing at least comparable with British conventional banks.

The opening of the first branch attracted much media attention, and therefore free publicity for the bank. The bank has a well designed website to attract business, plans to offer on-line services in the future, and has produced informative and attractive leaflets and other publicity material outlining its services. All the material at present is in English rather than Urdu or Arabic, as the costs of translation and printing have to be seen in the context of promotional benefits. Some staff members are fluent in Urdu and Arabic, but at varying levels of proficiency, and foreign language ability is not a prerequisite for appointing staff, but good English is important. Many staff members have previous banking experience, and most, but not all, are Muslim.

The Islamic Bank of Britain offers current, savings and treasury accounts, all of which are *shari'a*-compliant. No interest payments or receipts are made with current accounts, but a chequebook and a multifunctional bankcard is provided, these initially being simply cheque guarantee cards. Savings accounts operate on a *mudaraba* basis with £1 being the minimum balance. Profits on savings accounts are calculated monthly and have been held at 3 per cent since October 2004. No notice is required for withdrawals from basic savings accounts, which in other words can be designated as instant access accounts. Term deposit savings accounts, which are subject to a minimum deposit of £5000, pay higher rates. In March 2005, deposits for one, three or six months earned 3.5 per cent, 3.75 per cent and 4 per cent, respectively. Unique amongst Islamic banks, the Islamic Bank of Britain offers treasury deposits, with a minimum £100 000 for one, three or six months being invested.

These operate on a *murabaha* basis, with funds invested on the London Metal Exchange. This type of account, in other words, replicates for the retail market the type of wholesale or inter-bank deposit facilities first operated on a *shari'a*-compliant basis in London in the early 1980s.

The Islamic Bank of Britain offers personal finance, with amounts ranging from £1000 to £20 000 made available for 12 to 36 months. This operates through *tawarruq* with the bank buying *shari'a*-compliant commodities that are sold to clients on a cost plus profit basis. The client's agent, who is conveniently recommended by the bank, in turn buys the commodities and the proceeds are credited to the client's account. The client then repays the bank through deferred payments. Islamic mortgages have been offered since late 2005.

Islamic home finance and current accounts offered by conventional banks
It is a challenge for a new entrant such as the Islamic Bank of Britain to compete in a mature market for banking services with the major conventional banks offering Islamic products, notably HSBC, through its dedicated Amanah Islamic finance division (Khan, 2005) and Lloyds TSB, which has entered the market through Cheltenham and Gloucester, the former building society that it bought to create a focused mortgage and retail savings subsidiary.

It was the abolition of double stamp duty, as already discussed, that encouraged new entrants into the market for Islamic home finance, notably HSBC Amanah in 2004 and Lloyds TSB from March 2005.[6] At the same time the Al-Ahli United Bank, the successor of the United Bank of Kuwait, reached agreement with the West Bromwich Building Society for the distribution of Islamic mortgages through its extensive branch network. A similar agreement was concluded between the London-based Islamic finance subsidiary of Arab Banking Corporation, Alburaq (Qayyum, 2004), and the Bank of Ireland, for the distribution of Islamic mortgages through its English subsidiary, the Bristol and West Building Society (Smith, 2004, p. 12).

There are a number of different structures for Islamic home finance in the United Kingdom, the original Al Baraka and the United Bank of Kuwait Manzil scheme being *murabaha*-based with fixed monthly repayments to cover the cost of the house purchase that the bank undertook, plus the mark-up profit margin. In 1999, a second Manzil scheme was introduced based on *ijara*, with the United Bank of Kuwait, and its successor the Al Ahli United Bank, purchasing the property, but with the client paying a monthly rent, as well as a monthly repayment. The rent varied, but, rather than being calculated on the rental value of the property, which would have implied frequent expensive revaluations, the rent was simply benchmarked to LIBOR, the London Inter-Bank Offer Rate. As this was an interest-based rate, this was potentially controversial from an Islamic perspective, but the Bank's *shari'a* board approved its use as a benchmark, as LIBOR is often used in Islamic finance calculations because of its widespread acceptance in the banking community. The HSBC Amanah monthly home finance payments are also calculated in this way, as are those of the ABC Alburaq home financing facility marketed through the Bristol and West, although the latter is designated as a diminishing *musharaka* scheme as, over the life of the mortgage, the client's ownership share increases as repayments are made, and the share of the bank in the equity of the house correspondingly reduces.

One factor that appears to be limiting the uptake of Islamic home finance is that the cost is higher than for conventional mortgages. For Islamic financing worth £135 000 from Lloyds TSB over a period of 25 years, the monthly repayments were £883 plus £21 a month for buildings insurance in March 2005. This comprised a rental payment of £693 plus a capital repayment of £190. The total monthly payment was over £100 per month more than the cost of a Lloyds TSB conventional mortgage (Cumbo, 2005, p. 26). With HSBC Amanah for the same loan of £135 000 over 25 years the monthly repayments were £857, only £7 per month more than the bank's conventional mortgage, but the buildings insurance of £34 per month was obligatory with the Islamic financing as the property itself is owned by the bank, unlike the case of a conventional mortgage, where the bank simply has a charge on the property so that it can be repossessed in the case of payments default.

A survey of 503 Muslims in ten cities throughout England undertaken by Dr Humayon Dar of Loughborough University showed that many respondents had little knowledge of *shari'a*-compliant finance, but those who had enquired about Islamic home finance were deterred from proceeding by the higher costs.[7] These, however, partly reflect the limited scale of the market, and hence the higher costs per mortgage approved, as well as the costs involved in *shari'a* compliance, not least paying the fees and expenses of members of the *shari'a* committee. Of course the cost of a mortgage is not the only factor determining the level of business, as those Muslims who have signed contracts for Islamic finance have been prepared to pay a premium for *shari'a* compliance. Rather the issue seems to be the size of the premium, which greater competition in the market should reduce.

A further factor inhibiting the uptake of Islamic home finance is that a significant proportion of the Muslim population in the UK is in a low socioeconomic position and cannot afford to buy property. This applied in areas such as East London where many of those in the Bangladeshi community are quite poor, but property prices are relatively high. One solution might be co-ownership through Islamic housing associations, with the tenant, association and bank all owning a share in the property, but at present these do not exist in the UK.

Both HSBC Amanah and Lloyds TSB offer Islamic current accounts, these being linked to the Islamic home finance being offered, as clients make their repayments through these accounts. Neither HSBC Amanah nor Lloyds TSB pay or charge interest on these accounts, but the accounts offer normal transactions facilities such as cheque books, standing orders and direct debit facilities, monthly statements and multifunctional cards that serve as cheque guarantee and debit cards. With HSBC Amanah a minimum balance of £1000 is required to maintain the account, but with Lloyds TSB there is no minimum. At present savings and investment accounts based on *mudaraba* are not offered by either bank in the UK, as the liabilities to match the Islamic mortgage assets are generated elsewhere, notably in the case of HSBC Amanah through *shari'a*-compliant deposits in the Gulf.

Future outlook for Islamic finance in the United Kingdom
Although the UK has the most active and developed Islamic banking sector in the European Union, most activity until recently has been related to the role of the City of London as an international financial centre, rather than serving the retail banking needs of British Muslims. However, this is likely to change in the years ahead, especially if other major UK-based mortgage banks, notably Halifax Bank of Scotland (HBOS) and Royal

Bank of Scotland (RBS, which owns NatWest) enter the market for Islamic mortgages. United National Bank (UNB) launched an Islamic mortgage product in 2004, aimed at the Scottish market, with the international law firm, Norton Rose, providing advice on *shari'a* issues, and the mortgages being based on the diminishing *musharaka* principle.[8] HBOS and RBS have already sent representatives to several Islamic finance conferences in London, and it seems likely that the UNB Islamic mortgage aimed at the Scottish market, even though UNB is a minor player, may encourage the larger Edinburgh-based institutions such as Standard Life to bring forward their launch plans for Islamic financial products.

HSBC Amanah launched an Islamic pension fund in May 2004, where the assets held in the fund are screened for *shari'a* compliance, shares of companies involved in alcohol production and distribution, pork products and conventional banking being excluded, including ironically HSBC shares (Wilson, 2004). The pension fund is marketed to individuals and small Muslim family businesses. This may be a more promising way forward in the UK market than Islamic mutual funds, where there has been a history of failure, from the Kleinwort Benson Islamic unit trust of the 1980s to Flemings Oasis Fund and the Halal Mutual Fund of the 1990s, all of which failed to attract sufficient investors to ensure sustainability (Wilson, 2000).

The UK government is determined to create a level playing field for *shari'a*-compliant products. In the 2005 budget statement the same treatment was extended for *ijara* leasing mortgages and diminishing *musharaka* co-ownership mortgages as had already been applied to *murabaha* mortgages in the 2003 budget, with only a single stamp duty levy applying. The Chancellor of the Exchequer, Gordon Brown, announced at the Muslim News Awards for Excellence in March 2005 that a consultation paper would be issued concerning equal treatment for Muslim council tenants under the 'right to buy scheme', that at present is restricted to interest-based mortgages.[9] All this bodes well for the future, as a non-discriminatory system of taxation and regulation will encourage more competition in the market for Islamic financial services, reduce prices and margins, and make Islamic products more affordable. There is much that other European Union member states can learn from the quarter of a century of experience in the UK and, even if some of the lessons are cautionary, many in the Muslim community now believe that British Islamic finance is really taking off.

Islamic finance in the United States

Despite the American Muslim community being the largest in the West, Islamic banking remains in its infancy, with a few small and geographically dispersed institutions providing home and vehicle finance and small business funding. Unlike London, New York has not played a significant role as an international centre for Islamic finance, partly reflecting its geographical isolation from the Muslim world, which makes it more convenient for American institutions such as Citibank to locate their Islamic finance operations elsewhere, in the case of Citi Islamic Bank in Bahrain.

Insofar as the American population are aware of the existence of Islamic banking and finance, the events of 11 September 2001 were unhelpful to the industry. Some Americans, encouraged by often anti-Muslim media biases, have tended mistakenly to equate Islamic finance with terrorist funding (Pfeiffer, 2005). There is little appreciation or understanding of Muslim beliefs, and a lack of understanding of the meaning of *shari'a* law.

Fortunately, however, international relations issues have not had an impact on Islamic financial institutions at a local level, and home-grown banks and financial service providers run by American Muslims are much less likely to encounter hostility than institutions based in the Middle East.

As California has the largest Muslim population in the United States, estimated at more than 700 000 (Abdul-Rahman, 2005), it is perhaps appropriate to examine Islamic activity there first, focusing on LARIBA, the American Finance House, based in Pasadena. In Illinois, where an estimated 3.6 per cent of the population are Muslim, the Devon Bank serves as a community-based savings and financing institution. In addition the Shape Financial Group also provides mortgage products in the Mid-West through the University Bank of Ann Arbor, Michigan. The Guidance Financial Group based in Virginia also provides some Islamic home purchase financing, as does the United States operation of HSBC Amanah, which is potentially the largest player in the market.

LARIBA, the American Finance House
The oldest Islamic financial institution in the United States is LARIBA, the American Finance House, which designates itself as offering *halal* banking. LARIBA is the acronym for the Los Angeles Reliable Investment Bankers Association (www.lariba.com/company/index.htm). It was founded by a group of American Muslims in 1987 in Pasadena, a small community 18 miles north of Los Angeles. Although initially it was only licensed to operate in California, by 2005 it was registered to conduct business in every state of the union, excluding New York. LARIBA has an agreement with the Bank of Whittier, a self-designated 'Socially Responsible Bank', to distribute its products in all states of the union, including New York. The Bank of Whittier is based in the California town of the same name, where it has operated since 1982 (www.bankofwhittier.com/about.htm). It is a community institution that provides personal finance and home loans as well as small business finance, including leasing.

The major activity of LARIBA is home finance, both directly and through the Bank of Whittier. The financing is based on a lease-to-purchase model which it equates with *ijara wa iqtina* and diminishing *musharaka*, although it has only one structure rather than two contrasting between these potentially different types of Islamic financing, as *musharaka* involves a partnership, whereas pure *ijara* is an operational lease, the *iqtina* being the instalment purchase element. Under the LARIBA scheme the property is purchased jointly with the client, with the latter repurchasing the share of LARIBA over a predetermined period of up to 30 years. The client's initial share of the purchase can be as little as 5 per cent, although many opt for a larger share of 10 to 20 per cent of the purchase price.

The financing by LARIBA is based on the fair market value of the property, defined as the lease value if it was rented in the open market (www.lariba.com/home-financing.htm). The client is expected to obtain independent valuations from at least three estate agents, and LARIBA will also have the property valued separately. The client and LARIBA then negotiate over the mutually acceptable fair value, with the initial shares in this apportioned according to the amounts that each of the parties has contributed to the purchase. The lease value determines the monthly payment by the client to LARIBA and, as repayments of the amounts financed are also made to LARIBA monthly, the rental element in each monthly payment diminishes over time. The rental element is referred to as the return on capital (RonC), and the ownership instalments the repayment of capital (RofC). It should be noted that the structure of repayments can be flexible, with smaller repayments made initially when the client is perhaps financially constrained by the need to furnish his or her home at a time when perhaps they are starting a family on a limited income, with higher repayments made in later years when the client will, it is hoped, earn a higher salary.

Under the laws of California and most American states the transaction is simplified if the client takes immediate title to the property upon the initial purchase. As the client gives LARIBA an undertaking that he or she will repurchase the property, LARIBA authorizes the registration of title with the client. As in the United Kingdom, where Islamic housing financial transactions have to comply with English or Scottish law, in the United States the documentation has to comply with the laws of the state in which the home is purchased, otherwise the ownership of the title cannot be registered. Compliance with *shari'a* law has of course to be approved by the scholars comprising the *shari'a* committee, but the laws of California, and indeed of England or Scotland, do not recognize *shari'a* law in general; however, they can be, and have been, used in the resolution of disputes arising in contracts drawn up in compliance with *shari'a* law, provided the parties to the contract agree to *shari'a* provisions, as specified in the contracts, being used as the basis for settlements.

LARIBA also provides vehicle finance, using structures similar to that used for home finance, but over a much shorter period, typically three to five years (www.lariba.com/auto-financing.htm). The car finance is through a lease-to-purchase scheme, with the monthly rental payments determined through a survey of the rates offered by car rental companies and car dealers. This varies according to location, rather than being nationally determined, as is the case with interest. This process of determining the rental value is referred to as marking the item to the market, the crucial factor being the price of the car as a tangible asset, not the price of money or interest as with a conventional loan. LARIBA purchases the car jointly with the client, and the client then buys LARIBA's share at cost over time. The client has the title to the car from the start, but LARIBA holds a first-position lien, or in other words a legal claim, on the car. It should be noted that the financing involves two agreements, a loan agreement in which the original capital is returned without interest, and a lease agreement, which is the source of LARIBA's profit. Based on these agreements a promissory note is drawn up, in which the client guarantees payment. Under US law the monthly payments stream has to be calculated on a traditional amortization basis, so that clients can compare the percentage rate with those offered in conventional forms of financing. Such full and complete disclosure is in the interest of consumer protection. Similar provisions apply in the United Kingdom.

The Devon Bank

This old established community bank has been operating in the north side of Chicago since 9 June 1945 (www.devonbank.com/aboutus.html). Gradually over time the community it serves has changed, as northern Chicago has become one of the most multicultural and multiethnic populations in the United States, with a substantial Muslim community, mainly of South Asian or Arab origin. Many of the bank employees are Muslim and, as a self-designated caring community bank, there was a desire to provide financing in a *shari'a*-compliant manner. This was not for philanthropic reasons, although the bank has a good record of community endowment in this respect, but it made sound business sense given the demand by local Muslims for *riba*-free finance.

The Devon Bank does not have its own *shari'a* committee, but the *Shari'a* Supervisory Board of America has vetted all of its *shari'a*-compliant products, with respect both to the documentation and to the way the products are actually used. The guidance of other *shari'a* scholars is also sought on an ad hoc basis when necessary. All *shari'a*-compliant products of course have to conform to United States federal law and the laws of Illinois and the other 18 states where it is allowed to offer its services, and it is attempting to secure approval in a further 15 states (www.devonbank.com/availability.html). The Devon Bank stresses that it aims to make its Islamic products competitively priced, but adds 'where possible' in recognition that there are often higher costs in providing *shari'a*-compliant products that have to be passed on to the client.

As with LARIBA, residential finance is the major Islamic funding activity of the Devon Bank, as most American Muslims would like to own a home if they have sufficient income. The Devon Bank offers both *murabaha* and *ijara* home financing, the former being the cheaper and more popular facility. The *murabaha* home financing scheme works in the standard *shari'a*-compliant manner by making the home purchase a trading transaction, with the bank purchasing the property and reselling it to the client at a mark-up. The client makes an initial deposit payment, and then pays monthly instalments over a period of 15 to 30 years. With the *ijara* plan the client makes monthly repayments plus a rental payment, the latter determining the Devon Bank's profit. The rent can be varied over time with preset limits, set for the rental adjustment. The rent calculation is made in relation to an objectively measurable index, such as the rise in residential property values.

The Devon Bank also provides business financing using both *murabaha* and *ijara* structures. Terms for the *murabaha* finance run for up to seven years, with the client making an initial payment to the bank, followed by a series of monthly or quarterly payments, the total amount paid including the mark-up, the latter representing the Devon Bank's profit. The *murabaha* may be only valid for a single transaction, as is the case traditionally, but the Devon Bank has also developed a *murabaha* guidance line, that can be used repeatedly for equipment or traded goods purchases. In this case the *murabaha* resembles a revolving line of credit. The Devon Bank also provides *shari'a*-compliant letters of credit, in the form either of a standby facility, where a supplier of goods only seeks assurance that the bank's client is creditworthy, and will be able to make payments settlements, or of a documentary letter of credit, where the credit will actually be drawn upon to make the payment once the conditions of the bank's client regarding the goods being financed as specified in the documentation are met (www.devonbank.com/Islamic/BusFin.html). One of the advantages of *murabaha* is that, since the bank rather than the client is paying the supplier directly, letters of credit may not be required, as the bank is less likely to default on its obligations than a small or medium-sized business.

The Shape Financial Corporation
The employees of Shape are financial services and real estate professionals who design specialized products that represent *shari'a*-compliant alternatives to conventional financial products. Shape is the rebranded and refocused successor to SAMAD, which provided limited Islamic financial services until 2004 for American Muslims. Shape is not a bank and does not deal with the public directly; rather its clients are banks, credit unions

and mortgage providers who wish to develop products to suit the needs of their Muslim clients, but who lack the in-house expertise and, most crucially, the *shari'a* assurance that Shape can provide by issuing its own *fatwa* or Islamic guidance.

The strength of Shape is in the expertise of its own people, notably Abdulkader Thomas, an American Muslim graduate of the Fletcher School of Law and Diplomacy who has extensive experience of Islamic banking in the Gulf, London and New York, where he developed the Islamic mortgage products offered by the United Bank of Kuwait in the late 1990s (www.shapefinancial.com/team/abdulkader.asp). Shape's ethical advisory board includes the American *Shari'a* scholar, Sheikh Yusuf Talal DeLorenzo, a Cornell University graduate who also serves on the *Shari'a* advisory board of HSBC Amanah and the Dow Jones Islamic Indices, and Sheikh Nizam Yaquby, a graduate of McGill in Montreal, and a leading international *Shari'a* scholar. It is the credibility of these advisors that is crucial for Shape's reputation, together with the professionalism of Abdulkader Thomas, who can act as a bridge between the American Muslim community and mainstream bankers and real estate professionals.

The University Bank of Ann Arbor in Michigan (www.university-bank.com), with Midwest Loan Services providing back office processing and administration (www.mid-westloanservices.com), offers Shape Islamic mortgage products. Shape is not licensed to offer deposit facilities, but the *shari'a*-compliant profit sharing account that it designed is offered by the University Bank of Ann Arbor through its Mid Western branches. The deposits in the profit sharing account are invested in the Islamic home finance offered by the University Bank of Ann Arbor to residents of south eastern Michigan. The profit shares are derived from the rental income paid by those obtaining home finance, rather than coming from the income on interest-based loans and mortgages. The deposits are structured on a *mudaraba* basis, with the proportionate share of the profit paid out to the depositor depending on the period of notice required to withdraw funds. The rents on which the profit shares are based are very stable over time, providing an assured, but not a guaranteed, income, as that obviously depends on the performance of the overall home financing portfolio. Further products are currently being developed to complement the *mudaraba* deposits and the redeemable leases used for Islamic home finance.

Guidance Financial Group
The Guidance Financial Group is based in Virginia, and started operations in 2002. As with LARIBA and the Devon Bank, its major service is the provision of Islamic home finance, in the case of Guidance through a declining balance co-ownership financing structure. It can provide both new Islamic mortgage finance and the conversion of existing mortgages to Islamic products. It is not dependent on local deposits as the source of its Islamic mortgage finance, as it has extensive overseas connections, including a connection with the Abu Dhabi Investment Authority, on whose behalf it invests funds in a *shari'a*-compliant manner (Abdul-Rahman, 2005).

Under the declining balance co-ownership programme the client must put up at least 5 per cent of the value of the property as a deposit, with Guidance providing the remainder over a 15, 20 or 30-year period. Guidance does not charge any interest on its funding, and the amount of the total repayments does not exceed the financing made available. However the client pays a rent to Guidance for the use of the property, which represents the profit share. This is identical to the LARIBA home financing structure, which seems

to be increasingly accepted by American Muslims, as well as the regulatory authorities at
state and federal level.

Guidance has a *shari'a* supervisory board whose members represent much of the
Islamic World, with Justice Taqi Usmani of Pakistan acting as Chairman (www.
guidancefinancialgroup.com/sharia/ shariabios.asp). Other members come from Syria,
Bahrain and Malaysia, along with Sheikh Yusuf Talal DeLorenzo of New York, who, as
already mentioned, also serves as an ethical advisor to Shape. The Malaysian connection
is important, as Hasnita Hashim, who is well known as one of the leading women in
Islamic financial circles, serves on the senior management (www.guidancefinancialgroup.
com/company/management.asp). Dr Mohamad Daud Bakar, the internationally known
Malaysian *shari'a* scholar, serves on the Guidance Supervisory Board.

Prospects for Islamic banking in the West
Although Islamic banking is still in its infancy in both the United Kingdom and the
United States, it is evident that it can be self-sustaining in a non-Muslim financial environment where *riba*-based banks are dominant. In both countries the key driver for financial product development is client demand, and Islamic banks will emerge to provide for
the needs of the Muslim population if this is perceived to be profitable. This also applies
to conventional banks offering Islamic products, as there is no inherent objection or bias
against such products if the selling potential is favourable.

The problem to date, however, is that most of the initiatives have been supply rather
than demand driven, with the initiative usually coming from the Muslim world rather than
from Muslims in the West. Al Baraka was largely funded from Saudi Arabia, and even the
Islamic Bank of Britain had most of its capital raised in Bahrain and the other Gulf
states, although it does plan to secure a listing on AIM, the Alternative Investment
Market. Guidance and Shape financial services also have external backing from the Arab
Gulf states and Malaysia, and only the Devon Bank's Islamic products and LARIBA, the
American Finance House, can be regarded as home-grown. In the case of HSBC
Amanah, which offers home finance in both the United States and the United Kingdom,
the source of the *shari'a* funding is the Muslim world, the bank's role being to recycle
money into *shari'a*-compliant residential property financing. Only Lloyds TSB amongst
the major banks needs to attract *shari'a*-compliant deposits to fund its Islamic mortgages,
as it enjoys only limited access to Arab capital.

Although most Muslims in the West are aware of the Islamic prohibition of *riba*, they
are not necessarily willing to investigate Islamic savings and financing possibilities, especially if the services seem expensive compared to the conventional equivalents. The United
Kingdom possibly offers the greatest potential in the medium term, with two of the 'big
four' banks offering Islamic products, and the likelihood that Barclays and Royal Bank of
Scotland, which owns NatWest, will follow. In the United States, where the retail banking
system is much more fragmented, national initiatives are virtually impossible; hence the
enclaves in southern California and the Mid-West, where much of the Islamic banking
activity is focused on the Pakistani and Bangladeshi communities, and to a lesser extent
Arab Americans.

The Federal Reserve has been less proactive than the Bank of England and the United
Kingdom's Financial Services Authority in their support for Islamic finance, but the US
Treasury has been helpful and well disposed towards the industry, and the negative effects

of 11 September 2001 can be exaggerated. Less helpful have been continental European regulators, but this has been more because of a lack of awareness or knowledge of the issues rather than because of any inherent hostility. Banks in France and Germany have been uninterested in Islamic product development for their local Muslim communities, largely because of their lower socioeconomic position in relation to British Muslims, with many of the Arabs in France and Turks in Germany unemployed, or in casual and some-times illegal jobs, paying low wages. This is correctly, although unfortunately, not per-ceived to be a profitable customer base for the banks.

Furthermore, alternative banking models, notably ethical or socially responsible banking, are more developed and accepted in the United States and the United Kingdom than in continental Europe. The Devon Bank was a self-designated socially responsible bank long before it provided Islamic banking, and the development of these services was seen as a natural development of its community involvement. In the United Kingdom the Co-operative Bank, one of the top ten banks, is a self-designated ethical bank, and although it does not at present provide Islamic finance, it would certainly be well placed to enter the market. In contrast, in continental Europe, the Triodos Bank, the Dutch based ethical bank, is a very small and marginal institution with branches in Spain and Belgium, but an insignificant presence in any market. It does not offer Islamic finance, and has no plans for such an initiative.

The only substantial Islamic financial institution in continental Europe is Dar Al Maal Al Islami, the Geneva-based bank that was founded by a group of Saudi Arabian and Gulf investors headed by Prince Mohammed Bin Faisal in 1981. Dar Al Maal Al Islami caters largely for Arab clients based in the Middle East, and some wealthy Arab temporary resi-dents of Geneva, but not for the needs of Switzerland's small Muslim community, the majority of whom are of Turkish or North African origin, and have rather menial jobs.

Despite the limited extent of Islamic banking in the West, its development is already having a major impact on the Islamic finance industry worldwide. The climate for innov-ation is more favourable in the West than in much of the Islamic world, not least because of the better protection of intellectual property rights. The Shape Financial Corporation has registered trademarks for its Islamic financial products which limits their being repli-cated in the United States without permission. The Islamic Bank of Britain, although in its infancy, was the first Islamic bank anywhere to offer *murabaha* treasury deposit accounts. Similarly the emergence of Islamic home finance in the West has resulted in several different *shari'a*-compliant structures emerging, and much vigorous debate about the merits and drawback of each product, both from a *shari'a* and a financing perspec-tive. This has undoubtedly contributed to further product development. Dynamic economies usually have innovative financial sectors, and in this respect Islamic finance in the West stands an excellent chance of leading the way.

Notes

1. Al Baraka satisfied the ownership and control requirements of the October 1987 Banking Act. See Bank of England, *Quarterly Bulletin*, November 1987, pp. 525–6.
2. Editorial, 'Why London needs an Islamic Bank', *Islamic Banker*, London, February 1997, p. 2.
3. *New Horizon*, London, December 1995/January 1996, p. 24.
4. *New Horizon*, London, July 1996, p. 17.
5. 'Commentaries on the Finance Act of 2003 and Budget of 2005', Norton Rose law firm, London.
6. Islamic Finance Information Service, 'Lloyds TSB moves into Islamic home finance', *ISI Emerging Markets*, London, 22 March 2005.

7. New Millennium Publishing, 'Demand for Islamic finance in the UK is overvalued', *Islamic Banking and Finance Magazine*, London, 24 December 2004.
8. Islamic Finance Information Service, 'Norton Rose acts on the first ever Scottish Islamic mortgage', *ISI Emerging Markets*, London, 25 November 2004.
9. Mushtak Parker, 'Brown offers a level playing field for shariah compliant products', *Arab News*, Jeddah, 28 March 2005.

References

Abdul-Rahman, Yahia (2005), 'Development and growth of the US *shari'a riba*-free industry: prospects after 9–11', *Islamic Finance News*, 7 February.

Al-Omar, Fuad and Mohammed Abdel Haq (1996), *Islamic Banking: Theory, Practices and Challenges*, London: Zed Books.

Bank of England (1987), *Quarterly Bulletin*, November, 525–6.

Cumbo, Josephine (2005), 'Lloyds' Islamic mortgage increases buyer's choices', *Financial Times* (Money section), London, 26 March.

Fiennes, Toby (2002), 'The FSA and the UK regulatory environment', Euromoney 1st Annual Islamic Finance Summit, London, 23 and 24 January.

Hanlon, Michael (2005), 'Case study: Islamic Bank of Britain', Euromoney 4th Annual Islamic Finance Summit, London, 22 and 23 February.

Islamic Banker (1997), Editorial, 'Why London needs an Islamic Bank', London, February, p. 2.

Jarvis, Susan and Clive Whitfield-Jones (2003), 'Islamic home purchase finance', Council of Mortgage Lenders Islamic Home Finance Seminar, Jeffrey Green Russel law firm, London, 27 March.

Khan, Iqbal (2005), 'Revisiting the value proposition of Islamic finance', Euromoney 4th Annual Islamic Finance Summit, London, 22 and 23 February.

Maroun, Youssef Shaheed (2002), 'Liquidity management and trade financing', in Simon Archer and Rifaat Abdel Karim (eds), *Islamic Finance: Innovation and Growth*, London: Euromoney Books.

Paracha, Mohammed (2004), 'Islamic mortgage boom', *New Horizon*, London, June and July, pp. 15–17.

Pfeiffer, David (2005), 'Flight of capital from the United States following the 9/11 attacks', *Islamic Finance News*, 7 March.

Qayyum, Mohammed A. (2004), 'Seminar to introduce Alburaq', *New Horizon*, London, May, pp. 13–14.

Smith, Duncan (2004), 'Islamic banking in the UK – 2004 review', *Islamic Finance News*, Bahrain, 20 December, p. 12.

Wilson, Rodney (1994), 'The experience of Islamic banks in England', in Gian Maria Piccinelli (ed.), *Banche Islamiche in Contesto Non Islamico (Islamic Banks in a non Islamic Framework)*, Universita Degli Di Roma: Instituto Per L'Oriente.

Wilson, Rodney (2000), 'Challenges and opportunities for Islamic banking in the west: the United Kingdom experience', *Islamic Economic Studies*, **7** (1 & 2), 35–59.

Wilson, Rodney (2004), 'Screening criteria for Islamic equity funds', in Sohail Jaffer (ed.), *Islamic Asset Management: Forming the Future for Sharia Compliant Investment Strategies*, London: Euromoney Books, pp. 35–45.

Index